A HISTORY OF DIPLOMACY
IN THE
INTERNATIONAL DEVELOPMENT OF EUROPE

Volume II.

THE ESTABLISHMENT OF TERRITORIAL SOVEREIGNTY

A HISTORY OF DIPLOMACY

IN THE

INTERNATIONAL DEVELOPMENT

OF EUROPE

BY

DAVID JAYNE HILL

VOLUME II.

THE ESTABLISHMENT OF TERRITORIAL SOVEREIGNTY

WITH MAPS AND TABLES

HOWARD FERTIG

New York · 1967

First Published in 1906
by Longmans, Green and Co.

HOWARD FERTIG, INC. EDITION 1967
Published by arrangement with Catherine Hill Tillema

All rights reserved.

Library of Congress Catalog Card Number: 67-14185

PRINTED IN THE UNITED STATES OF AMERICA
BY NOBLE OFFSET PRINTERS, INC.

PREFACE

THE purpose of the present work, as explained in the preface to the first volume, is to offer the general reader an account of the political development of Europe, regarded from the international point of view, in which the emphasis is laid upon diplomatic policy and action rather than upon military operations. This book is, therefore, as the title indicates, a history of diplomacy, not in a purely technical sense, but as an influence affecting international life and relations.

In order to adapt its contents to all classes of readers, although based primarily upon authentic documents, the matter has been presented in the form of a synthetic narrative in which the more special details have been interwoven with facts already familiar. It is believed that the assignment of new matter to its proper place in the general order of events and the association of it with facts already known is preferable to a more abstract treatment. The life of history resides in the current of events, and its lessons should be drawn directly from the narrative.

For the same reason, definitions have their proper place at the end rather than at the beginning of historical studies. If we define diplomacy as it now exists, we shall, of course, fail to find it in the earlier periods; for, like the international system, it is a product of development. Having in mind the modern accessories of organized chancelleries and permanent missions, some historians have gravely denied its existence in the Middle Ages. But the essence of diplomacy does not lie in the character of its organs or its forms of procedure. Intrinsically it is an appeal to ideas and principles rather than to force, and may assume a great variety of specific embodiments. In the Middle Ages it was, no doubt, simpler in its elements and its instruments, for its aims were more direct and less obstructed than at present; but in no period has it been more resourceful or more fruitful of results. Without it mediaeval history would be almost devoid of permanent human interest. What other series of events in a period of a thousand years is to be compared with the marvellous growth of the Papacy, possessing in itself no material strength, building itself up and acquiring almost universal supremacy by skilfully acting upon the faith, hopes, fears, affections, and ideals of mankind; emancipating itself from Byzantine domination and frustrating the ambitions of the Lombard kings by its alliance with the Franks, reviving the Empire in the West for its own protection, curbing the German emperors by its treaties with the Normans and other powers of Italy, encouraging and then dividing the Italian republics to secure its own supremacy, and balancing and thwarting the forces opposed to its interests by dexterous manipulation until it became the most powerful and widely extended international institution that ever existed? What is to be said of the Italian cities winning their local liberties from the greatest emperors of the Middle Ages by means of their leagues and alliances? And what of the Republic of Venice, in particular, situated between powers of overwhelming magnitude, yet not only maintaining from the beginning its virtual independence but acquiring by its compacts a vast colonial dominion from the spoils of the Eastern Empire?

If these were not great feats of diplomacy, in what age shall we expect to find them? What power has ever been so nearly universal as that of Rome in the days of Innocent III? What modern state, except perhaps the Netherlands, has attained with such slender resources a position to be compared with that of Venice?

The importance of that period both for the international

development of Europe and for the part played in it by diplomacy cannot be overestimated. In it were elaborated and set in motion ideas and influences that have never ceased to affect the destinies of Europe. The rise of the Papacy, the revival of the Empire, its gradual absorption of the barbarian kingdoms, the struggle of the Papacy and the Empire for supremacy, the awakening of civic consciousness as a result of that conflict, and the rise of national monarchies are phenomena which cannot be left out of consideration as preconditions of the genesis of modern states.

But what is even more important to the international development of Europe is the fact that it was in the struggle between the Empire and the Papacy that Italian diplomacy was born, not as a mere technical art, but as an essential function of independent states exposed to the ambitions of coexistent political communities. It was from Italy, and in continuation of Italian policies, that Europe, as a whole, derived those conceptions of the State and those devices for its maintenance that have become classic in European statesmanship.

In the present volume the scene is filled with a group of semi-independent national powers in the process of transformation into modern states. The imperial idea—which, like a recurrent motive in a great orchestral composition, sometimes seems to dominate, then is swallowed up and lost in the general movement, only to reappear after an interval —is no longer as before the constant theme; but, for a time, the chief task is the further destruction of the great feudatories, particularly of those most affecting national consolidation, and the centralization of power in the hands of the national monarchs.

In the earlier period the political history of Europe consisted chiefly in the development and conflict of two opposing policies rooted in different conceptions of the imperial idea; but in that which we are now to traverse the field is occupied by the conflicts of national states, first for coherence and then for expansion. After they become disengaged from the fetters of feudalism, instead of two great antagonists contending for world supremacy, we behold a group of powerful monarchies struggling with one another for primacy. It is in this contest that Italy, designated as their prey, becomes their political teacher. Germany, France, Spain, and finally England all enter the arena of contention more or less under the influence of the imperial idea. Germany desires to recover its ancient preponderance in Italy; France pivots its international activity upon adventures of expansion; Spain, having obtained possession of Naples, aims at controlling the whole peninsula; and England covets the crown of France. But the Papacy and Venice frustrate for a time all foreign schemes to obtain supremacy in Italy; the system of Italian equilibrium becomes a model for Europe; and, as in the earlier period Italy was rescued from subjection to imperial power by diplomatic combinations, so the national monarchies, after aiming at indefinite expansion and striving to outstrip one another by drawing into their service the forces of their allies, finally adjust themselves to a system of balanced and co-ordinate power based upon the principle of territorial sovereignty.

If, in the present volume, the emphasis has been placed upon the transition from the Middle Ages to the modern system rather than upon the Thirty Years' War, which immediately preceded the Peace of Westphalia, it is because it is in this transition that the permanent traditions of Europe really have their origin. It is in the relations of France, Spain, Germany, and England to Italy and in the growth of the Reformation during the rivalry of Charles V and Francis I that were formed the most permanent international traditions of Europe. Italy was the battlefield, but the prize for which the contestants were contending was the primacy of Europe. The Thirty Years' War was, therefore, only the prolongation of a conflict whose strategic lines were drawn a century before it began, and the Peace of Westphalia was only the liquidation of still more ancient conflicts between the imperial and the territorial ideas.

As the efforts to realize the imperial idea gave character to the Middle Ages, so the motives and policies of the national monarchies have created modern Europe. Neither standing armies, nor modern navies, nor the financial systems that render them possible would have their being if these motives and policies had not brought them into existence. If political entities could live apart from rivals and enemies and possessed no instincts of expansion, there would be no occasion for diplomatic policies. In that case political history would be mainly confined to constitutional development; but no state is thus isolated, and in this fact lies the necessity of international relations in which diplomacy becomes a creative agent. Peace and war, defence and aggression, commerce and its protection, and, subsidiary to these, systems of revenue and industry, are all mere elements in the calculations and programme of diplomatic action. Ships are built and manned, frontiers are fortified, and armies are formed and moved in obedience to its theory and practice.

The narrative of brilliant campaigns and heroic military achievements may, indeed, at first glance, seem more attractive than the story of the reasons why battles have been fought; but, as after a storm the fallen trees in the forest, the fragments of wrecks upon the shore, and the general upheaval of nature, though more exciting, are of less abiding human interest than a knowledge of the atmospheric conditions out of which the tempest has been born, so the plans and purposes and policies of nations are intrinsically more important than the march of armies and the carnage of military conflicts. It is the psychological factor in moments of creative action that gives to history its highest instructive value and its most lasting social utility.

It is to history, and not to philosophy, that we must look for the real lessons of human experience. It is easy to theorize upon the swift realization of political ideals, to denounce war, to glorify peace, to propose a European federation, and to demand that all international differences be adjusted in an amicable manner; but armies will not be disbanded, navies will not cease to be built, and fortifications will not be demolished until the historic reasons for their existence have passed away. Those reasons cannot be dismissed until they are understood, and they cannot be understood until they are studied in the concrete setting of the events by which they have been produced. Only upon a somewhat broad background of general history can those events be shown in their full significance. Nor can they be rightly apprehended in the light of a single century, for they are rooted in a distant past.

The task of truthfully narrating the long story of international development is beset with peculiar difficulties. Some of these arise from the magnitude of the undertaking, others from its great complexity. It is only through the labors of a multitude of specialists that any high degree of success can be attained, for the field is too vast for the powers of any single investigator. If this work serves to guide others, and particularly the students of the author's own country, to the rich treasures contained in the works here cited as authorities, it will render a service which may, perhaps, in some degree palliate its own imperfection, and promote the cultivation of an aspect of history which is specially concerned with the progressive substitution of ideas for force in the wide field of international relations.

DAVID JAYNE HILL.

The Hague,
   October 1, 1906.

CONTENTS OF VOLUME II

CHAPTER I. — THE FORMATION OF MODERN STATES

	PAGE
The transition to the Modern State System	1

I. THE ANGLO-FRENCH DIPLOMACY AND THE PAPAL MEDIATION

The relations of France and England	3
Renewal of the conflict	4
Accession of Philip V	5
The Salic Law	6
The question of homage	7
The Anglo-French quarrel and the Papacy	8
The abdication of Edward II	9
Resumption of vassalage to France	10
Philip of Valois made King	11
The mediation of John XXII	12
Edward's quest for an ally	13
Lewis of Bavaria as Emperor	14
Papists and monarchists	15
The policy of Benedict XII	16
The English suspicion of the Pope	17
Edward's system of alliances	18
Edward's appeal to public opinion	19
The decisions of Rense and Frankfort	21
Edward III becomes Imperial Vicar	21
The papal intervention	22
The dynastic question	23
The legal claims of Edward III to the French crown	25
The war between France and England	25

II. THE DISMEMBERMENT OF CHRISTENDOM

The decline of papal influence	27
The ecclesiastical opposition to Edward III	28
The general disenchantment	30
The humiliation of Benedict XII	31

	PAGE
The fate of Lewis of Bavaria	32
The position of Germany under Charles IV	34
Cola di Rienzo	35
The coronation of Charles IV at Rome	36
The relation of Charles IV to his kingdoms	37
The Golden Bull of 1356	38
The Golden Bull and the Papacy	39
Effects of the Golden Bull	40
The unrest in Italy	41
Return of the popes to Rome	42
The Great Schism	42
The anarchy of Christendom	44

III. THE GROWTH OF NATIONAL SENTIMENT

The passing of mediaevalism	45
The rise of the Hanseatic League	46
Decline of the League	48
Difference between mediaeval and modern sovereignty	48
The Scandinavian kingdoms and the Union of Kalmar	49
The Teutonic Order in Prussia	50
The struggle with Poland	51
Dissolution of the Teutonic Order	52
Hungary the bulwark of Europe	53
The accession of Sigismund as King of Hungary	54
The isolation of Sigismund	55
Progress of the Hundred Years' War	56
Efforts to end the schism of the Papacy	57
The schism in the Empire	58
The Council of Pisa	59
Election of Sigismund as Emperor	60
The Council of Constance	60
The results of the Council of Constance	61
The mediatorial offices of Sigismund	63
Sigismund's mission of conciliation	63
The Spanish kingdoms	64
Sigismund's visit to France and England	65
The Truce of Paris	66
Civil strife in France	67
The Treaty of Troyes	68
The resistance of Charles VII	69
The diplomacy of Charles VII	70
The Treaty of Arras	70
Conclusion of the Hundred Years' War	71

IV. The Rehabilitation of the Papacy as an Italian State

	PAGE
The fortunes of the Papacy	72
Restoration of the papal monarchy	74
The struggles of Eugenius IV	75
The diplomacy of Eugenius IV	76
The compacts of Eugenius and the Empire	77
The fall of the Greek Empire	78
Authorities	80

CHAPTER II. — THE DIPLOMACY OF FRENCH EXPANSION

The state of France at the end of the Hundred Years' War . . . 83

I. The Instruction of France in Italian Diplomacy

The need of external alliances	84
The condition of Italy	85
The affairs of Italy become of European importance	87
The intervention of Charles VII	89
René of Anjou in Italy	91
Reoccupation of Genoa by the French	92
Sforza's opposition to France	93
The peril and relief of Genoa	95
The Congress of Mantua	95
The policy of Charles VII and the hostility of the Dauphin	97
Accession of Louis XI	98
The Kingdom and the Papacy	99

II. The Struggle of France with Burgundy

The "League of the Public Weal"	100
The policy of Louis XI in Italy	101
The diplomacy of Louis XI with his vassals	102
Isolation of Charles the Bold in France	103
The changed situation in Italy	104
The interview and Treaty of Péronne	106
Relations of Charles the Bold to Germany	107
Awakening of sentiment against Charles the Bold	109
The preparations of Louis XI	109
The war between France and Burgundy	111
The ambition of Charles the Bold	112
The negotiations at Trier	113
The triumph of Charles the Bold over the Emperor	115
The Emperor's humiliation of Charles the Bold	117

III. The Overthrow of Charles the Bold

	PAGE
The diplomatic situation in 1473	118
The Union of Constance	120
Invasion of France by Edward IV of England	121
The Peace of Picquigny	122
Louis' perfidy to his allies	123
Preparations for the attack on the Swiss	124
Defeat of Charles the Bold at Grandson	125
The ruin of Charles the Bold	127
The spoils of Burgundy	128
The attitude of the Burgundian deputies	129
Marriage of Mary of Burgundy with Maximilian	130
The partition of Burgundy	132
The trials of Maximilian	133

IV. The Efforts for French Preponderance in Italy

Conclusion of peace with Venice	134
The conspiracy of the Pazzi	136
The intervention of Louis XI in Italy	138
The attitude of Sixtus IV	139
The French mission in Italy	140
Negotiations with Sixtus IV	141
The intrigues of the Pope and the Emperor	142
The frustration of the French mission	143
Collapse of the negotiations	145
The isolation of Sixtus IV	146
Dissolution of the Triple Alliance	148
The death of Louis XI	149
The regency of Anne de Beaujeu	150
The use of diplomacy by Louis XI	152
The beginning of permanent missions in Italy	153
The influence of Louis XI on diplomacy	155
The subsequent importance of diplomacy	157
The idea of European equilibrium	158
Authorities	159

CHAPTER III. — THE IMPERIAL ASPIRATIONS OF FRANCE

Character of the *renaissance*	163

I. The Appeals of the Italians to Charles VIII

The mechanism of Italian politics	164
The Italian craving for foreign intervention	165

CONTENTS

	PAGE
The confidence of Italy in France	166
Attitude of the Papacy	167
Fluctuations of the papal policy	167
Election of Rodrigo Borgia as Alexander VI	169
The methods of Alexander VI	170
The personality of Charles VIII	171
The imperial tradition in France	172
The claim of Charles VIII to Naples	173
The projects of Charles VIII	175
The alliance of Charles VIII and Ludovico Sforza	175
Influence of Savonarola	177
Apparent isolation of Ferdinand	177
Relations of Charles VIII to the chief powers of Europe	178
The mission of Perron de Baschi	180
The casting of the die	181

II. THE EXPEDITION OF CHARLES VIII INTO ITALY

Reception of Charles VIII in Italy	182
Charles VIII at Florence	184
The prestige of Alexander VI	185
The Pope's negotiations with the Turks	187
Preliminaries to entering Rome	188
Entrance of Charles VIII into Rome	190
The demands of Charles VIII	191
The terms of settlement	193
Ratification of the treaty and act of obedience	195
Departure of Charles VIII from Rome	196
The occupation of Naples	197
The League of Venice	199
The deception of De Commines	201
Negotiations of Charles VIII to secure his return	203
Departure of Charles VIII from Naples	205
The retreat to France and loss of Naples	206

III. THE EXPLOITS OF LOUIS XII IN ITALY

The death of Charles VIII and accession of Louis XII	208
The rise of Modern Europe	209
The emergence of European problems	210
The state of Italy at the end of the fifteenth century	212
The Orléans claims to Milan	213
The search of Louis XII for allies	214
The diplomatic struggle of Ludovico Sforza	215

xvi CONTENTS

	PAGE
The diplomatic activity of Louis XII	216
The mission of Niccolò Alemanni in Italy	218
The *rapprochement* of France and Venice	219
Conclusion of the Franco-Venetian alliance	220
The transaction between Louis XII and the Pope	221
Ludovico Sforza's negotiations with Alexander VI	223
The conquest of Milan	224
The isolation of the Emperor	226
The diplomacy of Borgia	227
The conquest of Naples	229
Mediatorial policy of Cardinal d'Amboise	230
The loss of French prestige	232
Machiavelli's criticism of French diplomacy	233
Authorities	235

CHAPTER IV. — THE STRUGGLE FOR SUPREMACY IN ITALY

The destruction of Italian equilibrium 238

I. NEGOTIATIONS OF THE GREAT POWERS REGARDING ITALY

The policy and methods of the Borgia	239
The end of Alexander VI	241
The rivalry for the Papacy	243
The accession and policy of Julius II	245
Invasion of Romagna by Venice	246
Attitude of Julius II	247
The policy of Cardinal d'Amboise	248
The diplomacy of Julius II	250
The treaties of Blois	251
Motives and reception of the treaties of Blois	252
The progress of events in Italy	253
Temporary *rapprochement* of the Pope and Venice	254
The embarrassment of Julius II	255
The conflict over the government of Castile	256
The alliance of France with Ferdinand the Catholic	258
Dissolution of the treaties of Blois	259
Betrothal of Claude to Francis of Angoulême	260
Results of the new betrothal	262
Death of the Archduke Philip	263
The plans of Ximenes	264
Ximenes' rule in Castile	266

II. THE LEAGUE OF CAMBRAY

	PAGE
The decline of Venetian commerce	267
Project of a Suez canal	268
The growing prestige of Julius II	269
Relations of Julius II to France and Spain	270
The welcome of Julius II at Rome	271
The secret conference at Savona	271
Negotiations of the Pope with Maximilian	273
The attack of the Emperor upon Venice	274
Conclusion of the League of Cambray	275
The reserve of Julius II	277
The war of the League with Venice	279
Negotiations of the Venetians with the Pope and the Emperor	279
The appeal to England	280
The intervention of Henry VIII	283
Abandonment of the League by Julius II	284
Attempts to influence the Empire, and death of Cardinal d'Amboise	285
Rupture of the Pope with France	287
The plans and defeat of Julius II	288
Project of a league against the French	290
Maximilian's aspiration to the Papacy	290
Formation of the "Holy League"	291
The triumph and death of Julius II	292

III. THE EFFECT ON EUROPE OF THE CONTEST FOR ITALY

The corruption of international morals	294
Moral degeneration of the Papacy	295
Misfortunes of Louis XII	296
The pacific policy of Wolsey	297
The last days of Louis XII	298
The scheme of Ferdinand the Catholic	299
Accession of Francis I	300
Renewal of the alliance with Venice	301
The campaign of Marignano	302
Negotiations of Leo X and Francis I	303
The new coalition against Francis I	304
The Treaty of Noyon	305
The project of universal peace	306
The triumph of Wolsey	307
The institution of permanent embassies in Europe	308
The changed conception of the State	310

xviii   CONTENTS
                                                              PAGE
The political philosophy of Machiavelli 311
The maxims of Machiavelli 313
Machiavelli's purpose 315
Machiavelli's character and influence 315
Authorities 317

CHAPTER V. — THE ASCENDENCY OF THE HOUSE OF HAPSBURG

The revival of imperial ambition 321

I. THE RIVALRY FOR THE EMPIRE

The designs of Maximilian 323
The activity of Francis I 325
The efforts of the Hapsburgs 327
The Diet of 1518 328
Relations to Rome and attitude of the Pope 330
The second electoral campaign of Francis I 332
The vote of Bohemia 334
The candidacy of Henry VIII 335
The mission of Richard Pace 337
The hopes of Pace for Henry VIII 338
A bold financial venture 339
The rôle of the Fuggers 341
Preliminaries to the election 342
The electoral oath 343
The election 344
The electoral capitulation 345
The official notification 346
The ceremonies of installation 347

II. THE CONFLICT OF CHARLES V AND FRANCIS I

The transformation of the imperial idea 349
The task of Wolsey 350
Wolsey's plans for a meeting of the sovereigns 351
The visit of Charles V to England 352
"The Field of Cloth of Gold" 352
The meeting of Henry VIII and Charles V at Calais . . . 353
The attitude of Leo X 354
The Diet of Worms 355
Results of the Diet 357
The policy of Gattinara 358

CONTENTS

	PAGE
The pressure of Wolsey on Francis I	359
Obstructions to Wolsey's mediation	360
The Conference of Calais	362
Wolsey's visit to the Emperor at Bruges	364
The wreck of Wolsey's policy	365
The reasons for Wolsey's failure	366
Wolsey's hopes and disappointment	368
The masking of Wolsey's policy	369
The Anglo-Imperial alliance of 1522	370
The isolation and peril of France	370
The invasion of France	372
The crisis in the imperial alliances	372
The battle of Pavia and capture of Francis I	374

III. THE DIPLOMACY OF FRENCH REHABILITATION

Effect of the battle of Pavia	374
The courage of Louise of Savoy	375
The proposals of England to Charles V	376
The attitude of Charles V toward Henry VIII	377
The disillusionment of Henry VIII	378
The renewal of Wolsey's pacific policy	379
Reply of Charles V to Wolsey's proposals	380
Negotiations of the Emperor with Francis I	381
The diplomacy of Louise of Savoy	383
Relation of the English to the transaction of Charles V with Francis I	384
The captivity of Francis I	385
The Treaty of Madrid	386
The deliverance of Francis I	388
The fruits of the Regent's diplomacy	389
The attitude of the Emperor's former allies	390
Revelation of the King's intentions	391
The advice and proposals of Wolsey	393
Revival of Wolsey's mediatorial policy	394
The League of Cognac	395
The inefficiency of the League of Cognac	396
The degeneration of international morals	397
The matrimonial project of Henry VIII and the Treaty of Westminster	398
The sack of Rome and capture of Clement VII	401
Authorities	402

CHAPTER VI.— THE INTERNATIONAL INFLUENCE OF THE REFORMATION

	PAGE
Effects of the sack of Rome upon Europe	405

I. THE STRUGGLE OF CHARLES V FOR RELIGIOUS UNITY

The Emperor's valuation of religious unity	406
The period of hesitation in the policy of Charles V	408
The complications in Bohemia and Hungary	409
The diplomatic situation in the East	410
The threefold programme of Charles V	411
Negotiations of Charles V and Henry VIII with Clement VII	412
The diplomatic duel over the divorce	414
Nature of the English separation	416
The Peace of Cambray	417
The results of the Peace of Cambray	418
The coming of Charles V to Italy	419
The progress of Charles V in Italy	420
Coronation of Charles V at Bologna	421
The condition and problems of Germany	422
Nature of the reform	423
The development of Lutheranism	424
The policy of the Emperor at Augsburg	426
Formation of the League of Schmalkalden	427
The international aspects of the Protestant movement	428
The embarrassment of the Emperor's plans in Germany	430
The Emperor's appeal to Francis I	431
The failure of the Emperor's plans in Germany	432

II. THE LIMITATION OF THE HAPSBURG POWER

Relations of Clement VII to France	434
Expedition of Charles V against Tunis	434
Negotiations of Francis I with the Sultan and the Protestants	435
The relative strength of Charles V and Francis I	437
Attempt of Charles V to satisfy Francis I	438
The disappearance of religious solidarity	439
The diplomatic methods of Francis I	440
The aggression of Francis I upon Savoy	441
A diplomatic colloquy with Charles V	442

CONTENTS

	PAGE
The Emperor's arraignment of Francis I at Rome	443
Alternatives proposed by Charles V	444
The Emperor's explanation of his attitude	446
Invasion of France and mediation of Paul III	447
The illusory reconciliation of the two monarchs	448
The secret diplomacy of France	449
Entente of Francis I with the Sultan	450
Aims of the French diplomacy	451
The changed attitude of England	452
Success of the French diplomacy in the East	453
The Hungarian question	455
The project of a Hapsburg-Valois middle state	456
The murder of the French ambassador	456
The war of Francis I against the Emperor	457
Isolation of Francis I and invasion of France	458
The Peace of Crépy	460

III. THE RISE OF INDEPENDENT PROTESTANT STATES

Nature of the Protestant movement	460
Attitude of the German princes toward peace	461
Defensive measures of the Protestant princes	463
Opening of the Council of Trent	464
The Diet of Regensburg, 1546	466
The Emperor's diplomacy at Regensburg	467
War against the League of Schmalkalden	467
Death of Henry VIII and Francis I, and position of Charles V	468
The Interim	469
Ambition of Charles V for Philip and its failure	470
The growing hostility to Charles V	470
Attitude of Henry II of France	471
Diplomatic activity of Henry II	472
The defencelessness and peril of Charles V	473
Relation of Protestantism to the Emperor's misfortunes	474
The transaction of Passau	475
The disillusionment of Charles V	477
Marriage of Philip of Spain and Mary of England	478
The Peace of Augsburg	479
The abdications of Charles V	480
Prospects and purposes of Philip II	482
Death of Mary of England and accession of Elizabeth	483
The Peace of Cateau-Cambrésis	483
Authorities	486

CHAPTER VII. — THE DEVELOPMENT OF A SOVEREIGN STATE SYSTEM

	PAGE
The moral disintegration of Europe	489

I. THE CONCEPTION OF THE STATE AS SOVEREIGN

The non-existence of public law in Europe	491
Reasons for its non-existence	491
The gradual recognition of territorial sovereignty	492
The historic basis of the jurists	493
The Counter-Reformation and the Protestant resistance	494
The contest of Elizabeth and Philip II	495
The relations of England and Scotland	496
The international effect of the religious conflict	498
The contrasted qualities of Philip II and Elizabeth of England	499
The dynastic question in England	500
William the "Silent"	502
The revolt of the Netherlands	503
The statesmanship of the Prince of Orange	504
The triumph of Philip II in the Netherlands	505
Attitude of Philip II toward England	506
The conspiracies in England	508
The Protestant reaction	508
The alliance of France and England	509
The general paralysis of international activity	510
The new theories of the State	511
Theories of royal power	512
Bodin's conception of sovereignty	513
Significance of the principle of sovereignty	514
Case of the Bishop of Ross	515
Nature of a sovereign state	516
The State as a moral entity	517
The conception of the State as the basis of Elizabeth's policy	518

II. THE GENESIS OF INTERNATIONAL JURISPRUDENCE

The scheme of Don John of Austria	519
The Pacification of Ghent	520
The civic spirit in the Netherlands	522
Negotiations of William the Silent for foreign aid	523
The embarrassments of the Prince of Orange	524
William the Silent as a representative of the idea of the State	525
The right of sovereignty based on occupation	525

CONTENTS

	PAGE
The annexation of Portugal to Spain and the preponderance of Philip II	527
Elizabeth's policy of inaction	527
Formation of the "League" and Elizabeth's loss of the French alliance	529
The expulsion of Mendoza	529
Philip II assumes leadership against Elizabeth	530
Elizabeth's protectorate of the Netherlands	532
The Babington Plot	533
Discovery of the plot and execution of Mary Stuart	535
The Protestant concert against Philip II	536
The "Invincible Armada"	537
The aspiration of Philip II to the crown of France	538
Negotiations of the "League" with Philip II	539
The conversion of Henry IV	540
Negotiations of Philip II with the States General of France	541
The reconciliation of Henry IV with the Pope	542
The Peace of Vervins	543
The failure and death of Philip II	545
The state of Europe at the end of the sixteenth century	546
The foreign policy of Henry IV	547
The "Great Design"	550
The work of the jurists	551
The idea of a society of states	553

III. THE DISTURBANCE OF EQUILIBRIUM IN GERMANY

The state of Germany before the Thirty Years' War	554
Instability of the Peace of Augsburg	556
Reopening of the struggle	557
The Bohemian revolution	558
The international bearings of the revolution	559
The subjection of Bohemia and expulsion of Frederick V	560
The question of the Palatinate	562
The attitude of France toward the German situation	563
The ambiguous position of England	565
England's appeal to the Scandinavian powers	566
The attitude of Denmark and Sweden	567
The Danish intervention	568

IV. THE SIGNIFICANCE OF THE THIRTY YEARS' WAR FOR EUROPE

The work of Grotius on War and Peace	569
The nature of the system of Grotius	571

xxiv   CONTENTS
                                                                    PAGE
The influence of Grotius   572
The schemes of Wallenstein and the project of Urban VIII . .   574
The Edict of Restitution   576
The policy of Richelieu   577
The Diet of Regensburg of 1630   578
The negotiations of France with Sweden and the invasion of
    Germany   579
The diplomacy of Richelieu regarding Mantua   580
The plans of Gustavus Adolphus in Germany   582
The reception of Gustavus Adolphus in Germany   583
Victories and death of Gustavus Adolphus   584
Results of the death of Gustavus Adolphus   585
Attitude of France toward Protestantism   586
The dictatorship of Wallenstein   587
The Peace of Prague   588
The open intervention of France   588
The work of Richelieu for France   590
Preliminaries to a general peace   590
Arrangements for the Congress of Westphalia   592
Ceremonial impediments to negotiation   594
Organization of the Congress   596
Method of procedure   597
The political settlement   599
The religious settlement   602
Effect of the Congress upon Europe   603
Authorities   607

TABLES

I. A List of Popes and Emperors from 1313 to 1648, and of
     Ottoman Sultans from 1453 to 1648   612

II. Kings of France, England, and Scotland from 1313 to 1648   616

III. Rulers of the Spanish Monarchies and Portugal from 1313
     to 1648   618

IV. Rulers of the Scandinavian Kingdoms, Poland, and Hun-
     gary from 1313 to 1648   621

V. A Chronological List of Treaties and other Public Acts,
     from 1316 to 1648   624

INDEX   637

MAPS AT END OF VOLUME

I. Showing the Possessions of France and England in the Hundred Years' War.
II. Showing the Formation of Modern States.
III. Italy in the Sixteenth Century.
IV. Showing the Territorial Changes effected by the Peace of Westphalia.

CHAPTER I

THE FORMATION OF MODERN STATES

THE fruitless enterprise of the Emperor Henry VII and his tragic death on August 24, 1313, revealed the futility of the long struggle for universal empire which had agitated Europe since the coronation of Charles the Great. From its captivity at Avignon, the Papacy, which had become almost an appanage of the French monarchy, was able to strike a fatal blow to imperial hopes in Italy; but its earlier pretensions, if undiminished in theory, were far removed from realization in the sphere of practice.

The transition to the Modern State System

While these institutions, the Empire and the Papacy, which had for centuries given to Europe a sense of solidarity, were gradually losing their universal character, the national monarchies which had come into being in the thirteenth century had not yet acquired the attributes of modern states. Feudalism had begun to yield to the royal supremacy; but it not only continued to exist, it lent many of its qualities to the royal administration. Arbitrary force, as exercised by the local magnates, continued to be an element of government; and kings had still to reckon with their powerful vassals, whose union was sometimes able to defeat their will. As yet, the nations possessed only a vague sense of their rights, their limits, and their unity; and a long course of development was still necessary to create in them that intense national consciousness which characterizes the modern state.

An analysis of the sense of nationality as felt by modern nations discloses the fact that neither ethnical nor territorial considerations are the most fundamental elements of this sentiment. The conditions under which European peoples existed at the beginning of the fourteenth century did not admit of the formation of states founded exclusively upon community of race, language, or other personal affinities; nor were "natural limits" possible as lines of political demarcation. Modern states were founded primarily upon dynastic interests, around which have grown up sentiments of community among the local populations, who by long association and common action have gradually come to feel their essential oneness. No great European state possesses a population composed of an unmixed race. All have been formed by historical circumstances; among which the chief has always been the dynastic interest which the people, by choice or compulsion, have found it expedient to serve.

In the evolution of modern states two factors have proved of high importance: first, improved means of communication by which all parts of each political whole could be made to feel their community of interests; and, second, better instruments of defence, by which national rights could be asserted against foreign foes and private force compelled to respect public authority.

Both of these agencies came into action at about the same time. The use of paper early in the fourteenth century, the invention of printing by movable types in the middle of the fifteenth, — in connection with the Revival of Learning promoted by the fall of Constantinople and the diffusion of Byzantine scholarship over Western Europe, — and the establishment of royal postal services were to constitute long steps of progress toward that community of ideas and creation of public opinion upon which the modern state is founded.

But improvement in the arts of warfare was not less significant for human progress. The use of gunpowder deprived the mediaeval warrior of his physical superiority and raised the citizen-soldier to a plane of advantage. The use of artillery early in the fourteenth century placed a powerful and exclusive weapon in the hands of public authority, and in the next century the arming of organized troops with muskets rendered the prohibition of private war thenceforth effective. Finally, the organization of standing armies in the middle of the fifteenth century gave to war a public character that ultimately wrote upon the map of Europe definite national frontiers, consecrated by solemn treaties.

Thus, by means of ideas on the one hand, and public enforcement of the sovereign will on the other, the private relations of the feudal order were gradually swept away, modern states were brought into being, and organized diplomacy became essential to the protection of their rights.

The particular development of the several states of Europe does not concern us here, but the action of certain causes of an international character is of the highest importance to the comprehension of the political system of Europe as a whole. Among these the dynastic pretensions of France and England, the papal mediation in the interest of France, the resulting dismemberment of Christendom, the general growth of national sentiment, and the efforts of the Papacy to rehabilitate itself as an Italian state are influences of such far-reaching consequence that their place in the complicated process of transition from mediaeval to modern political conditions is essential to a comprehension of its nature. A brief description of that process will engage our attention in the present chapter.

I. THE ANGLO-FRENCH DIPLOMACY AND THE PAPAL MEDIATION

The central international incident of the first half of the fourteenth century in Europe was the controversy between France and England over the possession of Guyenne.[1] The military feebleness of both powers gave to the contest a distinctly diplomatic character, and the efforts of each contestant to overreach the other drew into the vortex of the quarrel nearly all the powers of Western Europe. The Empire and the Papacy, which in the Middle Ages had occupied the centre of the stage in the diplomatic drama, were now to

---

[1] The nature of this controversy has been explained in Chapter VIII of the first volume of this work.

play subsidiary parts as the aids and instruments of the chief contestants. The rôle of the Empire, rendered powerless by its old antagonist, and of the Papacy, vainly endeavoring to preside over the rising monarchies and to become the universal mediator and arbiter of Europe, only served to render conspicuous the expiring influence of mediaeval conceptions and the growing independence of the national states.

The Treaty of Paris of May 20, 1303, by which Philip IV of France and Edward I of England had temporarily settled their contentions in order to face the conflict with Boniface VIII, provided for the restoration to his English vassal of all that the King of France had taken from him in Guyenne, and the King of England was to do homage to his suzerain under the new title of "Duke of Aquitaine and Peer of France." When, in September, 1304, the day appointed for the new investiture arrived, an illness, — no doubt political, — prevented Edward I from appearing in Amiens, and his son Edward, Prince of Wales, was sent instead. Thus, the situation was in all respects the same as that created by the Treaty of 1259, when Henry III of England became the vassal of Louis IX of France.

Renewal of the conflict

The death of Edward I, on July 7, 1307, and the accession of Edward II to the throne of England would probably have reopened the question at that time, but for the marriage of the young king in 1308 with Isabelle, daughter of Philip IV of France.

Engrossed in his war with Scotland, Edward II was obliged to submit to the systematic encroachments of the French crown upon the fiefs of Guyenne operated under the obscure provisions of the Treaty of 1259. "Do you obey the English or the French?" was the question constantly asked of the inhabitants of Aquitaine by the royal bailiffs. If the response was "the English," the unfortunate vassal was haled before the royal tribunal to answer for his disloyalty. In 1310, the arrests and confiscations reached a point where the King of England was implored to intervene.

On April 27, 1311, the commissioners of the two kings met at Périgueux, furnished with all the acts, charters, and treaties issued since the Treaty of 1259, in the hope of arranging a new understanding; but all was in vain. The conditions continued for years essentially unchanged, for Philip IV and his successor Louis X had adopted the policy of recurrent encroachment, and Edward II was involved in domestic difficulties which prevented the protection of his rights.

So long as the conditions imposed by the Treaty of 1259 were in force, the King of France was in possession of a cunningly devised instrument of expropriation by which the King of England could be gradually divested of his estates. The problem was, therefore, how to escape its provisions; and that problem became the crux of English diplomacy for a hundred and fifty years.

The death of Louis X, on June 5, 1316, presented an opportunity extremely favorable to the interests of the King of England; for, at that time, there was neither a pope, nor a recognized emperor, nor a king of France. A strong manifesto on the part of Edward II might, perhaps, have enabled him to intimidate the regency into making a settlement; but he had just suffered defeat at the hands of the Scots at Bannockburn, and was not in a position to undertake a foreign war.

For the first time in its long history, the House of Capet had failed of a male heir in the direct line of succession; the only child of Louis X, at the time of his death, being Jeanne, heiress of Navarre. A new question was thus presented regarding the royal succession, namely, whether France would accept a queen. How far the possibility of the eventual inheritance of the French crown by the kings of England may have entered into the secret councils of the French nobles we have no means of knowing; but, it is clear that, if the principle of inheritance by a woman had been admitted, the rights of Isabelle, wife of Edward II, could not later have been denied.

At the time of the death of Louis X, his widow, Clemence, was expecting the birth of an infant. Until this event occurred the succession remained an open question, and Philip, eldest brother of Louis X, was named as regent. In expectation of the birth, the maternal uncles of Jeanne claimed that, if the child should be a girl, Jeanne's rights must be respected. An agreement was, therefore, signed, to the effect that, if the child proved to be a boy, he should inherit the crown of France; but, in any case, Jeanne's interests in Navarre, Champagne, and Brie were to be secured.

In November, 1316, a son was born to the widow of Louis X, but the child, — whose name figures in the list of French kings as John I, — lived only a few days. In the meantime, Philip had become well established in the regency and had made a favorable impression. The Duke of Burgundy, who had pressed the claims of Jeanne, was reconciled by a marriage with Philip's daughter and a rich dower; and the Regent was chosen king as Philip V.

The Salic Law At a later time, the reason for preferring Philip V to Jeanne of Navarre was sought in a passage in the ancient law of the Salian Franks which reads, "Of Salic land no portion of the inheritance shall come to a woman; but the whole inheritance of the land shall come to the male sex." The exclusion of women from the throne of France has, therefore, been commonly attributed to the so-called "Salic Law."[1] But, in the choice of Philip V, and afterward of Charles IV — brothers of Louis X — as kings of France, no such legal principle was invoked. The choice of Philip V and of his two immediate successors was purely political, and the question of the rights of women to inherit and transmit the crown of France was never juridical in the proper sense. Had it been made so, reasons for the exclusion of women might have been found with equal ease in the "Lex Voconia" of the Romans, which excluded daugh-

---

[1] See Henderson, *Select Documents*, pp. 176, 189, for an English translation of the Salic Law.

ters from the more important forms of inheritance; or in certain parts of the "Lex Feudorum," which excluded females from holding military fiefs. But, in truth, the legend of the "Lex Salica" is the creation of a later period, when jurists, engaged in argument, were in search of legal authority in support of an established custom.[1]

It was the conflict with England that led to questions of legality regarding the inheritance of the crown of France; but before the time for that discussion had arrived, another dispute had embittered the relations of the French and English monarchs.

The question of homage

Vassalage to the King of France, so long as it endured, never ceased to be a humiliation to the English kings, while the form of homage demanded by the King of France was especially obnoxious. Philip V explained the Treaty of 1303 as binding the King of England to "*hommage lige*," which involved the obligation of personal service against all the enemies of the suzerain, accepted by the vassal with the ceremony of kneeling, bareheaded, without gloves, without a sword, without spurs, and with his hands placed in those of his lord as a sign of complete subjection. The King of England, on the contrary, repudiating such subservience, contended that the only duty assumed by him was that of "*hommage simple*," by which he was only bound to recognize that he possessed fiefs pertaining to the crown of France.

Pressed by the exigencies of the situation in England, on June 29, 1320, Edward II reluctantly complied with the demands of Philip V and rendered homage to him at Amiens. But, upon the death of Philip V, in 1322, Edward raised technical objections to the summons which cited him to appear and repeat his homage to the new king, Philip's

---

[1] See Déprez, *Les préliminaires*, pp. 32, 33; Viollet, *Histoire des institutions politiques et administratives de la France*, II, pp. 55, 57; and Monod, *La légende de la loi salique et la succession au trône de France* in the Revue Critique d'Histoire et de Littérature, 26 December, 1892.

brother, Charles IV. His long delay provoked a new confiscation of his estates in Guyenne; but, through the influence of his Queen, Isabelle, sister of Charles IV, in 1325 a new convention was signed and ratified.

At this juncture, Queen Isabelle, proceeding to her brother's court in France, arranged with Charles IV the substitution of homage by the Prince of Wales in place of homage by the King, paying for the privilege a bonus of sixty thousand livres. Edward II was induced to accept the arrangement and to transfer his rights to the French fiefs to his young son, the Prince of Wales. On September 10, 1325, young Edward was, therefore, sent to France to receive the fiefs and do homage to his uncle.

In what manner the King of England was expected to profit from this arrangement does not appear; for he had simply transferred his rights to the Prince of Wales, for whom all the former embarrassments were in reserve. The advantage which France was to derive from this substitution, however, soon became evident; for the scheme was part of a conspiracy against Edward II, of which he appears to have entertained no suspicion.

The Anglo-French quarrel and the Papacy

The affair was further complicated by the part taken in it by the Pope. In 1314, Clement V had died at Avignon, and a new struggle had supervened between the French and Italian cardinals. Before the election of a new pope, the Italians had demanded that the next pontiff should return to Rome; for the authority of the Holy See, resting on the succession to St. Peter as Bishop of Rome, was imperilled by the choice of a foreigner residing permanently in a foreign land. The French cardinals, on the other hand, pleading the universal character of the Holy See and the disturbed state of Italy, refused to abandon Avignon. After more than two years of heated controversy, the French party triumphed; and, on August 7, 1316, a French prelate, Jacques d'Euse, was chosen pope, under the name of John XXII.

A man of high spirit and inflexible will, the new pope was soon found to be a disciple of the school of Boniface VIII, but inclined to use the papal influence to build up the political interests of France.

A letter written by Edward II to the papal legate, the Bishop of Orange, discloses the hand of John XXII in the transfer of the Duchy of Guyenne to the Prince of Wales, and proves his authorship of the entire programme weakly adopted by the King of England.[1] The confiding king, not suspecting the treason of which he was to be made the victim, had implicitly followed the directions of the Pope, whose plan embraced the sending of Queen Isabelle to France with the young prince, then only thirteen years of age; the arrangement of a truce, during which the King of France could take possession of Guyenne; and, finally, the substitution of the prince for Edward II. The ultimate purpose of the scheme never dawned upon the King of England until, after receiving the homage of his new vassal, Charles IV restored to him only a part of the fiefs in question and retained the others.

Thus, by the influence of the Papacy and court factions, the foreign policy of England was made to serve the interests of France. But a still deeper conspiracy was soon to be revealed. Painfully chagrined by the ambush into which he had fallen, Edward II was still unaware of the domestic treason that encompassed him, until Queen Isabelle, having accomplished her immediate purpose, refused to return to England. To add to her rebellion, young Edward, in defiance of his father's will, was detained in France. Wishing to undo as far as possible the mistake he had committed, the King replied by assuming the title of governor and administrator of his son's possessions, at the same time declaring war against Charles IV for the detention of his wife and son and the confiscation of Guyenne.[2]

---

[1] Letter of Edward II dated October 15, 1325. See Rymer, *Foedera*, II, Part II, p. 144.

[2] On September 10, 1326, Edward II ordered the arrest of all Frenchmen found in England. See Rymer, *Foedera*, II, Part II, p. 166.

Relying on the support of the dissatisfied English nobles and the unpopularity of the King and his favorites, Queen Isabelle returned to England to aid in the dethronement of Edward II and the accession of her son. Frightened by the depth of the conspiracy against him, the King fled to Wales, but was soon captured. In January, 1327, a parliament was assembled, and — being forced to confess himself no longer worthy of the crown — on January 20 he was deposed, and soon afterward was assassinated.

When this *coup d'état* had been accomplished, young Edward, now declared king under the regency of his mother, was permitted to retain as a vassal his remaining rights in Guyenne; and a new treaty, mediated by the papal legates, was signed at Paris, on March 31, 1327, in which the King of England agreed to pay a war indemnity of fifty thousand marks, while the King of France restored the *status quo ante* and proclaimed an amnesty.[1]

Thus, the vassal returned once more to his servitude, and even paid a price for the privilege; for the Treaty of 1327 simply renewed the entanglements of that of 1259, from which there seemed to be no egress.

Once again the web of feudal devices woven by the deft hand of St. Louis was spread over Guyenne by the equally deft hands of the French jurists and the papal legates; but, with the attainment of manhood, Edward III was not only to become aware of the inextricable nature of his position as a vassal, but of the guilty relations of his mother and her paramour, Mortimer, — who after his father's death ruled the kingdom during Edward's minority, — and to inflict upon him a tragic punishment. In the meantime, other events were, however, to complicate still further the compromised relations of France and England, by which the child who had played so conspicuous a rôle in the schemes of his French mother was destined, in the name of rights inherited from her, to end the long humiliation of the English kings with

---

[1] See Rymer, *Foedera*, II, Part II, p. 185.

the attempt to sweep aside the network of feudal entanglements that encompassed him, and claim for himself the crown of France.

The death of Charles IV, on February 1, 1328, reopened the question of succession to the throne of France in nearly the same form as in 1316; for a daughter, Marie, was his only living child. A short-lived infant, born five months after the King's death, proved also to be a girl. The nearest male relative of Charles IV was, therefore, Edward III, King of England. A new question was then presented: Can a woman transmit hereditary rights which she may not herself exercise?

The English envoys at Paris answered in the affirmative, and maintained that Edward III, grandson of Philip IV and nephew of Charles IV, was entitled to the throne.

On April 1, 1328, the peers of France, passing over the claims of Edward III, chose and crowned as king a cousin-german of Charles IV, Philip, Count of Valois. The choice was natural; for, setting aside the doubtful question of inheritance through his mother, under Edward III France would have become a mere appanage of England, while Philip VI was in every sense an exclusively national king.

Although the English at first affected to consider Philip VI a usurper, and their ambassadors duly protested against his assumption of the crown, there was at the time no alternative to submission except war; and for war the King of England was not yet prepared. It was only after long provocation, and as a necessary stroke of politics, that Edward III finally decided to assume the title "King of France."

Determined to follow out the traditional policy with reference to Guyenne, Philip VI, soon after his coronation, despatched envoys to summon Edward III to appear and do homage to him as suzerain. It was painful for "the son of a king to do homage to the son of a count"; but the threat of confiscation brought the young king to Amiens, where, on June 6, 1329, in the choir of the cathedral, the ceremony was observed; but not in the form of "*hommage lige.*"

CHAP. I
A. D.
1313–1453

Philip of Valois made King

CHAP. I
A. D.
1313–1453

The mediation of John XXII

In 1330, after many futile attempts to come to an agreement concerning the form of homage, with which Philip VI was not content, knowing France to be more powerful than England, — then fully preoccupied with its troubles with Scotland, — Edward III appealed to the Pope to intervene in his behalf. John XXII, eager to become the arbiter of Europe and also to restore good relations with England, cheerfully assumed the task; but made it a condition that Edward III should repair his delinquencies to the Holy See by resuming the payment of an annual tribute to the Papacy.

It was his war with Scotland and the alliance of France with the Scotch that paralyzed the arm of Edward III, both in the assertion of his claims to the French crown and the defence of his rights in Aquitaine. For him, therefore, peace with Philip VI was, for the time, to be sought at any price; and he gladly accepted the Pope's conditions.

A temporary *entente* between France and England was rendered more feasible by the ambition of Philip VI to lead a crusade to the Holy Land, and John XXII endeavored to employ this imaginary expedition as the basis of a reconciliation. But the papal mediation in no respect advanced the final solution of the problem; for, although Edward III was willing to join in the crusade, it was only on condition that his rights in Guyenne were respected. Philip VI, on the other hand, not only showed no intention to alter his policy toward his vassal, but adhered to his alliance with the Scotch, who were struggling to throw off the suzerainty of England.

In April, 1334, it was proclaimed at Paris that peace between France and England had been signed; but the English ambassadors were surprised to learn that peace with Scotland — which had not been mentioned in the negotiations — was an essential condition of the French king's signature. "Never," Philip VI is reported to have said to the indignant ambassadors upon their departure, "never will Christendom know peace until the King of France is recognized in England as judge and emperor for the kingdoms of France, England, and Scotland."[1]

Perceiving that Philip VI was determined to confiscate his lands in France, and that the Pope was more interested in maintaining his own influence than in ending the controversy, Edward III was compelled either to abandon his rights, or to form a system of alliances whereby he could restrain the action of his suzerain.

Edward's quest for an ally

The most available ally was the Emperor, Lewis of Bavaria, who was at this time anxious to strengthen his own position in his bitter conflict with the Papacy.

After the death of Henry VII, Robert of Naples, determined if possible to prevent the restoration of the Empire in Italy, had violently attacked the doctrine of Dante, pronounced the kings of Germany the natural enemies of Italy, declared the Empire to be the representative of brute force and oppression, and protested against further recognition of it by the Papacy.

The House of Luxemburg had hoped to continue its power by the election of John of Bohemia to the imperial office; but, finding itself unable to accomplish that purpose, had combined with the House of Wittelsbach to prevent the election of a Hapsburg by choosing Lewis of Bavaria. On October 20, 1314, five of the seven electors had assembled at Frankfort and proclaimed Lewis IV "King of the Romans." At the same time, the other two electors, the Archbishop of Köln and the Count Palatine of the Rhine, had met on the other side of the river and named Frederick of Austria. A bitter war had ensued, in which John XXII, — really favoring the candidature of the French king, and, therefore, opposing both contestants, — had named Robert of Naples Imperial Vicar in Italy; thereby assuming the papal right to declare a vacancy and administer the Empire.

Thus, a triangular quarrel had been provoked by which

---

[1] Quoted by Déprez, *Les préliminaires*, p. 97, with the comment, "Cette anecdote est sujette à caution."

Germany was rent with civil war and a rupture with the Papacy produced. The battle of Mühldorf, on September 28, 1322, had resulted in the capture of Frederick by Lewis and the subsequent reconciliation of the two rivals; but the success of the victor in rendering himself undisputed master in Germany only served to redouble the zeal of John XXII, who feared a similar success in Italy. Having appointed Castruccio Castracani Imperial Vicar south of the Alps, by an alliance with the Visconti of Milan, who with their friends held a great part of Lombardy in their power, Lewis of Bavaria had seemed on the point of effecting a Ghibelline restoration in Italy, when John XXII, dreading such a revival of imperial power, in 1323 had summoned Lewis to appear before him at Avignon and submit to his decision.

Lewis had refused to comply, excommunication had been pronounced against him, and open war had been declared. In 1327, he had received the iron crown at Milan and formed an alliance with King Frederick of Sicily to oppose Robert of Naples. On January 17, 1328, he had been crowned at Rome by four syndics representing the people, and consecrated by two excommunicated bishops. The civil character of the ceremony had been further celebrated by holding the coronation banquet in the Capitol.

Thus installed as Emperor, he had convoked a parliament in the square before St. Peter's Church at Rome, and caused to be read three edicts, in which it was decreed, first, that all who were convicted of heresy or *lèse-majesté* should be cited for judgment; second, that no future notarial act should be recognized as valid unless dated from the time of his accession; and, third, that all rebels against imperial authority should be severely punished.

It having then been decided that John XXII was a heretic, before another parliament, assembled on April 18, on a great platform erected in front of St. Peter's Church, the Emperor, — wearing the crown, holding a sphere in his left hand and the sceptre in his right, — in the midst of a multitude of magistrates and officers, had caused a Franciscan monk to ask if any one present would defend John XXII. When all was silent, a German abbot had pronounced a discourse, concluding with the imperial condemnation and deposition of the Pope as a heretic and anti-Christ.

After John XXII had been burned in effigy by the Roman populace, a Franciscan monk had been set up as an antipope, under the title of Nicholas V; but, Christendom having failed to ratify this revolution, a turn in the tide of popular feeling at Rome had soon occurred, and the newly chosen pontiff, expelled from the city together with the imperial partisans, had been made to confess his faults and do penance as a prisoner at Avignon.

This new conflict between the Pope and the Emperor not only disturbed relations with the papal court at Avignon, it produced a significant and enduring change in the world of thought. The national sentiment of Germany was deeply stirred, and the Emperor was sustained by a rising tide of civic feeling such as Germany had never known. Sagaciously utilized, the situation was full of promise for the creation of a national monarchy based on a sense of German unity; for the Pope — whose alliance with France was well understood — had both forced the issue between papal and royal authority and wounded the religious convictions of numerous Christian believers by his condemnation of the Minorites.

Originally organized in advocacy of clerical poverty, the Franciscans had acquired great wealth. The spiritual Franciscans, basing their teaching on the poverty of the primitive apostolic community, held that the Church should imitate its founders, and that corporate wealth was a detriment to spiritual ideals and influence. John XXII, whose avarice was thus condemned, had declared this doctrine to be heresy. Certain private views of the Pope, — particularly the dogma that the dead are not received into the divine presence until after the last judgment, — were, however, esteemed far more heretical, and a widespread hostility to his attitude was thus provoked.

CHAP. I
A. D.
1313–1453

The opposition to John XXII, therefore, assumed the double form of a defence of the civil as against the papal authority, and a repudiation of the spiritual supremacy of the Pope. Starting with the premises laid down by Dante, the jurists of the time began a critical examination of all the papal claims. Marsilius of Padua, — who had been rector of the University of Paris, and had taken refuge with Lewis of Bavaria, — in his " Defensor Pacis," [1] not only sustained the rights and powers of the Emperor as guardian of the public peace, but repudiated the authority of the Pope altogether, and sought to show that St. Paul, not St. Peter, was the first bishop of Rome; asserting that it could not even be proved that St. Peter had ever been in Rome. Examining the lives of the apostles, he declared that none of them had ever exercised any jurisdiction over rulers. Finally, the legend of the Donation of Constantine and the theory of the translation of the Empire by Leo III to Charles the Great were attacked and repudiated. The chief arguments later employed by Wiclif, Huss, and Luther in their work of reformation were at this time, in germ at least, produced and advocated. In England, William of Occam, in his book " Super Potestate Summi Pontificis," taught the same doctrines; and, having been excommunicated in 1330, he also sought asylum with the Emperor at Munich.

The policy of Benedict XII

It was not without great danger to his cause, therefore, that Edward III turned toward the Emperor for support. The act was long meditated before it was performed, and it was only after it became known that Philip VI was himself coquetting for an imperial alliance, that Edward III, having no other recourse, finally ventured to assume the risk.

The death of John XXII, at Avignon, on December 4, 1334, and the election of another French pope under the

---

[1] This remarkable book, composed in collaboration with another professor of the University of Paris, Jean de Jandun, not only advocated the practical separation of Church and State, but enunciated the doctrine of the sovereignty of the people as the true source of legislation in the religious as well as the civil sphere.

name of Benedict XII confirmed the necessity of a combination to resist the preponderance of French influence; but the known desire and efforts of the Emperor for a reconciliation with the new pope, and the alleged disposition of Benedict XII to accord it, seemed for a time to render an Anglo-Imperial alliance impossible.

But the Pope's anxiety for the salvation of the Emperor did not prevent the rejection of all his overtures, and the imperial ambassadors returned from Avignon again and again empty-handed. A lover of peace and at the same time a lover of power, Benedict XII was opposed to all alliances between temporal rulers; for he believed it easier to control them in isolation. Philip VI had been strongly inclined to forestall the union of the Emperor with Edward III by forming an alliance with Lewis in his own interest, but Benedict XII repeatedly interfered to prevent it. In the same spirit, the Pope opposed the execution of Philip's alliance with the Scotch, and in particular his wish to become the mediator between them and their English suzerain. That office Benedict XII preferred to reserve exclusively for himself.

Indefinitely postponing the crusade, which he perceived could not succeed while Christendom was rent by so many dissensions the Pope bent all his energies upon attaining an ascendency over all the kings. The ablest diplomatist of his time, he well understood how to paralyze their initiative and defeat their ambitions.

The English were deeply disturbed by rumors that the Pope was secretly bestowing largesses of money upon the King of France out of the papal treasury. It was known that loans had previously been made, and there was ground for anxiety lest the great fund collected for the crusade might be wholly diverted in this manner. Had Benedict XII been a weaker or less honorable man, this suspicion might have been justified. In April, 1337, Philip VI sent an envoy to ask of the Pope three favors: first, that he would defer his negotiations with the Emperor; second, that, in case of a war with England, the Holy See would loan him four hundred thousand livres from the contributions to the crusade; and, third, that, if Edward III invaded France, sentence of excommunication should not be fulminated against the King of France and his allies.[1]

Benedict XII replied, that he did not think it opportune to defer the negotiations with the Empire, which Philip had promised not to embarrass. Had not his envoys and those of the Duke of Normandy solemnly sworn not to touch the money collected for the crusade? The cardinals would certainly not permit it, for it would be a scandal against the Papacy to say, "The money raised to restore the Holy Places serves to shed the blood of Christians."

Convinced at last that there was no other defence of his rights than war, Edward III resolved to prepare for it by making friends on the continent. While negotiating an alliance with the Emperor, he sent his ablest diplomatists to make treaties with the Counts of Hainault, Brabant, Berg, Zeeland, Gelderland, Juliers, Limburg, Cleve, and Mark, and the Count Palatine of the Rhine. In May, 1337, conferences were held at Valenciennes, where the princes assembled in person to consolidate their league. Negotiations were opened with Philip VI to avert a war, but he replied that he "would never sign a peace"; and, on May 24, 1337, announced the confiscation of the Duchy of Guyenne. The die having thus been cast, Edward III prepared a fleet to make war on his suzerain.

The Pope had striven earnestly to prevent the Anglo-Imperial alliance; but, on August 26, 1337, notwithstanding his opposition, it was concluded.[2] In England, it was believed that the Papacy was in complete sympathy with France, even to the extent of supplying funds to Philip VI. In Germany, it was felt that it was the King of France who had prevented the favorable reception of the Emperor's over-

---

[1] See Déprez, *Les préliminaires*, pp. 145, 146.
[2] Rymer, *Foedera*, II, Part III, pp. 184, 185.

tures for peace, and Edward III did not neglect to deepen this impression. In his communications with Lewis of Bavaria, he referred to Philip VI as a "usurper" and "the enemy of the Empire."

When Benedict XII learned of the alliance with Lewis of Bavaria, he immediately sought to neutralize it by strenuous efforts to arrange an Anglo-French *entente*. His alarm was excessive, for he reported to Philip VI that Lewis of Bavaria was likely to content himself with becoming the national monarch of Germany, and that Edward III might be offered the crown of the Empire. For this purpose, it was alleged, vast sums of money had been sent into Germany intended for the purchase of the electors. All, except John of Bohemia, were said to be leagued with England against France.

It was true, that three hundred thousand florins in gold had been sent to the Emperor as the price of his assistance, and that relations had been established with many of the German princes; not, however, for the purpose of securing election to the Empire, but to form a coalition against Philip VI.

The tactics of the Pope in frightening Philip VI into an attempt at reconciliation were met by Edward III with rare diplomatic skill. On October 7, 1337, he announced his claim to the French throne; and, on the same day, appointed plenipotentiaries to treat with "the so-called King of France."[1] By this double play, he increased the motives for concessions on the part of his rival to avert so desperate a struggle, and gained time for completing his system of alliances.

During the progress of the negotiations that ensued, in which he placed but little confidence, Edward busied himself with strengthening his cause by an appeal to public opinion at home and renewing the pledges of his allies abroad.

The cities of Aquitaine and Gascony had always been favourable to the English connection, for the reason that they

---

[1] Déprez, *Les préliminaires*, pp. 171, 172.

not only enjoyed a profitable trade with England, but believed that English rule was more favorable to their commercial development than that of France. In announcing his intention to embark for Guyenne, Edward III informed the commune of Bordeaux that he had often offered to Philip a reasonable peace, but the "usurper" had illegally endeavored to appropriate all his possessions, even including his duchy.

In Flanders, English traders had long been treated with rigor, and finally arrested and imprisoned. Thus, was destroyed at one blow the chief market of English wool; for Ghent was at that time the Manchester of Europe, and Bruges the great trading *entrepôt* of the North in textile fabrics.

It was now possible, therefore, for Edward III to give a national character to the long feudal contest in which the kings of England had been engaged. Hitherto, public interest in the controversy with France had not been great in England, and bore no comparison with the intense feeling developed by the wars with Scotland. But now Edward III explained to his English subjects to what extent their interests were affected by the action of Philip VI in Flanders and the part he had taken in Scotland in sustaining the enemies of England. To the hostile conduct of Philip VI, Edward III had replied by prohibiting the exportation of wool to Flanders and the importation of Flemish cloth. The result was twofold: first, the migration of many clothmakers to England, who laid the foundations of the English manufacture of textiles; and, second, a popular rising in Flanders, led by Jacob van Artevelde, who declared that, without England, the Flemish cities could not live.

While thus strengthening his cause by an appeal to public opinion, Edward III renewed and enlarged his alliances on the continent. Among those with whom treaties were made to oppose Philip of Valois, were the Republic of Genoa, the Kings of Castile and Sicily, the Counts of Geneva and Savoy, the barons of Franche-Comté, the cities of Ghent, Bruges, and Ypres, the Duke of Brabant, and the Counts of Hainault and Gelderland. Thus reinforced with allies, on July 16, 1338, he sailed with his fleet for the continent.

Not less intense, but of a different character from that exhibited in England, was the state of public feeling in Germany. The relations of France and the Papacy, the part played by Philip VI in frustrating the Emperor's overtures for peace, and the obstinacy with which Benedict XII repelled the advances of the Emperor, combined to arouse the patriotism of the Germans. On July 15, 1338, the electors assembled in Lahnstein,— with the exception of the King of Bohemia,— and decided to uphold their rights and those of the Empire. On the following day, they met in the garden at Rense, on the other side of the Rhine, and resolved to assert their civil prerogatives and terminate the political pretensions of the Holy See. In a formal declaration, they affirmed that, by right and ancient custom, the person chosen by the whole, or the majority, of the electors required "no nomination, approbation, confirmation, consent, or authority of the Holy See," in order to undertake the administration of the possessions and rights of the Empire and to bear the royal title. The royal and imperial office was not a gift of the Papacy; and only the imperial coronation pertained to the Pope.

On August 6, a diet was convoked at Frankfort, and two laws were passed. The first declared, that the imperial dignity did not proceed from the Pope, but from God alone. The second placed the title and rights of the Emperor wholly in the choice of the electors. It was a declaration of unqualified national independence, but it was also the signal for a new move in the diplomacy of Benedict XII.

The way was thus opened for Lewis of Bavaria to make himself the representative of the national sentiment of Germany by seriously uniting his forces with those of Edward III in opposition to the Franco-Papal combination. It was owing entirely to the personal weakness and incapacity of Lewis that neither this nor any other consistent policy was pursued. Urged by the secular spirit of his earlier advisers, he had taken a positive attitude toward the Papacy, and entered into alliance with Edward III; but, left to himself by the death of Castruccio Castracani and Marsilius of Padua, his chief anxiety appears to have been to secure a reconciliation with the Holy See. Divided between the national policy already marked out and his quest for absolution and papal recognition, Lewis soon ceased to be a force, and began that course of wavering and tergiversation which was to end in misfortune for his reign.

On September 5, 1338, at Coblenz, Edward III, in a personal interview with the Emperor, obtained from him appointment as Imperial Vicar for Western Germany.

The meeting was celebrated with splendid fêtes, at which were present the Archbishops of Köln, Mainz, and Trier, the Count Palatine of the Rhine, the Duke of Saxony, and the Marquis of Brandenburg. Two thrones, sumptuously decorated, were prepared in the public place. One, twelve feet high, was reserved for the Emperor; the other, six feet lower, for the King of England. Richly dressed and surrounded by the electors and the knights of both realms, the two monarchs, — the Emperor wearing a crown of gold and precious gems, holding the sceptre in his right hand and a globe surmounted by a cross in his left, — were solemnly seated on the thrones. The Emperor declared before the assembly that Philip of France had forfeited his kingdom; then, handing Edward an imperial charter and a golden staff as a symbol of the vicariate, invested him as Imperial Vicar. After mass in the church of Coblenz, the Emperor solemnly swore that he would aid Edward III against Philip of France for seven years, and Edward took his oath of fidelity to the Emperor.

The papal intervention

Convoking the Counts of Liège, Hainault, Gelderland, and Brabant — vassals of the Empire — Edward III notified them of his imperial vicariate, and summoned them to his aid; but Benedict XII set his hand at once to dissolve the Anglo-Imperial alliance. His first step was to restrain Philip VI from executing his act of confiscation in Guyenne; his second, to forbid the imperial vassals, under threat of excommunication, to render aid or obedience to Edward, on the ground that, the Empire being vacant, they owed allegiance to himself alone; and, third, to plead with Edward III to abandon his unholy alliance with a heretical and excommunicated pretender to the Empire. In presenting this appeal, the Pope delicately touched the King's pride by insinuating that it was beneath the dignity of so great a prince to render himself subordinate to one who possessed no legal authority. "To sin is human," concluded this ingenious document, "but to continue in sin is diabolical."

In all these directions, the efforts of Benedict XII were not wholly without results. Philip VI was temporarily restrained from the execution of his purpose. Some of the imperial vassals refused to obey the summons of the Imperial Vicar, and John of Bohemia and Peter IV of Aragon promised the Pope their active support. On April 2, 1339, Benedict informed the King of France that ambassadors from the Emperor had been received at Avignon. On the sixth of the following May, he informed Philip that a second embassy, sent by the Emperor to treat of reconciliation with the Church, must pass through France, and asked for a safe conduct. Even Edward was induced to listen to propositions to resume negotiations with the King of France. The coalition, under the subtle influence of the Pope, seemed gradually melting away.

Benedict XII well understood that the question of Guyenne presented an insoluble problem, for the English were more and more disposed to make it a national issue, and the French were certain to regard it as vital to their national unity. Thus, by an inherent necessity, the expiring feudalism was creating a great question of international politics. The modern doctrine of "compensations" had not come into practice, and the Pope saw no other course to pursue than to gain time by a temporizing policy.

But Edward III, if he was, indeed, sincere in listening to proposals of peace, saw no prospect of a pacific solution. He

The dynastic question

could devise no other means of settling the controversy than a serious attack on Philip's rights to the crown; but, for this, a formidable front was necessary. On July 16, 1339, he addressed a letter to Benedict XII, in which he attempted to justify his own claims to the crown of France. He recited the manner in which Philip VI had obtained the throne, the injustice to which he himself had been subjected, and his own long-suffering; finally alleging that "natural justice, innate even in animals, permits that one defend himself against flagrant wrongs."

It was the herald of the coming storm, which all the sagacity of the Pope was unable to prevent. As if to excuse his indifference to the papal counsels, Edward complained that the money of the Holy See was providing armaments against him. The Pope denied this, but in England the assertion served as the moral justification of Edward's unalterable purpose to force the hand of his adversary.

Robert of Artois, banished from France on the charge of counterfeiting deeds of inheritance, had, in 1337, appeared as a refugee at the English court, where he had been kindly received. As it was known that he had recited with bitterness the wrongs he claimed to have suffered at the hands of Philip VI, and had tried to convince the English court that Edward III had been cruelly defrauded of his right to the crown of France, his presence there was regarded by the Pope and Philip of Valois as in itself a *casus belli;* and not without good reason, for, excited by Robert's eloquence, the English had cried, "By Holy Mary, we will make our king the King of France."

Edward had welcomed Robert and encouraged the national feeling, for it was necessary to the success of his cause. At a banquet, he is said to have sworn that, within a year, he would place on his queen's brow the crown of the Queen of France; and the nobles present had promised to support him. "*Dieu et mon droit!*" became the battlecry of England in that interminable war that Edward was about to carry into France.

So great an enterprise required a solid legal basis to commend it to the English mind. Nephew of Charles IV of France, while Philip of Valois was only his cousin, Edward's right seemed clear in English law. As Charles had died intestate, his inheritance naturally passed to the next of kin. But the French replied, that the King of England could not inherit the crown through his mother, because this was contrary to the law of France; and, even if he could legally inherit the crown, he had renounced his right by voluntarily doing homage to Philip VI.

But the English lawyers were not to be so easily confuted. Appealing to the Code of Justinian, they showed that the rights of nephews were superior to those of cousins. Even admitting that a woman could not wear the crown of France, it did not follow that her son could not inherit it; for his rights were derived, not from his mother, but from his grandfather; and, if his mother's sex prevented her from inheriting, that did not affect her son, whose sex permitted him to wear the crown. As for the alleged renunciation of rights, Edward III was a minor when he did homage to Philip VI in 1328, and, therefore, not responsible. Further, he did it involuntarily, and the *restitutio in integrum* of the Roman law rehabilitated minors with all the rights of which they had been illegally divested. Not only so, but even if Edward's vassalage had been competent, voluntary, and unreserved, the compact with his suzerain would be dissolved by the illegal expropriation of his lands and the destruction of his rights.

The English people were to pay a high price for the dynastic pretensions of their king. Depending largely upon foreign allies and mercenary troops to carry on the war, immense sums of money were exacted for their services, taxes soon became burdensome, and even the jewels of the crown were pawned to the Archbishop of Trier to raise necessary funds. Loans were made wherever possible,— in Flanders, in Germany, and in Italy. All Europe was laid under contribution. On August 27, 1340, the King of England besought the Republic of Venice to lend him forty galleys to increase his navy, and to exercise its good offices to induce Genoa, to whom Philip VI had applied for aid, to maintain at least a strict neutrality.

At the critical moment, the allies of England showed signs of weakness and defection; for the influence of the Pope had been steadily employed to dissolve Edward's coalition. The Emperor, still mastered by the mediaeval spirit, incapable of persistence in his devotion to the national ideals of Germany, and secretly hoping for absolution from the Pope, had busied himself with fruitless negotiations with Benedict XII; and, to improve his prospects of reconciliation, had afforded no aid to England. The imperial princes had been intimidated by the dread of papal anathemas, and even Flanders had felt the power of the papal influence.

To meet these difficulties, Edward III adopted a bold course. On February 21, 1340, his chancellery took the step of styling him "King of France," and caused a new official seal to be made in this sense, while the King changed accordingly the quartering of his royal coat of arms.[1]

This step secured for him the adhesion of Flanders; for the Flemish cities were now able to reply to the Pope that their duty called upon them, as subjects of the King of France, to take part in the dynastic controversy; and that they were serving Edward III, not as allies, but as their rightful sovereign.

On March 29, 1340, a new compact with Flanders was, therefore, concluded, in which Edward conferred upon Ghent and Bruges special commercial advantages in the manufacture and sale of woolen cloths. Other French vassals soon found it to their advantage to take sides with the English, and France was thereby plunged into a civil as well as a national conflict.

Thus began that Hundred Years' War between France and England which, with varying fortune and repeated renewals of negotiation, exhausted the energies of both countries

---

[1] Rymer, *Foedera*, II, Part IV, p. 69.

until the middle of the fifteenth century. Its chief significance for European history lies in the emergence from the conflict of two great powers, — one in possession of national unity on the land, the other in the exercise of faculties fitted for maritime supremacy. The war in France was for England a war beyond sea, and it could not be conducted without a strong naval armament. The naval battle of Sluys, fought off the coast of Flanders, on June 24–25, 1340, — in which the English fleet, aided by the Flemish ships, destroyed nearly two hundred French, Spanish, and Genoese vessels and thirty thousand lives, — was the first foreshadowing of that long struggle for supremacy on the sea which has created the British Empire.

II. The Dismemberment of Christendom

From the time when the barbarians entered the fold of the Catholic Church, Europe had possessed a certain moral unity under the guidance of the Holy See at Rome. The defection of the Greek Christians had, indeed, divided the Christian world; but nearly all Europe had acknowledged the spiritual authority of the Pope; and, in spite of sporadic outbursts of heresy, doctrinal union had remained practically unbroken.

The decline of papal influence

The hostilities which had divided the Guelf and Ghibelline parties in Italy, the controversy of Boniface VIII with the national monarchies, the resentment of the Germans awakened by the political claims of the Papacy, and above all the residence of the popes at Avignon, joined to the fact that they were French by nationality and in close intimacy with the French kings, had combined to diminish the influence which the Holy See had exercised in the time of Innocent III. By attempting to dictate the political relations of the world in the interests of France, the Papacy was losing its spiritual supremacy over other nations.

Benedict XII had placed himself in violent opposition, not only to the action of Edward III in claiming the crown of France, but to all the measures taken by him for the defence of his rights. In England, the suspicion was current, notwithstanding the papal denial, that the treasures of the Church were used against the cause of Edward and in favor of Philip VI. In addition to this, an unfortunate incident had occurred which appeared to render Avignon an unsafe place for residence and negotiation. On April 13, 1340, an ambassador of Edward III, — an Italian cardinal named Nicolino Fieschi, — was abducted from his apartment at night, hustled into a boat on the Rhone, and carried captive to France.

The report was circulated at Avignon that officers of the King of France had committed this outrage; but this story was proved false, and Philip VI took severe measures to discover the offenders. Investigation showed that, among the aggressors, were familiars of the pontifical court enjoying the confidence of the Holy Father. What was the condition of the papal capital, when ambassadors, engaged in negotiations for peace, were no longer safe within its precincts? Edward III affirmed that it was not possible to find persons at his court who had the courage to risk their lives at Avignon!

It was, thenceforth, difficult to convince the English and the Germans that the Papacy was not secretly conspiring to promote the political interests of France; and a deep chasm was, in consequence, opening between the Teutonic and the Latin peoples. A chronicler of the time, speaking of the great Anglo-Flemish naval victory at Sluys, reports: "All who speak the German language rejoice in the defeat of France."

It is not surprising that Edward III was, at last, wholly escaping from the influence of the Pope. On August 25, 1340, Benedict XII sought to impose peace by directing the archbishops of France and the Archbishop of Canterbury to cause processions to be formed and prayers to be made, to the end that God might terminate the war.[1]

---

[1] The Pope was moved to this measure by the fact that a general war against Christendom called for peace and unity in order to resist

Forced by such public manifestations, and by the lack of funds caused by the same influence, Edward III was obliged to declare his willingness to accept a truce; but never for a moment did he think of abandoning his claims. In all his frequent attempts at mediation, Benedict XII had never proposed any other basis of settlement than Edward's renunciation of his rights.

Archbishop John Stratford, who had conducted Edward's entire foreign policy, finally fell under the King's condemnation. It was the Archbishop who had repeated the remark attributed to Philip VI: "Everything will go badly while there are two kings, one in France the other in England."[1] It was he who had urged Edward to invade France, and had then failed to furnish his army with supplies. The subservience of the Archbishop to Benedict XII finally so affected the King, that he said: "I believe the Archbishop of Canterbury has wished to cause my ruin and my death by depriving me of resources. He has already tried to alienate from me the affections of the Queen."

Edward summoned his minister to London, but the Archbishop refused to appear. The breach between the Church and the State assumed the form of a dangerous rupture; for, when the King named his candidate for the vacant archbishopric of York, the Pope refused his sanction, while the King rejected the papal candidate on the ground that he was a homicide. For the first time in the history of England, a knight, Robert de Bouchier, was appointed chancellor, and ecclesiastics were systematically displaced from public office.[2]

---

it. The King of Morocco was about to invade Spain, the Turks intended to attack Roumania, and the Tartars Poland and Hungary. His mediation having proved fruitless, Benedict XII resorted to this form of intervention.

[1] See Déprez, *Les préliminaires*, pp. 351, 352, who discusses the conduct of the Archbishop.

[2] On November 30, 1340, the King arrived at the Tower of London about midnight, when he received the great seal from the Chancellor,

Chap. I
A. D.
1313-1453

When the royal agents traversed the kingdom to collect taxes, the bishops in return visited with excommunication, not only the King's officers, but those who were disposed to pay the assessments. Discontent was fomented on every side, and the royal authority was temporarily paralyzed. An influence emanating from Avignon thus defeated the foreign policy of the King by cutting off the sinews of war at home; and, deprived of the means of redeeming his financial pledges to his allies, Edward III saw his coalition against France end in dissolution.

The general disenchantment

While Benedict XII was able by his influence over ecclesiastics, reinforced by the disinclination to pay taxes for a foreign war, to cripple the resources of the King of England, he was not able to control entirely the King of France. The Pope had strenuously opposed all negotiations between Philip VI and Lewis of Bavaria, partly because he desired no interference in his own plans to humble the heretical emperor before the Holy See, partly because he wished to maintain absolute control of Philip. When, therefore, he learned that, on January 24, 1341, the Emperor, in the presence of the Chancellor and other officers of the Empire, had sworn upon the Gospel to be thenceforth for life the faithful friend and ally of the King of France, his indignation exceeded that of Edward III.

Philip hastened to make his excuses for the secret negotiations which had resulted in this startling *dénouement;* but the Pope, deeply chagrined that Christian princes should ally themselves with heretics, and that a beloved son should thus secretly conspire against the interests of the Holy See, administered to Philip VI his indignant rebuke and condemnation.

Stripped of the imperial vicariate which Lewis of Bavaria

Robert Stratford, Bishop of Chichester. On December 14, he appointed to this office Robert de Bouchier, and delivered the great seal to him at the Tower. See Rymer, *Foedera*, II, Part IV, p. 87; also Record edition, II, Part II, p. 1142.

had so ceremoniously conferred upon him, Edward III was now told that his own negotiations for peace had absolved the Emperor from his engagements; to which he replied, that he had only made a necessary truce, that he would never have concluded a permanent peace without conference with the Emperor, and that he regarded the alliance as binding until he was enthroned as King of France.

But to Edward's cup of misfortune still another bitter portion was soon to be added. The cities of Brabant and Flanders now informed him, that they were looking forward to an eventual reconciliation with the King of France; for Philip VI had promised them, on this condition, to secure from the Pope the revocation of the papal ban.

The King of France was now to receive his punishment for wounding the papal dignity. His envoys were informed at Avignon that His Holiness did not consider it opportune to revoke without sufficient reason a condemnation that had been pronounced by the Holy See. Fully committed to the excommunicated cities, Philip VI now suddenly found himself in the embarrassing position of trading in spiritual commodities which he could not deliver. Between the unaccomplished disloyalty of the cities — traitors both to himself and to his enemy — and the papal coolness, he presented the sorry figure of a trickster exposed in a game of confidence.

Cruelly disillusioned as he had been by the procedure of Philip VI, Benedict XII was to be still more deeply shocked and mortified. A letter from Lewis of Bavaria informed Edward III that he had been charged by Philip VI to terminate the disputes between France and England, and that he had hastened to accept the mission.

If this intelligence was a surprise to Edward III, it was torture for Benedict XII. The blow fell upon the aged and enfeebled pope like a bolt from heaven. After all his long endeavors for peace, the Papacy was, then, to be ignored in the reconciliation of two Catholic kings; and a heretic, under the anathema of the Church and disobedient to its authority, was to be called in as arbiter in composing differences which the Papacy had failed to terminate.

It was, perhaps, a relief, though still an unspeakable source of chagrin, when plenipotentiaries arrived at Avignon from the King of France to announce that Alfonso XI, King of Castile, was about to mediate with the King of England. That monarch had informed Philip VI that the Saracens were preparing an immense army for the destruction of Christendom, and had implored him to aid in resisting them. In order to undertake this expedition, Philip assured the Pope, he had given to the Castilian envoys full powers to arrange a peace between France and England. Thus, a second time, the Papacy had been rejected in the exercise of that office of mediation which it regarded as its own peculiar privilege.

The question of succession to the Duchy of Brittany soon arose, however, to cause the reopening of hostilities; the rival claimants united their fortunes with the contending kings, and the Castilian mediation fell by the wayside. On April 25, 1342, Benedict XII, whose vanity had been so deeply wounded by the disregard of the papal mediation, without having accomplished any of his great political purposes, passed from the scene of his misfortunes.

A new pope, Clement VI, heralded his accession by informing Edward III that he had been born in Guyenne, and as Archbishop of Rouen had taken an oath of fidelity to the King of England as his suzerain. "This is sufficient," he added, "to indicate what bonds unite me to him, and how much I desire the peace and prosperity of his kingdom."[1]

---

[1] Pierre Roger de Beaufort, who took the name of Clement VI, was born in the Castle of Maumont, in the diocese of Limoges, upon the very border of the English feudal territory. Although he had been technically subject to the King of England, he was in every sense a Frenchman. He not only greatly increased the number of French cardinals, but fixed the papal residence at Avignon by purchasing it outright and spending vast sums upon the decoration of his splendid palace there. To sustain his sumptuous court, he imposed excessive taxes upon the whole of Christendom, which provoked the opposition of England and Germany, whose contributions he loaned to France for

Edward III was pleased with these amicable words, but he was not long in learning that the new pope was the chosen candidate of Philip VI. In less than a month after his installation, the Holy Father, in conformity with Philip's wishes, revoked the ban imposed on Edward's allies in Flanders, who speedily fell away.

Toward the Emperor, however, Clement VI employed a different policy. As the representative of the national sentiment of Germany, Lewis of Bavaria had possessed the opportunity of founding a strong national state; but his wavering resolution, his preposterous claims in matters of religion, and his personal greed in expropriating the territories of others in the interest of his own family combined to ruin his career. His negotiations to procure absolution from the Pope were as futile as they were compromising to his professed principles. His interference in questions of religion destroyed at its foundation that distinction between the civil and the spiritual spheres upon which alone political independence could be logically based. His assumption of ecclesiastical prerogatives in granting a divorce to Margaret of Tyrol, in order that his own son, Lewis of Brandenburg, might obtain her estates by marriage, coupled with other acts of avarice, shocked the moral sense of Germany, excited the opposition of the Church, and provoked the union of the princes to drive him from the throne.

Clement VI, placing himself at the head of all these elements of hostility, secured a new imperial election; and, on June 11, 1346, all the electors, except Lewis' own son and

---

the purpose of carrying on the war. "From 1345 to 1350, Philip VI received 592,000 florins in gold and 5,000 crowns; John II borrowed the enormous sum of 3,517,000 florins in gold." See Pastor, *Histoire des papes*, I, p. 109. As Archbishop of Rouen, — which as a part of Normandy had ceased by the Treaty of Paris of 1259 to be subject to the King of England, — Clement VI had held certain ancient fiefs in England for which he rendered homage to Edward III. — Rymer, *Foedera*, I, Part IV, p. 72, under date of April 1, 1307, and II, Part I, p. 20, under date of November 20, 1312.

the deposed Archbishop of Mainz, chose Charles, son of King John of Bohemia, as "King of the Romans."

Although Charles IV was derisively called the "*Pfaffen-Kaiser*," or Priest's Emperor, his statesmanship not only secured for him a doubtful throne, but impressed upon Germany a permanent organization of the Empire. Hurried off to France immediately after his election, to aid Philip VI, he fled with the French king from the disastrous field of Crécy, where his blind father fell in battle, to find his cause almost lost in Germany.

The death of Lewis of Bavaria, on October 11, 1347, was favorable for the plans of the new emperor, but he was confronted with stupendous obstacles. The House of Wittelsbach possessed the whole of Bavaria, Brandenburg, Tyrol, the Palatinate of the Rhine, Hainault, Holland, Utrecht, Zeeland, and Friesland. A son of Lewis was at the head of the vigorous Suabian League; Albert II of Austria was allied with the Wittelsbachs; and the imperial cities were not favorable to Charles. In a secret treaty with Clement VI, Charles IV had yielded to all the Pope's demands, including the renunciation of Italy.

One by one, however, the new emperor swept these obstacles from his path. Siding at first with the "false Waldemar," — a pretender to the Margraviate of Brandenburg, — he was able to occupy the late emperor's son Lewis with civil war, until, by renouncing the pretender, he was successful in attaching Lewis to his cause. Four persons claiming the right of electors, in 1348, offered the crown to Edward III of England; but his preoccupation in the war with France and the objections of Parliament prevented his acceptance. After being several times rejected, the crown was at last offered to an obscure prince, Günther of Schwartzburg, who died in 1349. But, in the meantime, the cities, seeking to enlarge their municipal prerogatives, were won over to Charles IV by new privileges; both Albert II of Austria and the Elector Palatine were brought into alliance by marriage; and, in 1350, the

THE FORMATION OF MODERN STATES

King of Bohemia found himself the undisputed Emperor of Germany.

The reign of Charles IV was that of a statesman and diplomatist whose public acts were determined by practical considerations. His grandfather, Henry VII, had yielded to the seductive promises of the Italian Ghibellines and the expiring mediaevalism embodied in the ideals of Dante only to learn, too late, that the Ghibellines were inspired chiefly by their feudal interests in Italy, and that Dante was a dreamer. But Charles IV steadfastly refused to be made the pawn of Italian politics. His decision marks the end of the mediaeval conception of the Empire and the beginning in Germany of a great state of a unique type.

The new "King of the Romans" went to Rome, but in the spirit of peace and to receive a mere decoration. There, a tragic episode had startled Europe with its boldness and novelty.

When Clement VI was elected pope, among the ambassadors sent to bear the messages of the Romans and to invite the return of the papal court to Rome, was a young man — the son of a washerwoman — named Cola di Rienzo, whose eloquence and learning so pleased the Pope that he appointed him notary of the Apostolic Chamber at Rome. Inspired with a passionate admiration for the monuments of antiquity, Rienzo soon determined to restore its institutions. Having inflamed the minds of the citizens by his ingenious allegories and stirring appeals, which at first excited only ridicule among the aristocracy, by means of a conspiracy he was able, in May, 1347, to make himself master of Rome as "Tribune of the People."

For a time, the Pope appeared to approve of Rienzo's project of restoring the ancient Republic of the Romans, and the dictator rose to such a height of enthusiasm that he proposed to make Rome the head of an Italian confederation as the first step toward rendering it once more the capital of the world. Ambassadors had been sent to confer with him by several Italian cities, and he had finally ventured to cite the contending claimants to the Empire — Lewis of Bavaria and Charles IV — to appear before him.

Visionary in his plans, extravagant in his pretensions, and unpractical in executing his designs, Rienzo, after masquerading as a great reformer, was driven from Rome and excommunicated by Pope Clement VI; but his successor, Innocent VI, in 1354, released the fallen dictator from the prison in which he had been confined and sent him to Italy to revive the papal influence through his power over the people. After a brief success, during which he was chosen "Senator" and again exercised control, on October 8, 1354, having attempted in the midst of a riot excited against him to escape from the city in disguise, he was discovered and massacred by the mob.

The coronation of Charles IV at Rome

In the days of his exile from Rome, Rienzo had made a pilgrimage to Prague to beseech Charles IV to go to Rome, assert his imperial rights, and restore the supremacy of the Empire. The poet Petrarch, who had hailed the rising star of Rienzo as Dante had saluted that of Henry VII, had joined in the invitation; but the Emperor, unmoved by the fantastic schemes of the deposed tribune and the illusory fancies of the impassioned poet, had sent Rienzo a prisoner to Avignon as a heretic and a dangerous revolutionist.

Four years later, when the wild dreams of this unfortunate adventurer had ended in his tragic death, Charles IV saw and embraced his opportunity to receive the imperial crown at Rome.

The state of Italy presented a combination of circumstances extremely favorable for the restoration of imperial power. The anarchy at Rome seemed to demand the presence of a master. In the North, the Ghibelline family of Visconti had built up a powerful tyranny. After its defeat by Venice in 1353, Genoa had yielded to its local magnates and lost its municipal liberty. Florence, the last representative of Italian freedom, had vainly endeavored to unite Tuscany, Romagna, Rome, and Naples in a league under the papal protection, to resist the encroachments of the local despots; but now, at length, discouraged by the indifference of the Pope, the Guelf party was reduced to practical impotence and disposed to invoke once more the presence and authority of the Emperor to preserve the liberties which were rapidly disappearing.

In these circumstances, Charles IV, accompanied by only three hundred knights, in October, 1354, made his appearance in Italy. In January, 1355, he received the iron crown of Italy from the hands of Robert Visconti, Archbishop of Milan; and the cities of Tuscany, with Florence at their head, hastened to do him honor and present him with payments of money. With a modest retinue and without the customary ostentation of pomp and power, he then proceeded to Rome, where, after prayer and fasting, on Easter Sunday, 1355, he received the crown of the Empire from the hands of a cardinal, in the presence of the Prefect of the City, with the approbation of the Pope. Faithful to his promise to remain in Rome only a single day after his coronation, the Emperor promptly withdrew to Siena.

Disappointed by the pacific conduct of the Emperor, who steadily adhered to his determination not to pursue the policy of Henry VII in Italy, the Italians of the time expressed their contempt for the tame and mercenary spirit of Charles IV. "He is not an emperor," sneered Petrarch, "he is only a king of Bohemia." Others, displeased with his sale of regalian rights and his indisposition to enforce imperial authority, compared him to a "merchant at a country fair." But, Charles, who comprehended that the heroic age of the Empire had passed, had formed a policy of his own. Content to leave Italy to its own devices, he turned his attention to the reconstruction of the more coherent parts of his Empire.

As King of Bohemia, his first care was to establish peace, order, and prosperity within its borders, in the hope that, as Frederick II had planned to do in Sicily, he or his descendants might eventually render it the nucleus of a still more powerful monarchy. To this end, although he was also King of Germany, he strove to render his Slavic kingdom

CHAP. I
A. D.
1313-1453

an independent and self-centred power, a sure heritage to his dynasty and a powerful constituent of the Empire.

In 1365, by a journey to Arles he endeavored to revive the recognition of the imperial rights in Burgundy; but, although he assumed the crown of that kingdom with great solemnity and celebrated his progress by creating the Universities of Geneva and Orange, and by numerous imperial acts, his relation to Burgundy, like that to Italy, was only formal and perfunctory. To fix more definitely the claims of the Empire, he sought at Paris a French alliance and made the Dauphin, afterward Charles VI, an imperial vicar.

Even in Germany, the Emperor did little to assert his authority, but he clearly perceived the danger to which the kingdom was exposed, and attempted to supply a remedy. The disputed elections had been a primary cause of dissension and anarchy, and a fixed constitution was needed to avoid this confusion. In the subdivision of power, Germany was following in the course of development toward local tyranny which had destroyed all central government in Italy. To prevent this catastrophe, it was necessary that the kingdom should be provided with a constitutional head, supported by all the available forces of centralization; but to accomplish this result, it was important to consider the heterogeneous character of its constituent elements, which were certain to hinder the success of a monarchy resting on its own material force alone. The solution of the problem appeared to consist in legally providing for the choice of a sovereign by the votes of a few princes acting according to a precise mode of procedure, and in curbing the republican tendencies of the cities by placing them under the control of a strongly supported central authority.

The Golden Bull of 1356

This solution was embodied by Charles IV in his Golden Bull, which thenceforth became the fundamental law of the Holy Roman Empire until its end in 1806.[1] The number of

---

[1] A critical analysis of the Golden Bull shows that it was not entirely a newly composed organic law for the Empire, but a blending

electors was fixed at seven. Of these, the three ecclesiastics, — the Archbishops of Mainz, Köln, and Trier, — were, respectively, chancellors of the three kingdoms of Germany, Italy, and Burgundy. Of the four lay princes, the King of Bohemia was Chief Cup-bearer, the Count Palatine Chief Seneschal, the Duke of Saxony Chief Marshal, and the Margrave of Brandenburg Chief Chamberlain. The place of election was Frankfort, a majority of the votes was necessary to election, the solemnity of coronation was to be observed at Aachen, and the first diet of future emperors was to be held at Nuremberg.

The electors were to rank above other princes of the Empire, enjoy the right to coin money, and exercise exclusive jurisdiction over their subjects. Elaborate rules were laid down for the escort of the electors, the procedure of election, the seating of the archbishops, the rights of particular electors, and the duties of each. The immunity of the King of Bohemia and his subjects is provided for in a separate article.

It is a notable indication of the great change that was passing over Europe, that no mention was made in the Golden Bull of the papal claims regarding the Empire in respect to the right of veto, coronation, or acting during a vacancy. The crown of Milan was to be borne before the Emperor-elect at Frankfort, together with that of Aachen; but the crown of Rome and the right of the Pope to confer it are passed over in silence. All that had been decided at Rense was tacitly assumed in this written law of the Empire.

The Golden Bull and the Papacy

---

of more ancient documents. The number of Italian words contained in it shows the influence of Italian statesmanship in its composition. Among the Italian notaries in the service of Charles IV were Andreas Paynellus, Johann von Arezzo, and Angelus von Arezzo. A thorough reform of the imperial chancellery under Italian influence occurred soon after the coronation of Charles IV. See Hahn, *Ursprung und Bedeutung der Goldenen Bulle Karls IV*, pp. 37, 39. An English translation of the text may be found in Henderson, *Select Documents*, pp. 220, 261. Some of its provisions will be discussed in later chapters.

Pope Innocent VI, who had regarded Charles IV as a model son of the Church, did not fail to express his displeasure with this imperial independence; but the Emperor did not waver. When, afterward, the papal nuncio endeavored to secure a tenth of the clerical revenues for the papal court, Charles IV held firmly to his rights; and, following the example of Philip IV of France, threatened to confiscate the property of the Church. Unable to prevent, or even mollify, the slight to the Papacy inflicted by the silence of the Golden Bull, the Pope finally ceased his complaint that the new organic law of the Empire ignored the papal pretensions.

Effects of the Golden Bull

The provisions of the Golden Bull were not adapted to the creation of a strong monarchy, for the indivisibility of the electoral territories and the principle of primogeniture imposed upon them to preserve their unity prepared the way for their permanent independence rather than their absorption by a single ruler. But, although historians have criticised the policy of Charles IV as the "legalization of anarchy," it was only by such a compromise that the dissolution of Germany could be arrested; for a strictly national monarchy was then impossible. It is doubtful if Charles IV expected the new organization of the Empire to be more than transitional, and it is possible that in his mind it was only a temporary step toward rendering the imperial office hereditary in his family, with the ultimate hope of abolishing the electoral machinery and subordinating the princes as the kings of France had succeeded in absorbing the great fiefs. That the House of Luxemburg was not able to accomplish this result should not be regarded as decisive against this supposition; for the final success of the Hapsburgs in rendering the Empire practically hereditary in their house proves that the provisions of the Golden Bull were capable of being used to the advantage of a powerful dynasty. They at least gave a definite constitution to a unique and persistent form of political organization in which many of the imperial traditions were preserved.

The means employed by Charles IV to secure the succession to his son Wenzel show that he did not intend that the free choice of the electors should be exercised; but that, if possible, the possession of the imperial office should be secured to his own house. It was soon perceived, however, that an institution had been created which rendered the electors the virtual masters of the Empire; and, by the "*Wahlcapitulationen,*" — or concessions of new rights and privileges wrung from the candidates at the time of election, — they were able to raise themselves to practically sovereign power. Without military force, fixed revenues, or supreme judicial authority, the Emperor was, in reality, the mere president of a confederation of princes able to defeat his will by their joint opposition. The immense interval between the dignity of his rank and his actual limitations made it necessary to augment his influence by bestowing his chief attention upon his private estates, and reduced him to the necessity of gaining the support of the princes by every device of negotiation and compromise.

While Charles IV was endeavoring to accomplish the work of German unity, Italy, under the ineffectual supervision of an imperial vicar, was practically lost to the Empire and passing through an agony of unrest. Pope Innocent VI, realizing the intolerable condition of the Papal State, had confided to Cardinal Albornoz the difficult task of restoring the papal authority, and this able diplomatist and warrior had achieved a notable success. Abandoning the mediaeval conception of government, this eminent statesman formed the plan of uniting the Italian ideals of liberty with the papal authority, and endeavored to build up a solid system by placing municipal self-government under the aegis of the Papacy. Not only was Rome restored to the control of the Holy See, but the local tyrants of Romagna were held in check by awakening the population to a sense of their oppression.

But the long absence of the popes in Avignon and their foreign nationality had seriously weakened the papal influence in Italy, and neither the spiritual fulminations nor the

Return of the popes to Rome

The Great Schism

patriotic inspiration of a power so foreign to Italian sympathies could effectually excite the fears or arouse the enthusiasm of the Italians. While Rome sent up its cry for the return of the Pope, the Visconti are said to have compelled his legate to eat the seal and parchment of the bull of excommunication sent to them from Avignon.

In response to the urgent prayers of the Romans and the entreaties of Albornoz, aided by the influence of Charles IV, Urban V, who, in 1362, had succeeded Innocent VI, in 1368 went to Rome, accompanied by the Emperor; but the feebleness of the support furnished by Charles IV, the death of Albornoz, and the difficulty of restoring the papal authority in Italy combined to weaken his resolution, and in 1370 he returned to Avignon.[1] His successor, Gregory XI, who was chosen in the year of Urban's return with the conviction that he would remain away from Italy, was, nevertheless, prevailed upon to visit Rome in 1377, where in the midst of deep tribulation he died in the following year.

During this period of indecision, a great controversy had been precipitated in which national sentiment was deeply stirred. A French monk had ventured to answer the urgent appeals for the presence of the Pope in Italy with a pamph-

---

[1] The desire to revisit the "beau pays de France" was irresistible to Urban V and the majority of his cardinals, of whom eighteen out of twenty-one were Frenchmen. Commenting on this desire, Pastor says: "The Franciscan monk Peter of Aragon pointed out to him the possibility of a schism, if he abandoned the tomb of the Apostles; the Romans implored him, Petrarch adjured him to remain at Rome; St. Brigitte predicted that if he deserted Italy, his death would soon follow his departure; but all efforts were in vain. Nothing could alter his determination, and he departed for Avignon, to the great despair of the true friends of the Papacy and of the Church." — Pastor, *Histoire des papes*, I, pp. 112, 113. Upon his arrival at Avignon, the Duke of Anjou was awaiting him, with a demand for a subsidy to enable France to carry on the war with England. The pious pontiff was too weak to refuse, and by a bull of November 2, 1370, accorded to France the privilege of collecting a tithe upon the ecclesiastical revenues of Languedoc. — Archives of the Vatican, register 260, folio 112, No. 378.

let containing a fierce diatribe against Rome, which was pictured as a den of thieves, while Avignon was held up as an asylum of safety. To this attack upon the Eternal City Petrarch replied with a glowing panegyric upon the glories of the Roman past, while France was treated with contempt as the home of barbarism.

The death of Gregory XI furnished the occasion for the Romans to demand the elevation of a Roman prelate to the papal throne, and during the election the conclave of cardinals was surrounded by an armed mob to influence the decision. After a night of terror, on April 8, 1378, the Archbishop of Bari was chosen; but, as the mob still demanded a Roman, the cardinals were afraid to announce their choice. The hall of the conclave was entered by force, an aged Roman, Cardinal Tibaldeschi, was hastily crowned with a mitre; and, believing him to be the Pope, the Roman mob fell at his feet in reverence, while the cardinals fled from the place. When, afterward, it was officially announced that the Archbishop of Bari had been elected, the Romans, satisfied that they at least possessed an Italian pope, hastened to accept him and assure themselves that he would remain in Rome.

But the French cardinals were no sooner safely out of Rome and under the protection of hired *condottieri*, than they openly repudiated the election of the Archbishop of Bari — who had been proclaimed and recognized as Pope Urban VI — on the ground that he had been chosen under intimidation. The Archbishop of Arles, chamberlain to Gregory XI, had carried off the papal crown and jewels to Anagni, where the cardinals soon afterward assembled; and, a few weeks later, having proceeded for greater security to Fondi, on September 20, they elected to the Papacy Cardinal Robert of Geneva as Clement VII.

Thus was inaugurated the Great Schism,[1] which for forty

---

[1] The fundamental cause of the Great Schism was the antagonism of Rome and Avignon. Urban VI declared his determination to

years divided Europe into hostile camps, each under the headship of a series of rival popes. A national question had completely disrupted the Papacy, already long weakened by national controversies.

The anarchy of Christendom — The residence of the popes at Avignon and their close intimacy with France had gone far to excite the feelings of the rest of Europe, but so strong was the instinct of unity in the Church and so powerful was the influence of the Papacy that so long as there was but one canonically elected pope, his power with the masses of the people was irresistible. Antipopes there had often been, and local and temporary divisions had before existed; but when, for the first time in history, two claimants of papal authority, both chosen by the main body of cardinals, passionately disputed each other's pretensions, the unity of Europe was impossible.

Regularly chosen by the College of Cardinals, and duly recognized and enthroned by them, Urban VI possessed indisputable claims to the Papacy. Clement VII, on the other hand, chosen by a majority of the same cardinals, and even in the presence of the Italian minority, who made no protest although they took no part, could well defend his pretensions also. Left to decide a doubtful case, and sometimes tempted to seek special favors in return for recognition, nations and

---

remain in Rome, to institute reforms in the Church, and to destroy the preponderance of the French cardinals in the Sacred College by increasing the number chosen from other countries. The French cardinals, on the other hand, dreaded the proposed reforms, which were directed at themselves, desired to continue Avignon as the papal residence, and were strongly supported by Charles V, King of France, who, according to the unpublished testimony of Franciscus Aguzzonis, in the Codex Vaticanus No. 4927, folio 146, promised to sustain their action, if necessary, by sending an army into Italy, even at the cost of abandoning the war with England. Upon learning of the election of Clement VII, the King of France is said to have exclaimed, "Now *I* am Pope!" — Pastor, *Histoire des papes*, I, p. 149. A single writer, Cornelius Zantflied, has accused the cardinals of wishing to elect to the Holy See King Charles V himself. See Gayet, *Le grand schisme*, II, p. 267, who discusses at length all the circumstances of the double election.

prelates settled the question as their national prejudices or their personal interests inclined them.

Unhappily for the Church, neither pontiff could command that sincere devotion which the nature of his office implied. At Rome, Urban VI was cold, rude, selfish, and impolitic. At Avignon, Clement VII was worldly, ambitious, and devoted to the interests of France. The universal shepherd was no more; and the Church, whose discipline had relaxed and whose prelates had become corrupt, was rent by every form of dissension. The blow to faith was not inconsiderable, but to the organization of the Church the schism was fatal. In the efforts to rally round a common standard, it was the nations that were thenceforth to afford the fixed points of attraction.

III. THE GROWTH OF NATIONAL SENTIMENT

The practical restriction of the Empire to the Kingdom of Germany, the disruption of the Papacy by the Great Schism, and the triumphs of the national monarchies over feudalism mark the decline of those institutions which distinctively characterize the period known as the Middle Ages, — the ten centuries intervening between the dissolution of the Roman Empire and the organization of modern national states.

In the Middle Ages, life and society were essentially corporate. Neither the state as a political organism nor the individual as a social unit had any proper existence. The most universal corporation was the Church, in which every person had an assigned position. Kings and princes were its instruments, but their authority was conceived of as derived, not inherent; and, in isolation from its communion, even they were outcasts. Next in importance to the Church was the feudal relation, by which every man took his place in the social hierarchy. Even in that transformation by which feudalism was disintegrated and finally destroyed, the principle of association formed the medium of deliverance; for in the

CHAP. I
A. D.
1313-1453

process of emancipation from feudal servitude the corporate idea, as embodied in the commune, the trade guild, and the municipality, furnished the only avenue of escape from spoliation by armed force.

The modern world, on the other hand, is characterized by the freedom and initiative of the individual, unfettered by corporate restrictions, and rendered secure by organized public protection. Thought, literature, art, industry, and commerce, which in mediaeval times were subject to the rules of special societies formed to promote and protect them, with the advent of the modern era derived their chief impulse from untrammelled individual intelligence pursuing its own unobstructed path.

The transformation implied in the transition from the mediaeval to the modern era was, in great degree, a destructive process, by which the corporate forms of society were dissolved; but it was also a constructive process, by which new conditions were created.

Among these conditions, the most important was, perhaps, the formation of a civil system under which the individual could receive the guarantee of personal liberty. To think, to work, and to trade without the constraints of a conservative body existing for the perpetuation of its own interests and traditions, had become the ardent aspiration of men in the later centuries of the Middle Ages. The ambition of kings furnished the means of its partial realization. Throughout the fourteenth and fifteenth centuries, the most notable phenomenon in the greater part of Europe is the tendency toward the formation of commonwealths in which the kings, — too remote from the people, and often too magnanimous, to impose upon them a crushing servitude, yet powerful enough to afford them effective protection, — were gladly made the sole trustees of individual rights and liberties.

The rise of the Hanseatic League

Nothing, perhaps, could better illustrate the real significance of this transition than the fortunes of the Hanseatic League. The merchants of the thirteenth century were at the mercy of the feudal lords through whose territories they conveyed their merchandise and of the pirates who infested the northern seas. To guard against their depredations, protective associations called *hansas*, formed by the traders themselves, had long been in existence, but these afforded only a precarious protection. Two of the more important mercantile cities, Lübeck and Hamburg, influenced by the guilds of merchants, in 1241, concluded a formal treaty to protect the trade between the Elbe and the Trave and police the waters leading to the ocean, providing ships and soldiers for this purpose; but this was only one of many local compacts. In 1259, Lübeck, Rostock, and Wismar formed a confederation with a larger purpose and destined to a far wider expansion. Rapidly augmented by the accession of other cities, this union had developed by 1282 into a powerful association called the "Hanseatic League," finally numbering more than eighty adherents, grouped under four "quarters," or "circles," — the Wendish, for the southern and eastern coasts of the Baltic; the Westphalian, for the cities of Western Germany; the Saxon, for the interior of Germany; and the Prussian or Livonian, for the cities of the Northeast. Its principal magazines in foreign countries were Bruges for Flanders, London for England, Bergen for Norway, and Novgorod for Russia. Once in every three years a diet of delegates assembled to make laws, usually at Lübeck, which was regarded as the capital of the League. Its wealth and prestige gave to this government without territory an influence surpassing that of most of the kingdoms within whose borders it carried on its trade. Maintaining armies and navies, it gained victories over Denmark, Norway, and Sweden, whose extortions it resisted with success, and in 1332 practically suspended the Danish monarchy for eight years. A disastrous war with Waldemar III of Denmark, in 1362, nearly destroyed the League; but, in 1367, it resolved that, if any town failed to give support to the common cause, all commerce should be cut off from it, and no harbor privileges should be granted to its ships. The next year, Copenhagen was taken, the Danish king was driven into exile, and by the Treaty of Stralsund, of May 24, 1370, the control of the Sound and the fisheries, with the right to confirm the title to the Danish throne, passed into the possession of the League.

So great had the power of the Hanseatic League become, that the Emperor Charles IV, though desiring to support the cause of Waldemar III, was unable to humble the pretensions of the conqueror, and upon his visit to Lübeck, whither he journeyed in 1373 to conciliate the cities of the North, he is reported to have addressed the burghers in terms that practically recognized their sovereign powers.

Decline of the League

But the fifteenth century, at whose beginning the Hanseatic League had risen to an unprecedented height of power and arrogance, witnessed the decline of this great cosmopolitan corporation, which had been able to dictate its will to the kings of the North. Neither in Germany nor in Scandinavia could the League hold its own against the rising tide of national hostility, which opposed itself to the non-territorial authority of this international monopoly. The great geographic discoveries of the century altered the routes of trade, even the fish migrated from the Baltic to the coasts of Holland, and this powerful federation of merchant princes, in competition with the traders who disputed its supremacy under the protection of the national states, then struggling for primacy in the commerce of the world, gradually lost its pre-eminence and finally dwindled into impotence.

Difference between mediaeval and modern sovereignty

To the modern mind, it appears a singular fact that a power without territorial domain should exercise the rights of sovereignty on both sea and land; but it serves the better to disclose the difference between the mediaeval and the modern conception of authority. The modern state possesses definite frontiers, and its claim to sovereignty is based upon this fact; but the mediaeval kingdoms, like the mediaeval empire, had only vague and uncertain boundaries. Authority went with the land, but its source was from above. In the earlier period, the Emperor conferred it upon kings, as God had delegated it to him; and the King passed it on to his feudal vassals, as they in turn subdivided it among theirs.

In the time of Frederick Barbarossa, all the lands of Northern and Eastern Europe which had not been brought under his suzerainty were regarded as the legitimate field of German expansion. The kings whom Otto III had suffered to establish monarchies on the northern and eastern borders were all brought into vassalage to the King of Germany as Emperor. Svend of Denmark was his obedient vassal; Boleslav IV of Poland was forced to own his superiority; and Vratislav of Bohemia was permitted only by his grace to be crowned a king.

But, at the end of the fourteenth century, Germany, while failing of consolidation as a national kingdom, had lost its prestige as an empire; and on the shores of the Baltic, which had once promised to become a German lake, a league of merchants had built up the only power that offered security to German trade. Where the feudal empire of the mediaeval period had once claimed the homage of dependent kings, formidable national monarchies were coming into being, and the King, representing the nation, claimed the ownership of his entire realm, identified his royal authority with possession of the land, and finally ruled it as an absolute proprietor.

The formation of the Hanseatic League undoubtedly tended to check the national consolidation of Germany; for the cities, finding themselves capable of self-protection, were less disposed than they otherwise might have been to submit to a central royal authority, and gloried in their independence.

The Scandinavian kingdoms and the Union of Kalmar

But the existence of the League had a similar retarding effect upon the development of the Scandinavian kingdoms also; for prior to the Treaty of Stralsund it either allied itself to one or more of them against the remainder, or left them a prey to one another's violence, while after the peace imposed by that treaty its will became for a time their law.

In 1387, Margaret, daughter of Waldemar III, King of Denmark, and widow of Hakon, King of Norway, — called the "Semiramis of the North," — obtained by election the succession to the throne in both kingdoms. Soon afterward, the Swedes, dissatisfied with their king, Albert of Mecklenburg, offered their kingdom also to this enterprising princess, who, in 1397, assembled the estates of the three realms at Kalmar for the incorporation of the three kingdoms under a single crown.[1] The Hanseatic League did not prevent this union, and the diet of the three kingdoms ratified the compact in perpetuity; but, although the Union of Kalmar lasted for half a century, national discontent contantly disturbed the relation, and at the end of that period Sweden regained its independence. At the same time, the permanent union of Denmark and Norway was confirmed, and this connection endured until, as a punishment to Denmark, it was arbitrarily severed in 1815, by the Congress of Vienna.

Fettered by feudalism within, and held in tutelage by the Hanseatic League during the period of its power, these kingdoms, destined to play a large part in the subsequent history of Europe, for nearly three centuries pursued their way with little influence upon the fortunes of Christendom, yet serving to set limits to imperial expansion and rendering the Baltic the scene of future contests for preponderance.

The Teutonic Order in Prussia

Far different in purpose and methods from the rôle of the Hanseatic League was the work of the Teutonic Order. Established at the end of the twelfth century to serve as soldiers and nurses in the Holy Land, the "German Knights of St. Mary" — composed exclusively of German crusaders — received numerous benefactions from pious persons, and had become a great and powerful organization, when, in 1226, they were invited to undertake the extension of Christianity among the Slavs in that region on the shores of the Baltic between the Vistula and the Gulf of Finland where Prussians, Lithuanians, Livonians, and Esthonians still retained their heathen rites and primitive customs.

The Grand Master of the Order, Hermann von Salza, friend and adviser of the Emperor Frederick II, saw in the founding

---

[1] The text of this act may be found in a French translation in Mallet, *Histoire de Danemark*, IV, pp. 293, 300.

of a new German state in the North a field of enterprise far more promising than that afforded in the Holy Land, and gladly accepted the invitation. A diplomatist and statesman of the first rank, he obtained from the Emperor for the Order a formal right to all its future conquests; and, to avoid any opposition by the Holy See, induced Pope Gregory IX to claim these heathen lands as the property of St. Peter, and then to bestow them upon the Teutonic Knights in return for a small annual tribute.

The conquest of Prussia proved an arduous task; but, in alliance with the "Knights of the Sword," whose field of operations was in Livonia, the Teutonic Knights were able to make rapid progress. The rigorous rule of the Order, however, soon excited the opposition of the dukes and bishops who had invoked its aid, and the Poles resented the creation of a German state which cut them off from the Baltic. To meet the resistance that arose from this awakening of national feeling, recruits were sought in every part of Europe, and enthusiastic youth journeyed to Prussia to lend their aid to the crusade against the Slavs.

As the aims of the Teutonic Order became more and more political, the Papacy, which had at first promoted its designs, was placed in an attitude of hostility, and in the bitter wars which followed threw its influence on the side of Poland. But Germany, seeing its advantage in the progress of the cause of the Knights, gave its support to their conquests; and, in 1343, Casimir the Great, King of Poland, was compelled in the Treaty of Kalisch to confirm the cession of Pomerellen and other Polish territories to the Knights. By 1346, the Order had acquired by war and purchase the whole of Prussia, including Pomerania, as well as Samogitia, Courland, Livonia, and Esthonia, together forming an immense territory extending along the whole eastern coast of the Baltic from the Vistula to the Gulf of Finland. A new German state, governed by a close corporation at Marienburg, had thus been brought into existence, bidding fair to become the greatest power of the North.

The death of Casimir the Great in 1370 and the accession of Lewis, King of Hungary, to the crown of Poland favored the progress of the Teutonic Order; for Lewis took no interest in the fortunes of the Lithuanian peasants who were suffering most from the German invasion. But, upon the death of Lewis in 1382, the Polish nobles, moved by a great wave of race feeling, resolved to end the union with Hungary and the indifference of a foreign king. By the marriage of Hedwig, daughter of Lewis the Great, with Jagellon, a powerful prince of Lithuania, a great ruling house was founded, and Poland was redeemed from the humiliation of defeat and foreign rule. As a condition of his elevation to the throne, Jagellon accepted the Catholic faith, and was crowned under the name of Ladislas V. His people followed him in accepting the Catholic faith, thus removing the alleged reason for the conquests of the Teutonic Knights, who had hitherto enjoyed the sympathy of Christendom on the ground that they were engaged in a work of religion. This transaction secured for centuries the preponderance of Poland in the North, for Russia had not yet thrown off the Mongol domination. Although perpetually weakened by its feudal organization, Poland was thenceforth able to curb the power of the Teutonic Order, which from that time passed into a gradual decline.

Dissolution of the Teutonic Order

Although it maintained its existence for another century, the Order of the Teutonic Knights was, nevertheless, doomed to certain extinction. Even within its more limited confines it soon became an anachronism. Without close relations with the inhabitants and wholly separated from the public interests of Prussia, this oligarchy of militant monks, dedicated to celibacy, could not maintain its control over the industrial and commercial forces of the population, which became weary of its pious pretensions and public inefficiency. A "Prussian League" was formed by the nobles and towns, the country was plunged into civil war, Poland interfered, and the greater part of Prussia was annexed to the Polish kingdom. The Knights looked in vain for aid from Germany; and, after a heroic resistance, accepted vassalage to Poland. The grand masters of the Order were required to do homage to the Polish kings, but allowed to sit on their left in the Polish Diet. By the artifice of selecting their officers from among the princes of Germany, the total submergence of Prussia in the Polish monarchy was prevented, until Albert of Hohenzollern, having become grand master, finally ceded Western Prussia to Poland and retained Eastern Prussia as a hereditary duchy, which, falling later to the direct line of the Hohenzollern electors of Brandenburg, gave its name to a German state destined, five centuries afterward, to become the predominant force in accomplishing the unity of Germany.

To the south of Poland, the Magyars, who had once devastated Europe by their incursions, having been converted to Christianity about the year 1000, had built up a kingdom of peculiar historic interest and importance. Their king, St. Stephen, to whom Pope Sylvester II sent a celebrated crown called the "Angelic," was commissioned as an apostle of the Catholic faith and clothed with all the authority of an apostolic vicar. The Hungarians attached extreme importance to this crown and to the ecclesiastical attributes bestowed by the Pope, and the act of royal coronation was, therefore, esteemed in Hungary as a ceremony of exceptional dignity and solemnity.

Notwithstanding the high honor pertaining to the royal authority, the Hungarians have never ceased to regard with singular pride their public institutions; for St. Stephen, in addition to a thorough ecclesiastical organization, gave his people a civil code and recognized the value of the preexisting assembly of the estates; thus founding a government essentially constitutional in an age when in the greater part of Europe the public powers were in a state of anarchy [1]

---

[1] The Golden Bull of Andrew II, formulated in 1222, only seven years after the Magna Charta of England, was the formal embodiment in a written constitution of these earlier liberties by which the

CHAP. I
A. D.
1313-1453

At the beginning of the fourteenth century, Pope Boniface VIII, claiming Hungary as a fief of the Papacy, endeavored to impose upon the country an Angevin prince, Charles Robert, — known in Hungarian history as Charobert, — who was at first opposed, but afterward chosen king. Under the rule of this dynasty, the kingdom rose to a high degree of power, and comprised, besides Hungary proper, Dalmatia, Croatia, Bosnia, Servia, Wallachia, Transylvania, Moldavia, and Bulgaria.

The geographic position of Hungary rendered it for centuries the bulwark of Europe against the Ottoman Turks, who had succeeded the Saracens in Western Asia, and from the commencement of the fourteenth century began to encircle with their armies the remains of the Greek Empire. By 1360, the invaders had permanently established themselves on European soil, and soon afterward began their attack on the Slavonic territories, Bulgaria, Servia, and Bosnia, — extending their dominions to the Danube.

The accession of Sigismund as King of Hungary

In this perilous situation, it was to the Empire that Christendom naturally looked to beat back the tide of invasion; for the war with the Infidel had now lost the aggressive character it had possessed in the period of the crusades, and had become, on the part of Christendom, a struggle for its own defence.

To meet and master the double peril of invasion from without and schism within, Christendom was in need of a firm and heroic leader; but Wenzel, the son and successor of Charles IV as "King of the Romans," was a feeble and brutal ruler, weakened by the vice of drunkenness, while Germany was in a state of anarchy. Even in the time of Charles IV, the cities of the Suabian and other leagues had vindicated their right of association for their own protection against the protests of the Emperor, and under the

---

annual assembly of the nobles was solemnly legalized. In case of royal violation of the rights guaranteed in this constitution, the lawfulness of resistance is recognized.

nerveless rule of Wenzel all central authority seemed to have disappeared.

In the midst of this crisis, Lewis the Great, King of Hungary and Poland, dying in 1382, left two daughters, Maria and Hedwig, for whom he succeeded in procuring the recognition of both kingdoms. The elder, Maria, who thus became Queen of Hungary, was affianced to Sigismund, the second son of the late Emperor, Charles IV. This ambitious prince claimed for his future queen, on the ground of seniority, the crown of both kingdoms; but the Poles, who, as we have seen, had felt the evils of subordination to Hungary, resolved to maintain an independent Slavic state, called Hedwig to Poland, and arranged her marriage with Jagellon of Lithuania.

Before he had recovered from his disappointment in the loss of Poland, Sigismund was forced to make an unexpected struggle for the crown of Hungary. The Queen Mother, Elizabeth, widow of Lewis the Great, indisposed to accept the secondary place assigned to her, was inclined to make another marriage for the future queen of Hungary; but a faction of the nobles invited Charles of Durazzo, then occupying the throne of Naples, to accept the crown. Sigismund hastened to the scene to vindicate the rights of his fiancée, and the Queen Mother having joined her forces with him against the rebels, the marriage was solemnized in October, 1385. Charles of Durazzo was then assassinated by the order of Elizabeth, but his friends captured both queens, put Elizabeth to death, and kept Maria in prison until Sigismund, in 1387, having received the crown by election of the nobles, obtained her release.

By the accession of Sigismund to the throne of Hungary, a new kingdom was brought under the control of the House of Luxemburg, which thereby became possessed of a vastly augmented territory. But this brought no great advantage to a family whose elevation had already aroused the hostility of the German princes. If in Germany Wenzel was scorned as a mere drunken king of Bohemia, in Bohemia he suffered for being a German prince; and the latent fires of the Slav spirit, stirred at this time even more deeply than in Poland, were soon to burst forth in all their fury against the King.

It was Sigismund, therefore, who, as king of Hungary, became almost single handed the champion of a dissolving Christendom against the steady encroachments of the Turks. With the exception of Venice, whose immense commercial and colonial interests were at stake, Europe, absorbed in local quarrels, was but feebly interested in the advance of the Infidel. In the East, as we have seen, the conflict of dynastic pretensions prevented a union under any common leadership; while in the West, the relations of France and England were not favorable for united action. Upon the King of Hungary, practically unaided, therefore, devolved the defence of Europe against the Ottoman invasion.

Notwithstanding the English capture of Calais in 1347 and the success of English arms at Poitiers in 1356, the Hundred Years' War had dragged on its weary course, while anarchy prevailed in France. Worn out by the evasive tactics of his foe, which left him with a wasting army in a foreign land, Edward III, at last, had abandoned the struggle, and by the Treaty of Brétigny,[1] of May 8, 1360, surrendered his claims to the crown of France, and contented himself with full sovereignty at Calais, — which he populated with Englishmen, — and in that heritage of Aquitaine brought by Queen Eleanor to Henry II. By the same compact, France was to withdraw all support from Scotland, England was to renounce the alliance with Flanders, and King John II of France, who had been taken prisoner at Poitiers, was to be released on payment of three million crowns.

Thus, Charles V of France came into a kingdom which, under his practical rule, at first gave promise of a peaceful reign. Humiliating as the Treaty of Brétigny had been to

---

[1] The text of this treaty is found in Cosneau, *Les grands traités*, pp. 33, 68.

France, King John II had studiously endeavored to fulfil its obligations, and gave utterance to the noble sentiment, "If justice and good faith were banished from the world, it would be necessary to seek them in the heart of kings."

But Charles V, desirous of retrieving the lost position of his kingdom, was eager to take advantage of every sign of discontent with English rule and to cultivate the national feeling which had unexpectedly developed when France was thus vitally divided. A pretext for renewing the war with England was found in the complaints of the Gascon nobles regarding the payment of taxes levied by Edward, Prince of Wales and Duke of Aquitaine. Relying on help from the aspirant to the throne of Castile, Henry of Trastamara, and on cutting off from the English the aid of their ally, Charles the Bad of Navarre, Charles V, in violation of the Treaty of Brétigny, had in 1368 given ear to the rebellious nobles of Edward III, accused him of failure in executing his renunciation of the crown as required by the treaty, and in January, 1369, had cited the Prince of Wales to appear before the Court of Peers. In the following April he had sent his Breton valet to England with a curt message to the King, in the hope of stinging him into commencing hostilities. Edward III had disregarded the insult, but promptly resumed the title "King of France," and actively prepared for war; which, however, though not decisive, proved favorable to the French and resulted in a series of truces lasting till June 24, 1377. Edward III had died three days before the final expiration of the truce; and, after having renewed the war, Charles V also had died, on September 20, 1380, leaving his kingdom to his feeble-minded son, Charles VI.

Even more serious for the peace and protection of Europe than the dynastic contentions that were filling it with strife was the schism of the Papacy, and it was evident to all thoughtful men that the only hope for the restoration of peace and a combination against the Infidel lay in the deposition of both the papal claimants, — the Spaniard, Benedict XIII, who had succeeded Clement VII at Avignon, and the Italian, Boniface IX, who had succeeded Urban VI at Rome.

The University of Paris, then the chief centre of intellectual influence in Europe, had resolved to end the existing situation, and two of its professors, Jean Gerson and Pierre d'Ailly, had, accordingly, urged upon King Charles VI of France a union with the Germans to force the abdication of both popes. In execution of this plan, Wenzel and Charles met at Reims, in 1398, to regulate the affairs of Christendom. The interview was embarrassed by the frequent intoxication of Wenzel, who, when invited to a banquet by the King, was found in his quarters under the table too drunk to be disturbed, while Charles was subject to recurrent fits of insanity; but, notwithstanding these royal infirmities, an agreement was reached engaging Wenzel to obtain the abdication of Boniface IX, and the King of France to demand that of Benedict XIII.

The schism in the Empire

The intermeddling of Wenzel with the schism of the Papacy was the signal for bringing to the surface all the latent opposition against him in Germany. Although he had not been crowned at Rome, his imperial title had been confirmed by Boniface IX; but his engagement with Charles VI to unseat the Sovereign Pontiff sealed his doom. The offended pope encouraged revolt against the ill-starred king; and the four Rhenish electors, assembled at Lahnstein, in 1400 deposed Wenzel, and elected Rupert, Count Palatine, "King of the Romans" in his place.

France, in the meantime, had taken the initiative in demanding the resignation of Benedict XIII; but, in executing this purpose, was obliged to besiege Avignon and capture the person of the Pope. Finding no support from the other nations, France, divided into factions, in 1402, released Benedict, who promised to solve the problem of papal unity by direct negotiations with Rome.

Death having ended the claims of Boniface IX before any conclusion was reached, he was succeeded by Innocent VII in 1404, and he by Gregory XII in 1406, without a settlement of the controversy, and it was not until 1407 that a definite appointment was made for the rivals to meet at Savona, near Genoa; but, although Gregory XII had been elected with a promise to resign when Benedict XIII could be disposed to do so, the two popes never met. The one, as a contemporary wittily said, like a land animal, refused to approach the sea; the other, like an aquatic creature, refused to seek the shore.[1]

The long duration of the papal schism and the strained relations it was producing throughout Europe had, at last, become unendurable, and the impotence of the Papacy to cure the evil had led to the search for another seat of ecclesiastical authority. The University of Paris forced upon the King of France the final repudiation of Benedict XIII, who replied with a bull of excommunication, and retreated to his native town of Perpignan, still supported by the Spanish kingdoms, while Italy adhered to Gregory XII, and the remainder of Europe was divided.

At this juncture the cardinals of both parties, seeing the hopelessness of the struggle, abandoned their respective popes; and, following the instinct of self-preservation, called a general council at Pisa. Here, in March, 1409, both popes were sent a list of charges and summoned to appear for trial before the Council. Failing to reply, both were solemnly deposed, and a new pope, under the name of Alexander V, was chosen.

Although it is remarkable as indicating a radical change in the conception and government of the Church, the Council of Pisa produced no immediate effect, except to add a third claimant to papal supremacy; for neither Benedict XIII nor Gregory XII would recognize its legality or the rights of Alexander V. The death of Alexander in 1410 left the controversy where it was before his election, and the choice by the cardinals of John XXIII — an Italian military prel-

---

[1] Leonardo Bruni, Apostolic Secretary, in his *Commentarius Rerum Suo Tempore* (1378–1440), Venice, 1475.

ate of doubtful character — as his successor, only precipitated the contest by creating a new scandal in the Church.

To meet the encroachments of the Turks, Sigismund, King of Hungary, had in 1396 taken the field against them; and, although defeated in his first attempts, he had displayed qualities which seemed to mark him as the ablest available leader for the protection of Germany against the advance of the Infidel. After the death of Rupert, Jobst of Moravia had been elected to succeed him, but the death of the latter in 1411 opened the way for the unopposed recognition of Sigismund. Wenzel was induced to accept the assurance of his title as King of Bohemia, — to which Moravia was added by way of sustaining his dignity, — and, on July 21, 1411, the schism in the Empire was ended by conferring the imperial office upon the King of Hungary.

The new emperor brought to his task a high conception of his duties and prerogatives and an eager ambition to restore the imperial prestige both in the defence of Christendom and the reassertion of imperial authority over it. Unfortunately for his fame, his plans were often wanting in coherence, and so fertile was his invention that one enterprise was barely conceived before another was brought forward to displace it.

Terminating with a truce his war to punish the Venetians for invading Dalmatia, he undertook to reclaim Lombardy from the ambitious imperial vicar, Filippo Maria Visconti, but finding the power of Visconti too strongly intrenched, he abandoned his Italian expedition without results. But his negotiations with John XXIII while in Italy enabled him to engage that pontiff in a promise to call a general council, and thus to place himself in the position of a great conciliator of the Church.

On November 5, 1414, the Council of Constance met to compose the dissensions of Christendom. The primary problem was the restoration of unity, but there was a large party favorable to a general programme of reform. The teachings of John Wiclif at Oxford, repeated by John Huss at Prague, had not only deeply agitated both universities but created a popular movement for reform both in England and in Bohemia.[1] These students of the Christian Scriptures believed themselves to have found in them a conception of religious life and doctrine in striking contrast with that imposed by the Roman Church and implied in the institution of the Papacy, whose contentions for power seemed to them at variance with the apostolic teachings. At the University of Prague, the Bohemians had upheld and the Germans had opposed the doctrines of Huss. By a gradual absorption of power, the Germans controlled three out of four votes in the University, and a contest over the doctrines of Huss had led to their condemnation by the Germans, although generally accepted by the Bohemians. The intervention of Wenzel had been invoked, he had decreed three votes to the Bohemians, and the Germans, after an indignant protest, had abandoned the University in a body, numbering several thousands.

The incident not only marks the rise of national feeling in Bohemia in relation to the Empire — of which since the accession of Charles IV Prague had been the capital — but, in connection with the papal controversy, it became a political question of the first magnitude; for it was the commencement of that revolt against papal supremacy which was later to shake the whole of Europe to its foundations.

The condemnation and execution of Huss, who had been invited to Constance with a promise of safe conduct by the Emperor, became in its influence an event of European importance; for the reform party, although it was strong enough in numbers to deserve consideration, was entirely crushed and silenced in the Council.

After a session of more than three years, the Council brought forth no other results than the deposition of

---

[1] The marriage of Richard II of England to Anna, sister of Wenzel and Sigismund, had brought many Bohemians to the English court. Huss obtained through this channel the writings of Wiclif, which contained the germs of his own later teaching. See Loserth, *Geschichte*, p. 458; also his *Huss und Wiclif*.

John XXIII, after a tragic flight and capture, the trial of Jerome of Prague in connection with that of Huss, and the election of Cardinal Oddo Colonna, a Roman prelate, who was made pope under the name of Martin V.

It is worthy of note, that, at the Council of Constance, the " nations " were the recognized powers in the determination of the questions that arose. A vote by members would have given John XXIII the preponderance, since the Italians were in the majority; but the Council was organized into " nations," — English, French, Germans, and Italians, to which the Spaniards were afterward added, — each nation having one vote.[1] It was this form of organization that deprived John XXIII of control and enabled his opponents to overthrow him. Before the election of the new pope, it was decided that future councils should be held at regular intervals, thus creating a representative body within the Church to regulate its important interests. Nor was the choice of the pope confided entirely to the cardinals. The electoral conclave was composed of thirty delegates from the Council — six having been chosen from each of the " nations " — to serve as adjuncts to the twenty-three cardinals. While the Papacy was not abandoned, it was subordinated in principle to the will of the Church. But the Council had furnished to the new pope an unexpected instrument for defeating the party of reform. By concluding separate concordats with the " nations," Martin V was able to defeat the programme for general reform; but he, in turn, by thus disregarding the unity of the Church, laid the foundation for future reprisals by the " nations " when the question of national churches should arise.

If the Council of Constance had any real heroes, they were Jean Gerson, Chancellor of the University of Paris, who eloquently defended the rights of the Church against the pretensions of the Papacy; and Frederick of Hohenzol-

---

[1] Among the Germans were included Bohemians, Hungarians, Poles, Danes, Scandinavians, and Scotchmen!

lern, whose capture of John XXIII was rewarded by the Emperor with the gift of the Electorate of Brandenburg,[1] destined to form the nucleus of that Kingdom of Prussia which has proved to be the most powerful of all the German states.

Chap. I
A. D.
1313–1453

In the Council itself, the central figure was, without doubt, the Emperor Sigismund, who posed as the regulator of Christendom; but, notwithstanding his triumph in dethroning John XXIII, the superior tactics of his opponents virtually accomplished his defeat as the leader of the reform party. Not only was his safe conduct to Huss disregarded, but after a violent expression of his indignation at the treatment of his *protégé* and a threat to leave the Council if the person of Huss was not respected, he was induced to break his promise, and left him to his fiery fate. For this perfidy he paid a costly penalty in the Hussite Wars that soon afterward devastated Bohemia, and alienated from him the loyalty of a powerful party in the Empire.

The mediatorial offices of Sigismund

The revelation of the Emperor's mistakes was, however, reserved for the future, and during the session of the Council he seemed at least to dominate the situation. Filled with confidence in his imperial mission, he undertook a journey of more than a year for the purpose of detaching Europe from the support of Benedict XIII and Gregory XII, to which he added the enterprise of composing the factional dissensions in France and averting the renewal of the war with England. For the first time in a century, it seemed as if a really great emperor had arisen, and that the utility of the imperial office was, at last, to receive a vindication.

Proceeding directly to Perpignan, in Spain, while the Council suspended its business to await the result of his endeavors, Sigismund, accompanied by a staff of dignitaries, visited Benedict XIII in his fortress of Peniscola in the hope

Sigismund's mission of conciliation

---

[1] Sigismund was financially indebted to Frederick, and the gift of Brandenburg was partly in liquidation of this debt, its redemption being fixed at four hundred thousand florins.

of securing his abdication. Negotiations having proved fruitless on account of the obstinacy and extravagant demands of Benedict, the Spanish princes were besought to desert him; and the Kings of Aragon, Castile, and Navarre sent ambassadors to join in demanding his resignation. When the persuasion and menaces of all combined had proved unavailing, a capitulation was drawn up at Narbonne, on December 13, 1416, in which the estate of Benedict's cardinals was assured, his adherents were invited to attend the Council at Constance, and measures were proposed for his deposition in case of continued contumely. Benedict, completely deserted, still remained unmoved, and replied to the threat to depose him by excommunicating the Church Universal. The Spaniards, faithful to their engagements, sent representatives to the Council, thus forming a fifth "nation,"—much to the distress of the Portuguese, who protested against the denial of the same privilege to themselves,—Benedict was formally deposed, and the new adherents of the Council joined in the election of Martin V.

The Spanish kingdoms

The grouping of the Spaniards as a single "nation" was not in strict conformity with the existing political conditions, and resembled the classification of Germans, Danes, and Poles in the same general group; for the three kingdoms, Castile, Aragon, and Navarre, were not yet united in one monarchy. The long and weary strife between the nobles and the kings had filled the period of a hundred and fifty years since the Moors had been confined to their strongholds in Grenada, but Aragon and Castile were emerging from the struggle of the nobility against the monarchies as compactly consolidated states.

In the development of Aragon, Peter IV had already done for his kingdom what the kings of France and England had yet to accomplish in the consolidation of political control. This remarkable man, who had ruled Aragon from 1336 to 1387, had annexed Majorca and taken Sardinia from the Genoese. His depredations went so far as to covet a part of Castile, but here his intentions were defeated. More of a diplomatist than a warrior in his nominal respect for law and his preference for duplicity rather than force in the accomplishment of his ends, he was more modern than any of his contemporaries, — a Machiavellian before Machiavelli, — and well merited the surname the "Ceremonious" which his love of form obtained for him. Cool, calculating, insinuating, and treacherous, he measured every movement in advance, struck his blow with unerring precision, and treated the victim of his guile as best suited his convenience. Having destroyed with his own hands the "Privilege of Union," — the Magna Charta of Aragon, — he became the absolute ruler of his realm. As a Spanish writer has well said of him, "No king before him had ever so dominated and destroyed the work of force with the invisible key of intelligence, nor had any absolute ruler so obsequiously prostrated himself before the law in order to wring from it the sanction of his deeds."[1]

An alliance between Peter IV of Aragon and Charles V of France had resulted in placing a new dynasty on the throne of Castile in the person of Henry of Trastamara, who succeeded Peter the Cruel in 1369. From this king were descended the great monarchs who were later to rule not only a united Spain but a great part of Europe and America.

In 1412, the grandson of Henry of Trastamara, Ferdinand I, King of Aragon, had become actual ruler of both Castile and Aragon. The union was at that time only personal and temporary, but the possession of Sicily, then lately acquired by the crown of Aragon, made Ferdinand one of the most powerful sovereigns in Europe, and rendered the accession of this monarch to the plans of Sigismund of the first importance.

From Spain the Emperor continued his journey to France, and was received at Paris with great magnificence. During

CHAP. I
A. D.
1313–1453

Sigismund's visit to France and England

---

[1] Emilio Castellar, *Estudios historicos sobre la Edad Media*, Madrid, 1875, p. 147.

his visit to King Charles VI, he was not only sumptuously entertained, but permitted to exercise sovereign prerogatives, — holding a court of justice in the Parliament, creating knights, and elevating Amadeus, Count of Savoy, to the dignity of Duke and Prince of the Empire.

In marked contrast to these honors was his reception in England, which he visited during his sojourn in France in the hope of preventing the renewal of the war. Before the boat that bore him had touched the shore, several nobles rode into the water to inquire whether he intended to exercise any authority in the land. After receiving his disclaimer, the Emperor was permitted to disembark with due honor; but so persistent was the imperial tradition in the minds of that age, that even in England Cuthbert Tunstall thought it necessary a century later to assure Henry VIII that he was "not a subject of the Empire, but an independent king." Eighty years after that, it was solemnly debated in the University of Saragossa whether or not the Emperor was really the lord of the whole world.

The relations of France and England were not opportune for the enterprise of Sigismund as the arbiter of nations. During the reign of Charles VI in France and Richard II in England, the war had continued, with frequent interruptions, until the Truce of Paris,[1] of March 9, 1396, which stipulated peace for twenty-eight years, and was confirmed by the marriage of Richard II to Isabelle of France. But the peace was not destined to a long continuance. In August, 1399, Richard II was overthrown by Henry of Lancaster, who became king as Henry IV. That revolution, followed by the death of Richard II in 1400, had revived hostilities between France and England. The truce had afterward been several times renewed, but on July 28, 1415, Henry V — who had succeeded his father in 1413, and had entered into negotiations with the Duke of Burgundy for their mutual advantage — cited the King of France to execute the Treaty of

---

[1] The text is found in Cosneau, *Les grands traités*, pp. 69, 99.

Brétigny, and the following month invaded France and recommenced hostilities.

The war, which had not recommenced when the Emperor Sigismund started from Constance on his mission of conciliation, had made great progress before his arrival at Paris. The battle of Agincourt, fought on October 25, 1415, had been won by the English, but without any great advantage to the English cause; for Henry V had hastened to Calais, whence he soon returned to England. The occasion was, therefore, not beyond the reach of negotiations, if Sigismund had possessed the skill and influence to reconcile the antagonists. Instead of persisting in his purpose of effecting a reconciliation, however, on August 15, 1416, — the day of the English victory at Honfleur, — he concluded a separate alliance with Henry V at Canterbury.

Unfortunately for the French, they were suffering from a worse misfortune than the defeat at Agincourt. A civil strife had arisen from the rivalry of the French nobles, which left the country exposed to the mercy of its enemies.

Before the death of King John II, the Duchy of Burgundy had escheated to the crown, and the King had bestowed it upon his fourth son, Philip, a companion of his battles and his captivity, surnamed the "Bold." His brother, Charles V, had afterward augmented the possessions of Philip by arranging his marriage with Margaret, heiress of the Duchy of Flanders, whose inherited estates made the Duke of Burgundy one of the most powerful princes of his time.

The vast wealth and influence of the dukes of Burgundy laid the foundations, first of a formidable rivalry with the future kings of France; and, later, of a project to build up between France and Germany an independent state of dangerous proportions.

When, in 1380, Charles VI, at the age of twelve, had come to the throne of France, his uncles, the Dukes of Anjou, Berry, Burgundy, and Bourbon had formed a regency and conducted the government, but with more regard to their personal advantage than to the interests of France. The feuds and crimes of this period, which, owing to the insanity of Charles, continued with impunity throughout his reign, had led to the formation of two principal parties, — the Burgundians in the North and East, and the Armagnacs in the South and West. In the conflicts of these parties the spirit of nationality seemed, for a time, entirely quenched, and private vengeance took the place of national defence. In these circumstances, Henry V of England resolved to press to achievement his pretensions to the crown of France.

The Treaty of Troyes

When, therefore, Sigismund returned to the Council of Constance, not only having failed in his mission of conciliation, but having left the King of France to his fate, he found his own influence in the Council much diminished, the Empire agitated by the religious excitement in Bohemia that was about to burst forth in armed conflict, the opposition to reform strengthened by the influence of the Spaniards, and the English and French delegates rendered hostile by the renewal of the war.

In France, the murder of John the Fearless, Duke of Burgundy, on September 10, 1419, by the adherents of the Dauphin, Charles, completely turned the Burgundian party from the support of the French dynasty and rendered easy a triumph for Henry V by means of diplomacy which could not have been won in the field against a united France. On December 2, 1419, he was able to conclude a treaty of alliance with Philip the Good, the new duke of Burgundy, followed by a union against the Dauphin on December 25. By the terms of this arrangement, Henry V was to marry Catherine, daughter of Charles VI, to be recognized as heir to the crown of France, and until the death of the King to govern the kingdom as regent.

On April 29, 1420, these arrangements were made known by the Chancellor of France before a great assembly held in the Parliament of Paris without evoking a protest. The Duke of Burgundy procured from Charles VI full powers to negotiate the marriage and a peace with England; on the following day the King of England arrived at Troyes; and on May 21 was signed the Treaty of Troyes,[1] which delivered France to the English and formally conferred the succession to the crown upon Henry V.

The victory of Henry V, based on his alliance with a French faction, was, however, far from a complete triumph; for the Dauphin, opposing the humiliating transactions at Paris and Troyes, although confronted with the military superiority of the united forces of England and Burgundy, established himself at Bourges; and, upon the death of both Henry V and Charles VI, in 1422, laid claim to the throne of France as Charles VII.

While the child Henry VI of England ruled at Paris through the regency of his uncle, the Duke of Bedford, Charles VII represented the national sentiment of France at Bourges.

Three problems lay before the young king, — to kindle into a flame the embers of national feeling, to form an array of external alliances, and to detach the Duke of Burgundy from England. Although his efforts were in a great degree paralyzed by the factions of his own court, — led by his own favorites, Pierre de Giac and Georges La Trémoïlle, to whose malign influence he was strangely subjected, — he was aided by unexpected agencies which eventually achieved his success.

At the lowest ebb of his fortunes a peasant girl, Jeanne d'Arc, filled with mingled sentiments of religion and patriotism, fired the spirit of the French people, raised and commanded armies, and created for France a new age of heroism crowned by victories in the field among the most astonishing in history. Urging upon the King his duty to his country, Jeanne finally, with the aid of Yolande of Aragon, his mother-in-law, induced Charles to be crowned at Reims, on July 17, 1429.

The effect upon the French nation was instantaneous, for

---

[1] The text is found in Cosneau, *Les grands traités*, pp. 100, 115.

CHAP. I
A. D.
1313-1453

at last it appeared to have found a leader; but the efforts of Jeanne were soon frustrated by a court conspiracy, and the King was influenced to waste his opportunity for a successful advance on Paris by empty negotiations with the Duke of Burgundy until it was too late. The intrepid maid was captured, tried by an infamous tribunal, mercilessly put to death, at Rouen, on May 30, 1431, and the final victory of France was postponed for twenty years.

The diplomacy of Charles VII

While Charles VII was thus frittering away the support of his best ally, the French people, he was engaged in busy negotiations with foreign powers which proved of little value to his cause. At the beginning of his reign he sought to tighten his bonds with Pope Martin V, Castile, Scotland, the Duke of Milan, and Venice, and to detach the Emperor from the English alliance, although he had afforded no aid to his ally.

To oblige Sigismund, Charles VII had, on several occasions, endeavored to arrange a peace with Venice, with which since 1409 the Emperor had been at war over the Venetian depredations in Dalmatia; but no result was realized, and Sigismund was too deeply embroiled in the Hussite war in Bohemia to render aid in return for good offices that had wholly miscarried. It was not until 1435, therefore, after Philip of Burgundy had aroused the indignation of Sigismund by his appropriation of imperial territory and refusal to do homage for it, that Charles VII succeeded in obtaining the alliance of the Emperor.

The Treaty of Arras

Although his diplomatic adventures were fruitless in Italy, and in Germany only won for him the tardy alliance of the Emperor, in another direction Charles VII was more fortunate, for Yolande of Aragon had proved herself a more astute diplomatist than the King. Seeing that it was of primary importance to detach the Duke of Burgundy from alliance with England, after long negotiations she had obtained the intervention of Amadeus VIII, Duke of Savoy and uncle of Philip the Good, John V, Duke of Brittany, and Arthur, Count of Richemont, for the accomplishment of this purpose. Although these efforts failed, Yolande steadily pursued her purpose. Through her influence Pope Martin V and his successor, Eugenius IV, attempted mediation, and Cardinal Sainte-Croix, legate of the latter, on December 13, 1431, succeeded in arranging a truce for six years between Charles VII and the Duke of Burgundy. The quarrels of the latter with the Duke of Bedford facilitated the *rapprochement*, temporarily postponed by the discovery of a conspiracy formed by La Trémoïlle against the Duke of Burgundy; but, in June, 1433, Queen Yolande, having aided in the overthrow of La Trémoïlle, succeeded in establishing the supremacy of Count Richemont as Constable of France, and after long negotiations a conference was called at Arras on August 5, 1435. The negotiations lasted six weeks, and, although the English plenipotentiaries did all in their power to obstruct the purposes of France, the Duke of Burgundy finally consented to treat without England. On September 21, 1435, the Peace of Arras[1] was signed between Charles VII and Philip the Good. France was, at last, in principle, united; and, although the Duke of Burgundy aided in nothing but neutrality, there was left in the field only a single enemy.

The Peace of Arras did not, however, interrupt the war between France and England; but it rendered easier a final conclusion of the conflict. The prospect of a united France and the ascendency of a strong monarchy excited the jealousy of the great nobles, and the "Praguerie" — a conspiracy between the nobles to prolong the war in the interest of their own independence — became for a time the greatest danger to France. Even the Dauphin, Louis, who was afterward to become the most absolute of kings, joined in this plot to restrict the power of the Crown. But Charles VII, severely disciplined by his earlier experience and aided by an able *bourgeois* ministry, now rose to the height of administrative greatness, reorganized his army, appealed to the

---

[1] The text is found in Cosneau, *Les grands traités*, pp. 116, 151.

French people to pay the new taxes required for its support, became in 1436 the master of Paris, with consummate skill and patience beat down the recrudescence of feudality, and rendered war with France, eagerly responsive to his leadership, a serious enterprise.

The English, pressed by difficulties at home and less inclined to pursue this dynastic adventure in a foreign land against an overpowering foe, became more easily disposed to peace. William de la Pole, Earl of Suffolk, removed the principal obstacle to negotiation by consenting that the conferences should be held on French soil. At Tours, a settlement was arranged by which Henry VI, who would not yet recognize Charles VII as King of France, was affianced to Margaret of Anjou, and a truce was signed on May 28, 1444.[1]

The marriage proved unpopular in England, and the war was renewed; but the national pride of France was now keenly touched, and its military organization — the first in Europe that could be called modern — soon proved its superiority. One after another the strongholds fell into the hands of the French. With the progress of victory the whole French nation rose to its opportunity, and with the capitulation of Bordeaux, on October 19, 1453, the cause of Henry VI was lost. Excepting the small territory of Calais, nothing was left to England upon the continent. With the expulsion of the English France took its place as a modern state, a type and representative of those powerful monarchies for which the growth of national feeling had opened a new period of history.

IV. The Rehabilitation of the Papacy as an Italian State

The fortunes of the Papacy

The awakening of national feeling in every part of Europe was promoted by the conflicts of the Great Schism. As in the twelfth century thought had been stimulated by the

---

[1] The text is found in Cosneau, *Les grands traités*, pp. 152, 171.

quarrel of the Empire and the Papacy, so in the fifteenth a new agitation of mind had accompanied the mutual recriminations of the papal factions. For the defence of its pretensions appeals had been made by each party to history, to canon law, and to natural reason; and Europe was thus converted into a vast forum of political debate. The new humanism that was beginning to be cultivated by a few select scholars had produced a class of writers well adapted to participate in this controversy, and the age was prolific in treatises and pamphlets attacking or defending the claims of the two popes, and even assaulting the institution of the Papacy.

On both sides the papal chancelleries had called to their aid skilled writers familiar with the literature of the classic period. At Rome, the famous Bracciolini Poggio, though at heart a pagan, had been chosen by Boniface IX to be his apostolic secretary; while the University of Paris had opened to all its faculties a formal competition for the best plan of ending the division of the Papacy. "Discourses in a beautiful style became so much in fashion that they were the essential accessories of all the treaties of peace, of all the embassies, and of all the public and private solemnities. Every court, every government, sometimes even rich families had their official orators." In this tide of public discussion the nature and constitution of the Papacy had received a more searching examination than any to which it had ever been subjected.

While the thought of Europe was still busy in analyzing the Papacy as an institution, after the Council of Constance Martin V, with great energy and sagacity, had endeavored to evoke order from the chaos into which the Patrimony of St. Peter had fallen during the absence of the popes at Avignon. Unable to enter Rome, which was then occupied by Juana II, Queen of Naples, he had found the estates of the Church in the hands of petty sovereigns who were indisposed to surrender them, and had taken refuge as a guest at Florence.

Realizing that nothing could be accomplished by violence,

CHAP. I
A. D.
1313–1453

Restoration of the papal monarchy

Martin V set his hand to the difficult task of restoring the papal power by diplomacy. On October 28, 1419, he concluded with the Queen of Naples a compact by which, in exchange for her aid in regaining the lost territories of the Church and the gift of important fiefs to his brothers, the Pope recognized her royal rights and bestowed upon her the papal consecration. By a convention with Braccio da Montone, a bold *condottiere* who held half of Central Italy in his power, he procured his efficient services in restoring order. Rewarded by the gift of a few small fiefs under the papal suzerainty and the title of "Vicar of the Church," this hardy warrior restored to the Papacy the conquests he had previously made, and reduced to subjection the city of Bologna, which had become an independent republic. In the month of September, 1420, Martin V was so far victorious that he left his asylum at Florence and in triumph entered Rome, then almost in ruins. By the aid of his *condottieri* and of members of the Colonna family placed in high positions, the State of the Church was finally reduced to obedience, and the papal monarchy was so completely re-established that one of the Pope's biographers was able to say, "So great were the calm and peace that one might easily imagine himself transported to the time of the great Augustus."

But while Martin V was converting the Papacy into a well consolidated Italian state, national sentiment north of the Alps was planning to curb the absolute power of the papal monarchy and confine it to constitutional limits. Unable to maintain possession of the Papacy, the partisans of Avignon were determined to strip it as far as possible of its ancient prestige and authority by asserting the rights of the nations and of the Church as a self-governing body. At the same time, the Hussites were fighting for independence in Bohemia, the leaven of Wiclif's teaching was spreading in England, and Alfonso V of Aragon, hoping by his attitude to wring from the Pope the recognition of his claims to the Kingdom of Naples against Louis of Anjou, to whom

Juana II was disposed to bequeath her rights, stood aloof from the Pope in Spain, and even set up an antipope.

When, therefore, Eugenius IV succeeded Martin V, in 1431, a serious conflict awaited him. Martin V had soon disposed of King Alfonso's antipope, but he had vainly resisted the convocation of a general council at Basel, which had been all the more violently urged because of the crusades he had organized against the Hussites, his nepotism, his incessant demands for money, and his inaction in accomplishing reforms in the Church.

But the refractory prelates beyond the Alps were not the only enemies with which Eugenius IV had to contend. While the Council of Basel assembled to reform the Church "in its head and in its members," Rome and the State of the Church rose against the new pope, whose political capacity was inferior to that of his predecessor and for whose faults he was made to suffer. Local jealousy of the revived power of the Papacy combined with the spirit of revolt to resist the authority of the Pope; and his *condottieri*, Sforza, Vitelleschi, and Scarampo, although successful for a time in the enforcement of obedience, finally proved an inadequate support, and Eugenius was obliged to take refuge at Florence.

At no period of its history was the papal power exposed to greater danger. Determined to crush the pretension that the authority of a council is greater than that of the Pope, Eugenius, on December 18, 1431, published a bull announcing the dissolution of the assembly at Basel, which had met in the previous July, transferring the Council to Bologna, where, by the predominance of Italian prelates, he hoped to control its action. It was the signal of a battle that was to continue through the whole of his pontificate. The Council refused to be transferred; and, after long negotiations, on January 24, 1438, decreed the suspension of the Pope, and on June 25, 1439, pronounced him a heretic and declared his deposition. In these same years the "Pragmatic Sanctions" of Bourges (1438) and Mainz (1439) mark the determined steps taken in France and Germany toward the formation of national churches. With the view of ending the supremacy of Rome, on November 5, 1439, the Archbishop of Arles and thirty-two delegates of the Council of Basel elected Amadeus VIII, Duke of Savoy, as pope, under the name of Felix V; but in 1444, Felix V, who was left without financial aid, quarrelled with the Council, abandoned Basel, and set up his court at Lausanne.

Two problems thus presented themselves to Eugenius IV, — the pacification of Italy, and the dissolution of the Council of Basel.

A single transaction went far toward the solution of both these problems. In the war between Alfonso V of Aragon and René of Anjou, to whom Juana II had finally bequeathed the Kingdom of Naples, Alfonso had won a decisive victory and become master of that kingdom. By a treaty signed on June 14, 1443, the new king of Naples agreed to recognize Eugenius IV as the only legitimate pope, to aid him in regaining control in the State of the Church, and to furnish ships for the war against the Turks, on condition that he receive the papal consecration.

From that moment the fortunes of the Pope in Italy revived; and on September 28, 1443, he was able to return to Rome in triumph. But the changed situation in Italy was not the only result of the new alliance. Alfonso, who had been among the Pope's most powerful opponents at Basel, recalled the Aragonese ecclesiastics from the Council, whose retirement was soon followed by that of the delegates of Scotland.

In the meantime, other events had conspired to favor the fortunes of Eugenius IV. In 1431 the Emperor Sigismund had made his long coveted journey to Italy, to receive the imperial crown from the hands of the Pope. In opposition to the will of the Council of Basel, which had directed him not to receive the crown from Eugenius until the Pope had recognized the Council, Sigismund had, after long negotiations, in May, 1433, accepted the supremacy of Eugenius as the price of his coronation. His death in 1437 had left the House of Luxemburg without a male heir to the crowns of Germany, Hungary, and Bohemia; and, in 1438, in the person of Albert V of Austria, the son-in-law of Sigismund, the House of Hapsburg had again come into possession of the imperial office. Two years later, by the election of 1440, Frederick of Austria had been chosen as Albert's successor, and the way was opened for dealing the Council of Basel a fatal blow.

The pacific and pliant character of Frederick III, whose chief aim was to strengthen his own dynasty, rendered easy an accommodation with the Pope. Through the co-operation of the imperial chancellor, Gaspard Schlick, Eugenius IV was soon able to achieve an *entente* with the Emperor himself, by which the latter received the right to collect a tithe upon all the ecclesiastical benefices of Germany, the appointment of numerous bishops, and a sum of money, in return for his obedience. Progress in reconciling the German princes and prelates was more difficult, but the talents of Frederick's secretary of the imperial chancellery, Aeneas Sylvius Piccolomini, who became the mediator between the Pope and the Emperor, surmounted this obstacle also.

By skilful secret negotiations, based on the understanding that Frederick III should exercise his influence to secure the supremacy of the Holy See in Germany in exchange for the imperial crown at the hands of the Pope, after an exciting struggle in which the Archbishops of Köln and Trier were deposed, this able diplomatist succeeded, with the aid of money, promises, equivocation, and the enforcement of mutual concessions, in obtaining the general recognition of the Pope. In February, 1447, was achieved by means of four papal bulls the "Concordat of the Princes"; by which, in terms chosen with consummate ingenuity and with considerable attenuations, the demands of the princes were appeased. A few days afterward, surrounded by the envoys who knelt at his bedside to take their vows of obedience, Eugenius IV passed from the scene of his struggles and his victories. The last of the popes to be obliged to leave Rome as a refugee, until the time of Pius IX, four centuries afterward, he was also the last to be opposed by an antipope. Felix V was soon placated by the bestowment of a cardinal's hat from Rome, and the remnants of the opposition were gradually reconciled to the Papacy. In 1450, under Nicholas V, the papal triumph, more real in appearance than in fact, was celebrated at Rome by a great jubilee. Thenceforth, the Papacy was to assume a different character. Based on the material foundation of an Italian state, it assumed more and more the properties of an Italian principality. Although the international influence of the Papacy did not cease to be important, the wounds of the Great Schism were never to be entirely healed.

The fall of the Greek Empire

It marks the revival of the Papacy that, at the time when Europe was losing its moral unity and the sentiment of national interest had almost extinguished the idea of Christendom, the Holy See, from the depths of its weakness and humiliation, sounded the note of union. Even in exile, Eugenius IV imposed a tithe upon the revenues of all the churches, to aid in the war against the Turks; and in an encyclical of 1442 exhorted all Europe to aid the Hungarians in their struggle to resist invasion. Having concluded the Treaty of Szegedin, after the battle of Nisch, in which the Christians solemnly swore on the Gospel and the Turks on the Koran to keep the peace, the Hungarians, believing that the Pope would dispense them from keeping their oath, reopened the war at the instance of Cardinal Cesarini, the papal legate. The battle of Varna, fought on November 10, 1444, in which the Turkish troops carried as a standard the violated treaty, resulted in the overwhelming defeat of the Hungarians, the death of their king, and the exposure of Constantinople to attack.

The Greeks had long realized their danger, and had sought to effect a reconciliation with the West. For this purpose, the Greek Emperor, John Palaeologus, had come to Italy, attended by a numerous suite, and was present at the council which Eugenius IV had convoked at Ferrara and afterward transferred to Florence as a counterpoise to that assembled at Basel. There, urged by the necessity of seeking aid against the Turks, after long debates, the Greeks, in bitterness of spirit, humbly bowed before the papal throne, solemnly accepted the supremacy of the Pope, and subscribed to the Roman creed; but, upon their return to the East, the clergy and the people rejected with scorn the humiliation of this compromise, and saw the last gleam of hope fade into darkness, as the steady advance of the Infidel brought on the siege of fifty-three days amid whose horrors Constantinople fell.

On March 18, 1452, while the Turks were encircling Constantinople with their armies, the papal contract with Frederick III was fulfilled by his coronation in St. Peter's Church at Rome at the hands of Nicholas V, — the last ceremony of imperial coronation ever celebrated in that city. The "Doll Emperor," as Poggio calls him, though destined to become the founder of one of the most enduring dynasties of Europe, fitly symbolizes the decadence of the Empire and the transfer of leadership to the national monarchies.

On May 29, 1453, Constantinople fell before the assaults of the Ottoman Turks, and the Greek Empire, which had preserved the traditions of the ancient world throughout the Middle Ages, came to an end. In the political development of Europe it was also the beginning of a new era. The Papacy and the Empire, the two most general institutions of the Middle Ages, had alike shown their inability either to rule the world or to preserve that unity of Christendom which was the object of their existence. Thenceforth, it was the nations which were to play the leading part in the organization of mankind.

AUTHORITIES

Documents — The more important treaties and other public acts referred to in this chapter may be found in Dumont, *Corps universel diplomatique*, Amsterdam and The Hague, 1726–1731; Rymer, *Foedera*, The Hague, 1739, and other editions, to which Hardy, *Syllabus*, London, 1869, furnishes a chronological index; and Henderson, *Select Historical Documents of the Middle Ages*, London, 1892.

Many documents concerning the relations of England and France are found in Bliss, Johnson, and Twemlow, *Calendar of Entries in the Papal Registers relating to Great Britain and Ireland* (1198–1362), London, 1893–1897; and Viard, *Documents parisiens du règne de Philippe VI de Valois* (1328–1350), Paris, 1900.

Documents regarding the controversy of the Papacy with Lewis of Bavaria are found in Riezler, *Vatikanischen Akten zur deutschen Geschichte in der Zeit Kaiser Ludwigs des Bayern*, Innsbruck, 1891; and Ficker, *Urkunden zur Geschichte des Römerzuges Kaiser Ludwigs des Bayern*, Innsbruck, 1865. Other papal documents are found in the *Lettres des papes d'Avignon se rapportant à la France* in course of publication at Paris by members of the École Française de Rome, including those of John XXII (1316–1334), Benedict XII (1334–1342), Clement VI (1342–1352), Innocent VI (1352–1362), Urban V (1362–1370), and Gregory XI (1370–1378) from the registers of the Vatican.

Relations with the Empire are shown in Böhmer, *Regesta Imperii*, Innsbruck, 1881 et seq., edited by Huber for 1346–1378, and Altmann for 1410–1437.

For the Great Schism, see Gayet, *Le grand schisme d'Occident d'après les documents contemporains déposés aux archives secrètes du Vatican*, Florence and Berlin, 1889.

The documentary history of Bohemia, Poland, and Hungary is found in Theiner, *Vetera Monumenta*, Rome, 1860–1864, which contains in separate volumes documents relating to each of these countries.

For the Teutonic Order, see Töppen, *Akten der Ständtage Preussens unter der Herrschaft des Deutschen Ordens*, Leipzig, 1878–1881.

Kaiser, *Der Collectarius Perpetuarum Formarum des Johann von Gelnhausen*, — a Strasburg dissertation, 1898, — contains a collection of forms of the chancellery of Charles IV, from the manuscript records.

Documents relating to the Hanseatic League are found in the immense collection of *Hansarecesse* published by the Historical Commission of the Verein für Hansische Geschichte, Leipzig, 1870 et seq.

The principal treaties between France and England during the Hundred Years' War are found in Cosneau, *Les grands traités de la guerre de cent ans*, Paris, 1889, with introductory comments.

The general history of the whole period is well covered by Loserth, *Geschichte des späteren Mittelalters von 1197 bis 1492*, Munich and Berlin, 1903, with an exhaustive bibliography.

On the diplomacy preceding the Hundred Years' War, the masterly study of Déprez, *Les préliminaires de la guerre de cent ans*, Paris, 1902, is a *résumé* of all the sources.

For the history of the Papacy during this period, besides Baluze, *Vitae Paparum Avenionensium*, Paris, 1693, see Gregorovius, *Geschichte der Stadt Rom im Mittelalter*, Stuttgart, 1894; Pastor, *Histoire des papes depuis la fin du Moyen Age*, Paris, 1901, translated from the German edition of earlier date, with valuable bibliography; also Norden, *Das Papsttum und Byzanz*, Berlin, 1903.

For the conflict of Edward III and Philip VI, besides Déprez, Longman, *The Life and Times of Edward III*, London, 1869; Mackinnon, *The History of Edward III (1327–1377)*, London, 1900; Viollet, *Histoire des institutions politiques de la France*, II, Paris, 1898; and Lehugeur, *Histoire de Philippe le Long*, Paris, 1896.

On the relations of Lewis of Bavaria with England, France, and the Papacy, see Leroux, *Recherches critiques sur les relations politiques de la France avec l'Allemagne de 1292 à 1378*, Paris, 1882; Sievers, *Die politischen Beziehungen Kaiser Ludwigs des Bayern zu Frankreich in den Jahren 1314–1337*, Berlin, 1896; Müller, *Der Kampf Ludwigs des Bayern mit der römischen Curie*, Tübingen, 1879–1880; Riezler, *Die literarischen Widersacher der Päpste zur Zeit Ludwigs des Bayern*, Leipzig, 1874.

The history of the time of the Emperor Charles IV is given by Wernusky, *Geschichte Karls IV und seiner Zeit*, Innsbruck, 1880–1893. The origin of the "Golden Bull" is discussed by Harnack, *Das Kurfürstenkollegium bis Mitte des 14ten Jahrhunderts*, Giessen, 1883; and Hahn, *Ursprung und Bedeutung der Goldenen Bulle*, Breslau, 1902.

The most detailed treatment of Cola di Rienzo is that of Papencordt, *Cola di Rienzo und seine Zeit*, Hamburg and Gotha, 1841.

The relations of the popes at Avignon before the return to Rome are discussed by Prou, *Étude sur les relations politiques d'Urban V avec les rois de France Jean II et Charles V*, Paris, 1888; the motives and circumstances of the return of the popes to Rome, by Mirot, *La politique pontificale et le retour du Saint-Siège à Rome en 1376*, Paris, 1899; the condition of Italy after the return, by Guiraud, *L'état pontifical après le grand schisme*, Paris, 1896; and the history of the papal elections is given, in a spirit of hostility to the Papacy, by Petrucelli della Gattina, *Histoire diplomatique des conclaves*, Paris, 1864.

The development and decay of the Hanseatic League are discussed by Lindner, *Die deutsche Hanse, ihre Geschichte und Bedeutung*, Leipzig, 1898; Daenell, *Geschichte der deutschen Hanse in der zweiten Hälfte des 14ten Jahrhundert*, Leipzig, 1897; Stein, *Beiträge zur Geschichte der deutschen Hanse bis um der Mitte des 15 Jahrhundert*, Giessen, 1900; Schäfer, *Die deutsche Hanse*, Leipzig, 1903; and Denicke, *Die Hansestädte, Dänemark, und Norwegen (1369-1376)*, Halle, 1880.

The Union of Kalmar is discussed by Erslev, *Dronning Margrethe og Kalmarunionens Grundlaegelse*, Copenhagen, 1883.

The struggle between the Teutonic Order and Poland is considered by Thunert, *Der Krieg zwischen Polen und den Deutschen Orden*, Regensburg, 1886. A good account of Hermann von Salza is found in Koch, *Hermann von Salza*, Leipzig, 1885. Joachim, *Die Politik des letzten Hochmeisters in Preussen, Albrecht von Brandenburg*, Leipzig, 1890 et seq., is an important publication based on the Prussian archives.

A general sketch of Austrian and Hungarian history is found in Leger, *Histoire de l'Autriche-Hongrie*, Paris, 1895; for Bohemia, Loserth, *Huss und Wiclif*, Prague, 1884, gives what is necessary. See also Burrows, *Wiclif's Place in History*, London, 1881, for the beginning of the Hussite movement.

The great councils of this period are discussed by Stuhr, *Die Organisation und Geschäftsordnung des Pisaner und Konstanzer Konsils*, Schwerin, 1891; and Creighton, *A History of the Papacy*, London, 1882, of which volumes I and II treat of the councils of Constance and Basel.

The policy and negotiations of the Emperor Sigismund are discussed by Göller, *König Sigismunds Kirchenpolitik 1404-1413*, Freiburg, 1902; Gierth, *Die Vermittlungsversuche König Sigismunds zwischen Frankreich und England*, Halle, 1896; Lenz, *König Sigismund und Heinrich der Fünfte von England*, Berlin, 1874; Kingsford, *Henry V*, London, 1902.

On the closing events of the Hundred Years' War, see Zeller, *Charles V et Du Guesclin, la diplomatie et la guerre*, Paris, 1886; Petit-Dutaillis, *La diplomatie française et la traité de Brétigny*, Paris, 1897; Benoist, *La politique du roi Charles V*, Paris, 1886; Lowell, *Joan of Arc*, Boston, 1896; Beaucourt, *Histoire de Charles VII*, Paris, 1881-1891; and the various histories of England.

On the fall of Constantinople, Pears, *The Destruction of the Greek Empire*, London, 1903.

CHAPTER II

THE DIPLOMACY OF FRENCH EXPANSION

WHEN France emerged from the century of conflict with England, it had acquired more completely than any other country of Europe the essential qualities of a modern state. The administration of Charles VII, aided by able ministers, had developed a financial and military organization superior to any other then existing. The "Ordonnance sur la Gendarmerie," passed by the States General at Orléans in 1439, was designed to end the robberies and atrocities committed by the undisciplined levies which had previously constituted the only defenders of the country. That act and a series of measures extending to 1445 placed the whole organization and control of the army in the hands of the King, forbade pillage, and provided for the regular payment of the troops. After suffering from the intolerable atrocities of an unpaid soldiery, the people were glad to pay the *taille*, or national tax collected by the King's own agents for the support of the army.[1]

The state of France at the end of the Hundred Years' War

Before the close of the war with England these new measures had resulted in the creation of a standing army — composed of infantry, cavalry, and artillery — supported by a fixed revenue administered exclusively by the Crown. The possession of this formidable and flexible instrument of power subsequently enabled the French kings to exercise an almost despotic sway over their people, and to carry on enterprises of territorial expansion and foreign adventure which previous to that time were impossible.

---

[1] It was the *bourgeois* minister, Jacques Cœur, who rendered permanent the *taille*, — a tax supplementary to the *aides* and the *gabelle*, — thus laying the foundation for the modern budget.

The initiative of France soon created a rivalry for power that gave a new character to the relations of all the European states. The increased necessity for information regarding the activities of friends and enemies led to the multiplication of diplomatic missions; and the constant contact with Italy, where a system of relative political equilibrium had already been built up by diplomacy, opened the way for the adoption of Italian methods of statecraft.

I. The Instruction of France in Italian Diplomacy

The need of external alliances

Although the English had been expelled from France, with the exception of Calais, in 1453, the kingdom was still flanked by the practically independent duchies of Brittany on the one side and Burgundy on the other. In 1349, a great area lying between the Rhone and the Alps, called Dauphiné, had been added to the French Crown by Philip VI; but, aside from this important acquisition, nearly all of that great realm north of the Alps which at the partition of Verdun was assigned to the kingdom of Lothair, then belonged to the Duke of Burgundy. From Lyons on the south, Orléans on the west and the Rhine on the east, practically all of the lands, except Lorraine [1] and Champagne, as far as the German Ocean were ruled by this powerful prince. Flanders, Artois, Franche-Comté, Nevers, and Rethel had been acquired by marriage with Margaret of Flanders. Namur had been obtained by purchase; Brabant and Limburg, by inheritance; Hainault, Holland, Zeeland, Friesland, and Luxemburg, by conventions with Jaqueline of Hainault and Elizabeth of Brabant. Containing within their limits excellent seaports and important centres of manufacture and commerce, these extensive territories, though subject by feudal law to obligations of vassalage, partly to the King of France and

---

[1] A part of the ancient Lotharingia shown on Map III of Volume I. See Map II in the present volume.

partly to the Emperor, made the Duke of Burgundy a formidable rival to both his suzerains.

By the Treaty of Arras Philip the Good had obtained the suspension during his own lifetime of the French suzerainty over the fiefs held of the King of France, and had diligently employed his time in building up his own exclusive authority within his realm. His policy was, in effect, a total separation from France, and plainly revealed his intention to create an independent kingdom. To this purpose, Charles VII, wholly absorbed in his war with England, was unable to raise opposition; and even when the Dauphin, Louis, took refuge with Philip the Good to escape from his father's wrath on account of his conspiracies with the French nobles, the King of France did not deem it prudent to make demands upon his disloyal vassal which he was unable to enforce. Contenting himself, therefore, with the caustic comment that Philip was "nourishing the fox that would one day devour his chickens," he steadily pursued his course of strengthening the kingdom, and left a settlement with the Duke of Burgundy for a future time.

But, while avoiding an open issue with his too powerful vassal, Charles VII, knowing that the coming conflict would require all his resources, did not neglect preparation for it. On every side, he sought to make alliances that would be of service to his cause and leave his enemy unprotected.

In Italy, after a century and a half of incessant diplomatic activity in pursuit of a durable system of equilibrium, five powers of considerable magnitude had been formed, embracing within their limits nearly the whole peninsula. In the South, the Kingdom of Naples, together with Sicily, had fallen to the rule of Alfonso V of Aragon. In Central Italy, the State of the Church, reconstituted by Martin V and Eugenius IV, had been consolidated into a compact principality including most of the territory between Rome and Ravenna. Florence had united the greater part of Tuscany under the rule of the Republic, then practically governed by the Medici. In the North, Francesco Sforza, a successful *condottiere* of humble origin who had married an illegitimate daughter of Filippo Maria Visconti, Duke of Milan, had made himself master of that powerful state, which then comprised nearly the whole of Lombardy. Finally, the Republic of Venice, having extended its dominion on the mainland as far west as the river Adda, had become a competitor with Milan for the possession of Lombardy; and, relying upon its great wealth and powerful navy, aspired to the chief place in Italy.[1]

In 1379, Pope Clement VII, of Avignon, in the hope of regaining possession of the papal estates in Italy then passing into the hands of the local princes or becoming independent republics, had planned an extension of the Angevin rule by creating for Louis of Anjou, brother of Charles V of France, a new kingdom to be called the "Kingdom of Adria," — so named from the city of Adria, situated on the Adige southwest of Venice, from which the Adriatic takes its name. The proposed kingdom was to be formed primarily from territories that had belonged to the Papacy extending from Ancona to the Po, and containing the cities of Bologna, Ravenna, and Ferrara.[2] This plan for the papal recovery of Italy was never executed; but it excited the apprehensions of Venice, whose interests would have been seriously men-

---

[1] A glance at Map III, at the end of this volume, shows in addition to the five chief powers of Italy just described, the Marquisates of Saluzzo, Montferrat, and Mantua; the Duchies of Modena and Ferrara; and the Republics of Genoa, Lucca, and Siena. These were, politically, of less importance than their area on the map would indicate, which is somewhat exaggerated in order to indicate their locality. Their part in the movements about to be described will be noticed when necessary; but, not being fully independent powers, a minute account of them would render the subject of Italian politics more complicated than their importance justifies.

[2] Commenting upon this project, Pastor regards it as an illustration of the extent to which the sentiment of French nationality had taken possession of the Pope, since he was willing to bestow upon a French prince the greater part of the State of the Church. *Histoire des papes*, I, p. 148.

aced by its success, and made that republic the vigilant antagonist of French influence in Italy.

The attitude of Venice toward France was strengthened by the efforts of its ancient rival, Genoa, then overwhelmed with misfortunes by the loss of its eastern trade and by its internal dissensions, to throw itself into the arms of France. After long negotiations, in November, 1396, a capitulation had been made on the part of the Genoese by which that republic had become a French protectorate, and a French governor had been placed over it. The abandonment of Genoa by France and its surrender to the Duke of Milan, in 1421, while relieving in part the apprehensions of Venice regarding French intentions, had created a far greater immediate danger to the peace of the peninsula; for the acquisition of Genoa had given to Milan the preponderance in Northern Italy.

Once possessed of Genoa, Milan had not failed to realize the danger that might arise from too close dependence upon France. Made a prisoner of war by Filippo Maria Visconti in 1434, Alfonso V, King of Aragon, had pointed out to his captor that, if the domination of the House of Anjou should replace his own at Naples, the French would hold Italy at their mercy. So impressed was the Duke of Milan by this observation that he not only released his royal prisoner from captivity, but made an alliance with him.

The death of Filippo Maria Visconti, Duke of Milan, in 1447, had given the affairs of Italy an interest for the whole of Europe which they had not possessed for more than a century. Five claimants disputed the succession of this great duchy: the German emperor, who claimed it as a fief of the Empire;[1] King Alfonso V of Aragon, who posed as sole heir by the last will of the late duke;[2] Charles, Duke of Orléans,

---

[1] Frederick III was in Italy at the time of the dispute over the succession, but did nothing more than proclaim his rights.

[2] It was pretended that Filippo Maria Visconti had executed a codicil to his will bequeathing the duchy to Alfonso V. The existence of this codicil, the original of which has never been produced,

who was the next of kin through his mother, Valentine Visconti; Francesco Sforza, husband of Blanche, the natural daughter of Filippo Maria Visconti; and finally, his widow, the duchess dowager, daughter of Amadeus VIII, by whose influence her brother, Louis, Duke of Savoy, hoped to be made Duke of Milan.

Although distinctly warned by Charles VII not to interfere with the rights of the Duke of Orléans — whose claim was thus recognized by the King of France — Louis had prepared to press the pretensions of Savoy;[1] and for this purpose had made a compact with a party of the Milanese in November, 1446, nearly a year before the death of Filippo Maria Visconti. Supported at first by the approval of his father, Amadeus VIII, then antipope under the name of Felix V, — who from the beginning perceived the magnitude of an enterprise which if successful would make his son ruler of a realm extending from Lake Léman on the north to Venice on the east and the Mediterranean on the south, — Louis endeavored to raise an army, in order to make good his pretensions; but his lack of pecuniary resources, for which he made almost frantic appeals to his father, left him without sufficient military strength to carry out his plans, and led him at last to form an alliance with the Duke of Orléans for the partition of the Milanese territory between them.

But even this combination was not sufficiently strong to counterbalance the energetic movements of Francesco Sforza. While Sforza's rivals were busily negotiating with Venice for its support, that republic, secretly hostile to the ambitions of both Savoy and Orléans, was on the point of concluding an alliance with Alfonso of Aragon as the least objectionable claimant; when, suddenly convinced of the certain triumph

---

has been strongly contested. See Cipolla, *Storia delle signorie italiane*, p. 427; and Perret, *Histoire des relations de la France avec Venise*, I, p. 194.

[1] The text of the letter of Charles VII to Louis of Savoy is in the Geneva Archives, "Affaires Etrangères," No. XXIV; see also Gaullier, *Correspondance du Pape Félix*, p. 55.

of Sforza, it hastily signed a treaty with him on October 18, 1448, at Rivoltella, by which Venice was promised a small territorial compensation for its friendship.

But the Signory of Venice, which had allied itself with Sforza only to avoid his enmity and share in his expected spoil, doubting for a time of his success, reversed its policy and went over to the Republican party of Milan by a treaty signed at Brescia, on September 24, 1449; when, to the surprise and chagrin of the Venetians, Sforza entered Milan in triumph. Florence, which had joined Venice in supporting him, remained faithful; and Venice was thus left in isolation. No time was lost, however, in averting the effects of this miscalculation. Uniting with Sforza's enemies, the Duke of Savoy and Alfonso V, a triple alliance was promptly formed for the partition of Italy between the signatories.

In this emergency, Florence, which had been traditionally the friend of France, resolved to invite the aid of Charles VII; thus affording an opportunity for making French influence preponderant in Italy.

Angelo Acciajuoli, one of the ablest diplomatists of that period and a personal friend of Sforza, being already in relations with René of Anjou, — who, as the representative of the Angevin claims to Naples, was then aspiring to the throne of that kingdom, — was sent by the Florentines in September, 1451, to congratulate Charles VII upon his victories over the English, to assure him of the faithful devotion of Florence, and to procure his aid in preventing the secretly arranged partition of Italy between Venice, Savoy, and Alfonso of Aragon. Thus, once more, after a long period of independence sustained by leagues and alliances among the Italian states, the system of equilibrium was destroyed, the presence of the foreigner was again invoked, and Italy became the prey of European avarice.

At Milan, counsels were at first divided. The King of France, it was suggested, would assemble his States General at Lyons, obtain their assent to an invasion of Italy, take possession of Genoa, make himself master of the peninsula, demand the imperial crown, transfer the Papacy once more to Avignon, and take vengeance upon the Dukes of Burgundy and Savoy, and others who had shown themselves favorable to England in the Hundred Years' War. To avert this disaster, Italy should unite, compose its own dissensions, and by presenting a solid front to the foreigner preserve its own peace and unity.

However wise this programme of Italian independence may have been, it was not the one accepted by Francesco Sforza. As a usurper of rights which the King of France might be disposed to sustain against him, his personal advantage was, without doubt, to join with the Florentines and secure if possible a French alliance. On his way to France, Acciajuoli visited Milan, assured himself of Sforza's acquiescence, and made haste to fulfil his mission.

The ambassador was received by Charles VII with caution, and days elapsed before his answer was returned. Having finally, on December 21, accepted in principle the proposition of alliance, the King still hesitated to furnish forces from France, where they were needed to protect the country against the English. He called attention to the fact that Genoa — then once more independent — had, on November 4, concluded a treaty with Florence and Milan in which its independence had been guaranteed by them against Alfonso V, and suggested that this obligation might, perhaps, in future be turned against himself.

The opponents of the alliance had pointed out the small advantage of an adventure in Italy during the unsettled state of the kingdom, the utility of supporting the rights of the Orléans family rather than the claims of Sforza, and the impossibility of establishing the House of Anjou at Naples without a larger sacrifice than France was prepared to make. But neither these arguments nor his own mental reservations convinced the King. The influence of René overcame them all, and on February 21, 1452, at Montils-les-Tours, a treaty was signed with Florence and Milan, in which the two Italian states agreed to sustain the interests of Charles VII in

Italy; and he in return to protect them, if molested, against all enemies, except the Emperor and the Pope, and to send a prince of his blood with an army for their defence.

To the Treaty of Montils-les-Tours Venice and Alfonso V responded promptly by a declaration of war. Sforza, already on the defensive, was able to hold the Venetians in check; but the Florentines were exposed to grave danger from the large army sent against them by Alfonso V. The efforts of Charles VII to detach Louis of Savoy from the Venetian alliance, though temporarily successful, were of no practical use to the Florentines; who, after urgent appeals for aid to the King of France, then fully occupied at home, sought it directly of René of Anjou.

The treaty made by Florence with this claimant to the throne of Naples on April 11, 1453, while ostensibly a contract engaging the Republic to support him in his royal pretensions, was in effect only a bargain to pay him in cash for his military services, and placed him upon the footing of a mere hired *condottiere*.[1] Having been signed without any obligations on the part of the King, the treaty permitted Charles VII to claim all the prestige which might result from René's success, and in the event of failure to disavow having taken any part in the expedition.

Both René and Charles VII were, however, to receive important lessons in Italian politics. After having been refused passage for his troops by Louis of Savoy, who in spite of the King's insistence caused a long delay, René finally arrived in Italy to learn that Sforza and the Florentines were endeavoring privately to arrange a peace with the Venetians, and intended to cancel their contract with him without reference to his Neapolitan expectations. When these negotiations were divulged, to appease the indignation of René, Sforza assured him that no arrangement with Alfonso V had been contemplated, and that he was ready to die for him.

---

[1] The treaty has been published by Lecoy de la Marche, *Le roi René*, II, p. 265.

A few days afterward, the Duke informed an agent of the King of Aragon that, now he had become Duke of Milan, he was opposed to any solid establishment of the French in Italy, for he would always be threatened with the claims of the Duke of Orléans!

Notwithstanding the secrecy of the constant negotiations for a peace to be so concluded as to eliminate him from the scene, René gradually became aware of the deception practised upon him. His efforts to isolate Alfonso V by arranging a separate peace between Venice, Florence, and Milan proved unavailing. His wish to lead his troops southward and confront the King of Naples in open conflict was defeated by the Florentines' concentration of their own troops in the South; insisting that René, thus confined to the North and separated from his chief antagonist, should defend them against Venice. At length, the unsophisticated ally discovered that the chief problem that remained to his confederates was how to get rid of him without aiding his cause against the King of Naples. When he had clearly perceived this, with mingled irony and courtesy, René withdrew to France, promising to send his son, John of Anjou, Duke of Calabria, to take his place. After a short and ineffectual campaign, the Duke of Calabria also abandoned an enterprise so obviously hopeless. Venice and Sforza concluded a peace by the Treaty of Lodi, on April 9, 1454; Florence acceded to it on April 23; on January 26, 1455, Alfonso V added his adherence; and the Pope subsequently joined the concert. Charles VII, chagrined at the manner in which the Duke of Anjou had been duped, disclaimed responsibility for the failure of his adventure; and the Italians, satisfied, for the time, that the French had not acquired a foothold in Italy, transformed the Peace of Lodi into a league nominally intended to promote a crusade against the Turks, but really to prevent the progress of French influence south of the Alps.

Reoccupation of Genoa by the French

In the formation of the league for the protection of Italy against France, the Republic of Genoa, formally excluded from participation in it, was reserved as a prey to the Duke of Milan and the King of Aragon. Menaced on land by the former and on the sea by the latter, the Republic once more attempted to preserve its existence by surrendering itself to France.

On his journey homeward, John of Anjou, in March, 1456, was authorized by Fregoso, Doge of Genoa, and Fiesco, Admiral of the Genoese navy, to request the King of France to resume the government of the Republic, in the same manner as in 1396. Charles VII accepted the invitation, and John of Anjou was promptly appointed the future governor.

Although the transaction was intended to be secret, both Sforza and Alfonso V became aware of the negotiations, and combined to prevent the execution of the plan. Simulating a fervent friendship for Charles VII, and attempting to disarm suspicion by unusual gifts and courtesies, Sforza steadily prepared to carry out his engagements with the King of Aragon, at the same time secretly fomenting opposition to the French among the Genoese themselves. While the Milanese ambassador, Tibaldo, was flattering the King and busily reporting every movement made in France, Alfonso V was fitting out a naval expedition against Genoa, which Sforza was to support by land. In the meantime, the Duke of Calabria was concluding a treaty with the Genoese by which their rights and privileges were to be maintained; and on May 11, 1458, he entered the city, received the oath of fidelity from the inhabitants, and assumed the task of government.

The moment was critical, for the forces sent by Sforza were approaching by the mountains, the malcontents incited by his emissaries were ready to resort to arms, and the Neapolitan fleet had concentrated to assault the city; but in the midst of his preparations for resistance, John received the news that Alfonso V had suddenly died on June 27; that the fleet had, in consequence, dispersed, and the Milanese troops turned homeward.

The death of the King of Aragon created an entirely new situation; for, while John of Navarre thereby became Alfonso's successor in Aragon, the succession to the crown of

Sforza's opposition to France

Naples was again thrown open. In Italy, the attitude of the Duke of Milan became of the highest importance; since, if he sided with the Aragonese claimant, Ferdinand, the natural son of Alfonso V, he would be able to frustrate the efforts of the House of Anjou in the North while Ferdinand resisted its advances in the South.

At this juncture, a new element entered the contest in the person of Pope Calixtus III, who had succeeded Nicholas V in 1455. Calixtus had been friendly to Alfonso V, but he was the declared adversary of Ferdinand, whom he refused to recognize, and, by his bull of July 12, 1458, declared that the Kingdom of Naples had reverted to its original suzerain, the Holy See.

Strongly inclined toward the House of Anjou, Calixtus III perceived the necessity of propitiating Sforza,— now become the head of the opposition to France and the arbiter of Italy, — and offered him every inducement to support the claims of René of Anjou; but the Duke of Milan, while assuring René of his cordial friendship, and even felicitating him upon the success of his son at Genoa, obstinately resisted the Pope's importunity, and declared his purpose to sustain the pretensions of Ferdinand.

In the midst of these negotiations, on August 6, Calixtus III died, and was succeeded by Aeneas Sylvius Piccolomini, who assumed the pontificate as Pius II. Resolute antagonist of the House of Anjou, the new pope replied to the request of Charles VII for René's investiture with the Kingdom of Naples, that the throne was already occupied by another prince, that the great interest of Christendom was to oppose the progress of the Turks, and that to render that movement successful it was necessary to pacify all the Christian princes. A short time afterward, he gave the investiture to Ferdinand, discreetly adding the formula, "save the rights of another."

Notwithstanding the action of the Pope, Charles VII sent embassies to press upon the Duke of Milan and the Republic of Florence the support of René. Both replied with polite refusals, pleading in excuse their solemn treaty engagements with the late king of Aragon. But the official reply of Florence was only intended to preserve appearances. Secretly, Cosimo de' Medici, then practically the dictator of Florence, fearing the continuance of Alfonso's policy by Ferdinand, desired the establishment of the House of Anjou at Naples, and used his influence with Sforza to change his policy. But the remonstrance of Charles VII and the persuasion of Cosimo were alike unavailing. The political instinct of Sforza was not at fault, for the greatest danger to his own ambitions was the predominance of France in Italy.

The pacific mood of the new king of Aragon, John II, who was anxious to confirm the union of Aragon and Navarre, enabled Charles VII to disembarrass himself of hostile action from that quarter against Genoa by forming a treaty of alliance with him at Valencia, on June 27, 1459, but, in the meantime, Sforza had made good the loss of his old ally by a secret compact with Ferdinand, the new king of Naples.

While John of Anjou was consolidating his power at Genoa, a conspiracy to crush him had been formed by these new confederates. Counting on the support of the citizens, the former Doge, Fregoso, and the Admiral, Fiesco, won over and provided with troops by Sforza, had plotted an attack by land, while a Neapolitan fleet was to make an assault by sea; but the inhabitants were loyal to their new governor, Fiesco was slain, Fregoso forced to retreat to Lombardy and afterward killed, and the triumphant Duke of Calabria acquired complete ascendency at Genoa. In October, 1459, confiding in the loyalty of the Genoese, he decided to attempt the conquest of Naples, and embarked with his fleet upon that enterprise.

While John of Anjou was engaged in his ill-starred adventure in trying to dispossess Ferdinand and acquire the Kingdom of Naples, Pope Pius II was opening the general congress of princes he had called at Mantua for the purpose of pacifying Christendom and organizing a crusade against

CHAP. II
A. D.
1453–1492

The peril and relief of Genoa

The Congress of Mantua

the Infidel. From the commencement to the end, the Congress was not only a disappointment but a bitter revelation both of the disregard into which the Papacy had fallen as an international influence, and of the national and personal ambitions by which the princes were then inspired. Convoked for June 1, 1459, the Congress did not open until the end of September; and was attended by none of the sovereigns, while only a few of them even sent ambassadors.

But there were particular reasons why neither the German emperor nor the King of France was disposed to join in the proposed crusade. Frederick III was not only devoid of military talent, but he was offended with the Pope, who had once been his secretary and had served him as a diplomatist, because of his attitude toward Hungary and Bohemia. In the conflict of Hungary with the Turks, a native leader, John Hunyady, had made a brilliant record and won the unbounded admiration of the Hungarians. When the young king, Ladislas Postumus, died without descendants, the Hungarian nobles, disregarding the hereditary claims of the House of Austria, in January, 1458, had chosen Matthias Corvinus, son of Hunyady, to be King of Hungary. In Bohemia, a similar national feeling had elevated to the throne, in March, 1458, the popular leader, George Podiebrad. Frederick III, deeply disappointed by the loss of these two thrones, which he had confidently hoped to occupy, had vainly appealed to Pius II to support his claims. Resenting the Pope's recognition of Matthias Corvinus, the Emperor sent no ambassadors to the Congress, and only a few German princes were represented.

Charles VII had a similar cause of dissatisfaction, but was still anxious to win the Pope's support. In the hope of employing their influence in pressing upon Pius II the Angevin claims to Naples, he wrote to his allies, — the Kings of Castile, Aragon, Scotland, and Denmark, — asking them to join with him in sending ambassadors to Mantua. The kings took no interest in the Congress, and even the embassy of France did not make its appearance until the middle of November. With a fine show of dignity, Pius II then kept the six ambassadors waiting for an audience; and it was not until December that their business was discussed. With skill and eloquence the ambassadors then presented the claims of the House of Anjou to the Kingdom of Naples; but the Pope with firmness adhered to his attitude and complained bitterly of the "Pragmatic Sanction," so detrimental to the authority of the Holy See and the unity of the Church.

Left thus without support by the monarchs of Europe, Pius II saw the Congress of Mantua and his plan for a general crusade against the Turks end in dismal failure. On January 18, 1460, the assembly was adjourned, but not until the Pope had formally declared war upon the Turks and issued the Bull "Execrabilis," by which he condemned as heresy an appeal from a papal decision to a general council.

The foreign policy of Charles VII had been constantly hampered by his relations with the English, with whom no definitive peace had been concluded, and by the independence and jealousy of the Dukes of Burgundy and Brittany. Until the King's death, these conditions did not wholly change; although in 1460, — through the dissensions of the Houses of York and Lancaster in England, then devastated by the Wars of the Roses, and the good offices of Margaret of Anjou, the French wife of King Henry VI, and her victories over the Duke of York, — the fear of hostilities had subsided; while his good understanding with the German princes and the possession of Genoa seemed to have prepared the way for that final subjection of his vassals which was necessary to the security of France.

The quarrel with the Dauphin, Louis, who, though once forgiven, had proved a serious disturber of his father's plans, had only deepened until his final flight, in 1456, to find asylum with the Duke of Burgundy. Married to Charlotte, daughter of Louis, Duke of Savoy, the future Louis XI had for ten years ruled at Grenoble, in Dauphiné, almost as an independent monarch; forming alliances on his own account, encouraging his father's enemies, and laying plots to frustrate his father's policy. Even before his marriage, he had offered his assistance to the Duke of Savoy in his scheme to become the possessor of Milan, carried on against the solemn injunction of the King; and had concluded with the Duke an offensive and defensive alliance without regard to his father's interests.[1] In his marriage contract, he had stipulated for the possession of Nice in a manner that revealed his intention to sway the future destinies of Savoy.[2] For years he had been in secret negotiations with Venice, Florence, and Francesco Sforza, for whom he conceived a warm admiration, accepting him as a model and master in the arts of diplomacy. By his constant and intimate relations with Italians, Louis had learned their language, penetrated their motives, and acquired all their *finesse*. All the traditions which had passed from Byzantium to Venice, and from Venice to the rest of Italy, were now to be made European by this apt and astute pupil. A Milanese ambassador spoke truly when he said of Louis, " It seems as if the King has always lived and been brought up in Italy."[3]

Accession of Louis XI

When, therefore, Charles VII died, on July 22, 1461, and the Dauphin became King of France as Louis XI, a radical change of policy was to be expected, and in this the world was not disappointed. Already accomplished in statecraft through his intimate contact with Italian politics, wholly devoid of conscientious scruples, and naturally endowed with the spirit of intrigue, this disciple of Francesco Sforza, though lacking in his military qualities, was to apply all the lessons of Italy to the problems of France and to open thereby a new era in the history of Europe.

Proceeding to Paris, after his coronation at Reims, in company with his friend the aged Duke of Burgundy, who played a conspicuous part in the ceremonies of his installation, the

---

[1] Geneva Archives, "Affaires Etrangères," No. XXIV, and Gaullier, *Correspondance*, pp. 58 et seq.

[2] The same, as above.

[3] " Pare que questo re sia sempre stato e elevato in Italia."

exile of Genappe dismissed his father's ministers, permitted the retention of the Duchy of Berry by his brother Charles, placed the government of the region between the Lower Seine and the Loire in the hands of the Duke of Brittany, and that of Normandy in those of Charles, Count of Charolais, son of Philip the Good, and heir to the vast estates of Burgundy.

For a time, it seemed as if the young king intended to apply in practice the conception of government which he had held as a supporter of the "Praguerie," and to restore the power of the feudal nobles. Not content with these revolutionary changes, he astonished France by the abolition of the "Pragmatic Sanction," — the charter of ecclesiastic independence of the nation. In thus restoring at the same time the power of the feudal lords and the authority of the Papacy, it appeared as if the reckless monarch was ruthlessly sacrificing all the national interests of France and reinvoking the Middle Ages.

But the policy of Louis XI was not inspired by motives upon the surface. Vast and far-reaching plans underlay his apparently malicious reversal of his father's system. Aiming at absolute control in France, he hoped to attain also unlimited preponderance in Italy. With Genoa as a military and naval base, the Orléans family established at Milan, the House of Anjou in possession of Naples, and the Pope friendly to his ambitions, he might become greater than any other sovereign of his time.

The key to this spendid enterprise was the pacification of France and an alliance with the Papacy. To compose the affairs of his kingdom, he sought to make himself the source of generous benefactions to those who might otherwise oppose his schemes. The next step was to make the Pope the instrument of his ambition.

Eager to procure the abolition of the hateful "Pragmatic Sanction," Pius II had named the accomplished Jouffroy, impatient for the hat of a cardinal, as his legate in France. This able emisssary pointed out to Louis that the effect of the "Pragmatic Sanction" was to place regalian rights over the

Church in the hands of the great nobles, and that its abolition would restore them to the King. But Louis required little persuasion, for he wished to engage the Pope. Accordingly, with the understanding that Pius II would sustain his interests in Italy, the act was abolished, and the King believed he had made a master stroke.

If Pius II had been a less astute diplomatist than himself, his end would, no doubt, have been accomplished; but, although His Holiness was exultant over the acquiescence of the King, and Rome was made red with bonfires at the Pope's command to celebrate the triumph, embassy after embassy vainly employed its eloquence at the papal court to obtain recognition of the House of Anjou. Showering upon the King of France the most extravagant praises for his virtue, justice, charity, fidelity, and generosity, and confirming the proud title of "*Roi Très-Chrétien*" which Louis claimed as derived from Charles the Great, Pius II either evaded the question or postponed his final answer; until at last, forced by Louis' threat to restore the previous relations, he complained that he was the victim of the unanimous wishes of Italy and his solemnly pledged engagements with Ferdinand of Naples, ending with an obstinate *non possumus*.

II. THE STRUGGLE OF FRANCE WITH BURGUNDY

Thus defeated in the stratagem most essential to his purpose, Louis XI, whose absolutism had rudely shocked the churchmen and nobles of France, now realized the error of judgment he had committed in confiding in his ability to manipulate the Pope. "The universal spider," as Chastellain has called the King, had laid his web with consummate skill; but his invitation to enter it was marred by the revelation of his deep designs at the centre of the entanglements he had so deftly spread. The Parliament refused to register his act of revocation; the nobles cried out at being deprived of their valuable privileges with the revenues of the Church; and Francis II, Duke of Brittany, stubbornly refused to surrender to the King the prerogatives which he claimed over the abbeys and bishoprics of his domain. The Pope sent a legate to intervene in the dispute; and the King, furious at the intrusion of a foreign power between him and his vassal, replied by causing his arrest and the seizure of his papers.

Not content with his quarrel with the Duke of Brittany and his rupture with the Pope, Louis XI, suspecting secret relations between Francis of Brittany and Charles of Charolais, the future Duke of Burgundy, deposed the latter from the government of Normandy; and, in order to weaken his influence in the Burgundian realm, began fomenting disturbances against him. By the aid of his friends Antoine de Croy and Jean de Chimay Louis induced the aged Duke Philip to permit the restoration of the towns on the river Somme ceded by France to Burgundy by the Treaty of Arras, for the sum of four hundred thousand crowns; but Charles was able to procure the disgrace and expulsion of Louis' friends.

Under the name of the "League of the Public Weal," a coalition of the aggrieved nobles was formed in 1465 to resist the absolute rule which the King was aiming to impose. His brother, Charles of Berry, fled to Brittany; the dismissed adherents of Charles VII rallied round the rebellious duke; and Charles of Burgundy, — soon to acquire the surname the "Bold," — joined with the Duke of Brittany in opposition to the King. Closed in by hostile vassals on every side, and betrayed by secret enemies everywhere, his situation was soon rendered most precarious. Fearing above all the revival of the Burgundian alliance with England, he now resolved to crush the nobility and unify France by every means within his power.

Holding steadily before him the fixed purpose to effect the unification of France at any cost, Louis XI now resolved not to favor the Anjou policy of pursuing phantoms in Italy, and to concentrate all his forces upon France. Before his accession, Genoa had revolted from John of Anjou, and the expedition to Naples had since proved a vain adventure.

By abandoning to Sforza Genoa, — a dependency that was in revolt and had to be reconquered, — he won the support of that astute ruler; but, in order to give the appearance of value to his concession, he first announced his intention of reconquering Genoa, and afterward entered into active negotiations with all the states of Italy. Venice was made to feel the power of France by the proposal to aid in the war against the Turks, then threatening the destruction of Venetian commerce, on condition that Genoa be made the port of shipment for the troops. Florence was already the friend of France, and Ferdinand of Naples was anxious to end the contest with the Angevins. When all these circumstances had added their full weight to increase the desire of Sforza for the undisturbed possession of Genoa, Louis XI, on December 22, 1463, signed a treaty with the Duke of Milan by which, in exchange for his alliance, Genoa and Savona were ceded to him.

By this convention Louis XI gained from the Italian situation, without any real cost, all it had to give; for he secured the military support of Sforza — who sent his eldest son, Galeazzo, with a body of five thousand men to the King's aid — and quieted Italy by abandoning the claims of Anjou and Orléans, already hopeless through the unwillingness of Pius II to pay the price promised for the abolition of the "Pragmatic Sanction." While the policy of concentration temporarily alienated from the King the Angevin and Orléans princes at a moment when their co-operation would have been useful, and his inaction in the crusade against the Turks offended Venice, his conduct had the merit of being both national and prudent. In the great struggle with Burgundy upon which he was soon to enter, Louis XI was endeavoring to cut off from Charles the Bold a group of possible alliances which might determine the fate of France.

The diplomacy of Louis XI with his vassals

Another benefit derived from the alliance with Sforza was the practical advice of which Louis XI, notwithstanding his aptitude in statecraft, then stood in need: "Divide your enemies by temporarily satisfying the demands of each," — was Sforza's counsel to his friend and pupil; — "then destroy them, one by one, without giving them a chance for combination."

This precept not only pointed out the defect in Louis' previous procedure in creating so many enemies at once, but it was in harmony with his genius for deception and intrigue. Opening separate negotiations with his different adversaries, on October 5, 1465, he concluded with his rebellious vassals the Treaty of Conflans, by which the fiction of the "public weal" was exposed, and the personal greed of the confederates revealed.[1] Regardless of the public interests, for which they had been nominally contending, each of the allied nobles was solicitous only for a generous share in the distribution of favors with which the wily king was now beguiling his enemies. The towns on the Somme were restored to Burgundy; Normandy was promised to Charles of Berry; Montfort and Étampes, with the coveted rights regarding church revenues, went to appease the Duke of Brittany; John of Anjou was placated by the promise of funds for his cause in Italy, while the mercenary and treacherous Count St. Pol was permitted to fill the high office of Constable of France.

At the moment, it seemed like a complete defeat of the purposes and policy of the King; but this conclusion, which temporarily disarmed his foes, was altogether delusive. In reality, he had dispensed at Conflans nothing but empty promises; and on his return to Paris, after new engagements made at St. Maur, on October 27 and 29, he procured the refusal of Parliament to register them, on the ground that they had been made under forcible constraint and not of his own free will.

Having thus separated his opponents, in January, 1466, Louis XI took possession of Normandy, arranging with his brother Charles for the arbitration of his rights by John of

Isolation of Charles the Bold in France

---

[1] For this and the later treaties of Louis XI with his vassals, see Léonard, *Recueil*, I.

Anjou and the Count St. Pol, — who were then in the King's pay, — and an annual pension until the case was settled.

The death of Pius II in 1464, hastened by his chagrin over the failure of Europe to support his plans against the Turks, had not ended the controversy of Louis XI with the Papacy, which was continued with the new pope, Paul II. But, following out his policy of concentration, and wishing to arm himself once more against the nobles, and to strengthen himself in Italy, on July 24, 1467, the King revoked his numerous ordinances against the papal authority, and even permitted the collection of a tax to aid in the "Holy War."

On September 10, 1468, he made a convention with the Duke of Brittany, by which the Duke promised to enter into no alliance against the King, and especially with the Duke of Burgundy.

Thus isolated in France, Charles the Bold, who, by the death of Philip the Good in 1467 had become Duke of Burgundy, was the adversary against whom all the King's strength was now to be directed.

The changed situation in Italy

Although Charles of Burgundy was now isolated from his former allies in France, he was far from being without support elsewhere. In Italy, important changes had occurred which affected the position of the King of France, while the proposed marriage of Charles the Bold with Margaret of York, sister of King Edward IV of England, and the quarrel of Bohemia with the Papacy threatened Louis XI with new embarrassments.

The death of Cosimo de' Medici, on August 1, 1464, had thrown Florence into a tumult, in which his son Piero de' Medici was menaced with the triumph of his opponents, the Soderini, and had been obliged to seek support by forming a league with Galeazzo Sforza, — who had succeeded to the Duchy of Milan upon the death of his father in March, 1466, — and Ferdinand of Naples, the chief enemy of France. The death of Francesco Sforza had again aroused the hopes of Savoy for the Milanese succession; and Philip of Bresse, brother of the reigning Duke of Savoy, Amadeus IX, supported by Venice, had secretly woven a web of tentative alliances directed equally against the King of France and Galeazzo Sforza, the King's only active ally in Italy, from whom Philip hoped to win Milan. Already in league with Charles of Burgundy, Philip of Bresse was plotting an open union with him against Louis XI, to become effective at the opportune moment, when, deprived of support by the fall of Sforza, the King of France would be unable to resist their plans.

In the midst of these complications, George Podiebrad, King of Bohemia, having been cited to appear at Rome to answer for his contumacy toward the Holy See, had refused to respond, arrested the pontifical envoy sent to coerce him, and declined to publish the bull against heretics. While Paul II, who had inherited this quarrel from Pius II, was endeavoring to subdue the King of Bohemia with the aid of the Emperor Frederick III, Podiebrad sent ambassadors to Louis XI, asking for his support in calling a general council; at the same time pointing out the peril in which the royal authority everywhere was placed by the pretensions of the Pope.

Offended by these negotiations with his enemies, and especially by Louis' promise to sustain the compacts of the Council of Basel, Paul II made strenuous efforts to procure the publication in France of the bull in which he deposed Podiebrad and his son for levying taxes upon ecclesiastics without the consent of the Pope. Supported vigorously by his parliament, Louis refused to permit the publication of the bull in France, on the ground that none of his predecessors had ever recognized a superior in temporal affairs.[1]

But the necessity of disarming opposition in Italy soon afterward induced Louis XI to invoke once more the good offices of the Pope, who not only held the balance of power

---

[1] For the details, see Combet, *Louis XI et le Saint-Siège*, p. 75.

as between the combination of Milan and Florence on the one hand, and of Venice and Savoy on the other, but would be able to prevent a conflict in which Galeazzo Sforza might either lose Milan or become so preoccupied with Venice as to fail to hold in check the devices of Savoy.

The interview and Treaty of Péronne

Hoping to gain time and complete his preparations for the final issue, Louis XI, to the astonishment of Europe, now took a step so rash in conception and so humiliating in its consequences as to imperil his political existence. Having first obtained a safe conduct from Charles of Burgundy, he ventured upon a personal interview with his formidable enemy. In October, 1468, accompanied by a small retinue, he met Charles at Péronne, where he hoped to beguile him into the permanent abandonment of his former allies in France, whose previous submission, Louis appears to have thought, would dishearten him.

Unfortunately for Louis XI, he had quite overlooked the consequences that might result from the fact, that, at that very moment, his own emissaries were at Liège actively engaged in exciting rebellion against Charles of Burgundy. While the King was receiving the hospitality of his enemy at Péronne, the news arrived that the Bishop of Liège had been seized, and that several members of his chapter had been murdered. Rendered furious by this barbarity, Charles was on the point of making Louis answer for it with his life, and was dissuaded only by the intervention of his advisers. Recalling the fact that the King's father had been accused of instigating the murder of John of Burgundy, Charles the Bold might, perhaps, have felt justified in a crime so foolishly provoked; but, he chose, instead, to use his power over the person of his unhappy guest. While the citizens of Liège were shouting "Long live the King," the captive monarch was forced to accompany the Burgundian army and lead an expedition against his own friends.

But this humiliation was not enough. Preferring to consolidate his own domain rather than to create a new coalition of the French nobles, Charles the Bold required the King to cede to his brother, Charles of Berry, instead of Normandy, the estates of Champagne and Brie; thus forming a bridge of friendly territory between his northern and southern possessions, by which he hoped to unite them more effectively. Louis consented, but his alert intelligence, ever ready to repair an error, led him to suggest before he was set at liberty that Charles of Berry might prefer another arrangement. To this Charles the Bold carelessly replied, that the King would be expected to satisfy his brother. To evade the fulfilment of his promise, Louis, taking his opponent's answer as a permission, offered to Charles of Berry, instead of Champagne and Brie, the richer Duchy of Guyenne. The bribe was accepted, the design of Charles the Bold was defeated, and the King's two enemies, so formidable together, were thus kept apart. The death of Charles of Berry a few years later permitted the reversion of Guyenne to the Crown of France, and thus finally removed the last substantial consequence of the King's rash performance.[1]

Thus outwitted by Louis XI, Charles the Bold was apparently counterbalancing his defeat in France by his negotiations in Germany. The troubled state of the Empire, then in a condition of anarchy, afforded to the Duke of Burgundy an inviting opportunity. While the Turks were menacing the eastern frontier of Christendom, the rivalries among the German states were not less threatening. Podiebrad, deposed by Paul II, was scheming to form a coalition between Austria — then ruled by Duke Sigismund — Bohemia, Hungary, and Poland for defence against the Turks, and at the same time in defiance of the Pope and the Emperor. Frederick III, in turn, was trying to detach Matthias Corvinus, King of Hungary, from alliance with Podiebrad by tempting him with the Kingdom of Bohemia and the succession to the imperial

---

[1] The Treaty of Péronne, signed on October 14, 1468, does not contain the promise regarding Champagne and Brie; but Commines, *Mémoires*, I, pp. 172, 173, is so explicit upon this point as to leave it beyond doubt.

office. On May 3, 1469, the King of Hungary accepted the crown of Bohemia, and allied himself with the Emperor, the Elector Palatine, and the Duke of Bavaria.

Thus deserted, Podiebrad turned toward Charles the Bold, and proposed, for a consideration of one hundred thousand florins, to use his influence to procure for the Duke of Burgundy the imperial crown. His plan was to win over the Electors of Brandenburg and Saxony, together with the Archbishop of Mainz, whose votes, with his own as legal King of Bohemia, would constitute a majority in the Electoral College. This visionary scheme of Podiebrad had, however, no other effect than to infuse a new ferment into the active mind of Charles the Bold; but it was a ferment fatal to the success of all his plans.

The House of Hapsburg had long possessed a group of territories in Southern Elsass, generally known as the Sundgau and the Breisgau, so far removed from Innsbruck, the capital of the Hapsburgs of Austria-Tyrol, that they had been exposed to predatory encroachments by the local nobles, and the inhabitants had sought protection of their neighbors. Mülhausen was particularly exposed to these ravages, and for its defence a treaty had been made in 1466 with Berne, whose militia had restored order there. Desiring to extend its territories to the Rhine, Berne, — which then, together with Schwytz, Uri, Unterwalden, Lucerne, Zürich, and Zug, having thrown off the suzerainty of Austria, formed the Swiss Confederation, — had laid siege to Waldshut; and Sigismund of Austria, having previously failed to secure the protection of Louis XI, visited Charles the Bold in person, offered to cede to him the territory of Upper Elsass and the Rhenish towns for fifty thousand florins, subject to future redemption, and held out the glittering attraction of a marriage for his daughter Mary with Maximilian, son of the Emperor Frederick III, and the prospect of the imperial crown at the emperor's death. Pleased with the opportunity of acquiring territories connecting separated parts of his domain, and dazzled by the brilliant future opened before him, the Duke of Burgundy accepted the offer, signed the Treaty of St. Omer, on May 9, 1469, and entered upon that path of eastward expansion that was to lead to unforeseen disasters.

Although Frederick III had no serious intention of allowing the arrangements of Sigismund to determine the imperial succession, he was ready to accept the services of Charles the Bold in defending the Austrian possessions, and to act upon the compact of St. Omer.

The first step of the Emperor, after this transaction, was to annul the treaty with the Swiss; and the second, to order Charles the Bold to protect the newly acquired territory from aggression, in case the Swiss should resent the denunciation of the treaty. Thus, the new possessor of Upper Elsass, who had hitherto lived in good relations with his eastern neighbors, was suddenly weakened for his conflict with the King of France by assuming the rôle of an aggressive and dangerous prince, the natural enemy of those against whom his ambition was soon to be directed. The Swiss were at once converted into a hostile camp, and measures of resistance were discussed at Berne; while the large towns of the Rhine, — Basel, Colmar, and Strasburg, — long habituated to an independence of which they were proud, regarded with suspicion and hostility a neighbor who seemed disposed to become their master.

Had Charles the Bold been a more astute diplomatist, he would have felt the necessity of winning the good will and confidence of this population, which might have proved as useful to his cause as it afterward became obstructive of his purposes. But the Duke of Burgundy, feeling only contempt for the free towns of the Rhine and the "cowherds of the Alps," took no pains to cultivate their friendship and set over his new province Peter von Hagenbach, a governor armed with full powers, but devoid of capacity for a task so delicate.

The opportunity thus offered to Louis XI was not neglected, and circumstances rendered it of vast importance to his cause. On December 3, 1470, having finally resolved to make use of the permanent army which the prudent policy of his father had provided, Louis publicly repudiated the Treaty of Péronne before an assembly of notables held at Tours. The hour for conflict had struck at last.

But Louis XI was too cautious a statesman to throw down the gage of battle without deliberate preparation. The mountaineers of the Swiss cantons, for whom Charles the Bold felt only disdain, were esteemed by the King of France worthy of his confidence and friendship. As shown by documents preserved at Berne, at the time when Sigismund was making to Charles the Bold the offer which Louis had already rejected, the King took into his employ three active and intelligent Bernese, Nicholas von Diesbach and his two cousins, upon whom he lavished those seductive attentions with which he knew how to charm those whom he wished to attach to his service. From that time forward, there was at Berne a predominant French influence, which resulted in the signature, on September 23, 1470, of a treaty of friendship pledging the neutrality of the Swiss in case the King of France should be at war with the Duke of Burgundy.

In order to weaken the German support of his enemy, Louis XI opened negotiations with Sigismund of Austria. When this prince had explained to the Emperor his plans for the marriage of Mary of Burgundy with Frederick's son Maximilian and the promise of succession to the Empire, the price of the Burgundian alliance had seemed to the Emperor too high; and he had endeavored to lower it by offering merely to erect for Charles the Bold a kingdom to be held in vassalage to himself. Chilled by this dissipation of his dream of empire, the proud duke in January, 1471, declined to make an abatement of his claims, and a period of coolness toward Sigismund and the Emperor supervened.

Even in England, the star of Louis XI seemed to be in the ascendant; for the Earl of Warwick, who had preferred a French marriage for King Edward IV, offended by Edward's union with Elizabeth Woodville, had resolved to drive him from the throne; and the royal fugitive, taking refuge in

Holland, was forced to seek the protection of his brother-in-law, Charles the Bold.

In Italy, a combination of circumstances had deprived the Duke of Burgundy, for the moment, of all hope of aid. The death of Amadeus IX had placed Savoy in the hands of his widow, a sister of Louis XI, Yolande of France, who at that time preferred the dangerous protection of her brother to the domination of her ambitious brother-in-law Philip of Bresse and the Counts of Geneva and Romont; and, on March 11, 1470, at Amboise, the King solemnly took her under his protection. Although Galeazzo Sforza was wavering in his allegiance to Louis XI, his defection did not constitute an immediate danger; and Venice, — whose attention was chiefly bent upon the conflict with the Turks, soon to take possession of Greece by the fall of Negropont, — was not then in a position to sustain the cause of Charles the Bold. Louis XI, on the other hand, was so firmly established that, in treating with the Republic, he took pains to show his superiority by expressly commanding the replies to the Venetian ambassador to be composed in French, instead of Latin.[1]

Having thus isolated his foe diplomatically, in the autumn of 1470, the King sent his forces against the Duke of Burgundy. Taken by surprise, Charles made haste to muster an army and advance to the Somme; but, notwithstanding his powerful artillery, he failed before Amiens, and was glad, on April 4, 1471, to sign a truce for three months, by which Louis XI retained his conquests.

But a series of events soon proved favorable to the cause of Charles the Bold. On May 4, 1471, the battle of Tewkesbury restored Edward IV to the throne of England; the birth of a dauphin, which destroyed all hopes of the crown for Charles of Berry, threw that prince into a new alliance with the Duke of Burgundy, who promised him the hand of

---

[1] See Perret, *Histoire des relations de la France avec Venise*, I, p. 546.

his daughter; Francis II of Brittany joined the new coalition; while Venice made a secret treaty with Charles the Bold on June 18, 1472; and Louis XI was thus confronted with the most perilous situation of his reign.

The campaign of 1472 was an incident of critical moment in the history of France; for the Duke of Burgundy, advancing across the Somme with a great army, laid waste the country with fire and sword, while Charles of Berry was in arms in the South, and Francis of Brittany marching toward Paris from the West. But Louis XI was able to prevent the junction of the Burgundian forces with those of Brittany; the patriotism of the French people was inflamed by the outrages committed by the invaders; and, on November 3, 1472, Charles the Bold made an excuse of the desertion of his alliance by Francis of Brittany to sign a truce at Senlis. Charles of Berry had died during the campaign; and the King of France was once more relieved from open opposition.

The direct advantage of the war to Louis XI was not great, for his chief adversary was by no means destroyed; but the national feeling awakened by the wise policy and good administration of the King, fired by the public indignation against the offending dukes, now came to the aid of the royal cause, thenceforth regarded as representing the peace and unity of France in its desperate struggle with feudalism. The invasion thus proved to be the decisive turning point in the long contest with the King's refractory vassals.

The ambition of Charles the Bold

While France was thus profiting by a policy of concentration, the power of Burgundy, which had almost vindicated its capacity for independence, was to be dissipated in the pursuit of mere chimeras. Dreams which only an ancient dynasty could hope to realize awoke in Charles the Bold an aspiration to become the chief personage in Europe. Vassal of both France and the Empire, he repudiated his subordination to both, and aimed to rise to a height to which neither of his suzerains had yet attained.

An ambition so extravagant was not a quality to promote the confidence of others. While his governor, Von Hagenbach, was alienating by his treatment the cities of the Upper Rhine, the Swiss were preparing to oppose his plans of conquest and to support the policies of France. At this critical time, Charles the Bold concluded with Arnold of Cleve a bargain for his doubtful claims to Zutphen and Gelderland, thereby offending the legitimate heirs, and outraging the public conscience by the use of force to obtain possession.

But the acquisition of a new province was a small episode in the vast programme of Burgundian aggrandisement. By the death of Charles of Berry, to whom Mary of Burgundy had been betrothed by her father, the sole heiress of all the Burgundian realm had become once more an available chattel in the matrimonial market; and, with her to trade upon, the Duke hastened to reopen negotiations with the Emperor.

Having appointed Peter von Hagenbach to represent his interests, he offered bribes to Rudolf von Sulz, the commissioner of the Emperor, to promote his cause. The instructions of Hagenbach set forth, that the abdication of Frederick III would not be demanded, but Charles the Bold was to be at once named "King of the Romans," in order to become emperor after the death of Frederick; Maximilian would marry Mary of Burgundy, in time become "King of the Romans," and after the death of Charles the Bold would, in turn, become emperor. To consummate these arrangements, Charles the Bold now asked for a personal interview with Frederick III.

After elaborate preliminaries, in October, 1473, it was arranged for the Emperor and the Duke of Burgundy to meet at Trier. The Duke, anxious to impress Frederick with his great wealth and power, was accompanied by a large force of troops, including artillery, and bore in his train the sumptuous tents, the magnificent vessels of gold and silver, and the elaborate costumes inherited from the

The negotiations at Trier

former dukes of Burgundy, whose taste for luxury had profited for generations from the great marts of the Netherlands, where the Hanseatic and Venetian ships had long met to exchange the products of the North with those of the Orient; but neither the coveted heiress nor any Burgundian lady attended an interview the chief business of which was a betrothal. The Emperor, accompanied by his son, young Maximilian, came with a simple escort, in striking contrast with the magnificence of his ambitious vassal.

But neither of the participants in this portentous meeting, in which the deepest interests of Europe were involved, had any other purpose than to gain a personal advantage; the Emperor to secure for his son and successor the rich heritage of the Burgundian estates, the Duke to acquire the crown of the Empire.

The Archbishop of Mainz, Chancellor of the Empire, pronounced a long discourse in Latin in the Cloister of St. Maximin, in which he spoke of the necessity of Christian union in view of the insolence and victories of the Turks. To this oration the Burgundian Chancellor, Guillaume Hugonnet, replied, also in Latin, saying that the cause of the disunion of Christendom was the perfidious King of France, after whose destruction the Duke of Burgundy would be ready to use all his force against the Infidel. But the princes in attendance well understood that it was not of the Turks, but of their own interests, that both Emperor and Duke were thinking.

The question of a crusade having been submitted to the care of a commission appointed to study the subject, the principal negotiators approached the real purpose of the interview. In the meantime, the commission concluded that the first step toward effective resistance to the Turks was the reconciliation of the King of France and the Duke of Burgundy. The method of solving this hopeless problem having been referred to a second commission, the diplomatic contest between the Emperor and the Duke was then resumed.

To display his magnificence, Charles gave a sumptuous

banquet, preceded by a solemn mass, and endeavored to impress the imagination of the Emperor by the exhibition of his splendid ancestral plate. To stimulate still further the avidity of Frederick for the marriage, rich gifts were presented to him. For nearly a month, — much to the perplexity of the German nobles, who became curious regarding the real purport of the secret proceedings, — the personal interviews of the Emperor and the Duke were renewed from day to day, without reaching a satisfactory conclusion.

The prospect of the imperial succession appears to have vanished early in the month, and even the demands of Charles for an independent kingdom now seemed to the Emperor extravagant; for they included sovereignty over the Rhenish cities, Gelderland, Lorraine, the Swiss cantons, and Savoy, all of which, not already lost, were to be detached from the Empire. Eager for the prize he had in mind, Frederick had neither the firmness to end the negotiations nor the courage to discuss the overtures with his counsellors. The splendor with which the Duke was surrounded acted like a spell upon the avarice of the impecunious emperor, and its effect was heightened by the arrival of ambassadors who came from England, Italy, and the princes of Germany to transact business with his ambitious vassal rather than himself. Even the King of Hungary sent an embassy to ask the aid of the Duke of Burgundy in his conflict with the Turks. In all but the empty title the Duke already seemed greater than the Emperor.

Although fascinated by the magnificence of Charles, Frederick, whose faculty of calculation was his most characteristic attribute, could not fail to see the danger of encouraging an ambition so extravagant. When all the resources of persuasion had been exhausted, and the interest of Europe in this mysterious and thus far fruitless encounter had begun to be oppressive, toward the end of October, the Duke demanded a definite reply. The Emperor hesitated; then proposed a triple alliance between the Empire, Burgundy, and France, to be sealed by a double marriage, — Mary of

The triumph of Charles the Bold over the Emperor

Burgundy to be affianced to Maximilian, and Frederick's daughter Kunigunde to the Dauphin of France, — with the confirmation of Gelderland and Savoy as gifts to the Duke of Burgundy.

Disgusted with such an anticlimax to his elevated hopes, Charles suddenly broke off the negotiations, and prepared to take his departure, accompanied by the envoys of the King of Hungary, the Count Palatine of the Rhine, and the Archbishop of Köln.

The possible consequences of such a rupture, however, overcame the wavering will of the Emperor, and he urgently besought another interview. With renewed confidence, Charles the Bold now returned to his earlier demands. Unwilling to sacrifice the project of marriage, Frederick appeared to yield; but affirmed that, before concluding a definite engagement, he must consult the electors. Two were present, the Archbishops of Mainz and of Trier, as well as the representatives of the Elector of Brandenburg. On November 5, the Emperor laid before them the following plan: Mary of Burgundy would be affianced to Maximilian; the Duke would lead an army of ten thousand men against the Turks, as soon as the disputes between him and the King of France were settled; the Burgundian estates would be erected into a separate kingdom, to which regalian rights over the bishoprics of Liège, Utrecht, Toul, and Verdun, and the duchies of Lorraine, Savoy, and Cleve would be conceded; this kingdom would be transmissible by heredity in the male or female line of the House of Burgundy, and, like Bohemia, would be attached to the Empire.

The two electors present considered that a project of such gravity should be submitted to the electors as a body, and proposed that further discussion of the subject be referred to the imperial diet soon to meet at Augsburg. The Emperor in reply pointed out that the decision could not be postponed; for the Duke of Burgundy, disappointed in his plans, might ally himself with the King of France against the Empire! The two electors continued to insist upon discussion by the diet; but the Emperor, indignantly affirming his authority to act alone, at once solemnly confirmed to Charles possession of Zutphen and Gelderland, and declared himself ready to name the day of coronation. Charles agreed not to sustain the threatening coalition of Bohemia, Hungary, and Poland against the Emperor, the arrangements for the coronation were begun, and his triumph appeared to be assured.

But, at heart, neither the Emperor nor the Duke was satisfied with the proposed arrangement. The latter had discovered the weakness of the Emperor, yet had failed to realize his highest hopes. The former had learned to dread the dominating character of the Duke, now an avowed candidate to succeed him in the imperial office, for which his impatient temperament might impel him to make a premature demand. On both sides, therefore, the relations were already strained; and the Emperor's counsellors, who were suspicious of the Duke's ambitions, arrayed themselves against the execution of the plan.

The Emperor's humiliation of Charles the Bold

Although the documentary evidence of it is not available, it is probable that the agents of Louis XI, certain to be interested in these secret and prolonged negotiations, did not miss so excellent an opportunity to expose the dangers and arouse the fears of the German princes, whose estates were the natural prey of Burgundian expansion. But, whatever the truth may be, in some manner, the zeal and self-confidence of the Emperor soon perceptibly declined. For the personal conversations with the Duke in which the negotiations had previously been conducted was now substituted the less favorable mediation of the Emperor's advisers; and even those of Charles, distrustful of the validity of the Emperor's acts unsupported by the ratification of the electors, pressed for their provisory confirmation of his promises.

While these complications were threatening the *entente*, active preparations were made for the coronation which was to take place at Trier before the final separation. The Cloister of St. Maximin, decorated with rich tapestries and costly ornaments, was garnished for the approaching fête, and two thrones awaited the presence of the Emperor and the expectant King of Burgundy, while even the royal crown, which Charles had prepared for the occasion, was in readiness.

The time of the coronation had been fixed for November 25; but when that morning came, Charles learned on awakening that the Emperor had stolen silently away in the previous night, without leaving a word of farewell, or even paying his debts! Von Hagenbach was despatched in haste to beg for another audience; but, Frederick, overtaken, after promising the messenger to return, resumed his journey without explanation, and left the angry duke to pack up his coronation trappings in the midst of his furious indignation.[1]

III. The Overthrow of Charles the Bold

It is unnecessary to recount the schemes of conquest by which Charles the Bold endeavored to build up through the power of the sword the kingdom which the Emperor had refused to legalize. Thenceforth, his attitude became a constant menace to the independence of his neighbors, and they in return prepared to resist his encroachments. The Swiss and the cities of Elsass united to guarantee the safety of their territories; and Louis XI, taking advantage of his opportunity, kept his emissaries constantly in the field to combine the Swiss, the cities of the Rhine, and the German princes against the designs of Burgundy.

For a time, however, the diplomatic contest was not unequal. The agents of Charles found means to divide the councils of the Swiss cantons, some of which felt themselves secure from his encroachments; and even Berne was treated by him with a seductive courtesy that might have disarmed its opposition had it not been for the activity of Nicholas von Diesbach.

In Savoy, the success of Charles was still more decisive.

---

[1] Under the heading "Tagebuch für die Zuzammenkunft in Trier," Rausch, *Die burgundische Heirat*, pp. 185, 193, gives a digest of the occurrences of each day during the conference.

The Duchess Yolande, fearing the cupidity both of her brother-in-law, Philip of Bresse, and of her protector, Louis XI, even more than the ambition of the Duke of Burgundy, was long in secret negotiations with the Duke, and in June, 1473, formed an alliance with him.

The defection of Savoy was for the King of France a blow that shattered his entire system of alliances; for it was immediately followed by the total loss of effective allies in Italy.

Anxious to procure the papal support, Louis XI had resolved to divide with Pope Sixtus IV, — who, in 1471, had succeeded Paul II, — the government of the Church in France by concluding with the Holy See the Concordat of 1472, through which he expected to conciliate the Pope, at the same time hoping, by his own superior skill in the interpretation of its provisions, to secure for himself the chief advantages. But Sixtus IV, like his predecessors, had shown himself an astute politician, and Louis had not been able through the papal intervention to dissolve the Italian league against himself. On the contrary, the Pope, invoked as mediator, had held the King of France absolutely at his mercy; for he could easily, with Venice and Naples on his side, hold the balance of power against Milan and Florence, — the only Italian states upon whose friendship Louis could at any time depend.

When, therefore, Savoy — whose territories were on both sides of the Alps, half French and half Italian — deserted France, the influence of Louis XI over the Duke of Milan was diminished by the fact that the latter was left between two hostile camps, Venice on the one side and the combined force of Savoy and Burgundy on the other. The Duchess of Savoy could safely balance her interests between France and Burgundy, for each of them would oppose the absorption of Savoy by the other; but Milan, cut off from France by the defection of Savoy, was left without support except from Florence. In this emergency, Galeazzo Sforza secretly endeavored to make terms with Venice, and through the good offices of the Republic to enter into friendly relations with Charles the Bold, and Louis XI was thus rendered powerless in Italy.

Until the defection of Savoy could be repaired by France, the situation in Italy was beyond remedy. It was to the region north of the Alps and east of Burgundy, therefore, that the King of France now turned his serious attention. By the King's mediation, the Swiss and Sigismund of Austria, although hereditary enemies, were now brought into alliance, together with the cities on the Upper Rhine; and, on March 30, 1474, was signed at Constance the "Ewige Richtung," or "Eternal Compact," by which Sigismund recognized the independence of the Swiss cantons.[1] On the following day an alliance for mutual defence was formed.

Among the provisions of this union was the repurchase of the territory of Elsass which had been conveyed by Sigismund to Charles the Bold with the privilege of redemption; but Charles refused to listen to this proposition. The Emperor was soon drawn into the contest; the populations of Gelderland, Flanders, and Franche-Comté seized the occasion to revolt; the Duke of Lorraine resented the designs of Charles upon his estates; and a general war was thus unchained. In the meantime, Charles had invaded the territories of the Archbishopric of Köln under the pretext of defending the Archbishop's authority, and was engaged in the siege of Neuss. Obstinately determined to take the town, notwithstanding the stubborn resistance of the citizens, he wasted more than a year in a fruitless siege. While thus engaged, his own possessions were attacked by his enemies; and, in May, 1474, Elsass was invaded by the Swiss and Von Hagenbach put to death.

While the Swiss and Germans were making ravages in Burgundy, the army of Louis XI was strangely inactive; but his gold and his agents were constantly doing their silent

---

[1] See *Amtliche Sammlung der älteren eidgenössischen Abschiede*, II, pp. 473-485.

work. Philippe de Commines, the ablest counsellor of Charles the Bold, had been bought over by Louis in 1472, Nicholas von Diesbach was busy encouraging the Swiss, and Jost von Silinen stirred up the zeal of the German cities. The defensive treaties with France were soon converted into offensive alliances, the Swiss carried the war into Franche-Comté, and ended the campaign of 1475 by the conquest of Vaud from the Duchess of Savoy.

At war with nearly all his neighbors, and profiting from his Italian relations only to the extent of receiving from Italy a few mercenary troops, Charles the Bold knew that the organizing cause of these hostilities was the King of France; and that if he could deal him a fatal blow, he would thereby destroy the coalition.

The opportunity for this revenge seemed to be presented by the alliance of Charles with Edward IV, King of England, who was now disposed to renew the pretensions of Henry V to the crown of France. Charles the Bold, in return for his assistance, was to round out his territories by the addition of Champagne and Brie, and to be emancipated from vassalage to the crown of France, with the privilege of establishing a separate kingdom.

Nearly all Europe had now been drawn into the Franco-Burgundian quarrel; and, diplomatically, the balance was not far from equal. To offset the Emperor, Charles the Bold was in alliance with the King of Hungary and Bohemia, the Archbishop of Köln, and the Elector Palatine; against the Swiss, he could oppose Savoy and Milan; while France was threatened on the West and South by the Duke of Brittany and the King of Aragon. With the weight of an English invasion thrown into the scale, it seemed as if the ambitious duke might finally realize his plans.

If, in the summer of 1475, when Edward IV landed his army at Calais, Charles the Bold had promptly joined him with a strong force and St. Pol had surrendered the French troops as he had promised, it is not impossible that the plans of the two allies might have been in great part realized; but

Chap. II
A. D.
1453-1402

The Peace of Picquigny

the preoccupation of Charles on the Rhine, his late arrival at Calais without an army, and the double treason of St. Pol, joined with the difficulties of the undertaking, which became to the mind of Edward more insuperable the longer he considered them, tended to discourage the English king.

The skill and cunning of Louis XI did not desert him, however, in this moment of supreme danger, rendered the more imminent by a recent reconciliation of the Emperor with Charles the Bold.

The first move of Louis was to convince the King of England that the conquest of France was a hopeless enterprise; and the second to take advantage of his impaired fortunes, so rudely shattered by the civil wars of England.

The unfulfilled promises of the Duke of Burgundy and the treachery of St. Pol had shaken the faith of Edward IV in his ally, and this blow was soon followed by a revelation of the strength of France and the weakness of Burgundy which wholly disheartened him. The splendid gifts sent to him by Louis XI, as expressions of his good will, convinced him of the King's resources, while the reports of the revolts against Charles the Bold created doubts of the Duke's hold upon his subjects. In a letter addressed to his ally, Edward IV pointed out to Charles that the state of his possessions and the disposition of his people, habituated to industry and commerce, and not to war, did not justify his military pretensions.

Edward IV being thus inclined to peace, the friendly overtures of Louis XI were not disdained; and the King's *entourage* was not insensible to generous presents of choice French wine and liberal gifts of money. A proposition to pay to the King of England seventy-five thousand crowns in cash, and the arrangement of a marriage between the Dauphin of France and the eldest daughter of Edward IV, with the revenues of Guyenne to be paid annually in London for her maintenance, prepared the way for a personal interview between the two kings in which the amiability of Louis rendered easy the negotiation of a peace.

On August 29, 1475, the two sovereigns met in the castle of Picquigny, near Amiens; which, it was recalled, had been designated in an ancient prophecy as the place where a great peace would be made between France and England. After a friendly conversation in the French language, the kings placed their left hands on a missal and their right hands on a holy cross, while they solemnly swore to live at peace with each other for seven years, sealing their engagement by the betrothal of their children and a defensive alliance against their enemies.[1]

When this ceremony was concluded, Louis invited Edward to come to Paris, where he promised to fête him with fair ladies; adding that he would commend to him the Cardinal de Bourbon as a confessor, since he was easy in granting absolution, if one had committed sin.

The King of England entered heartily into the humor of his host; and replied, that he would with pleasure take the Cardinal as his confessor, for he knew him to be a "gay companion."

When Louis asked if the Duke of Burgundy should be included in the truce, Edward responded that he would leave that to the King of France; but for Francis of Brittany he asked the King's grace, because he "had always found him a true friend in adversity."[2]

When Charles the Bold learned of the treaty, he was furious with the King of England for the desertion of his cause; but Louis XI, preferring to permit him to be destroyed by others, celebrated his diplomatic victory by including the Duke of Burgundy, together with the Duke of Brittany, in the peace.

Louis' perfidy to his allies

Generous as this act may appear upon the surface, its cynical selfishness was deeply felt by those whom the intrigues of the King had involved in war with Charles

---

[1] The treaty is in Rymer, V, Part III, p. 65 et seq.
[2] See Philippe de Commines, *Mémoires*, I, p. 318, who was present at the negotiations at Picquigny.

CHAP. II
A. D.
1453–1492

the Bold. The only excuse for his total abandonment of his allies is to be found in his abnormal fear of the treachery of his generals; for which the treason of St. Pol gave, perhaps, some real foundation.

It was, in fact, the desire for the capture and punishment of this traitor that turned Louis XI from his true interest and his plain obligations, and led him to make easy terms with Charles the Bold. St. Pol had taken refuge with the Duke of Burgundy, whom also he had betrayed, and it was in order to secure his person that the King of France was ready, on September 13, 1475, to sign the secret Truce of Souleuvres, erroneously called Soleure, by which his former allies were abandoned. Delivered to the King by the Duke of Burgundy, the Constable was tried before the Parliament of Paris, condemned, and executed.

But the punishment of St. Pol was bought at the price of the King's honor; for René of Lorraine, whom Louis had instigated to oppose the encroachments of Charles the Bold, was the first object of his vengeance. Instead of supporting the Duke of Lorraine in the defence of his estates, Louis XI feigned astonishment at the procedure of Charles, and perfidiously permitted him to make the conquest of the duchy.

The next of Louis' allies to receive the attacks of Charles the Bold were the Swiss, who had invaded the estates of the Count of Romont and wrested Vaud from the possession of Savoy, terminating their conquests at Geneva on the west and St. Maurice on the east. Deserted both by Louis XI and by the Emperor, the Swiss now found themselves in peril of division by the insidious representations of the Duke of Burgundy, preparatory to his invasion of their country. Intoxicated with his conquest of Lorraine, his purpose was, first to separate, and then to subdue, the cities of Elsass and the Swiss cantons.

Preparations for the attack on the Swiss

Although a campaign in the midst of winter was opposed by his wisest counsellors, Charles the Bold could not be restrained from his summary vengeance upon the Swiss. Relying upon the revolt of the territories conquered from

Savoy and the support of the Duchess, he made haste to overwhelm the "cowherds of the mountains," for whose military qualities he expressed a serene contempt. Berne, whose exposed position placed it in peril of the first attack, now abandoned the territories taken from Savoy, in order to concentrate its defence on the lakes of Neuchâtel and Bienne. The Duke of Burgundy left Nancy on January 11, 1476, with some ten thousand men, the Count of Romont resumed control in Vaud, and, in the end of February, the Duchess of Savoy crossed the Alps by the Mont Cenis pass, to watch her interests from Lausanne.

In the meantime, Louis XI, having tardily sought to arrest the course of Charles by means of a personal interview at Auxerre, which the latter avoided, took up a post of observation at Lyons, whence he sent funds to the support of Berne, while he offered to confirm Philip of Bresse in the regency of Savoy, if he would oppose the Duchess; but took no active part in offering military aid to his friends and allies.

Charles the Bold, by incredibly swift marches, notwithstanding the season of the year, hastened to take the enemy by surprise. The messengers sent out from Berne to summon aid from their German neighbors returned to report that no aid was to be expected from them. But, while the Duke was awaiting the appearance of their envoys to implore peace at any price, the Swiss were courageously fortifying two lines of defence, and making ready to meet the coming storm.

An attack on the Castle of Grandson having failed on February 18, 1476, on the twenty-first a general assault, supported with artillery, was ordered; but, to the surprise of the invader, the little garrison of four hundred men succeeded in checking the advance of the Burgundian army for ten days. Forced to capitulate on the twenty-eighth, the besieged had understood that their lives would be spared upon their surrender; but the conqueror, after causing them to pass disarmed in front of his tent, designated certain of

Defeat of Charles the Bold at Grandson

their number to hang the others. When, under the aim of the Burgundian soldiers, this murderous work had been accomplished, the executioners were likewise slain.

The purpose of this barbarity was to intimidate the Swiss, but its effect was to unite and infuriate them. On March 3, the Confederates made their descent upon the Burgundian army, which fled from the field, leaving immense booty behind it. Even the formidable artillery, the horses, and the ammunition fell into the hands of the sturdy mountaineers.

His army scattered and his equipment captured, Charles the Bold bore his defeat with fortitude. Hastening to reorganize his attack, he made his headquarters at Lausanne, where he strove to retain the support of Savoy against the blandishments of Louis XI, then busily engaged in trying to detach the Duchess Yolande from the Burgundian cause.

The defeat of Charles at Grandson revealed the pitiable emptiness of his large pretensions. Stripped of soldiers by the dispersion of his army, it was with difficulty that he was able to extort money for a new campaign from his reluctant subjects, who had little sentiment of nationality and slight sympathy with his ambitious projects. With his misfortune, his allies fell away. The Duke of Milan hastened to renew his old relations with Louis XI, while Venice was inactive, and Savoy was wavering in the balance.

At this moment of the Duke's humiliation the Emperor Frederick III, comprehending how acceptable his friendship might now be regarded, considered the occasion opportune for procuring the hand of Mary of Burgundy for Maximilian. Imperial envoys soon arrived in the camp at Lausanne; Charles was led to believe that the Emperor would be able to negotiate a favorable peace with the Swiss; and, on May 6, 1476, Charles the Bold placed his hands between those of the Bishop of Forli, who represented the Emperor, and solemnly promised to give his daughter in marriage to Maximilian, at the same time arranging a personal interview with Frederick III to be held at Aachen.

In this engagement there was no promise of the imperial

crown, nor even of a Burgundian kingdom. The wily old emperor offered valuable counsel when he wrote to the Duke to dissuade him from further wars, assuring him that "there would be small glory in vanquishing a troop of peasants, but much shame in being vanquished by them"; but, besides mere words, he offered no remuneration for the rich heritage of the Burgundian estates that were soon to be added to the possessions of the Hapsburgs.

But a more terrible catastrophe than that of Grandson was about to befall the humbled Duke of Burgundy. Having by supreme efforts assembled another army, he concentrated his forces between the deep Lake of Morat and the mountain-wall that rises above it. There, on June 22, 1476, sixty thousand Burgundian soldiers became the almost helpless victims of Swiss revenge for the massacre of Grandson. An avalanche of thirty-five thousand mountaineers, armed with terrible pikes and powerful crossbows, swept down the steep slopes, concealed and protected by the foliage, dealing death on every side. The power of Charles the Bold was broken forever at one blow; and a vast ossuary, composed of more than twelve thousand skeletons, for three centuries stood on the shore of Lake Morat as a monument to the heroism of the Swiss and the rashness of their adversary.

In the excitement of his disaster, Charles the Bold took the impolitic step of trying to force the Duchess Yolande of Savoy, who had retired to Gex to await the result of the conflict, to accompany his retreat to Burgundy. Failing to persuade her, he ordered her to be kidnapped by his officers, and she with one of her children, on June 27, was captured at Grand Sacconnex, on the road from Gex to Geneva, and carried to Dijon, whence she was rescued by Louis XI. Thus separated at last from the cause of Charles the Bold, the rescued duchess was received by her brother, the King, at Plessis-les-Tours with a smile of triumph and the words. "Madame of Burgundy, you are welcome!" Deeply ashamed of her disloyalty, she was restored to her estates, and Savoy returned to the French alliance.

By all except the Duke of Burgundy himself, the tragic defeat of Morat was considered a final humiliation; but nothing less than death could subdue his indomitable will. Appearing in person before the States General of Franche-Comté, with eloquent exhortations he appealed to their loyalty for money with which to raise a new army. The delegates replied, that, after so many disastrous wars, the nobility was discouraged, the fields were barren, commerce had been destroyed, and the peasants were dying of hunger; still, if he would provoke no new wars, they would make new sacrifices.

Exhausted by the long struggle to support the ambitions of the Duke, the only hope of Burgundy lay in peace; but it was difficult to preserve it where so many seeds of war had been already planted. The Duke of Lorraine, who had been cruelly stripped of his rights, was recalled by his people, who rose in revolt to restore him. The Swiss had declared that they would not sign a peace until the Duke of Burgundy had renounced his usurpations; and, supported by them, René had retaken and fortified Nancy. To prevent the union of René and the Swiss, Charles the Bold made haste to besiege the capital of Lorraine. Before its walls, after the treason of his Neapolitan general, Campobasso, overwhelmed by superior numbers, when three-fourths of his army had deserted him, on January 5, 1477, the Duke fell, slain upon the field of battle. With him perished the illusory dream of restoring the unity of that middle kingdom which had been erected between France and Germany by the Treaty of Verdun, and of winning back the imperial crown that Charles of France and Lewis the German had then conceded to Lothair.

The spoils of Burgundy

Although a popular belief sprang up that Charles the Bold was not dead but concealed in some secret hiding place, and loans of money were even made payable on the day of his return, plans to appropriate his possessions were not long delayed.

The Burgundian territory comprised, in addition to the Duchy of Burgundy, held originally as a fief of France, and the County of Burgundy, — known as Franche-Comté, —

held as a fief of the Empire, lands acquired by marriage, by purchase, and by conquest, even greater in extent. These included Holland, Gelderland, Zeeland, Flanders, Artois, Brabant, Hainault, Namur, Rethel, Luxemburg, the cities of Upper Elsass, and, until the restoration of Duke René, the Duchy of Lorraine.

Although Louis XI had taken no active part in the final overthrow of Charles the Bold, the moment his death was announced the King of France hastened to seize those portions of his domain that were most accessible, and to lay his plans for the eventual appropriation of the whole.

The simplest method of giving to this enterprise an appearance of justice was, of course, the marriage of Mary of Burgundy to a member of the royal family, by which her rights would be legitimately acquired. Unfortunately for Louis XI, however, the Dauphin was only eight years old, while the heiress of Burgundy was twenty-one.[1] To further the fortune of a French noble of suitable age and rank by securing for him the hand and estates of the wealthy princess, would have involved the risk of substituting for his old enemy a new one with equal power. Forced, therefore, to postpone the complete expropriation of the Burgundian possessions until a way should open, Louis XI was content to demand the immediate surrender of all the fiefs pertaining to the French crown, and to await his opportunity to bring the other estates under his control.

While the King of France was claiming the restoration of the French fiefs, four deputies of Flanders, representatives of the States of Holland, and those of Brabant and Hainault met at Ghent, in February, 1477, to safeguard the interests of their country.

The first step taken by this assembly was to secure the "Great Privilege" of February 11, 1477, by which all ducal

---

[1] Louis XI did, however, seriously consider a marriage of Mary of Burgundy with the Dauphin. See Vaesen and Charavay, *Lettres de Louis XI*, VI, p. 112.

encroachments upon the ancient communal rights were swept away, and an organism created for their future protection. The Grand Council, organized on a representative basis, became the depositary of public power, including with the princes of the dynasty twenty-four other members chosen for life by the sovereign from the several provinces, half of their number being nobles and the other half lawyers and publicists.

The movement thus initiated was, in effect, a union of the nobles and the cities to preserve their local liberties, not only against a future ducal ruler, but especially against the pretensions of the King of France. With this purpose a new army was organized for the defence of the land, and preparations were made to control the future action of the Duchess.

Fully realizing the dangers to which she was exposed, Mary of Burgundy, joined by her stepmother, Margaret of York, had, on January 18, written a pathetic letter to the King of France, her relative and godfather, imploring in a spirit of humble helplessness his clemency and protection. Alarmed by his encroachments upon her territories, she had followed this appeal with an embassy, offering to the King the towns he had already taken; but Louis demanded in addition Arras, Franche-Comté, and the fortresses of Artois, at the same time working privately upon her envoys, some of whom virtually passed to his service, among them the Chancellor, Hugonnet.

Marriage of Mary of Burgundy with Maximilian

But the pretensions of the King of France and the action of the Burgundian leaders were not the only embarrassments to which the young duchess was subjected. René of Lorraine and the Swiss, who had overthrown her father, were planning to obtain indemnity by extending their borders at the expense of her territories, while the Count Palatine of the Rhine and the Duke of Bavaria were claiming Holland, Zeeland, Friesland, and Hainault as belonging to them by legitimate inheritance, and the Duke of Cleve was pressing upon her a marriage with his son.

All these circumstances combined to favor the designs of the Emperor Frederick III; for the Duchess, left without protection, resolved to end the situation by marriage with the Archduke Maximilian, — a courageous prince, then eighteen years of age. This decision was strengthened by her own personal preference and the wishes of the Flemish cities, as well as by the engagement made between the Emperor and her father at Lausanne. On February 12, Frederick had written to press the early fulfilment of this pledge, at the same time promising his aid; and on March 26, the young duchess had implored the Archduke to come at once to her rescue. An imperial embassy started out to conclude the arrangements for the marriage, and the impatient bride, learning that the envoys were not provided with sufficient funds to continue their journey, pawned her jewels to supply the necessary means. Arriving at Ghent on April 16, the embassy was formally received on the eighteenth; and, in the presence of her public officers, Mary of Burgundy solemnly concluded her betrothal by procuration to Maximilian of Austria. To give the ceremony still greater *éclat*, it was repeated at Louvain, and the embassy then returned to Germany.

While the King of France and the King of Hungary were plotting to prevent the marriage, Frederick III, through avarice or poverty, failed to provide the means for his son's journey to Ghent, now rendered urgent by the interests working to obstruct the union. Begging a sum of money insufficient for his purpose, Maximilian started from Gratz on June 5, received some useful presents at Augsburg, and reached Frankfort on July 1; but was obliged to remain at Köln until his *fiancée* could send him money to complete his journey. Well received at Louvain, Brussels, and Ghent, he took an oath to respect the liberties of Flanders; and on August 19, 1477, the marriage was celebrated at Ghent, with extreme simplicity. Son and heir of an emperor, Maximilian was indebted to the generosity of his bride, not only for the expenses of his journey, but for the six thousand crowns with which he procured the papal dispensation for his marriage; and even, it is said, for his wedding garments.[1] While her marriage with Maximilian was for Mary of Burgundy, in a sense, a deliverance from pressing dangers, for her people he was always a stranger, sometimes obeyed with respect as the chief representative of public authority, but often treated with suspicion, and even openly opposed. A month after his marriage, on September 17, he was required to renounce by testament all the duchies, principalities, and private property derived from his union with Mary of Burgundy, in case it should prove childless. The estates of Burgundy had no thought of losing their autonomy by subjection to foreign rule.

The partition of Burgundy

The unity of Burgundy was, however, from the hour when Charles the Bold fell before the walls of Nancy doomed to permanent dissolution. Based on no foundation of racial or national sentiment, and composed of incoherent parts brought together by chance or compulsion, the Burgundian realm had no essential principle of perpetuity. By a singular combination of circumstances, Flanders, which had been a fief of France, passed into the system of the Empire; while Franche-Comté, which was an imperial fief, fell into the hands of Louis XI along with the Duchy of Burgundy

---

[1] The traditional stories regarding the impecunious condition of Maximilian appear in substance to be true, notwithstanding the efforts to redeem the reputation of Frederick III. The documents printed by Chmel, *Monumenta Habsburgica*, I, show that Maximilian was obliged to beg money of Duke Sigismund (No. 46), while the Emperor also endeavored to raise loans by pawning his estates (Nos. 47, 93, and 99); also that he gave Maximilian a part of what he had thus raised for his journey (No. 46). The same authority further shows, that Maximilian remained nearly a month in Köln, without other apparent reason than the need of money; and, after obtaining it from the ambassadors of Mary, proceeded to Aachen, where he received more presents. See also Rausch, *Die burgundische Heirat*, pp. 173 et seq.

The part played by marriage in the growth and power of the House of Austria is well and wittily expressed in the following Latin verses:

"Bella gerant alii; tu, felix Austria, nube;
Nam quae Mars aliis, dat tibi regna Venus."

proper. René of Lorraine had invaded the Comté in the hope of enlarging his dominion, and the Swiss claimed the right to subject and annex it to their Confederation; but, by force of arms and the free use of money, René was held within the limits of his duchy, and the Swiss were induced to abandon their designs.

As the result of the long struggle with Charles the Bold, the diplomacy of Frederick III had finally borne off the principal prize by the marriage of Maximilian to Mary of Burgundy; but it was Louis XI whose spoils were most valuable and enduring. The loss of Flanders, which had become almost inevitable, opened a question which was to be in some way involved in nearly every subsequent European war; but the acquisition of the Duchy and the County of Burgundy, Charolais, Nevers, Artois, and parts of Namur and Hainault rounded out the territory of France in a manner to add greatly to its security, and to realize in a high degree its doctrine of "natural limits." On the other hand, the fateful marriage of Maximilian and the heiress of Burgundy involved the House of Austria in complications that frequently threatened its ruin, and sowed the seed of that bitter hatred that for centuries did not cease to pursue the Hapsburgs.

From the beginning, the husband of Mary of Burgundy had occasion to realize the disquietude of the heritage he had acquired and the perils to which it was exposed. Receiving no substantial aid from his lethargic father, the Emperor, too prudent to follow the advice of the Duchess Dowager, Margaret of York, and form an alliance with England for the invasion and partition of France, harassed by the recurrent revolts of his jealous subjects, and constantly exasperated by the intrigues and encroachments of Louis XI, Maximilian was put to the most trying tests. After the birth of a son, Philip, and a daughter, Margaret, — by which the estates of Charles the Bold were secured to the Hapsburgs, — on March 27, 1482, the Duchess Mary died from injuries received in falling from her horse, and the position

134   A HISTORY OF DIPLOMACY

Chap. II
A.D.
1453-1492

of Maximilian became still more precarious; for he was deprived, for a time, of the care of his children, and almost excluded from a share in the government. To complicate the situation still further, parts of the ancestral lands of the Hapsburgs in Austria fell into the hands of the King of Hungary, Matthias Corvinus, and the nerveless emperor was unable to reclaim them. Chiefly anxious for peace and the retention of their municipal liberties, the nobles and burghers of Flanders opened negotiations with Louis XI; and, on December 23, 1482, the Peace of Arras was concluded with the King, providing for the marriage of young Margaret and the Dauphin of France, with Artois and Burgundy for her dowry.[1]

But this legitimation of his previous annexations was not the only triumph of the wily king. It was further conceded by the Treaty of Arras that young Philip should do homage to him for the Duchy of Flanders, thus becoming once more the nominal vassal of France. Almost excluded from participation in the management of public affairs, Maximilian was compelled to accept the provisions of the treaty, and to see his daughter Margaret surrendered to the guardianship of the King of France, and on June 23, 1483, publicly betrothed to the Dauphin.

IV. The Efforts for French Preponderance in Italy

Conclusion of peace with Venice

Substantially triumphant in his designs upon the Burgundian realm, Louis XI was for a time not less successful in his relations with Italy. During the whole of his struggle with Charles the Bold, he had never ceased to be served by trusted agents at Rome, Milan, Florence, and Naples, whose

---

[1] According to Philippe de Commines, Edward IV of England, whose daughter Elizabeth had been betrothed to the Dauphin at Picquigny, suddenly died of melancholy upon receiving the news that the Dauphin, Charles, was affianced to Margaret of Burgundy. — *Mémoires*, I, p. 454; and II, pp. 58, 63, and 91.

correspondence kept him fully informed of the state of Italy. Unable to secure from that quarter any practical aid against his enemy, he had nevertheless succeeded by his diplomacy in depriving Charles the Bold of advantages that might otherwise have accrued from his Italian alliances. The Pope, Sixtus IV, had been favorable to the cause of Burgundy, Venice had been in formal alliance with Charles the Bold, and the Duke of Milan had followed Savoy in going over to his side; but none of these had proved of any marked utility to the Burgundian cause. On the other hand, Florence, under the control of Lorenzo de' Medici, had never ceased to remain loyal to the interests of Louis XI.

With the news of the defeat of Charles the Bold at Morat, the Duke of Milan had hastened, as the Duchess of Savoy had done, to renew the ancient friendship with the King of France. Soon afterward, on December 26, 1476, Galeazzo Sforza fell by the hand of assassins. "It is all over with the peace of Italy," Pope Sixtus IV is said to have exclaimed, when he heard of Galeazzo Sforza's death. Following a ruler whose personal influence had aided in preserving the equilibrium of Italy, the regency of Galeazzo's widow, the Duchess Bona of Savoy, rendered inevitable new designs and fresh intervention on the part of France.

But the death of Charles the Bold, even more than that of Galeazzo Sforza, opened a new era in Italian politics. Even Venice now realized the necessity of changing its attitude toward Louis XI. "The death of the Duke of Burgundy is of the greatest gravity," said the Venetian Signory to the Milanese Ambassador; "the disappearance of a prince who held in his hand the fate of so many political questions is of an import to absorb for more than a year the attention of every intelligent and prudent man."[1] "If ever Italy had need of peace it is to-day," said a member of that body; "she has two dragons upon her back, the Turk and the King of France, who aim only to enslave her. Let us, therefore, imitate

---

[1] Gingins-la-Sarraz, *Dépêches*, II, p. 397.

nature, and raise about us mountains almost inaccessible between the rest of the world and ourselves."[1]

It was, no doubt, a mark of clear insight to foresee the danger of French preponderance in Italy; but, following the instinct of commercial advantage, the Republic of Venice hastened to procure an *entente* with France. In May, 1477, Gradenigo was despatched as ambassador to Louis XI, under instructions to watch closely the relations with Burgundy, but above all to make peace with France.[2] On January 9, 1478, after negotiations rendered easy by the King, a treaty was signed by which both signatories agreed to respect each other's commerce and to offer no aid to each other's enemies.

For Louis XI it was a diplomatic victory whose consequences were soon to become evident. Already sure of Savoy, Milan, and Florence, it opened to him a period of predominant influence in which he was to attain the long desired end of becoming the arbiter of Italian politics.

The conspiracy of the Pazzi

Situated in the geographical centre of Italy, the Republic of Florence was exposed to the hostility of the Kingdom of Naples and the State of the Church on the one side, and of Milan and Venice on the other. Under the domination of the Medici family, a sagacious foreign policy had served to protect the Florentine interests, particularly under the rule of Lorenzo de' Medici, called the "Magnificent," who had sought to secure the equilibrium of Italy by forming against the dual alliance of the Pope and Ferdinand of Naples the triple alliance of Florence, Milan, and Venice, concluded by the treaty of November 2, 1474.

Under the cover of friendly appearances, another Florentine family, the Pazzi, rich, numerous, and engaged as the Medici were in trade and banking, had become a powerful

---

[1] Venetian Archives, "Potenze Estere," Feb. 17, 1477.

[2] A most interesting despatch of the Milanese ambassador disclosing the real feelings of the King of France toward Venice, and at the same time most piquantly illustrating his marital virtue and his diplomatic guile, may be found in Baschet, *La diplomatie vénitienne: les princes de l'Europe au XVIe siècle*, pp. 298, 300.

rival. Lorenzo de' Medici had been the financial depositary of the funds of Pope Sixtus IV; but, wishing to purchase for his nephew, Girolamo Riario, the lordship of Imola, which Lorenzo de' Medici intended to annex to the territory of the Republic, the Pope, being unable to borrow the necessary money from Lorenzo, sought to obtain it of Francesco de' Pazzi, who had a bank in Rome. Lorenzo endeavored to dissuade Francesco from making the loan; whereupon the Pope, deeply offended, transferred all the funds of the Holy See to the Pazzi, who advanced the money for the purchase of Imola. Thus sprang up a personal quarrel that did not end until it had involved all Italy in its angry passions, and provoked the intervention of Louis XI.

The immediate occasion of this intervention was a tragedy of the most dramatic character. Determined to constitute a principality in Romagna for the benefit of Girolamo Riario, — who had married a natural daughter of Galeazzo Sforza, and aspired to be a great prince, — Sixtus IV had attempted to secure his end by force, the Medici had opposed him, and war had become inevitable between the Republic of Florence and the Holy See, unless the government of the Medici could be overthrown. With the purpose of accomplishing this result, a conspiracy was formed by the Pazzi and Riario, — of which Sixtus IV not only had previous knowledge but which he was believed to sanction, — for the destruction of the Medici at Florence.[1] In order to accomplish this result, it was

---

[1] On this point, see Perret, *Histoire des relations de la France avec Venise*, II, p. 125; Cipolla, *Storia*, p. 583; and Pastor, *Histoire des papes*, IV, pp. 279, 281. Sixtus IV desired to affect the revolution without bloodshed. He still advocated the change of government, however, even after being informed that it probably could not be accomplished without the murder of Lorenzo : "Io non voglio la morte de ninn per niente, perchè non è offitio nostro aconsentire alla morte de persona: e bene che Lorenzo sia un villano e con noi se porte male, pure io non vorria la morte sua per niente, ma la mutatione dello stato si." — Capponi, *Storia della repubblica di Firenze*, II, Florence, 1876, p. 552; and Franz, *Sixtus IV und die Republik Florenz*, Regensburg, 1880, p. 199.

decided to assassinate Lorenzo de' Medici and his brother Giuliano. The occasion chosen for this deed was the celebration of mass in the cathedral of Florence, on April 26, 1478, where it was known that the intended victims would be present. Francesco de' Pazzi and Bernardo Baroncelli were selected for the murder of Giuliano, while two priests undertook the assassination of Lorenzo, the signal for the action being the elevation of the host at the end of the mass. Giuliano fell under the blows of the assassins; but Lorenzo, throwing off his assailants, sought refuge in the sacristy, whose bronze doors were closed against his pursuers by his faithful friend Poliziano.

Francesco Salviati, by favor of the Pope successor of Filippo de' Medici as archbishop of Pisa, in revenge for the proscription of his family at Florence had undertaken the capture of the Palace of the Signory; but the people, instead of supporting the Pazzi as had been expected, rose in defence of the Medici; the conspirators were massacred; the Archbishop of Pisa and four of his accomplices were hung from the windows of the palace; and Cardinal Raffaello Riario, who had celebrated mass in the cathedral on the day of the assault, was held as a hostage.

Defeated in the scheme for overthrowing the government of the Medici at Florence, Sixtus IV began an open war against the city. Not satisfied with the liberation of Cardinal Riario, the Pope demanded reparation for the violation of the immunities of the Church in the summary execution of the Archbishop of Pisa together with the exile of Lorenzo de' Medici. To give force to these demands, Florence was put under the ban of the Church, and a commission of five cardinals was appointed to sit in judgment upon its delinquencies.

The political designs of Sixtus IV and of his ally, King Ferdinand of Naples, were so evident in this quarrel with the Florentines that all these events immediately assumed a European importance. On May 2, Lorenzo de' Medici besought the intervention of Louis XI; on the twelfth, Philippe de Commines was despatched to Florence; and, soon afterward, an embassy composed of the Seigneur de Clermont and the jurist Gabriel Vivès was sent by the King of France to Rome.

Equally balanced in material force with the league of the Pope and the King of Naples, the triple alliance of Florence, Milan, and Venice endeavored to preserve peace by uniting in the demand for French intervention. On June 19, Venice sent Bertucio Gabriel as ambassador to France, Florence was already represented there, and Milan hastened to send an envoy. The fate of Italy seemed now to hang upon the action of the King of France.

But it was at Rome that the great diplomatic battle was to be fought upon which depended not only the destinies of Italy but the question of preponderance in the affairs of Christendom. Louis XI had already threatened the Pope with the convocation of a council at Lyons; and, supported by three of the powers in Italy, it appeared as if he was easily master of the situation.

With half of Italy under the leadership of the King of France, the position of Sixtus IV, already compromised by acts which might easily visit upon him the reproaches of the Church Universal as inconsistent with the duties and character of the Supreme Pontiff, was one of apparent weakness and even helplessness; but the astute obstinacy of the Pope never quailed in the presence of the dangers that beset him, and his skill and dexterity soon proved his superiority to the craft of Louis XI.

Assembling at Bracciano, whither the Pope had retired to escape the pest at Rome, on August 1, 1478, the ambassadors of France and the Triple Alliance met in the castle of the Orsini to form their plans. As a result of their deliberations, a document was prepared protesting against the scandal to Christendom of preventing the union of Italy against the Turks, and closing with a demand for a council to be held in France for abolishing the abuses of the Roman court.

The Florentines and their allies had believed that this step would bring Sixtus IV to terms and force him to cease his persecution of the Medici and his war against the Republic, but they had wholly miscalculated the Pope's tenacity.

On August 16, the King of France forbade his subjects to send money to the Holy See, and in the following September a French council was convoked at Orléans, which extended the prohibition of August 16 to all the allies of France.

Moved by the prospect of this general abandonment, Sixtus IV sent an embassy to Louis XI, "to present considerations tending to peace and union." Louis received the envoys with cordiality; but, enlightened upon the situation in Italy, probably by the return of Philippe de Commines, he resolved to send to Rome an embassy composed of eight distinguished personages of the highest rank, accompanied by two hundred cavaliers, charged with the mission to offer his services as arbitrator in the pacification of Italy.

In order to give force to his proposition, the King provided that the instructions to this embassy should be submitted to the representatives of the Triple Alliance, and they were authorized to propose modifications. With the conviction that the Pope's neglect to unite Italy against the Turks was one of the weakest points in his position, Louis XI, who had never shown any enthusiasm for a crusade, now made himself the champion of the defence of Christendom against the Infidel, and exhorted Sixtus IV to show himself the true Head of the Church and compose his difference with the Florentines, in order that Italy might be united for the prosecution of a war against the Turks.

Unfortunately for the success of the French mission, the troops of the Pope and Ferdinand of Naples had been successful in the field, while Venice had been preoccupied with its war in the East, Milan had been disturbed by the revolutionary measures of Ludovico Sforza, — called "Il Moro," or "The Moor," — brother of the late Duke Galeazzo Sforza, and Florence, thus left to its own resources, had been unable to defend its interests.

When the French embassy arrived at Milan, on December 27, 1478, — although efforts had been made by the King of Hungary, son-in-law of the King of Naples, to detach the Milanese from the Triple Alliance, — assent was readily procured to the proposed mediation of Louis XI. At Florence, on January 15, Lorenzo de' Medici expressed grateful acknowledgment of the good offices proposed, and Venice soon ratified the acceptance of its allies.

At Rome, however, unexpected difficulties were to be encountered. Not only was it necessary to overcome the obstinacy of Sixtus IV, whose dearest passion, the preferment of his nephew, was involved; but to meet the hostile influence of the Emperor Frederick III and the Archduke Maximilian, who were bitterly opposed to the success of the King of France, now threatening to rob the House of Hapsburg of that headship of Christendom which had hitherto belonged only to the imperial office.

Having arrived at Rome on January 24, 1479, the French embassy delivered its credentials, and on the twenty-sixth the ambassadors were presented to the Pope. After assuring His Holiness of the filial obedience of their master, they requested a public audience, which was accorded for the following day. As orator of the embassy, the jurist, Antoine de Morlhon, in the presence of the Sacred College, described the dangers to which Europe was exposed by the divisions of Italy; explained that it was to avert these dangers that the King of France had convoked the council at Orléans; and stated that, with the assent of the ambassadors of the Triple Alliance, those of the King of Naples, and of the Holy See, Louis XI offered his arbitration in the differences that were desolating Italy; ending his discourse with the petition that the Pope would not, by repelling this arbitration, expose himself to more rigorous measures.

During the public audience, Sixtus IV replied only in vague terms; but, in the course of private conversations, he let it be known that he would consent to peace only on condition of the public humiliation of Lorenzo de' Medici, the surrender of certain places to the Holy See as indemnity for the expenses of the war, and the engagement of the Triple Alliance not to concern itself with the affairs of the Church. In no case would he listen to arbitration by the King of France.

Disconcerted, but not discouraged by the apparent futility of their mission, the French ambassadors sought to convince the Pope of the extravagance of his demands, to intimidate him with the hostilities he was provoking, and to protest that he was bound by the action of his envoy in France, the Bishop of Fréjus, who had in his name accepted the arbitration of the King. In reply, Sixtus IV disavowed the authority of his envoy, and in a fit of anger stripped him of his office and placed him in disgrace. At the same time he declared that he would not submit to the arbitration either of the King of France or of any other, for the Vicar of Christ should not submit to be judged by any man.

While thus repudiating the idea of arbitration, the Pope professed his readiness to accept mediation, and for that purpose a commission of cardinals was named to discuss with the French ambassadors and with those of the Triple Alliance the conditions of a peace.

The intrigues of the Pope and the Emperor

On February 25, the envoys of the Triple Alliance arrived at Rome, and a memorandum containing the Pope's demands was laid before them. They were more severe than those at first proposed. Not content with the humiliation of Lorenzo de' Medici, Sixtus IV now demanded that the Florentines should implore pardon for having hung the Archbishop of Pisa, and that they should construct an expiatory chapel in memory of their fault. In addition, he exacted an indemnity of one hundred thousand ducats to be used in the war against the Turks, and the restoration of independence to the Genoese.

The secret of these new and exaggerated claims is found in the fact that the Emperor was at that moment endeavoring to enter upon the scene. During his mission to Italy, Philippe de Commines had procured by order of Louis XI a renewal of homage on the part of Genoa, and the papal demand for its independence was an evident encroachment on the rights of France. The probable purpose of this new demand was to give color to the proposition of Frederick III, who, on January 26, 1479, affecting to consider that Louis XI and the Pope were adversaries, had offered to become the arbitrator between the King of France and the Triple Alliance on the one hand, and the Holy See on the other.

While Frederick III was less anxious to arbitrate the affairs of Italy than he was to defeat the preponderance of the King of France, Sixtus IV, indisposed to accept the arbitration of either, was only too eager to embroil the negotiations in such a manner as to obstruct the purposes of Louis XI. Perhaps it was for this reason that the plenipotentiaries of the Emperor were permitted to be present at the conferences with the French ambassadors. On March 5, they complained that the credentials of the representatives of the Triple Alliance made mention only of the King of France. Some days afterward, they expressed to Badoer, the ambassador of Venice at Rome, the surprise of the Emperor at seeing attributed to the King a rôle which rightly belonged solely to His Imperial Majesty.

Not content with these intrusions, which were encouraged by the Pope, the imperial ambassadors endeavored to disturb the harmony of the French with the representatives of the league. Every device was employed to create distrust among the allies and to destroy the influence of France. It was not until April 16, however, after the ultimatum of the Triple Alliance had been placed in the hands of the Pope, that the plenipotentiaries of the Emperor and Maximilian, who as usual had taken places in the conference of that day, were excluded upon the imperative demand of the allies, on the ground that the business in hand did not concern them.

Left alone to sustain the war against the Turks, the Republic of Venice, after a series of defeats, on January 25, 1479, had made peace with the Sultan. From that time onward the Republic was able to take a more vigorous part

The frustration of the French mission

in the conflict with Sixtus IV. On March 26, an ultimatum was presented to the Pope by the Triple Alliance, demanding a suspension of arms. At the end of a week, in a public consistory, all the cardinals implored him to accede to the demands of the allies; but Sixtus IV dismissed the assembly without definitive action. Two facts had revealed to his quick apprehension the advantages he now possessed, — the peace between Venice and the Sultan rendered united action by the allies in the crusade against the Turks impossible, and the certainty that Louis XI would confine his intervention to merely diplomatic channels rendered easy his defeat.

In an audience accorded on April 28, the Venetian ambassador presented the final refusal of the allies to accept the conditions of the Pope. To destroy as much as possible its force, the imperial ambassador immediately rose and laid claim to Milan as a fief of the Empire, declaring that he could not comprehend how Genoa could belong to the King of France. Thus, by an ingenious turn, in place of appearing as an impartial arbitrator, Louis XI was made the object of accusation before the Pope.

The reinforcement of Louis XI's intervention by that of the King of England, who at first sent a single doctor of laws accompanied by one of Louis' secretaries, and afterward an embassy of four persons, only increased the determination and the advantage of Sixtus IV.

On May 11, he announced in the consistory that he had determined to proclaim the liberty of Genoa; and at the same time admitted some Genoese envoys, who presented their credentials from Baptiste Campofregoso, "by the grace of God Duke of Genoa."

The French ambassadors rose to protest against this invasion of their sovereign's rights; but the Pope commanded silence, and proceeded to receive the oath of Campofregoso as Duke of Genoa. The French ambassadors then presented their solemn protest, while Sixtus IV met them with reproaches, affirming that the allies were not sincere, that he had recommended union against the Turks, and that one of their number had already made peace with them. To cap the climax of this unexpected scene, the imperial ambassador disputed the right of the King of France to the title "*Roi Très-Chrétien*"; which, he declared, better suited his master, the Pope's ally, and the audience was dissolved in the midst of a bitter altercation between the plenipotentiaries of the King and the Emperor.

Sixtus IV well understood that his victory thus far was only one of strategy; and, to avoid decisive action by the allies, he let it be known through Girolamo Riario that, if Borgo San Sepolcro were ceded to him, he would make peace without arbitration. This being contrary to their instructions, the ambassadors of the allies, on May 22, so informed the Pope, and announced that if they did not receive his definite reply to their ultimatum within eight days, they would leave Rome. The French and English plenipotentiaries added that, if the joint arbitration of their kings was not accepted, they also would abandon Rome at the end of the period named.

On the day fixed for their departure, Sixtus IV convoked the ambassadors, read a long explanation of his conduct, and ended with a vague invitation to continue the negotiations. The Venetian ambassador then explained the reasons that had led the Republic to conclude a peace with the Turks, and made an appeal for justice to a general council as superior to the Pope. Antoine de Morlhon wished also to read a public protest against the conduct of the Holy See; but Sixtus IV, after once more expressing his inclination to prolong the negotiations, silenced the French orator, and abruptly ended the audience.

All hope of peace seemed finally to have vanished, when, on June 2, the Pope again assembled the ambassadors, and announced that he would refer the matters in dispute to the Kings of France and England for adjudication, and, in case of a difference in their views, would add to them the Emperor and Maximilian as joint arbitrators. With this understanding he would sign a convention suspending hostilities until the final decision was pronounced.

The French ambassadors, ignorant of the way in which Louis XI would regard this proposition, were so completely deceived by it that they believed themselves to have won a great victory, and proceeded to draw up a *modus vivendi* pending the sentence of arbitration.

Although the Venetians were suspicious of the Pope's designs, believing that he intended to embroil them with the Turks during the litigation, and then take advantage of their embarrassment before the promulgation of the sentence, on July 3, at Milan, an agreement was prepared accepting the terms of the arbitration as proposed.

When, however, Louis XI learned of what his ambassadors had done at Rome, his indignation was such that the hope of pacification seemed illusory. Having already yielded a point in respect to his own prestige in admitting the King of England as joint arbitrator, he was furious at the proposed addition of the Emperor and Maximilian. Alleging that his war with Maximilian, then waging in Burgundy, required all his attention, he declined to take any action. Refusing to listen to the papal envoy, he poured the vials of his wrath upon the French orator, Antoine de Morlhon, treating him as an imbecile, and even declining to hear his justification. It was only after a desperate endeavor that the King could be induced to discuss the subject; but, finally, seeing that the matter would otherwise elude him altogether, he ratified the agreement, and hastened to press for the formal acceptance of the Pope. On August 17, Sixtus IV threw off his mask and announced that he would not execute the *modus vivendi*.

The isolation of Sixtus IV

Baffled in his attempt to compose the affairs of Italy, Louis XI now resolved to isolate the Pope by strengthening the Triple Alliance and detaching from his cause the King of Naples.

The first step in this direction was the support given to the intrigues of Ludovico Sforza, uncle of the young Duke

Gian Galeazzo Sforza, in his attempt to possess himself of the regency of Milan. The friendly relations at that time existing between Ludovico and Ferdinand of Naples held out the hope that the new regent might prove the instrument of winning over the latter to the Triple Alliance, thus depriving the Pope of his only Italian ally.

Exposed, as he was, to the attacks of the Turks, the King of Naples had derived no substantial advantage from his support of the Pope, while the conduct of Sixtus IV in rejecting peace furnished to Ferdinand an excellent pretext for abandoning his cause. To promote this desertion of the Pope, Louis XI sent one of his agents, Pierre Palmier, to Italy with the ostensible mission of winning the adhesion of Sixtus IV to the compromise for peace, but with the real intention of reconciling the King of Naples with the Triple Alliance.

The appearance of Palmier in Italy was the signal for a series of tergiversations that furnish an instructive commentary upon the character of Italian politics. Fully disposed to sacrifice Lorenzo de' Medici, and having formed the idea of a system in which he should himself hold the balance of power, Ludovico Sforza had, however, resolved to make a separate peace with the Pope in behalf of Milan, and, by joining the league of Sixtus IV and Ferdinand of Naples, to destroy the Triple Alliance. To further this design, Ludovico proposed to Venice and to Florence the recall of all the Italian ambassadors from France.

Both Venice and Florence opposed this proposition, but the mere fact that Ludovico had made it awakened suspicions not easily allayed. Florence, suddenly alarmed, imagined in the mission of Palmier a project of Louis XI to advance the cause of Milan with the King of Naples; but it proved, on the contrary, to be for the purpose of effecting a *rapprochement* between Ferdinand and Lorenzo de' Medici, and was so successful that a truce between Florence and Naples was signed on November 24, 1479, and on December 5 Lorenzo left Florence in person to visit Ferdinand.

Thus, completely isolated, the Pope, unable single handed to continue hostilities, was forced to ratify the peace between Florence and Naples; which, in March, 1480, put an end to the war.

Dissolution of the Triple Alliance

While engaged in reconciling Naples with Florence, Louis XI had not neglected to use his powerful influence with Ludovico to prevent the dissolution of the Triple Alliance; but, when Venice saw that she was no longer a participant in the negotiations for peace, — which were conducted exclusively by Lorenzo de' Medici in co-operation with the King of France, — and beheld with dismay the vast increase of influence thus acquired by Florence, the Republic could not resign herself to the subordinate place to which she had been reduced in the league, and, although invited to join in the peace between Florence and Naples, began to seek a new combination. On April 17, 1480, persuaded by the papal legate, Cardinal Foscari, that both Milan and Florence, in spite of their constant protestations to the contrary, intended to nullify the triple compact, Venice concluded a dual alliance with Pope Sixtus IV, and on the twenty-fifth of the same month Girolamo Riario was named as the captain-general of the new confederation.

The wily pontiff, emerging from his isolation almost at the moment when it had been accomplished, with the Republic of Venice as his ally, had again baffled the King of France, while Milan was thus left alone as the sole remnant of the Triple Alliance.

Ludovico Sforza, whose unfruitful treason to his allies was the real cause of this situation, lost no time in the effort to repair his mistake. Not yet fully settled in the seat of power, — since he was still only acting as regent for his young nephew, Gian Galeazzo, — he was now placed in extreme embarrassment through fear of displeasing the King of France. In order to cultivate the King's friendship and ascertain his intentions, he promptly renounced his purpose of recalling the Milanese ambassadors, who on the contrary were ordered to remain at the court of France. But his em-

THE DIPLOMACY OF FRENCH EXPANSION

barrassment was rendered still more painful when his envoys soon afterward informed him that Louis XI had, in person, and in the presence of others, announced his own wish to seek an *entente* with Venice and the Pope, reproached Ludovico with having selfishly thrown himself into the arms of Ferdinand of Naples, — which he had not really done, — and ended his voluble denunciation of their master by practically dismissing them.

Finding himself entirely without support, and embittered by the desertion of Venice to the Pope, only one course was now open to the Regent of Milan. On August 24, 1480, his union with Naples and Florence in a new confederation was publicly announced.

Thus, by the agile action of the Italians, Sixtus IV had escaped submission to the arbitrament of Louis XI, the dangers of Florence had been averted, peace had been restored, and a new political adjustment had reproduced the original contra-position of two evenly balanced confederations — a dual and a triple alliance — quite able, if not disturbed, to maintain the equilibrium of Italy.

The descent of the Turks upon Otranto, by exposing Ferdinand of Naples to grave danger, furnished a new occasion to the King of France for regaining his predominance in Italy by becoming the champion of the war against the Infidel; but Venice stood firmly in the way, and even the influence of her ally, the Pope, was unable to change her policy. The war between Venice and the new triple league of Naples, Florence, and Milan over the possession of Ferrara presented another pretext for French intervention; but after Venice had stirred once more the spectre of the old Angevin pretensions to the Kingdom of Naples and the Orléans claims to the Duchy of Milan, with the double purpose of inciting France and intimidating her opponents, the incident ended without results. Just at the critical moment when by supporting these claims his word might have been decisive in Italian affairs, the announcement of the death of Louis XI, on August 30, 1483, and the regency of his daughter, Anne de

Beaujeu, during the minority of young Charles VIII, shattered all plans for the exercise of French predominance in Italy.

But, although Louis XI did not live to exercise in Italy that supremacy which had once belonged to the emperors, his diplomacy was fertile in consequences for the future. On the one hand, he had established a new system of French intervention beyond the Alps by soothing Italian suspicions through his apparent moderation and disinterestedness; until, at last, as an historian has well observed, the Italians "gradually habituated themselves to regard the King of France as an equitable mediator."[1] On the other hand, he had laid the foundations for a future national policy of aggrandisement at the expense of Italy that was to determine in a large degree the fortunes of France and the destinies of Europe.

The regency of Anne de Beaujeu

Although the daughter of Louis XI was not able to pursue the plans of her father in Italy, her personal talents and the spirit and principles derived from him enabled her to apply to the government during the eight years of her regency the policy by which he had built up the monarchy.[2] Happily for her rule, he had left France at peace. By the Treaty of Arras, of December 23, 1482, young Philip as Count of Flanders had been made to do homage to the King, and the daughter of Maximilian had been delivered to his hands. The death of Louis XI furnished an occasion for the Archduke to declare the authority of the Council of Flanders at an end, and to make a new struggle to regain the mastery; but after a heroic effort, in January, 1485, he was unsuccessful in holding Ghent, and his power was soon confined to Brabant and Hainault. A revolt of the people of Ghent against the French, however, enabled him to recover the city in the following June, and he was then so far master of the situation as to find it possible to leave the Netherlands under the rule of his lieutenants and depart for Germany.

---

[1] Perret, *Histoire des relations*, II, p. 218, regards this as a great gain for the diplomacy of Louis XI.

[2] Louis XI had said of her: "She is the least foolish woman in the kingdom, for there is no wise one."

THE DIPLOMACY OF FRENCH EXPANSION 151

A movement of the feudal lords to regain their power after the death of Louis XI only served to strengthen the hands of Anne de Beaujeu. Under the leadership of Louis, Duke of Orléans, the nobles, thinking thus to control the Regent, demanded the convocation of the States General. Opposing the will of the nation to the schemes of the nobility, in 1484 Anne gladly convoked the assembly; but took care to give it a really national character. The result was her overwhelming victory; for the national sentiment was now clamorous for the unity of France, and the designs of the nobles were completely frustrated. Only two powerful fiefs, aside from Flanders, still remained in France, — the Duchy of Brittany, and the Duchy of Bourbon. Both were soon to feel the power of the Crown.

The death of Francis II, Duke of Brittany, in 1488, leaving this great duchy to his only daughter, Anne, having opened the question of succession, the Archduke Maximilian of Austria, who had just received the title "King of the Romans," — being a widower since the death of Mary of Burgundy six years before, — offered his hand to the young duchess, and in 1490 they were formally espoused by procuration. The engagement opened for Maximilian the prospect of possessing territories on both sides of France, by which he hoped to renew the policy of Charles the Bold; and for the Duchess Anne it offered the distinction of sharing with him the honors of the imperial crown. But, for France, this union was freighted with dangers that rendered it intolerable. Asserting the rights of the Crown over the young duchess, the Regent forbade the marriage, and marched an army into Brittany to prevent it. One after another the strongholds fell into the hands of the royal troops; and, in December, 1491, Anne of Brittany was required to sign a contract of marriage with young Charles VIII, by which her duchy was preserved to the French monarchy.[1]

CHAP. II
A. D.
1453–1492

---

[1] For many years Margaret of Burgundy had resided in France as the betrothed wife of Charles, and his marriage to Anne of Brittany,

CHAP. II
A. D.
1453-1492

To the political unity of France was now added territorial unity. From the English Channel to the Mediterranean, from the Atlantic to the Jura and the Alps, France had become a consolidated state. Calais was still held by the English, the Kingdom of Navarre still possessed lands north of the Pyrenees, and the Netherlands were already in effect lost to France; but the great fiefs, except those of the House of Bourbon, had now been gathered in, and the transformation of feudal into national sovereignty was almost complete.

The use of diplomacy by Louis XI

If the reign of Louis XI had proved full of consequences for the unity of France, it had not been less significant for the affairs of Europe. No monarch had ever before made so large an employment of the arts of diplomacy. Inheriting from Charles VII the finest army in Europe, he had preferred to hold his military power in the background, and to accomplish his purposes by more peaceful means.

From the imperfect records of the time it is possible to discover the names of more than seventy persons who served Louis XI in a diplomatic capacity, and it is certain that his secret agents far exceeded this unprecedented number. Among his servitors it is interesting to note the numerous Italians who brought to his aid the capacity for negotiation and intrigue for which that race had long been distinguished. Sometimes these were permanently in his employ, sometimes hired to serve his purposes while in the employ of others. Among them are to be specially noted the names of his chancellor, Pietro Doriolo, the brothers Valpergi, the jurist

---

already married by procuration to Maximilian of Austria, not only appeared to that prince an unpardonable injury, but became a great scandal throughout Christendom. Pope Innocent VIII was induced to find the marriage of Maximilian by procuration "null and void," but hesitated to grant a formal dispensation for the union of Charles VIII and Anne of Brittany, responding to the request for it by three times sending his simple "benediction." Finally, after long efforts, the French ambassador at Rome procured a dispensation, upon the condition that it be kept an absolute secret. For the details, see De Maulde, *La diplomatie*, I, p. 28; and for the documents, Dumont, *Corps diplomatique*, III, Part II, pp. 274 et seq.

Raimondo Marco Montepessulano, the Milanese Alberto Magaloto and Panicharola, and the Florentine Francesco Nori.[1] Wherever information could be found or co-operation inspired, there his emissaries spread the seduction of his gold and insinuated the advantages of his friendship. Among his sayings was the declaration that "he would burn his hat if he could suppose it to guess the secret of his head." "To reign is to dissimulate," is the principle laid down as the basis of his policy. In sending Dubouchage and De Solliers to the Dukes of Guyenne and Brittany, his instructions were: "If they lie to you, lie still more to them."

It was the example of Louis XI, even more than the precepts formulated a quarter of a century afterward by Machiavelli, that made the "*raison d'etat*" the foundation of European politics for centuries. In his vocabulary, "corruption" was pronounced "liberality," and all men were only pawns to be moved in the interest of the state. Without scruples of conscience, he seduced from the service of other men their ablest advisers, when he could not use them in the councils of his enemies. Philippe de Commines, the two chancellors Rochefort, and D'Esquerdes, afterward a marshal of France, were thus drawn into his vortex, and employed as effective instruments against their former masters.

Although Italy had long maintained active diplomatic intercourse between the states of the peninsula, permanent missions were never established until the fear or hope of French intervention had rendered them important.[2]

---

[1] The part played by these persons may be followed in the pages of Perret, *Histoire des relations de la France avec Venise*, and other works on the diplomacy of the time. Baschet says: "Louis XI fut réellement en France le premier prince qui donna de grandes et actives besognes à la diplomatie européenne." — *La diplomatie vénitienne: les princes de l'Europe*, p. 296.

[2] "C'est du reste l'époque où la diplomatie vénitienne s'établit régulièrement auprès de toutes les cours importantes: le mouvement général des affaires exigeait cet établissement. Jusqu' alors, sauf auprès du Saint-Siège, la République des Vénitiens n'avait été représentée

CHAP. II
A.D.
1453-1492

The earliest permanent diplomatic relations of which we have record were those of Francesco Sforza and Cosimo de' Medici. As early as 1446, before Sforza became Duke of Milan, he sent Nicodemus de' Pontremoli to reside permanently near Cosimo de' Medici at Florence. But this affable envoy, who from his powers of insinuation was called "Sweet Nicodemus," did not become a diplomatic agent in the proper sense until 1450; for, prior to that date, Sforza was not a sovereign, and his representative was, therefore, only a private agent.[1]

If, as appears to be the case, permanent diplomatic representation begins with Nicodemus, that institution dates in Italy only from 1450. About the same time, Florence began to maintain a permanent representation at Milan. Soon afterward, similar relations were established between Milan, Venice, and Naples. In Milan, not only the official representation but also the official representatives assumed a permanent character, and in that state a class of public officers first came into being whose lives were devoted to diplomacy.

In 1463, had begun the permanent representation of Milan at the court of France, and the example was soon followed by other states of Italy. Venice, however, for political reasons, was not continuously represented, but the unbroken representation of Florence began in 1474 with the mission of Francesco Nasi.[2]

---

qu'extraordinairement auprès des princes, c'est à dire, selon le besoin des circonstances." — Baschet, *La diplomatie vénitienne*, etc., p. 300. It was not, however, until 1498 that the Venetian embassies to France became continuous. See Krauske, *Die Entwickelung der ständigen Diplomatie*, pp. 32, 34.

[1] Schaube, in his learned article on the origin of permanent embassies, appears to have overlooked this fact. The so-called "despatches" of Nicodemus for this earlier time have, indeed, been published by Buser and Sickel; but, until Milan became an actual possession of Sforza, Nicodemus was not in the official sense a diplomatic representative. See Schaube, *Zur Entstehungsgeschichte der ständigen Gesandtschaften*, pp. 508, 509.

[2] See Schaube, *Zur Entstehungsgeschichte*, pp. 525 et seq.

THE DIPLOMACY OF FRENCH EXPANSION   155

With the reign of Louis XI conditions were created which demanded increasing watchfulness on the part of all the European powers, but the institution of permanent missions was not yet established by them.

The methods of Louis XI changed the entire character of European diplomacy, not only in spirit but in form. To meet such agencies as he employed, every nation was compelled to form a definite foreign policy, and either to devise a "system" of its own or passively take its place in systems imposed by others. The *régime* that had long been customary in Italy was thus made necessary throughout Europe.

As the international mechanism set in motion by the King of France became more complicated, the time was soon to come when no nation, no princely house, could well dispense with a diplomatic establishment. Determined in this as in other respects to crush out the independence of his vassals, Louis XI required from the Duke of Orléans a formal oath not to ally himself to any prince against his successor.[1] Every resource was thenceforth used to render diplomatic action the monopoly of the monarch, and to deny the right of embassy to powerful vassals.

As correspondence between court and court became more and more necessary, the royal postal system was developed, and was largely the outgrowth of diplomatic needs.[2] In 1480, Louis XI first gave it effective organization, and made it directly subservient to his interests.[3] Under penalty of

CHAP. II
A. D.
1453–1492

The influence of Louis XI on diplomacy

---

[1] De Maulde, *La diplomatie*, I, p. 179.

[2] For a long time the postal service existed solely in the interest of the sovereign, and private persons were forbidden to make use of it. In France, it was first introduced by royal edict in 1464. In England, royal messengers were employed in carrying letters as early as 1252; but it was not until 1470, under Edward IV, that regular post stations, at intervals of twenty miles, were established, for the purpose of quick communication with Scotland.

[3] The improvements effected in the rapidity of communication between 1474 and 1498 were remarkable. A courier sent from Rome to Paris in April, 1474, promised as a great feat to traverse the distance in thirteen days. See Gingins-la-Sarraz, *Dépêches*, I, pp. 3, 4. In

capital punishment, masters of the post were forbidden to furnish horses to any one without a special order from the King or his minister. At each frontier a clerk was instructed to open and read all suspected correspondence; and to withhold it, if it was prejudicial to the King. A courier who attempted to pass the frontier otherwise than by the royal highway, and thus escape the King's officers, was liable to "the confiscation of his body and his goods." Only the private couriers of foreign princes were, "conformably to the ordinances," exempt from examination; those of French princes being subject to search and arrest.

In Germany, Maximilian soon endeavored to establish the same monopoly in diplomatic privileges for the Emperor; but with less success, owing to the power and independence of the German princes. In Italy, even the inferior princes continued to maintain their immemorial rights of diplomatic intercourse.

To insure secrecy of communication, cryptography, which had been known and practised in Europe as early as the time of Julius Caesar, was now developed into a more perfect art; and every chancellery had its expert, not only in enciphering despatches, but in deciphering stolen or intercepted correspondence by ingeniously working out the underlying code.[1]

1498, news of the death of Charles VIII, which occurred at Paris on the evening of April 7, reached Rome on the evening of the fourteenth, just seven days after the event. See De Maulde, *Diplomatie*, III, p. 116. A table prepared by Marino Sanuto in 1500, showing the time required for despatches to pass between Venice and other places, may be found in his *Diarii*, III, under date of October 3.

[1] See De Maulde, *La diplomatie*, III, pp. 132, 135; and Fumagalli, *Istituzioni diplomatiche*, I, pp. 170, 171. For the extent to which the art of decipherment was perfected, see Perret, *Les règles de Cicco Simonetta pour le déchiffrement des écritures secrètes 4 juillet, 1474*, in the Bibliothèque de l'École des Chartes, 1890, p. 516 et seq. As examples of codes thus reconstructed, see those of Cardinal d'Amboise and the Sire de Chaumont in De Maulde, III, p. 134; and for the modern use made of the principles of decipherment, Meister, *Die Anfänge der modernen diplomatischen Geheimschrift*, Paderborn, 1902.

It was in this period also that Latin, which during the Middle Ages had been the sole international medium, began to yield a place in diplomatic intercourse to the national languages. Each nation thenceforth carried on its correspondence with its own agents chiefly in its own tongue, though Latin continued to be employed in strictly international documents. By the close of the fifteenth century, even the reports of the papal nuncios were written in Italian.[1]

With the reign of Louis XI and the diffusion of Italian methods and conceptions north of the Alps, began a period of political history in which the whole of Europe underwent a radical transformation. At the death of Louis XI, the Papacy had largely lost its power as a supreme and universal magistracy, the consolidation of the French monarchy had created a formidable rival to the Empire, and the minor states of Europe perceived the necessity of such mutual intelligence and combination as would protect them from absorption by one or the other of these great protagonists. Italy, Savoy, Switzerland, and the Netherlands, — the fragments of that imperial domain which had been assigned to

---

[1] The use of national languages in the public acts of the chief countries of Europe was a necessary consequence of the growth of national sentiment. In England, Edward III in 1362 forbade the use of Norman-French in public acts and established the use of English. In Germany, Rudolf of Hapsburg ordained the publication of state documents in the German language, and by 1320 the use of Latin had greatly diminished. It was the Emperor Frederick III, however, who, at the request of the Germanic body, ruled that all notarial acts should be in German; Latin being retained for strictly imperial acts. In Spain and Portugal, the change occurred at about the same time. In Italy, Latin continued much in use, owing to the influence of the Roman See; but Italian was frequently employed in secular correspondence, and finally in that of the papal nuncios. In France, Latin was confined chiefly to particular classes of acts as early as the beginning of the fifteenth century. In 1512, Francis I ordained the sole and exclusive use of French in all public and private acts; but it was not until 1539 that this decree became wholly effective. Latin long continued to be, however, owing to its universal character, the language of treaties and of strictly international communication.

CHAP. II
A. D.
1453–1492

Lothair by the Treaty of Verdun, — could find safety only in such adjustments as would prevent the entire domination of either France or the Empire. The interests of England, of the Scandinavian and Slavic kingdoms, and of Spain and Portugal, — soon to open to royal ambition new fields of conquest, — were still grouped round the destinies of Italy; for Rome had not ceased to be the titular seat of moral authority and the centre of an influence still almost universal.

Left without a common bond, except the memory of institutions already fallen into decay or rapidly changing their character, instincts which the combined forces of the Empire and the Church had once molded into a great European community, had now grouped the peoples of Western Christendom into independent nations, each with its own prejudices, interests, and ambitions. Confronted with the problem of maintaining their own existence against the organized encroachments of their neighbors, the states of Europe were in much the same position as that in which the Italian municipalities had found themselves when struggling to preserve their liberties by the formation of defensive leagues.

The idea of European equilibrium

The idea of political equilibrium, which had long served to preserve the peace of Italy, was soon to dawn upon the nations of Europe also as their only hope of safety. The events of the fifteenth century brought to light the principle — so clear as to be worthy of recognition as a law of history — that, as in the constitution of single states the dissolution of monarchy presents no other alternatives than anarchy or self-government; so in the relations of independent sovereignties, war and diplomacy become the inevitable substitutes for empire. When the Empire had ceased to be a protection and the Papacy was no longer universally recognized as a tribunal, the security of nations became wholly dependent upon armed force on the one hand, or intelligent association for mutual safety on the other. Unhappily for Europe, the aspiration after imperial power became the

THE DIPLOMACY OF FRENCH EXPANSION

passion of the greater states at the very moment when the ancient guardians of peace, the Empire and the Papacy, were least able to defend the rights and liberties they were theoretically intended to protect. That universal monarchy which, if realized, might have given repose to the world, was still to be the elusive phantom of princely ambition. Wars of aggression and wars of resistance were still to follow one another in the ceaseless struggle to reconcile the ideals of imperial dominion and of local sovereignty, but a new and powerful agency had been brought into action. Diplomacy, made the instrument of both these opposing principles, was to work out the problem of controlling by intelligent association that lust for imperial domination which has made of human history an unending tragedy.

AUTHORITIES

We have now reached a point in the history of diplomacy where the archives of governments begin to have great value as repositories of authentic documents. It may, therefore, be useful in this connection to offer some observations upon the more important of these collections.

The Archives of Venice begin to be exceedingly useful for general European relations in the reign of Charles VII of France. The "Libri Pactorum" furnish many originals and transcripts of treaties; the "Commemoriali," beginning with 1295, supply memoranda of important events; the "Registri Misti," or miscellaneous deliberations of the Senate, run from 1295 to 1440, and contain references to diplomatic incidents; and the "Registri Secreti," covering the period 1401–1630, include the instructions to ambassadors, and, therefore, possess great historical value. The existing "Relazioni" begin in 1493, but the "Dispacci," which Baschet calls "*la lumière dans l'histoire*," do not regularly begin until 1554. The most ancient despatch preserved is that of Jacopo Tiepolo, ambassador at Constantinople, addressed to the Doge, Pietro Ziani, and is dated in December, 1219. The *Annali Veneti*, compiled by Domenico Malipiero, and published in the Archivio Storico Italiano of Florence, contain many despatches of the period 1457–1500. The so-called "Corti" do not begin until a later period. A list of the documents most useful for the present chapter may be found in Baschet, *Histoire de la chancellerie secrète*, Paris, 1870, pp. 257, 260. On the nature and contents of the Archives of Venice, see further Baschet, *Les archives de la Sérénissime République de Venise*, Paris, 1857; and *La diplomatie vénitienne*, Paris, 1872; and Brown, *L'archivio di Venezia con riguardo speciale alla storia inglese*, Venice, 1865. Brown, *Calendar of State Papers* and *Manuscripts relating to English Affairs*, I (1202-1509), London, 1864, gives valuable extracts. Lamansky, *Secrets d'état de Venise*, St. Petersburg, 1884, does the same for relations with the Greeks, the Slavs, and the Ottoman Empire. Toderini and Cecchetti, *L'archivio di stato in Venezia nel decennio 1866-1875*, Venice, 1876, shows the use made of the Venetian archives by historians down to 1875. The monumental *Diarii* of Marino Sanuto does not begin until January 1, 1496.

The Secret Archives of the Vatican, opened for the use of historical research by Pope Leo XIII in 1879, contain few unpublished diplomatic documents of importance prior to the return of the Papacy from Avignon.

The Archives of Milan are particularly rich in materials for the period covered in this and the following chapter. Their published contents are found in De Gingins-la-Sarraz, *Dépêches des ambassadeurs milanais sur les campagnes de Charles-le-Hardi, Duc de Bourgogne* (1474-1477), Paris and Geneva, 1858; Chmel, *Briefe und Aktenstücke zur Geschichte der Herzoge von Mailand von 1451 bis 1513*, Vienna, 1856, published in the "Notizenblatt" of the Academy of Vienna; and Osio, *Documenti diplomatici tratti dagli archivi milanesi*, Milan, 1864.

The most important diplomatic documents of Florence have been published by Desjardins and Canestrini, *Négociations diplomatiques de la France avec la Toscane*, Paris, 1859.

Other archives particularly valuable for the period covered by the present chapter are those of Turin and Geneva, which contain much information preserved by the House of Savoy. See, for the contents of the former, Armingaud, *La maison de Savoie et les archives de Turin*, Paris, 1877. The Archives of Geneva, "Affaires Etrangères," No. XXIV, contain the original manuscripts or authentic copies of the correspondence of Pope Felix V (Amadeus VIII of Savoy) with his son, Louis, Duke of Savoy, and many copies of treaties relating to the League of Milan (1446-1449). For some account of this correspondence, see Gaullier, *Correspondance du Pape Félix et de son fils, Louis, Duc de Savoie, au sujet de la Ligue de Milan, d'après des documents inédits*, Zürich, 1851, in the Archives pour l'Histoire Suisse, VIII; and Sickel, *Die ambrosianische Republik und das Haus Savoyen*, Vienna, 1856.

The collections of Dumont and Rymer continue to be useful for the treaties of the time; and to these may be added, particularly for the treaties made by Louis XI, Léonard, *Recueil des traitez de paix*, etc., Paris, 1703.

Other valuable collections of documents for this period are *Amtliche Sammlung der älteren eidgenössischen Abschiede*, Lucerne, 1839–1874; Duclos, *Recueil de pièces pour servir de suite à l'histoire de Louis XI*, The Hague, 1746; Vaesen and Charavay, *Lettres de Louis XI*, Paris, 1883–1885; *Mémoires de Philippe de Commines*, the best edition being that of Mandrot, Paris, 1901, in the Textes pour servir à l'étude et à l'enseignement de l'histoire; Kervyn de Lettenhove, *Lettres et négociations de Philippe de Commines*, Brussels, 1867; Trinchera, *Codice Aragonese*, Naples, 1860.

On the general development of France in this period, see Paquier, *Histoire de l'unité politique et territoriale de la France*, Paris, 1879.

For the reigns of Charles VII and Louis XI, Basin, *Histoire de Charles VII et de Louis XI*, Paris, 1855 et seq.; Beaucourt, *Histoire de Charles VII*, Paris, 1891, based on recent and exhaustive research; Desjardins, *Louis XI, sa politique extérieure, ses rapports avec l'Italie*, Paris, 1874, dealing chiefly with the relations of France to Florence; Moufflet, *Étude sur une négociation diplomatique de Louis XI*, Marseilles, 1884.

On the history of Italy during this period, Cipolla, *Storia delle signorie italiane dal 1313 al 1530*, Milan, 1881; Perrens, *Histoire de Florence depuis la domination des Médici jusqu' à la chute de la République* (1434–1534), Paris, 1888; Cappelletti, *Storia della Repubblica di Venezia*, Venice, 1850; Romanin, *Storia documentata di Venezia*, Venice, 1854 et seq.; Corio, *Storia di Milano*, Milan, 1851.

On the diplomatic relations of France with the Italian states, Buser, *Die Beziehungen der Mediceer zu Frankreich während der Jahre 1434–1494*, Leipzig, 1879; Buser, *Lorenzo de' Medici als italienischer Staatsmann*, Leipzig, 1879; Reumont, *Lorenzo de' Medici il Magnifico*, Leipzig, 1883; Baschet, *La diplomatie vénitienne*, Paris, 1862; Perret, *Histoire des relations de la France avec Venise du XIIIe siècle à l'avènement de Charles VIII*, Paris, 1896, founded upon admirable original researches; and Combet, *Louis XI et le Saint-Siège* (1461–1483), Paris, 1903, also based on original sources, particularly those of the Vatican. To these should be added for the papal diplomacy, Gregorovius and Pastor, as previously cited.

For Charles the Bold and the relations of France to Burgundy, Kirk, *History of Charles the Bold*, Philadelphia, 1863; and, particularly, Toutey, *Charles le Téméraire et la Ligue de Constance*, Paris, 1902, representing the most recent and careful research.

For the relations of France with the Swiss, Mandrot, *Relations de Charles VII et de Louis XI avec les cantons suisses*, Zürich, 1881; and Rott, *Histoire de la représentation diplomatique de la France auprès des cantons suisses*, I (1430–1559), Berne and Paris, 1900.

On the marriage of Mary of Burgundy with Maximilian of Austria, see Rausch, *Die burgundische Heirat Maximilians*, Vienna, 1880.

For the development of diplomacy in general, see, besides the works of Baschet cited above, Krauske, *Die Entwickelung der ständigen Diplomatie vom 15ten Jahrhundert*, Leipzig, 1885 ; De Maulde-la-Clavière, *La diplomatie au temps de Machiavel*, Paris, 1892, who has collected a multitude of curious details relating to this period; and Schaube, *Zur Entstehungsgeschichte der ständigen Gesandtschaften*, in Mittheilungen der Instituts für österreichischen Geschichtsforschung, Band X, pp. 501, 551; Flassan, *Histoire générale et raisonnée de la diplomatie française*, Paris, 1811, gives to the reign of Louis XI only the most meagre treatment. See the reply to his critics in his *Apologie de l'histoire de la diplomatie française*, Paris, 1812.

CHAPTER III

THE IMPERIAL ASPIRATIONS OF FRANCE

THE closing decades of the fifteenth century present a strange commingling of mediaeval traditions and modern ideas. The institutions of the Middle Ages had been profoundly modified, but they had not disappeared. Although the Pope had ceased to be the undisputed head of the Church, he joined to the obedience of a great part of Christendom the sovereignty of a temporal prince in Italy. If the Emperor had been rendered practically impotent south of the Alps, and had been hedged in by the rise of powerful national states in the North and the East, the imperial crown had not lost its glamour, nor the imperial title its immemorial distinction. But a multitude of events had occurred, each in itself sufficient to create an epoch of history, to justify the bold figure of speech by which historians have agreed to portray this period of transition as a new birth of humanity.

Character of the renaissance

As in every form of natural evolution, so in this era of the *renaissance*, the new was in large degree a rehabilitation of the old; but the revival of ancient knowledge in art, letters, and government would have had a greatly diminished effect upon the world if it had not been aided by forces entirely new.

While the employment of gunpowder and artillery was working a revolution in the art of warfare, the printing press was creating a still more significant revolution in the human mind. Force and thought, the essential rulers of the world, were both deriving new efficiency from their better organization; but the chief distinction of the period is, that they were thenceforth to enter the service of really colossal

164   A HISTORY OF DIPLOMACY

Chap. III
A. D.
1492–1502

nations, all aiming at the same object, the primacy of the world.

Beside the struggles of these giant nations, — France, Spain, and England, — the petty rivalries of the Italian states were to become almost contemptible; yet it was from Italy, as a primary school of politics, that the great nations were to derive their first lessons in the arts of statecraft. Here, as nowhere else in the world, had been developed the art of checking the preponderance of any particular political community by artificial combinations. Too distrustful of one another's designs to unite in permanent confederations, the Italians had learned to preserve their local independence by a system of diplomatic equilibrium. In the conflict for pre-eminence which was soon to fill the broader arena of Europe, the experience of Italy was to furnish the method by which the nations were to maintain their local sovereignty against imperial aspirations so colossal in their proportions as to render the pretensions of the past comparatively insignificant.

I. The Appeals of the Italians to Charles VIII

The mechanism of Italian politics

In the breaking up of Christendom into national states, Italy had never ceased to be regarded as the central seat of power. Although irreparably divided since the collapse of the Empire by the fall of the Hohenstaufen in the thirteenth century, it was still agitated by the imperial traditions and the claims of the Papacy. In these claims and traditions still survived contradictory hopes of Italian unity. Since the return from Avignon, the Papacy had unceasingly striven to expand the Papal State and obtain the mastery of Italy; while Naples, Milan, and Venice had entertained conflicting ambitions for primacy in the peninsula.

To defeat these designs for the union of Italy under the domination of a single master, Florence had taken the lead in so combining the rival aspirants for power against one another as to hold all of them in check.

Sometimes, as in the case of Charles VII and of Louis XI,

when the system of balanced power seemed in desperate danger, the foreigner had been invoked; but in every instance the instinct of self-preservation had finally come to the rescue before it was too late, and the independence of the five chief powers of Italy had been preserved.

Such were the three principles which, for centuries, had constituted the mechanism of Italian politics. Unification, equilibrium, and intervention, — these were the mainsprings of the three alternating systems by which the Italians had sought to solve their political problems. A fourth, confederation, might have proved, had it been practicable, the salvation of the peninsula; but the political union of the Italian states was, in fact, not less impossible than the federation of Europe would be to-day.

So long as they were left to their own reciprocal counteraction, Italy was safe; for the independence of all the states was secured by averting the preponderance of any single one through the combinations of the others. Lorenzo de' Medici had made himself the champion of this system, and by his skilful statesmanship he had been able to obtain for Italy a period of security; but his death on April 8, 1492, followed by the rule of his incapable son, Piero, rendered inevitable calamities which his genius for statecraft might possibly have averted.

During the lifetime of the great Florentine, repeated attempts had been made to invoke foreign intervention. After the death of Louis XI the French court had become a busy centre of intrigue on the part of the Italians, who sought to find support from the regency for their respective interests. In the hope of gaining some advantage, the ambassadors of Venice, Naples, Milan, and the Holy See hovered like birds of prey about the court of France; but, during the minority of young Charles VIII, the government of Anne de Beaujeu wisely adhered to the policy of building up the internal interests of the monarchy.

Even the Turks had been approached as a means of promoting schemes for supremacy in Italy, for the mediaeval idea of the solidarity of Christendom against the Infidel had given place to political conceptions in which the only standard of conduct was success. Devoid of idealism in the intellectual as well as in the moral meaning of the term, Italian politics had become frankly realistic, positive, and opportunist. Public power in Italy, having ordinarily been acquired by crime and maintained by the brute force of hired *condottieri*, recognized no obligations and hesitated before no moral obstacles.

It is not strange, therefore, that when Lorenzo de' Medici's restraining influence was removed, a general appeal, actuated by widely different motives, was made to young Charles VIII to come to Italy. The conservative policy of Charles VII in Italian affairs, and the beneficent effects following from the moderate interventions of Louis XI had created among the Italians a curious illusion regarding the disinterested motives of the French monarchy. Philippe de Commines assures us that, at the time when Charles VIII was invited to Italy, the French were generally regarded there "as saints." True, it is, that Italy had then suffered less from the French than from others, and the French kings before that time had shown their wisdom in renouncing temptations to foreign conquests; but the Italians were soon to learn that invading armies are not essentially dissimilar, and that ambition is not confined to particular races.

That which is most astonishing in the general enthusiasm with which Charles VIII was invited to cross the Alps is the almost universal blindness to the fact that small political communities were making themselves the prey of great powers, whose cupidity and antagonisms were certain to be aroused by the armed intervention of France. It is a striking instance of the manner in which the gravest political dangers may be concealed by the most petty immediate interests. In calling for Charles VIII, Italy was bidding farewell to her independence, and fixing her destiny as the victim of foreign depredations for centuries to come.

With the accession of Sixtus IV to the Papacy, the Holy

See had definitely taken its place as an Italian principality, whose motives and principles of action differed in no respect from those of purely secular princes, such as the Sforza, the Medici, and the Aragonese dynasty at Naples. While the office of Holy Father and Head of the Universal Church gave to the Pope incalculable advantages in his contest with his rivals, it modified in no degree his political policy or methods. Nepotism and corruption in public affairs and the most despicable vices in private life are among the faults which the most stalwart defenders of the *renaissance* popes do not pretend to deny or even to conceal. The Church had fallen a victim to private ambition, its highest office had become a chattel in the market, and its august mission was made to serve as a cloak for the lowest passions.

Attitude of the Papacy

Selfish and unprincipled as Sixtus IV had shown himself to be, his immediate successors were to surpass him in both public and private perfidy. To him, to Innocent VIII, and to Alexander VI, Italy was merely a field for conquest, and their chief ambition was to become its master.

It was Sixtus IV who set the example of plunging Italy into the horrors of war for the sake of building up the temporal power of his nephew, Girolamo Riario, whose greatness lasted no longer than his uncle's life. It was this same pope who, enraged with his former ally, Ferdinand of Naples, made overtures to France to recognize the Angevin claims to that kingdom, which by the death of René of Anjou in 1480 had passed to Charles of Maine, and a year later to Louis XI, together with the estates of Anjou, Maine, and Provence. Preoccupied with his struggle with Maximilian over Burgundy, Louis XI was not disposed to undertake the enterprise of deposing Ferdinand; whereupon the Pope, hoping to exercise more power over him as his ally than as his open enemy, hastened to make peace with the King of Naples, and to enter the league which had been formed with Florence.

The real interests of the Papacy lay, no doubt, in keeping the French out of Italy; but the papal office was too much at the mercy of rival factions to maintain a consistent policy.

Fluctuations of the papal policy

With the death of Sixtus IV on August 12, 1484, the dangers to which the Holy See was exposed as an elective office came plainly into view. Good candidates were to be found among the cardinals, but the spirit of faction and intrigue had become so prevalent that it was impossible to elect any of them. The first act of the electoral conclave was the adoption of a capitulation giving new powers to the cardinals. Dominated by an intriguing prelate, Cardinal Giuliano della Rovere, nephew of Sixtus IV, who wished to elect a pope subject to his own control, aided by Cardinal Ascanio Sforza, brother of Ludovico, the electoral body was beguiled into choosing Giambattista Cibò, who humbly subscribed to the conditions imposed upon him. After a night of secret negotiations, his opponents were confronted in the morning with a solid majority, who in exchange for various offices and emoluments had been pledged to the support of Cardinal Cibò while the others slept.

But Innocent VIII, as the new pope chose to be called, had no sooner firmly seated himself upon the papal throne than he began to show an unexpected independence. The first pope to make public acknowledgment of his natural children, he understood too well the worthless character of his son Franceschetto, who married a daughter of Lorenzo de' Medici, to make him a cardinal; although he conferred the red hat upon Giovanni, son of Lorenzo, at the age of thirteen. The Pope is said to have found more profitable employment for his offspring in bartering ecclesiastical offices and in the sale of pardons.[1] Father and son are reported to have founded a "bank for indulgences," where even the crime of murder received the papal pardon.[2] Every sin had its price, which was divided between the Pope and Franceschetto. The failure of Ferdinand of Naples to pay his annual tribute

---

[1] Infessura reports that when the Vice Chancellor, afterward Pope Alexander VI, was asked why criminals were allowed to pay instead of being punished, he replied, "God wills not the death of a sinner, but rather that he should pay and live."

[2] Burckhardt, *Geschichte der Renaissance*, p. 138.

at last aroused the anger of Innocent, who in 1486 and again in 1488 secretly appealed to France. But the Pope had no real intention of displacing Ferdinand. Without officially recognizing the French rights to Naples, which would have been the only really effective measure for dispossessing the King, Innocent VIII contented himself with vague threats to depose him by offering the crown to the son of the King of Hungary, or even to Ludovico Sforza, keeping in reserve the more dangerous menace of French intervention.

To the end of his life, Innocent VIII, although holding the Angevin claims as a sword of Damocles over the head of Ferdinand, never took decisive action against him, and toward the end of his reign formed an open alliance with him. On July 25, 1492, while Franceschetto, knowing that he would be of no importance after his father's death, hovered about the bedside of the expiring pope planning to lay hands on his treasures, the blood of three boys, at the price of a ducat each, is said to have been vainly sacrificed to prolong the life of the Pontiff by transfusion. His death was the signal for the most active traffic for the papal office known to history.

Having secured their places in the College of Cardinals by the use of money, many of the papal electors of 1492 were ready to realize a dividend on their investment by selling their support. Cardinal Rodrigo Borgia, a prelate of Spanish origin, set himself to the task of ascertaining the price of each; and, being the richest and shrewdest of the candidates, he was able to secure a majority of the votes. To Ascanio Sforza went the office of Vice Chancellor; to Cardinal Colonna, the Abbey of Subiaco and its fortresses; to Cardinal Orsini, the Borgia palaces at Rome and certain coveted castles; to Cardinal Savolli, Civita Castellana; and so on down the list. When the available assets of the papal office had been thus distributed among the more influential cardinals, those of minor importance were bought up with gold. For this purpose, Borgia is said to have sent four mules laden with coin to be distributed among the voters. The result

CHAP. III
A. D.
1492-1502

was his triumphant election, only Giuliano della Rovere, — who had himself expected the papal office, — and a few other cardinals, refusing to sell their votes.

When, on August 11, 1492, the election of Alexander VI was announced, Rome was delirious with joy. Handsome in person, courtly in manner, royal in bearing, generous in his largesses, Rodrigo Borgia was the embodiment of a majestic prince, while his vigor of intellect, his brilliancy as an orator, and his accomplishments as a scholar and statesman promised a reign of exceptional power and prestige for the Papacy. Among the panegyrics that voice the admiration of his time, one pictures him as fitted "to adorn the seat of the Apostles with his divine form in the place of God."

While retaining his "heroic beauty of body" at the age of sixty-two, when he entered upon his pontificate, Alexander VI had been disciplined by a large experience of the world. Having personally lived through the great transformation of Europe in the middle of the fifteenth century, he had witnessed the disappearance of the mediaeval ideals, the decay of faith, and the revival of ancient paganism, all of which were represented in his own life and character. As legate to various courts, he had thoroughly studied the political conditions of his time, and entered upon his office with the fixed purpose of using it to promote his own ambitions. Of these the chief was the advancement of his family, especially of his son Cesare.

The methods of Alexander VI

The incredible crimes by which Alexander VI endeavored to accomplish his cherished purpose are too well known and too little edifying to be recounted for their own sake; but they represent a phase of political development too important to be passed unnoticed.

"Alexander sells the keys, the altars, Christ himself," — runs the epigram; "well, he bought them, so he has the right to sell them!"[1]

---

[1] "Vendidit Alexander claves, alteria, Christum:
Emerat ille prius; vendere jure potest."
See Sanuto, *Diarii*, V, 96.

But this crafty trader, taking a lesson from the pagan emperors at Rome, not only sold benefices and indulgences; when he had loaded the purchaser with honors and possessions he secretly poisoned him, and sold his belongings over again. Five cardinals are said to have been murdered by his orders, and many others did not dare to remain within reach of his power. "Every night," writes a Venetian ambassador, Paolo Capello, "they find in Rome four or five murdered men,— bishops and other prelates." To an ambition such as that of Alexander VI the intervention of the King of France could not be a matter of indifference.

The legend that Charles VIII of France was kept in ignorance and isolation by his father, Louis XI, because the King was jealous or suspicious of his young son, may be dismissed, not only as devoid of proof but plainly contradicted by authentic documents.[1] The secret of his neglected education and his seclusion from society in his childhood is to be found in the King's apprehension that the feeble brain of this constitutionally abnormal prince, upon whom the future of his dynasty depended, might be overtaxed by serious studies, and that his person might be made the victim of designing men.

The anxiety of Louis XI for his son and heir proved to be well founded; for, having arrived at the age when he claimed the right to rule in his own name, his natural weakness of mind not only left him without a clear perception of his highest duties as a ruler but exposed him to the influence of self-seeking counsellors.

The assertion has been made that the invasion of Italy by Charles VIII was but the natural fruit of the traditional policy of the kings of France.[2] It would be more accurate

---

[1] See Delaborde, *L'expédition de Charles VIII*, pp. 155, 156.

[2] See Delaborde, *L'expédition*, and other writers cited by Lemonnier in Lavisse, *Histoire de France*, V, Paris, 1903; who points out that neither Charles VII nor Louis XI attempted conquests in Italy, or even strongly supported the Anjou and Orléans claims, but regulated their relations with Italy in view of the unification of France.

to say that it was the first important departure from that policy. "The grandeur and repose of the kingdom," said Crèvecœur to Charles VIII, "depend on the possession of the Netherlands." This was not only the solid judgment of the time, but it was the conviction of the real founders of French preponderance, Charles VII and Louis XI. The abandonment of the policy of eastward expansion and the substitution for it of adventures in Italy in fact created a period of arrested development in the history of France, and has been well characterized by a modern historian as "one of the most dangerous aberrations of French policy."[1]

The imperial tradition in France

But it was not merely the incomplete intelligence of Charles VIII nor the selfish motives of his counsellors that changed the foreign policy of France. Although the mystical element in the young king had been cultivated by the romances of chivalry whose fascination had most provoked the activity of his mind, there was a deeper cause for interest in Italy. Two forces had never ceased to operate upon the soul of the French nation, — the legend of the French claim to the glory of Charles the Great, and the sophisms of the French jurists who endeavored to sustain by an appeal to Roman law the right of France to perpetuate the rule of the Roman Empire. From Philip IV to Napoleon Bonaparte, these forces have spasmodically entered upon the scene to influence the course of French foreign policy.

The vigorous intelligence of Philip IV, notwithstanding his ambition for the imperial crown, perceived the chimerical nature of the splendid programme presented to him by Pierre du Bois, in which the Carlovingian legend and the digest of Justinian were skilfully woven into a vast scheme of universal dominion to be executed by the King of France.[2]

---

[1] Sorel, *L'Europe et la révolution française*, I, p. 261.

[2] The title of Du Bois' work was *Traité de l'abrégement des guerres et des procès* ; its purpose, to end the conflicts of Christendom by bringing all Europe under the sway of France. Philip IV, more practical

Philip was to render the imperial crown hereditary in his family, the electors of the Empire were to be compensated for their loss of dignity by the secularization of ecclesiastical property in Germany, the Pope was to be made the creature of the Emperor, in order that his spiritual authority could be employed to make the monarchy universal, and the thrones of Europe and the East were to be given to French princes, who would loyally represent the Emperor throughout the world.

So magnificent a programme could not fail to impress the imagination and inspire the cupidity of France, and none the less because it rested upon popular tradition and formal legal argument combined with the assumption that, because of its virtue, justice, and nobility, France had been divinely chosen to execute the will of God in exterminating the Infidel, reforming the Church, and bestowing peace upon the world.

The history of France is, in great measure, the story of the struggle between this and affiliated dreams of glory with the sober ideas of practical national interest; and the diplomacy of Europe for three hundred years was destined to revolve around this struggle as the central axis of its movement.

Prematurely, but with perfect confidence in himself as the embodiment of the imperial heritage of France, Charles VIII set out to realize its dreams of glory. The natural starting point of his imperial career was Italy, for there was the ancient seat of empire, and from Italy must of necessity begin the conquest of the East. The claim to the Kingdom of Naples was a sufficient pretext for this great enterprise, and the first step was, therefore, to give it the appearance of validity.

That Louis XI attached no great value to his inherited rights to the Kingdom of Naples is evident from the little

---

and less visionary than Du Bois, was, nevertheless, much influenced by his schemes of French predominance; but he perceived that the first task was the internal consolidation of his kingdom.

CHAP. III
A.D.
1492-1502

attention he paid to them. During the regency, Anne de Beaujeu ceded them to René of Lorraine to win his adherence to her government, but gave him no practical support. It was a cheap way of gaining his friendship, while allowing him to waste himself in fruitless adventure. When, however, an excuse was needed by Charles VIII for the invasion of Italy, an attempt was made to give these claims a definite legal character, and for this purpose jurisconsults were employed to gather evidence with which to sustain them. An elaborate treatise was prepared in which arguments for their validity were presented, but it does not bear impartial analysis. If the French title is based upon the gift of Naples as a fief by the Papacy to Charles of Anjou, nothing is easier than to dispute it on the ground that the kingdom was transmissible only to his actual descendants within four degrees of relationship, which excludes Charles VIII, and leaves the fief at the disposition of the Pope. If, on the other hand, the French title is founded on the alleged adoption of Louis I of Anjou by Queen Juana I in 1380, or the bequest of the kingdom by Juana II to René I of Anjou in 1435, it may be answered that such acts were not legal under the constitution of the kingdom, and that, besides, the alleged will of Juana II was apocryphal.[1]

It did not, however, require a faultless argument to convince Charles VIII of his rights in Italy, and it was in

---

[1] The relation of Charles VIII to the Anjou claims on Naples may be seen from the following genealogical table:

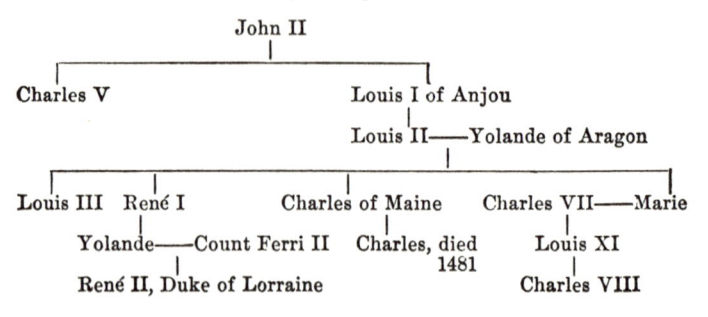

```
                         John II
          ┌─────────────────┴─────────────────┐
       Charles V                        Louis I of Anjou
                                              │
                                      Louis II──Yolande of Aragon
                                              │
          ┌─────────────┬───────────────┬─────────────────┐
     Louis III   René I        Charles of Maine      Charles VII──Marie
                    │                   │                   │
                Yolande──Count Ferri II  Charles, died      Louis XI
                    │                      1481               │
           René II, Duke of Lorraine                      Charles VIII
```

accordance with his temperament to start out in pursuit of them.

When, therefore, Italy seemed to hold forth a hand of welcome to the King of France, his desire for adventure, his imagined rights, and the wishes of his favorites all conspired to urge him forward. Having escaped from the authority of his sister, Anne de Beaujeu, by a *coup d'état*, the young king fell under the influence of one of his servants, Étienne de Vesc, who became Seneschal of Beaucaire, and Guillaume Briçonnet, soon to be made Bishop of St. Malo, whose personal ambitions impaired the value of their advice. To please his youthful majesty became the principal business of these and of secondary courtiers. Not only was the glory of vindicating his alleged rights in Italy commended to him, but imperial aspirations were implanted in his bosom. Did not the kings of France possess a claim to the imperial crown superior to that of the kings of Germany? Was not he already a greater monarch than Maximilian, from whom by the valor of his armies he had won his bride, the coveted Anne of Brittany? Should not the King of France in other achievements also surpass his rival? Visions of recovering Constantinople from the Turks were soon added to his project for asserting his claims in Italy. This was expected to lead on to a glorious crusade, in which he would not only drive the Ottoman power from Europe, but restore to Christendom the Holy Places. Borne onward by the current of his romantic imagination, these fancies grew into a passion for chivalrous exploits that swept aside the cold reflections of reason and prepared the young monarch to enter upon a course of foreign adventure in which the substantial interests of France were sacrificed to his vagaries.

To the motives already in the mind of Charles VIII for crossing the Alps was added the assurance that his coming would be acceptable in Italy.

Since 1479, Ludovico Sforza had ruled at Milan as regent during the minority of his nephew, Gian Galeazzo. Married to Beatrice d' Este, the ambitious daughter of the Duke of

Ferrara, Ludovico, who had long coveted the ducal honor, was now resolved not only to retain his power in the Duchy of Milan, but if possible to found a new kingdom in Northern Italy. The betrothal of the young Duke Gian Galeazzo and Isabella, granddaughter of Ferdinand of Naples, presented a serious obstacle to the schemes of Ludovico; for, so long as his nephew could count upon the protection of the King of Naples, it would be difficult to exclude him from his inherited rights at his majority. Without a trustworthy ally in Italy, Ludovico was, therefore, not only anxious to destroy the power of Ferdinand of Naples, but to establish such relations with the King of France as would ensure him against the assertion of the dormant Orléans claims to Milan, or the King's intervention on behalf of Gian Galeazzo through the influence of his mother, Bona of Savoy.

In October, 1490, Ludovico's secretary, Brasca, had been sent to France to solicit the investiture of Genoa. On the side of Charles VIII, it was important that the most powerful state in Northern Italy should not oppose his Italian project, and in January, 1491, his ambassadors were sent to Milan; but it was not until January 24, 1492, that an alliance between Milan and France was signed.

Although Charles VIII had already paid well for this alliance by reinvesting Milan with Genoa, Ludovico was not quite satisfied with his success. Disturbed in conscience by his plans for the future, and determined above all to make them secure, he wished to render his relation with Charles VIII more strictly personal. For this purpose, an embassy was sent to France, charged to impress upon the King the great sacrifices Ludovico had made in concluding an alliance with him at a time when all Europe was seeking the friendship of Milan, and to demand a secret treaty by which Ludovico's personal control of Milan would be guaranteed.

Although the heir presumptive to the crown of France, Louis of Orléans, who had inherited the Orléans claims to Milan, was already agitating his rights to that duchy,

Charles VIII, through the liberal bribery of those who en- joyed his confidence, was induced to yield to Ludovico's wishes; and, on April 29, 1492, the Regent of Milan was not only accepted as a personal ally, but his illegal demand for the continued government of the duchy was guaranteed against the rights of young Gian Galeazzo, nephew of both contractants.

At Florence, Lorenzo de' Medici, in the crisis of his last illness, in April, 1492, sent for the fiery reformer, Savonarola, — whose arraignment of the corruption of the clergy, the pride of princes, and the destruction of Florentine liberty had already moved Florence almost to revolt, — in the apparent hope of reconciling the reformer to the government of his son Piero. But the stern censor of decadent morals not only formed no alliance with the Medici, but publicly invoked the presence of Charles VIII as an instrument of divine justice in punishing the sins of the Florentines.

Influence of Savonarola

The attachment of Piero to the cause of Naples together with his utter incapacity for the task of government soon raised Savonarola to the height of supreme influence in Florence; and, in the spirit of Dante invoking the Emperor, the eloquent priest predicted and implored the coming of Charles VIII as the scourge of God and the renovator of Italy. It needed, therefore, only the actual presence of the invader upon Italian soil to fulfil the prophecies of the Prior of San Marco and place him in command of Florence as heaven's chosen oracle.

With the friendship of Piero de' Medici for Ferdinand thus neutralized by the loss of his influence at Florence, and with both Venice and the Pope in friendly relations with Ludovico Sforza, the King of Naples appeared to be without the hope of an effectual ally. To the mind of Charles VIII all Italy, except the adversary against whom he was to march, was now ready to welcome him.

Apparent isolation of Ferdinand

Even Venice, the traditional opponent of French influence south of the Alps, was not only friendly with Milan, but now seemed well disposed toward France. The embassy sent by the Venetians to Charles VIII in January, 1493, gave every assurance of friendliness, notwithstanding its secret instructions to observe and report with special care the condition of affairs at the French court; and, above all, to enter into close relations with Louis of Orléans, with a view to obtaining his aid if necessary in frustrating the designs of Ludovico Sforza.

The attitude of Alexander VI was at the time even less obstructive of the plans of Charles VIII than the watchful neutrality of Venice; for, in order to bring pressure upon the King of Naples, who had greeted his accession to the papal throne with lamentations, in February, 1493, the Pope had inspired Cardinal Savelli to exhort the King of France to undertake his enterprise in Italy.

Thus, so far as Charles VIII could perceive, at the beginning of 1493, Ferdinand was helplessly isolated, and all the rest of Italy was eager to receive the French with open arms.

Relations of Charles VIII to the chief powers of Europe

With his more powerful European neighbors, however, the situation was quite different; and before a foreign expedition could be undertaken important preliminaries were to be arranged. The project of Charles VIII for the conquest of Naples was not only known to England, Spain, and the Emperor; but this enterprise, added to the old hostility of Maximilian, based on the double offence of the King of France in repudiating Margaret of Burgundy and marrying Anne of Brittany, had provoked the Archduke to plan a coalition against him. If opposed by the union of the three greatest monarchies in Europe outside of France, the Italian expedition would plainly be impossible. Before setting out upon his path of conquest, therefore, it was necessary to conciliate these powers at any cost.

Between France and England the animosities of the Hundred Years' War were not yet extinguished, and on neither side could peace be regarded as permanent. The accession of Henry Tudor, Earl of Richmond, representing the House of Lancaster, to the throne of England in 1485 and his victory of Bosworth had virtually ended the Wars of the Roses; while his marriage with Elizabeth of York had united the rival houses whose bitter strife for the throne had so long divided and desolated England. The reign of Henry VII had begun that period of national consolidation and development under the Tudor dynasty by which the greatness of England was to be established. Not indisposed to popularize his reign by a successful foreign war, on October 6, 1492, in alliance with the discontented nobles of Brittany, he landed his forces at Calais, and Boulogne was besieged; but, on November 3, was concluded the Treaty of Étaples, by which Charles VIII purchased peace with the payment of seven hundred and forty-five thousand crowns of gold.

After centuries of struggle, the Spanish peninsula had become the seat of one of the most powerful monarchies in Europe. By the marriage of Isabella of Castile, who had come to the throne in 1474, to Ferdinand of Aragon, whose rule began in 1479, the two realms formed a personal union that was soon to be merged into the Kingdom of Spain. The expulsion of the Moors by the fall of Grenada on January 2, 1492, left this great state without a rival in the peninsula, except Portugal. The discovery of America by Columbus in the name of Ferdinand and Isabella in that year was to pour into the treasury of the Spanish monarchy resources hitherto unknown in Europe. So great a power had to be conciliated at any price. By the Treaty of Barcelona, signed on January 19, 1493, Roussillon and Cerdagne, which geographically belonged to France,[1] were ceded to Ferdinand, and soon

---

[1] The counties of Roussillon and Cerdagne had been delivered to Louis XI in 1462 by John II of Aragon as a pledge for a loan of three hundred thousand crowns. Charles VIII restored them without receiving the payment for which they were held as security, and without really obtaining the promise of Ferdinand not to oppose his enterprise in Italy. See the treaty in Dumont, III, Part II, pp. 297 et seq. Their recovery was regarded by the Spaniards as of great importance, as they had opened to the French the passes of the Pyrenees.

afterward the little kingdom of Navarre, half Spanish and half French, was permitted to become a protectorate of Castile.

Only the Empire now remained to be conciliated, or more strictly Maximilian himself, who as "King of the Romans" was upon the death of his father, Frederick III, on August 19, 1493, about to become Emperor.[1] Already master of the heritage of Charles the Bold, he had even taken possession of Artois, Charolais, and Franche-Comté, — the marriage portion of Margaret of Burgundy, which had been ceded to France in 1482. To avoid the detention of a war for the recovery of these possessions, and to propitiate Maximilian, by the Treaty of Senlis, of May 23, 1493, these territories were surrendered to the "King of the Romans," and the princess Margaret was delivered to her father. It was the price of permission to the King of France to pursue his adventures in Italy.

The mission of Perron de Baschi

The diplomatic preliminaries having been thus completed north of the Alps, the time seemed ripe for the march to Naples; but clouds were already rising on the horizon. The loyalty of Ludovico Sforza was brought in question by his purchase from Maximilian of the investiture of the Duchy of Milan for himself, without regard to Galeazzo's rights, in exchange for four hundred thousand ducats and the hand of Ludovico's niece, Blanche Sforza. His closer relations with Venice and the Pope also gave ground for fear that he might abandon his alliance with the King of

---

[1] The title "King of the Romans" had long been the proper designation of a future emperor *prior* to his coronation by the Pope. Since the time of Henry II the German kings had not only exercised the rights of the Emperor before their coronation at Rome, but had added to the title "*divina favente clementia Rex*" the word "*Romanorum.*" See Von Borch, *Ueber die Entstehung des Titels Romanorum Rex*, Innsbruck, 1885. Maximilian I was never crowned by the Pope, but practically became emperor upon the death of his father, Frederick III. Although it was not until February 4, 1508, that he assumed the title "Emperor-elect," it is convenient to refer to him after Frederick's death as the Emperor, in conformity with general usage.

France, and Charles VIII felt obliged to threaten him with the Orléans claims if he proved disloyal.

It was time for the suspicions of the King to be aroused; for, after the Treaty of Senlis, Ludovico had entirely changed his tactics and was disposed to seek his safety in a union with Venice and the Emperor. To resolve all doubts concerning the state of Italy, Perron de Baschi, a skilful negotiator born in Provence of an Italian family, was sent on a mission to report upon the situation and prepare the way for action.

At Milan, he received solemn assurances of friendship. At Venice, where the wife of Ludovico had preceded him to strengthen the bonds of amity between her husband and the Republic, he received the evasive answers habitual with the Signory. At Florence, Piero de' Medici endeavored to cover his real hostility by means of presents and polite attentions. At Rome, where he had more definite demands to make, the French ambassador encountered a more obstinate evasion. As to the investiture of Naples, Alexander VI replied, that it was not he, but Pius II and Innocent VIII, who had granted it to Ferdinand; and that, as Head of the Church, the interests of peace and justice required him to observe existing conditions. As to free passage and the purchase of provisions for the army of the King of France, these implied the right of investiture.

But the death of Ferdinand of Naples, on January 24, 1494, and the accession of his son Alfonso to the throne soon forced the complete disclosure of the Pope's position. He not only invested Alfonso II with the kingdom, but addressed a bull to Charles VIII, in which he expressed his astonishment that the King of France was about to attack a Christian power at a time when Christendom should present a united front against the Turks. Should he persist in his intention, might not the King of Naples be compelled to ask aid of the Infidel to defend his throne? Finally, if Charles VIII believed himself to possess rights concerning Naples, he had only to submit them to the judgment of the Pope!

The casting of the die

CHAP. III
A. D.
1492-1502

The alternatives now were either to abandon the claims upon Naples altogether, or to defy the opposition of Alexander VI. In the mind of Charles VIII, in spite of the opposition of many of his counsellors, the decision was not difficult; for the thought of his expedition had become a ruling passion. With the purpose of securing the concurrence of Maximilian in giving to the Italian campaign the character of a mission to reform the Church, an effort was made to procure a personal interview with him; but the wily emperor was indisposed to aid an enterprise which he felt to be directed in part against himself, and which he secretly hoped would end in failure.

At Lyons, where Charles VIII was assembling his forces and making his preparations for the descent into Italy, the great purpose of his plans during the summer of 1494 was almost forgotten in the amorous indulgences with which the King and his courtiers amused themselves. But the arrival at Lyons of Giuliano della Rovere, who believed his life to be threatened by Alexander VI, and had taken refuge in France, recalled the King to the object of his preparations. Received on June 1 with great honor by Charles VIII, the energetic cardinal, burning with hatred toward the Neapolitan dynasty and Pope Alexander VI, became from this moment the soul of the enterprise. Aroused from his self-indulgence and inspired anew by the influence of this great personality, in spite of the lack of funds, which had been dissipated rather than amassed at Lyons, toward the end of August, 1494, Charles led his army into Italy.

II. THE EXPEDITION OF CHARLES VIII INTO ITALY

Reception of
Charles VIII
in Italy

On September 9, the principal army of Charles, including many Swiss and Italian mercenaries, and numbering more than thirty thousand men, marching by the Mont Genèvre pass, arrived at Asti. The artillery had been sent by sea with about ten thousand men. So powerful an armament had never before appeared in Italy.

THE IMPERIAL ASPIRATIONS OF FRANCE

With characteristic ingenuity, Alexander VI had prepared a singularly seductive scheme to divert the young king from his march to Naples. Andrew Palaeologus, brother of the last emperor at Constantinople, and therefore supposed to have some hereditary right to the imperial throne of the East, in an act of cession dated September 6, 1494,[1] had been induced, in consideration of proposed annual revenues to the value of ten thousand ducats and the principality of Servia, to assign his right to Charles VIII, on condition that he would lead his army against the Turks. Although a papal notary was present to witness the signature of Charles, the relation of Alexander VI to this transaction, mediated through Raimund Peraudi, Cardinal of Gurk, was such that, if the venture succeeded, he could claim the glory of it; while, if it failed, he could disavow all responsibility for it.[2]

A severe illness which attacked the King soon after his arrival at Asti may have influenced his decision; which was, without definite action upon the offer, to proceed at once to the conquest of Naples; but the imperial illusion appears to have taken firm possession of his fancy.

Borrowing money from the Marquis of Montferrat to meet his immediate needs, he entered the territories of Milan, where Ludovico Sforza gave him a cordial reception, but was soon convinced that his guest was likely to become his master. After a triumphal reception at Pavia, where the young Duke Gian Galeazzo languished in virtual imprisonment, the King — touched by the sight of his afflicted nephew and the pathetic prayers of his wife, the Duchess Isabella, for her husband and her father, Alfonso II of Naples — seemed on the point of renouncing his support of Ludovico and even his own enterprise of conquest. Fear-

---

[1] The act may be found in *Mémoires de l'Academie Royale des Inscriptions et Belles Lettres*, Paris, XVII, p. 572.

[2] See Schneider, *Die kirchliche und politische Wirksamkeit des Legaten Raimund Peraudi*, pp. 37 et seq.

CHAP. III
A. D.
1492-1502

Charles VIII
at Florence

ing the consequences of further exciting the King's sympathies, Ludovico hastened the departure of Charles from Pavia, and took care to surround him with new diversions. A few days afterward, Galeazzo, — it was believed not without assistance, — suddenly died, and Ludovico Sforza was promptly proclaimed Duke of Milan.

While Philippe de Commines was sent to Venice to quiet the apprehensions of that republic and to secure at least the continuance of its neutrality with a loan of fifty thousand ducats, plans were formed for the advance of the invaders toward the South. As Florence, though under the influence of Savonarola, was officially in alliance with Alfonso II, it was necessary to prevent aid being rendered by the Florentine government to the Neapolitan army that had been sent northward to resist the approach of the French. The defection of the Tuscan cities which had been subjected to the rule of Florence was to be expected. Among these, Pisa, weary of its long humiliation, was waiting to throw itself at the feet of the conqueror.

On October 26, Piero de' Medici, unaccompanied by ambassadors to support his action, set out in person from Florence to negotiate with Charles VIII. On October 31, at San Stefano, in order to maintain his government of Florence, he agreed to surrender six Tuscan cities to the conqueror, as a pledge that a loan of two hundred thousand ducats would be made to him. Before the conditions accepted by Piero were known at Florence, an embassy of seven citizens was sent to Charles VIII, but he refused to receive them. When, after his return to Florence, Piero presented himself at the public palace, on November 6, he found it locked and guarded. It was the signal for his overthrow.

Savonarola, delighted to see his prophecies fulfilled, now became the spokesman of the city. On November 17, the King of France entered Florence with great pomp, amid the salutations of the people, "Welcome, restorer of liberty!" and "*Viva Francia!*" as, wearing over his armor a long cloak of blue velvet blazing with precious stones, a crown surmounting his great white bonnet with black plumes, and covered by a canopy borne by members of the College, he followed his splendid cavalry, mounted on his magnificent black charger.

Suddenly, in the course of the following days, a great fear fell upon the Florentines. Rumors were set afloat that Piero de' Medici, whose palace had been pillaged by the infuriated people and who had fled to Bologna, was to return under the protection of Charles VIII. The indignation of the people was at once aroused. When the king demanded of the city a hundred and fifty thousand ducats and the right of his representative to be present at the secret meetings of the Council, resentment rose to a still higher pitch. On November 24, the shops were closed, and the people prepared to expel the French.

Savonarola's influence with the King seems to have already ended, but a joint commission of the French and the Florentines was appointed to prepare a treaty. The report of the commission was an unexpected firebrand. When on the twenty-fifth it was read in the King's presence, filled with anger because the tribute demanded had been reduced to one hundred and twenty thousand ducats, he rose from his seat uttering words of menace. Instantly, the chief commissioner of the Florentines, Piero Capponi, before the face of the King, tore the manuscript of the treaty into a hundred pieces, and exclaimed, "Most Christian Prince, sound your trumpets, then, and we will sound our bells!"

On the same day the treaty was signed, and on the following, the King and the Signory in the Church of Santa Maria dei Fiori solemnly swore to observe it. On the twenty-eighth, after an urgent appeal by Savonarola to hasten his departure from Florence, Charles VIII and his army resumed their march toward Rome.

The essentially mediaeval character of the King was plainly revealed as he approached the Eternal City. In France, he had thought of reforming the Church, and even of deposing

The prestige of Alexander VI

the Pope; but when he found himself face to face with this great task, its immensity overpowered his feeble faculties.

In his mind the necessity of the papal investiture of the Kingdom of Naples assumed increased proportions, and the traditional fear of the Pope became an obstacle to his progress. At Florence, on November 22, he had issued a manifesto designed to appease the Papacy, quiet the fears of the Italians, and calm the apprehensions of the great powers of Europe, who now began to distrust his purposes. In that document, which was printed in both French and Latin and circulated broadcast, he announced that his predecessors had twenty-four times received the papal investiture of Naples, that he aimed at no other conquest, and that his ultimate intention was to ruin the power of the Turks and deliver the Holy Places.[1] He gave solemn assurances that he intended no harm to the city of Rome or the Papal State, and that he only demanded free passage and the right to purchase supplies for his army.

Although the Papacy was on its secular side only an Italian principality, it claimed, and the claim was in great degree respected, that its pontifical authority was the highest general law of Europe. In the dispute that had arisen between Spain and Portugal over the results of their explorations and discoveries, Alexander VI, superseding the bulls of Nicholas V, Sixtus IV, and Innocent VIII, had issued a series of decrees which furnished a basis of settlement for the Treaty of Tordesillas, of June 7, 1494, by which those countries had agreed upon a partition of their respective spheres of discovery.[2]

The essential element of all these bulls is, the *de jure* sovereignty of the Holy See over the lands in question. When that had been delegated by the papal act, the possessors of this authority, bound by this grant and their own

---

[1] A copy still exists in the Bibliothèque Nationale at Paris.

[2] The subject is fully discussed by Harrisse, *The Diplomatic History of America.*

agreement, esteemed themselves guaranteed against the intrusions of other Christian princes. Thus, a line was to be drawn from pole to pole, that is from North to South, at a distance of three hundred and seventy leagues west from the Cape Verde Islands, astronomers were to be sent to fix this line, and the Pope was to be requested to confirm the compact. Portugal, therefore, was supposed to control, thenceforth, the route to the East Indies by the Cape of Good Hope which Bartholomew Diaz had discovered in 1486 with the lands found by its navigators, while to Spain belonged all those countries which were believed to be bathed by the Atlantic Ocean on the eastern coasts of Asia. At the time, no power raised objection to this wholesale apportioning of the earth; and it was reserved for Francis I of France, born in the year of the partition, to exclaim, " What! the King of Spain and the King of Portugal quietly to divide between them all America, without allowing me to take a share! I should much like to see the article of Adam's will that gives them this vast inheritance."

But, while Charles VIII was vainly hoping to procure the papal investiture of Naples, which, as a fief of the Papacy, according to the public law of the time, Alexander VI had a right to bestow or withhold, the Pope was busily occupied in planning his defeat. As the guardian of Djem, brother of the Sultan Bajazet II, the custody of whom he had inherited from Innocent VIII, Alexander VI had a powerful hold upon the Sultan. In order to prevent the return of Djem to the East, where his presence might have proved fatal to Bajazet's supremacy, the Sultan had for many years paid an annual pension of forty thousand ducats to the Pope for holding as a prisoner his rival to the throne. In June, 1494, Alexander VI had sent his agent, Buzardo, to collect a year's pension in advance, and had embraced the opportunity to demand of Bajazet his aid in sustaining Alfonso II of Naples and his urgent pressure upon Venice, with which he was in cordial relations, to oppose Charles VIII.

The Turk had every reason to accept the invitation, for

the King of France had plainly announced his purpose to destroy his power, and just before Charles departed from Florence, three Turkish ambassadors landed at Ancona. One took the road to Venice, a second proceeded to Alfonso's camp, and the third, accompanied by Buzardo, set out for Rome, bearing the forty thousand ducats to Alexander VI.

The money never reached its destination, for Giovanni della Rovere, Prefect of Rome and brother of the Cardinal, claiming it in payment of a debt owed him by the Pope, seized the treasure on its way and captured Buzardo; while the Turkish emissary, having a swift horse, made his escape to Ancona. Of far greater importance than the loss of the money was the fact that the correspondence of the Pope with the Sultan fell into the hands of Della Rovere, who promptly joined his brother and passed into the service of Charles VIII.[1]

The other ambassadors were more successful. One was warmly welcomed by Alfonso II, and the other had an equally cordial reception at Venice. With their habitual finesse, the Venetians represented to the Sultan's envoy that their friendship with the King of France did not permit their doing more than to continue their efforts in the interest of peace; but the embassy that was sent by them to Charles VIII was instructed to explain to him, that the heavy expenses of the Venetians in defending themselves against the Turks prevented their making the loan of fifty thousand ducats which the King had ordered Philippe de Commines to demand!

The practical failure of Alexander's negotiations with the Sultan and the capture of his correspondence with him placed the Pope in a position of extreme danger; for he was not only without adequate defence against the armed force of Charles VIII but his enemies were now in possession of

---

[1] On the authenticity of this correspondence, see Pastor, *Histoire des papes*, V, pp. 411, 412; also Villari, *The Life and Times of Niccolò Machiavelli*, I, p. 184, note.

evidence to show that, in addition to being a usurper of the papal throne through the purchase of his election, the Pope was also a traitor to the Church, having sought an alliance with the Infidel.

Trembling, therefore, lest his enemies call a council and depose him for simony, hypocrisy, and perfidy, of which they had such ample evidence, Alexander VI, while at the same time entering into active negotiations on every side, made preparations for both flight and resistance. All his treasures were packed for a hasty retreat, and Rome was soon occupied by six thousand Neapolitan soldiers for his protection, while the Spaniards and Germans were implored to hasten to his assistance. In the meantime, the King of France was steadily advancing. On December 4 he left Siena in his march toward Rome, arriving without opposition at Viterbo on the tenth; for the papal cities, equally with the others, received him with marks of honor.

In the hope of inciting Maximilian to action, the Pope represented to the imperial ambassador at Rome, Rudolf of Anhalt, that Charles would soon usurp the title of Emperor. The ambassador promised to implore his master to come to the rescue; but, fearing that he might otherwise be compelled to abandon Rome while waiting for assistance, and thereby lose the tiara altogether, Alexander secretly provided the Castle of St. Angelo with food and munitions for a long siege.

On the other hand, Charles, though possessing every material advantage, was indisposed to offend the Pope, whose investiture he was seeking. Before reaching Viterbo, he had sent an embassy to solicit free passage, the right to purchase provisions, the delivery of Djem, — for whose immediate murder he already knew that the Sultan, through his intercepted ambassadors, had proposed to pay two hundred thousand ducats, — and his own investiture with the Kingdom of Naples.[1]

---

[1] See Gregorovius, *Geschichte*, VII, p. 349, note.

On December 30, the Pope publicly dismissed the French ambassadors under a guard of papal troops, with the declaration that he would grant neither passage nor provisions. At the same time, Cardinal Ascanio Sforza, with whom Alexander VI had lately been in negotiation for his mediation with Charles VIII, with other distinguished personages, was placed under arrest.

Thus provided with hostages, the Pope, in reply to the indignant protest of the King, with the intention of prolonging negotiations until aid from the Emperor could arrive, sent three legates to Charles VIII to explain the grounds on which he had refused to accede to his demands.

Entrance of Charles VIII into Rome

The effect of the Pope's conduct was not, however, what he had expected it to be. Ludovico Sforza, though secretly unfaithful to Charles VIII, was now indignant with Alexander VI on account of the arrest of his brother; while the King of France, regarding all negotiations at an end, hastened his march to Rome.

Realizing the inability of the Neapolitan troops then in Rome to protect the city, Alexander first urged, and finally demanded, their withdrawal. The draft of a treaty still exists, signed only by the son of Alfonso II, Ferdinand, Duke of Calabria, in which Alfonso II proposed to receive the Pope in his kingdom with his prisoners, with a pension of fifty thousand ducats and a guarantee for the security of Djem.[1] At the last moment, however, although it had been previously approved by him, Alexander VI refused to sign this treaty. The fear of being deposed by a council, augmented by the fact that the Colonna and the Orsini had joined forces with Charles VIII, induced him to brave the dangers that surrounded him in Rome; and, in order to prevent an assault of the city by the French, he resolved to dismiss the Neapolitans and depend upon diplomacy for his security.

On Christmas morning, furnished with a safe conduct from Charles VIII by which he was permitted to retire without

---

[1] See Theiner, *Codex Diplomaticus Dominii Temporalis*, III, p. 510.

attack, the son of Alfonso II withdrew his troops from the city. On the following day, three French envoys were received by the Pope. When their suite unceremoniously took possession of the seats intended for the prelates, to the great disgust of the master of ceremonies, Burchard, who remonstrated at the indignity, the Pope, fearing to offend them, ordered that they be allowed to sit where they wished.

The negotiations were rendered difficult by the King's demand that Djem be immediately surrendered to him, and that four strongholds within the city be delivered for his occupation. The Pope refused to comply, but the envoys ended the discussion by fixing January 1, 1495, as the date when the King would enter Rome, with the assurance that he would do no harm to the spiritual or temporal authority of the Pope. Alexander was obliged to yield, and the Palace of San Marco was designated for the residence of the King, while the Pope and his *entourage* retained possession of the Vatican. On December 27, fifteen hundred French soldiers quietly entered the city. On December 31, at nightfall, the King made his entrance into Rome by the Porta del Popolo, in the midst of a general illumination, the houses being decorated with French flags, while the people uttered cries of "*Francia,*" "*Francia!*" Charles VIII, without striking a blow, had made himself master of Rome.

The King of France was now apparently in a position to impose his will upon the Pope. Not only so, but Alexander VI had become the victim of his own excited imagination. His disturbed conscience placed him in mortal terror of being cited to appear before a council to answer for his deeds. For religious faith, which appears to have been entirely dead within him, he had substituted a belief in divination and astrology; and certain prophecies had convinced him that Charles VIII was predestined to become the ruler of a universal monarchy. Incapable of placing confidence in the promises of others, he found little assurance in the pledges already given by the King not to encroach either upon his temporal or his ecclesiastical authority. His mental state was, therefore, one of abject despair, until events revealed to him the moral weakness of his adversary, and the powerful allies he possessed in the greed and ambition of the King's advisers.

Two days after the arrival of Charles VIII in Rome, Alexander's son, Cesare Borgia, then known as the Cardinal of Valencia, accompanied by many other cardinals, — all carrying the trains of their robes with their own hands, as a mark of respect never shown except in the presence of the Supreme Pontiff, — presented himself in the Palace of San Marco before the King. It was then ascertained that the claimant to the throne of Naples made only three demands: (1) that the Cardinal of Valencia should follow him to Naples, in the capacity of papal legate; (2) that the Castle of St. Angelo be surrendered to him for occupation by French troops; and (3) that Djem be delivered to his keeping.

The disclosure of the King's moderation at once inspired the Pope with new confidence; for it was not only evident that Charles had no intention of denying his authority, but that there were reasons for his not boldly exacting the investiture of Naples.

Although disturbed by the demand for the surrender of the Castle of St. Angelo, to which he expected to retire in case of necessity, Alexander's passion for bold negotiation was now excited by the prospect of a diplomatic game from which the chief stake, his immediate deposition, appeared to have been already eliminated.

Encouraged by the fact that the influence of his former rival and implacable enemy, Giuliano della Rovere, was not the dominant power in determining the purposes of Charles, his keen intelligence soon divined the existence of supporters in the camp of the enemy. The spoils of Naples and high honors in the Church were evidently more attractive to the French nobles and prelates than the reformation of the Holy See, which would involve long delays and unforeseen contingencies. His evident policy, therefore, was to make friends of the courtiers and ecclesiastics who accompanied the King.

With them as his allies, even the moderate demands of
Charles VIII might be abated; if not, the victory would
seem all the greater to the King and his counsellors if it
were not too easily won.

Resolved to stand bravely upon the dignity of his holy
office, Alexander soon received so many French barons who
came to kiss his feet and beg for his blessing, that he is
said to have fainted from physical exhaustion, and to have
been obliged to take to his bed.

His reply to the demands of Charles VIII tended to win
for him the influence of those who were anxious to hasten on
to Naples or to receive honors from his hands. Denying
everything that had been demanded, he loftily asserted that
the designation of a legate to accompany the King required
an act of the Consistory of Cardinals; as to the surrender of
the Castle of St. Angelo, it was the last fortress of Christianity, and belonged to the princes of the Church alone as an
asylum for their safety; with regard to the surrender of
Djem, the moment had not arrived to deliver from captivity
this pledge of the peace of Christendom against the attacks
of the Infidel! As Head of the Church Universal, charged
with all these obligations, he could not yield to the King's
demands.

The existence of two parties in the councils of Charles
VIII rendered it difficult for the young king to form and
execute a consistent policy. He had left France with the
intention to dignify his Italian campaign with a reformation
of the Church, and at that time his advisers united in adding
this to the other motives for his expedition; but, when Briçonnet, Bishop of St. Malo, found himself in Rome, his mind
was chiefly preoccupied with his ambition to obtain the hat
of a cardinal, while De Vesc and others were looking anxiously forward to duchies to be carved out for them from the
spoils of conquest in Southern Italy. Against the influence
of these intimates was the voice of Giuliano della Rovere,
who hoped to be made pope in case of Alexander's deposition,
and the intrigues of other cardinals who were watching for

chances of advancement. But it was naturally his earlier French advisers who seemed to the King nearest to him, and it was these who finally won the day in their efforts to procure an understanding with the Pope and hasten the march to Naples.

When Charles VIII first learned of the refusal of the Pope to grant his requests, mortified and indignant, he brusquely dismissed the cardinals who accompanied his envoys. On January 7, 1495, Alexander thought it prudent, on account of disturbances by the French soldiers in the city, to retire by his covered passage from the Vatican to the Castle of St. Angelo, where he was guarded by his Spanish soldiers. The party hostile to him urged that artillery be brought to bear upon the castle, if the Pope did not at once yield to the King's demands; but, after cannons were twice drawn up before the castle for an assault, Charles declined to resort to violence against the Supreme Pontiff.

On January 11, after interviews with Briçonnet, the Pope signified his willingness to make a compromise with the King, and on the fifteenth, the terms of a treaty were definitely settled. The relations of Alexander VI and Charles VIII are represented as having suddenly become those of "father and son." The King agreed to defend the Holy See, if attacked by the Turks! Free passage was, in return, assured to the French army; Civita Vecchia was to remain in the King's hands, and Ostia was to be garrisoned by his troops; the cities of the March of Ancona and of the territory about Rome were to receive governors named by Charles VIII; the cardinals who had been dispossessed of estates or honors, including Giuliano della Rovere and Ascanio Sforza, were to be restored to favor; Cesare Borgia was to accompany the King to Naples as papal legate; Djem was to be delivered to the French as security against an attack by the Turks; and, finally, Charles VIII was publicly to pledge his filial obedience to the Pope. As to the papal investiture of the Kingdom of Naples, that was not even mentioned in the treaty, but a vague promise was orally made to the Count de Bresse that the Pope would give to the King the crown of Naples "without prejudice to the rights claimed by others."

When all was thus arranged, on January 16, a personal interview occurred in a secret corner of the Vatican garden between the Pope and the King. Affecting not to perceive him until Charles, uncovered, had knelt to the ground three times, Alexander then raised him up, kissed him, and began that course of flattery by which he completely won the heart of the young king. The one request of Charles was a cardinal's hat for the Bishop of St. Malo, which was immediately granted. That night, Charles VIII, under the surveillance of his Scotch guards, slept in an apartment of the Vatican next to that of Alexander VI. On the eighteenth, after long discussions, particularly regarding the unfortunate Djem, whose return to the Pope after six months was demanded under heavy guarantees, two copies of the treaty, in French and in Latin, were duly signed, and certified by two notaries.[1]

On January 19, Charles VIII publicly performed his act of obedience. Conducted before the papal throne, he kissed in succession the foot, the hand, and the cheek of the Pope. At that point, before pronouncing the formula of obedience by the mouth of De Ganay, President of the Parliament of Paris, three acts of grace were implored: (1) the confirmation of all the privileges conceded to the kings of France by previous sovereign pontiffs; (2) the investiture of Naples; and (3) the cancellation of the article of the treaty regarding guarantees for the return of Djem. Alexander replied, that he gladly accorded the first; that the second, affecting the interests of a third party, ought to be carefully considered by the cardinals; and that he was ready to agree to the third, on condition that the Consistory assented. The King then repeated the formula of submission to the Holy See.

The victory of Alexander VI was already considerable; but, having so completely won over the King, he hoped for

---

[1] For the treaty, see Dumont, I, Part II, p. 318.

Departure of Charles VIII from Rome

a still more brilliant termination of his negotiations. To this end, he entered into the most intimate relations with Charles VIII, passing portions of every day in his society. A solemn mass in St. Peter's Church, — in which, however, the Pope displayed his painful want of familiarity with the service,[1] — the exhibition of holy relics, and the hypnotic influence of the Pope's charms of manner and conversation were calculated to bring the impressionable nature of the young king completely under the spell of Alexander, who hoped to deflect him entirely from the conquest of Naples. Reports were current at Rome that the Pope was about to effect a reconciliation between Charles VIII and Alfonso II. The King was informed through Briçonnet that Alfonso II was ready to pay him an indemnity of a million ducats and an annual tribute of at least a hundred thousand francs. Alexander subsequently in person pressed this offer upon him, and added his promise to sanction the cession of the rights of the Palaeologi by crowning Charles Emperor of Constantinople. But the influence of the French nobles, who perceived more flattering chances of reward in the conquest of Naples, was naturally opposed to an enterprise so uncertain as the expulsion of the Turks; and Charles is said to have replied, "I wish first to conquer it, and then I will take the title of Emperor."[2]

The scarcity of provisions at Rome was an urgent reason for the speedy departure of the French; and, having secured by treaty the permission of Alexander VI to pursue his plan of conquest, with the practical assurance that he would receive the investiture when he was master of the Kingdom of

---

[1] See Cherrier, *Histoire de Charles VIII*, II, p. 93.

[2] Sanuto, *La spedizione*, p. 188. Romanin, *Storia documentata di Venezia*, V, p. 60, citing as authority Malipiero, asserts that the silver plate taken by the army of Charles VIII at Rome was coined into money with the inscription: *Carolus imperator*, which excited the jealousy of the King of Germany; but this appears to be an error, often repeated by other historians. See Delaborde, *L'expédition de Charles VIII*, pp. 522, 523.

Naples, on January 28, accompanied by Cesare Borgia as legate of the Pope, and by the miserable Djem as a defence against the Turks, Charles VIII, with these two companions riding on either side, passed out of the Porta San Giovanni on his march to Naples.

Had Alfonso II possessed courage as a warrior in proportion to his vices as a king, he might, in conjunction with the coalition which was already forming against Charles VIII, have been able to save his kingdom; but, overwhelmed at the moment of danger by a sense of his incapacity as a military leader and the merited disaffection of his people, he at once abandoned his throne in favor of his son Ferdinand, Duke of Calabria, and fled to Sicily to expiate his sins in a monastery.

Although the infidelity of Alexander VI to Charles VIII was soon made evident by the flight of Cesare Borgia two days after the departure from Rome, leaving his empty baggage behind him, soon followed by the death of Djem,[1] the march of Charles VIII and his army toward Naples was little more than a triumphal progress. Ferdinand II was not prepared to do more than momentarily check the advance of the King of France, and the nearer the French army approached to Naples the weaker his support was seen to be; for the popular discontent with the Aragonese dynasty had reached an intensity that secured a joyful welcome to the conqueror.[2]

---

[1] Djem, according to Sanuto, did not die immediately or of poison, as has generally been believed, but of a fever unskilfully treated. The Pope had no motive to cause his death, he being thereby deprived of the pension for detaining him; and the reward for Djem's murder, offered by the Sultan, was contingent on the delivery of his body See also Cherrier, II, p. 137; and Creighton, *History of the Papacy*, III, p. 208.

[2] Charles VIII was surprised but not disconcerted at Velletri by the ambassadors of Ferdinand and Isabella, who were sent to inform him that their sovereigns would not permit the overthrow of the Neapolitan dynasty. Alexander VI had hoped by this intervention, which he rewarded by conferring upon Ferdinand of Aragon the title

On February 19, Charles VIII made his entry into Capua, amid the rejoicings of the people. Obliged to retire to Naples, Ferdinand II found the population in revolt, the palaces of the Aragonese pillaged, the crowds crying " *Viva la Francia!* " Forced to abandon his newly acquired crown, he pointed out that he had wished to give the people a better government; that he had been betrayed by an undeserved defection; and added, that, if, when his subjects had experienced the arrogance and exactions of the stranger, they should desire his protection, he would face the greatest dangers to respond to their appeal. With these brave words, he retired to Ischia.

On February 20, the King slept in the castle of Poggio Reale, the favorite pleasure palace of the Aragonese kings, situated in the midst of a magnificent park filled with rare trees and curious birds and animals. Here a deputation of the Neapolitans came to welcome him to the city. His coming, the deputies affirmed, had been awaited "as the coming of the Messiah had been awaited by the Jews."

On February 22, Charles VIII made his entry into Naples. Some cannon shots were delivered from the Castel Nuovo by the partisans of Ferdinand II, — which seem to have done more damage to the city than to the invaders, — but the French artillery soon silenced them. Practically without opposition or resort to force, the occupation was completed. " Never did a people show so much affection for a king or a nation," says Philippe de Commines, " as they show to ours." The only indication that the occupation was also a conquest was the fact that the great offices of government were filled by Frenchmen. The Count de Montpensier, who is described by De Commines as " a good knight and brave, but not very wise, who does not rise till midday," was made Viceroy; Briçonnet took the first place in the Royal Council;

---

of "the Catholic," to check the course of Charles VIII. Rejecting the proposal to submit his rights to the Pope's arbitration, Charles reproached the ambassadors with the perfidy of Ferdinand, whereupon they tore up the Treaty of Barcelona in his presence.

and De Vesc added to the office of Grand Chamberlain the Duchy of Nola and other valuable estates.

Two important consequences resulted from the brilliant success of Charles VIII in making himself master of Naples. The ease with which that success was attained led the young king to trust entirely to the good fortune that had thus far attended him, and no pains were taken to secure the confidence and affections of the people who had so lightly delivered themselves to the power of the King. His unmeasured indulgence in sensual pleasures, the ruinous luxury of his court, the haughtiness and insolence of his ministers, the evident contempt for the Neapolitans, the drunkenness of the soldiers and their familiarity with the women of the country all combined to destroy the illusion previously entertained regarding the saintliness of the French, and to embitter the people of Naples against their new masters.[1]

The effect of the occupation upon the other Italian states and upon the great powers of Europe was even more signifi-

---

[1] "Naples was now destined to ruin for Charles whatever nerve yet remained to his festival army. The witch too, while brewing for the French her most attractive potions, mixed with them a deadly poison — the virus of a fell disease, memorable in the annals of the modern world, which was destined to affect the nations of Europe from this centre, and to prove more formidable to our cities than even the leprosy of the Middle Ages." Symonds, *The Age of the Despots*, London, 1902, p. 444. See, besides his bibliographical note on the history of the disease, Delaborde, *L'expédition*, p. 576, and Cipolla, *Storia delle signorie*, p. 712. The French called the infection "*mal de Naples*"; but the Italians returned the compliment by declaring that it was imported from France, and called it "*morbo gallico.*" See Guicciardini, *Storia d'Italia*, I, pp. 362 et seq. "Notwithstanding popular rumor," says Cipolla, "it is certain it did not come either from France or from the countries touched by Christopher Columbus," — as others have alleged. He proves these assertions by the fact that the disease was known at Genoa two years before the coming of Charles VIII, and by the existence of a sepulchral stone in the Church of Santa Maria del Popolo at Rome recording the death of a youth from it in 1485, seven years before the discovery of America by Columbus.

Chap. III
A. D.
1492-1502

cant. None of these had really believed that the enterprise of Charles VIII would ever end successfully. His own incapacity, the incompetence of his advisers, and the expected resistance by the Aragonese dynasty, aided by the Turks, had all been counted upon to render his adventure fruitless and perhaps ruinous. When, therefore, the occupation of Naples was announced, its suddenness and the ease with which it had been accomplished filled all Europe, and in particular Italy, with surprise and consternation. With Charles VIII in undisputed possession of Naples, and the Duke of Orléans at Asti ready to lead an army against Milan for the enforcement of hereditary claims to that duchy, it appeared not impossible that the French might soon reduce all Italy to the condition of a French province.

Against this contingency the Republic of Venice had long been making secret preparations. While congratulating Philippe de Commines upon his master's brilliant fortunes in Southern Italy, with its accustomed skill and activity the Signory had been for months busy in exciting the apprehensions of all the possible opponents of the French, and in combining these enemies into a coalition to expel the invaders from Italy.

Long before Charles VIII had arrived at Rome on his march to Naples, Ludovico Sforza had fully disclosed to the Venetian ambassadors his anxiety to renew the ancient league against the ambitions of France. When the news of the occupation of Naples reached him on February 27, while ordering public demonstrations of joy in Milan, he hastened to renew negotiations with Venice for prompt action against Charles VIII.

Alexander VI was, if possible, even more disturbed by the announcement of the King's success than either Sforza or the Signory of Venice; for he knew that the investiture of Naples would now be promptly demanded. On March 28, a French ambassador, the Count St. Pol, arrived in Rome for this purpose, with a message that His Majesty "*Très-Chrétienne*" would arrive in Rome during Holy Week to receive the crown of Naples from the hand of the Head of the Church.

While the Consistory was divided as to the action to be taken, it was decided that the investiture should be refused. The ambassador replied that his master would come in person and take the crown. "I will give it," replied the Pope, "only in conformity with the sacred canons, and after having heard those who present claims to it. Further, inform your master that he might not find me in Rome, if he came. Tell him also that I am strongly solicited to enter into a confederation which is forming between the chief powers of the world."[1] He might have added, had he deemed it prudent, that his legate was already at Venice with orders to join, and as far as possible promote, the league then practically concluded.

The ambassador of Charles VIII at Venice, Philippe de Commines, has himself left us a graphic account of his experience there during the formation of the league.[2] It was, of course, apprehended that the Emperor Maximilian and Ferdinand the Catholic of Spain, as well as the states of Italy, would be concerned for the fate of Naples; but assurances had been repeatedly given that the intentions of the King of France did not include any other projects than the recovery of his rights in Southern Italy, and afterward a crusade against the Turks. The false report that money had been coined at Rome bearing the inscription "*Carolus Imperator*,"[3] and the suspicion that the King was about to resume the rôle of Charles the Great, were, however, sufficient to excite the fears of Maximilian; while the expectation that the next step might be the conquest of Sicily, and perhaps Sardinia, disturbed the apprehensions of the King of Spain.

On January 5, a Spanish embassy had arrived in Venice, headed by one of the ablest of Spanish ambassadors, Lorenzo

---

[1] See Sanuto, *La spedizione*, p. 103.
[2] *Mémoires*, II, pp. 216, 230.
[3] See note 2, page 196.

Suarez de Mendoça y Figueroa, to be followed soon afterward by a second delegation. On February 15, just a week before the entry of Charles VIII into Naples, an imperial embassy, composed of four persons, led by Ulrich von Lichtenstein, Bishop of Trent, was also received at Venice. The curiosity of De Commines was excited, but the solemn assurances of the Signory, as well as of the ambassadors themselves, — especially those of Milan, in whom he had the right to repose some confidence, — for a time disarmed his suspicions. About March 1 a rumor was abroad in the city that a league was forming against the King of France; but the Doge, Barbarigo, with his habitual suavity, replied, that "one should not believe what is said upon the street where every one may say what he pleases"; that "the Venetians had never thought or heard of a league against the King, but on the contrary wished to join with him and the other powers against the Turk!"[1]

On March 5, the news reached Venice that Charles VIII had entered Naples. Admitted to the private apartment of the Doge, who was ill, De Commines was received in the presence of fifty or sixty persons. While Barbarigo displayed a "joyful countenance," the others, less accustomed to dissimulation, revealed the sadness of their hearts. It was evident to De Commines that he had been deceived, but his knowledge was now of little value. In vain he informed the King at Naples and the Duke of Orléans at Asti of the hostility at Venice. Although the negotiations were not without serious difficulties, the league was concluded with little delay. On March 31, at two o'clock in the morning, the treaty was sealed and sworn to by the ambassadors of the Pope, the Emperor, Ferdinand and Isabella of Spain, the Duke of Milan, and Venice.[2] It bound the contracting powers to a defensive confederation for the preservation of their estates for a period of twenty-five years, each signatory

---

[1] *Mémoires*, II, p. 219.
[2] The treaty is found in Lünig, *Codex Italiae Diplomaticus*, XXIV.

THE IMPERIAL ASPIRATIONS OF FRANCE 203

to furnish, in case of need, eight thousand horsemen and four thousand infantry.[1]

The next day, De Commines was summoned before the Signory, to be informed of the coalition and its purpose, which was declared to be, (1) the protection of Christendom against the Turks; (2) the defence of Italy; and (3) the preservation of their estates. The ambassadors "held their heads high and made good cheer." De Commines, dejected, began to doubt if his master would ever be able to leave Italy alive and without the loss of his army.

That evening, after dinner, from his window, the French envoy saw the ambassadors of the league disporting themselves at the expense of the Signory in a gala festival in some forty decorated gondolas upon the water, while cannons were fired and the city was illuminated. For three days he remained shut up in his apartment. Meanwhile, the celebration continued, ending with the solemn proclamation of the league, in commemoration of which a stone of red porphyry was placed at the corner of the Church of San Marco. To cap the climax of De Commines' humiliation, Spinola, the ambassador of Ferdinand II of Naples, who had remained at Venice in a private capacity, laid aside his garments of mourning, put on a resplendent robe, and after April 1 was regularly summoned to the Council and treated as the representative of a recognized power.

The events which had afforded to Philippe de Commines an initiation into the resources of Italian diplomacy were to be for all Europe the revelation of a new system. The secret of national self-preservation was disclosed, and the remedy for dangerous ambitions was seen to lie in the principle of association.

CHAP. III
A. D.
1492-1502

Negotiations of Charles VIII to secure his return

To Charles VIII, notwithstanding the warnings of De Commines, the conclusion of the league was a painful surprise. When, on April 5, he was informed of it by the

---

[1] There were additional secret articles. In consideration of the spiritual arms the Pope was able to employ, he was bound to furnish only half the force required of the others.

Venetian ambassadors at Naples, although assured by them that its purpose was merely the protection of the Italian states against the Turks, he at once perceived that it was really directed against himself. "What!" cried the King, "have not I also states in Italy?" Repeating the exclamation, "It is a great shame!" he approached the window where he had left De Vesc and Della Rovere. The former was as furious as himself, but the latter tried to calm him. "The King of Spain!" he burst forth, "to whom I have given Perpignan and Elne! Maximilian! whom I could restrain with a single letter!"[1] "But now," he continued, "since the Signory has seen good to form this league without a word to us, we shall do what we please without letting it know our intentions." The ambassadors, almost unnoticed by the King, withdrew from his presence and immediately asked for their recall.

Recovered from his first indignation, before their departure from Naples Charles VIII declared to the Venetians that he still counted on their friendship, that without it he would not have come into Italy, and announced that he would send one of his secretaries to the Signory.

This step was prompted by his anxiety lest his return to France might be cut off, and in the hope that he might still break the force of the league, whose military preparations were already under way, by giving new assurances and by proposing to organize an expedition against the Turks.

On May 22, Jean Bourdin appeared at Venice, and on the next day De Commines and he presented to the Senate the complaint of their master relative to the formation of the league, declared that on account of his friendship for the Republic the King had been unwilling to accept the overtures of a great personage in an affair directed against them, justified the conduct of the French while in Italy, and concluded with a statement that, being now disposed to return to

---

[1] The allusion was, no doubt, to Maximilian's proposal of a year previous to unite with him against Venice.

France, the King was counting on a free passage in order to meet in person the Emperor, with whom he hoped to arrange an expedition against the Infidel, and would be pleased to know what part the Republic was willing to take in that enterprise.

In reply, the Venetians gave assurance, with their usual courtesy, that if the King kept his engagements with the Pope and the Florentines, he could retire without anxiety; but added that the magnitude of his army and the assembling of fresh troops at Asti compelled them to make provision for their own safety. As for the intentions of the "great personage," the Venetians plainly understood the allusion, but intimated with dignity, that they had always been able to defend their possessions against their enemies.

Unable to secure from Alexander VI the investiture of the kingdom, Charles VIII humbly wrote to him a personal letter in which he begged the Pope not to place faith in malevolent rumors regarding his intentions.[1] Having done this, he resolved that before departing for France he would at least make his solemn entry into Naples. Withdrawing to Poggio Reale, on May 12, 1495, a triumphal procession was formed of the French officers and the Neapolitan nobility and clergy, in which Charles VIII, arrayed as an emperor, rode under a canopy borne by the chief dignitaries of Naples, wearing the crown, and holding the imperial globe in his right hand, the sceptre in his left.

It was an indication that he had abandoned none of his pretensions, but the triumphal entry and the symbols of world dominion were not sufficient to satisfy his mind. A last desperate effort was made to obtain the investiture from Alexander VI, and for this purpose an embassy was despatched to Rome. But the time had passed when the Pope needed to dissimulate his opposition to the King of France, for the confederates were now ready to begin hostilities. A

---

[1] The letter of Charles VIII is printed by Lamansky, *Secrets d'état de Venise*, pp. 291, 292.

Chap. III
A. D.
1492-1502

Spanish fleet was bringing Ferdinand II to the coast of Calabria, the Milanese were marching to drive Louis of Orleans from Asti, and the fickle Neapolitans were preparing to welcome their exiled king. At Rome, the herald of the French embassy was attacked and robbed; and an unfortunate cook, sent forward to make preparations for the arrival of the ambassadors, was killed by the pontifical guard. Fearing to enter the city, the embassy halted and awaited the formal permission of the Pope. On May 20, the offer of Charles to pay his annual tribute of fifty thousand ducats for the Kingdom of Naples, together with the arrears owed by Ferdinand II, was presented by his ambassadors but failed to propitiate the Pope, who now frankly gave them to understand that the hope of investiture was chimerical.

In the meantime, Charles VIII had decided to leave Naples under the government of his Viceroy, the Count de Montpensier, and on May 20 took his departure from that city with an army of about ten thousand men. As he approached Rome, he learned that Alexander VI, accompanied by the Sacred College, had retired on the twenty-seventh to Orvieto. Entering Rome on June 1 without opposition, he was informed that the Pope had retreated from Orvieto to Perugia.

The reason for his presence in Rome being thus removed, the King now proceeded on his march toward the North. At Siena, he met De Commines, who had taken his departure from Venice early in June. Coming from Florence, he had just heard the denunciation of Savonarola, — who could not forgive the neglect of Charles VIII to reform the Church, — "God has already sentenced him."

The retreat to France and loss of Naples

The prediction was even then in process of fulfilment. By a secret article of the League of Venice it had been agreed that the King of France should be expelled from Italy, and that he should not be allowed to retain Naples. That agreement was already receiving its enforcement.

Ludovico Sforza had demanded of Louis, Duke of Orléans, the evacuation of Asti and the renunciation of his pretensions to Milan; but Louis had surprised Novara, where Sforza held him besieged. In the meantime, the confederates had assembled an army of some thirty-five thousand men to arrest the progress of Charles. Wearied with dragging their cannons and their heavy baggage trains through the defiles of the Apennines, on July 5 the French emerged into the plains of Lombardy near the village of Fornovo. Here, on July 6, an attack was made upon them by the allied forces. After a battle in which the Italians lost between three and four thousand men and the French only a few hundred, the army of Charles VIII held the field; but the confederates claimed the victory. Judged by the results, it was really theirs, for his army retreated to Asti, where it idly rested, without offering aid to the Duke of Orléans at Novara. Through the mediation of the Duchess of Savoy, a treaty was signed on October 10, at Vercelli, by which Charles VIII agreed not to support the Orléans claims to Milan, while Ludovico offered fifty thousand ducats to the Duke in compensation, promised free passage through his territories for the French troops, and accepted a renewal of vassalage to the King of France for Genoa. Having concluded these arrangements, Charles VIII led his army back to France, and at Lyons, reached on November 9, plunged again into his accustomed pleasures.

In less than a week after Charles VIII had departed from Naples, Ferdinand II, with an army of Spaniards and Sicilians, entered his kingdom. An additional force was soon sent by Ferdinand the Catholic under the command of the famous general, Gonsalvo de Cordova. The day after the battle of Fornovo, Ferdinand II entered Naples amid the salutations of his delighted subjects, who remembered his prophecies concerning their treatment by the French.[1] Although the French garrisons could not be at once dislodged, before

---

[1] The League of Venice was renewed at Rome, on July 18, 1496, with the addition of Henry VII of England, and proclaimed anew with public rejoicing on July 31. — See Brown, *Calendar*, I, No. 712.

the end of 1496 the former dynasty was once more completely master of the kingdom, and the traces of the conquest had practically disappeared.

In Italy, the only state to sustain a serious loss was the Republic of Florence, whose alliance with the King of France resulted in the independence of Lucca and Siena, and of Pisa, to whose citizens the French garrison surrendered the citadel instead of delivering it as promised to the Florentines.

For France, the results of the Italian expedition were financial disaster, loss of prestige, the wasting of a great army that might have been employed for securing the natural frontiers of the kingdom, the hatred of the Italians, and a bitter rivalry with Spain and Austria as contestants for territory in Italy. The only positive asset of this ill-starred adventure was the red hat of Briçonnet, Cardinal of St. Malo.

III. The Exploits of Louis XII in Italy

After his return to France, Charles VIII often dreamed of renewing his claims upon the Kingdom of Naples, but his councils were now divided. Étienne de Vesc, in the hope of recovering his lost duchy, urged a new expedition to Naples. On the other hand, the Cardinal of St. Malo, having secured the chief object of his ambition, exercised a restraining influence upon the King, who now declared his intention "to live according to God's commandments."

But the efforts of De Vesc were unceasing, and the condition of Italy, and of Europe generally, was promising for his designs. The Pope now hoped to engage the King of France in the advancement of Cesare Borgia; the Venetians were anxious to form an alliance against Ludovico Sforza; the Emperor Maximilian was planning to punish the Venetians for disregard of his rights; Ludovico Sforza also had schemes in which he wished to secure the King's assistance; and even Ferdinand the Catholic was disposed to invite his participation in an Italian project. Thus, on every side, circumstances appeared favorable for a new campaign; when on April 7, 1498, in passing through a doorway in the Castle of Amboise, Charles VIII struck his head against the stone casement, and died of apoplexy a few hours afterward, at the age of only twenty-eight.

The previous death of the children of Charles VIII left the throne of France without a direct heir; and Louis, Duke of Orléans, great-grandson of Charles V, as heir presumptive, now claimed and received the succession as Louis XII. Uniting, for the first time, in the person of a king of France the doubtful claims of the House of Anjou to the Kingdom of Naples and the Orléans pretensions to the Duchy of Milan, Louis XII was to make Italy once more the centre of European interest.

But it was a new Europe that had come into existence in these closing years of the fifteenth century. A new order of things, moral, social, intellectual, and political had silently supervened, and the Middle Ages were no more. The expedition of Charles VIII may justly be regarded as the last great mediaeval adventure and the first military campaign of modern times. With equal truth, it may be taken to mark the birth of international politics.

The Europe which confronted Louis XII of France was in all its great essentials modern. The map of the year 1500 contains the names of the chief political powers which are to-day in existence. Their frontiers have been repeatedly modified, but the great national entities themselves remain essentially the same. Portugal, Spain, France, England, Germany, Denmark, Sweden, Norway, Hungary, Poland, even Russia, and the Ottoman Empire were at that time established powers; and most of them are still in some sense identical with the nations of the fifteenth century. Only in that middle Kingdom of Lothair where Holland, Belgium, Switzerland, and Italy now appear, and in what was Poland and the Balkan and Grecian realms, have stupendous territorial changes taken place.

And what is true of the physical configuration of the great national states is true also of their inherent elements and affinities. The sense of nationality had already pervaded them and impressed upon them a permanent unity. The Pyrenees, the Alps, the Rhine, the Channel, the Baltic are not, in truth, the chief separating barriers in Europe. The real causes of national cleavage are not to be found in these merely physical boundaries, to which imagination has attributed the name of "natural limits." Far deeper and more impassable are the purely psychical affinities and repulsions based on race, language, and tradition. Though none of these may be insuperable, they have proved practically determining; and even the powerful forces of economic interest have been thus far unable to destroy their effectiveness. The division of Europe into national states was the necessary compromise between the forces of racial and territorial coherence on the one hand, and on the other that large conception of human solidarity which gave both vigor and dignity to the imperial idea. Since Europe could not be united under one law and one ruler, efficiency of government demanded the system of national states.

The emergence of European problems

Although they have come into view only with the progress of events, nearly all the great problems of European politics were already implicitly involved in the international relations of that time.

The partition of the unknown portions of the world by Spain and Portugal had for its first result the rivalry of those two countries, whose ethnographical differences and national antipathies were thus rendered more difficult to reconcile. But its effect upon the world at large was of far greater importance, for it created that most lasting and complicated of international problems, the Colonial Question. It was inevitable that the rest of the world should at some time assert its rights to a portion of the maritime trade and colonial possessions by which Spain and Portugal were then enriched. Thus, after the frontiers of European states were practically settled, the struggle for colonial supremacy was to open new conflicts, to be fought out in Asia and America and upon the sea.

It was, without doubt, in great measure, the colonial question that increased the bitterness of the rivalry between France and Spain, and later between England and Spain. But it was the wars of Italy which precipitated a contest that was to endure for centuries between nations of similar ethnic qualities and of the same religion.

It was not, however, Spain alone whose interests were affected by the pretensions of France in the Italian peninsula. For Germany the success of France implied not only the eventual loss of the imperial title, but encroachment along the whole line of its frontiers, in the effort to extend French dominion to and, perhaps, beyond the Rhine. For England also the preponderance of France would create a neighbor too powerful to be tolerated. The ambitions of France were thus provoking an issue of general European interest.

More remote, but not less certain to arise, were the problems of the Baltic and the East. As the Mediterranean had been the theatre of contention between rival powers, until Rome encircled it with her dominions, so the Baltic was predestined to become in time the scene of a desperate struggle for predominance.

But Eastern Europe, forced to face the problem of the Russian and the Ottoman advance, was to be the scene of a still more vast and enduring conflict; for there was the meeting place of wholly antagonistic forces, and there were Poland and the Balkan lands, the certain prey of future conquest or expropriation. Thus was already posed the great Eastern Question, at first the mere problem of fixing the frontiers of Christendom, but finally to become, in union with the colonial question, the supreme issue of world politics, with India, China, and the Pacific islands as the pawns, when new nations, then unknown and even non-existent, should enter the arena of dispute.

From this larger point of view it is not difficult to see how Italy, the ancient seat of empire, was still, at the end of the

CHAP. III
A. D.
1492-1502

The state of Italy at the end of the fifteenth century

fifteenth century, the centre of Europe; for it was in Italy that imperial honors were yet to be sought, and it was Italy that possessed the secret of the method by which imperial ambitions could be restrained.

There, when the armies of Charles VIII had been expelled from Italian soil, the old local rivalries and animosities flamed up anew, and the splendid triumph of the League of Venice was soon followed by fresh schemes of intervention.

When Louis of Orléans came to the throne of France his first thought was the prosecution of his claims in Italy, particularly to the Duchy of Milan. He, therefore, did not hesitate to proclaim his hostility to Ludovico Sforza and his intention to divest him of the duchy. In the circular letter announcing his accession, he took pains to style himself "King of France and Duke of Milan."

In Ludovico Sforza Louis XII was, however, to meet an antagonist whose great ability gave to the contest a highly dramatic character. To meet the defensive tactics of this crafty and untiring Italian,—called by his fellow-countrymen "the wisest sovereign of the earth," and without doubt the most perfect embodiment of the ideal statesman of that time,— Louis XII was obliged to employ all his immense resources.

In Italy, Ludovico had made himself easily preponderant. Of all the Italian rulers he, who was the most responsible for the expedition of Charles VIII, had suffered least from its consequences.

Ferdinand II of Naples had died on October 7, 1496, in the midst of his efforts to expel the French; and he had been succeeded by his uncle, Frederick of Altamura. His kingdom, greatly weakened by its desperate conflict, was slowly recovering from the effects of the French invasion and was still too feeble to count for much in Italy.

Alexander VI, suffering from loss of prestige on account of his political perfidy during the French expedition, was practically friendless in Rome. Opposed by the Orsini and the Colonna, he had been brought into strained relations with the new king of Naples, troubled with the fear of deposition through the influence of Savonarola at Florence, estranged from Ludovico Sforza through his quarrel with his brother Cardinal Ascanio, embroiled with Venice over territorial questions, and placed in extreme danger on every side through the ambitions of Cesare Borgia.

The Republic of Florence had been divided into factions by the expulsion of the Medici and the theocratic mysticism of Savonarola, enfeebled by the loss of the emancipated cities, and plunged into a bitter war with Pisa to reclaim its vassalage.

Venice and Milan were, therefore, the only powers in Italy possessing a real vitality; and this fact alone made them almost of necessity antagonists. Although Ludovico Sforza had profited by the Treaty of Vercelli, in which Venice was ignored, the Republic had derived no particular advantage from the success of the League of Venice, while the relations of the Venetians and the Emperor were already strained.

Alone in Italy, Ludovico possessed a powerful ally. His family relations with Maximilian gave him a close intimacy with the imperial court, and his ambassadors lost no opportunity to extend his influence. A common hostility to France furnished the basis for an *entente* between Ludovico and the Emperor, valuable to the impecunious Maximilian because it enabled him to replenish his empty treasury with Milanese gold, and to the Duke of Milan because it secured to him preponderance in Italy.

Nothing could be more obscure or equivocal than the Orléans claims to Milan. Such as they were, they depended upon rights inherited from Valentine Visconti, sister of Duke Filippo Maria. If the Sforzas were usurpers, so also had been the Visconti. If the Visconti could claim legitimation by the investiture of Milan as a fief of the Empire, so also could Ludovico Sforza. The inheritance of the Orléans family by the will of Gian Galeazzo Visconti in favor of his daughter Valentine, if established, was clouded by doubt if

The Orléans claims to Milan

Chap. III
A. D.
1492–1502

the duchy, as an imperial fief, could be transmitted by him to a daughter. So doubtful was the inheritance that, to sustain its legality, fictitious genealogies were invented. The most plausible of these represented Valentine Visconti, the sister of Duke Filippo Maria, as his legitimate daughter through his marriage to a French princess![1]

It was, therefore, in reality, not the vindication of unquestioned rights but a veritable war of conquest which Louis XII was about to undertake against the Duke of Milan. It is true, that the claims of the Orléans family, slender as they were, were somewhat better founded than the claimants knew, that they were believed to be real even in Italy, and that Ludovico Sforza had attempted to destroy evidence of them "which would be of great value to the Duke of Orléans"; but all this does not establish the good faith and justice of what was in substance a mere dynastic adventure, as foreign to the national interests of France as the expedition of Charles VIII. Unhappily for Europe, it was to fix in the usages of Western Christendom the principle of foreign conquest at the expense of passive populations, with new and deplorable practices of partition and "compensation" destined to retard the movement of normal national development and create antagonisms that have never ceased to bear their bitter fruits.

The search of Louis XII for allies

The designs of Louis XII upon Italy were not, however, so easily executed as might at first appear; and the efforts of the King of France to prepare the way reveal the progress that had then been made in the development of European politics. Embroiled with the Emperor and the Archduke Philip over the affairs of Burgundy, exposed to the hostility of the King of England because of the French alliance with the Scotch, and estranged from Ferdinand the Catholic on account of the protection Spain had furnished to the kings of

---

[1] On the legality of the Orléans claims to Milan, see Pélissier, *Louis XII et Ludovic Sforza*, I, pp. 80, 95, and p. 98. His conclusion is : "Rien n'était donc plus inconsistant et plus vague que la base des prétentions des Orléans à l'héritage des Visconti."

Naples, Louis XII was compelled to realize that, thenceforth, in carrying out his Italian projects, France had to reckon with the rest of Europe.

The experience of Charles VIII had proved that Italy was not incapable of organizing its own defence. Ludovico Sforza not only maintained embassies at the courts of the Empire, England, and Spain, but he possessed the skill and the influence to arouse the Italian states to a sense of the danger of a new invasion. It was, therefore, not without strenuous exertions that the King of France could hope to escape from the apprehension of an opposing coalition in case he should attack the Duchy of Milan.

The pacific inclination of the other powers was, however, favorable for the efforts of Louis XII to secure their neutrality. Although at first coldly received by Henry VII of England, his friendly overtures were with the aid of liberal subsidies at last successful, and in spite of the persistent opposition of the Duke of Milan, in July, 1498, a treaty was signed between France and England which was at least equivalent to a promise of neutrality.

The *rapprochement* with Spain was more difficult; but Ferdinand the Catholic had little regard for Ludovico Sforza, and saw many advantages in an *entente* with France. Accordingly, while pledging to the Italians his endeavors to secure the peace of Italy by his influence with Louis XII, in the same month a treaty was signed between France and Spain by which the opposition of Ferdinand was practically averted.

The support of the Emperor thus became essential to the safety of the Duke of Milan. Could he depend upon it? For a time, the availability of his ally was a source of deep anxiety. Urged by the Milanese ambassador to wage war with the King of France upon his Burgundian frontiers, Maximilian, whose military preparation was insufficient, was soon forced to declare a truce. Displeased on this account with his Italian ally, he now declared his intention to disengage himself from the affairs of Italy, and Ludovico was thus left to defend himself alone.

The diplomatic struggle of Ludovico Sforza

A war of the Emperor against the Swiss proved fortunate for Ludovico; for, in serious need of funds, Maximilian was obliged to turn to him for aid. Inclined, as the suzerain of Milan and the enemy of France, to oppose the conquest of the duchy by Louis XII, Maximilian was almost inevitably the ally of his endangered vassal. To what extent his support would prove effective was, however, a subject of concern.

A double interest secured the alliance between the Emperor and Ludovico; for Savoy, also a vassal of the Empire, was wavering in the balance. An attack on Milan required the passage of a French army across its territory, and if Milan were conquered Savoy also was likely to be annexed to France.

Turin, therefore, became the seat of arduous negotiations to secure the adhesion of Savoy to the cause of the Emperor and the Duke of Milan. For a time, the loyalty of the young Duke Philibert seemed assured, but the influence of France soon proved triumphant, and Savoy not only permitted the French troops to pass without opposition, but the Duke accepted service in the French army.

The essential feebleness of the imperial organization as compared with the solidarity of a strong national monarchy was now brought into view. The inability of the Emperor to support his vassal in Italy was revealed not only by the defection of Savoy, but by his fruitless exertions to rally to his aid other portions of the Empire. In August, 1499, an imperial diet was held in which it was voted that the Emperor was absolutely under obligation to rescue the Duke of Milan; but no effective aid was offered to support him in this task. While France had become modern the Empire was still mediaeval, and its feudal organization left the Emperor without the means to support his policy. By the force of circumstances, therefore, the Empire was effectively in a state of neutrality.

The diplomatic activity of Louis XII

A still more striking exhibition of the feebleness of the Empire was afforded by the success of the King of France in detaching its forces in his own interest. At the time of his accession, the Archduke Philip of Austria, — son of Maximilian and Mary of Burgundy, — had shown a disposition to settle amicably the question of his inheritance. Louis XII had conducted with him long negotiations, ending in the Archduke's consent to sign with him a treaty of peace and amity on condition that three towns situated in Artois, on the frontier of Picardy, be ceded to him. Louis XII accepted this proposition, and Philip promised to withdraw his troops from his own frontiers, to render homage to the King of France, and to place at his command his entire army if he were attacked, "without excepting any man in the world." The Emperor was irritated beyond measure, and declared to the imperial diet that he considered "that peace as a personal affront"; yet, on June 6, 1499, the prime minister of Louis XII, Georges d'Amboise, restored the promised cities, and the Archduke took his oath of fidelity before the royal chancellor.

The King of France was not less fortunate in effecting other alliances. Of these, that negotiated with Ladislas VI, King of Bohemia and Hungary, soon afterward sealed by his marriage with a niece of Louis XII, was of great importance; for the Kingdom of Hungary possessed the double advantage of bounding the Austrian realm upon the East and of touching the Venetian possessions on the South. Its attitude was, therefore, of strategic value to the enterprise of the King of France.

But a still more useful ally was to be found in the Swiss Confederation. Commanding the routes of communication between Germany and Italy, the Swiss were also useful in furnishing brave and hardy mercenary troops. The contest for an alliance with them was not dissimilar to an open market in which the purchasers outbid each other. At first Ludovico made great progress in his negotiations with the cantons, but the war of the Swiss with the Emperor rendered Ludovico's relations with them offensive to his ally, and he was thenceforth obliged to treat with them in secret only. On March 16, 1499, a compact was concluded at Lucerne by which the cantons and the King of France agreed to oppose each other's enemies. For France it was a brilliant diplomatic victory over the Duke of Milan, and for the Swiss a source of immense pecuniary gain as mercenary troops.

Thus, by his well directed activity, in little more than a year Louis XII had practically isolated Ludovico Sforza in Europe. This great diplomatic triumph was to be completed by an equally brilliant one in Italy.

The expedition of Charles VIII had left the name of France without prestige beyond the Alps. Florence, the one traditional friend of France in Italy, was rendered politically impotent by its factional divisions and its struggle with Pisa and the other Tuscan cities lost to the Republic by the French invasion. Both Milan and Naples were now the objects of French aggression. Only Venice and Rome remained, therefore, as possible allies in the coming contest.

Soon after his accession Louis XII sent Niccolò Alemanni to Italy with letters to all the princes and republics, except the Duke of Milan and the King of Naples. The instructions of the French envoy were "to cheer and encourage the old clients of France in Italy, and to recommend peace among them." The real purpose of the mission was to ascertain the sentiments of the Italians toward Ludovico Sforza and to restore the lost prestige of France.

The appearance of the embassy was the cause of general disquietude in Italy, but it was not unfavorable to the cause of France. The smaller princes, like the Dukes of Mantua and Ferrara, and the family of Bentivoglio at Bologna, who were inclined to support the Duke of Milan, were suddenly thrown into an attitude of practical neutrality. Venice and Rome, perceiving that a French invasion was imminent, began to consider how they could best profit from the situation. Seeing the peril in which he was placed, Ludovico Sforza now made a supreme effort to rally and unite the Italians against the French.

Since the Treaty of Vercelli between Ludovico Sforza and Charles VIII, the relations of the Duke of Milan to the

Republic of Venice had been strained. With the accession of Louis XII, diplomatic relations between the Republic and France, which had been suspended since the departure of Philippe de Commines from Venice, were renewed; for it was evident to the Venetian statesmen that their interests would be involved in the contemplated action of the King of France, with whom, as the Duke of Orléans, they had sustained intimate relations in the past. Their first envoy, Stella, who hastened from Savoy to announce to Louis XII that the Venetian government would soon send a solemn embassy to felicitate him upon his accession to the throne, was received with extreme cordiality by the King, who granted him an immediate reception, embraced him affectionately in the presence of his courtiers, overwhelmed him with marks of welcome, and inquired familiarly, "*Comment va la Seigneurie? Comment va le Doge?*"[1]

In due time the more formal embassy arrived in France, composed of three patricians headed by Antonio Loredam, which was also welcomed with unusual warmth. When Loredam entered the King's presence, Louis laughingly said in Italian, "This is our good father!" and when the ambassador raised his *berretta* to salute him, the King interrupted his movement with the words, "*Mettez votre bonnet!*"[2]

The rumors of this reception of the Venetian ambassadors in France soon filled Italy with commotion, and reports were set afloat that an alliance had been formed between the King and the Republic for the conquest and partition of Milan; but the *rapprochement* was not to be so easily effected. Venice was divided in opinion, distrustful of the King's intentions, and prudently disposed to put a price upon its alliance. The King, on the other hand, after his first spontaneous advances, was inclined to secure the support of the Republic at as little cost as possible. The offer of his protection seemed to him a sufficient reward for all he demanded

---

[1] For Stella's letter of June 3, 1498. see Sanuto, *Diarii*, I, 979
[2] See Sanuto, the same, 1050.

of the "Most Serene Republic," and his message sent by Stella, — "Say to the Signory that, if it is with me, it has nothing to fear from any other power," — was the basis of his negotiations.

Conclusion of the Franco-Venetian alliance

All the skill of Ludovico Sforza was now exercised to defeat the threatened Franco-Venetian *entente* and to prevent its ripening into an alliance. Venice was reminded of the danger it incurred by trusting the "barbarians," who were meditating nothing less than the subjugation of all Italy. For a time, the traditional hostility of the Republic to French intervention in Italy prevailed; but, at length, after long and serious consideration, at ten o'clock at night, on September 6, 1498, the question of the French alliance *in nomine Domini* was settled, and the opponents of Ludovico Sforza won the day.

But the Venetians were now to make the discovery that they were dealing with a great power, and that their methods of negotiation were less effective than they had been with their Italian neighbors. Reports circulated and supported by Cardinal Giuliano della Rovere, to the effect that Louis XII was about concluding a treaty with Ludovico Sforza by which the Duke of Milan was to cede Genoa and a part of the duchy to France, and to pay half a million ducats for the remainder, filled the Venetians with apprehension. The King's demand of a hundred thousand ducats, to be advanced by Venice for the expenses of the war, accompanied by the menace that, if his terms were not accepted within twenty days, "he would know what to do," rendered the situation of the Venetian ambassadors still more uncomfortable. Their audiences with the King became less frequent and his attentions less flattering; till, finally, his remark, that the Venetians were "merchants" and made their friendship "merchandise," revealed the contempt with which he regarded them. Soon afterward Georges d'Amboise angrily informed them, that "the King is king, in war as in peace!" When the ambassadors insinuated that it was unworthy of the King's honor to receive money, "Attend to the honor of the Signory," cried Marshal Gié, "and leave undisturbed the honor of the King!"

After suffering much humiliation and many asperities, the ambassadors induced Cardinal della Rovere to intervene in their behalf. "The plenipotentiaries cannot exceed their instructions," pleaded the Cardinal with the King. "If pressed too hard, all Italy will unite to form a league." "It will not last two years," replied the King. "Yes," argued the Cardinal, "but Your Majesty will not be able to make his expedition, and with three hundred thousand ducats a year that league will oblige Your Majesty to expend a million to defend himself against the Emperor."

But the King remained inflexible, and on February 9, 1499, a treaty of "perpetual confederation" was signed by the Venetian ambassadors upon the King's own terms.[1] The considerations advantageous to Venice were the cession of Cremona and the Ghiara d'Adda.[2] Although the signature of the treaty was celebrated at Venice with public rejoicing, its terms, which remained secret, were not received with satisfaction by the Signory. While not publicly disgraced, the ambassadors received no honors. For the first time in its history, under the appearance of success, the diplomacy of Venice had endured a real humiliation.

While the desire to despoil Ludovico Sforza furnished the basis for the Franco-Venetian alliance, the personal interests of Louis XII and Alexander VI offered a foundation for an *entente* between the King of France and the Papacy.

Wishing to marry the widow of Charles VIII, Anne of Brittany, whose duchy was in danger of becoming independent and falling into the power of another, Louis XII was planning his divorce from Jeanne, daughter of Louis XI, whose deficiency in personal charms was not in the King's

---

[1] The text of the treaty is given by Sanuto, *Diarii*, II, 522.

[2] The Ghiara d'Adda is the country between the Adda, the Po, and the Oglio.

eyes compensated by her acknowledged virtues. To render effective this separation and remarriage, the King stood in need of a papal dispensation, rendered the more difficult to procure by the fact that there was no just or legal ground upon which it could be granted.

On the other hand, Pope Alexander VI was at that time seeking to procure for his son, Cesare Borgia, a temporal sovereignty and a marriage with a royal princess. The life of a cardinal being too tame for the ambitious young prelate, whose scandalous habits rendered his succession to the Papacy improbable, Alexander VI had procured his secularization, and had thus far sought in vain for the matrimonial alliance and principality which he coveted for his son. Frederick of Naples had refused to grant the request for the hand of his daughter, saying, "Arrange for the Cardinal to marry while still retaining his hat, and then I will give him my daughter." Ludovico Sforza had also incurred the Pope's displeasure by his half-hearted support of his designs.

The way having been prepared by the negotiations of secret agents, on October 1, 1498, Cesare Borgia set out upon a journey to France. From his window in the Vatican Alexander VI watched with pride the departure of his now fully "secularized" son as he rode away on horseback, in a robe of white damask with a golden border, covered with jewels and surmounted by a cape of black satin, wearing upon his head a black plumed *berretta*, quite in the French fashion. Four cardinals accompanied him, followed by a long train bearing his costly treasures.

The transaction he went to complete involved, on the one hand, the concession of a papal bull dissolving the marriage of Louis XII and Queen Jeanne, and the cardinal's hat for Georges d'Amboise; on the other, the erection of the Comté of Valence, in Lower Dauphiné into the Duchy of Valentinois in favor of Cesare Borgia. The new Duke of Valentinois brought the papal bull from Rome, and also the red hat for Georges d'Amboise. On December 17, the dissolution of the

King's marriage was pronounced, and on January 6, 1499, the marriage with Anne of Brittany was celebrated.[1]

Invested with his new duchy, Cesare Borgia now only awaited his promised marriage. The proposed bride was not, however, to be readily found, and the impatience of the Pope, who had fulfilled his part of the contract, had to be appeased by fulsome praises of Cesare's noble qualities, for whom it was difficult to find a worthy mate!

In the meantime, the question of the Pope's adhesion to the Franco-Venetian League became the centre of interest in Italy. If Ludovico Sforza could unite with himself the King of Naples and the Pope, there was still a chance for checking the designs of Louis XII, notwithstanding the ambiguous alliance of France with Venice.

Accordingly, the Duke of Milan set his hand to the task of securing for Cesare Borgia a principality and a marriage alliance in Italy. The delay of Louis XII in finding for the Duke of Valentinois the promised princess opened the way for intrigues with Alexander VI, to which the Pope gave such countenance that, in February, 1499, the project of a treaty was prepared providing for a defensive coalition between the Pope, Milan, Naples, and Florence. The three allies of the Pope were to contribute conjointly a hundred thousand ducats for the purchase of the Duchy of Suessia, the office of Grand Constable, and all the possessions of the Duke of Gandia, in the Kingdom of Naples, for the benefit of Cesare Borgia, together with certain "rights of aggression by the person whom the Pope should designate" in Romagna.

Alexander VI, whose chief object was to create a sovereignty for his son, approved the terms of the treaty, but

---

[1] The details of this transaction are given in the *relazione* of Polo Capello, Venetian ambassador at Rome, presented to the Senate on September 28, 1500. It is reproduced by Sanuto, and a brief digest of it is given by Ranke, *History of the Popes*, III, pp. 3, 8. Among the provisions of the agreement was the renunciation by Louis XII of all attempts on Naples, *except in aid of the Pope*, from which Ranke infers that Alexander VI had at that time designs on Naples.

with the secret purpose of using it for his own account in treating with Louis XII. With this intent, he insisted upon the insertion of a clause providing that, in case Cesare Borgia was not able to return from France within two months, the treaty should be inoperative.

Frederick of Naples plainly perceived the equivocal attitude of the Pope and his intention to force the hand of Louis XII; from whom, by threatening to revoke the bull authorizing the divorce and ally himself with the Duke of Milan and the King of Naples, he could now extort still further concessions in favor of Cesare Borgia.

More optimistic than the King of Naples, Ludovico Sforza, relying on his power of seduction with the Duke of Valentinois, proposed to him "great things" in Italy, where Ludovico knew he was anxious to consolidate his power. The result was, that Cesare Borgia divulged these proposals to Louis XII, and was thus able, in the most natural manner, to place the papal alliance in the market to be bought by the highest bidder.

Artfully proposing his return to Rome and the resumption of the office of cardinal in view of the long deferred marriage, Cesare Borgia sought to quicken the pace of the King of France, who at once showered upon him every honor and attention. With unexpected celerity a marriage contract was negotiated with Alain d'Albret for the hand of his daughter Charlotte, sister of Jean d'Albret, King of Navarre; and on May 10, 1499, the marriage was celebrated. Cesare was loaded with gifts and honors by the King and Queen of France, aid was promised in his enterprise for the subjugation of Romagna, and the Pope, who had thus been rendered "entirely French," immediately joined the Franco-Venetian League.

The conquest of Milan

The storm that had thus slowly gathered was now about to burst. The Pope and the Republic of Venice, — the natural and traditional opponents of French intervention, — were at last in league with France for the dismemberment of Italy. Florence, rent with factions, and the scene of a papal triumph by the excommunication and execution of Savonarola in May, 1498, was powerless to prevent the designs of the conquerors. Milan and Naples, allied for mutual defence, were thus left alone to resist the forces combined to destroy them.

On July 29, 1499, a list of the allies of Louis XII was published. All Europe seemed to be in collusion with him for the subjugation of Italy. England, Scotland, Spain, Portugal, Sweden, Norway, Denmark, the Swiss, the Pope, Venice, and even the Archduke Philip and certain electors of the Empire, were all in the catalogue of his diplomatic triumphs.

Events now marched with great rapidity. The general of Louis XII, Trivulzio, able, fearless, and experienced, — politician and *condottiere* at once, — knowing Italy and himself an Italian, was already at Asti. An army of fifteen thousand men soon marched against Milan. The tactics of the day were to paralyze opposition by the sudden massacre of whole populations, — a method of intimidation which was at least effective. Begun in August, 1499, the campaign was ended in October, Ludovico a refugee at Innsbruck, Milan in possession of the French, and Trivulzio governor of the duchy.

The return of Ludovico in February, 1500, with aid furnished by the Emperor, resulted in the recapture of the city of Milan; but Cardinal d'Amboise came to Italy as plenipotentiary, and in April Ludovico was taken prisoner and sent to languish in the Castle of Lys St. Georges in the heart of France. There, attended by a single family servant, he was to await his end. His brother, Cardinal Ascanio, soon shared his captivity, though afterward released, and thus was accomplished the ruin of the family of Sforza, together with the conquest of Milan.

Bellinzona soon afterward fell into the hands of the Swiss as their share of the spoil in the conquest of Milan, and still forms a part of the Swiss canton of Ticino.[1] But this was

---

[1] The acquisition of Bellinzona by the Swiss was long believed to have been the reward paid them by Louis XII, according to treaty,

226   A HISTORY OF DIPLOMACY

Chap. III
A. D.
1492–1502

not the only gain of the allies of Louis XII. In September, 1499, Maximilian had been forced to dispense the cantons from all taxes and contributions to the Empire and from the jurisdiction of the Imperial Chamber, thus substantially, though not formally, recognizing their virtual independence. The accession of Basel, Schaffhausen, and Appenzell soon increased the strength of the Confederation, which had already become an autonomous political community.

The isolation of the Emperor

But these were not the only blows inflicted upon Maximilian. At the Imperial Diet of 1500, the Emperor complained that the King of France, not content with his conquests in Italy, was raising opposition to him in Hungary and Poland, and making efforts to secure the imperial crown.

The charge was not without foundation. Having already secured an *entente* with the Scandinavian kingdoms, Louis XII was now negotiating for closer alliances in the East, with the purpose of literally surrounding the Empire with a circle of confederates.

On July 14, 1500, a treaty was signed with Ladislas VI, King of Bohemia and Hungary, and with John Albert, King of Poland, in which the three signatories pledged their united strength against their common enemies; thus setting bounds to the expansion of Germany on the East as well as on the West.[1]

Europe was soon excited by the report that the King of France was to place himself at the head of a great movement for the expulsion of the Turks, and an expedition was actually organized. Twelve ships and four royal galleys

---

for their alliance against Ludovico Sforza. De Maulde has, however, undertaken to show: (1) that the Swiss pretensions to Bellinzona were anterior to 1500; (2) that the occupation in 1500 was effected by the force of the Swiss, and not the generosity of Louis XII; and (3) that Louis XII regarded that occupation with regret, and would, if possible, have been pleased to prevent it. See De Maulde, *La conquête du canton du Tessin par les Suisses*, Turin, 1890.

[1] See Dumont, III, Part II, pp. 442 et seq.

proceeded to the East, to act in concert with Pierre d'Aubusson, Grand Master of the Knights of Malta; but, through the delays of the Grand Master, an attack on the stronghold of the island of Mitylene was repulsed, and the fleet was forced to return to France. It was a futile attempt of the French king to revive the spirit of the crusades and outbid the Emperor as a champion of Christendom against the Infidel.

The conquest of Milan was for the Borgia family a triumph almost equal to that of the King of France, for it prepared the way for the realization of those political aspirations on behalf of Cesare which formed the nucleus of the Pope's diplomacy.

That the idea of Cesare's elevation to the Holy See had at one time been seriously entertained seems more than probable.[1] The obstacles to this ambition were, however, so numerous and formidable that the project of an hereditary kingdom to be created for him out of the papal domain was finally substituted for it. This scheme may have been at first suggested by the plan for the Kingdom of Adria,[2] for which the necessary territory was to be found in the fiefs of the Papal State, held in great part by half independent vassals of the Papacy. This bold conception was, doubtless, intended to supersede altogether the temporal sovereignty of the Pope, leaving to the Supreme Pontiff only his purely spiritual functions.

It is in the light of this project that we can best comprehend the fascination that Cesare Borgia exercised upon Machiavelli, who saw in him the ideal agent for the destruction of the temporal power of the Papacy and the unification of Italy under a single secular ruler.

The capture of Milan by Louis XII furnished an exceptionally auspicious occasion for the execution of this plan. The nephew of the Pope, Giovanni Borgia, was promptly named as legate for Northern Italy, under the pretext of

---

[1] See Burckhardt, *Geschichte der Renaissance*, pp. 142, 143.
[2] See page 86.

placing all the ecclesiastical terrors at the disposition of the King of France. While Cesare began in person the conquest of Romagna with an army of eight thousand soldiers, including many Swiss furnished by Louis XII, his sister Lucrezia, who had lately married her second husband in the person of Don Alfonso of Bisceglia, — a natural son of King Alfonso II of Naples, — was made regent of Spoleto and put in possession of the estates of the Gaetani, whose chief had been murdered in the Castle of St. Angelo.[1]

Soon Imola, and after a cruel siege Forli, fell into the hands of Cesare. The heart of Alexander VI was overwhelmed with joy, and in the reception he gave to the conqueror in the Vatican "he wept and laughed in the same instant."[2] With great pomp, in St. Peter's Church he bestowed upon Cesare the "Golden Rose" and named him Gonfaloniere of the Church, while Rome shuddered to behold such honors conferred upon this "virtuoso in crime," already known as a ruthless murderer.

Pesaro, Rimini, Faenza, Cesena, and Fano were rapidly brought under Cesare's power. Bologna and Florence were to be the next objects of his ambition, but at this point Louis XII intervened to protect them from subjugation.

---

[1] The much maligned character of Lucrezia Borgia has been more generously appreciated by Roscoe, *Life of Leo X*, I; and Gregorovius, *Lucrezia Borgia*, Stuttgart, 1874. The cruel murder of Alfonso of Bisceglia, to whom Lucrezia was tenderly attached, is thus described by Polo Capello: "He was nursed by his wife and sister, who was married to the Prince of Squillaci, another son of the Pope; they remained with him and prepared his food in a small vessel with their own hands for fear of poisoning, because of the hatred felt toward him by the Duke of Valentinois, the Pope causing him to be guarded lest the Duke should kill him; and when the Pope went to visit the sick man, the Duke did not accompany him, once only excepted, and then he said: 'What has not been done at dinner shall be done at supper.' Accordingly, — it was on August 17, — he entered the room, the patient having already risen, and made the wife and sister go out; then Michiele came in, as if called, and strangled the said youth."

[2] Sanuto, *Diarii*, III, 105.

The time had now come, therefore, to check the power of France in Italy, whose utility to Borgia had already reached its climax. In October, 1500, Alexander VI, while still nominally adhering to the Franco-Venetian alliance, resumed his diplomatic relations with the great powers of Europe, sending Cardinal Alessandrino to the Emperor, Santa Croce to England, Santa Pressede to Hungary, and a Spanish cardinal to Spain.

While yet in formal alliance with Louis XII, whose favor was still necessary to the plans of Cesare, Alexander VI thenceforth devoted his energies to preventing the further progress of the French in Italy.

The first fruit of this policy was not long delayed. On November 11, 1500, in the secret Treaty of Grenada, Louis XII and Ferdinand the Catholic agreed to conquer and divide the Kingdom of Naples.[1]

For this partition there was no sufficient reason, and the transaction can be explained only by the intrigues of Alexander VI, who on June 25, 1501, issued a bull by which he deposed Frederick and gave the kingdom to the kings of France and Aragon. But the Treaty of Grenada was, in truth, a compromise which revealed the hollowness of all the empty pretensions regarding the Kingdom of Naples. Louis XII was ready to trade the Angevin claims for a portion of the spoil; Ferdinand the Catholic, after having repeatedly recognized and supported the ruling branch of the House of Aragon at Naples, was eager to possess himself of the kingdom on the ground that the reigning dynasty was of illegitimate origin; and Alexander VI was prepared, for reasons of his own, to sacrifice a vassal more worthy than most of his predecessors of the Pope's protection. Thus the conspiracy to despoil a peaceful monarch was easily concluded, and the principle of "partition" became thenceforth a favorite device of dynastic aggrandizement in Europe.

But, if from the point of view of morals the Treaty of

---

[1] Dumont, III, Part II, pp. 441 et seq.

Grenada was a crime, from that of diplomacy it was for France a humiliating blunder. While in June, 1501, a French Army took possession of Naples, a superior Spanish force under Gonsalvo de Cordova, known as the "Great Captain," landed in Apulia. King Frederick, astonished at the perfidy of Ferdinand and Alexander VI, upon whom he had relied for support against the French, indignantly renounced the crown and sought the protection of the King of France, by whom he was received as a prisoner of state and kindly treated.

Mediatorial policy of Cardinal d'Amboise

Alexander VI was now in possession of means for checking the progress of the French in Italy, and the victory at Milan was soon balanced by defeat at Naples. The attempt to execute the treaty of partition revealed the inherent incompatibility of the French and Spanish pretensions. The two armies fell upon each other, the French were overpowered, and for nearly four years France and Spain were engaged in a bitter contest over the division of their spoils.

The position of Louis XII, which at the beginning of the year 1500, seemed so promising, was now suddenly seen to be full of dangers. Milan, being a fief of the Empire, was certain in due time to be claimed by Maximilian, as Naples was already claimed by Ferdinand the Catholic. These rulers, uniting with the Pope, would be able to drive the French from Italy, as the League of Venice had expelled them under Charles VIII.

In these circumstances, the true policy for Louis XII was to unite with Venice to hold all three of his rivals, — the Emperor, the Pope, and Ferdinand the Catholic, — effectively in check. But from this moment forward it was the personal ambition of Cardinal d'Amboise for succession to the Papacy, not the dynastic interests of Louis XII, which controlled the devices of French diplomacy.

Throughout his entire career, the Archduke Philip of Burgundy had been pacifically inclined toward Louis XII. For this there was a substantial reason, since France intervened between the two realms which he hoped at some future day to unite in his own person, — Castile, the heritage of his wife, Juana, daughter of Ferdinand and Isabella, and the Austrian possessions of his father, Maximilian, whom he expected to succeed as " King of the Romans."

In expectation of personally filling the papal office, Cardinal d'Amboise was interested in a policy of conciliation which would place him at the centre of a great international combination. Without absolute treason to the King of France, therefore, all his powerful influence was thrown in the direction of a general peace in which the great peacemaker would stand forth as the virtual head of Christendom and the logical candidate for the Papacy.

Accordingly, on August 10, 1501, at Lyons, was signed with the Archduke Philip a treaty by which Louis XII promised in marriage his only child, Claude, then two years old, to Charles, the infant son of Philip and Juana, thus uniting by a family alliance the future destinies of France, Spain, and the Empire.[1] By the negotiation of supplementary treaties with Maximilian and Ferdinand the Catholic, it was expected by Louis XII that the imperial investiture of Milan might be obtained on the one hand, and the possession of Naples settled on the other.

On October 3, 1501, therefore, Cardinal d'Amboise, accom-

---

[1] See Le Glay, I, pp. 28, 34, for the treaty. Had this arrangement become effective, the Archduke Charles, later known as the Emperor Charles V, might, perhaps, have united France to the House of Hapsburg. The sources and extent of his inheritance are shown by the following table:

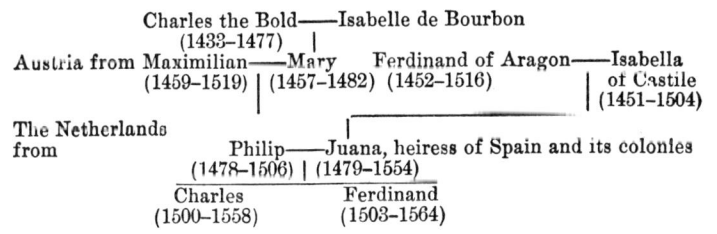

```
          Charles the Bold——Isabelle de Bourbon
               (1433-1477)   |
Austria from Maximilian——Mary    Ferdinand of Aragon——Isabella
          (1459-1519) | (1457-1482)  (1452-1516)    |  of Castile
                                                    |  (1451-1504)
The Netherlands              |
from              Philip——Juana, heiress of Spain and its colonies
          (1478-1506) | (1479-1554)
                Charles         Ferdinand
               (1500-1558)     (1503-1564)
```

The dates in the table indicate the birth and death of the persons named above them.

CHAP. III
A. D.
1492-1502

The loss of French prestige

panied by a royal train, arrived at Trent, in the Tyrol, to seek the investiture of Milan at the hands of Maximilian. On the thirteenth of that month, a treaty was signed by which the marriage was confirmed, the investiture of Milan promised, and Louis XII agreed to sustain Maximilian's pretensions to the crowns of Hungary and Bohemia.[1] On December 13, in his oath of ratification of this treaty, Louis XII solemnly renounced all claims to the imperial title.[2]

With this event began the splendid dream of a United Europe in which the houses of Hapsburg and Valois should combine in one great confederacy under their joint rule nearly the whole of Christendom, thus constituting an empire greater than had ever before existed. The infant Charles, by adding France to the Hapsburg heritage in Germany, the Netherlands, Spain, and Italy, might thus become the fulfilment of his great-grandfather's prediction that Austria was destined to rule the world.[3]

Returning from a visit to Spain with full powers from Ferdinand and Isabella, the Archduke Philip next signed a treaty with Louis XII, at Lyons, on April 5, 1502, in which it was stipulated that each of the two contestants should renounce in the interest of their children, Charles of Burgundy and Claude of France, — whose marriage was again confirmed, — all their conquests in the Kingdom of Naples.[4]

Thus, at last, a general peace appeared to have been concluded; but when Gonsalvo de Cordova was informed of this compact, professing to have no orders for its execution from Ferdinand the Catholic, and having received, on the

---

[1] See Dumont, IV, Part I, p. 16.

[2] The words were: "Que nous n'entreprendrons jamais pour occasion que puissons avoir ou ymaginer d'estre empereur."

[3] Frederick III, who was fond of devising heraldic titles and inscriptions, had chosen as the device of the House of Austria the vowels, A. E. I. O. U.; in German, *Alles erdreich ist Oesterreich unterthan;* in Latin, *Austriae est imperare orbi universo.*

[4] See Dumont, IV, Part I, p. 27.

contrary, as is believed, secret instructions to disregard the treaty,[1] he continued his operations in the field against the French.

While the Duke of Valentinois was rendering himself master of Romagna, and Louis XII was preparing the fatal Treaty of Grenada, Niccolò Machiavelli, who had been sent by Florence as an envoy to France, did not hesitate to point out the errors of statecraft by which Louis XII was accomplishing his own ruin in Italy. In reply to a remark of Cardinal d'Amboise at Nantes, that the Italians knew nothing of the art of war, Machiavelli bluntly informed him that the French knew nothing of diplomacy; and in his book on "The Prince" he has given us the reasons for this observation.[2]

After having conquered Lombardy and regained for France the reputation that Charles VIII had lost in Italy, every circumstance was in favor of Louis XII. Genoa had submitted to him, Florence had become his ally, and all the small princes and republics had sought his protection. In order to maintain his ascendency he had only to protect his numerous friends; who, weak and trembling, threatened on the one hand by the Papacy and on the other by Venice, were obliged in their own interest to remain faithful to him. But hardly had he arrived at Milan, when he began to aid Alexander VI and Cesare in the conquest of Romagna, thus committing the double error of destroying his own friends and strengthening the papal power to be used against himself. When, having too tardily perceived the dangers resulting from Cesare's conquests, the King of France offered his protection to the Tuscan cities, he thereby only aroused the opposition of the Pope, who was then disposed to drive him out of Italy. Nor was this all. Not content with aggrandizing the Borgias and depriving himself of friends, burning to possess the Kingdom of Naples, he fell into the trap of

---

[1] See Le Glay, I, p. LVIII.
[2] *Il principe*, cap. IV.

Chap. III
A. D.
1492-1502

dividing it with the King of Spain, in such a manner that, instead of remaining the sole arbiter of Italy, he had himself introduced a rival to whom all the ambitious and the malcontent could rally; and when he could have left upon the throne a king that would have been happy to be tributary to France, he had overthrown him in order to share his kingdom with a prince who was able to make himself the master of all Southern Italy. With inexorable logic the Florentine diplomatist exposes the imbecility of Louis' procedure. If, then, he says, the King of France had the force to attack the Kingdom of Naples, he should have done so; if he had not, it was folly to divide it with a stronger monarch.

The partition of Lombardy with Venice, Machiavelli continues, was excusable, because it provided France with the means of obtaining a foothold in Italy; but the partition of the Kingdom of Naples, being in no respect necessary, was without excuse. Thus, Louis XII committed five mistakes in Italy: (1) he ruined the weak who were ready to be his friends; (2) he increased the power of one already too powerful; (3) he introduced there a powerful rival; (4) he did not make Italy his residence; and (5) he did not colonize it with his own people.

These five mistakes, remarks Machiavelli, would not have been ruinous, if he had not also committed a sixth, namely, that of afterward trying to despoil Venice, his ally. If he wished to enfeeble the Venetians, he should not have aggrandized the Borgia or called Spain into Italy; but having done both, his true policy was to unite with Venice to maintain their mutual interests against the Pope and Ferdinand the Catholic.

But even this keen analysis of the faulty diplomacy of Louis XII does not exhaust the catalogue of his political errors. Machiavelli calls attention to the promises made by Louis XII to Alexander VI for the purpose of dissolving his marriage and securing the cardinal's hat for Georges d'Amboise, which he thinks might properly have been broken; but he does not point out how the policy of France was continually paralyzed by the intrigues of that prelate to procure his own election to the Holy See. With eleven Spanish votes in the Sacred College, Cardinal d'Amboise, — then the virtual ruler of France and the first of those great cardinal-ministers whose influence was to determine the destinies of Europe, — found it difficult to carry on a war with Spain. Thus, the Kingdom of Naples was again lost to France, and another great power was drawn into the conflict for predominance in Italy.

AUTHORITIES

Of the printed collections already cited, Dumont, *Corps universel diplomatique;* Desjardins and Canestrini, *Négociations de la France avec la Toscane;* Léonard, *Traitez;* Trinchera, *Codico Aragonese;* and Chmel, *Briefe und Aktenstücke,* are the most important.

For the Italian expedition of Charles VIII, Philippe de Commines, *Mémoires,* is an indispensable contemporary authority. To this may be added *Divers traitez, contracts, testamens, et autres actes, et observations, servans de preuves et illustration aux Mémoires de Philippe de Commines,* The Hague, 1682; also an earlier edition, Paris, 1614. Mandrot's edition of the *Mémoires* contains valuable critical notes. The military details are to be found in Pilorgerie, *Campagne et bulletins de la grande armée d'Italie commandée par Charles VIII, 1494–1495,* Nantes, 1866. Many original documents are published in Molini, *Documenti di storia italiana,* Florence, 1836. Marino Sanuto, *La spedizione di Carlo VIII in Italia,* Venice, 1883, is a practically contemporary account.

The state of Italy, the condition of the Papacy, and many interesting facts are given in the *Diarium* of Burchard, papal master of ceremonies, 1483–1506, Paris, 1883–1885, and other editions. Many curious incidents are reported by Infessura, *Diario della città di Roma,* in Muratori, Scriptores, III, and in Tommasini's edition, Rome, 1890; but his diatribes against the Papacy must be taken with allowance.

For the reign of Louis XII, the most important documents may be found in Le Glay, *Négociations diplomatiques entre la France et l'Autriche durant les trente premières années du XVIe siècle,* Paris, 1845, which covers nearly the whole period of the present chapter, and contains biographies of the leading French and Austrian diplomatists of the time. De Maulde, *Procédures politiques du règne de Louis XII,* Paris, 1885; and Baudier, *Lettres de Louis XII et du cardinal d'Amboise,*

Brussels, 1712, contain additional sources. For the period 1499-1513, Pélissier, *Documents pour l'histoire de la domination française dans le Milanais*, Toulouse, 1891, is exceedingly valuable, and the same author's *Louis XII et Ludovic Sforza*, Paris, 1896, contains the most important results of researches in the Italian archives. The last named is so perfect an abstract of all the documents, — which he has published separately, — as to render reference to them unnecessary for the period April 8, 1498, to July 23, 1500.

From their beginning, January 1, 1496, to their end, June 30, 1533, the *Diarii* of Marino Sanuto, published at Venice, 1879-1902, in fifty-eight quarto volumes, furnish a rich mine of facts and documents regarding the diplomacy of Europe, standing without an equal in any period as the result of one man's labors.

On the general character of the *renaissance* period, see Gebhart, *Origines de la Renaissance en Italie*, Paris, 1879; and Burckhardt, *Geschichte der Renaissance in Italien*, Stuttgart, 1867, also in French and English translations.

For the history of the Papacy in this period, Gregorovius VII, Pastor V, and Creighton III, as already cited, present different points of view, but in the main agree as regards the personal characters of Sixtus IV, Innocent VIII, and Alexander VI.

The older lives of Charles VIII have been entirely superseded by Cherrier, *Histoire de Charles VIII, roi de France*, Paris, 1868; and Delaborde, *L'expédition de Charles VIII en Italie*, Paris, 1888, both of which are based on a careful study of documents. See, however, Chotard, *Charles VIII et l'expédition d'Italie*, Paris, 1865, based on the letters of the King and his secretary, Robertet. Here may be mentioned also Schneider, *Die kirchliche und politische Wirksamkeit des Legaten Raimund Peraudi*, Halle, 1882.

For the partition of the new world between Spain and Portugal, see Harrisse, *The Diplomatic History of America: its First Chapter*, London, 1897.

Maximilian I is studied from original documents in Ulmann, *Kaiser Maximilian I*, Stuttgart, 1884-1891.

For the diplomacy of Louis XII, no adequate work exists. De Maulde, *La diplomatie*, Paris, 1892, has many useful details. His *Histoire de Louis XII*, Paris, 1892, is incomplete; and the earlier lives and histories are insufficient. Pélissier, already cited, is admirable for the period covered.

For Cardinal d'Amboise, Legendre, *Vie du cardinal d'Amboise*, Rouen, 1726, contains some documents, but requires to be supplemented.

Other important biographies for this chapter and the next are Leonetti, *Papa Alessandro VI secondo documenti e carteggi del tempo*,

Bologna, 1880; Alvisi, *Cesare Borgia, duca di Romagna*, Imola, 1878; Yriarte, *César Borgia, sa vie, sa captivité, sa mort*, Paris, 1889; Gregorovius, *Lucrezia Borgia nach Urkunden und Correspondenzen ihrer eigenen Zeit*, Stuttgart, 1874; Villari, *Life and Times of Girolamo Savonarola*, London, 1860.

On the alliance of Alexander VI and Louis XII, see also Pélissier, *Sopra alcuni documenti relativi all' alleanza tra Alessandro VI e Luigi XII* (1498–1499), Rome, 1895.

The results of the participation of the Swiss in the campaign against Milan are discussed by De Maulde, *La conquête du canton du Tessin par les Suisses* (1500–1503), Turin, 1890.

For the part played by Savoy in the Milanese campaign, see Carutti, *Storia della diplomazia della corte di Savoia, 1494–1663*, Turin, 1876; and Pélissier, *Le traité d'alliance de Louis XII et de Philibert de Savoie*, Montpellier, 1893.

CHAPTER IV

THE STRUGGLE FOR SUPREMACY IN ITALY

The destruction of Italian equilibrium

THE French invasions had brought upon Italy a double foreign occupation that now converted the peninsula into the battlefield of Europe. While France and Spain were respectively in possession of Milan and Naples, the Emperor held fiefs in Italy, and by virtue of his feudal rights still laid claim to the duchy which the French had conquered.

Three great powers, therefore, were now to dispute with one another over their Italian spoils. In the midst of this triangular controversy, the Papacy, morally so enfeebled as to exercise little authority except through its alliance with one or another of the contestants, in the hands of Alexander VI had become a mere instrument for advancing the private interests of Cesare Borgia.

The system of equilibrium, which for nearly two centuries had preserved Italy from the ravages of the foreigner and given a semblance of solidarity to its interests, was now entirely broken down. Venice, — whose maritime supremacy was already threatened by the transfer of commerce to the Spaniards and the Portuguese, and the opening of new trade routes on the Atlantic, — was the only independent Italian power still remaining; for Florence was internally divided and dependent for its safety on French protection.

In these circumstances, Cesare Borgia, sustained by the influence of the Pope and supplied with resources from the treasures of the Church, as Duke of Romagna was able by his double relations with the French and Spaniards to make rapid progress in the conquest of Central Italy. The destiny of the peninsula was, therefore, in great measure dependent upon the action of the Holy See. Once more Rome had become the centre of European interest, and the Pope a leading actor in the diplomatic drama.

I. Negotiations of the Great Powers regarding Italy

The keynote of the papal policy regarding foreigners in Italy was sounded by Alexander VI in a conversation held in November, 1502, with Antonio Giustinian, the Venetian ambassador at Rome, when he declared that the only safety of Italy had thus far lain in the "jealousy of Spain and France." Having pointed out the manner in which the ambitions of France had been checked by the intervention of Spain, with deep emotion he pleaded with the ambassador for the support of the Republic, saying, "For the love of God, let us lay aside our differences; let us have an understanding, and provide for the safety of Italy."[1]

The policy of the Pope was now by an alliance with Venice and Florence, which had sent Niccolò Machiavelli, then Secretary of the Council of Ten, to the camp of Cesare for the negotiation of an *entente*, to prepare the way for expelling both the French and the Spanish from Italy. But the accomplishment of this design required both time and the reinforcement of the Borgia power. Machiavelli has left us the record of the cool calculation and merciless cruelty with which the Duke of Romagna was establishing his tyranny, — qualities which so deeply impressed him as an observer and theorist that he afterward made them the basis of his celebrated political system. "This lord never reveals anything except when doing it," writes the Florentine envoy. "This morning Messer Rimino," — Cesare's trusted instrument in Romagna, — "has been found cut into two pieces, on the Piazza, where he still lies. . . . The cause of his death is not well known, excepting that such was the pleasure of

---

[1] Giustinian, *Dispacci*, I, pp. 242, 243.

the prince, who thus shows us that he can make and unmake men according to their deserts."[1]

But the cruelty of the Duke had excited a wide-spread conspiracy against him, and the chief nobles had resolved to end his career. Knowing of the plot, Cesare entrapped them with messages of courtesy at Sinigaglia, where, on December 31, 1502, they accompanied him to the house in which his counterplot was to be revealed. At the given signal, Paolo Orsini, Oliverotto Fermo, Vitellozzo Vitelli, and the rest were seized and strangled, and at the same moment their soldiers were overwhelmed by his troops. Before midnight the bloody work was over. In his despatch of January 1, 1503, Machiavelli describes to the Council of Ten his interview with the Duke, "who with the brightest face in the world expressed his satisfaction at this triumph, adding wise words and expressions of exceeding affection toward our Florence. He said that this was the service which he had promised to render you at the fitting moment. And as he had declared that he would offer you his friendship all the more pressingly the surer he was of himself, so now he kept that promise; then he expounded all the reasons inducing him to desire this friendship in words that excited my admiration."

On the same day the news of the massacre was received at the Vatican. After mass, the Holy Father summoned the ambassadors and announced the news, affecting to be surprised by it, although he had known what was intended weeks before the event;[2] adding that "the Duke never

---

[1] Machiavelli's letter of December 6, 1502, *Opere*, IV. In chapter seven of the "Prince," Machiavelli explains that, having subdued the population by the ferocious cruelty of this man, "in order to persuade men that the severities inflicted had in no way proceeded from himself, but solely from the wicked nature of his minister, he caused the latter to be found one morning hacked in two pieces with a bloody knife beside him." See also Giustinian, *Dispacci*, I, p. 293.

[2] Giustinian had written from Rome on November 24, that the first blow would be struck at Sinigaglia; that the Pope was busy collecting money for Cesare, — who spent about one thousand ducats a day besides what he got by plunder; — and that Alexander was so

forgives his enemies." The cardinals present offered their congratulations, then "retired, shrugging their shoulders and wondering what would happen next."[1]

They had not long to wait. On January 3, the Pope summoned Cardinal Orsini to the Vatican, when he was at once arrested and sent to the Castle of St. Angelo, where he soon afterward died from poisoning. His property was immediately appropriated. Other arrests and deaths, — followed by confiscation, — succeeded one another; and so completely effective was the system of terror at Rome that the Apostolic Secretary, the Bishop of Chiusi, is said to have died from fright.[2]

To carry on the operations of Cesare, large sums of money were necessary. On March 29, the Venetian ambassador reports the creation of eighty new offices in the Curia, which were sold for seven hundred and sixty ducats each.[3] On May 31, he notes the nomination of nine new cardinals, — one German, three Italians, and five Spaniards, — at twenty thousand ducats for each promotion.[4]

The excessive number of Spaniards and the absence of Frenchmen in the list of promotions indicates the intention of the Pope to attach his fortunes to Spain and to abandon France, until the moment should arrive to expel both nations from Italy. Among those who coveted the honors thus placed in the market, Troches, or Troccio, "one of the Borgia's most trusted assassins,"[5] having been refused a red hat, is said to have fled from Rome on being told by the Pope that Cesare had made the list, and that the Duke would know what to do if he complained. Having resolved to inform the King of France of the Pope's secret intrigues with Spain,

---

impatient for the progress of events that he cursed Cesare in Spanish for delaying at Cesena.

[1] Giustinian, I, p. 298.
[2] Gregorovius, VII, p. 475.
[3] Giustinian, I, p. 453.
[4] Giustinian, II, p. 30.
[5] Villari, *Life and Times of Niccolò Machiavelli*.

Troches took ship for Corsica. Captured and brought back to Rome, the poor wretch was confined in a tower in Trastevere, where Cesare, after a conversation with him, from a secret post of observation witnessed his death at the hands of another professional assassin, Don Micheletto. The murdered man's property was then distributed according to the orders of the Pope.

Although Alexander VI was negotiating with Spain to complete the discomfiture of the French in Italy, he at the same time proposed to the King of France, with whom he was still in formal alliance, that he would aid him with money to drive the Spaniards from the Kingdom of Naples, provided Louis XII would give that kingdom, or Sicily, to the Duke of Valentinois, and indemnify himself by further conquests in Northern Italy.[1]

While thus negotiating with both invaders, the Pope was still pressing upon Venice an alliance for the expulsion of all foreigners.[2] Not content with this duplicity, he was urging upon the Emperor Maximilian, who at that time was anxious to come to Italy to receive the imperial crown, the investiture of Pisa for Cesare; declaring that, otherwise, he should be compelled to throw himself into the arms of France, now ready, he declared, to give him the Kingdom of Naples in exchange for Romagna![3]

What might have been the ultimate result of this reckless fishing in all waters, had Alexander VI been able to carry out his purposes, must remain unknown. In the midst of these desperate endeavors to found a kingdom for his son at the expense of the Holy See, a call from that other world of which his holy office made him the representative on earth suddenly terminated all his tangled schemes.

His death was at the time attributed to the unguarded taking of poison mixed by his order for another, and the

---

[1] Giustinian, II, pp. 34, 36.
[2] Giustinian, II, p. 24.
[3] Giustinian, II, pp. 34 and 91.

subject is still left in much obscurity. Signor Gar, director of the Archives of Venice, claims to have demonstrated that Alexander VI died from natural causes, and the despatches of Giustinian seem to sustain this view.[1] On August 5, 1503, the Pope, with Cesare and a number of cardinals and ambassadors, took supper in the vineyard of Cardinal Adriano da Corneto in the rear of the Vatican, from which exposure many of the guests were soon stricken with Roman fever. On the eighteenth, at the vesper hour, death came upon Alexander VI in the presence of the Bishop of Carinola, the datary, and a few serving men.[2]

Cesare was also ill, and unable to come to his father's bedside; but his armed men were sent to seek the Pope's treasures, of which gold and jewels to the value of about three hundred thousand ducats, were secured by threatening the chamberlain with instant death if he did not surrender the Pope's keys. When the pillage was over, the doors were thrown open, and the death was publicly announced.[3]

The eyes of all Europe were now anxiously turned upon Rome and the action of the Sacred College. Louis XII wished to sustain the ambition of Cardinal d'Amboise, Fer-

---

[1] For Signor Gar's article, see the Archivio Veneto, I, p. 1 et seq., 1871. The manner of Alexander's death has given rise to much controversy. See Lamansky, *Secrets d'état de Venise*, pp. 315, 357; Ranke, *History of the Popes*, III, pp. 8, 11; and Villari, *Life and Times of Niccolò Machiavelli*, I, pp. 325, 328.

[2] Giustinian, II, pp. 107, 120.

[3] In his work on "The Prince," Machiavelli has devoted a large part of the seventh chapter to an analysis of Cesare's plans. Fearing the opposition of a future pope after Alexander's death, he had resolved: (1) to destroy completely the race of lords he had dispossessed, so that a new pope could not restore them; (2) to win over the gentry of Rome, in order to control the next pope by means of their power; (3) to attach to himself as far as possible the Sacred College; (4) to render himself sufficiently powerful to resist the first shock. "At the moment of Alexander's death," says Machiavelli, "three of those things had been accomplished, and the fourth he regarded as nearly so. . . . If his health had not failed at the moment of Alexander's death, all would have been easy for him." The whole of the seventh chapter should be read in this connection.

dinand the Catholic the candidacy of a Spaniard, Cesare Borgia the accession of the most pliant instrument of his will. So precipitate was the haste of the cardinals to elect a successor to Alexander VI that one of them, the Cardinal d'Este, broke his leg on his journey.

The illness of Cesare Borgia rendered it possible for the cardinals, in conjunction with the ambassadors of the different powers, to take the initiative; and the Duke, with enforced humility, in exchange for the concession that he should continue Gonfaloniere of the Church, consented to withdraw from Rome during the election. As a guarantee that his interests would not suffer, however, on September 1 he concluded a compact with the representatives of Louis XII by which the possessions he had already acquired in Italy were secured to him.[1] On the nineteenth, the Florentine envoy, Nasi, wrote from Macon, "His Majesty has received letters from Rome, from Cardinal d'Amboise, which inform him that Valentinois is at Nepi, and that the Duke has assured him of his order to the Spanish cardinals to name His Most Reverend Lordship as pope; avowing that, if these cardinals do not keep their promise, he would cause them all to be cut in pieces, as he had caused so many others!"[2]

The unexampled credulity of Cardinal d'Amboise, who not only believed that Italy would, in the circumstances, accept a French pope, but that the Spanish cardinals, and even Ascanio Sforza, — now restored at Rome, — would cast their votes for him, was soon to receive a rude shock. When the trial vote was taken, on September 21, it became evident that Cardinal d'Amboise could muster only thirteen votes; while Giuliano della Rovere had fifteen; twenty-four being necessary to an election.[3] When told that the

---

[1] Giustinian, II, pp. 462, 463.
[2] Petruccelli della Gattina, *Histoire diplomatique des Conclaves*, I, p. 449.
[3] Sanuto, *Diarii*, V, 93, 94.

THE STRUGGLE FOR SUPREMACY IN ITALY   245

Spaniards and Italians did not wish a French pope, Cardinal d'Amboise said to the Venetian ambassador, " Our generals are informed of the matter; they will not permit that such an insult be offered to their King."[1]

But the Cardinal's menace was only a momentary outburst of indignation. The complaisance toward Spain which had prompted the fatal Treaty of Grenada was still to control the policy of Louis XII's prime minister, in the hope of finally securing the Papacy by the aid of Spanish votes.[2]

Seeing that his election was at that time impossible, on September 22, in order to gain time for improving his chances, Cardinal d'Amboise proposed to the conclave the name of a nephew of Pius II, Francesco Piccolomini, an aged prelate then confined to his bed with illness, having lately endured a surgical operation. No one of the other contestants being able to succeed, Piccolomini, known as the Cardinal of Siena, was unanimously elected; and, in honor of his uncle, took the name of Pius III.

In less than a month after his election, this devout and benevolent successor of Alexander VI quietly passed away. It was not, however, Georges d'Amboise who was to gather the fruit of his scheme of postponement. Even before the meeting of the conclave, the election of Giuliano della Rovere was assured. Either a French or a Spanish pope being out of the question, Cardinal della Rovere, a Genoese by birth, while appealing to the Italians to rally to the defence of Italy, had won the French as the most likely from his past affiliations to be favorable to France, Cesare Borgia by the

---

[1] Giustinian, II, p. 195.

[2] Having abandoned for the time the idea of becoming emperor, the rôle of Louis XII at this period was that of " *Roi Très-Chrétien.*" " Dans une lettre adressée à la commune de Bologne," says De Maulde, " il parle comme ' protecteur de l'église ' ; il couvre de cette même idée sa campagne en faveur de César Borgia. La fiction se poursuit assez bien jusqu' à la mort d'Alexandre VI. Louis XII veut alors la consacrer (et il pensait, d'ailleurs, agir dans l'intérêt de l'église) en faisant élire à la papauté le cardinal d'Amboise." *La diplomatie*, I, p. 64.

CHAP. IV
A.D.
1502-1518

promise that he should continue as Gonfaloniere and lodge in the Vatican,[1] and the Spaniards through Cesare's influence, supplemented by various gifts and concessions to individuals. Perceiving how the tide was turning, even Cardinal d'Amboise helped to make the vote for Cardinal della Rovere unanimous; and, on October 31, 1503, that prelate was chosen pope under the name of Julius II. Two days afterward, the Duke of Valentinois took up his residence in the Vatican, where he continued to reside, but "with little reputation."[2]

Two qualities had enabled Cardinal della Rovere to triumph over his rivals, his recognized ability as a leader and the confidence men had in his word. "Della Rovere has all the vices, except lying!" Alexander VI had once said of the Cardinal. To dissemble was not beyond his powers; but to his word, once pledged, he was accounted loyal. In the midst of the deceptions to which Italy had become accustomed, veracity was a virtue so exceptional that it went far toward securing his success.

The conception that Julius II entertained of the pontifical office was in diametrical contrast with that of Alexander VI. Hating Alexander for his nepotism and his greed, Julius II resolved to turn all his energies toward the aggrandizement and glorification of the Church. No pontiff had ever lifted the Papacy to such a height of visible magnificence. Patron of the new forces furnished by the Revival of Learning, he aimed to render them all subordinate to the princely dignity of the papal office. Art, letters, statecraft, diplomacy,—all were to be loyally employed to reconstitute, expand, and ornament the temporal power of the Holy See.

Invasion of Romagna by Venice

The direction in which the energies of Julius II were to be exercised was soon made evident. On November 5, the revolt of Imola against the Duke of Valentinois and the ad-

---

[1] Machiavelli considers Cesare Borgia's support of Julius II for the Papacy the one mistake in his career.
[2] Sanuto, *Diarii*, V, 291 and 342.

vance of the Venetians into Romagna were known at Rome. The news was soon followed by the report that Faenza had been taken and Rimini annexed to the Republic.

The action of Venice in laying hands on these cities of Romagna had been induced by the fear that, if this step were not taken, a powerful and hostile neighbor would soon menace its political existence. It was not denied that these strongholds of Romagna belonged to the Holy See, and Venice was ready to hold them in strictly feudal relations; but the Republic had determined not to permit them to form a part of a hostile principality, or to continue longer as objects of contention.

The probable attitude of the Papacy toward this summary action was well understood at Venice, and was promptly signified by the Venetian ambassador in his despatch of November 6, in which he counselled prudence; for he well understood that Julius II was engaged in exhuming the papal titles to the whole of Romagna, and would soon resuscitate the rights of the Holy See to all of Cesare's conquests. But, while the Republic understood that a papal protest was to be expected, it had no suspicion of the gravity of its own action, destined to furnish the pivotal point of the diplomacy of Europe for more than a decade. Machiavelli, who had been sent to Rome as the envoy of Florence,[1] possessed a clearer vision; for, in his despatch of November 24 to the Ten, he remarks, with prophetic foresight, that the attack of the Venetians upon Romagna "will either be the gate opening all Italy to them, or prove to be their ruin."

The secret wish of Julius II would have been best realized if the circumstances of the time had permitted him to force all foreigners out of Italy, in order to make the Holy See the predominant power in the peninsula; but the unexpected action of Venice rendered this hope impossible, for it con-

---

[1] The word "envoy" is here used with intention, for Machiavelli never rose to the rank of ambassador. His salary was only ten lire per diem even when on special mission at Rome, where living was extremely dear; for which a special allowance was granted.

CHAP. IV
A. D.
1502-1518

fronted him with a problem that could be solved only by using the great powers against the offender.

At first, the Pope endeavored to induce Venice to desist from its course by professions of friendship, claiming to love Venice "as if he were himself a Venetian." This course having proved unavailing, on November 28, he protested in an assembly of cardinals against the conduct of the Republic. The following day, writes Giustinian, he spoke before the Consistory in violent terms, and threatened to demand the support of France and Spain in asserting the rights of the Holy See. Soon afterward, the offer of Venice to make no further advances in Romagna, and to hold the strongholds taken as fiefs of the Papacy, was rejected, on the ground that the Pope preferred to appoint as governors of those cities persons who had grown up in the service of the Church rather than entrust them to a powerful neighbor.

Of the rights of the Duke of Valentinois there is henceforth no further consideration; for the Pope had determined to reintegrate the territories of the Church without reference to the pretensions of Cesare, now reduced to a secondary rôle, forced to surrender his conquests, and soon to be wholly eliminated from the scene. Deserted by all, after being for months a virtual prisoner of the Pope, he fled to Naples, where, by the Pope's request, he was put under guard, and by order of Ferdinand the Catholic conveyed to Spain. Four years later, after escaping from a hard captivity, he was killed while fighting for his brother-in-law, Jean d'Albret, in Navarre.

The policy of Cardinal d'Amboise

Even more energetic than Julius II in his denunciation of Venice was Cardinal d'Amboise; who, as prime minister of France, might have been expected to find his chief interest in regaining possession of the Kingdom of Naples, for which the alliance of Venice would have been of great value. But his cherished hope of yet succeeding to the Papacy made the minister more concerned for the votes of the cardinals and the interests of Rome than for the pretended rights of the French dynasty, and his diplomacy was entirely controlled by his own ambitions. When Cardinal Grimani offered a plea in behalf of the Venetians as "faithful sons of the Church," it was Cardinal d'Amboise who rose in the Consistory to denounce their usurpation.[1] Nor did Julius II neglect his opportunity to render France useful to his cause. Writing to Louis XII, the Pope referred to his election as the work of Cardinal d'Amboise,[2] whom he not only confirmed as papal legate in France but chose also for the legation of Avignon, while his nephew was at the same time made a cardinal. To those who opposed this advancement of the prime minister, Julius II frankly declared, that "it was necessary to propitiate him at a time when His Holiness had need of the King of France, on account of the conduct of the Venetians."[3]

It is Rome, therefore, which now becomes the mainspring of French diplomacy, rather than the immediate interests of France. Already divested of Naples, Louis XII, who had so hopefully set out upon the conquest of Italy, was now to relinquish all he had acquired, and to use all his influence for preventing the encroachments of Venice upon the cities of Romagna. Cardinal d'Amboise was not only ready to enlist France in this enterprise but to visit the Emperor in person for the purpose of arranging a coalition.[4] On January 11, 1504, the Venetian ambassador writes from Rome: "The Pope awaits with all earnestness the union of the kings of Spain and France, giving them to understand that their mutual discords are aggrandizing the Republic of Venice in such a manner that it will some day drive them from Italy, and become its master. He has tried also to win over the King of the Romans, promising him a part of the money raised in Germany for the war against the Turks."[5]

---

[1] Sanuto, *Diarii*, V, 481.
[2] Sanuto, *Diarii*, V, 349.
[3] From the *relazione* of Costabili, of November 27, 1503, in the Archives of Modena.
[4] Sanuto, *Diarii*, V, 481, 505, 512, 520, 545.
[5] Giustinian, II, pp. 387, 388.

CHAP. IV
A. D.
1502-1518

The diplomacy of Julius II

The disproportion of the means thus set in motion to the end to be attained reveals the deeper purpose of Julius II in forming a union of the three great powers; which was, to limit the pretensions of each by those of the others. To arrest the expansion of Venice by so formidable a coalition was a fine stroke of diplomacy; but to balance the interests of France, Spain, and the Emperor, and thereby place a limit to their progress in Italy was a far more brilliant conception.

With the intention of carrying out this double design, in March, 1504, papal envoys were sent to the three great powers. In Spain, the nuncio, Cosimo de' Pazzi, met a complete rebuff, Ferdinand the Catholic even refusing to receive him. On March 31, a truce for three years between France and Spain was signed,[1] but it proved, as it was no doubt intended to be, altogether illusory for the French so far as an equitable division of Naples was concerned. In the following August, Ferdinand the Catholic, from alleged scruples of conscience, refused to ratify the marriage of Claude of France with the Archduke Charles, with Naples as their inheritance, proposing, on the contrary, to restore it to the Duke of Calabria, son of the former king, Frederick, on condition that he would wed Ferdinand's niece, Juana of Aragon.

Carlo di Carretto, Marquis of Finale, who was sent as papal nuncio to France, to act in unison with Cardinal d'Amboise, was accorded a far different reception. Although the consolidation of the three powers in a great coalition, acting in the interest of the Holy See, was rendered impracticable by the indisposition of Spain to renounce its conquest in Italy, there yet remained the possibility of uniting the forces of France and the Emperor. To this task Cardinal d'Amboise now set his practiced hand. The difficulties were, however, not inconsiderable; for, while the Papacy had everything to gain, and Maximilian would be profited

---

[1] Dumont, IV, Part I, p. 51.

by the recognition of his feudal rights over Milan and the ratification of the marriage of his grandson with Claude of France, it is difficult to see what advantage France was to obtain from a convention in which nothing was to be secured that Louis XII did not already possess.

Inspired by the papal nuncio, Bartolini, — who had been sent for this purpose in the previous March, — on July 10, 1504, the Emperor despatched ambassadors to Louis XII with full powers to settle all disputes and regulate all interests between the two monarchs.[1] On September 22, three treaties were signed at Blois, in which a significant compact was formed between Maximilian, the Archduke Philip, and Louis XII.[2]

In the first, an indissoluble alliance was concluded between the three signatories, who were to be as "*one soul in three bodies*"; investiture with the Duchy of Milan was to be accorded within three months to Louis XII and his male descendants, — who did not exist, — or, in default of these, to Charles as husband of Claude; peace with Ferdinand the Catholic was to be concluded only in accord with Maximilian; Ferdinand was to have the privilege of adhering to the treaty, on condition that Naples be placed in the keeping of Philip until his son Charles was married to Claude; the Italian allies of Louis XII were to receive amnesty and be admitted to the alliance; and, finally, the electors of the Empire were to be conservators of the compact.

In the second treaty, provision was made that, if Louis XII died without male heirs, Brittany, Burgundy, Milan, Genoa, and the counties of Asti and Blois were to be assured to Charles, as the husband of Claude. In case the marriage failed, the Duchy and County of Burgundy, Milan, and Asti were to be ceded to him.

The third treaty, intended to be secret, was a compact be-

---

[1] For the instructions, see Le Glay, I, pp. 61, 72; for details of the negotiations, Höfler *Das diplomatische Journal des Andrea del Burgo*, pp. 9 et seq.

[2] For the treaties, see Dumont, IV, Part II, pp. 55 et seq.

tween the Emperor and the King of France with the Pope, directed against Venice, and may justly be regarded as the first prognostication of the later League of Cambray.

Motives and reception of the treaties of Blois

The motive for engagements so prejudicial to the national interests of France has always remained obscure. The latent hostility of Anne of Brittany to Louise of Savoy, mother of Francis, Count of Angoulême, the heir presumptive to the throne of France, — who had been previously intended for the husband of Claude, — has been usually assigned as a reason for this family alliance with the Hapsburgs, and the proposed alienation of Brittany, along with the Italian possessions; but this explanation is insufficient. It is to be sought, rather, in the purposes of Cardinal d'Amboise, whose aspiration for the Papacy had in other instances deflected the policy of France from its normal course. In a conversation with Philibert Naturelli, one of the imperial ambassadors who negotiated these treaties, Cardinal d'Amboise frankly stated, that the agreement regarding the investiture of Milan was "nothing for the French"; that the French did not wish the marriage of Claude with the Archduke Charles; that numerous French opponents of the entire negotiation were anxious to break it up, particularly the Admiral of France; yet, without referring in any manner to the wishes of the Queen, the Cardinal concluded the interview with the words: "Come what may, I shall bring the matter to a good conclusion, and set great hopes upon the love of the Emperor and the Archduke."[1] In his report of another interview, in which the negotiations came near being broken off, Naturelli says, that the "French cursed," and the "Cardinal was in the greatest embarrassment, and complained even to Heaven."[2] Throughout the entire negotiation, his personal eagerness to conclude the transaction is most evident.

After the signature of the treaties, on September 22, all

---

[1] Höfler, *Das diplomatische Journal*, p. 36.
[2] Höfler, p. 38.

the plenipotentiaries betook themselves to the royal garden, where they found the King, the Cardinal, and the Italian envoys, with many nobles, in the vestibule of the chapel. They were received with great respect and manifestations of pleasure, and mass was said; whereupon the King retired to an anteroom, where the Cardinal held the missal and the Chancellor read the form of the oath, while the King and the assembled plenipotentiaries placed their hands in those of the Cardinal, who, after the oath was taken, turned toward the Italian envoys and others present, and with a serene air said: "Now there are no more difficulties to dispute about, everything is arranged." The King, whose health was much broken, proceeded to the vestibule of the chapel, and there, alone with the Cardinal and the plenipotentiaries, pronounced a discourse, in which, among other things, he said he now had what he desired, namely, this friendship, and asked of the Almighty nothing more than to see the face of his brother, the King of the Romans. He then spoke of the elevation of the Houses of Valois and Hapsburg as if they were no longer rivals.

It is only in relation to the affairs of Italy that this extraordinary performance can be understood; for Italy was at that time, in the words of Ascanio Sforza, "the inner court in the palace of the world."

From the archives of Venice we now know that the indisposition of Ferdinand the Catholic to enter into the combination Julius II had planned and Cardinal d'Amboise had endeavored to realize, was based on his determination to retain possession of the Kingdom of Naples, and that he had already proposed to Venice an alliance to defend his conquest.[1] From the same source is revealed the ineffectual efforts of Cardinal d'Amboise to secure the adhesion of Ferdi-

---

[1] Ciustinian, III, p. 282; and Romanin, *Storia documentata*, V, pp. 170, 171, who cites the passage from the "Secreta" of the Senate of April 22, 1504, to show that the Republic at that time already knew through Don Lorenzo Suarez, the Spanish ambassador, of the machinations against Venice.

nand to the treaties of Blois, by which the papal plans would have been accomplished.

Defeated in this great enterprise, on January 11, 1505, Julius II despatched Francesco Dentici, Bishop of Cariati, upon a special mission to France, to urge upon the King the prompt execution of the Treaty of Blois against Venice; but Maximilian had not yet ratified the treaties, and the negotiations still remained a dead letter.

Despairing of aid from the coalition upon which he had depended, the Pope was now disposed to accept the overtures of Venice made on February 10, to restore a part of the conquests in Romagna, and so to dispense with the intervention of the great powers, whose discords and delays had left him without support. On February 21, the Venetian Ambassador writes from Rome to the Signory, that he has learned from letters of the Marquis of Finale, papal nuncio in France, that His Holiness intends to displace Cardinal d'Amboise as legate. "The Pope," continues the ambassador, "is not willing to have other popes than himself in the world"; and adds, "as the Cardinal sees himself without hope of that legation, he will cease to offer incense to the Pope as he hitherto has done."

Temporary rapprochement of the Pope and Venice

On the same day with the previous announcement, the Venetians are assured that the Pope is well disposed toward the proposals of the Republic, in which the Signory had said, "We are content and freely promise to deliver to His Holiness the places taken by us from Valentinois, except Rimini and Faenza, with the territories belonging to them."[1] On March 6, this assurance takes the form of an open invitation by the Pope to restore friendship, in which Julius II calls the Venetians "good and well beloved sons of the Apostolic See,"[2] declares his constant neutrality between the Spaniards and the French, and asserts that he has not wished the Italians to be either French or Spanish.[3]

---

[1] Giustinian, III, p. 429.
[2] Romanin, V, p. 176.
[3] Giustinian, III, p. 536.

It was, perhaps, the urgency of the situation thus created that prompted Cardinal d'Amboise, whose prestige at Rome was now seriously endangered, to hasten the ratification of the treaties of Blois by Maximilian. In the month of March, he made a journey to Hagenau, attended by a numerous company of bishops and other magnates of France, and twenty-four archers, each of whom carried in his coat four thousand crowns for the investiture of Milan, to obtain from Maximilian the ratification of the treaties.

On April 6, the Cardinal in person took the oath of homage in behalf of his King, pledging him, as Duke of Milan, to remain "the faithful and obedient servant of you, the King of the Romans, his true lord, to give notice of plots formed against you, to accomplish without fraud or deceit all that is required of a faithful prince, vassal of you and the Empire." On the next day, Maximilian gave the formal investiture of Milan to the Archduke Philip for his son Charles in default of male heirs of Louis XII.[1]

Thus vanished the imperial aspirations of France, which saw its king become a vassal of the Empire, its conquests alienated, and its territorial integrity threatened by the prospective loss of Brittany. Between the ambitions and the humiliations of the kingdom, its national interests seemed wholly in abeyance, while its glory was sacrificed for private ends on the altar of a feudal fiction.

The ratification of the treaties of Blois was known at Rome on April 17, 1505, as well as the secret mission to Spain of Andrea del Burgo, secretary to Maximilian, for the purpose of attaching Ferdinand the Catholic to the League.[2] The position of Julius II was thus rendered exceedingly embarrassing, for he was now fully launched upon his peace negotiations with Venice, while the coalition was still forming against the Republic. The triple alliance, whose aid he had

---

[1] See Le Glay, I, pp. 78 et seq., who, however, doubts the authenticity of this act of investiture.
[2] Giustinian, III, p. 436.

despaired of securing, was moving forward under the leadership of Cardinal d'Amboise not only without his aid, but even in opposition to his plans.

It was, in truth, Cardinal d'Amboise who had now taken up the threads of the papal diplomacy in defiance of the Pope; for an unexpected event had renewed the prospect of a vacancy in the Holy See. On March 27, Julius II had experienced a temporary fainting spell, and Rome had been startled with rumors of his death. The arrival of a French embassy on April 15, — nominally to perform the ceremony of obedience to the Pope, but really to support the cause of Cardinal d'Amboise, — increased the disquietude of Julius II; for, in the letter of credence, the King of France assumed the title of "King of Naples," which threatened to force the Pope's hand on the question of neutrality.

While the Spanish ambassador protested against the assumption of a title prejudicial to the claims of Ferdinand the Catholic, Julius II calmly ignored the incident, addressed the French envoys only as representatives of the "King of France," and promptly ended the consistory.

To the intrinsic difficulties of a reconciliation with Venice was now added the obstruction created by the new alliance against the Republic between Louis XII and Maximilian; and the papal negotiations with Venice soon ended in the recall of Giustinian from Rome and the failure of the concord so hopefully begun. But new and unexpected occurrences were suddenly to change the situation.

The conflict over the government of Castile

In France, a recoil from the national abasement to which the policy of Cardinal d'Amboise had condemned the kingdom was certain to be felt; and the death of Queen Isabella of Castile, on November 26, 1504, had become the occasion of a series of events which permitted the sentiment of France to find expression.

While recognizing the hereditary rights of her daughter, Juana, wife of the Archduke Philip of Burgundy, whose mental condition forbade her taking up the government, the Queen's testament placed the regency of Castile in the hands of her husband, Ferdinand the Catholic. Isabella had been devotedly attached to Ferdinand, who had led her to believe that after her death he would never marry, and she not only made him regent of her kingdom, whose importance he had done so much to enhance, but bequeathed to him a million crowns, half of the revenues of all the discoveries in America, and a life tenure as Grand Master of the rich and powerful orders of St. James, Calatrava, and Alcantara. But the Archduke Philip, however, claiming Castile as his wife's inheritance, and counting upon Castilian antipathy to Aragon, proclaimed himself "King of Castile"; and, with the aid of a strong party in the kingdom, determined to enter upon immediate possession.[1]

The mental incapacity of Juana being evident, the Cortes of Castile decided to guard that fact as a secret, and to approve of the late Queen's wish that Ferdinand should act as regent in his daughter's place.[2]

To obtain the approval of Juana and the Archduke Philip to this arrangement, two envoys were sent to the Netherlands. One of these, Lopez Conchillo, adroitly secured from Juana secret letters to Ferdinand in which she implored him not to abandon her kingdom, and offered to confirm him in the regency even in opposition to the will of the Archduke.

Conchillo having confided these letters to his colleague,

---

[1] The children of Ferdinand and Isabella were five in number: a son, John, and four daughters, Isabella, Juana, Catherine, and Mary. John married Margaret of Burgundy, daughter of the Emperor Maximilian, and died in 1497, the only issue of the marriage being a child born dead. Isabella was married to Alfonso of Portugal, and upon his death to Emmanuel, who became King of Portugal in 1495. Isabella having died in 1498, the king married her younger sister, Mary, with the design of continuing the friendship with Spain. Juana, who after 1498 became the heiress of both Castile and Aragon, married the Archduke Philip of Burgundy. Catherine, — destined to play so conspicuous a part in English history as "Catherine of Aragon," — was first married to Arthur, eldest son of Henry VII, and afterward to his brother, Henry VIII.

[2] On the question of Juana's insanity, see the fifth paragraph under the head of Literature at the end of the present chapter.

Miguel Ferreyra, the latter imprudently placed them in the Archduke's hands; who at once threw Conchillo into prison as a conspirator, at the same time substituting Flemish women for the young queen's Spanish attendants, — except two trusted maids, — by whom she was thenceforth carefully guarded.

The alliance of France with Ferdinand the Catholic

To meet the crisis that had thus arisen, Ferdinand the Catholic promptly sought to form an alliance with Louis XII of France. The general revulsion from the treaties of Blois, the cost and humiliation of which were now becoming evident to the King, prepared the way for a favorable reception of Ferdinand's overtures; while, for Ferdinand, the alliance proposed had the double advantage of withdrawing support from the Archduke Philip and settling his own outstanding differences with the King of France. On October 12, 1505, a treaty was signed between the two monarchs by which Ferdinand the Catholic, although then fifty-three years of age, was to marry the eighteen-year-old niece of Louis XII, the beautiful Germaine de Foix; Louis was to renounce in favor of the children that might be born of this union his rights in the Kingdom of Naples, which by the treaties of Blois were intended to be transferred to the Archduke Charles as future husband of Claude; and Ferdinand, in recognition of Louis' rights in that kingdom, was to pay him one million ducats "in good gold," in ten annual payments.[1]

Although this compact was at the time kept secret, the open dissolution of the treaties of Blois was not to be long delayed. At the time of making the treaty with Ferdinand the Catholic, Louis XII sent a messenger to inform the Archduke Philip and the Emperor that the "Most Catholic King" had asked in marriage the hand of Germaine de Foix; and, since the welfare of Christendom depended upon the peace, union, and concord of Christian princes, "knowing the joy they would feel," he communicated to them the

---

[1] See Dumont, IV, Part I, pp. 72, 74.

fact that he was signing an ordinary treaty of peace with Ferdinand.

Even this act was in violation of the treaties of Blois, which provided for the negotiation of a peace between Ferdinand and Louis XII only in union with his allies. It plainly indicated, therefore, that, in the struggle between Philip and Ferdinand, the King of France intended to be on the side of the King of Aragon. A copy of the treaty, soon afterward secretly placed in the hands of the Archduke by a "high personage," revealed the additional fact that, instead of an ordinary peace, an offensive and defensive alliance had been concluded, together with the transfer of the French rights in Naples.

In possession of this knowledge, the Archduke resolved to hasten his voyage to Castile, and on January 7, 1506, accompanied by Juana, he set sail for Spain. A fire at sea and a tempest drove his vessel upon the shores of England; where, being mistaken for pirates, he and his crew were for a time in danger of violence. Representing himself as captain of the fleet of the King of Castile, he obtained communication with King Henry VII, who received the royal pair at Windsor Castle. There, in the course of a visit of two months, a treaty of commerce between England and the Netherlands was signed by the King and the Archduke.[1]

It was now evident on both sides that the treaties of Blois were effectively at an end. The French learned with irrita-

[1] A circumstantial account is given in the despatches of Quirini, Venetian ambassador. See Brown, *Calendar*, No. 864. A letter, now regarded as a forgery, was published by certain chroniclers, purporting to have been sent by Louis XII, requesting the King of England to hold Philip as a prisoner. See Le Glay, I, p. LXXV. Henry VII did not omit, however, to engage Philip to deliver any traitor or rebel taking refuge in his states. In making this compact, Philip had not thought of Edmund de la Pole, Duke of Suffolk, called the "White Rose," whom he delivered to Henry VII with great regret. The King kept his promise to spare the Duke's life, but Henry VIII celebrated his accession to the throne by putting him to death. The treaty was commercially so unfavorable to the Netherlands that it was called the "*malus intercursus*," in contrast with the "*magnus intercursus*" of 1496.

tion that Maximilian was preparing to seek the imperial crown at the hands of the Pope at Rome, and was intending to revive all the ancient pretensions of the Empire. With the House of Austria in possession of Castile, France would be encompassed by Hapsburg influences on every side.

A letter from Rome, written on April 22, 1506, by Philibert Naturelli, the imperial ambassador who had negotiated the treaties of Blois, reveals the utter emptiness of these extraordinary compacts. In this letter, Naturelli notifies the Archduke Philip that Cardinal d'Amboise has " marvellously and dishonestly changed his disposition " toward him; and that he is supporting with all his power Ferdinand the Catholic, " because he hopes to be pope by means of this same King of Aragon, who has promised him that, in case of the death of the present pope, he will receive the votes of all the Spanish cardinals." [1] In the same letter, the ambassador informs the Archduke, that the Pope is deeply offended because the King of France has formed a secret league with Venice to prevent Maximilian's journey into Italy for his imperial coronation. To withstand this new combination, the Pope, indignant with the French, not only gives assurance of his attachment to the cause of the Archduke in his conflict with Ferdinand the Catholic, but of his hope to form an alliance with him, with Florence, and the Emperor, to punish the Venetians for their aggressions upon the cities of Romagna. In view of the alleged alliance of France with Venice, however, Naturelli advises Maximilian not to venture into Italy; with the result that the imperial coronation was postponed.

Betrothal of Claude to Francis of Angoulême

But a dramatic incident was now to destroy all hope of union between the House of Hapsburg and that of Valois. In May, 1506, an imperial envoy appeared at Plessis-les-Tours to solicit the payment of the hundred thousand francs still due for the investiture of Milan. The coldness of his reception did not augur well for the success of his mission;

---

[1] Le Glay, I, pp. 112, 113.

and, on May 14, a national demonstration proved how deeply the French nation had been moved. In the great hall of the palace the deputies of the States General assembled to have audience of the King. Seated on his throne, on his right hand Cardinal d'Amboise, the Cardinal de Narbonne, the Chancellor, and a number of high prelates; on his left the Duke of Valois, with the great lords and barons of the kingdom; the King received them in high state. Before the assembly then rose Thomas Bricot, a learned doctor of the Sorbonne, who, after recognizing in the name of the clergy, the nobility, and the people that "no prince had ever so worked for the happiness of his subjects," declared the King worthy of being proclaimed "*le Père du Peuple.*" "Sire," continued the speaker, "we are here, by your good pleasure, to make a request for the general well-being of your kingdom, which is, your most humble subjects pray, that you may be pleased to give my lady your only daughter to the Sieur d'Angoulême, here present, *who is all French!*" The orator then, in eloquent words, touched the hearts of the assembly with such a love of country that all present were moved to tears.[1]

On the sixteenth, the King having in the meantime taken counsel, the assembly was reconvened, and the Chancellor solemnly announced the royal decision, "after mature deliberation," that the betrothal of Claude and the Count d'Angoulême should take place on the following Thursday.

On the twenty-first, in the presence of the royal family and the high nobility, the Princess Claude was carried before the throne in the arms of young Gaston de Foix, accompanied by Francis, Count of Angoulême, then twelve years of age. The Chancellor read the marriage contract, the King offered as a dowry, to become available when the marriage should be consummated, the counties of Asti and Blois, and the lordships of Soissons and Coucy, to which the Queen added a gift of a hundred thousand francs. Cardinal

---

[1] See *Lettres de Louis XII*, I, p. 43.

CHAP. IV
A. D.
1502-1518

Results of the new betrothal

d'Amboise then solemnly consecrated the betrothal, and for more than a week the event was celebrated with public rejoicings.[1]

While dissipating by this act the idea of a union between the houses of Hapsburg and Valois, Louis XII was disposed to conciliate his late allies as far as possible, and for this purpose embassies were sent to Maximilian and the Archduke Philip. The ambassadors, François de Rochechouart and Antoine Duprat, were more than two months in finding the Emperor, who sent them word that he would meet them first in Carinthia, then in Austria, then in Styria; until, finally, after threatening to return to France without discharging their mission, they found him near Leoben, in the last named country.

Although Maximilian habitually wrote French, he would consent to hear them only in Latin. In that language Duprat then informed him how "the King, for the good and utility of his kingdom, at the request and by the deliberation of the estates of France, had given in marriage Madame Claude, his daughter, to Francis of Orléans, Count of Angoulême; of which fact he wished to give notice to the King of the Romans, with whom he desired to have good peace and love."[2] Finally, he asked if the Emperor wished to maintain the investiture of Milan in favor of Claude and her posterity, on condition that the one hundred thousand francs still due were paid. Maximilian replied with vague assurances of friendship, and after a merely formal exchange of courtesies, without making any engagement, dismissed the ambassadors, who returned to France.

The extent to which the *raison d'état* was at this time accepted as a principle of public law in Europe is instructively disclosed by the decision of the three doctors of Louvain, to whom the following questions were submitted for their opinion: (1) Are the King and Queen of France guilty

---

[1] See Höfler, *Das diplomatische Journal*, p. 89.
[2] Le Glay, I, p. LXXXI.

of perjury for not having accomplished the obligation contracted by them, under oath, to marry their daughter to the Archduke Charles? (2) Is the promise made by them to abandon to the said Charles the duchies of Burgundy and Milan and the county of Asti legally binding, in case, by their voluntary act, the marriage of Claude and Charles should not take place? (3) If the second question is answered in the affirmative, has the said Charles the right to claim the duchies and county mentioned?

To the first question the learned jurists answered, that, at present, the King and Queen of France have not committed perjury, in case a circumstance independent of their will, before the betrothed had arrived at legal age, should create a necessary obstacle to their marriage; to the second, that the clause by virtue of which the King and Queen have become responsible for the future accomplishment of the marriage of their minor daughter with the Archduke Charles is immoral according to the civil law, *but that immorality is nullified when the contracting parties are sovereign princes or communities, which recognize no superior;* to the third, that, although it is now certain that the marriage cannot take place, Charles has not the right to demand the penal execution of the clause which assigns to him the lands in question.[1]

While these proceedings were annihilating the last vestiges of the treaties of Blois, the Archduke Philip and Queen Juana were received with honor, first at Valladolid, then at Burgos, by the Cortes of Castile. If the Archduke felt resentment toward Ferdinand the Catholic for his conduct in destroying his relations with France, the grandees of the kingdom he went to govern felt not less aggrieved by Ferdinand's marriage with Germaine de Foix. The hostility entertained by Castile toward Aragon had been mollified during the lifetime of Queen Isabella, and the personal union of the two kingdoms had brought them great advantages; but, now that Ferdinand's marriage suggested new dynastic pretensions, the

---

[1] Le Glay, I, pp. 195, 198.

Castilians revived their animosity toward him as a foreign king. An attempt on the part of Francisco Ximenes de Cisneros, Archbishop of Toledo, who had been the chaplain of Queen Isabella, to reconcile the Archduke and the nobles to Ferdinand the Catholic, though adroitly managed, failed to be effective, and the "Most Catholic King" found it expedient to withdraw from Castile to his own kingdom of Aragon.

It was to the great ability and fidelity of Ximenes that Ferdinand owed all future relations with the Kingdom of Castile. On September 25, 1506, the Archduke Philip, after having been recognized by courtesy as King of Castile, and entrusted with the regency for his insane wife, Juana, suddenly died. The Archduke Charles being too young to govern, and Queen Juana being utterly incapable, the kingdom was thus thrown into a dangerous state of disorder. The nobles, divided into factions, were plotting against each other, and the realm was reduced to a condition bordering upon feudal anarchy, when Ximenes, with admirable tact and coolness, used his personal prestige to procure his own election as regent.

After a pompous funeral, the embalmed body of the Archduke was buried in an abbey near Burgos until it could be carried to the royal chapel at Grenada; but the demented queen, whose jealousy of her husband was ferocious during his lifetime, would not permit him to rest even in his tomb, exhumed the body, placed the coffin upon a great chariot draped with black, and began a restless journey from city to city, travelling only at night by the light of torches; and, when only a nunnery was available for shelter, camping in the open air, for fear some woman might touch the coffin of the prince.

The plans of Ximenes

Suspecting his great captain, Gonsalvo de Cordova, of treason, Ferdinand the Catholic had gone to Naples to administer in person the affairs of that kingdom; whence, later, he brought back Gonsalvo, loaded with illusory honors, soon to be rescinded, to a virtual imprisonment in Spain.

In these difficult circumstances, Ximenes sought and obtained from the nobles authority almost absolute, which he employed with diligence to procure the restoration of Ferdinand to power in Castile. In order to prepare the way for the King's return, according to a contemporary writer, he invented the ingenious scheme of securing from Queen Juana a mandate for the recall of her father. He announced that there were only two persons capable of composing the affairs of the kingdom, — Maximilian, father of the late Archduke, and Ferdinand, father of the Queen; and proposed that a choice between them be left to Her Majesty.

To procure this decision from the mad queen was not an easy task, but Ximenes was equal to the emergency. A chosen deputation went to the grated window of the Queen's apartment, behind whose bars she was then sequestered, and placed the alternative before her. Her reply was calm and reasonable. She preferred to live in retreat; she did not feel capable of attending to affairs of state; her son Charles was, unfortunately, not of sufficient age to assume the government; Maximilian was already heavily taxed with the affairs of the Empire; her father, Ferdinand, knew the needs of the kingdom, and above all "the talents and merits of persons within the realm"; her wish was, therefore, that he would return and resume the reins of government.[1]

Nothing favorable was said of Maximilian, who from the first was out of the question. The wishes of the Queen and the public needs pointed, therefore, toward Ferdinand's return. To render it the more urgent, Ximenes refused to fill the vacant bishoprics and other offices until a proper authority existed, and Juana would sign nothing. The Queen's observation that Ferdinand knew "the talents and merits of persons," coupled with the fact that no offices could be filled till his return, created a party urgent to procure it. Ximenes and Ferdinand were in constant correspondence, and each

---

[1] Peter Martyr, *Opus Epistolarum*, 17, Book 19.

knew the advantages of delay. Finally, having preceded his arrival with letters of amnesty for his former enemies, while Ximenes raised an army to repress revolt, toward the end of 1507 Ferdinand returned to Spain, and soon afterward entered Castile. The clergy and nobles eagerly sought to welcome him, his civility won numerous adherents, and the cardinal's hat he brought from Rome for Ximenes proved that he was not unmindful of his great services.

Ximenes' rule in Castile

The King of Aragon soon came to realize, however, that it was the Regent, and not himself, who had accomplished his restoration in Castile. The hatred which he afterward displayed toward his great servitor was the natural fruit of his feeling of dependence; for it was the minister who upheld the king, not the king the minister. Although Ferdinand, by the influence of Ximenes, was again entrusted with the regency, it was the Cardinal who continued to be the power behind the throne.

By a single stroke of policy, Ximenes made himself the real master of Castile. Early in the thirteenth century, an ecclesiastical tribunal known as the "Holy Office" had been established for the suppression of heresy. In 1478, under the protection of Ferdinand and Isabella, this tribunal had been reorganized in Spain for procedure against Jews and Moors, and sanctioned by Sixtus IV, — though not without a protest against the extent of its powers, — under the name of the "Great Inquisition." Intended solely for the suppression of religious error, Thomas de Torquemada, had employed it for this purpose with wonderful effect. Seventeen thousand persons are said to have been "reconciled" by him to the Church, two thousand burned, and the number of fugitives is unknown. As a great French Catholic prelate has remarked, "The people had some difficulty in accustoming themselves to that new form of law, and to a procedure by which children were punished for the sins of their parents, in which the accuser did not appear, in which the witnesses were neither named nor confronted, and in which the penalty of death was inflicted for the slightest reason; but they were made to understand that the laws of the Church change according to the times."[1]

Such was the instrument which Cardinal Ximenes brought to the service of the State by causing himself to be named "Grand Inquisitor," — an office of which the Archbishop of Seville was divested for this purpose.

In the disturbances which followed Ferdinand's re-entrance upon the regency, castles were razed, nobles were executed, and armed force was applied without restraint; but the power of a prime minister armed with a secret weapon reaching every individual in the kingdom, and against whose secret exercise there was no protection, did not chiefly depend upon those visible agencies of power by which nations are accustomed to be awed into obsequious silence.[2]

II. THE LEAGUE OF CAMBRAY

At the beginning of the sixteenth century, Venice, which had before that time possessed a monopoly of Eastern trade, had reached the zenith of its prosperity, and was already confronted with the symptoms of decline. The fall of the Byzantine Empire and its occupation by the Turks involved immense losses to the Republic, thenceforth menaced with the total extinction of its trade in the Orient, and even with the destruction of its entire Mediterranean commerce. The discoveries of Vasco da Gama, who had rounded the Cape of Good Hope in November, 1497, and arrived at Calicut on May 20 of the following year, gave to Portugal a maritime position for which Henry the Navigator had so faithfully labored, and stripped Venice of that commercial supremacy

The decline of Venetian commerce

---

[1] Fléchier, *Histoire du cardinal Ximénès*, I, p. 341.
[2] The interest of the monarchy in maintaining and controlling the Inquisition as an instrument of power in the State is evident from the action of Ferdinand the Catholic in issuing his decree of August 31, 1509, in which he ordained the death penalty against persons guilty of obtaining from the Pope or his legate a bull or other document unfavorable to the Inquisition in Spain.

which it had thitherto enjoyed. While Camoëns was soon to celebrate in jubilant verse the good fortune of the Portuguese, the Venetians beheld with consternation the shifting of the world's centre from the Mediterranean to the Atlantic, now suddenly become the highway of nations as a result of the Spanish and Portuguese discoveries.

In the summer of 1501, a Venetian ambassador at Lisbon sent to the Signory a detailed report of Vasco da Gama's explorations, showing the dangers and the advantages of the new route to India. "The wise," says a Venetian chronicler of that time, " regard it as the worst news that has ever reached them; for they see in it the ruin of their own commerce." Their fears were well grounded. Three hundred ships then floated the standard of San Marco, but in another century Venice had almost ceased to be of maritime importance.

Project of a Suez canal

In 1502, a commission was appointed to study the question of reviving the commercial supremacy of Venice, and the Venetian ambassador in Egypt, Benedetto Sanuto, was ordered to treat with the Sultan and point out to him how much his own commerce was endangered by the progress of the Portuguese.

In the fourteenth century, Marino Sanuto the Elder had advised the conquest of Egypt as a naval base; but in 1504 a still more brilliant enterprise was conceived for the rescue of the declining trade of Venice. Classical writers had mentioned a canal which at one time had connected the Nile with the Red Sea, and thus opened a water communication with the Mediterranean. Necho is said to have commenced it in the seventh century before our era, but it was closed because an oracle had declared it would prove chiefly for the benefit of the barbarians. The enormous difficulty of maintaining the canal and the spoiling of the water of the Nile for other uses by mingling it with the water of the Red Sea may have led to the abandonment of this enterprise. But the plan proposed by the Venetians was superior to the ancient one. They thought of cutting the isthmus of Suez in such a manner as to open a direct passage for ships between the Mediterranean and the Red Sea, thus shortening by thousands of miles the route to India discovered by Vasco da Gama, which required the circumnavigation of the entire coast of Africa.

Bernardino Giova was sent as a special ambassador to discuss this proposition with the Sultan, but either the magnitude of the undertaking or failure to convince the Sultan of its importance appears to have prevented the realization of the scheme.[1]

All the more desperately because of its failing fortunes on the sea, Venice was determined to fortify its security upon the land. For this reason, the Signory had never yielded to the constant pressure of Julius II for the surrender to the Papacy of the strongholds of Rimini and Faenza, rescued from the power of Cesare Borgia. For the same reason, taking advantage of the military weakness and preoccupation of Maximilian, the Republic had encroached upon territories formerly embraced within the Empire.

Necessary as these measures may have seemed as means of securing the safety of the Republic, they were certain to arouse the indignation of the Pope and the Emperor, and to expose the aggressor to the danger of assault.

Weary of the dissensions of the great powers, which had rendered ineffectual the vast schemes of Cardinal d'Amboise, Julius II, while abiding his time for dealing with Venice, resolved to take in hand the refractory possessors of estates pertaining to the Holy See in Romagna and subdue them by main force. Proceeding in August, 1506, at the head of his little army, augmented by the Swiss mercenaries, he established peace at Viterbo, entered Perugia in triumph, wrested Bologna from the haughty Giovanni Bentivoglio, and invested his own name with the title "Renovator of the States of the

---

[1] For the Venetian projects of an Isthmian canal, see the documents presented by Fulin in his article on *Il canale di Suez e la Repubblica di Venezia* (1504), in the Archivio Veneto, II, Part I, Venice, 1871.

CHAP. IV
A. D.
1502-1518

Church." Clothed in his pontifical vestments and preceded by the sacrament, this fearless priest and warrior filled with awe the entire population, as he moved from city to city asserting the rights of the Holy See, made terrible once more by the majesty of his presence. Carefully avoiding a collision with Venice, for which he was not yet prepared, by the summer of 1507 Julius II had secured by his own exertions a prestige that rendered the Papacy once more the leading power in Italy.

Relations of Julius II to France and Spain

Realizing, as he had from the first, the value of the co-operation of France and Spain in his dealings with Venice, the Pope made every effort to win them to his cause. The Sacred College, fearing the consequences of the success of Cardinal d'Amboise as a candidate for the Papacy, in which they imagined lurking the danger of a new transfer of the Holy See to Avignon, opposed the increase of his power; yet, to appease him, Julius II not only confirmed him once more as papal legate in France, but conferred the cardinalate upon three of his relatives and granted to Louis XII the privilege of collecting in Milan revenues belonging to the Holy See.

In the same spirit of conciliation, the Pope had sent the red hat to Ximenes, but Ferdinand the Catholic was little disposed to serve the purposes of Julius II. Nor was Louis XII now wholly inclined to requite the favors bestowed upon himself and his prime minister. As a Genoese, the Pope was believed to be in sympathy with the Republic of Genoa, at that moment endeavoring to throw off the suzerainty of France. In February, 1507, the King declared to the ambassador of Florence: "I wish the Pope to understand that, if he sustains the Genoese, I will place Giovanni Bentivoglio back in Bologna. It is only necessary for me to write a letter, and I shall have the benefit besides of a hundred thousand ducats from Bentivoglio for my trouble. In fact, the Pope is sprung from a race of peasants, and it is necessary to manage him with a stick."[1]

---

[1] Desjardins, *Négociations*, II, p. 220.

It was, in truth, the obstinate courage of the Pope which had appealed with such force to the Italians, so long deprived of a veritable leader. When Julius left Bologna on February 22, 1507, to return to Rome, the population was deeply moved and could hardly be prevailed upon to permit him to depart. His progress through Imola, Forli, and Cesena revealed the devotion with which he was regarded. As he approached the Eternal City, great crowds came forth to welcome him, garlands and tapestries were spread along the streets, inscriptions in his honor covered the arches of triumph, and all Rome was filled with jubilation. It was the hero rather than the Holy Father, however, who was celebrated in the songs with which poets praised the success of his arms against Bologna. In the address of welcome pronounced by Cardinal Raphael Riario, the sentiment of the Sacred College was expressed in the words: "From the moment Your Holiness made known his intentions regarding Bologna, it was impossible not to approve the excellence of the project of reducing that city to real obedience to the Apostolic See. . . . By doing so, Your Holiness has marvellously augmented and strengthened the prestige of the State of the Church, and assured to its name an immortal glory."

Judged by the standards of that time, an increase of temporal power was of vital import to the dignity of the Papacy and Julius II had rendered it this service. From that day to the end of his career, with increasing boldness, this great pontiff bent his titanic energies to the fulfilment of that task.

If the Pope had defended the rights of the Holy See to Rimini and Faenza in the period of his relative helplessness, it was not to be expected that he would now abandon them; but the attitude of France and Spain required caution on his part. The ground for the hostility of France has already been noted, but the relation with Ferdinand the Catholic was not less threatening. His nearest neighbor on the South, Ferdinand had not yet settled with the Pope the question of investiture and tribute for the Kingdom of Naples, and in Spain he had encroached upon the papal prerogatives by his appointment of bishops in Castile.

In June, 1507, the Pope journeyed to Ostia to meet Ferdinand on his voyage from Naples to Savona, where he was to confer with Louis XII and Cardinal d'Amboise; but the King went on his way without an interview.

At Savona a secret conference between Ferdinand and Louis XII occurred, in which Cardinal d'Amboise figured as "the real king of France,"[1] and questions of "reform," in the Church were there discussed. Ferdinand had long desired the undisputed right to the Kingdom of Naples, and had caused the nobles of the kingdom to take the oath of allegiance, not to Germaine de Foix, as had been expected, but to Queen Juana. Cardinal d'Amboise, on the other hand, was eager to receive Ferdinand's support for succession to the Papacy. The King is reported to have assured the Cardinal that "nothing could so much contribute to the general good of Christendom as the elevation of a man of good will like himself to the pontificate; but that, while his great desire was to see him in the Chair of St. Peter, it would be difficult to elevate him to it, if certain articles were not changed which were displeasing to the cardinals, — his subjects and his friends."[2]

Although, notwithstanding the discovery of new documents, a veil of obscurity still hangs over the secret conference at Savona, it is presumable, since the two kings separated "friendly and satisfied," that the hopes of Cardinal d'Amboise were once more confirmed, and it is probable that upon this basis the first plans for the League of Cambray against Venice were definitely laid.[3]

The report of the proceedings at Savona furnished to Julius II by his legate, Cardinal Pallavicini, who had been

---

[1] Secret Archives of the Vatican, cited by Pastor, *Histoire*, VI, p. 272.

[2] Fléchier, *Histoire du cardinal Ximénès*, I, p. 328.

[3] See Filippi, *Il convegno di Savona*, and de Maulde in Revue d'Histoire Diplomatique, IV, pp. 583, 590.

sent to intercede with Louis XII in behalf of the Genoese, was not of a nature to reassure him. While the unnecessarily large army brought into Italy by the King of France for the subjection of Genoa, composed of fifty thousand troops and the *élite* of the French nobility, excited the fear that he had further designs, the treatment accorded to the Pope's envoy, especially by Cardinal d'Amboise, indicated that it was not intended to be used for the benefit of Julius II.

Negotiations of the Pope with Maximilian

The appearance of Louis XII in Italy with so large an army and his secret negotiations with Ferdinand the Catholic excited the apprehensions of Maximilian also, who now exclaimed to the diet at Constance: "The King of France wishes to wrest the imperial crown from the German nation! I intend to conduct an army into Italy to secure it. Then I will drive the French from Italy." Provided with thirty thousand soldiers, in July, 1507, his early attempt to execute his purpose was expected.

The threads of diplomacy had now fallen entirely from the grasp of Julius II. On the one hand a secret Franco-Spanish combination, on the other the Italian campaign of Maximilian, who would demand of him the bestowment of the imperial crown, threatened to place him at the centre of an impending conflict from which he could foresee no sure advantage, and which promised wholly to escape his control.

On August 5, 1507, therefore, Cardinal Bernardin Carvajal was despatched as papal legate to prevent the coming of Maximilian into Italy, and for this purpose to present to him two propositions: first, that he should receive his coronation in Germany at the hands of two cardinal-legates; and second, that he should join in a general alliance against the Turks and a special alliance with the Pope against Venice.

The purpose of the Pope in sending this mission was, by anticipating the Franco-Spanish designs, to place himself at the centre of action and divert the movements of all the powers to the advantage of the Papacy. The opportunity had at last arrived to secure from Venice the satisfaction of the papal claims by combining all the powers against her.

CHAP. IV
A. D.
1502-1518

The next step would be to block the further progress of all the contestants in their schemes for spoils in Italy. For this purpose the Pope must be at the centre, not at the circumference, of the diplomatic battle.

The legate met the King of the Romans at Innsbruck, in September; but Maximilian, while ready in a general way to join in a universal alliance against the Turks and a specific one against Venice, was not inclined to be reconciled to the King of France, nor to abandon his coronation at Rome at the hands of the Pope himself.

Resolutely determined to fulfil his mission, Cardinal Carvajal did not rest, however, until Maximilian, finding that Venice was determined to oppose his passage through its territories, in February, 1508, finally sent a secret envoy to France to invite an offensive and defensive alliance against the Republic.

At the same time, Maximilian took a step intended to settle definitively the question of his imperial pretensions. On February 4, 1508, in the cathedral at Trent, his confidential counsellor, Matthias Lang, solemnly proclaimed that Maximilian had adopted the title " Roman Emperor-elect."[1]

Too feeble in a military sense to march to Rome, the "Emperor-elect" took pains to make a formal announcement that he meant no prejudice to the Pope's prerogatives, and that he would proceed to Rome for his coronation when he had chastised the Venetians.

The attack of the Emperor upon Venice

Julius II, who had thus succeeded in keeping Maximilian away from Rome, in a letter of February 12, 1508, recognized his title, commended his decision, and ended with the

---

[1] From this time onward the King of Germany was called "*Erwählter Kaiser*" after his German coronation; but none was ever crowned by the Pope, except Charles V, and he at Bologna, not at Rome. The qualification "Erwählter," or "Elect," was usually dropped, and the title "Emperor" thus became customary without any adjunct. The expression "German Emperor," or less correctly "Emperor of Germany," became natural when the imperial power was practically confined to Germany, and grew out of the fact that the "*König*" (*Germaniae rex*) was also "*Kaiser*."

advice to conclude an immediate arrangement with France, and when he should make his journey to Rome to imitate the example of his father, Frederick III, and come with a modest escort.

Indisposed to encourage the appearance of any great power in Italy with an armed force, the Pope comprehended the advantage of bringing Venice to terms by a union of the powers, whose ambitions he then hoped to curb by balancing one against another; for he clearly perceived, as Alexander VI had already pointed out, that the safety of Italy lay in the mutual jealousy of the powers.

But Maximilian was too much irritated by the opposition of Venice to be restrained. On the day that he proclaimed himself "Emperor-elect," hostilities were begun. For the first month, it appeared as if the Venetians would be forced to yield; then, aided by the French, as Julius II had foreseen, the Republic took a terrible revenge. Friuli and Istria were invaded; in May, Trieste and Fiume were taken; and by June, the Emperor was ready to conclude a truce of three years, leaving the victorious Venetians in possession of all their conquests.

Although the inconvenience of Maximilian's presence in Italy had been averted, the general situation had not been improved; for the old fear that Venice, flushed with victory, might press her primacy upon Italy to the disadvantage of the Papacy as well as the foreign powers, now returned. Unfortunately for the Republic, in its determination to increase its security by extending its frontiers, encroachments had been made upon all its neighbors, who were now ready to combine against it. The French, who had just aided in arresting the advance of the Emperor, having been ignored in the subsequent negotiations, were now disposed to renew that hostility to Venice which only jealousy of Maximilian had led them to abandon, and which he in the previous February had invited them to resume. Maximilian was burning to inflict vengeance, and Ferdinand the Catholic had injuries to resent. The Papacy, dreading the augmented power of Venice, and eager to obtain redress for past encroachments, was now ready to humiliate the proud Republic.

Accordingly, toward the end of November, 1508, at Cambray, was formed the first great European coalition for the total extinction of an independent state. Cardinal d'Amboise, acting at the same time as minister of Louis XII and as papal legate, Matthias Lang, as plenipotentiary of Maximilian, and Margaret of Burgundy [1] — who since the death of her brother, the Archduke Philip, had been Regent of the Netherlands — as representative of Ferdinand the Catholic, met to dismember and divide the Venetian territory. A nuncio of Julius II and envoys of Spain and England were present at Cambray, but they took no part in the negotiations.

On December 10, the conspirators signed a series of treaties which together form the notorious compact known as the "League of Cambray." All but one of these were secret. The public agreement was a convention concluding peace between the Emperor and the King of France, which purported to be the sole object of the conference, renounced the marriage of the Archduke Charles with Claude of France, confirmed the investiture of Milan to Louis XII, and provided for a war against the Turks on condition that Venice previously restore all its conquests.[2]

But the real purpose of the League was contained in its secret engagements, comprising an alliance of the Emperor, the Pope, Louis XII, and Ferdinand the Catholic for the dismemberment of Venice, from which none of the contractants could recede until the Republic had surrendered to the Emperor Roveredo, Verona, Padua, Vicenza, and

---

[1] Margaret was successively affianced to Charles VIII, John of Spain, and Philibert of Savoy; and is frequently referred to as "Margaret of Austria" and "Margaret of Savoy." It is considered more convenient to refer to her as Margaret of Burgundy. She was practically the ruler of the Netherlands from 1506 until her death in 1530.

[2] See Dumont, IV, Part I, p. 109 et seq.

Treviso, cities of the ancient March of Friuli, the key to the imperial descents of the Middle Ages into Italy; to the Pope, Ravenna, Rimini, Faenza, and other cities of Romagna "with their districts"; to the King of France, Brescia, Crema, Bergamo, Cremona, and the Ghiera d'Adda, taken from the Duchy of Milan; and to Ferdinand the Catholic, Trani, Brindisi, Otranto, and Gallipoli, ports that had been ceded to Venice by King Frederick of Naples in the time of his extremity.[1]

Provision was made also for other powers to adhere and share in the spoils. The King of Hungary was expected to take Dalmatia; the Duke of Savoy, — as heir of the Lusignan family, expelled by Venice, — the island of Cyprus; and the Duke of Ferrara, the city and province of Rovigo. The Signory of Florence, unauthorized by the allies, invited the Sultan Bajazet to take possession of the oriental dominions of the Republic; but the suspicious Sultan, considering the conspiracy incredible, refused to participate in the spoliation.

In order to release Maximilian from his truce of three years with the Venetians, it was arranged that the Pope should summon him as the official "Defender of the Church" to aid his Holiness in recovering the territories taken from the Patrimony of St. Peter. By this ingenious artifice, Maximilian was to ease his conscience in fighting his enemies in the name of the Church, while keeping his pledges on his own account!

If Julius II must be regarded as in some sense responsible for the League of Cambray, he was so only in a qualified degree. Wishing to obtain from Venice the restoration of the strongholds once possessed by the Holy See, he had no desire to destroy the Republic or to bring upon Italy a foreign domination.[2] His plan of action was, on the contrary, to constrain Venice to make the concessions he

The reserve of Julius II

---

[1] See Dumont, IV, Part I, p. 225 et seq.
[2] See Maximilian's letter to Margaret, of March 22, 1509, in Le Glay, *Correspondance*, I.

demanded, yet to prevent the predominance of any single foreign power by uniting all in a common action.

Before adhering to the League by his bull of March 23, 1509, Julius II had used every means of persuasion to induce the Venetians to surrender to him Rimini and Faenza. The papal nuncio present at Cambray, as we have seen, had really taken no part in the negotiations, in which Cardinal d'Amboise, as legate, had assumed to act as the plenipotentiary of the Pope. A week previous to his final adherence to the League, Julius II had made a proposition which reveals his disinclination to bring the curse of foreign invasion upon Italy. In the previous November, he had been stung by the haughty obstinacy of Pisani, the Venetian ambassador, to say, "I shall not cease till I have reduced you to the humble fishermen you once were"; to which Pisani had flung back the answer, "And you, Holy Father, if you do not take care, we will make you only a little curate." Still, the testy envoy was allowed to remain in Rome; and in the following March, the Pope, during a pleasure trip in company with the ambassador, is reported to have said to him: "Can you not insinuate to the Signory the idea of proposing some Venetian to whom Rimini and Faenza might be given in fief?" To this the ambassador is said to have replied, that Venice did not make kings of its citizens; and the subject was not even mentioned to the Signory.[1]

When, therefore, Julius II finally adhered to the League of Cambray, he believed that he had exhausted every resource of diplomacy to obtain from Venice the restoration of the cities in dispute. It is true, that when, on April 7, he learned that the Republic was ready to surrender them, he refused to accept its offer; for, at that time, hostilities had already been announced, and he had formally joined the League. On April 27, therefore, he launched against the Republic the thunders of his interdict and excommunication.

---

[1] See Pastor, *Histoire*, VI, p. 287.

The menace of the Pope to reduce the Venetians to their primitive condition of fishermen was soon perilously near fulfilment. The war against Venice opened on April 1, 1509; by the middle of the month a French army had invaded Venetian territory; on May 9, Louis XII was in person on the banks of the Adda; and on the fourteenth, he gained the decisive battle of Agnadello.

The war of the League with Venice

Forced to abandon their possessions on the mainland by the determined onslaught of the French, the Venetians were now driven across their lagoons and shut up in their islands.

For a time, it seemed as if the Republic was destined to complete annihilation. The military force of the French alone had been sufficient to rout the Venetian army and wrest from it all the territories in dispute. The magnanimity of Louis XII in refusing to take for himself the cities claimed by the Emperor when surrendered to the French troops is said to have so touched Maximilian that he burnt his "red book," in which he had recorded the injuries received from France, and resolved to stand by the French alliance.

But the superiority of Venetian diplomacy was soon to make itself felt. The League was based upon no principle of justice capable of being erected into a doctrine of public law. If the territorial rights underlying the claims of the allies had been at any time well-founded, all, except, perhaps, those of the Holy See, had become nugatory by circumstances that rendered them ineffective. Those of the Emperor had long been a dead letter, passing with the fiction of imperial supremacy on which they rested. The territories now claimed by France had for the most part been ceded to Venice by solemn treaties connected with the conquest of Milan. The ports in Southern Italy claimed by Ferdinand the Catholic had been placed in pledge to the Republic for sums of money due by the former king. Finally, all three of the great powers were interlopers in Italy whose pretensions had no other foundations there than force or fraud. Venice, on the contrary, as an Italian state, was contending

Negotiations of the Venetians with the Pope and the Emperor

for its means of independent existence as a political community against a secret conspiracy to destroy it.

Founded on cupidity alone, the League had no moral solidity, and the Venetian diplomatists, who so well understood the art of creating discord among their enemies, bravely undertook the task of dissolving this powerful coalition.

Knowing that division would begin as soon as the spoils were in the hands of the conspirators, the Venetians issued a decree releasing all their Italian subjects from their allegiance, abandoned to Ferdinand the Catholic the seaports in Southern Italy, and offered their humble submission to the Emperor. On July 2, a Venetian embassy composed of six persons entered Rome at night, — the excommunicated not being permitted to enter the city except in darkness. On July 8, Julius II, by special grace, consented to withdraw the excommunication from Girolamo Donato, one of the ambassadors previously known to him, and to receive him in audience; but the conditions imposed on the Republic rendered peace at that time impossible. They included the renunciation of all possessions on the mainland, of all interference in questions of the Church, of all right to tax the clergy, and of the exclusive navigation of the Adriatic. The Senate was enraged, and the Doge exclaimed that, rather than accede to the demands of the Pope, he would prefer to send an embassy to ask aid from the Turks.

Turning next to the Emperor, Antonio Giustinian was sent by the Senate to appease him; but the attempt proved futile. In the meantime, however, the Italians who had been released from their allegiance to Venice, weary of their new masters, who cruelly oppressed them, joined their forces with the army of the Republic, Padua was retaken, and a few months later the imperial army was repulsed.

The appeal to England

In seeking for friends at this critical moment, the Signory naturally turned its eyes toward England, whose envoy had been present at Cambray when the League was formed, but had taken no part in the negotiations. In a communication to Lorenzo Giustinian, its consul at London, then the only official representative of Venice in England, on January 30, 1509, the Signory had set forth its theory of the League of Cambray in an argument which ran as follows: "The plain fact is, that Cardinal d'Amboise, the author of these negotiations, aspires *per fas et nefas* to the Papacy, on obtaining which they,— Cardinal d'Amboise and Louis XII, — purpose, moreover, getting possession of the universal monarchy; and by divers stratagems they are inveigling the Emperor into this detestable undertaking, trying to deceive him as they often have done, and bring matters to such a pass that it will then be impossible to prevent the two swords, spiritual and temporal, from being the one in the hand of Rouen,— Cardinal d'Amboise,— the other in the hand of the King of France; who together are one flesh, and would consequently act together, a result never yet witnessed, but of easy realization unless speedily thwarted by such princes as have received greater power and authority from the Almighty than the rest."[1]

King Henry VII is then urged to interfere, "both of his goodness, and also for the safety of the Christian world, which the Infidels are invited by these disturbances to attack." The consul is personally and privately to communicate all these things to the King; but, if unable to

---

[1] Brown, *Calendar*, I, No. 920. In the author's copy of this work, which was Rawdon Brown's own personal one, with his autograph annotations, he has appended to the quotation cited the words: "See Mutinelli's and Toggenburg's prohibition against my having this document, 12th January, 1855, at pp. 291, 292, of my transcript of Michiel & Surian despatches." Fabio Mutinelli was the curator of the Archives of Venice from 1847 to 1861. Toggenburg was the Austrian governor of Venice. In 1855, Mutinelli had himself prepared from the archives an anecdotal history of Italy; but the Austrian government at that time would not permit a sheet of it to be printed until it was sent to Vienna for examination. The manuscripts were held for months, as Baschet says, "soumis à la haute approbation, sans doute, de quelques employés subalternes qui les retournaient stigmatisés par le crayon rouge en de très-nombreux et intéressants passages absolument historiques." — *Histoire de la chancellerie secrète*, pp. 68, 69.

obtain an audience, is to make the communication through Pietro Carmeliano of Brescia, Latin secretary of Henry VII.

At the same time, Andrea Badoer, a Venetian nobleman, was chosen as ambassador to England, with an allowance of one hundred ducats per month for his expenses "without the necessity of accounting," under orders "to keep five servants and as many horses." Unable, on account of the danger of the roads, to make the journey in his proper character, Badoer travelled as an English gentleman, which his knowledge of the language enabled him to do, without carrying upon his person either credentials or instructions.

These, bearing the date of February 12, 1509, and to avoid capture sent to London by another means of conveyance, directed the ambassador to secure the intervention of Henry VII in behalf of Venice with the Emperor, "with whom the Republic is ready to make a perpetual peace," pointing out to him that, should Cardinal d'Amboise attain to the Holy See, "France would become monarch of the universe by the occupation of the Empire, which would certainly follow." Interposition on the part of Henry VII with the King of France and with the Pope is also requested, and the ambassador is to assure "The Reverend Pietro Carmeliano, who has not been found wanting hitherto, how much he is loved and appreciated" by the Signory, which will "see that he has the fruit of his good and faithful services!"[1]

Such was the beginning of the permanent diplomatic relations between Venice and England, soon to result in drawing that kingdom into the international politics of Italy. But the death of Henry VII on April 20, 1509, and the accession to the throne of his son, Henry VIII, left these efforts without immediate effect.

The germ of future policies was, however, soon apparent to the keen perception of the Venetian ambassador in the young king's ill-concealed hostility toward France. The Abbé de Fécamp having arrived in England as ambassador from

---

[1] Brown, *Calendar*, I, No. 922.

Louis XII, Badoer reports in his despatch of September 9, 1509, that the King, being in his palace of Westminster, determined to give him audience and sent for him. The Abbé announced the receipt by Louis XII of a letter from King Henry requesting friendship and peace, and stated that he had been sent to confirm it. " What," cried the young monarch, " who wrote this letter ? *I* ask peace of the King of France, who dare not look me in the face, still less make war on me !! " With this he rose, nor would he hear more ; so the ambassador withdrew. At a joust that followed, the French ambassador was invited to be present ; but, no seat having been reserved for him upon the stage erected for the guests, he departed offended. The King, however, caused him to be recalled and a cushion given him, and he sat down. " In short," concludes the despatch, " King Henry holds France in small account."

The arrival at Rome of Christopher Bainbridge, Archbishop of York, as the ambassador of the King of England to Julius II, on November 24, 1509, marks an important step on the part of King Henry VIII. The Venetian envoys at Rome hastened to inform the English ambassador that they would have been pleased to go forth to meet and welcome him, had not their state of excommunication forbidden their doing him this honor. The Archbishop gave them a cordial greeting, accepted their apologies, and assured them that the King was for the Signory and would attack France. He had also brought a letter from King Henry to the Pope in favor of the Signory. "The Pope was ill," write the Venetian envoys at Rome. " Some said," they continue, " he fell sick on seeing the letter." [1]

While the Signory was urging through its ambassador that King Henry VIII should suggest to his father-in law, Ferdinand the Catholic,[2] to beware of rendering the King of France so powerful, lest thereafter detriment might ensue to

---

[1] Sanuto, *Diarii*, IX, 293.
[2] Henry VIII had married Catherine of Aragon on June 11, 1509.

CHAP. IV
A. D.
1502-1518

the Spanish possessions in Italy, and that he himself should not neglect so great an opportunity for the conquest of a crown whose title he bore, it assured him that in any operations he might undertake against the King of France, they would so " straiten him in Italy " that an easy victory might be won by Henry VIII, who would thereby " gain as much praise and glory as have ever fallen to the lot of any other king of England."

Thus, by the astute diplomacy of Venice was prepared that sudden shifting of the scene by which France, which at the end of the year 1509 was the arbiter of Italy, before the close of another year found itself practically isolated from its allies, who in turn were arrayed against it.

Abandonment of the League by Julius II

Always apprehensive of the excessive power of France, Julius II already shrank from the consequences of the threatened French predominance in Italy. With England as a probable ally, with Ferdinand the Catholic practically satisfied with the fruits of the League of Cambray, and likely to be wholly won over by the investiture of Naples in his own name, the Pope saw that it was time to pardon Venice and to unite the powers in an effort to curb the growing ascendency of France.

On February 15, 1510, therefore, he made peace with Venice, which humbly bowed to the legality of the papal censures, guaranteed full ecclesiastical power to the Pope, and accorded to the subjects of the Papal State the right of navigation in the Adriatic. On February 24, absolution was solemnly granted in the vestibule of St. Peter's Church, — the ambassadors swearing to observe the provisions of the treaty with their hands resting on the Gospels held by the Pope in person.[1] In form and appearance, the Republic accepted the terms imposed by the Holy See; but, in secret,

---

[1] In a letter of March 2, 1510, from the Doge and Senate to Andrea Badoer, the credit for the change in the attitude of Julius II toward Venice is ascribed to the letters of Henry VIII to the Pope and "the good operation of his ambassador at Rome." — Brown, *Calendar*, II, No. 45.

the Venetians prepared for their revenge by recording a protest that they had acted by constraint.

To his confederates, particularly the King of France, the act of Julius II in making peace with Venice appeared an unpardonable desertion, since the Treaty of Cambray bound the signatories to continue their alliance until all its provisions were realized. Determined if possible to prevent the defection of the Pope, Louis XII despatched to Rome a plausible Savoyard, Albert Pio, Count de Carpi, to remonstrate with His Holiness, charging him to use every art of flattery to win the Pope's confidence for France. But this effort was in vain, for every argument was met by the Venetian ambassador, Donato, now firmly established in the confidence of Julius II; who, moreover, having just secured from Venice the claims of the Holy See, was resolved to procure the complete independence of the Republic. To this end, Venice itself was his necessary ally; and to effect the realization of his purpose, France, — the master of Milan, the patron of Florence and Ferrara, and the recent conqueror of Genoa, the Pope's native city, — must be expelled from Italy.

Against the argument that the Treaty of Cambray had not yet accomplished its purposes, Julius II replied, that all its terms had been already complied with; for France, the Holy See, and Ferdinand the Catholic were all in actual possession of the territories claimed by them. Only the Emperor remained unremunerated, but this was because Padua had been lost by him after its occupation. In reply, the League, it was said, specified no limit of time; to which the Pope responded, that it was certainly never intended to guarantee the perpetual retention of the spoils, when once secured.

Deeming himself thus absolved from further participation in the League of Cambray, the Pope now looked for aid in expelling the French from Italy. His first thought was to detach the Emperor from the coalition. Unable to accomplish this result directly, he sent the Bishop of Pesaro to the diet at Augsburg, to dissuade the princes from granting the

Attempts to influence the Empire, and death of Cardinal d'Amboise

subsidies for the imperial army; but Louis XII having commissioned one of his counsellors, Luigi Eliano, an Italian poet and orator, to act in the opposite sense, this personage addressed the assembly of princes at Augsburg with such persuasive eloquence that the Venetians were put under the ban of the Empire, and a subsidy of three hundred thousand crowns was voted to prosecute the war.

It was in the midst of these efforts of France to fan into a flame the hatred against Venice, that word was received of the death of Cardinal d'Amboise on May 25, 1510, at Lyons. Andrea del Burgo, then imperial ambassador near Louis XII, wrote to Margaret of Burgundy, "Your house has sustained a great loss . . . , and it would be well to send a present to Monsieur the Treasurer Robertet; . . . for it will be he who will have the most credit."[1] The loss to Louis XII was still more important; for, as Machiavelli, then Florentine envoy in France, has said, "The King, not being accustomed to enter into the details of business, always forgot a part of it, and those who governed him dared neither act for themselves nor recall to him what he ought to do."[2] Wise and able in the internal administration of the kingdom, the Cardinal had shared with Louis XII both the powers of the crown and public appreciation in France as a "father of the people"; but his foreign policy, turning always upon his aspiration to the Papacy, had involved his country in deep humiliations and extravagant exploits. Yet, such was his force and prestige as a leader, that Robertet, when shown a portrait of the dead cardinal, exclaimed: "O, my master, if thou hadst lived, we should now be at Rome with our army!" Ambitious to rise to the height of power, Cardinal d'Amboise was modest in seeking rewards from his king; and, while the majority of French prelates were loaded with bishoprics and abbeys, he had been content with his single benefice, the archbishopric of Rouen.

---

[1] *Letters of Louis XII*, I, pp. 233, 234.
[2] Machiavelli's report of his third legation in France.

While Louis XII, who now undertook to carry on his war in Italy with the aid of Robertet as his minister, but without confiding to him more than a secondary rôle, was crippled by his irresolution, Julius II, armed with an inflexible constancy of purpose, began to seek allies against France. At the time when Louis XII was summoning and preparing to attack the spiritual powers of the Pope through a general council, Julius II was negotiating with the Swiss, with Henry VIII of England, and with Ferdinand the Catholic. On July 3, 1510, Ferdinand the Catholic was invested with the Kingdom of Naples in his own name, without regard to the Valois claims. Henry VIII was honored with the "Golden Rose" and the elevation of Bainbridge to the cardinalate was promised. But it was the Swiss who were now expected to furnish to the pontifical army the needed force for the desperate struggle into which the Pope was soon to plunge.

Rupture of the Pope with France

In the heart of Valais, in the valley of the Rhone, rise the heights of Sitten, or Sion, where Matthias Schinner, priest and warrior, held his bishopric. Fervent champion of the Holy See, and bitter enemy of France, the Bishop of Sion exercised by his eloquence and by the force of his character a marvellous influence over the sturdy mountaineers of the Confederation. Resolved to oppose the schemes of Louis XII, when in 1509 the treaty of the Swiss with France expired, Schinner had made a journey to Rome to confer with the Pope, and returning so moved the Confederates against the French that on March 14, 1510, the twelve cantons and the country of Valais ratified a treaty of alliance with Julius II for a period of five years, in which these allies placed at the disposition of the Holy See, whose rights they undertook to defend, six thousand men, to be used against his enemies, "whoever these might be."

Assured of the support of the Swiss and allied with the Venetians, Julius II now boldly declared on June 19, 1510, "These French wish to make me the chaplain of their king; but I intend to be pope in spite of them." Ten days later, Cardinal Clermont, who had endeavored to leave Rome for

France against the Pope's prohibition, was imprisoned in the Castle of St. Angelo, and the other French cardinals who came to complain of this action were threatened with a like discipline if they refused to obey. In the beginning of July, the French ambassador, having taken the Pope to task for remonstrating against the French domination in Genoa, Julius showed him the door, with the declaration that the King of France was his personal enemy, and thus the rupture became complete.

Thenceforth, till the day of his death, Julius II was at open war with France. His plan of campaign included an uprising at Genoa, an attack of the Swiss upon Milan, an assault by the Venetians at Verona, and a movement of the papal troops upon the Duke of Ferrara. Taking the field in person at the head of his army, in August, 1510, Julius II proceeded to Bologna, where he learned that the Swiss had been induced to renounce the expedition at Chiasso by the intrigues of France and the Emperor.

Menaced with a council by the combination of France and Germany, where the national spirit had deeply affected the clergy, confronted with a schism in the Sacred College, and finally overtaken by fever, the winter of 1511 bore heavily upon the pontiff of seventy years in his battle for the supremacy of the Papacy in Italy.

A conference having been called by the Emperor at Mantua, where representatives of France, England, and Spain were assembled to consider propositions of peace, on March 10, 1511, Julius II, in the hope of securing additional influence, created eight new cardinals, including the English Archbishop Bainbridge and Matthias Schinner, Bishop of Sion. A ninth nomination, *in petto*, was reserved for the Emperor's chief plenipotentiary, Matthias Lang, through whom the Pope hoped to detach Maximilian from the French alliance.

Meeting the imperial envoy at Bologna, on April 10, Julius II soon discovered with what refractory material he had to deal. Although an ecclesiastic, Lang, who was Bishop of

Gurk, much to the disgust of the master of ceremonies, Paris de Grassis, in order to emphasize the fact that his authority was derived from the Emperor, insisted on wearing the dress of a civilian. When complaint was made to the Pope, he recommended to the master of ceremonies to close his eyes. Dissatisfied with his seat immediately after the cardinal-deacons, Lang expressed his views in an arrogant discourse, in which he laid down the principle that the essential condition of peace was to impose upon the Venetians the surrender of all territories occupied by them which had ever belonged to the Empire or the hereditary estates of Austria. Refusing to negotiate with any one except the Pope himself, in whose presence he remained seated with his hat on his head, the Bishop of Gurk shocked the cardinals by declining to discuss business with them, designating three German nobles to represent him. With the airs of a king and the manners of a barbarian, Lang brusquely took his departure from Bologna on April 25, and hostilities were soon reopened. On May 14, Julius II also departed from that stronghold, which he left under the command of his legate, Alidosi, by whose cowardice and ineptitude the city was allowed to be retaken by the Bentivogli. It was the heaviest blow that had ever fallen upon the aged pontiff, but still other misfortunes were awaiting him.

On May 28, 1511, a citation was posted on the doors of the Church of St. Francis, at Rimini, near the lodgings of the Pope, summoning him to appear before a general council to be held at Pisa, on September 1. The document was signed by eight cardinals.

A war of pamphlets was now opened, in which the Pope was represented as unworthy of the tiara, and Louis XII exalted as a divinely appointed reformer of the Church.

Beaten in the field, discredited by the Emperor and the King of France, menaced with an invasion of the State of the Church and deposition from the Papacy, Julius II, who had so boldly endeavored to expel the French from Italy, re-entered Rome on June 26, 1511, broken in body and with-

CHAP. IV
A.D.
1502-1518

Project of a league against the French

Maximilian's aspiration to the Papacy

out ground for hope, yet as firmly resolved as ever to drive out the "barbarians," as he now called the French.

In the previous year, Venice had proposed the formation of a league against France, which England, Spain, and the Emperor were to be asked to join; but the time had not then arrived for this combination. In November, 1510, Archbishop Bainbridge had advocated such a coalition, which the Pope, relying upon support from Venice and the Swiss, then thought unnecessary and declined on account of the expense.[1] To promote the rescue of the Holy See and expel the French from Italy, the King of England was at that time ready to attack France north of the Alps, if the Pope and Venice could put into the field two thousand men-at-arms and ten thousand infantry.

When, however, Julius II found himself defeated and exposed to still greater peril, he turned with eagerness toward the plan which Bainbridge had proposed; and early in July, 1511, the Venetian ambassador at Rome was able to report to the Signory that a league between the Pope, England, and Spain was in process of negotiation, but with the exclusion of Venice unless the Republic made terms with the Emperor.[2]

This apparently strange provision had no other object than to prepare the way by a reconciliation of Venice and Maximilian for securing his adhesion to the proposed general alliance against France. But, in the meantime, Maximilian was forming plans of his own. Having learned of the Pope's impaired state of health, on September 18, 1511, he wrote to his daughter Margaret that he was about to charge Matthias Lang with a special mission to Rome, for the purpose of arranging with Julius II to accept him, Maximilian, as his coadjutor in the Holy See, with a view to becoming pope upon the death of Julius. In this letter he declares that he had asked the support of Ferdinand the Catholic, who had

---

[1] Brown, *Calendar*, II, No. 89.
[2] The same, No. 108.

THE STRUGGLE FOR SUPREMACY IN ITALY

promised to secure for him the votes of the Spanish cardinals, upon condition that the imperial crown be accorded to his grandson, the Archduke Charles. He had commenced already, he continues, "to work the cardinals," and a contribution of two or three hundred thousand ducats would render him great service in this respect. In another letter, the Emperor authorizes Paul von Lichtenstein, Marshal of the province of Tyrol, to pawn his jewels and imperial ornaments for a loan of three hundred thousand ducats with the bankers Fugger to be used in securing a papal election.[1]

The prompt recovery of Julius II rendered futile this and all other schemes for grasping the tiara, and with renewed vigor the Pope continued his efforts to form a coalition against France. On October 4, 1511, he signed with Venice and Ferdinand the Catholic a compact known as the "Holy League," having for its object the expulsion of the French from Italy. On November 13, Henry VIII of England joined the League, and on December 20 signed with Ferdinand a treaty for a combined attack on France.[2] Although the Emperor did not formally sign the "Holy League" until November 19, 1512, his adhesion was from the first provided for, and his letters to Margaret of Burgundy reveal his utter inutility to France. Thus, Julius II was again made the arbiter of European politics, and France completely isolated.

The military genius of young Gaston de Foix was now the only dependence of the King of France. In October,

---

[1] The first named letter is found in Le Glay, *Correspondance*, II, p. 37; and the second in Goldast, *Politische Reichshändel*, Frankfort, 1614, pp. 428, 429. The subject of Maximilian's real intention has given rise to controversy. Ulmann, *Maximilians I Absichten auf das Papstthum*, considers that the real purpose of Maximilian was to secularize the State of the Church. On the other hand, see Pastor, *Histoire* VI, pp. 350, 357, whose valuable note on p. 350, gives an excellent *résumé* of the controversy. The recent tendency has been to give the letters of Maximilian a literal interpretation. For the financial conditions of Maximilian's loan from the Fuggers, see Ehrenberg, *Das Zeitalter der Fugger*, Jena, 1896, p. 94.

[2] See Dumont, IV, Part I, p. 137.

1511, ten thousand Swiss poured into Italy from the St. Gothard, a little later Don Ramon de Cardone led an equally strong force of Spaniards into Romagna to secure Bologna, and the Venetians advanced their troops to Brescia. For a few months the feats of Gaston de Foix covered the French with glory, but his death in the battle of Ravenna, on April 11, 1512, deprived Louis XII of his great leader. In May, the Swiss had entered Milanese territory; in June, La Palice led the French army back to France; in July, Ferdinand the Catholic had taken possession of Navarre, and Henry VIII was intending to send ten thousand men for the conquest of Guyenne, thus threatening the reopening of the old contest for the crown of France.

The triumph and death of Julius II

In the meantime, five cardinals, supported by Louis XII and less earnestly by Maximilian, were endeavoring to convoke a council at Pisa for the deposition of the Pope; who, in return, in order to prove the movement only schismatic, called another council to meet at Rome in the Lateran. The war of pamphlets was again reopened, and all the tactics of the Great Schism were renewed; but the Italians were loyal to Julius II, the handful of French prelates and jurists who met at Pisa found the doors of the cathedral barred against them, while the Lateran Council assumed an ecumenical character, and toward its close received representatives even of the Emperor, who had then become an adherent of the "Holy League."

In the temporal as well as in the spiritual field, Julius II had achieved a triumph over all his foes. The Swiss had driven the French from Milan, which had fallen under the condominium of the Pope, Venice, Ferdinand, and the Confederates. This was in itself a grave danger. The Swiss would gladly have retained Como and Novara, and the Venetians the territories formerly occupied by them; while the Emperor, to whom the investiture belonged by feudal law, proposed as duke of Milan his grandson, the Archduke Charles; but the Pope, supported by the Swiss and the Milanese themselves, secured the recognition of Maximilian

Sforza, son of Ludovico. At the same time, the Medici were restored to Florence, and Genoa was once more free. Thus, the French, who had lost everything for which they had so long struggled in Italy, saw all their work undone.

When the Pope heard of the liberation of Genoa, his triumph seemed complete. "Now," he said, "we have nothing more to ask of God!" All Rome rejoiced with him, and poets celebrated him as the "Liberator of Italy." "Never," wrote the Venetian ambassador, "has a victorious general or emperor on his entry into Rome been the object of honors equal to those the Pope has received to-day." He saw the State of the Church enriched with Parma, Piacenza, and Reggio in addition to its former subject cities. At Rome itself monuments to the greatness of his reign rose on every side. The Church of St. Peter crowned with the dome of the Pantheon in the mind of Bramante, the vault of the Sistine Chapel made alive with heroic forms by the hand of Michaelangelo, the stanze of the Vatican populated by the imagination of Raphael, — such were the creations which sprang from his wish to glorify the Church with every sign and symbol of immortal power.

Yet, when on February 21, 1513, Julius II passed from the scene of his heroic existence, he had not accomplished the great task which would have made him one of the creative forces of modern Europe, — the liberation of Italy from the foreigner. No one of the great powers was satisfied with the fruits of the "Holy League." Spain had been permanently entrenched in the possession of Naples, Milan was to be an apple of discord for future contestants, and the whole of Italy to be made the scene of unending strife. The temporal power of the Papacy had, indeed, been revived; but its spritual influence had been seriously impaired. Unwilling to appeal to the nations as a kingdom not of this world, the augmentation of its political power did not increase its authority as an instrument of truth.

III. THE EFFECT ON EUROPE OF THE CONTEST
FOR ITALY

The corruption of international morals

The wars of Italy and the diplomatic negotiations connected with them rested upon no fixed principles whatever. Neither national interest, nor public morality, nor religious zeal had any place in them. Personal ambition, rivalry, or resentment was their only spring of action. The infantile diplomacy of Louis XII, actuated wholly by a passion for the conquest of Milan and Naples and the candidacy of Cardinal d'Amboise for the Papacy; the brutal selfishness of Ferdinand the Catholic, ill concealed by his flimsy hypocrisy; and the impotent greed of Maximilian, always insatiable as he was impecunious; — these were the elements that gave direction to the international development of Europe for an entire generation.

Of the four great sovereigns of the time, only Henry VII, — cautious, prudent, avaricious, and eminently practical in building up his kingdom, — managed to hold aloof from the deplorable intrigues and conspiracies which filled the first decade of the sixteenth century. In the trio of competitors for the first place in Italy, Maximilian had proved the feeblest, Louis XII the most unfortunate, and Ferdinand the Catholic the most successful. The secret of Ferdinand's relative success lay in his unswerving purpose to hold fast to a single object, the Kingdom of Naples. His falsehoods had at least the advantage of being systematic, while the infidelity of Louis and Maximilian was often inconsequent. All of them promised where they had no intention to fulfil, Louis and Maximilian where there was nothing practical to gain, but Ferdinand applied deception only where it counted for his interest. Upon one occasion, when he was informed that Louis XII had complained of his deceiving him, "What," he cried with contempt, "does he complain of that? Why, I have deceived him ten times without his knowing it!"[1]

---
[1] Voltaire says of Ferdinand: "On l'appelait en Espagne, le sage, le prudent; en Italie, le pieux; en France et à Londres, le perfide."

The methods of diplomacy borrowed from Italy not only suffered from being imperfectly understood and clumsily applied, but when exercised by great powers seemed to acquire a different character. As developed and practised by the little states of Italy, diplomatic intrigue was a natural and necessary means of self-preservation. In the intercourse of great nations, however, it seemed petty and ignoble. In the long history of rivalry between the Italian states, no outrage had ever been perpetrated equal to that for which the League of Cambray was organized; nor had any transaction ever involved more deplorable methods and motives. The hypocritical fiction of a war against the Turks was used to mask a gigantic conspiracy of secret attack and ruthless spoliation. When asked by the Venetian envoys if the League had any relation to Venice, Cardinal d'Amboise had solemnly assured them that it had not. In the name of the last remnant of European unity, the pretence of hostility to the Infidel, the one European power which had persistently opposed the Turk until it was abandoned by the others, had at last become the prey of a coalition between the three most powerful Christian states.

Moral degeneration of the Papacy

The complete wreck of Christendom as a moral organism is now evident. The Papacy, which represented its inner life, had degenerated into a mere temporal power, exactly equivalent in its motives and purposes to the other Italian principalities. Instead of reforming the Church, the Lateran Council had merely celebrated and confirmed the victories of Julius II; and instead of arresting the secularization of the Holy See as a political and military power from which spiritual authority had practically departed, it approved and sanctioned a policy which was soon to alienate from it the half of Europe. The *renaissance*, — notwithstanding its glory in the arts, in letters, and in the humanities, — by its revival of Roman Paganism, essentially imperial and pre-Christian, had engulfed the elements of evangelical morality which had conquered barbarism and created the grandeur of the Church.

CHAP. IV
A. D.
1502-1518

Misfortunes of
Louis XII

The events immediately following the death of Julius II, who has too often been condemned as the evil genius of the time and responsible for most of its aberrations, reveal the utter inconsequence of the international politics of that period, and serve to illustrate the observations already made.

The election of Cardinal Giovanni de' Medici, son of Lorenzo the Magnificent, to the Holy See, at the age of only thirty-eight, under the name of Leo X, in no respect altered the attitude of the Papacy, except by the substitution for the intense personality of Julius II of a will less resolute and an intelligence less vigorous. In princely ambition and secular policy no change was introduced.

Still opposed by the coalition of the Pope, the Emperor, the King of Spain, the King of England, and the Swiss, — Louis XII disclosed the hollowness of his claims against Venice by forming an alliance with the Republic in a treaty of March 14, 1513, for the partition of the northern part of the Italian peninsula, France to take the Milanese territories and Venice those claimed by the Emperor.

About the same time, on April 1, a truce was concluded by Louis XII with Ferdinand the Catholic, by which the King of Spain retained possession of that portion of Navarre lying south of the Pyrenees, which has since remained Spanish, and Louis was thus left free to pursue his plans in Italy.

In May, 1513, a French army again crossed the Alps to recover Milan. Alexandria was captured without a battle, and Maximilian Sforza retreated to seek refuge with the Swiss; but on June 5, an army of twenty-four thousand Swiss fell upon the French at Novara, and inflicted upon them a definitive defeat.

But the misfortunes of Louis XII were not to end with Novara. Driven from Italy, he was promptly attacked upon his own frontiers. On July 1, the King of England landed a force at Calais, and on August 16, in concert with Maximilian, defeated the French at Guinegatte. On September 7, under the direction of Margaret of Burgundy, a large army of

Swiss and imperial troops appeared at Dijon. The French general, La Trémoïlle, was obliged to make a hasty treaty promising to the Swiss four hundred thousand crowns, the abandonment of Milan and Asti, and the restitution to the Pope and the Emperor of all the other places that had been held by France in Northern Italy. The King refused to ratify the treaty; but, except the payment to the Swiss, the accomplished facts were equivalent to its ratification. At the same time, the defeated monarch learned that his ally, James IV of Scotland, had been beaten and killed on September 9 by the English at Flodden Field.

Following swiftly upon these military reverses, the death of Anne of Brittany, on January 9, 1514, added to the King's afflictions, but opened the way for the operation of new influences upon him.

Leo X had effected a reconciliation between the Emperor and Venice, and was able to win the adhesion of Louis XII to the decisions of the Lateran Council; but he could not divert him from his fixed purpose to recover Milan. Clinging with greater tenacity than ever to that idea, the King of France was still hoping to form an alliance for that purpose.

To this end, on March 13, 1514, he signed a new truce with Ferdinand; but without an understanding with Henry VIII he could not hope to renew with success hostilities in Italy.

An apparent obstacle to an *entente* with the King of England lay in the fact, that Margaret of Burgundy had obtained from Henry VIII an engagement not to conclude a peace or even a truce with France without consulting her; and Margaret's price for her consent was the surrender of Franche-Comté. "Other princes," she complained, "are farther removed from their enemies than we, and there are mountains or seas between them."

But a powerful influence was working in England for a peace with France. Since 1513, Thomas Wolsey, who had won the King's favor by his devoted activity and great ability in the campaign of that year against the French, had become the power behind the throne. Intelligent, not too scrupulous, and faithful to the royal interest as he apprehended it, Wolsey had conceived the vast and fruitful project of making England the arbiter of Europe by holding the balance of power between the continental monarchies. An ecclesiastic by choice and training, he had been rewarded for his services to the State by high preferment in the Church, being already Archbishop of York, while holding several other sources of church revenue, and soon to become a cardinal.

On June 9, 1514, the gossip of the Venetian ambassador includes the announcement, that the King of England had abandoned his intention of invading France, and that an alliance with Louis XII was about to be concluded. On the thirtieth, it is reported that when the French ambassador had refused King Henry's demand for a million and a half ducats and the cession of three towns in France, the King had gayly replied, — " Well, if he wishes to marry my sister, the widow of the King of Scotland, the agreement shall be made." [1]

On August 14, Badoer describes from London the ceremony of betrothal, at which he was present, the alliance having been determined after conference with the Pope, who was to be included in it. Of the Emperor there was no mention, and neither his ambassador nor the ambassador of Spain was invited to be present at the ceremony, " which caused much comment universally." The *fiancée*, however, was not the widow of the King of Scotland, as Henry had suggested, but the King's younger sister, Mary. So pleased was she to become Queen of France, says the ambassador, that she " did not care for the French King's being an old man of fifty-two, whereas she is a young maiden of seventeen."

If the Anglo-French alliance was a wise stroke of diplomacy for both France and England, it was a happy event for the whole of Europe; for it created an equilibrium of the powers which stood for peace. For the first time in its

---

[1] Brown, *Calendar*, II, No. 436.

history, England, while pursuing a course conducive to its national interest, was in a position to exercise that mediatorial influence which, dating from the triumph of Wolsey's policy, was to be its frequent rôle in international affairs for centuries to come.

It was time for England and France to become friends, for their interests were in many respects identical, and their enmity had for years been traditional rather than vital. It was natural, perhaps, for Henry VIII to oppose Louis XII so long as he menaced Europe with a universal monarchy and the control of the Papacy; but in 1513 both these dangers had ended with his defeat. Happy with his beautiful young queen, — described by a contemporary as "*rien mélancolique ains toute récréative*," — though he could not abandon the thought of a new campaign for the recovery of Milan, Louis XII was never able to carry it into execution. "In the spring," he said to his courtiers, "in the spring, we shall march to Italy." But when the spring came, the poor king had been three months dead.

In the earlier part of his reign, Henry VIII had been much influenced by Ferdinand the Catholic through his daughter, Queen Catherine. Devoted to her father's interests, she had since her marriage with Henry VIII acted as Ferdinand's ambassador at the English court, and regarded England almost as a part of his domains. But Henry had been led to realize the selfishness and perfidy of Ferdinand's conduct toward him, and Wolsey had fathomed his secret designs.

To form a kingdom in Italy for his grandson, Ferdinand, by the union of Milan, Venice, Genoa, and Florence under Spanish rule; to draw Maximilian into his plans; and to deceive France until it was too late to oppose them, — such was the ambitious scheme of Ferdinand. To execute it, on March 13, 1514, he had renewed his truce with France, and Maximilian had joined in it; but Venice had comprehended its import, Wolsey had formed the Anglo-French alliance, and the establishment of Austro-Spanish predominance in Italy was thereby frustrated.

Chap. IV
a. d.
1502-1518

Accession of Francis I

Scarcely more than twenty years of age, Francis of Angoulême, brave, chivalrous, and ambitious, the pride of his mother, Louise of Savoy, from whom he inherited his brilliant intelligence and lively sentiment, in January, 1515, ascended the throne of France. As husband of Madame Claude, whom he had married in the previous May, he had secured her inheritance of Brittany to the monarchy, and after his consecration at Reims, the young king was prepared to turn his thoughts toward Italy.

Preliminary to a campaign, however, diplomatic arrangements were necessary; for the Emperor, the Pope, Ferdinand the Catholic, and the Swiss were ready to defend Milan against the French.

By acknowledging a debt of a million crowns to Henry VIII, peace with England was easily maintained, and Francis conceived the idea that by the generous use of money the friendship of England could always be ensured.

Although only fifteen years old, the Archduke Charles of Burgundy five days after the accession of Francis was declared to have reached his majority; and thus, at the very beginning of his reign, the King of France and the future King of Spain entered upon that rivalry which was to continue throughout the tragic careers of these two young monarchs, each destined to be the chief impediment to the other's plans. From the first, the aversion and contempt of Francis toward his young "vassal," as he chose to call him, were manifest. On hearing of the Archduke's release from tutelage, Francis declared that he would never be led by him as the late king had been led by the Emperor and the King of Aragon.

Still, eager to begin his campaign against Milan, Francis was ready to make an arrangement with his neighbors of the House of Austria. At first it was proposed to renew the provisions of Cambray, supplemented by the marriage of the Archduke Charles to Renée, second daughter of Louis XII, with Milan and Asti as her wedding dowry. The cession of Franche-Comté to the Archduke was also suggested, but all these proposals were rejected by the counsellors of Francis as unreasonable. Finally, on March 24, 1515, a treaty was signed at Paris, by which the marriage of the princess with Charles was arranged with the Duchy of Berry and two hundred thousand crowns as a marriage portion; while Abbeville, Amiens, Montdidier, Péronne, and Ponthieu were pledged as a forfeit, if the marriage should not be consummated.[1]

Needing the aid of Francis I to oppose the designs of Ferdinand the Catholic and the demands of the Emperor, Venice was only too eager to renew its alliance with France; and despatches preserved in its archives present us with a detailed description of the ceremonies accompanying this solemnity, which may serve to illustrate the diplomatic usages of that time.

On March 25, the Venetian ambassadors, Pietro Pasqualigo and Sebastiano Giustinian, were received in solemn audience by the young king. Two bishops and the Seneschal of Toulouse conducted the magnificently attired envoys from their hotel to the great hall of the palace, where Francis I awaited them in state. Seated under a canopy, robed in white brocade, the King had on his right the Duke of Alençon, — husband of the King's sister "and the second person in France," — the Constable de Bourbon, and all the princes and lords of royal blood; on his left the Chancellor, Antoine Duprat, and a number of high prelates; while behind the throne stood the Grand Master of his household, Arthus de Boisy, — who was virtually his prime minister, — the Marshal de la Palice, the Treasurer Robertet, and other councillors and courtiers.

As the ambassadors entered the King arose, holding in his hand his *berretta*, and courteously declined to permit them to kneel or kiss his hand. When he had effusively embraced them, the ambassadors presented their letters of credence, after which all sat down upon invitation from the King.

---

[1] Dumont, IV, Part I, p. 200.

In a flowery Latin oration, Giustinian then expressed the condolences of the Republic upon the death of Louis XII and its felicitations upon the accession of Francis, for whom, he declared, it had a great affection, which it had always entertained for the royal house of France.

After a response by the Chancellor in the name of the King, also in Latin, Francis himself arose, led the ambassadors to a window, and asked if they had anything secret to communicate to him. Pasqualigo replied, that the Signory desired to preserve the existing alliance, and urged the King to send an army into Italy.

The King answered that he had always felt a great affection for the Republic, now greater than ever since it had pleased God to raise him to the throne, and promised soon to march to Italy in person with his army.

The campaign of Marignano

Having secretly obtained from the Doge of Genoa a new recognition of French suzerainty, Francis was now prepared to invade Italy for the reconquest of Milan.

A league composed of the Pope, Ferdinand the Catholic, the Swiss, and their Italian allies was disposed to dispute his passage; but Francis was confident, and, though the ordinary passes were held by the Swiss, he led his army over the Alps by roads cut in the rocks. On September 14, aided by the troops of Venice, the battle of Marignano made him master of Lombardy. On October 4, Maximilian Sforza renounced his rights for a small indemnity and an annual pension, and Milan passed into the hands of Francis I.

Leo X had relied upon the Swiss and the Spanish to drive back the young invader, and on the first day of the battle had announced to Marino Giorgi, the Venetian ambassador, the total defeat of the French army. Early in the morning of the following day, the ambassador hastened to the Vatican, where he found the Pope only half dressed, to whom he said: "Holy Father, yesterday Your Holiness gave me bad news which was false. To-day, I bring you good news which is true." When the Pope had read the letter reporting the victory of the French, he said, "What will become of us, and of you?" "As to us," replied the ambassador, "we are with the Most Christian King, and Your Holiness has nothing to fear from him." "We shall see," replied the Pope, "what the King of France will do; we shall place ourselves in his hands and ask for mercy."

Francis had believed, and even boasted, that he would be able to get the better of the Pope; but Leo X, though wanting in the military qualities of Julius II, was a better practical diplomatist. Ludovico da Canossa, Bishop of Tricarico, was sent to make peace with the King of France but was obliged to abandon to him Parma and Piacenza, because the King's "sense of honor" demanded that they be restored to the Duchy of Milan. The Medici family, however, received his protection at Florence, and the rule of the Pope's brother Giuliano and his nephew Lorenzo was thus guaranteed.

But it was in his personal interview with Francis at Bologna that Leo X showed his diplomatic skill. The dignity of the Pope might have seemed better sustained had he received the young conqueror at Rome; but Rome was too far on the way to Naples, and to prevent Francis from going there was of capital importance. At Bologna, therefore, the young king was received by Leo X on December 12. There, after a formal audience, in which Francis appeared in a robe of cloth-of-gold and the Pope sat upon his throne with his tiara on his head in the presence of the whole papal court, several days were spent in each other's society, lodging in the same palace. Francis began by demanding that Modena and Reggio should be restored to the Duke of Ferrara, but ended by abandoning his intended campaign against Naples, and annulling the "Pragmatic Sanction" of 1438, which had so long maintained the liberties of the Gallican Church. To dissuade the young king from the invasion of Naples, the Pope pointed out the inconveniences that might be avoided by waiting till the death of Ferdinand the Catholic, which could not be far removed. By the Concordat of Bologna the Pope and the King resumed a divided control over the clergy of France, and thereby re-established relations which Louis XI had once so inconti- nently restored and afterward revoked.[1]

The new coalition against Francis I

The military success of Francis I in Italy reopened the entire Italian question, for the Emperor saw himself about to be stripped of his Italian possessions, Ferdinand the Catholic feared for the fate of the Kingdom of Naples, and Henry VIII was so chagrined by the success of the King of France that he was moved to tears.

A desperate effort was now made to oppose the progress of Francis I. Henry VIII and Ferdinand the Catholic sent money to the Emperor to raise a powerful army, Richard Pace was despatched from England to confer with him at Innsbruck and to stir up the Swiss, while the relentless Cardinal of Sion once more appealed to the cantons to recover Milan from the French.

On the other hand, Francis sent his agents to negotiate with the Swiss cantons for an alliance, for which they were to receive enormous sums of money. Ten cantons had made this engagement, but Schwytz, Uri, and Unterwalden held off; and, joined by Zug and Zürich, soon decided to serve the Emperor. Finally, eight cantons stood for Francis and five for the coalition. Thus divided, the Confederation, capable by its military force of playing a determining rôle in the politics of Europe, neutralized its influence and fell from the position of political importance which it had previously enjoyed.

In March, 1516, at the head of an army of thirty thousand men, the Emperor descended into Venetian Lombardy; but his military skill and personal bravery were not equal to the situation. Wasting his resources without definite gains, he was finally altogether disconcerted by an ingenious stratagem. A letter was prepared purporting to be a secret communication from the Swiss of the French party to those adhering to the Emperor, in which a pretended conspiracy

---

[1] The Concordat may be found in Dumont, IV, Part I, p. 229.

between them was revealed. Believing himself abandoned by his mercenaries, Maximilian is said to have dreamed that night of his ancestor, Leopold of Austria, killed by the Swiss at Sempach, and of Charles the Bold, fallen before the walls of Nancy, who, covered with blood, warned him of his danger. So impressed was he by this nocturnal vision, that he left his camp and returned to Germany. His army, unpaid and without a leader, gradually melted away, the French and the Venetians advanced, and soon nothing but Verona was left to the Emperor in Italy.

The death of Ferdinand the Catholic on January 23, 1516, placed the young Archduke Charles in a position requiring extreme circumspection. Through his mother, Juana of Castile, — still living but incapable of governing, — he became the heir of Castile, Aragon, and the "Two Sicilies," that is, the Kingdoms of Sicily and of Naples, which Ferdinand had united under his own rule. The probability of discord in these realms, combined with their hesitation to coalesce into a single monarchy, and their wide separation from the estates inherited by Charles from Mary of Burgundy through his father, Philip, in the Netherlands, rendered necessary an *entente* with France, geographically so centrally situated and so solidly unified as to place these possessions in constant peril.

By the labors of Guillaume de Croy, Seigneur de Chièvres, who had been chosen as the chief adviser of Charles, and Arthus de Boisy, prime minister of Francis I, the Treaty of Noyon was concluded on August 13, 1516, by which, instead of the Princess Renée, the infant daughter of Francis was espoused to the King of Spain, with a relinquishment of French rights in the Kingdom of Naples as her dowry.[1] As the marriage could not be consummated for a long time to come, Charles was to pay his prospective father-in-law an annual tribute of one hundred thousand crowns of gold, thus acknowledging French rights in the Kingdom of Naples.

---

[1] See Dumont, IV, Part I, p. 224.

An indemnity was also to be paid to Catherine, widow of the late King of Navarre, who had been an ally of France.

To render this treaty more secure, the Emperor was invited to adhere to it; but his animosity toward Francis was difficult to overcome, and it was not until December 3, 1516, that, after strenuous efforts, he was induced to make peace by the Treaty of Brussels, and cede Verona to the Venetians for two hundred thousand ducats.[1]

The project of universal peace

Thus, at last, the Emperor was entirely excluded from Italy, Venice restored to its position on the mainland, and peace concluded between the Kings of France and Spain. In a treaty of November 29, 1516, the thirteen cantons of the Swiss Confederation had concluded with France a "perpetual alliance." On March 11, 1517, the Emperor, Charles, and Francis I confirmed at Cambray their previous agreements by an alliance for the mutual guarantee of their possessions and a union to prevent the further encroachments of the Turks.[2]

For a time it seemed as if the Anglo-French *entente* of 1514 might become abortive, for several of its provisions still remained unexecuted; but the well directed activity of Wolsey soon changed the situation. Raised to the cardinalate on November 17, 1517, in spite of the reluctance of Leo X, who hated him, the Archbishop of York was so powerful in England that the papal legate, Campeggio, was forbidden to enter the realm except on condition that his dignity and powers be shared by the great minister. Rebuffed by the treaties of Noyon, Brussels, and Cambray, which had disregarded England, the Cardinal-legate opened negotiations for a new *rapprochement* with France.

The possession of Tournay by the English since 1513 was an open wound in the pride of Francis I, and Wolsey, who

---

[1] Léonard, II, p. 158. In adhering to the Treaty of Noyon, Maximilian had no intention of keeping his engagements. "My son," he said to Charles, "you will deceive the French, and I will deceive the English." — Brewer, *Letters and Papers*, II, No. 2930.

[2] See Dumont, IV, Part I, p. 256.

had been made Bishop of Tournay as a reward for his services to Henry VIII, found this a convenient starting-point for opening negotiations. Openly and stoutly opposed by the chief nobles of England, who wished for no alliance with France, he steadily pursued his course of conciliation, aided by a secret understanding with his king. The task was long and difficult, but his patient efforts not only resulted in two separate treaties, of October 4, 1518, whereby Tournay was surrendered to France in exchange for six hundred thousand crowns of gold, and a marriage arranged for the new-born dauphin, Francis, with Henry's daughter, Mary, then two years old;[1] but, by his resolute insistence, the new alliance was made to include acceptance of the principle of a universal peace, to be guaranteed by the two signatories and those who might afterward adhere to the compact.

In October, 1518, the treaties were solemnly ratified in St. Paul's Cathedral by Henry VIII and the French plenipotentiaries, and on December 12 in Paris, by Francis I. Wolsey was rewarded with an annual pension of twelve thousand livres as indemnity for the loss of Tournay, but it cannot be justly said that he was "bought."[2] The victory of Wolsey's diplomacy for England and for himself was too palpable to require a bribe for accepting it. Charles of Spain reluctantly, but quite inevitably, adhered to the general peace on January 14, 1519; and Leo X, though deeply mortified that the office of mediator and peacemaker had thus passed from the

---

[1] The text is found in Rymer, VI, Part I, p. 147; and also, as ratified by the King of Spain, in Dumont, IV, Part I, pp. 269, 275.

[2] Mignet, *Rivalité*, I, pp. 236, 237, regards Francis I as having "acheté l'avide monarque et son ministre Wolsey, non moins avide que lui." Money compensation had become a recognized mode of settling international differences, certainly quite as honorable for both disputants as war. As to Wolsey's alleged acceptance of bribes, it was customary at that time to receive gifts from foreign monarchs. In Wolsey's case the grant was open and in recognition of vested rights surrendered by him. On Wolsey's motives and practices, in this respect, see the judicious remarks of Creighton, *Cardinal Wolsey*, pp. 58, 59.

CHAP. IV
A. D.
1502-1518

Holy See to the Chancellor of England, was also compelled to join in the compact of universal peace. In the audience of March 16, 1519, when the papal legate and the ambassador of Charles bearing the ratifications were received by Henry VIII at London, the opportunity was used to celebrate the triumph of Wolsey in winning for England, thitherto regarded as a third-class power, the acknowledged primacy in the diplomacy of Europe. In the public speeches made upon that occasion, the King of England was alluded to as the head of the alliance, and the Pope merely as a member of it, whom the King would magnanimously be pleased to see become its chief! "The principal author of these proceedings," wrote the Venetian ambassador, "was the Legate of York, whose sole aim was to procure incense for his king and himself. No one could please him better than by styling him the arbitrator of the affairs of Christendom."

To the end of his life the Emperor Maximilian secretly resented this general pacification, for it left him stripped of Milan and without revenge upon Venice; but his death, on January 12, 1519, while it opened a new cause of contention, left the chief affairs of Europe in the hands of three young monarchs, the kings of England, France, and Spain. Under the fraternal rule of these three sovereigns, all under twenty-seven years of age, it seemed as if Europe might enjoy a long period of repose, and bring to perfection an international system based on equity and national security. It was, however, an illusory prospect; for the imperial succession was now to make all Europe the theatre of a struggle beside which the wars of Italy were insignificant.

The institution of permanent embassies in Europe

Among the results of the rivalry for supremacy in Italy, the most important and the most enduring was the establishment of permanent diplomatic relations between the chief European countries. From the fall of the Roman Empire occasional embassies had always been customary, but the continuous residence of diplomatic agents in foreign capitals was unknown until the affairs of Italy rendered it imperative. The Italian states had, indeed, long enjoyed a diplomatic system, made obligatory by the abdication of the Empire as a general authority over them and by their mutual rivalries; but until the wars of Italy had awakened the monarchs of Europe to the necessity of constant vigilance and associated action, even the great powers were hardly more advanced in their international intercourse than the barbarian kingdoms of the early Middle Ages. The plans of Charles VIII of France for the conquest of Italy suddenly brought Europe to a consciousness of its peril and of the need and value of alliances between the powers. In close connection with the great coalitions which followed was developed the institution of permanent diplomatic representation.

Although Philippe de Commines was designated by Malipiero as "resident" at Venice when he took his leave on May 24, 1495, this mission can hardly be regarded as the beginning of that institution on the part of France; since it was of short duration and followed by a long suspension of diplomatic relations with Venice. Between that time and the end of the fifteenth century, however, permanent embassies were generally established by France and by nearly all the powers of Western Europe. During the reigns of Louis XII, Ferdinand the Catholic, and the Emperor Maximilian, diplomacy thus became an organized institution, by which the chief powers were brought into closer and more vital relations with one another.

Thus came into being in the "*Corps Diplomatique*," the first permanent international representation of sovereign states. Without organization and possessing no code except its own usages, which gradually took the form of customary law, the diplomatic body was an aggregation of living molecules without vital relations and without a soul. Questions of form, ceremony, and precedence quite inevitably became the chief objects of its interest, until a later age gave its existence a new significance through the regulation of its functions by principles of jurisprudence and conventional agreement. Had this body been from the first an association of authorized agents for the maintenance of international justice and equity, the history of Europe might have been altogether different; but the political theory of that time made no provision for a rule of law among the nations.[1]

The changed conception of the State

In the early Middle Ages, two political conceptions had predominated, — that of feudality, and that of imperial authority. Both of these conceptions were rooted in the idea of "obligation" as an essential social bond. In the feudal hierarchy there was an unbroken series of correlative rights and duties extending from the lowest vassal to the highest suzerain. The imperial idea was in substance nothing less than the assertion of a universal right of command and a universal duty of obedience. However violent and lawless the spirit of the Middle Ages may have been in practice, in theory all its institutions were founded on ethical ideas, and all its public life was inspired by morality and religion.

With the rise of the independent city-states in Italy and of the national monarchies in the rest of Europe, new political principles came into action. All the rights that had formerly been comprised in the idea of "*imperium*," or "sovereignty," were assumed by the head of each individual state, as if that state were universal and not merely local and particular; while, at the same time, with the abolition of feudalism disappeared that conception of duties as reciprocal which had animated the feudal organization. As a result of this double evolution, appeared a new conception of mon-

---

[1] Although permanent missions became practically universal before the close of the sixteenth century, the expression "*Corps Diplomatique*" did not come into use until about the middle of the eighteenth. Its origin is thus explained by Vehse : " Der Name ' Diplomatisches Corps ' für die Wolke von fremden Gesandten, die in Wien von vielen grossen, kleinen, und kleinsten weltlichen und geistlichen Kur- und Fürsten Deutschlands und Italiens und von den auswärtigen grossen und kleinen Höfen zusammengeschaart waren — dieser sehr bezeichnende Name kam unter Maria Theresia auf. Der Kanzler Fürst schreibt in seinem Hofbericht vom Jahre 1754 : ' Corps diplomatique, nom qu'une dame donna un jour à ce corps nombreux de ministres étrangers à Vienne.' " — *Geschichte des österreichischen Hofs und Adels und der österreichischen Diplomatie*, Th. VIII, Hamburg, 1852, p. 113.

archy, ever tending to become more and more absolute, holding itself responsible to no law, and above all obligation. Since the will of the prince is law, everything is lawful which the prince wills. Upon this hypothesis, when the wills of princes collide,— there being no law above them, and the sovereignty of each being unlimited,— it only remains for them to endeavor, by ruse or by armed force, to destroy one another.[1]

The political thought growing out of this conception finds its most complete expression in the writings of Niccolò Machiavelli, whose career as diplomatic agent and secretary of the "Ten" at Florence had well fitted him to become an exponent of the age in which he lived. Having entered the service of the Republic as a clerk of its government at the time of the expulsion of the Medici in 1494, he was constantly engaged in political activity as envoy or secretary till their restoration in 1512.

Having then retired to his farm near San Casciano, he led the life of a country gentleman, spending his afternoons at cards with low companions in the village inn; while, in the

---

[1] At Rome, all secular rulers were regarded as subordinate to the Holy See, but the supremacy of the Emperor over kings was not maintained.

Numerous writers have attributed to Pope Julius II an ordinance fixing the relative rank of the principal sovereigns in an order of precedence. A list of rulers, evidently intended for this purpose but not implying their subordination, is found at the beginning of the *Diarium* of Paris de Grassis, Master of Ceremonies at the Pontifical Court under Julius II; but it is now regarded as an unofficial draft intended for his personal use. It is found in the British Museum, "Additional MSS.," Nos. 8440, 8444, and is as follows:

ORDO REGUM CHRISTIANORUM Imperator Caesar; Rex Romanorum; Rex Franciae; Rex Hispaniae; Rex Aragoniae; Rex Portugalliae; Rex Angliae, cum tribus discors praedictis; Rex Siciliae, discors cum rege Portugalliae; Rex Scotiae et Rex Ungariae, inter se discordes; Rex Navarrae; Rex Cipri; Rex Bohemiae; Rex Poloniae; Rex Daniae.

Another list of Paris de Grassis, containing numerous names of no importance and some of them unknown, is preserved in the Vatican, — See Nys, *Les origines du droit international*, pp. 332, 334.

Chap. IV
A. D.
1502-1518

evening, laying aside his coarse garments and "arrayed in courtly attire," he sought the society of great minds in his library, where he devoted himself to study and composition. Thus was brought forth his famous work, "Il Principe" or "The Prince," destined to become a favorite textbook of statecraft for European rulers.[1]

Pining for a return to the excitement of public life, "if it were only the work of rolling a stone," Machiavelli hoped to procure his reinstatement in office by the Medici, to whom with this purpose he dedicated his book. Two hundred years earlier, Dante had said in exile, "If Florence cannot be entered honorably, I will never set foot within her walls." But Machiavelli was ready to return at any price.

It is not from "The Prince" alone, but from the whole of his writings that the political philosophy of Machiavelli can best be gathered. His fundamental premise is the depravity of mankind. Because the bad prevails over the good in human nature, there is no sufficient law of human conduct in the constitution of man. Rules of right action must, therefore, be imposed upon men from without; for, since their prevailing impulses prompt them to disorder, without laws life would be chaotic. If men were not corrupt, the best form of human government would be a free republic; but, because the strength of a state lies in its unity and authority, in a corrupt condition of society a republic cannot exist and a prince is necessary.[2] As the creator of law and order, the

---

[1] This remarkable work was written in 1513, but was not published until 1532, five years after Machiavelli's death. The book then made great progress. The Emperor Charles V and Philip II of Spain were close students of it. Catherine de' Medici introduced it into France, and both Henry III and Henry IV are said to have had it on their persons when they were murdered. Richelieu esteemed it highly; it was well known and studied at the English court; Pope Sixtus V, who condemned it publicly, made a summary of it in his own handwriting; and Queen Christina of Sweden has left curious marginal annotations upon it. See Villari, II, p. 193; and pp. 522, 530.

[2] Machiavelli is not always consistent. In the fifty-seventh chapter of the first book of his "Discourses," he defends the wisdom and con-

prince is not bound by conventional morality; for such a limitation would defeat his purpose. Whatever he finds it necessary to do in order to establish his authority is, therefore, proper for him. Force, deceit, falsehood, and even murder may be necessary in establishing this authority; but, while these are not commendable in themselves, as necessary means to so great an end they are permissible. Being the source of moral order in society, the prince is not, then, subject to ordinary rules of morality. The State is essentially non-moral. As between states, therefore, there is no law or obligation; for, since there is no superior authority to impose rules of action upon them, each sovereign power is a law to itself.

The cold-blooded philosophy of Machiavelli has been condemned by his critics as a shocking example of intellectual perversity; but this severe judgment overlooks both the origin of his doctrines and the practical purpose he had in view.

The maxims of Machiavelli

As to the origin of his doctrines, his writings are only a faithful exposition of practices already actually embodied in the art of government. His method was based upon observation, analysis, and induction; imperfect it may be, but still entitling him to a place as the first founder of modern political science. With remorseless accuracy, though with undisturbed conscience, he reduced to formulas the principles adopted by those who in his time had achieved political success.

If all men were perfectly good, argues Machiavelli, all government would be superfluous; but, since men are bad, it is a necessary evil. Only a despot can create a strong state, and he will fail if he shrinks from the use of force or is

stancy of the multitude in comparison with princes. After arguing against the observations of Livy, he says: "A people which commands, under a good constitution, will be as stable, as prudent, as grateful as a prince. What do I say? It will be still more so than the wisest prince." With regard to fidelity in keeping engagements, he says in the fifty-ninth chapter: "I am convinced that peoples are less subject to error than princes, and that they may be more surely trusted."

governed by moral scruples. "The belief that if you remain idle on your knees, God will fight for you in your own despite, has ruined many kingdoms and many states." "Our religion has glorified men of humble and contemplative life, rather than men of action. Moreover, it has placed the *summum bonum* in humility, in lowliness, and in the contempt of earthly things; Paganism, on the contrary, placed it in highmindedness, in bodily strength, and in all the other things that make men strongest." "No country was ever united or prosperous, unless the whole of it had passed beneath the sway of one commonwealth or one prince, as has happened in the cases of France and Spain." "Let the prince, then, determine to conquer and maintain his state; the means employed by him will always be deemed honorable and universally praised, for the popular mind is always caught by appearances and by the final result of things." "A certain prince of these days, whom it is not well to name, never preaches anything but peace and faith, while yet most adverse to both; and had he observed either the one or the other, he would frequently have lost his reputation or his state."[1] "A prince should know how to play both the beast and the man, both the fox and the lion. . . . Those that merely play the lion do not understand the matter. Therefore, a prudent lord neither could nor should observe faith, when such observance might be to his injury, or when the motives that caused him to promise it are at an end. . . . Since men are bad, and would not keep faith with you, you are not bound to keep faith with them." "It is necessary, however, to give a good coloring to your nature, and be a great dissembler and dissimulator, because men then readily allow themselves to be deceived. Alexander VI did nothing but deceive, . . . nevertheless he succeeded in everything." It is not necessary for a prince to have "piety, faith, humanity, integrity, and religion," but it is necessary to *seem* to have them. "It is well to have your mind so

---

[1] The reference is, without doubt, to Ferdinand the Catholic.

trained that when it is expedient not to have these qualities you may know how to become entirely different." "Accordingly, a prince should be very careful to let nothing escape his lips that is not pregnant with the five qualities above described, and nothing is more necessary than to *appear* to possess religion."

The end to which Machiavelli would apply his science of successful government was the redemption of Italy, " more captive than the Jews, more enslaved than the Persians, more divided than the Athenians, without a head, without discipline, bruised, despoiled, lacerated, ravaged, and subjected to every kind of affliction." The deliverer who would rescue her from her abyss of ruin, he thinks, must possess the qualities of the prince described by him. "The Prince" of Machiavelli was confessedly the portrait of Cesare Borgia, who knew how to be "gloriously wicked," and "whose crime has something of grandeur and nobility in it." Reprehensible as his whole career seems to us, Machiavelli pleads, he had given Romagna a brief period of peace and unity, he had destroyed only his opponents, and had not been more cruel than the Republic of Florence toward Pisa and Pistoia. He had come nearer than anyone else to the realization of the dream of Italian nationality, so dear to Machiavelli, who had studied during Cesare's campaigns that "ferocity, courage, and shrewdness," which but for the Pope's sudden death and his own illness, he believes, "would have triumphed over every difficulty."

It was easy for Macaulay to say of Machiavelli: "The whole man seems to be an enigma, a grotesque assemblage of incongruous qualities, selfishness and generosity, cruelty and benevolence, craft and simplicity, abject villany and romantic heroism";[1] but justice requires us to ask: What, then, is to be said of the age in which Machiavelli lived? Not only so, but what shall be said of the history of Europe in that age?

---

[1] *Essays*, I, p. 63.

Villari has affirmed, "It is beyond doubt that 'The Prince' had a more direct action upon real life than any other book in the world, and a larger share in emancipating Europe from the Middle Ages."[1] Would it not be more exact to say, that Machiavelli's work was the most perfect expression of an emancipation already far advanced? Certainly, the author of "The Prince" proposed nothing more perverse than the practices upon which his theories were based. His influence upon Europe has sprung in no degree from the purely subjective spirit of his work, but solely from its strict conformity to the facts of history and the lessons they seemed to teach. The revival of Paganism had already destroyed for that age the Christian idealism of the Middle Ages; the customary grounds of obligation had already been swept away; new conceptions of the State, of life, of the future, and of nature, — both human and physical, — had been introduced; and the spiritual corruption of the Holy See had paralyzed those moral energies which had once redeemed Europe from barbarism and created Christendom.

Without an ethical standard in which sincere faith could find support, Italy had become what Machiavelli pictured it, — the prey of nations. Instead of seeking its redemption in a revival of faith, Machiavelli sought it in a revival of what had once made Rome the mistress of the world, — heroic daring in the building of a state. "Had the Christian religion been maintained as it was instituted by its founder," he writes, "things would have gone differently, and men would have been greatly happier. How much, on the contrary, it has been changed and corrupted is proved by this, that the peoples nearest to Rome are those having least faith in it."

The gospel of Machiavelli, then, is the unity, strength, and authority of the civil state under the control of one man as the only sure ground of moral order. For its consummation everything else must be sacrificed. It is best secured

---

[1] Villari, *Life and Times*, II, p. 184.

through the efforts of a prince who knows no other aim than success, no other law than his own intelligence. With keen analysis the Florentine philosopher then exposes the methods by which this success may be attained, the procedure by which intelligence must operate.

But Machiavelli little dreamed of the immortality of infamy reserved for him. In composing an esoteric doctrine for the guidance of the Medici he had become, unconsciously, the "legislator of ambition" for all succeeding centuries. But it was not for the occult use of princes alone that he disclosed the secret formulas of absolute power and the false assumptions on which it rested. In laying bare the inner mechanism of princely pretences he was also preparing a manual for future revolutions, which found in this exposition of the principles of despotism a justification for the overthrow of authority based upon them. When, in a subsequent age, Grotius taught that a law for the regulation of nations was to be found in the nature of mankind, the absolutism of princes was confronted with a limitation for which Machiavelli's philosophy made no provision. When, in a still later time, Rousseau laid down the dogma that human nature in a state of freedom is essentially good, his argument gathered force from the fact that the theory of absolutism assumed that it was essentially bad. Thus Machiavelli, whose doctrines were held responsible for a political system which he had analyzed and expounded but which later ages found intolerable, served at last to reveal the false postulates upon which that system had been founded, and to indicate the methods by which it was to be attacked. By systematically epitomizing the theory of personal despotism, Machiavelli made an important contribution to its final overthrow.

AUTHORITIES

The principal treaties and negotiations may be found in the collections of Dumont, Léonard, Rymer, and Le Glay, already mentioned. The most important single source is, however, Marino Sanuto, *Diarii*, which contains a vast storehouse of facts and documents.

A general but imperfect digest of treaties is given in *Cronologia dei principali trattati di pace, di alleanza, etc., dal 1496: manuele di storia diplomatica*, Turin, 1887.

Some important details regarding the treaties of Blois are found in Höfler, *Das diplomatische Journal des Andrea del Burgo und des Philippe Haneton* (1498–1506), Vienna, 1885.

An important original source for events at Rome, and incidentally in Europe generally, during the years 1502–1505, is the *Dispacci di Antonio Giustinian, ambasciatore Veneto in Roma*, edited by Villari, Florence, 1876. The *Legazioni* of Machiavelli also furnish important contributions to our knowledge of the time. These, together with his *Istoria fiorentina*, may be found in all the complete editions of his works. The most available, perhaps, are the Italian editions of 1782, 1796, and 1813, and the French translation of the complete *Opere* in twelve volumes, published by Michaud, Paris, 1823–1826. The great edition of Passerini, commenced at Florence in 1873, has never been completed. It contains, however, the history of Florence and the *Legazioni*. The works of Guicciardini, especially his *Storia d'Italia*, *Storia fiorentina, and Recordi politici*, are of very great value. The more important of his writings are found in the edition of Canestrini, Florence, 1857–1859, several of them being then published for the first time.

The correspondence of Margaret of Burgundy (Marguerite d'Autriche) with Maximilian I, published by Le Glay, Paris, 1839; and with her friends, published by Van den Burgh, Leyden, 1847, throws much light on the period.

A digest of manuscripts in the Venetian Archives on the relations of Switzerland with Venice, and incidentally other Italian states during the wars of Italy, is found in Ceresole, *Relevé des manuscrits des Archives de Venise se rapportant à la Suisse*, Venice, 1890. It contains a complete list of the doges from 1289 to 1797.

On the conference of Louis XII, Ferdinand the Catholic, and Cardinal d'Amboise at Savona, see Filippi, *Il convegno di Savona*, Savona, 1890; and De Maulde, Revue d'Histoire Diplomatique, IV, pp. 583–590, for documents and discussion.

For the League of Cambray, Paul de Musset, *Voyage pittoresque en Italie, (partie septentrionale)* Paris, 1863, contains original documents from the Venetian Archives translated by him. See also the observations of Baschet, *La diplomatie vénitienne: les princes de l'Europe au XVI*^{e} *siècle*, pp. 366, 368, particularly on the lost *relazione* of Condulmer.

For the English relations, during the period of this chapter, and incidentally much besides, Brewer, *Letters and Papers*, in the series of Calendars of State Papers, I and II, London, 1862–1864, now becomes important; as well as Brown, *Calendar of State Papers and Manuscripts relating to English Affairs, existing in the Archives and Collections of Venice, etc.*, I and II, 1864–1867.

For the Spanish relations, during this period, see Bergenroth, *Letters, Despatches, and State Papers relating to the Negotiations between England and Spain, preserved in the Archives of Simancas*, I and II, London, 1862–1866, and *Supplement*, London, 1868.

A brief general sketch of the present period is contained in Fischer, *Geschichte der auswärtigen Politik und Diplomatie im Reformationszeitalter, 1485–1556*, Gotha, 1874.

For the Papacy, Gregorovius and Pastor, as before; with Ranke, *History of the Popes*, I, London, 1896, whose third volume contains valuable extracts from the sources; and Petruccelli della Gattina, *Histoire diplomatique des Conclaves*, Paris, 1864. For Pope Julius II, see also Brosch, *Papst Julius II und die Gründung des Kirchenstaates*, Gotha, 1888; and for Pope Leo X, Roscoe, *Life and Pontificate of Leo X*, London, 1846; Nitti, *Leone X e la sua politica*, Florence, 1892.

The Spanish relations are discussed by Prescott, *Ferdinand and Isabella*, Philadelphia, 1847, and later editions; Mariejol, *L'Espagne sous Ferdinand et Isabelle*, Paris, 1892; Häbler, *Der Streit Ferdinands und Philips um die Regierung*, Dresden, 1888; Fléchier, *Histoire du cardinal Ximénès*, Paris, 1693; Hefele, *Der Cardinal Ximénès*, Tübingen, 1851; Lea, *A History of the Inquisition of the Middle Ages*, New York and London, 1888.

The history of Juana of Castile has given rise to much controversy. In 1868, Bergenroth denied the insanity of Juana, and alleged that she was the victim of persecution on account of heresy. See the supplement to Bergenroth, *Letters, Despatches, and State Papers*, London, 1868. These conclusions were promptly disputed by Gachard, *Sur Jeanne la Folle*, Brussels, 1869; and Rösler, *Johanna die Wahnsinnige*, Vienna, 1870. Maurenbrecher, *Studien und Skizzen*, Leipzig, 1874, confirms this dissent, pp. 75, 99, in an interesting *résumé* of the discussion, in which he says the result is entirely destructive for Bergenroth's conclusions, and affirms the insanity of Juana to be beyond all doubt and her alleged heresy without foundation.

Brewer and Gairdner, *The Reign of Henry VIII, from his accession to the death of Wolsey*, London, 1887.

For the part played by the Swiss in the French wars in Italy, see Kohler, *Les Suisses dans les guerres d'Italie de 1506 à 1512*, Geneva, 1897.

For the League of Cambray, Dubos, *Histoire de la ligue faite à Cambray*, Paris, 1709, is the only special history of this conspiracy, but needs to be supplemented. A short account of the League is given in Romanin, *Storia documentata di Venezia*, V, Venice, 1856; and also by Cappelletti, *Storia della Repubblica di Venezia*, VII, Venice, 1851; but both are inadequate. Fraknoi, *Ungarn und die Liga von Cambray*, Budapest, 1883, throws new light on the relations of Hungary to the League, and shows the injury caused by it to that country. Fulin, *Il canale di Suez e la Repubblica di Venezia*, in the Archivio Veneto, II, Part I, Venice, 1871, gives the history of the plans of Venice regarding a Suez canal. An excellent general account of the peril and defence of Venice may be found in Cipolla, *Storia delle Signorie Italiane*.

On Maximilian's ambition for the Papacy, see Ulmann, *Kaiser Maximilians I*^{ten} *Absichten auf das Papstthum*, Stuttgart, 1888.

For Francis I, see De Maulde, *Louise de Savoie et François I*^{er}, Paris, 1895; Gaillard, *Histoire de François I*^{er}, Paris, 1819; Mignet, *Rivalité de François I*^{er} *et de Charles-Quint*, Paris, 1875.

The literature regarding Wolsey belongs chiefly to the next chapter, but the lives by Cavendish, London, 1641; Fiddes, London, 1724; Howard, London, 1824; Galt, London, 1846; and Creighton, London, 1902, may be mentioned here.

On the origin of permanent missions, besides Krauske, De Maulde, and Schaube, cited under chapter II, see Nys, *Les origines de la diplomatie et le droit d'ambassade jusqu' à Grotius*, Brussels, 1884.

For Machiavelli, Villari, *The Life and Times of Niccolò Machiavelli*, London, 1878, and later editions, is the most important. The best edition of "The Prince" is Burd, *Il Principe*, with introduction by Lord Acton, Oxford, 1891, containing a good bibliography of lives, studies, and translations. The Machiavelli literature is immense, as shown by this bibliography and the earlier work of von Mohl, " Die Machiavelli Literatur " in his *Geschichte und Literatur der Staatswissenschaft*, Erlangen, 1855–1858. The following works may be named as of special utility: Ferrari, *Machiavel juge des révolutions de notre temps*, Paris, 1849; Mundt, *Machiavelli und der Gang der europäischen Politik*, Leipzig, 1853; Fester, *Machiavelli*, Stuttgart, 1900.

CHAPTER V

THE ASCENDENCY OF THE HOUSE OF HAPSBURG

THE death of the Emperor Maximilian created a situation which served to reveal the latent impulses of the time and thereby mark the beginning of a new epoch in the history of Europe. "Emperor-elect," but never able to obtain the papal coronation, Maximilian left vacant by his death the imperial office, by theory and tradition the symbol of universal monarchy.

As held and exercised by him that office had been in effect a symbol only. Heir and ruler of the lands comprised in the heritage of the House of Austria, — sufficient in themselves to form, if properly organized, a substantial kingdom, — Maximilian was a prince entitled by his position to great influence in the German Empire, and much had at first been expected of him; but his pitiable poverty in ready money, his lack of administrative capacity, his inconsequent foreign policy, and his preference of dynastic aggrandisement to imperial consolidation had united to defeat his plans and complicate his purposes. Even in his own eyes, his inferiority to the rulers of the great national monarchies was evident. With good-humored frankness he once said, "I am a king of kings, for no one regards himself bound to obey me; while the King of Spain is a king of men, since men, though they raise objections, render him obedience; and the King of France is like a king over animals, for no one ventures to dispute his authority."

In effect, the aphorism of the Emperor expressed the truth. The princes of the Empire, though nominally his subjects, were in reality not only his equals but by their union had become his masters. Instead of a monarchy, Germany had become a federation of almost autonomous and independent states, while Italy had passed out of the imperial system and France and Spain had become Italian powers.

The German Imperial Diet was divided into three chambers, — (1) the six electors;[1] (2) the non-electoral princes, lay and ecclesiastical; and (3) the deputies of the free imperial cities. Brandenburg, Saxony, the Palatinate, Würtemberg, and Bavaria stood on nearly the same plane as Austria, each under the headship of a powerful family. It was chiefly through the Suabian League — formed in 1488, and composed of Würtemberg, the margraviates of Baden, the Hohenzollern principalities, and thirty-one imperial cities — that Maximilian had asserted such authority as he had exercised. In 1495, the Diet took advantage of Maximilian's financial necessities to obtain from him constitutional concessions which added to the power of the princes, especially in the organization of the Imperial Chamber, or supreme court of justice, thitherto appointed by the Emperor, but thenceforth — except the president — chosen by the estates. In 1500, the Council of Regency, based on representation of the estates, was charged with the chief executive power. The later division of Germany into ten circles, over each of which a captain was appointed to enforce the execution of the laws, completed the organization of the Empire; but none of these reforms greatly affected the position of the Emperor.

Notwithstanding the limitations of the imperial prerogatives, the office of Emperor still implied the highest secular dignity in the world; and, in the hands of a prince whose resources were sufficient for the task, would have presented an opportunity for the exercise of enormous power. To such a prince as Francis I, if once clothed with the imperial authority, Germany as well as Italy seemed to offer a promising field of territorial expansion. Already powerful in Italy, young, ambitious, and boasting that his resources were what-

---

[1] The King of Bohemia took no part in the Diet.

THE ASCENDENCY OF THE HOUSE OF HAPSBURG

ever he wished to extract from his people, the King of France had already set his heart upon the imperial succession at Maximilian's death. King Henry VIII of England also was secretly ambitious to mount the imperial throne. But the King of Spain, heir to the estates of the House of Austria in both Germany and Burgundy, was already in the field as Maximilian's chosen candidate. With these three young monarchs all coveting the imperial title, the election of 1519 was destined to be the most hotly contested that Europe had ever known.

I. The Rivalry for the Empire

To the imagination of Maximilian, who had always indulged in exaggerated projects for augmenting the Hapsburg power, the imperial possibilities of his grandson Charles could not fail to appeal with an irresistible attraction. Death had wonderfully multiplied the hereditary possessions of this heir of the House of Hapsburg. Besides the rich territories of the Burgundian realm inherited through his father, Philip, and Castile and Aragon derived through his mother, Juana, from Ferdinand and Isabella, the "Kingdom of the Two Sicilies" gave him a foothold in Italy if he could resist the claims of Francis I, while the American colonies promised untold treasure for carrying out his schemes. If, in addition to all this, Charles were invested with the Austrian estates in Germany, and raised to the imperial dignity, he might not only become the most potent monarch of his time; but, by welding together all these vast resources, eventually realize the dream of a universal empire.

A prospect so dazzling could not be materialized without skilful manipulation, and Maximilian had long labored upon this problem. To strengthen the House of Hapsburg on the East, he had sought to obtain for it the crowns of Bohemia and Hungary. The weakness of the child Lewis II, only son of Ladislas VI of the House of Jagellon, who possessed both these thrones, rendered probable a succession through the female line; and Maximilian's second grandson, Ferdinand, was, accordingly, affianced to the heiress, Anna, through whom the two crowns were to pass to the Hapsburg family. To break down the opposition of the brother of Ladislas — Sigismund I, King of Poland — Maximilian had formed an alliance against him with Albert of Brandenburg, Grand Master of the Teutonic Order, whom he abandoned as soon as Sigismund was driven to make terms. In order to retain his influence over the heritage of Lewis II, Maximilian had made a secret treaty on July 20, 1515, by which he adopted the young prince, and conferred upon this child of nine years the office of "Vicar General of the Holy Empire"! Still further to assure the devotion of the prince, it was solemnly ordained that Lewis II, on the death of Maximilian, should succeed him in the Empire; and the secret document containing this promise requested the electors " to choose and crown him as King of the Romans and Emperor."[1]

This intrigue of Maximilian in trading with the expectation of the imperial succession emboldened him to repeat his experiment with Henry VIII of England. While the promise to Lewis II was still in the secret archives, Sir Robert Wingfield, the English ambassador to Maximilian, was convinced by him that he wished to establish the King of England in the Empire. On May 17, 1516, the ambassador in good faith laid before his royal master the Emperor's project that Henry VIII should meet him at Trier with an armed force, whence they would proceed together to Frankfort, where Maximilian would renounce the throne, and the King of England would be elected as his successor, with investiture of the Duchy of Milan, after which they would march to Rome for the imperial coronation.[2]

Richard Pace, who was then on special mission to the Emperor, was sagacious enough to discredit this fanciful scheme,

---

[1] On the details of the transaction and genuineness of the document, see Liske, *Der Congress zu Wien*. For the treaty itself, see Lünig, *Codex Germaniae Diplomaticus*, I, p. 599.

[2] Brewer, *Letters and Papers*, II, Part II, No. 1902.

THE ASCENDENCY OF THE HOUSE OF HAPSBURG 325

which had no other purpose than to flatter Henry VIII and aid in securing subsidies.[1] In October, 1516, the subject was reopened through the Cardinal of Sion, who was despatched to London to obtain money for the Emperor.[2] In February, 1517, when a special embassy was sent to the Netherlands with reference to the Emperor's proposed visit to England, the Cardinal of Sion again gave assurance of Maximilian's wish to have Henry VIII assume the imperial crown; but Cuthbert Tunstall opposed the idea on the grounds, that, if made emperor, Henry VIII would have to become a German; that the crown of England was of greater value than the German crown; and that during the Emperor's lifetime Henry VIII would be only "King of the Romans," but even this dignity could not be obtained until after Maximilian had himself been duly crowned by the Pope. In conclusion, he informed the King that the Emperor's real design was to obtain a sum of money.

While Maximilian, still cherishing his secret intention to secure the succession of his grandson Charles, was devising means for accomplishing his purpose, Francis I was busy in promoting his own candidacy for the imperial crown. The German electors were not only ready but eager to enhance the value of their votes through the competition of an aspirant so powerful as the King of France, and it needed only an intimation of his ambition to awaken interest in Germany.

More than two years before the death of Maximilian, several of the electoral princes opened negotiations with the King of France, and even made solemn promises to support him. In November, 1516, Richard von Greifenklau, Archbishop of Trier, sent his chancellor to pledge his influence to Francis I.[3] On June 27, 1517, the Margrave Joachim of

---

[1] Brewer, *Letters and Papers*, II, Part II, Nos. 1878 and 1923.
[2] The same, No. 2463.
[3] Weicker, *Die Stellung der Kurfürsten zur Wahl Karls V*, p. 2, relying upon the documents printed by Kluckhohn, *Deutsche Reichstagsakten*, I, pp. 20 et seq., maintains that the first direct proposal came from the French side. In the autumn of 1516, the German knight Franz

Brandenburg concluded a convention with the King of France by which a close alliance was formed between them, providing for the marriage of the princess Renée, the eight-year-old daughter of Louis XII, to the Electoral Prince, with a dowry of one hundred and fifty thousand crowns of gold and a pension of four thousand livres, with other gratifications, in exchange for his support of Francis as a candidate for the Empire at the death of Maximilian. The Margrave's brother, Albrecht, Archbishop of Mainz and Archchancellor of the Empire, through the negotiations of his plenipotentiary, the famous Ulrich von Hutten, was also soon bound by a written promise of support.[1] The adhesion of Lewis V, Count Palatine of the Rhine, to whom was promised an annual pension of twelve hundred livres and the expectation of adding to his domain Hagenau and Ortenau, — of which he had been deprived by the Emperor, — gave Francis I a majority of the electors; and thus, in January, 1518, a year before Maximilian's death, the election had seemed virtually won.

But the apparently secure possession of four out of seven electoral votes neither fully represented the strength of Francis I in Germany nor set a limit to his further negotiations. Among his less prominent friends and supporters were Antoine, Duke of Lorraine; Robert de la Marck, Duke of Bouillon and Lord of Sedan; his brother Eberhard, Bishop of Liège; the warlike Duke of Gelderland; and many others, including the great *condottiere* of the Rhine, the famous Franz von Sickingen, who commanded two thousand cavalry, ten thousand *landsknechts*, and some formidable artillery.

---

von Sickingen came to Francis I and offered his services in securing for the King of France the next imperial election. Soon afterward, Claudius de Baudoche was sent to negotiate with the Archbishop of Trier, who sent to Francis I Heinrich Dungin von Witlich with full powers, dated November 18, 1516. See Kluckhohn, I, p. 21; and Vaissière, *Journal de Jean Barrillon*, I, p. 251.

[1] The credentials of Ulrich von Hutten are in the Archives Nationales at Paris, J. 965, No. 1. See Vaissière, as before, I, p. 253.

Sustained by all these powerful allies in the Empire, served by a multitude of lesser adherents already in his pay, while others pressed forward eagerly for his gold, and with the Dukes of Bavaria open to influence, the King of France appeared to be certain of his election long before the Emperor was dead.

The sudden discovery of the progress that Francis I was making had roused to activity both Charles and Maximilian. In August, 1517, Jean de Courteville, a Burgundian confidential agent, was instructed to win for the young King of Spain the most wealthy princes,— those of Saxony, Bavaria, and Brandenburg,— by holding out to them the expectation of the coveted order of the Golden Fleece. But Maximilian, who knew the character of the princes, quickly perceived that it was vain to attempt competition with the King of France by balancing against his solid gold mere empty honors, however highly prized; and Charles, who had thought to conduct his campaign with a paltry ninety-four thousand florins, to be distributed in presents and pensions, was frankly informed that only money, much money, and that in hard cash, not in drafts on bankers, could win the day.[1] The Count Palatine alone must have at least eighty thousand florins. The spiritual electors would scorn his offers of two or three thousand florins each, when Francis I was ready to pay them ten times as much. The Swiss, too, would demand much money, and their alliance must be had. Realizing the price the electors would put upon their votes, Maximilian informed his grandson that more than four hundred and fifty thousand florins would be necessary to carry the election.

Cost what it would, however, Charles was determined to be emperor; while Francis let it be known that he was ready to spend half his income — then estimated at three million livres — to secure his own election. In the midst of this reckless competition, the price of the crown quite naturally rose, for the electors saw their opportunity of exhaust-

---

[1] See Ehrenberg, *Das Zeitalter der Fugger*, I, p. 101.

ing the resources of both contestants before finally deciding for whom they would cast their votes.

For Maximilian the raising of ready money was impossible. So poor was he that, in 1518, Jacob Fugger loaned him first two thousand florins, and afterward one thousand more, "without which His Majesty would literally have had nothing to eat."[1] It was to Charles, therefore, that the Emperor looked for the means to carry on his campaign; but the young King of Spain had just ungratefully dismissed Cardinal Ximenes, who had secured for him his Castilian throne; all Spain was in revolt against his Flemish advisers and opposed to his imperial ambitions; and, to express their displeasure, his new subjects were refusing to grant him subsidies unless he would agree to recognize their liberties and remain in Spain. For Charles, therefore, as for his grandfather, ready money — beyond the ninety-four thousand florins he had sent from the Netherlands before he set out for Spain — was absolutely unattainable. If he were to compete with Francis, it was only by means of credit that he could hope to outbid his rival.

The Diet of 1518

When, therefore, in February, 1518, the Diet began to assemble in Augsburg, the chances of Francis I for the imperial succession seemed well assured; and Leo X, determined if possible to unite Christendom in a campaign against the Infidel, was ready to throw his influence upon the side of the candidate most likely to promote this cause. To preach the holy war, a papal legate, Thomas de Vio, Cardinal Cajetan, was present, by whose well-known eloquence the Pope expected to revive the spirit of the crusades. A moment more inopportune could not, however, have been chosen; for Germany, on the point of insurrection against the Papacy, was not in a mood to accept the plans of Leo X, whom the followers of Martin Luther — whose work as a reformer had just begun — were disposed to regard as an enemy more worthy of opposition than the Turk.

---

[1] See Ehrenberg, *Das Zeitalter der Fugger*, I, p. 100.

THE ASCENDENCY OF THE HOUSE OF HAPSBURG 329

In truth, it was felt that it was Francis I who was really most likely to be the chosen leader in a great enterprise against the Infidel, and not the mere boy who had just become King of Spain. But the day had passed when the German princes wished either to be drawn into adventures in the East or to be controlled by a too powerful superior. The friends of Francis boasted of his military strength, his maturity of vigor, his commanding qualities, his enormous power derived from the wealth and unity of France, and his consequent ability to play the rôle of a great ruler. On the other hand, Charles was regarded as young, modest, possessed of too widely scattered territories to become a really potent sovereign, and reputed to be of no great intelligence. It was, on the whole, a nominal rather than a real ruler whom the princes desired; and, from this point of view, it was Charles rather than Francis who would best suit their purposes. If the King of France were to be chosen emperor, he at least had not yet paid a sufficient price.

At Augsburg, therefore, a great revolution was produced. By means of marriage arrangements and promises of money the engagements of the electors were suddenly changed. The Electoral Prince of Brandenburg was to marry Catherine, sister of Charles, with a dowry of three hundred thousand florins; the Archbishop of Mainz was to receive through Maximilian's influence the cardinal's hat, and thirty-one thousand florins in gold, with a pension of ten thousand; Hermann von Wied, Archbishop of Köln, demanded less, his reward being twenty thousand florins and a pension of six thousand, with liberal gifts of office and money to his brothers; the offended Count Palatine of the Rhine was reconciled to Maximilian by his brother Frederick — who got twenty thousand for his pains — at the price of a hundred thousand florins in exchange for his claims on Hagenau and Ortenau, and a yearly pension of six thousand.

Accordingly, on August 27, 1518, the electors of Brandenburg, Mainz, Köln, the Palatinate, and the representative of the King of Bohemia, in the presence of De Courteville and the imperial chancellors, Villinger and Renners, signed a solemn compact to elect Charles upon the death of Maximilian; and, on September 1, the Emperor took the five signatories under his protection in case objection were made to their action by the Pope, the King of France, or any others.

When this victory was joyfully announced and celebrated, Francis I was left with only one adherent, — the Archbishop of Trier, — while Frederick, Elector of Saxony, held aloof from all promises, on the ground that they were in violation of the Golden Bull, which provided that the electors take an oath that their choice was free and uninfluenced by personal rewards or compacts.[1]

Relations to Rome and attitude of the Pope

The defeat of Francis I now seemed as inevitable as his election had before appeared certain. De Courteville was despatched to Spain to secure the King's assent to the marriage of Catherine to the Electoral Prince of Brandenburg and arrange for the payment of the sums of money pledged, while Maximilian retired from Augsburg in the best relations with the electors, including Frederick of Saxony, to whom he displayed unusual courtesy, even accompanying him to the door at his departure.

Maximilian would have been pleased to proceed at once to the election of Charles as "King of the Romans," but the Electors of Trier and Saxony objected that, as the Emperor was himself only "Emperor-elect," — since he had not received the papal coronation, — he was, in reality, only "King of the Romans"; and where there was no vacancy there could be no election.

To overcome this difficulty, it was proposed to have the imperial crown sent from Rome; or, if that were not possible, that the Pope should himself come to Trent, since he had already met Francis I at Bologna. The answer that the coronation could properly take place only in Rome, revived

---

[1] The form of the oath was: "And my voice and vote, or said election, I will give without any pact, payment, price, or promise, or whatever such things may be called. So help me God and all the saints."

THE ASCENDENCY OF THE HOUSE OF HAPSBURG 331

the desire of Maximilian to visit the Eternal City; but the expenses of the journey and the ceremony, the fear of armed opposition by Francis I, and the requirement of the Pope that he should come unattended by an army, combined to present an insuperable obstacle to the realization of his wish.

In the midst of these complications the attitude of Leo X remained equivocal. Since Charles was King of Naples, his election to the Empire would be contrary to the traditional papal contention that that kingdom should never be a possession of the Emperor. On the other hand, as compared with Francis I,—who actually occupied Milan and had claims to Naples which, as emperor, he would probably try to enforce,— the young King of Spain was likely to prove a more docile son of the Church.

But, in truth, while secretly inclining toward Charles as on the whole less formidable than Francis; yet, fearing to antagonize the King of France, on account of his ability to affect the further aggrandisement of the House of Medici, Leo X would have preferred, but for a single consideration, to see a less powerful prince than either of the royal candidates raised to the throne of the Empire. Such princes were available in the persons of Ferdinand — the younger brother of Charles — and Frederick of Saxony, whose high character and practical wisdom were generally recognized; but the Pope's objection to such secondary candidates was, that an emperor having no power in Italy would be useless to the Holy See and to the Medici in securing either their protection or their territorial aggrandizement. Eager to obtain possession of Parma, Piacenza, and Ferrara, Leo X desired an emperor too weak to curb the Papacy, yet able to change the *status quo* in Italy upon terms advantageous to his interests. From these conditions arose the fluctuations and apparent contradictions in the conduct of the Pope.[1]

---

[1] The real purpose of Pope Leo X in regard to the imperial election has been the subject of much controversy, on account of the ambiguity

CHAP. V
A. D.
1518–1527

The second electoral campaign of Francis I

The death of Maximilian on January 12, 1519, gave the negotiations a new character; for Francis I could now publicly and officially announce his candidacy for the vacant throne. At last, the battle between the House of Valois and the House of Hapsburg was fairly on, but not divested of its bitterness by the friendly interchange of notes in which the two candidates were represented as two friends seeking the love of the same lady, whose mutual affection should not be disturbed by their generous rivalry.

The rumor that a secret dispensation for Charles to hold the Kingdom of Naples, even though chosen emperor, lay in the papal chancellery, excited the apprehensions of the King of France, and his agents set about the task of holding back the Pope from further action. The chief aim of Leo X was now, apparently, to mystify all parties; seeming to be for Francis I, yet not seriously employing his resources to advance his cause. Thus, he doubtless hoped to make terms with all factions, when the time should come to play the loser against the winner in the interest of the House of Medici.

Convinced by a letter of the Pope to the Swiss, in which he had declared the possession of both Naples and the imperial office by the King of Spain to be incompatible with the security of the Holy See, and by a like communication to the Archbishop of Mainz, that the Pope was laboring in his interest, Francis I counted also on the good will of Henry VIII of England, of which he believed himself to possess assurances. Thus encouraged, he began in earnest to undo the work of Maximilian by a second electoral campaign in Germany.

The prospect soon became most promising. The Archbishop of Trier had remained faithful to the King of France, and now four of the five electors who had solemnly bound

---

of his conduct. Even as late as March 12, 1519, he wrote to Francis I promising to do all in his power to secure his election. The letter is in the Archives Nationales, J. 952. See Vaissière, *Journal*, II, p. 145, where a part of the text is cited.

THE ASCENDENCY OF THE HOUSE OF HAPSBURG   333

themselves to Maximilian at Augsburg regarded themselves as liberated from their promise by his death.

Even during the Diet at Augsburg, the Count Palatine had given new pledges to the French at Nantes, and immediately after Maximilian's death a French embassy hastened to Heidelberg to confirm his vote for Francis I. The Elector was available, but his demands had risen to four hundred thousand florins.

The hesitation of Charles to approve of the proposed marriage of his sister Catherine to the Electoral Prince of Brandenburg afforded an opportunity to reopen the negotiation for the hand of Renée of France, and the former contract with Francis I was soon renewed, on condition that the amount of the dowry previously named be raised to four hundred thousand florins in gold, the first half to be paid in Berlin, on May 1, the other half at the time and place of the election, with an annual pension of twelve thousand crowns during the lifetime of Joachim and his son. But even these terms did not comprise the whole of the greedy margrave's exactions: in case of the election of Francis I, Joachim was to become his stadtholder in Germany; in case he failed, the King was to aid the Margrave to obtain for himself the imperial crown![1] In any event, Brandenburg was to be guaranteed French protection. Shocked as the King was by the exorbitance of the Elector's demands, he wrote: "I wish that the Margrave Joachim be entirely satiated."[2]

Following in his brother's train, Albrecht, Archbishop of Mainz, went over to the side of Francis I in response to an offer of thirty thousand florins and a pension of nine thousand, although a hundred thousand more was subsequently demanded. At the same time, the Archbishop requested that Francis obtain from the Pope his appointment as perpetual legate, and a bull for the bestowment of this honor was procured and held by the King of

---

[1] See Rösler, *Die Kaiserwahl*, p. 70.
[2] See Mignet, *Rivalité*, I, p. 251.

France, to be published "when the end contemplated has been attained."[1]

Through the mediation of the Duke of Gelderland, the Archbishop of Köln was counted upon; for a papal bull for his elevation to the cardinalate, as well as one for the same office for the Archbishop of Trier, was in the hands of Francis I.[2] Thus, the King of France was again counting upon the votes of four or five members of the Electoral College.

The vote of Bohemia

Two suffrages were still to be sought. That of Bohemia was involved in much uncertainty; for, during the minority of Lewis II, according to the Golden Bull, his uncle, Sigismund, King of Poland, might legally claim the right to cast it.

The negotiations were, therefore, long and difficult. Secret agents were sent by both sides to Sigismund, who discreetly took the position that he had bound himself to Maximilian at Augsburg, and before giving another pledge he must consult the estates of Bohemia and Hungary.

The candidacy of Lewis II for the imperial crown, promised by Maximilian, was now once more revived in Bohemia; but not in an effective form. The King himself and his Bohemian counsellors would gladly have pressed it, but decided to make it contingent upon the disposition of the other electors toward Charles and Francis. Two envoys, Cuspinian and Saurer, were sent to Buda to represent the Hapsburg interests, and afterward Andrea del Burgo; and, in due time, a French embassy also appeared there in behalf of Francis I.[3]

The contiguity of the Austrian possessions to those of Lewis II made it evident that he had more to gain from the friendship of Charles than from that of Francis I. If his

---

[1] See Le Glay, *Négociations*, II, p. 380, and Mignet, *Rivalité*, I, p. 238.

[2] See Weicker, *Die Stellung*, p. 190, and Mignet, *Rivalité*, I, p. 237.

[3] New documents throwing light upon the negotiations of Cuspinian and Saurer at the court of Lewis II are fully summarized by Weicker, *Die Stellung der Kurfürsten*.

own candidacy should prove impossible, it was, therefore, to his advantage that the vote of Bohemia should be cast for the Hapsburg candidate. If Charles should become emperor, it would be desirable that he, rather than his brother Ferdinand — who was already betrothed to the King's sister, Anna — should be his brother-in-law; for, in that case, though Lewis II would fail of being emperor, his sister at least would become empress.

It was not difficult, therefore, for the Hapsburg envoys to gain a substantial victory, and the expectation of this marriage — in which Ferdinand and not Charles was, however, destined to be the future bridegroom — became at once the mainspring of the Hapsburg influence and the secret motive of the King of Bohemia's policy, which was, in view of his minority, to abandon his own candidacy;[1] to avoid irritating Francis I; but, finally, to cast the Bohemian vote for Charles, and bring about, if possible, his sister's marriage to the future emperor.

But the King was a minor, and the Bohemian estates had notions of their own. It was they who finally chose and named to the King the representatives who went to Frankfort in Bohemia's name, and the action they would take was thus left in a state of uncertainty.

There were, therefore, until the electors met in Frankfort, two votes that were in reality unpledged.[2] Bohemia was not finally committed; and Frederick of Saxony remained unshaken in his position that the Golden Bull forbade all bargains and compacts, and steadfastly reserved his electoral intentions.

The chances of Charles now seemed desperate, indeed; and his warmest partisans almost despaired of his success. Margaret of Burgundy, the shrewdest and wisest of the

The candidacy of Henry VIII

---

[1] Lewis II was then only thirteen years old.
[2] The Bohemian estates were not disposed to recognize the right of Sigismund to pledge the vote of Bohemia for Charles and were inclined to sustain the candidacy of Lewis II.

King of Spain's advisers, so far abandoned hope for him as to counsel the substitution of his brother Ferdinand as the Hapsburg candidate; but the young king earnestly and scornfully refused to listen to this proposal, and prepared to fight his battle to the end.

The story of the struggle which then ensued is one of deep intrigue and strenuous endeavor, but only its main features and final result can be recounted here.

Without perhaps intending it, a letter of Leo X, written on February 19, 1519, to his legate, Campeggio, then resident in England, brought into the contest a new competitor. In terms of most solemn secrecy, Campeggio was instructed to sound Cardinal Wolsey on the project,—which the Pope professed to approve,—of throwing over both Charles and Francis in favor of a third candidate, "either one of the electors *or some other person.*"[1]

Of the Pope's sincerity there can be no doubt, since the Venetian ambassador at Rome, Marco Minio, who knew the real desire of Leo X as well as any man could know it, informs the Signory on March 13, that "the Pope did not wish either of the two kings to obtain the crown," being desirous "that King Francis should condescend to favor some third candidate"; for the support given by the Pope to France, the ambassador continues, "had for its object to prevent the Catholic King from being elected Emperor."[2]

In his reply, Wolsey recommended to the Pope the policy of neutrality regarding the election thitherto pursued by England, and intimated that, if a choice must be made between Charles and Francis, the King of Spain would be the lesser evil.[3]

But the expression of the Pope, "some other person," appealing to the vanity of Henry VIII, was interpreted by

---

[1] Full details may be found in Rösler, *Die Kaiserwahl Karls V*, pp. 176, 182; and the Archivio Storico Italiano, XXV, pp. 383, 384.

[2] See Brown, *Calendar*, II, No. 1219.

[3] See Martene and Durand, pp. 1285, 1287.

him as an insinuation that he himself would constitute an acceptable third candidate.[1] Although it was toward the Papacy, not toward the Empire, that Wolsey's aspirations were directed, he was obliged to humor the ambition of his royal master, knowing full well that there was little chance of his success; and, on May 13, Richard Pace was sent to Germany to study the prospects for his king's election.

The reports of Pace regarding his journey and conversations reveal in an interesting manner the state of affairs on the eve of the imperial election. Although bearing two letters from Henry VIII addressed respectively one to Frederick of Saxony and the other to the rest of the electors, in which the King admonished them to make a unanimous choice, and promised in case of discord to protect their rights,[2] the English ambassador, through an omission that discloses the indifference of Wolsey, started on his mission unprovided with full powers; which were so long delayed that they did not reach him until the month of June.

Only fragments of the ambassador's instructions still remain to us,[3] from which we learn that he was (1) to sound the intentions of the electors; (2) to give them assurances up to a certain amount, — not named in the instructions, but fixed in another document at fifty or sixty thousand florins,

CHAP. V
A. D.
1518–1527

The mission of Richard Pace

---

[1] The Venetian ambassador, Sebastian Giustinian, presents the following portrait of Henry VIII at this time: "King Henry is twenty-nine years old, and much handsomer than any other sovereign in Christendom, — a great deal handsomer than the King of France. He is very fair, and his whole frame admirably proportioned. Hearing that King Francis wore a beard, he allowed his own to grow, and as it was reddish, he then got a beard which looks like gold. He is very accomplished and a good musician; composes well; is a capital horseman, and a fine jouster; speaks good French, Latin, and Spanish; is very religious; hears three masses daily when he hunts, and sometimes five on other days, besides hearing the office daily in the Queen's chamber. He is fond of hunting, and never takes that diversion without tiring eight or ten horses." Brown, *Calendar*, II, No. 1287.

[2] See Brewer, *Letters and Papers*, III, Part I, Nos. 215 and 216.

[3] The same, Nos. 240 and 241.

— to be paid after Henry was chosen; and (3) while ascertaining the exact disposition of the electors toward Charles and Francis, to maintain neutrality between them. Thus, the King hoped to keep the electors divided and to urge his own candidacy upon them as a final compromise.

The little interest taken in the enterprise by Wolsey is further evidenced by the fact that only once, and that so late as on the ninth of June, did he communicate with the ambassador.

At Köln, on May 30, Pace concluded that the Archbishop was inclined to favor Charles. At Mainz, a week later, he had a secret audience at night of Archbishop Albrecht, from whose own mouth he heard that both he and his colleague of Köln were opposed to Francis, although his brother Joachim remained attached to him. There also he met the Archbishop of Trier, who professed to approve of the candidacy of Henry VIII, particularly since the dead emperor had indicated him as his successor. The Count Palatine was still inclined toward Francis. During an interview with the Margrave of Brandenburg at Mainz, in which he felt his way by first suggesting a German prince and then commending Charles, the French envoy, Bonnivet, heard the entire conversation from behind a curtain, and afterward reported it in France.

Relying upon the co-operation of Leo X, who was expected to aid the cause of Henry VIII, Pace had hoped for a postponement of the election, in order that he might secure for his king the necessary suffrages; but the Pope had taken no steps to procure delay, and the electoral session at Frankfort was now imminent. Still, accepting as sincere the inquiry of the Archbishop of Mainz for evidence that, if chosen, Henry VIII would accept the crown, and the flattering intimation that the Archbishop might be inclined to cast his vote for the King of England and that the Archbishop of Köln would probably follow him, the courage of Pace was raised to a point where he hoped that, with the Archbishop of Trier, as he believed, already favorably disposed, and

THE ASCENDENCY OF THE HOUSE OF HAPSBURG 339

letters from Leo X in support of Henry hourly expected, he might even yet succeed.

CHAP. V
A. D.
1518–1527

On June 20, more extended powers arrived from England, directing him to unite with the envoys of the Pope to obstruct the choice of either Charles or Francis; to the end that either Henry, "who is of the German tongue," or some German prince, should be chosen, so as to prevent the Empire from passing to a "foreign power."

Keen and experienced diplomatist as he was, Pace fully realized that without money he could do nothing. Urgent in his appeals for funds, for whose transfer he had arranged with Hermann Ring, a merchant of Köln, he used every art and influence to secure his king's election. Wolsey, while humoring the King's ambition, no doubt sincerely believing it to be against the interest of England, made no strenuous efforts for its realization; but Pace, loyal to his master's will, employed every means to promote it within his reach. His last desperate measure was, on June 25, to send to Frederick of Saxony a memorial in which he said that, since the electors intended to choose neither the King of France nor the King of Spain, the King of England had intimated that he was not indisposed to accept the Roman Empire, was ready to risk his person and his resources for the good government and protection of Germany, and prepared to expend from fifty to sixty thousand florins upon the enterprise.[1]

If Richard Pace had fully known all that the secret archives of Europe have since revealed, he could hardly have written to Wolsey from Mainz: "I look hourly for some tidings of the King's own promotion to the Empire." That he knew of the corruption of the electors, is evident from his correspondence; but beside his own modest offer of from fifty to sixty thousand florins, the sums already promised were overwhelming.

A bold financial venture

Notwithstanding the boasts of Francis I regarding the

---

[1] Neudecker and Preller, *Spalatins Nachlass*, p. 109.

extent of his financial resources, at the critical moment they proved inadequate; partly because of their insufficient amount, and partly because of their immobility.

Francis had not succeeded in obtaining subsidies or even a loan from Genoa, which was not disposed to contribute to the extension of his power. Lyons also failed to supply him with cash, because of the controlling influence in that financial centre of the Florentines, who at that time had the same reason for withholding aid as the Genoese. It was, in truth, from his rich mother, the Duchess of Angoulême, — best known as Louise of Savoy, of whom it was said, "Though Francis wishes the Empire, his mother wishes it still more," — that most of his ready money came. As late as May, 1519, according to a contemporary chronicler, the gold that Francis had obtained was slowly journeying to Frankfort in sacks upon the Rhine, belated for its purpose because the Fuggers and other bankers refused to accept French drafts.

Poor as Maximilian had always been, and straitened as Charles then was in Spain, the business foresight of that time perceived in the young king a profitable debtor. In January, 1519, the financial agent of Charles, Paul von Armersdorf, had been able to procure upon the credit of the Spanish government from the bankers of Antwerp and associated houses in Genoa, Florence, and Germany, drafts to the amount of three hundred thousand florins, payable "on condition that Charles should be chosen King of the Romans"; and with this hypothetical paper as his main reliance, the anxious agent had proceeded to Germany.

In the meantime, the prodigal promises of Francis I had greatly enhanced the price of votes, and it became a question whether the sum represented by Armersdorf's drafts would be sufficient to insure success, without which they were wholly valueless. The transaction was further complicated by the fact, that, by the middle of May the French expected to have five hundred thousand ducats in gold available in Germany. Who, then, would take the risk of cashing the Antwerp drafts?

Unwilling to be deceived by empty promises, the electors had refused to accept any payments except in cash or the assurances of reputable Augsburg bankers, of whom the firm of Fugger was by far the richest and the most esteemed. Francis I offered to the Fuggers enormous premiums for their accommodation; but these bankers, professing loyalty to the House of Hapsburg, refused to deal with the French agents. Repulsed by this powerful firm, the French sought the good offices of other bankers and merchants, but in vain.

Beneath the candidacy of Charles — who was esteemed as at least the grandson of a German prince and emperor — a tide of national feeling was rising which it was dangerous for even the electors to resist. The favor believed to have been shown to Francis I by the Pope, his French blood and interests, his open threat to use armed force if necessary to attain his end, — all combined to arouse the Germanic spirit and create the feeling that his candidacy was not only an impertinence but a veritable danger. The Suabian League became so excited over the report that German merchants were clandestinely advancing money in the interest of the King of France, that it urged upon the municipal council of Augsburg the adoption of an ordinance prohibiting the cashing of a French draft under penalty of death.

While public opinion was thus intensifying the contest, a faithful servitor of the dead emperor, Max von Zevenbergen, had been plying the electors with offers of the money Armersdorf was hoping to procure from his conditional drafts. Unfortunately for the economy of these transactions, the inability of the French agents to raise ready money induced them to exaggerate their promises for the future; and thus the price of votes had been constantly augmented. Nevertheless, confiding in the prospects of Charles, Jacob Fugger accepted the Antwerp drafts; but the growing demands upon his resources threatened at last to extinguish the Hapsburg credit and his own. Before the election finally set a limit to the bidding for votes, the engagements of the Hapsburg candidate had risen to the enormous sum of eight hundred thousand five

Chap. V
A. D.
1518-1527

Preliminaries to the election

hundred florins,—nearly twice the amount the Emperor Maximilian had predicted,—of which the house of Fugger had advanced five hundred and forty-three thousand, the house of Welser one hundred and forty-three thousand, and Genoese and Florentine bankers the remainder. In the money market, the King of Spain had found credit where the King of France could not procure it; and was thus able to place the solid gold in the palms of the Swiss, of the *condottiere* Franz von Sickingen, of all the innumerable servitors who lined the avenues of approach to the seat of influence, and finally in the treasure chests of the electors themselves.[1]

Having thus measured the influences secretly acting upon the electors, we may now turn to the description of their work.

Early in June, the electoral princes began to assemble in Frankfort, the seventeenth having been named as the day for choosing an emperor. By a regulation of the Golden Bull, during the election the city became inviolable ground, from which all strangers were legally excluded; while through the civil authorities the citizens of Frankfort took an oath to preserve the conditions of a free choice by guaranteeing that none of the electors had a greater number of armed forces outside the walls than the ordinances permitted.[2] So little, however, were these solemnly ordained precautions observed, that Frankfort was not only surrounded with large bodies of infantry and cavalry, but in the guise of servants a plenipotentiary of France, Admiral Bonnivet, and others penetrated to the lodgings of the electors and held conversations with them. From Mainz, where the Austrians had their head-

---

[1] "Niemals hätten die deutschen Kurfürsten Karl gewählt, wären die Fugger nicht für diesen mit ihrem Baarkapital und namentlich mit ihrem gewaltigen Credite eingetreten. Dies geht mit völliger Klarheit aus dem Verlaufe des ganzen Handels hervor." Ehrenberg, *Das Zeitalter der Fugger*, I, p. 100.

[2] The limit was two hundred horsemen without and fifty within the city walls for each elector.

THE ASCENDENCY OF THE HOUSE OF HAPSBURG 343

quarters, and Höchst, which was populous with agents of both sides, an incessant stream of correspondence flowed into the electoral city, plying the electors with new fears, hopes, and promises intended to determine their decision.

On June 15, the Bohemian delegation arrived, and on the following day the commission of Sigismund, King of Poland. According to the Golden Bull, the vote of Bohemia appears to have belonged rightfully to Sigismund, as the legal representative of Lewis II; but the Bohemians contended that that provision referred only to the electoral princes and could not be applied to the Bohemians, whose liberties were untouched by it.[1] Accordingly, Ladislas von Sternburg was finally admitted to participate in the election as the representative of Bohemia; but not without special formalities and an evident misinterpretation of the Golden Bull in substituting for the prerogatives of Sigismund privileges which properly applied only to the choice of a king of Bohemia and not to an imperial election.[2]

The Electoral College being thus duly organized, the solemnities of its high function now began. On June 17, according to the requirements of the Golden Bull, the six electors and the Bohemian delegate mounted their horses and rode in state from the "Römersaal" to the Church of St. Bartholomew, where the mass *De Spiritu Sancto* was solemnly celebrated, to the end that the Holy Spirit might "illumine their hearts and infuse the light of his virtue into their senses; so that, armed with his protection, they might be able to elect a just, good, and useful man as King of the Romans and

---

[1] The provisions of the Golden Bull are: (1) in case a lay elector dies without male heirs, the power of electing shall devolve upon his eldest lay brother descended from the true paternal line; (2) in case a minor male heir survives, the eldest lay brother of the deceased lay elector shall be his tutor and administrator until he attains the age of eighteen years.

[2] Rösler, *Die Kaiserwahl*, pp. 188, 189, regards this result as a diplomatic victory won by the skill of Andrea del Burgo; but this idea is rejected by Weicker, *Die Stellung*, pp. 319, 321.

future emperor, and as a safeguard for the people of Christ." After divine service, the electors retired into the choir before the high altar, where, the archbishops with their hands on their breasts, the lay princes with their hands on the Gospel of St. John, took from the Archbishop of Mainz the oath "to elect a temporal head of the Christian people ... without any pact, price, or promise." This oath having been taken, instead of proceeding in the usual manner to an immediate choice, the electors caused a protocol to be made by a notary, stating that, for certain reasons relating to the welfare of Christendom and the Roman Empire, they had agreed to postpone further action for ten days, during which time they were free to negotiate while awaiting their final "inspiration."

Notwithstanding all the previous negotiations, on June 17, therefore, the outcome of the election was far from certain. The papal legate, Orsini, as late as the twenty-first gave assurance that the Pope was opposed to the choice of Charles, and would ratify the election of another, even although he were chosen by only three electors.[1] The difficulty was, however, to obtain even three votes for Francis I; for only the Archbishop of Trier and the Margrave of Brandenburg were ready to support him. Brandenburg much desired his own election, but received no encouragement from the other electors. The nomination of Frederick of Saxony by the papal legate obtained some support, but the proposition was silenced by Frederick himself. On June 24, to the surprise of all, the papal legate communicated the information that, for the sake of peace, and in the hope that the Catholic King would prove the most faithful son and defender of the Church, the Pope had decided that the rights of the Holy See in Naples should not stand in the way of the election of Charles.[2] A recently discovered document explains this change in the attitude of Leo X. On June 17, at Rome,

---

[1] See Weicker, *Die Stellung*, pp. 348, 349.
[2] The same, pp. 354, 355.

a treaty had been concluded between the Pope and Caroz, the plenipotentiary of Charles, by which the Holy Father dispensed the King of Spain from the prohibition of receiving the imperial office on account of his possession of Naples.[1]

On June 27, there was another solemn mass, but no action was taken. On the following day, at seven o'clock in the morning, still another mass was celebrated. The night had given counsel. When the conclave was opened, the Archbishop of Mainz, presiding, asked first the Archbishop of Trier to name his choice. The Archbishop answered, that he gave his voice for King Charles of Spain, in the hope that he would prove useful and suitable. One after another, the votes were given, all for King Charles of Spain; and the Archbishop of Mainz led the electors from the electoral chapel to the chancel of the church, where the Dean of the Cathedral of Mainz read the formal announcement to the assembled people.

The King of Spain had, at last, won the imperial crown; but the future was to justify the remark of Richard Pace, that it was "the dearest merchandise that ever was sold!"

As the Emperor-elect was still in Spain, a mandate prepared on March 8, in Barcelona, was now presented, appointing Cardinal Lang, the Count Palatine Frederick, the Margrave Casimir, Henry of Nassau, Max von Zevenbergen, and others, as his plenipotentiaries. These at once took their oaths of office and proceeded to execute the "*Wahlcapitulation*," or electoral concession.

The electoral capitulation

The aim of the princes was to render the new emperor strong for the defence of the Empire from without, but as weak as possible within its borders. Maximilian had been feeble outside of Germany because he had been unable to concentrate its power; but the programme of the princes, fearing the strength that the immense territorial possessions

---

[1] This treaty was discovered by Nitti at Florence. See his *Leone X e la sua politica*, p. 212.

of Charles might yet afford him, was, to reduce the imperial authority to still lower terms.

Already drawn up in outline at Mainz, the capitulation took final form in thirty-four articles.[1] The Emperor promised to protect the Empire, all its separate members, and the Church, and to secure to them peace and justice; to observe the regulations of the Golden Bull; to confer no office upon any one not a German; not to make alliances with other states without the knowledge and consent of the electors; not to dispose privately of estates falling to the Crown, but to use them as imperial possessions; to introduce no foreign military forces into the Empire; to impose no taxes, and to call no diet, against the will of the electors; to use only the German or the Latin languages in official communications, except in places where another tongue was already usual; and to aid in improving the financial status of the electors. In brief, the Emperor assumed entire responsibility for the safety and prosperity of the princes, without receiving in return any equivalent whatever, or any means of procuring it.

Thus handicapped in the exercise of the imperial office, it was difficult to see that Charles V had gained much by his election. In France, although Francis I had striven desperately for the prize that now seemed so hollow, and his mother had even ordered the jewels in which she had expected to shine at her son's coronation, the sentiment of the French court was that it was a great weal for France that its king had not been chosen emperor; "for, they say, if he had been, it would have put him to an infant business, and impoverished and undone his subjects."

On November 19, 1519, an embassy headed by the Count Palatine Frederick arrived at Barcelona, to tender to the King of Spain the crown of the Empire; but the Spaniards were opposed to his acceptance. The cities of Castile remonstrated, an armed brotherhood was organized to prevent his

---

[1] See Dumont, IV, Part I, pp. 296, 303.

departure from Spain, and the Cortes of his kingdom would have refused him subsidies but for the fear, aided by bribes and promises on the part of the court, that a revolution of the commons would overturn the power of the nobles if the commotion were not at once subdued. It was not until May 22, 1520, however, almost a year after his election, that Charles V was able, by promising to exclude from office his Netherlands advisers, to leave Spain, still deeply agitated, and later bitterly resentful because, — contrary to his promise, — the King's former tutor, Cardinal Adrian, was appointed regent.

In person only a slight figure, a prey to epilepsy, counselled not to make the sea voyage, from which he suffered much, not expected by his physicians to live two years, Charles V had, indeed, secured the crown of the Empire before he was able to bear its weight. Overwhelmed with debts that menaced him with perpetual impoverishment; loaded with obligations to the princes of Germany; exposed to aggression on every side by an antagonist whose compact territories intervened between Spain and the Netherlands, threatened him in Navarre, pressed upon him in Germany, and separated his possessions north of the Alps from his inheritance in Italy; Charles V began his lordship of the world with the largest outfit of unrealized assets that any ruler of Europe had ever possessed, yet impotent to assert his will in any one of his vast dominions. Such was the unprepossessing youth of only twenty years, marked with the pendulous lower lip characteristic of the Hapsburgs, not distinguished for intelligence, thitherto the passive ward of Flemish tutors and counsellors, knowing no word of German and an indifferent scholar in any branch, who was now to mount the throne of the Caesars.

Before this youth could enter upon his office it was still necessary to be crowned at Aachen. The pompous ceremonies of this solemnity — which did not occur until October 23, 1520 — were four in number. First, came the "*Sessio*," when the Emperor-elect was conducted into the domed cathedral over the tomb of Charles the Great and solemnly seated upon the imperial throne in the chancel, when the sword was laid across his knees, the imperial gauntlets were put upon his hands, in which were then placed the globe and the sceptre, and finally the crown of Charles the Great was deposited upon his head by the Archbishop of Köln. Next, came the "*Deambulatio*," or tour of the cathedral by the Emperor, weighted with all these glittering insignia. Finally, the ceremonies in the church ended with the "*Processio*," when, surrounded by every circumstance of sovereign pomp, escorted by the entire Electoral College led by the Archbishop of Trier, — before whom the crowns of Germany and Italy were borne, — who was followed by the Elector of Saxony holding high the sword of the Empire, the Count Palatine with the globe, and the Margrave of Brandenburg carrying the sceptre, the Emperor, between the Archbishops of Köln and Mainz and followed by the King of Bohemia, or his representative, was shown to the people in a solemn march. After these exercises, the festivities were closed by the "*Prandium*." The table having been blessed by the three archbishops in succession, the Margrave of Brandenburg, as grand chamberlain, accompanied by trumpets and timbals, descended to the open place in front of the Römersaal, mounted upon a horse, and went to fetch with great pomp a basin, a ewer, and a towel, to be placed before the Emperor. The Count Palatine, as seneschal, also on horseback, then went to bring from the kitchen, installed upon the open square, four silver plates filled with choice meats, which he placed on the Emperor's table, elevated above the others by a height of six feet. Then, the King of Bohemia, or his representative, as cup-bearer, rode up with a great goblet of silver containing wine and water, which, descending from his horse, he offered to the Emperor. As each of the electors finished his part in the ceremony he passed to his place at his own table and remained standing until the others had performed their parts, when they all sat down together.

Having thus celebrated the installation of the new emperor, the next task of the princes was, to see that the supreme authority which these splendid ceremonies implied was reduced to a minimum in the realm of reality.

II. THE CONFLICT OF CHARLES V AND FRANCIS I

The events connected with the reign of the Emperor Maximilian and the accession of the Emperor Charles V bring to light the fact that, in the course of European development, an important transformation had occurred in the imperial idea. In conception, and by ancient law and tradition, the imperial office represented a universal sovereignty, resting on no territorial basis, but derived from the relation of human nature to its divine origin. To the mediaeval mind the Emperor was God's representative on earth for the execution of justice among men. By the close of the fifteenth century that conception had almost entirely passed away, and in its place had been substituted the idea of territorial sovereignty; not, indeed, as a definitely established principle of public law, but as a practical condition. Whoever held a particular territory in his actual possession assumed over it the rights which the Emperor had formerly exercised. The kings and peoples of England, France, and Spain, as well as those of the Scandinavian and Slavic countries, acknowledged no subordination whatever to the Emperor. Even in Germany, the imperial authority had been reduced to a merely nominal supremacy, while in practice the great princes ruled their lands as independent sovereigns.

And yet the old Roman idea of "*imperium*" had not entirely passed away. It was the national monarchs, however, who now clothed themselves with its attributes and exercised its powers. Henry VIII was more absolute in England and Francis I in France than Charles V would have dared to be in Germany.

In substance, therefore, an order of fact had superseded the order of theory, and at least two great monarchs disputed

CHAP. V
A. D.
1518-1527

with the Emperor pre-eminence in Western Europe. There were, in truth, three competitors for supreme power not only before but after the choice of the electors had fallen upon Charles V. Francis I and Henry VIII were disposed to divide with its nominal possessor that supremacy for whose title they had previously striven as candidates for the Empire; and, having failed to attain that pre-eminence by the forms of imperial law, were resolved to acquire its substance by war or diplomacy. The heritage of world dominion was no longer to be safeguarded by obsolete theories of its sacred character and formal unity; for national imperialism had now entered the arena, and three practically co-equal sovereigns were to contend with one another for primacy in Europe.

The task of Wolsey

Looking forward with eagerness to his own future promotion to the Papacy, Cardinal Wolsey, already a kind of lay pope through his mediatorial influence, — of whom a Venetion ambassador had said, " He is seven times more powerful than the Pope," — was now confronted with the difficult task of holding these rival sovereigns to the observance of their pledges in signing the universal peace. His own sovereign, Henry VIII, was ready at any favorable moment to assert his claims to the territory and crown of France; Francis I was determined to extend his power in Italy, recover Naples, and humble the new emperor; while Charles V was likely to assert the prerogatives which pertained to his newly acquired eminence. The position of Wolsey as peacemaker and arbiter of Europe seemed, therefore, invested with peculiar difficulties.[1]

---

[1] The power possessed by Wolsey at this time and the spirit in which he used it are well portrayed by Sebastian Giustinian, the Venetian ambassador at London, in the following character sketch : " He rules both the King and the entire kingdom. On my arrival in England he used to say, '*His Majesty* will do so and so.' Subsequently, he gradually forgot himself, and began to say, '*We* shall do so and so.' He has now (September 10, 1519) reached a pitch where he says, '*I* shall do so and so'!

" About forty-six years old, very handsome, learned, eloquent, indefatigable, and of vast ability, he transacts alone the same business as

The certainty that a collision between Francis I and Charles V could not be long averted, opened the way for England's continued mediation, and rendered possible the prolongation of peace by throwing the weight of English influence against the aggressor, whoever he might be. Whichever of the powers should be inclined to begin hostilities would be disposed, as a first preliminary, to seek England's aid, or at least an assurance of neutrality. Upon this necessity was based the power which Wolsey was soon to exercise with the will of an autocrat.

A plan for a personal interview between Henry VIII and Francis I had long been under discussion, and Wolsey now resolved not only to hasten its realization, but to arrange a similar meeting with Charles V, and if possible to secure a reunion of all three monarchs. The project was one of extreme delicacy, and its execution required not only all the rare skill of the Cardinal but all the force of his character. In order to overcome any prejudices Francis I might entertain regarding a journey across the Channel, the meeting with him was appointed to take place at Calais, England's only possession on the continent.

The visit of Charles V was far more difficult to arrange, partly because it was desirable that it should occur before the interview with the King of France, and partly because Wolsey wished it to take place in England. Afterwards, it was intended to have the three sovereigns meet at Calais.

Francis I, anxious for the promised interview with Henry VIII, made Wolsey his plenipotentiary for arranging it, and as a token of his friendship pledged to him the fourteen votes of the French cardinals when there should be a

*Chap. V
A. D.
1518–1527*

Wolsey's plans for a meeting of the sovereigns

---

that which occupies all the magistracies, offices, and councils of Venice. He is pensive, and has the reputation of being very just. He favors the people exceedingly, and especially the poor. He makes the lawyers plead gratis for all poor men. . . . He has a very fine palace, where one traverses eight rooms before reaching his audience chamber. . . . He is supposed to be very rich indeed in money and in household stuff." — Brown, *Calendar*, II, No. 1287.

vacancy in the Papacy. Not wishing to offend the pride of France, the Cardinal was obliged to propose conditions which the punctilious Spanish envoys felt to be derogatory to the dignity of the Emperor; but Wolsey, knowing well that the alliance of England was necessary to Charles, replied with arrogance, "Then do nothing and be gone!" Even the offer of the Emperor to secure his succession to the Papacy did not move the inflexible cardinal from the rigid prosecution of his plans, and he ended by fixing the conditions of the Emperor's visit upon his own terms.

For three weeks the ship that was to bear Charles V to the shores of England waited at Coruña for favorable winds, and not until May 26, 1520, was the thunder of the salutes to the belated emperor on landing at Dover heard on the coast of France. Not relishing this preliminary meeting between the yet uncrowned emperor and the King of England, the French had done all in their power to prevent it; but Wolsey's will had overborne all obstructions, and the King of France was obliged to await his turn.

Greeted at Dover by the Cardinal with a Latin speech,— which the imperial guest did not understand,— Charles V was met next morning by the King, who escorted him to Canterbury, where his aunt, Queen Catherine, had come to meet him. During two days, the two monarchs passed the time in friendly intercourse; and, on the twenty-ninth, the Emperor-elect rode to Sandwich, and embarked for Flanders, leaving the English delighted with "the benign manner and meekness of so high a prince," whose friendliness had given warning to France that her king had no monopoly in the fraternity with England.

In striking contrast with the simplicity of the Emperor's entertainment in Canterbury was the exaggerated splendor of the conference between Henry VIII and Francis I. On the meadows between Guînes and Ardres, near Calais,— the borderland of the French and English possessions,— *renaissance* art and mediaeval pageantry vied with each other in loading with gorgeous decorations the improvised palaces of

THE ASCENDENCY OF THE HOUSE OF HAPSBURG 353

wood that blazed under the sun of June with their prodigal gilt and gaudy colors. "The Field of Cloth of Gold" is the designation which English historians have bestowed upon that barbaric affluence of display which appealed to the vanity of both nations.

It was Wolsey's masterpiece of magnificence. The plenipotentiary of both kings, — his person resplendent in his cardinal's robes and costly jewels, — he was the central figure as well as the organizing intelligence of that royal encounter, the most spectacular, perhaps, in the history of Europe.

But while the curious of both nations assembled in multitudes to behold this theatrical exhibition of a friendship as dubious in fact as it was ostentatious in outward appearance, Wolsey was busily striving to give it reality. Had the two monarchs been as hearty in their feelings as the French and English spectators, whose pride and joy mingled in their sports and overflowed from their cups in pledges of eternal amity, the festivities would have terminated in a solid peace between France and England. But the two kings never for a moment forgot that they were rivals, and the treaty of June 6, 1520, was in effect only a reproduction of that of 1518.[1]

During the entire period of the royal fêtes, from June 4 to June 24, the Emperor was waiting in Flanders for a hint from Wolsey to join the conference; but the psychological moment never came. Francis I had no wish to take into fellowship the rival who had borne off the prize of the Empire, and against whom he was already plotting vengeance.

The meeting of Henry VIII and Charles V at Calais

As soon as he had taken leave of Francis, Henry VIII went to Gravelines to meet Charles V and bring him back as his guest to Calais. It was now the turn of Francis I to hover about the place of conference, curious regarding the secret negotiations in which he was not a participant; but he was not long left in suspense. Finding a union of the

---

[1] The treaty may be found in Dumont, IV, Part I, pp. 312, 313.

CHAP. V
A. D.
1518–1527

three monarchs in a confederation to preserve the peace impossible, Wolsey had resolved upon maintaining separate friendly alliances, in which England would hold the balance of power between the two contestants. Accordingly, on July 14, after four days of direct negotiation, a treaty was concluded between Henry VIII and Charles V, providing for the continuation of all former treaties, the maintenance of permanent embassies at each other's courts, and the convocation of a general conference within two years.[1] Charles V, although he was still affianced to a French princess and Mary of England to the Dauphin of France, proposed to seal the new alliance with a marriage contract with Henry's daughter. As she was then only four years old and Charles was twenty, the chief purpose of the proposal was, probably, to make it evident that England would stand with the Emperor and not with France. To prove to Francis I that he could throw his influence on either side of the scale, Henry VIII promptly informed the King of France of the Emperor's offer, which he falsely claimed to have repudiated. To hold the balance even, the King of England in escorting Charles V rode a charger presented to him by Francis I; and, to crown the position of England as the moderator of Europe, Wolsey obtained from the Emperor a promise that, when he went to Italy for the papal coronation, he would go unaccompanied by an army. Unable to secure peace by a general confederation, the Cardinal now sought to preserve it by siding with the power least inclined to war.

The attitude of Leo X

The discontent of Leo X with the proceedings of Wolsey, who had virtually assumed in Europe the position which the Pope had formerly enjoyed, was not long in becoming manifest. Nettled also because he was ignored by England, except when ecclesiastical favors were requested, he complained to his nuncio, Ghinucci, through whom he hoped to ameliorate

---

[1] The treaty does not appear in Dumont or Rymer, but exists in the British Museum, Cottonian Library, under the head of Vespasian, C. I, folios 307, 308.

the situation, that he had for six months received no communication from the English court except when promotions were wanted. Nevertheless, so important to him was England's friendship, that he remitted to Wolsey the annates of the bishopric of Badajoz, which the Cardinal had received through the favor of Charles V, and at King Henry's request conferred against his own will the cardinal's hat upon Sylvester de Giglis, Bishop of Worcester.

Had the security of the Holy See been the main solicitude of Leo X, he would have received thankfully the efforts of Wolsey to preserve a general peace; but his wish to increase his power as a temporal potentate would be promoted by a conflict between France and the Emperor, from which he could derive some benefit in Italy.[1]

The Pope possessed the great advantage that the new emperor had various favors to seek at his hands. He needed a new investiture for the Kingdom of Naples, a dispensation for his proposed marriage with Mary of England, and the papal assistance in securing an alliance with the Swiss and in quieting the uprisings in Spain. Above all, without the consent of the Holy See, an imperial coronation at Rome would be impossible. Until he had obtained his price for all these concessions, Leo X could refuse to accord them, with the assurance that his indisposition to accommodate the Emperor would in the meantime procure for himself and his family the protection of Francis I.

But a new and unmeasured force was entering upon the field of European politics, feeble in its beginnings, yet destined to work a profound revolution in the organization of

The Diet of Worms

---

[1] Baumgarten has emphasized the desire of Leo X to increase the power of the Medici in Italy; but Nitti, in his *Leone X e la sua politica*, opposes this view and sees in the policy of Leo X an effort rather to promote the independence of the Holy See. To this end, according to Nitti, he was allied to both Charles V and Francis I at the same time, with the intention of driving the French out of Italy. His secret treaty of October, 1519, with Francis I, while in close alliance with Charles V, was recently discovered by Nitti at Florence.

Europe. The Diet which assembled at Worms in April, 1521, confronted the young emperor with the problem of suppressing Martin Luther and the cause of reform of which he was the champion.

It has been truly said, "The Lutheran question made a man of the boy ruler." At Worms, for the first time in his life, Charles V came in personal contact with a force that made him tremble for all that he was and all that he represented. His encounter with Luther placed in violent contrast the powers of Rome and the aspirations of Germany, the mediaeval past and the instincts of modern freedom, the terror of mandates deriving their authority from the absolutism of Pope and Emperor and convictions based upon the reason and conscience of one fearless man.

The Pope, who had already condemned Luther, had wished that he be heard no further; but Charles V, aiming to conciliate Germany, had left the question to be settled by the Diet, and it was decided that he should have a hearing. When, on April 17, the heretical monk had finished his bold address before the Diet, in which he had not feared to condemn the Pope's iniquities, he departed from the presence of his judges with his hand raised in a gesture that betokened triumph and almost defiance. The Emperor saw in it, as in his teaching, a revolutionary spirit not less dangerous to imperial than to papal authority, and his proud nature was deeply stirred.

On the following day, the princes, hesitating what course to take, consulted first the will of the Emperor; who at once, with his own hand, wrote in French a declaration of his views. A German translation was then read to them. "My predecessors, the most Christian emperors of German race, the Austrian archdukes, and dukes of Burgundy" — ran the portentous document, — "were until death the truest sons of the Catholic Church, defending and extending their belief to the glory of God, the propagation of the faith, and the salvation of their souls. They have left behind them the Holy Catholic rites that I should live and die therein,

THE ASCENDENCY OF THE HOUSE OF HAPSBURG 357

and so until now I have lived, as becomes a Christian emperor. What my forefathers established at Constance and other councils it is my privilege to uphold. A single monk, led astray by private judgment, has set himself against the faith held by all Christians for a thousand years and more, and impudently concludes that all Christians up till now have erred. I have, therefore, resolved to stake upon this cause all my dominions, my friends, my body and my blood, my life, and my soul."

As the full meaning of the Emperor's words sank into the minds of the hearers, some of the princes became deadly pale. Better than he, they knew what this reassertion of imperial authority then meant for Germany. When the Archbishop of Mainz had wished to burn Luther's books, the leaders in his diocese had fervently dissuaded him. Not far from Worms was the camp of Franz von Sickingen and with him the scholar and humanist Ulrich von Hutten, who were united to defend Luther with sword and pen. Nearly all the new learning of Germany appeared to be on the reformer's side, including the lawyers and canonists, while the people were crying "Long live Luther." So hostile to Rome was the populace of Worms that Aleander, the papal nuncio, upon his arrival there had been threatened with death, could find no landlord willing to offer him hospitality, and was obliged to shiver in an attic.

Seeing what a storm was rising, the princes pleaded with Luther to recant. The Emperor's declaration had concluded: "I have now resolved never again, under any circumstances, to hear him. Under protection of his safe conduct he shall be escorted home, but forbidden to preach and to seduce men with his evil doctrines and incite them to rebellion. I warn you to give witness to your opinion as good Christians and in accordance with your vows."

Accordingly, on April 25, Luther was ordered to leave Worms. Two weeks later he had mysteriously disappeared, but his influence was never more powerful in Germany. Until 1522, in the Castle of Wartburg, under the secret pro-

Results of the Diet

tection of the Elector of Saxony, he was occupied in translating the Bible, which he believed to be the conclusive argument for his conduct and his cause.

But the condemnation of Luther was not the only important result of the Diet of Worms. Momentarily saved from a repudiation of its authority in Germany by the intervention of the new Caesar, the Holy See was now placed in a relation which almost forced its alliance with the Emperor; yet, as we shall see, not upon his own terms.

On the other hand, the unexpected revelation of character which the trial of Luther had occasioned had intensified the purpose of the princes to enfeeble as much as possible the power of the Emperor in Germany. Contarini reports that De Chièvres had once said to Charles V, "Do not fear the King of France or any other prince except your brother." To appease Ferdinand's ambition, and thus to guarantee his aid, the old Austrian provinces were conferred upon him, and his marriage to Anna, the heiress of Hungary and Bohemia, — which secured to Ferdinand the crowns of those kingdoms upon the death of Lewis II in 1526, — opened before him a great sphere of activity in the East. But this partition of the Hapsburg territories into Austrian and Spanish did not in fact diminish the power of Charles V, who soon afterward rewarded his brother's fidelity by intrusting him with the administration of his lands on the Upper Rhine, Elsass, and Würtemberg. The real restriction upon his authority was in his dealings with the princes concerning the organization of the Council, in which he was obliged to content himself with the appointment of the president and four out of twenty-two members, authorized to act in his absence. Although charged with the direction of foreign affairs, the Emperor was bound by his electoral concession not to form alliances affecting the Empire except with its consent.

The policy of Gattinara

The death of De Chièvres in 1521 and the accession of an Italian, Mercurino Gattinara del Arborio, a descendant of a noble Piedmontese family, as the chief counsellor of Charles V, mark a change in all the Emperor's policies. Thitherto

Burgundian influences had been uppermost, and these were favorable to peace with France. Gattinara, on the contrary, regarded all things as centring in Italy, and his ambition was to see his master assert his imperial prerogatives. For this purpose he must first obtain his crown from the hands of the Pope, then secure his hold on Southern Italy, and in time drive the French from the imperial fief of Milan. To realize these aims, this wily statesman, who in diplomatic skill proved himself the equal if not the superior of Wolsey, desired to draw the King of England into a close and exclusive alliance with the Emperor in the attempt to abase the power of France.

It is to the credit of Gattinara that he perceived from the beginning the inevitable struggle with Francis I. The attack of the King of France upon Navarre for the restoration of the House of Albret and the secret aid furnished to Robert de la Marck in his rebellion against the Emperor were indeed sufficient evidence that he would not hesitate to begin an open war as soon as he could assure himself of the neutrality of England.

In the matter of the Emperor's proposed marriage with the daughter of Henry VIII, Gattinara, with the purpose of forcing the hand of England, had urged procuring an immediate dispensation from the Pope; but Wolsey had opposed it. "The King of England," exclaimed the minister of Charles, "is like a man with two horses, one of which he rides, while he leads the other by the hand." But Wolsey was obdurate, and wrote to his king, that, when the time came, the Emperor would seek the friendship of England "on his hands and knees."

To incline the favor of England toward his side of the balance, Francis I sent his emissaries to make trouble in Scotland, evidently hoping to make Wolsey feel his power in that direction; but the Cardinal was imperturbable, and declared that, if the aggressions of France were not discontinued, England would throw its weight on the side of the Emperor. Charles V having already appointed the King of England mediator in his disputes with France, Wolsey was anxious to force Francis I into a like position. On May 28, the Venetian ambassador in England, Antonio Surian, writes that the Cardinal had said: "The King wants to recover Navarre; should he obtain it, he will lose France."[1]

For a time, there were rumors of secret negotiations between Francis I and Charles V, from which it was intended to be inferred that England would be isolated by their union; but Wolsey soon discovered that this was only a deception. To end the farce, he informed the French ambassadors that, if France did not at once accept English mediation, his king would cast his support on the side of the Emperor.

Astonished at this unexpected announcement, in the beginning of June, 1521, Francis I declared that the friendship of Henry VIII was more important to him than that of any other prince, promised a cessation of hostilities in Navarre, and agreed to submit his differences with Charles V to the mediation of England. In this connection he made one request, — that, owing to his relations to the Pope, a papal nuncio be allowed to participate in the negotiations. In his reply, Henry VIII accepted his proposal, and demanded a truce of from eight to twelve months between Francis I and Charles V, with authority to extend it. All was assented to, full powers were sent to Wolsey as mediator, and the Cardinal appeared to stand forth once more as the maker of peace and the arbiter of Europe.

Obstructions to Wolsey's mediation

But an influence adverse to peace had entered upon the scene of action not less potent than the great minister of England. Gattinara, who had shown compliance when Francis I was indisposed toward mediation, was now determined to pursue his policy of preventing a reconciliation and of forcing England to his master's side.[2]

---

[1] See Brown, *Calendar*, III, No. 225.

[2] In a communication to the Emperor dated July 30, 1521, Gattinara urged upon him the continuation of the war against Francis I, enumerating ten reasons for this course which he called the "ten commandments" and seven objections which he called the "seven deadly sins." — See Le Glay, II, pp. 473, 482.

THE ASCENDENCY OF THE HOUSE OF HAPSBURG 361

The first step in this direction was the negotiation of a secret offensive alliance with Leo X. The work of Luther naturally drove the Pope and the Emperor together; for, as their treaty expressed it, they were "responsible for the conduct and peace of Christendom." Urged by Gattinara to place his hand upon Italy, and cordially encouraged by the Pope, who did not neglect to provide for the recovery of Ferrara, Parma, and Piacenza, Charles V signed the compact of May 8, 1521, by which he engaged to restore those territories to Leo X.[1] With the Medici secure at Florence, Siena under the suzerainty of the Pope, — as was agreed, — his *protégé* Francesco Sforza II invested with Milan, and his ally Antoniotto Adorno in power at Genoa, Leo X, sustained by the Emperor, was likely to become more powerful in Italy than any pope had ever been.

It was a prudent precaution that the treaty was to remain secret until the gage of battle had been openly thrown down by Charles V; for, when it was discovered, the rage of Francis I, who had depended upon the Pope's friendship and had thought to derive advantage from the participation of the papal nuncio in Wolsey's work, was inexpressible. In the hope of vengeance, Louise of Savoy proposed through Margaret of Burgundy that Navarre be surrendered to Charles V by Francis, and that he take the Emperor's investiture of Milan; promising further that the payment of tribute owed by Charles for the Kingdom of Naples in accordance with the Treaty of Noyon would not be demanded, if the Emperor would only give Francis a free hand to punish Leo X.[2]

Such an arrangement might have been a settlement of the chief points in issue between the two monarchs; but Margaret replied, that the Emperor was willing to discuss all the matters in question except revenge upon the Pope, which he could not do with honor. How near the proposal of the

---

[1] See Dumont, IV, Part I, pp. 96, 99.
[2] Brown, *Calendar*, III, No. 266.

CHAP. V
A. D.
1518–1527

King of France came to being a basis of conciliation is evident from the words uttered by the Emperor himself many years afterward in his reproaches of Cardinal Giulio de' Medici for his ingratitude after he had become Clement VII. "His Holiness is well aware," runs the imperial indictment, "how, being a youth, and scarcely knowing what I was about, I entered upon this war for him alone: I do not say for Pope Leo, but for him; for he ruled Pope Leo.[1] Nor were the mutual injuries between the King of France and myself of such a nature as to preclude adjustment; but at his instigation I waged war; and he has had very good proof how far one and the other of us may be trusted."

By the Papal-Imperial alliance Gattinara had placed the first block in Wolsey's path; but another was disclosed when Charles V refused a truce during the negotiations, on the ground that his consent to mediation had been given before the attack of Francis I on Navarre, which now made resistance necessary.

Only by patient perseverance on Wolsey's part was a conference finally rendered possible. For the success of his work of mediation two conditions were indispensable: first, that Charles V should agree not to negotiate with Francis I during the efforts of Wolsey to effect a reconciliation; and, second, that full powers should be placed in his hands to order a truce during this period. In the hope of finally alienating Henry VIII from Francis I, these conditions were accepted by Charles V; but Gattinara proceeded to the conference with the fixed purpose not to accept peace through England's intervention, but to continue the war against Francis I with England's aid.

The conference of Calais

When, on August 2, 1521, Wolsey arrived at Calais to open negotiations, he bore from Henry VIII full powers either to establish a general peace between England,

---

[1] That he did not wholly do so is probable from Leo's greater decision of character. See Villari, *The Life and Times of Niccolò Machiavelli*, II, p. 443.

Charles V, Francis I, and the Pope; to make a separate alliance with Francis I; or, finally, to conclude a compact between Henry VIII and Charles V for the protection of their states against the aggressions of the King of France. So far as his own monarch was concerned, therefore, Wolsey's powers were unlimited.

The disclosures of the first few days revealed to him, however, the extent and difficulty of the work he had to do. The treaty of Charles V with Leo X made it obligatory upon the Emperor to accept no peace with Francis I in which the Pope was not included. When, at the first interview with Gattinara, the full powers of the Imperial Chancellor were made known, it was discovered that they provided for the conclusion of a marriage contract between Charles V and the child Mary and for an alliance against Francis I, but contained no word regarding a peace, a truce, or a compromise!

With perfect composure the Cardinal forbore to antagonize the imperial envoys, and turned his attention to the attitude of France. On August 4, the French plenipotentiaries arrived at Calais, headed by the Chancellor Duprat and Marshal La Palice, and presented their credentials. The position in which Francis I was now placed led Wolsey to hope that he could enforce an arrangement; for the imperial armies had been set in motion, the expedition to Navarre had already ended in a surrender of the country to the Spaniards, the Pope was preparing to turn his forces against Milan, the Swiss cantons were loyally under his influence, and the allies of Francis I in Italy were disposed toward peace.

In the first general session, however, the gulf which Wolsey had to bridge yawned wider than he had expected. Each side denounced the other as responsible for the beginning of hostilities, excused itself with a pretence of peaceable intentions, and demanded the aid of England to maintain its rights. Gattinara affirmed that he was there to demand an indemnity from Francis I for breaking the peace. The papal nuncio, Ghinucci, supported Wolsey's pacific aims, but regretted that he could not properly take part in the discussion, since he possessed no powers from His Holiness the Pope; to which Gattinara added, that the Emperor was bound by treaty to accept no agreement without the Pope's consent. Indignant at the attitude of the Emperor's envoys and the papal nuncio, the French ambassadors threatened to abandon the conference at once.

Wolsey's visit to the Emperor at Bruges

The supreme test of Wolsey's resources as a diplomatist was now to be made. He seemed equal to the emergency. Brushing aside the plenipotentiaries at Calais, on August 12, he set out on a journey to Bruges, to continue the negotiations directly with the Emperor.

His reception was a splendid tribute to the power that he wielded. Surrounded with all the pomp of a king, and royally greeted by the nobles and people on his way, he found Charles V in person waiting for him before the gates of the city. As the cardinal approached, the Emperor, hat in hand, advanced on horseback to meet him, and from his saddle embraced him as an equal. Lodged in the same palace, the princely guest was accompanied by his imperial host to the very door of his chamber.

Far different from this was the reception given by Wolsey to Christian II, King of Denmark, when that prince, who happened to be in Bruges, besought an interview. Asserting that his dignity as representative of the King of England forbade his calling upon a foreign prince, Wolsey suggested that, if the King would place himself in the garden at a place he was accustomed to pass on his way to see the Emperor, he would meet him upon that neutral ground as if by chance!

But, proud and resourceful as he was, Wolsey was now to enter upon a path whose unforeseen turning was to bring him into the labyrinth of Gattinara's wily diplomacy. In fixing the conditions for the marriage of Mary of England, the Cardinal was allowed to have his way; for that was from beginning to end only a snare to secure the English alliance, which, on August 25, was converted into a secret engagement to make war upon the King of France. In only one particular was Wolsey successful, — hostilities were not to be declared by England until March, 1523, although aid was to be furnished to the Emperor in the next November, if Francis I was still at war with him. In making this postponement Wolsey believed that he had accomplished all, for in the meantime he intended to restore the general peace; but, although the Cardinal bore away from Bruges the assurance of Charles V that he would receive the Spanish votes at the next papal election and was firm in the conviction that he would yet triumph by effecting a general peace, Gattinara knew that it was a Portuguese and not an English princess that the Emperor would eventually wed, that Wolsey would never have the votes of the Spanish cardinals, that Charles V would never make an uncompensated peace with Francis I, and that England would finally be forced to cast her lot with the enemies of France. Without the loss of honor, Wolsey could now no longer take the bold stand that had once made him the arbiter of Europe, and say to both contestants: England will withdraw her friendship from the one that persistently opposes peace.

For two months after the return of the Cardinal to Calais, the negotiations went on, but the real master of the situation was Gattinara. Leo X had been included in the recent coalition of Charles V and Henry VIII, but the secret was for a time well kept; for premature divulgence would have absolved England from rendering aid, since the time agreed upon had not arrived, and the whole force of Francis I would have continued to fall upon the Pope and the Emperor. But from the moment when Wolsey had changed his policy from an enforced peace to an eventual partnership with the enemies of France, Gattinara held in his hand the instrument with which he could ultimately strike the conference a fatal blow.

The fluctuation of the negotiations, the pressure for a truce by Wolsey, his illness, the concessions of Francis I, the obstinacy of Charles V, until November, have only an academic interest; for the die was already cast. The success of the imperial armies in the field strengthened the resolve to crown them with a diplomatic victory. Gradually the suspicion of a secret coalition between Henry VIII, the Emperor, and the Pope dawned upon the French. Thitherto, their part had been one of passive confidence in Wolsey's truth and loyalty, but thereafter this suspicion steadily undermined his influence. Soon the point was reached where the Cardinal was obliged to explain the surface indications and to deny the truth. Powerless at Rome, where his perfidy was known, he was distrusted by the ambassadors of France, and doubted even by his new allies. When the Spanish envoys at Rome communicated to their chief the Pope's opinion that Wolsey was really inspired by no other motive than his own ambition, Gattinara wrote on the margin of the despatch: "It is clear, that the Cardinal is betraying one side or the other."

The comedy was now drawing to a close. The impotence of Wolsey dated from the day when, abandoning his position as a possible ally to either contestant, he had placed his king in bonds to one to despoil the other. All his efforts to recover his lost position were in vain. In disregarding the principles of truth and justice on which the edifice of his greatness had been erected, he was doomed to fall from the greatest height of influence and power that any European statesman had yet attained.

On November 24, 1521, a new secret compact, the Treaty of Calais,[1] united the Pope, Charles V, and Henry VIII in a league against Francis I, by which Leo X should lay France under his interdict, the Medici were to be protected at Florence, the Swiss were to be won for the coalition, and no one of the signatories was to negotiate to the disadvantage of another. On the following day, November 25, the farce was ended; and the curtain fell upon the Conference of Calais.

The reasons for Wolsey's failure

In justice to Wolsey it must be considered that, while both contestants were anxious for the alliance of England, a

---

[1] See Brewer, *Letters and Papers*, No. 1802.

bitter war between them had become inevitable. Francis I was not only insisting upon the prompt payment of the Emperor's arrears on account of his tribute for Naples, and upon the possession of Flanders, which he claimed as a fief of France; but he demanded as a condition of a truce the maintenance of the military *status quo* and a promise that Charles V should make no new move in Italy. Refusing to accept these propositions, the Emperor made it known that he would not in any way be limited in the exercise of his sovereign imperial rights. So far as Francis I and Charles V were concerned, therefore, the conflict could not be arrested.

Even had Wolsey thrown the weight of England's influence on the side of France, the continuation of war could not have been averted. On the contrary, its intensity would, perhaps, have been increased; for Francis I would then have been free to use all his resources in attacking the Netherlands. In every approach to France, Wolsey had encountered a formidable opposition in England, inspired by hostile sentiment and business interest. The old animosity which the struggles with the kings of France had excited had never yet died away, and there were those who still believed it to be the duty of the King of England to renew his claims to the crown of France; while nothing but its impracticability restrained the King from sharing that conviction. It was, however, the commerce with Flanders — the great market for English wool — that touched most effectively the springs of English policy; for that commerce was more likely to thrive under imperial than under French predominance in the Netherlands. For every practical reason, therefore, since his lofty ideals of peace and confederation were doomed to perish, Wolsey had chosen as the English people wished him to choose in forming an alliance with the Emperor against the King of France. The splendid conceptions of peace and fraternity for which he had long nobly contended were swept away in the stream of passions which he was unable to resist.

Doubly defeated,— first by the antagonisms of the Emperor and the King of France, culminating in the diplomacy of Gattinara; and, second, by the hostility which then prevailed in England to an alliance with Francis I against the Emperor,— Wolsey had nevertheless drawn from the wreck of his policy of mediation a shrewdly devised support for his prestige in the future. The last article of the Anglo-Imperial alliance provided for a war against the Infidel, in which the kings of Portugal, Poland, Hungary, and Denmark, the Duke of Savoy, and the Swiss were invited to participate. To give unity to this movement, the King of England was called upon by the Pope and the Emperor to deal with Francis I for his violation of the universal peace.

Thus, in legal form, Wolsey still stood forth as the chief figure in European politics, and the Conference of Calais appeared to have been merely transferred to London; while the whole of Christendom under Wolsey's leadership was summoned to sustain the cause of peace within and to oppose its enemies without.

The sudden death of Leo X, on December 1, 1521, awakened in the breast of Wolsey a hope of soon transferring his office of mediator to Rome. Urgent letters were written to the Emperor, reminding him of his promises at Bruges regarding the Papacy; but, although hopeful answers were received, neither Charles V nor Cardinal Campeggio— to whom Wolsey intrusted the presentation of his name— did anything important to support his candidacy. A few votes on the first ballot were the only evidence that Wolsey had any friends at Rome. From the beginning, the Emperor had supported Cardinal Giulio de' Medici; but when Richard Pace, who had hurried to Rome to aid the ambition of Wolsey, arrived at his destination, the conclave was over, and the former tutor and minister of Charles V, Cardinal Adrian Dedel of Utrecht, had been chosen pope as Adrian VI. Regarded by all, though erroneously, as an imperial victory, the Romans posted up sarcastic notices of his election reading "Rome is to let!"

It was as first minister of Henry VIII, therefore, that Wolsey was to continue his rôle in European politics. The limitation thus imposed upon him was a narrow one; for the vanity and prejudices of the King, the Spanish affinities of Queen Catherine, the traditions of the court, and the commercial interests of the people all combined to favor the Emperor and to oppose the King of France. The true national policy of England was, without doubt, one of complete neutrality; but the conception of a strictly neutral attitude had not entered the minds of men in an age when so great a thinker as Machiavelli was counselling participation in every quarrel, on the ground that some profit could be derived from the misfortunes of those who needed aid. Yet it was the high distinction of Wolsey that he wished to hold the balance between the contestants rather than side with either of them. It was against his will that he had been drawn into forming an offensive alliance of England with the Pope and Charles V. His future task, difficult beyond any other he had yet undertaken, was to carry out his pacific purposes by rendering the alliance as little effectual as possible so far as England's action was concerned.

In this he was opposed not only by all the influences that have just been enumerated but by the French themselves, who now accused him of systematic perfidy in all his negotiations with them.[1] On December 28, Francis I concluded a new treaty of alliance with Scotland. Soon afterward, goods lying at Bordeaux for shipment to England were seized by the King's orders. In spite of Wolsey's wishes, public feeling could be no longer restrained; and, on May 28, 1522, war against France was formally declared.

During a visit of Charles V to England at the moment

---

[1] This is the position taken by Mignet, *Rivalité*, etc., I, pp. 282, et seq., who cites in proof of it Wolsey's correspondence with Henry VIII. It must be remembered, however, that Wolsey was mediating with Henry VIII as truly as he was with Francis I and Charles V. The truth upon this point is well developed by Busch, *Drei Jahre englischer Vermittlungspolitik*, pp. 174, 182.

CHAP. V
A. D.
1518–1527

The Anglo-Imperial alliance of 1522

The isolation and peril of France

when war was declared, a permanent treaty was elaborated by Wolsey and Gattinara, in which the Emperor undertook to pay the loss sustained by Henry VIII in the cessation of French tribute for Tournay, while Wolsey personally received a pension of nine thousand crowns in compensation for his lost bishopric with renewed promises of the Papacy at the next election.

The Cardinal had protested against the pressing demand of Charles V for the aid promised by England in the Treaty of Calais, but in vain. Reviving his earlier policy, he had proposed first a return to a universal peace, then the acceptance of a long truce, and finally the further postponement of England's part in the hostilities. In the end, however, Gattinara again prevailed in securing a renewal of the obligations entered into at Bruges, except that the alliance was no longer secret, and the time of united action against France was fixed for May, 1524.

Such were the terms of the Treaty of Windsor, signed on June 19, 1522; in which Wolsey, as papal legate, again appeared in the rôle of the high-priest of diplomacy, administering to the two sovereigns before the altar the oaths by which they bound themselves to observe their engagements.

Dazzled with the prospect of obtaining the French crown, the zeal of Henry VIII could not be restrained; and, in July and August of that same year, a premature and ill devised assault upon France was made by the allies, who invaded Picardy, devastated the country without permanent results, and by this wanton atrocity placed Francis I in the position of a national champion that every French patriot was ready to support. When, in October, the fruitless campaign was over, France was united, while the allies were already busy with recriminations against each other.

Excusing England from further immediate participation in the war so long as Scotland, aided by Denmark, continued to threaten hostilities in the North, Wolsey was nevertheless ready to widen the Anglo-Imperial alliance in the hope of thereby controlling it, and Pace was sent to negotiate for the adhesion of Venice. The siege of Rhodes by the Turks, soon followed by the fall of that bulwark of Christendom, presented a new reason for a general union; but, while still serving as a rallying cry, the Ottoman invasion was no longer a real element in the diplomacy of Europe. The defection of the Swiss from the cause of Francis I, the union of Savoy, Genoa, and Florence with the Emperor, and finally even the adhesion of Venice under the pressure of England in attacking Venetian commerce, all combined to give the imperial position unexpected strength in Italy. The death of Adrian VI and the election of Cardinal Giulio de' Medici to the Papacy as Clement VII, on November 18, 1523, by the influence of Charles V, — who again disappointed the hopes of Wolsey, — left Francis I still without support from the Pope, while Francesco Sforza II had rallied to his cause the Milanese and confined the French troops to the castles of Milan and Cremona.

At this perilous moment for the position of France, a new danger sprang up within the kingdom. Although the monarchy had nearly suppressed the power of the great feudatories, Machiavelli had pointed out that France had still something to fear from them. His prediction was verified in the revolt of Charles de Montpensier, Constable of France, who as Duke of Bourbon regarded himself as the victim of the King's cupidity in the confiscation of his estates.[1]

The occasion was opportune for Charles V. The Constable knew the value of his alliance to the Emperor, and demanded in exchange for it a marriage with his sister, Eleanora, the Queen dowager of Portugal, and an independent kingdom to be created in Central and Southern France.[2] This price was promised, and the Duke of Bourbon became the ally of Charles V.

---

[1] The origin of Bourbon's misfortunes, leading to his treason, has been sometimes imputed to the vengeance of Louise of Savoy, whose advances he is said to have repelled. She is vindicated from this imputation by Clément-Simon in his *Jean de Selve*, Tulle, 1901.

[2] See Le Glay, *Négociations*, II, pp. 589, 592.

Thus supported, in alliance with England, successful in Italy, with Spain now loyal to him as the defender of Spanish territory against the aggressions of the King of France, Charles V, nevertheless, made new proposals for a reconciliation; but Francis I would not listen to his terms. Unable to obtain satisfaction otherwise, the allies then formed a programme for the complete dismemberment of France.

The invasion of France

Totally isolated, but not disheartened, Francis I was now menaced with destruction. The crown of France was to be transferred to Henry VIII; a separate kingdom — composed of his own great duchy, Dauphiné, and Provence — was to be created for the Duke of Bourbon; while Charles V was looking forward to the undisputed command of the Mediterranean, thenceforth intended to be made a Spanish lake.

But it was impossible that a conspiracy so gigantic could succeed against a nation as spirited and powerful as France. Charles V never really intended that Henry VIII should wear the crown of that kingdom; and Wolsey, who could never have had faith in the enterprise, at the moment when, if ever, it might have succeeded, was already in secret negotiations with the French court; while Bourbon, rendered powerless in France by his flight to Italy, could only offer the aid of his sword as an exile. The patriotism awakened in France by the treason of the fugitive duke and the want of union between the principal allies rendered the invasion a ridiculous failure. Concentrating his forces at Avignon and driving Bourbon's foreign mercenaries from Provence, Francis I in person pursued his enemy beyond the Alps, recaptured Milan, and began the siege of Pavia. On October 29, 1524, Richard Pace wrote that the King of France had concentrated his forces for an attack on that stronghold. If victorious, he declared, his cause would be won in Italy; if defeated, it would be the end of his power there.

The crisis in the imperial alliances

The whole world realized that the crisis in the conflict between the Emperor and Francis I had now arrived. While the old allies of France in Italy were preparing to take advantage of a French victory and to return to their alliance, the imperial coalition was on the point of dissolution. Clement VII had long been neutral, and in the spring of 1524 he had sent Nicolas Schomberg, Bishop of Capua, on a mission to France and Spain, in the hope of effecting a general peace; but his efforts had proved unsuccessful. Following the general drift in Italy toward the King of France, on December 12, 1524, the Pope also made a secret treaty with him.[1]

Never more than half hearted in the war with France, Wolsey had striven to convoke a congress of the powers at London for a universal peace. Failing in this, his attitude was now equivocal to the point of contradiction. To Clement VII he wrote that, if the King of France were victorious, he would aspire to the Empire and make the Pope his chaplain. At the same time, the Venetian ambassador reported from London: "Cardinal Wolsey would fain keep the Emperor in such straits as to compel him to place the negotiations for peace or a truce in his hands; but the Emperor does not choose to be managed by him."

But the Cardinal's deeds were far more significant of his real intentions than any words he uttered. He had limited the promised contingent of troops sent to France to a handful of infantry; he had ceased to supply money for Bourbon's army; he was at that time negotiating in secret with French agents in London; and so inactive was he in the war that Pace complained of his conduct as disloyal, and declared that, if the King of England had sent his troops as agreed upon, Francis I would never have crossed the Alps.

The coldness of Wolsey toward the imperial alliance did not escape the sharp observation of De Praet, the imperial ambassador, who did not hesitate to report it to his master. Suspecting his action, the Cardinal intercepted his despatches, brought him before the Council, and charged him with false-

---

[1] This treaty is still unpublished. A copy exists in the Bibliothèque Nationale at Paris. See Jacqueton, *La politique extérieure de Louise de Savoie*, pp. 67, 68.

hood. De Praet pleaded his immunity as an ambassador; but Wolsey confined him to his house, forbade his communication with his own government, and complained to Charles V of his conduct.

The battle of Pavia and capture of Francis I

The time was ill chosen for a proceeding as rash as it was illegal, but Wolsey was more anxious to prove to his king the hollowness of the imperial friendship than for the success of the vast scheme of spoliation from which he was convinced England could derive no substantial benefit. Not ready to break openly with the Emperor, however, he was nevertheless disposed to impress him with the fact that the state of affairs was critical, not only in the field but in the cabinet; for the uncertainty of the situation promised the reopening of the way for diplomatic intervention, by which the Cardinal hoped to regain his old ascendency as mediator. But a complete surprise was awaiting him. On February 24, 1525, the French army was almost entirely destroyed at Pavia; nearly all the old heroes of the Italian wars were either killed or captured; and even the King, wounded in the face and in the hand, after a desperate charge led by him in person, was made a prisoner.

When a courier brought the news to Charles V in Spain, the Emperor — repeating abstractedly the startling announcement, " The battle is fought and the King is your prisoner " — retired to his apartment to fall upon his knees in prayer. Forbidding all public rejoicings, he calmly prepared his mind for the use to be made of the victory his generals and troops had won in Italy.

Without a king, without generals, without an army, without an ally, designated as the victim of a scheme of dismemberment, France appeared for the moment in danger of disappearing from the map of Europe as an independent state.

III. THE DIPLOMACY OF FRENCH REHABILITATION

Effect of the battle of Pavia

The announcement of the disaster that had befallen France in the battle of Pavia produced a sudden change in the attitude of England. The confidential agents of the mother of Francis I — Jean Joachim de Passano and Jean Brinon, President of Rouen — who for months had been in secret negotiations with Wolsey, had so far succeeded in their efforts for peace that an audience of the King had been promised them, to take place on March 9, the day on which the news of the capture of Francis I arrived in London. Awakened from sleep in the early morning of that day, the King received in his night-clothes the messenger who had been sent by Margaret of Burgundy, calling him a "holy Gabriel," serving him with wine in his own apartment, and overwhelming him with every honor. The next day, Wolsey ordered public rejoicings, and both King and Chancellor took pains to publish their satisfaction in the fall of the King of France. The French agents were not accorded the expected audience, and soon afterward returned to France, while Wolsey informed the Flemish commissioners present that, if three thousand cavalry and one thousand infantry were furnished in the Netherlands for an invasion of France, the King of England would make a descent in person upon Normandy at the end of May. On March 11, London was illuminated, the Mayor and aldermen marched in procession to the sound of trumpets, wine was distributed to the people, a banquet was given at the Tower to the ambassadors of the Pope, Venice, and Margaret of Burgundy, and on the following day Cardinal Wolsey celebrated the victory of the Emperor with a solemn mass in St. Paul's Cathedral, in the presence of the King and the court.

Chap. V
A. D.
1518–1527

If from the outside France appeared to be in a state of helpless humiliation, within its borders there were patriotism and hope. Placed in charge of the government as regent during the absence of the King, Louise of Savoy, trained in the school of domestic sorrow and adversity, and familiar with affairs of state, in the midst of her grief at the misfortune which had befallen her "glorious Caesar," as she loved to call her son, was not dismayed, and with the support of the whole nation bravely took up the problem of defending

The courage of Louise of Savoy

France. In the instructions to her agents in England written from Lyons,— which she made the seat of her government,— upon receipt of the news from Pavia, there was no word of concession to the demands for territory which Wolsey had exacted as a condition of peace, and even in the matter of money she held firmly to her previous proposals. "You will recommend me strongly to the Cardinal," she writes, "and say to him from me that the zeal and salutary affection which he has had for universal peace and to create between my lord and son and his master an indissoluble fraternity and friendship ought not to change on account of the fortune which has befallen us." With a firm tone she concludes: "And, if you are able, say to him, that, in case he does not wish to persevere in what he has begun, thanks to our Lord, the affairs of this kingdom are in such a state that its enemies will find its force equal to the resistance of former times, or even greater, and money to pay for it."[1]

The attitude of England was not reassuring, however, for the Regent of France. The signs all indicated that the King, the nobles, and even the Chancellor were for war. Two missions were promptly sent forth by Wolsey, one to the Emperor, composed of Cuthbert Tunstall, Bishop of London, and Sir Richard Wingfield, Chancellor of the Duchy of Lancaster; the other to Margaret of Burgundy, headed by William Fitzwilliam, to urge upon Charles V the claims of England to a share in the fruits of victory. At the same time, measures were taken for raising an army, the Duke of Norfolk was chosen to take command until the King could do so in person, and an appeal was made to the counties for an extraordinary subsidy. On the continent, it was regarded as certain that a new attempt was about to be made to invade and conquer the North of France.

The instructions delivered to the two embassies gave precision to the purpose of the King of England. In those issued to Cuthbert Tunstall and Sir Richard Wingfield,

---

[1] See Jacqueton, *La politique*, pp. 314, 316.

two possibilities were presented: (1) the dethronement of Francis I; and (2) his restoration by the payment of a ransom. In case the first alternative were acceptable to Charles V, a combined assault upon France should be made by the allies, the Emperor was to be reminded of his secret promises to place Henry VIII on the throne of Francis I, and any objections Charles V might make were to be met by showing him the advantages that would ultimately accrue to him through the English marriage. If, to assure this, Charles V should demand guarantees, the Princess Mary would either be delivered to him at once in exchange for the person of Francis I, who would be returned to the Emperor after the consummation of the marriage; or in Paris, after Charles V and Henry VIII had arrived there and Henry was crowned King of France. If, on the other hand, Charles V should be opposed to the dethronement of Francis I, England must be indemnified by extensive territorial concessions, including Gascony, Guyenne, Poitou, Anjou, Maine, Brittany, Normandy, and Picardy, — together forming the half of France. Charles V might take Provence and Languedoc, while the Duke of Bourbon should content himself with his patrimony and Dauphiné. In case all these propositions were rejected, the ambassadors were finally instructed to accept the cession of Normandy or Picardy in full sovereignty, and a pension of one hundred thousand crowns a year.[1]

The embassy to Margaret of Burgundy was instructed in a similar sense, and ordered to urge upon her immediate aid in the conquest of France.

The effect of these proposals upon Charles V did not prove encouraging for the success of Henry VIII in obtaining the crown of France. In the affair of his ambassador, De Praet, the Emperor had shown an admirable moderation and much diplomatic skill. Not wishing to break with England, of whose subsidies he was still in need, he had recalled

The attitude of Charles V toward Henry VIII

---

[1] See Brewer, *Letters and Papers*, IV, No. 1212.

De Praet; but, in order to sustain his own dignity, he had ascribed the blame for the treatment of his ambassador, not to the King of England, — which would have led to a rupture, — but to the personal action of the King's officials.

This prudent act of concession on the part of the Emperor in no respect effaced from his mind, however, the indignity to which he had been subjected; which revealed to him the hollowness of the alliance he had been at such pains to cultivate. With the King of France secure in his own power, the situation was now changed; for he could, he believed, make terms with Francis I that would render the English alliance thenceforth superfluous.

So complete was the alteration in the position of Charles V after the battle of Pavia, that it seemed opportune to execute the long cherished project of his marriage with a Portuguese princess, which was popular in Spain on account of the close commercial relations with Portugal, and acceptable to Charles V himself in prospect of a wedding dowry of a million crowns. To disengage himself from his betrothal to Mary of England was, therefore, the next step in this direction. Accordingly, an embassy was sent to London with a demand for the immediate transfer of his *fiancée* to Spain, with the prompt payment of her dowry and a subsidy of two hundred thousand ducats for the support of his army in Italy.

If, as has been suggested, the secret purpose of Wolsey's large demands for French territory was to place upon Charles V the responsibility of taking the first step in dissolving the Treaty of Windsor, the diplomacy of the Emperor repaid the Cardinal in his own coin; for the exactions upon England were undoubtedly intended to provoke refusal, and thus justify the Portuguese marriage.

Before the English embassy arrived in Spain, the imperial embassy had set out for London; so that each side knew the disposition of the other before an answer to its own proposals was received. When, therefore, on June 7, the imperial ambassadors communicated to Henry VIII their master's requisitions, the wide difference between his own wishes and those of the Emperor became evident. The impossibility of his securing the crown of France,—which Wolsey had long comprehended,—was now clear to the King of England also. With perfect loyalty, the Cardinal had strained every nerve to secure the means to prosecute the war in France, calling down upon himself the condemnation of the taxpayers of the realm for his efforts to secure new contributions, in which he had plainly violated the rights of Parliament. His device of the "Amicable Loan," which he had taken strenuous measures to enforce, had raised a storm of popular indignation. Even the King, who had allowed all the odium of this measure to rest upon his minister, now saw that, if his empty treasury precluded the prosecution of a war in France, it also rendered impossible compliance with the exorbitant and humiliating demands of the Emperor. He had vainly expected aid from the imperial alliance in carrying out his scheme of gaining new territories in France, and he was now convinced that he must radically change his policy. Turning once more to his personal pleasures and diversions, the King left the formation of a new system to his great chancellor; and Wolsey was again free to regain for England its former vantage ground as the moderator of continental politics.

Although by patiently awaiting the disclosure of conditions of whose existence he had long been conscious, the Cardinal had at last won a victory for his own pacific policy, he had in the meantime not only incurred general hostility but was now exposed to the danger of becoming also the victim of his master's displeasure. Still trusted by Henry VIII as his most capable servant, he wished, nevertheless, to give a new proof of his devotion and obtain a new assurance of royal favor. To show that, while others withheld the money of which the King stood in need, he was ready to make personal sacrifices, he offered to his sovereign as a gift his splendid palace of Hampton Court. The King accepted it, and Wolsey seemed mightier than ever.

The renewal of Wolsey's pacific policy

To his clear intelligence it was evident that the great peril for England now lay in the possibility of its isolation through a reconciliation of Charles V and Francis I. Holding Francis I in his power as a prisoner, it appeared to be easy for the Emperor to restore him to his kingdom upon such terms as to cement with him a perpetual friendship, thus leaving England to stand alone. Not only so, but, by an offensive and defensive alliance between the two monarchs, the trade of England might be driven from the continent.

Two purposes became, therefore, the mainsprings of Wolsey's policy: first, to avoid an open breach with Charles V by continuing with him amicable negotiations; and, second, to outstrip him in making an advantageous peace with France.

Accordingly, Wolsey eluded the Emperor's strategy by frankly assenting to the Portuguese marriage, on three conditions: (1) the conclusion of a peace with France by the Emperor that would be satisfactory to Henry VIII; (2) the payment of the debts that Charles V owed to England; and (3) the abolition of their previous treaties.

This procedure was intended to prevent a separate peace between the Emperor and France, through the suggestion of an arrangement in which England should participate. It was, in truth, a desperate attempt to restore the conditions that prevailed before the Conference of Calais.

Reply of Charles V to Wolsey's proposals

In one respect the calculations of Wolsey were realized, the proposals of England served to divide the imperial counsels and procure delay.

The success of Charles V at Pavia was, in a sense, a fruit of the diplomacy of Gattinara. It was he who had counselled war; it was he who had dragged England into the imperial alliance; and it was but natural that he, the chief of the Emperor's advisers, should now be heard. Centring his thoughts about Italy as the historic seat of empire, believing that it was the key to the universal monarchy which he wished Charles V to establish, Gattinara's system was,

THE ASCENDENCY OF THE HOUSE OF HAPSBURG 381

to crush France so completely as to prevent its ever disputing the authority of the Emperor; to ignore the claims of England, which had done nothing to secure the defeat of Francis I; and to reorganize Italy on the basis of a union of local freedom with supreme imperial authority. It was a revival of the old Roman idea, slightly modified by the lessons of experience; yet not recognizing the fact that the new temper of Europe rendered that idea chimerical.

Had Charles V been a man of more vivid imagination and less practical judgment, he might have attempted to follow Gattinara's wild dream of imperial restoration by the total subjection of France; but, although not unaffected by his chancellor's ideas, his early training in the fixed conceptions of his Netherland tutors and counsellors, his sense of his poverty, and his realization of the power that France might still possess, led him to adopt a different course.

Anxious to be liberated from his engagement to the Princess Mary, and fearing lest England, if rendered hostile, might unite with France and seek compensation in the Netherlands, Charles V thought it more prudent to reply to Wolsey, that he would pay his debts to England in their order; that he would admit the ambassadors of Henry VIII to the negotiations with Francis I, thereby safeguarding the interests of England in the treaty which he would make with him; and, finally, that he would consent to abolish all former treaties, thus releasing England from its earlier obligations to him.

The transfer of Francis I from Italy to Spain, on June 10, 1525, was not calculated to inspire Wolsey with confidence in the Emperor's intentions. A helpless prisoner in the hands of his enemy, Francis I, to save his life, could be forced to accede to almost any conditions which his captor might impose. In fact, however, Charles V was not absolutely cruel to his prisoner. Hunting in the Segovian forest at the time of the captive's arrival in Spain, the Emperor paid no attention to his presence until, on September 18, having heard that the King of France was dying in the

Chap. V
A. D.
1518–1527

Negotiations of the Emperor with Francis I

Alcazar at Madrid, he went to his bedside. "Here I am, my Lord Emperor, your servant and slave," exclaimed Francis I, as his captor entered his apartment. "Not so; you are my good friend and brother, and I hope that you will always be so," replied Charles.

Much agitation was produced in England by the news that the sister of Francis I, Margaret of Angoulême, accompanied by Robertet and armed with full powers by Madame Louise, had been sent to Spain and was lodged with her brother in the Alcazar; for it was feared that her charms might impress the Emperor, and induce him to make an easy peace to be celebrated by their marriage. Charles V had been solemnly exhorted by the English ambassadors not to receive her. "Being young and a widow," — runs the note of warning, — "she comes, as Ovid says of women going to the play, to see and be seen, that perhaps the Emperor may like her; and also to woo the Queen dowager of Portugal for her brother!" — a suggestion which, owing to the recent death of Queen Claude, was not preposterous.

The negotiations with Francis I were opened by Gattinara with an immense flourish of disinterred legal claims. The whole of France, asserted the Chancellor, had been forfeited to the Empire under a bull of Pope Boniface VIII; Provence had passed to the House of Aragon with the crown of Naples as a fief of its Anjou kings; Languedoc was an old Aragonese possession; Bourbon's wrongs justified the denial of Francis' sovereignty over his great duchy; the Duchy of Burgundy was an ancestral heritage of Charles V, from whose grandmother, Mary of Burgundy, it had been cruelly wrested in the moment of her weakness after the death of Charles the Bold; finally, to complete the effect, even the claims of England to the crown of France — though never intended to be pressed — were added to the long catalogue of juristic quibbles by which the tenure of the French throne by Francis I seemed to be reduced to an illegal impertinence.

The sober intelligence of Charles V set little value upon

the brilliant pettifoggery of Gattinara, but he was settled in the conviction that four points were to be insisted upon: (1) France must abandon all claims in Italy; (2) the suzerainty of Artois and Flanders must be relinquished; (3) the Duchy of Burgundy must be ceded to him in full sovereignty by Francis; and (4) Bourbon must be restored to his estates.

Hard as these conditions seemed to Francis I, — particularly in being forced to alienate the Duchy of Burgundy, so important in securing a safe frontier to France, — they would probably have been far more severe but for the negotiations of Louise of Savoy. Through a private letter to Thomas Lark, the confessor of Wolsey, at the instance of Madame Louise, Jean Joachim de Passano had caused it to be represented to the Cardinal that France was by no means defenceless; and he had expressed the hope that His Most Reverend Lordship might be again recognized as the promoter of universal peace.

In response to this overture, Wolsey had intimated his readiness to resume negotiations with the Regent; and on June 9, Madame Louise had commissioned De Passano and the President of Rouen to continue them with the Cardinal at London in behalf of France.

The moment was favorable for a peace with England, for the King had already decided that nothing further was to be hoped for from his alliance with the Emperor. Thenceforth, there was no further question of territorial cessions on the part of France. By June 28, De Passano was able to inform the Regent that the English government was ready to treat with France on the basis of a payment of two million crowns as the price of peace.

Although the sum was at first contested as exorbitant, it was finally accepted; and only questions of detail remained to be discussed. Of these the matter of hostages, guarantees, and ratification were vexatious; but, although the Chancellor of France, Duprat, raised technical objections, the firm resolve of Madame Louise to effect a peace and ameliorate the conditions of her son's deliverance brushed them all aside; and, on August 30, 1525, the Treaty of Moore was signed at Wolsey's castle of that name.[1] The great nobles and chief cities of France were made guarantors of the treaty, the ratification of Francis I was to be obtained, and Madame Louise was to be discharged from her personal obligation to pay the two million crowns when that ratification should have been procured.[2] On September 6, the result of these secret negotiations was publicly proclaimed in France and England; and the Regent's diplomacy proved to the world that France, with England as her defensive ally, was able to maintain her integrity, even while her king was a captive of the Emperor.

The Treaty of Moore bound Henry VIII to use his influence with the Emperor to secure the early release of Francis I; but, apart from substantially exempting the imperial authorities from further recognizing the claims of the King of England to the crown of France or to territorial compensation, this circumstance had no appreciable effect upon the negotiations of Charles V with the King of France. In order to create an appearance of regard for the promise to associate the English ambassadors in the transaction with Francis I, however, a few formal questions were put to them by Gattinara; but in the determination of the final conditions they were virtually excluded from any part. Only in the ordaining of a general truce on August 11, was their counsel of any practical effect; and during the secret negotiations with the French plenipotentiaries, the English ambassadors were kept in almost total ignorance of what was taking place.

Upon two points Wolsey had insisted: first, that no territorial concessions be made to the Emperor; and, second, that

---

[1] See Dumont, IV, Part I, pp. 436 et seq.

[2] Wolsey received for himself, besides the arrears of his pension as Bishop of Tournay, a present of one hundred thousand crowns from Madame Louise in reward for his services in making peace, as previously promised by her agents. — See Jacqueton, *La politique*, pp. 144, 146.

no arrangement of marriage between Francis and the Emperor's sister, Eleanora, be included in the peace. So close a union of the two monarchs as that marriage would imply, it was feared, would exclude England from all influence in continental politics. What Wolsey commended was the exaction by Charles V of a money indemnity to be paid by France, which he then hoped to find available as a resource for paying the Emperor's enormous debts to England. But in all these particulars, his wishes were to be entirely disregarded.

Besides the Anglo-French alliance, other considerations were urged upon Charles V as reasons for moderating his exactions from Francis I. His able general, Pescara, the real victor of the battle of Pavia, exposed to him the conspiracy of Girolamo Morone, Chancellor of Milan,— who had offered Pescara the crown of Naples as a reward if he would join the Italians with his army in establishing the complete independence of the Italian states, — and advised immediate peace with France and the liberation of Francis I, on the sole condition that he would abandon all claims in Italy.

The captivity of Francis I

Gattinara, on the contrary, hating France while loving Italy, pressed upon the Emperor the conciliation of the Italians, in order to isolate and dismember France; which he imagined was within the power of his master.

De Praet had well pointed out, that, in view of the strength France still possessed, it was indispensable either to retain the King as a perpetual prisoner, thus reserving him as a permanent hostage against further French aggression; or, by magnanimously according him liberty without humiliation, to win his grateful and loyal friendship.

None of these policies met with the entire approval of Charles V, who preferred to deal with Italy in his own way. By limiting his exactions from France to the concessions he had already determined upon, he hoped still to obtain the friendship of Francis I.

But the Emperor little realized the results of this composite programme, based on no clear principle of justice, of affection, or even of hostility. In desperation, a plot was formed for the King's escape, disguised as the negro slave who attended the fire in his apartment, and for his flight from Madrid by means of relays of horses previously stationed to receive him; but the plan was revealed by a *valet de chambre* made angry by a blow from a French noble. Charles V professed to be incredulous of a tale that assigned to so great a prince a rôle so ignoble, but care was thereafter taken that escape should be impossible.

Deeply concerned for the deliverance of her son, in November Madame Louise sent Chabot de Brion to authorize assent to any necessary terms which the Emperor might require. The envoy arrived after Francis I had signed a deed of abdication in favor of the Dauphin, Francis, appointing Madame Louise regent during the minority of his son, but reserving his own right of sovereignty by the *jus postliminii*, in case he should recover his liberty at a later time. Montmorency was about to carry this deed to France; but when the message of his mother was received, the resolution of Francis failed; and he announced that he was prepared to make every renunciation that had been exacted from him, even including the Duchy of Burgundy.

The sacrifice imposed touched most deeply the patriotic sentiment and national interest of a proud king and a proud nation, yet Charles V believed it possible to secure in full sovereignty the ancestral heritage to which he so tenaciously clung without danger to his peace with Francis I by placing him under most solemn bonds to himself as a man, as a king, and as a father.

The Treaty of Madrid

Perhaps with the intention of intimidating Francis I with the idea that the Duke of Bourbon might be named by the Emperor to succeed him as King of France if he were not tractable, the Constable was brought to Spain and magnificently fêted; although, with true Spanish loyalty, the grandee in whose palace he was lodged declared that he would burn the polluted place as soon as the traitor had quitted it. One

THE ASCENDENCY OF THE HOUSE OF HAPSBURG 387

object of these flattering attentions was to induce the Duke to surrender in favor of Francis I the promise of marriage with Eleanora, who was now needed to cement peace with France. The disappointed suitor demurred, but the lady herself settled the question by expressing her preference for the King.

On January 14, 1526, was signed the Treaty of Madrid, by which Francis I "restored" to the Emperor the Duchy of Burgundy, abandoning also his suzerainty over Flanders and Artois; renounced all claims in Italy; contracted an offensive and defensive alliance with Charles V; and agreed to accompany him with an army to Rome when he should go there for his coronation. French protection was withdrawn from Navarre and the imperial vassals in Germany; the Duke of Bourbon was restored to his estates in France, and promised by the Emperor investiture with the Duchy of Milan; Francis I was to marry Eleanora, and to send his two sons — the Dauphin Francis, and Henry, Duke of Orléans — to Spain, as hostages for the faithful execution of the treaty. If all the stipulations were not duly observed, he engaged to return and take the place of his sons as the Emperor's prisoner.[1]

To render these obligations as solemn as possible, an altar was placed in the King's apartment, mass was celebrated, and in the presence of the plenipotentiaries who had negotiated the treaty it was read aloud, after which Francis I, with his hand on the Gospel, swore to execute it faithfully. His plenipotentiaries did the same, and all signed it.

Then, as if to leave no bond unsecured, Lannoy, the Viceroy of Naples, in the name of the Emperor, asked that Francis I bind himself upon his honor as a knight. Without hesitation, the King, his head uncovered, his hand in that of the Viceroy, solemnly pledged his word of honor as "*gentilhomme à gentilhomme*" that, in case he should not

---

[1] See Dumont IV, Part I, pp. 399 et seq.

CHAP. V
A. D.
1518-1527

The deliverance of Francis I

accomplish the restitution of the Duchy of Burgundy to the Emperor within six weeks after he was set at liberty in his kingdom of France, and deliver all the ratifications and sureties within four months, he would return as a prisoner of war to the power of the Emperor. Letters were then exchanged between the two monarchs, in which each expressed his satisfaction that the treaty was concluded and a desire to see the other.

Six days after the conclusion of the Treaty of Madrid, the betrothal with Eleanora was solemnized by proxy in the apartment of the King; but the Emperor's "brother," as Francis I had now become, was still watched and guarded as a prisoner.

On February 11, Charles V ratified the treaty at Toledo, much against the will of Gattinara, who had wished to insist upon the delivery of the Duchy of Burgundy before the treaty was ratified. At Madrid, the two sovereigns met, tenderly embraced each other, and passed several days in fraternal intercourse. Although the treaty had been formally concluded, Charles V requested that Bourbon be allowed a pension until his claim on Provence could be legally adjusted, and be granted full sovereignty in his own estates. Francis I promised the pension, but refused to alienate the estates from dependence on the Crown.

On February 16, captor and captive set out together to visit Queen Eleanora at Torrejon de Velasco, whither she had come to meet them. There, for the first time, Francis I beheld his *fiancée*. Accompanied by Queen Germaine de Foix and attended by other ladies of the Court, as Francis I approached, she fell upon her knees to kiss his hand; but the King, raising her up, said gallantly, "It is not the hand that I should give you, Madame, but the mouth." The day was then spent in fêtes and dancing.

On February 19, the sovereigns parted; Francis I to return to Madrid preparatory to his journey to France, Charles V to proceed to Seville for his marriage with Isabella of Portugal. "I have never hated you," said the

Emperor, as they separated; "but if you should deceive me, — above all as concerns the Queen, your wife and my sister, — I would consider it so great an injury that I would seek every possible means to do you harm." "I swear to you," replied Francis I, "that I will perform all that I have promised."

On March 17, 1526, as arranged by special convention, near Bayonne, in the exact middle of the river Bidassoa, — the frontier between France and Spain, — a landing stage was anchored for the exchange of Francis and his sons. At seven o'clock in the morning, two boats, starting from opposite sides of the river at the same moment, advanced to the place of meeting. In one, under the charge of Lannoy, accompanied by ten armed knights, was the King of France; in the other, directed by the French general Lautrec, with a similar escort, were the two motherless children of the King, — Francis, aged eight years and a half, and Henry, aged seven. Disembarking upon the float, Francis I embraced his children, then delivered them to Lannoy, and stepped into the boat which had brought them from the shore of France. "Sire, now that Your Highness is free, do the promises hold good?" said the Viceroy. "Every thing shall be done as agreed," replied the King.

The boats parted as they had met; the children to their captivity as hostages in Spain, the King to freedom in France. When the shore was reached, Francis I leaped upon his horse with the cry, "Now I am once more a king!" and hastened to Bayonne, where his mother was waiting to receive him.

Not only had the administration of Louise of Savoy as regent maintained the territorial integrity of the kingdom, but her diplomacy had produced results of the greatest importance to the future of Francis I. As he rode to Bayonne, the English ambassador, Taylor, came out to greet him, to whom the King said with effusion: "I know perfectly the good intentions of my good brother of England; and, after God, I thank him for my liberty. During my

CHAP. V
A. D.
1518–1527

The fruits of the Regent's diplomacy

captivity he has done an act which merits eternal glory, and which obliges me and mine forever to do him service."

But it was not the alliance of England alone which Louise of Savoy had won for France during the King's captivity. All Italy was now ready to offer him support in checking the power of Charles V. The battle of Pavia had filled the Italians with terror lest the Emperor might soon completely dominate the peninsula; and, in less than a month after his victory, under the leadership of the Venetians, they had projected a "league for the defence of the liberties of Italy." Pope Clement VII, Venice, Florence, the Duke of Ferrara, and the lords of Siena, Lucca, and Mantua, had combined to prevent the re-establishment of imperial supremacy in Italy; and even the Duke of Milan had joined them. Henry VIII had perceived the value of the Italian movement in his negotiations with the Emperor, Madame had secretly promoted it without compromising herself at Madrid, and Charles V had undoubtedly been restrained by it from even greater severity in his transaction with the King of France.

When, therefore, Francis I returned to his kingdom, he found the materials for a formidable coalition against the Emperor already prepared for use. They needed only to be combined, in order to isolate Charles V in Western Europe, as France had been isolated in the previous year.

The attitude of the Emperor's former allies

The excitement produced in England and Italy by the deliverance and return of Francis I was intense; for the world was still uncertain upon what conditions the Treaty of Madrid had been concluded. If, as was at first suspected, a firm offensive and defensive alliance had been effected between Charles V and Francis I upon the lines proposed by Pescara, — by which France was to be left intact and Italy abandoned to Charles, — the Italians would have been exposed to the absolute supremacy of the Emperor; while Francis could have made his own terms with England.

When, however, the truth at last began to be known, a sense of relief was felt. To prevent the effacement of Italian liberties, the isolation of England, and the vassalage of

France, nothing was needed but the decision of Francis I not to keep his engagements with the Emperor. Neither Wolsey, nor Henry VIII, nor the Privy Council of England, nor the Pope believed that he would ever execute them.

When Clement VII learned of the terms of the Treaty of Madrid, he said to the English ambassador: "It is possible that the King of France has conceived the able design of recovering his liberty at any price, with the fixed purpose of not keeping his promises except so far as they are not contrary to the interests of his kingdom, those of the Christian Republic, and the public good." So convinced was the Pope of the secret intention of Francis I to violate his oath, that he predicted his evasion of his promise to marry Eleanora and his refusal to alienate Burgundy; and this course, he considered, was one to be commended.[1]

In the previous December, Clement VII had consented to a new treaty with the Emperor; but, in expectation of aid from Francis I, he now declined to conclude it, and together with the other Italian princes proceeded with military preparations. His secret instructions to his nuncio, Capino, were, to exhort the King of France not to observe the Treaty of Madrid, but to conclude an offensive and defensive alliance with the Italians.

Before he departed from Madrid, Francis I knew precisely what his future course would be; but, with perfect circumspection, he concealed his intentions. "When I shall have received the counsels of my dear brother and those of Monsignore the Legate," he said to the English ambassador soon after his deliverance, — referring to Henry VIII and Wolsey, — "I shall throw off the mask."

To Thomas Cheyney, one of the most trusted chamberlains of Henry VIII, who had been sent to France to compliment the King upon his deliverance, he showed every mark of honor and attention. Upon the occasion of the ceremonial entry into Bordeaux, on April 9, the Portuguese ambassador,

---

[1] See Brewer, *Letters and Papers*, No. 1956.

claiming precedence of Cheyney, took his place at the head of the diplomatic body with the imperial ambassador. Cheyney protested, and his complaints reached the ear of the King, who sent the Master of Ceremonies to the Portuguese with the order to take his proper place or retire. The ambassador resisted, and it was necessary to send the Grand Master to command him formally to leave the *cortège* and return to his lodgings. When he still refused to yield, Montmorency lost his temper and rudely told him that His Majesty did not intend to offer an affront to the King of England for the pleasure of honoring the King of Portugal. The ambassador still persisted in holding his place, alleging that, as the *cortège* was to pass his lodgings, he would obey by retaining his place until he reached there. At this the Grand Master became so irritated that he roughly pushed the ambassador from his place in the line, and ordered four halberdiers to put him out of the procession; while the ambassador of Charles V witnessed with the deepest mortification this insult offered to the representative of the Emperor's brother-in-law.[1] In the evening, Francis I declared to the English ambassadors, that he would care for the honor of their sovereign as for his own. "What!" he exclaimed, "an apothecary diplomatist would precede the representative of the King of England! Indeed, he would better go to Calicut and make laws for the spice trade, for he will not make them here!"

Soon afterward, when the papal nuncio, Capino, the Venetian secretary, Rosso, and the English ambassadors, Taylor and Cheyney,—whose business it was to prevent Francis I from keeping his promises to the Emperor,—were anxiously awaiting an expression of his mind, the King of France opened the subject by saying, that he had good reasons for protesting against the pledges he had been constrained to give, and that he entertained a fear that even if he ceded Burgundy he might not recover his children.

---

[1] Charles V had been married to Isabella of Portugal in the preceding March.

The King was now ready to discuss the formation of a Franco-Italian league, and expressed displeasure that Capino and Rosso were not provided with full powers to conclude it. On April 15, the Treaty of Moore received its formal ratification by Francis I, and later in the month the peace between England and France was celebrated with great solemnity at London. On May 10, Lannoy — who had come to France as special ambassador of the Emperor to supervise the execution of the Treaty of Madrid — was officially informed that the King could not detach Burgundy from the Kingdom of France, and that the only sacrifice he could make was the payment of a ransom in money.

Among the reasons for this bold declaration was the support that England professed to offer. Already certain of the Pope, of Venice, and of their Italian allies, Francis I was soon fortified with assurances that seemed to his mind to justify his repudiation of his treaty obligations to Charles V.

A document dated May 4, 1526, and signed by Wolsey in the form of instructions to the English ambassadors, furnished the formal opinion and advice which the King of France had requested of Henry VIII.[1] The King of England and his Council had carefully examined the conditions of the Treaty of Madrid and the circumstances in which it was signed. Their opinion was, that those conditions were impossible of fulfilment, contrary to reason and honor, and tended to the ruin of Christendom. They were impossible of fulfilment by the King, because the alienation of territory belonging to the Kingdom of France could be authorized only by the affirmative action of the Parliament, the Chamber of Accounts, and the States General, which would undoubtedly be refused. They were contrary to reason and honor, first, since they created a precedent for the imposition of unlimited obligations upon a captive sovereign, whereas usage required only the payment of a ran-

---

[1] The document exists in the British Museum, Cottonian Library, under the head of Caligula, D. IX, folios 190 et seq.

som in money; and, second, because the aid promised to Charles V when he should make his journey to Italy would deprive the kingdom of forces necessary to its defence. Finally, if Charles V were permitted to reduce Italy to submission, it would be possible for him to make himself master of France also by turning his arms against it, and thus to dominate the whole of Europe. Since the children of Francis I were to remain as hostages in Spain until every condition was fulfilled, there was no guarantee that they would ever be released. The succession of France would, therefore, be in the power of the Emperor. The conclusion was, that, since the treaty had been extorted from Francis I by terror and violence, it was in no sense binding; and should be abrogated. The advice of Wolsey was, therefore, to endeavor to procure the restitution of the French princes by paying a ransom for them, and to cancel the marriage contract with Queen Eleanora; which, if fulfilled, would bring upon France, it was declared, grave dangers in the future.

Revival of Wolsey's mediatorial policy

Notwithstanding all this urgency upon Francis I to break his pledges to the Emperor, the only substantial aid offered by Henry VIII for the execution of the programme proposed by Wolsey was a monthly subsidy of twenty-five thousand crowns, to be subsequently reimbursed by France. Besides this secret loan, Henry VIII promised to send to Charles V a special ambassador who, in the presence of the French representatives, would present a threefold demand: (1) the surrender of the French princes for a ransom to be named by the King of France; (2) the disbanding of the imperial army in Italy and the promise that no aggression should be made upon the independence of the Italian states, in case the Emperor should go to Rome for his coronation; and (3) the payment of the Emperor's debts to England and the recognition of the rights of Henry VIII to the kingdoms of Castile and Leon, derived through his marriage with Queen Catherine! If Charles V should accept the first and second demands, Henry VIII would waive his personal claims to Castile and

THE ASCENDENCY OF THE HOUSE OF HAPSBURG 395

Leon, and make easy terms for the payment of the money owed. If, on the contrary, the Emperor should decline to accept them, or resort to delay, he would be informed that the King of England would be constrained, at the end of three months, to become the protector of a Franco-Italian league.

Without the trouble or expense of war, Wolsey hoped by this mediation to restore the former preponderance of England, and thus to become a second time the arbiter of Europe. To this end, he placed his personal services at the disposal of the King of France; insinuated that the King could find a "younger, more amiable, more beautiful, and more virtuous wife" than Eleanora, — meaning thereby to indicate the Princess Mary of England, — and used all his arts to obtain the signature of a Franco-Italian alliance in England rather than in France, with Henry VIII as its protector. But, while the Cardinal was thus again gathering the threads of diplomacy into his own hand, the Italians, threatened with the immediate wrath of the Emperor, were pressing for the conclusion of a league against him to be signed in France.

It was Clement VII who, in conjunction with Francis I, bore off the honor of forming a coalition nominally organized to secure the peace of Christendom, but really intended only to serve their personal interests. On May 22, 1526, at Cognac, where the French court was assembled, a treaty was signed, alleging as its purpose universal peace, to which the Emperor could accede within three months, provided he should accept the following conditions: (1) the release of the French princes for a money ransom; (2) the independence of Italy; and (3) the payment of the sums due to England.[1] The signatories of this "League of Cognac" were the Supreme Pontiff, the King of France, the Republic of Venice, and Francesco Sforza II, Duke of Milan. All Christian princes were invited to adhere, and the King of

CHAP. V
A. D.
1518–1527

The League of Cognac

---

[1] See Dumont, IV, Part I, pp. 451 et seq.

England was named as "protector" of the League, with the privilege of accepting this distinction within three months. An apportionment of troops for the defence of Italy against the Emperor was agreed upon; Sforza was recognized as Duke of Milan; the expulsion of Charles V from Northern Italy and, if necessary, from the Kingdom of Naples was provided for; the Pope was to dispose of that kingdom as a papal fief in whatever manner might please him best, but a pension was to be paid to Francis I in recognition of his hereditary rights; and both Henry VIII and Cardinal Wolsey were to be assigned the revenues of rich estates within its borders.

Thus, in a few months, Francis I was able to oppose the Emperor with a powerful coalition, which enabled him to repudiate with comparative impunity the Treaty of Madrid. Now, as he had intimated to the English ambassador soon after his return to France, he was ready to throw off the mask. From the beginning, he had entertained no intention of keeping his elaborate promises to Charles V.

On the evening of January 13, before he signed the Treaty of Madrid, he had assembled in his apartment the plenipotentiaries of France, to whom, after binding them to secrecy by an oath, he had violently protested against the treaty, which he declared to be forced upon him, injurious to France, and derogatory to his honor. He had then reviewed the history of his captivity, condemned as unjust and dishonorable the restraint that was imposed upon him, and declared before God that, although he was compelled to sign the treaty, it was null and void; and that he would not observe it.

The inefficiency of the League of Cognac

Had Francis I energetically employed the advantages which the League of Cognac conferred upon him, the power of Charles V might have been effectively broken; but, having set in motion the forces of his allies, his whole life at this time seems to have been given up to sensuous pleasure. Absolved from his perfidy to the Emperor by a special dispensation of the Pope, Francis I saw his quarrel taken up

THE ASCENDENCY OF THE HOUSE OF HAPSBURG   397

by all Western Europe to a point that made him almost forget that it was his own. The papal nuncio complained that the King avoided everything likely to give him trouble or annoyance; and a contemporary French chronicler observed, that, while Alexander the Great saw women only when he had finished business, Francis I would attend to business only when he was tired of his amours.

Leaving to his generals the conduct of the war against Charles V, the King of France did not appear in person upon the field of battle;[1] and the irresolute character of Clement VII left his allies in painful uncertainty regarding his constancy;[2] while the Duke of Urbino, who commanded the forces of Venice, possessed neither military skill nor the quality of decision. Through his incapacity as a general, the faction of the Colonna was able, on September 20, to make the Pope a prisoner; and he was compelled to sign a truce with Ugo de Moncada, who represented the Emperor, only to break it at a moment most inopportune.

But the weakness of the League of Cognac was only a symptom of a general decay in the vitality of Christendom as a moral organism. The Pope had become a political partisan, the Church was rent by schism and heresy, and the ancient foundations of moral obligation had been swept away. The rude passions that agitated the Middle Ages were at least tempered by a sense of knightly honor, and for the most part possessed the merit of sincerity; but the ambitions of the sixteenth century had degenerated into a sordid lust for power ennobled by no sentiment of chivalry, and dignified by no large conception of public duty. Nations, full grown in magnitude and organization,

The degeneration of international morals

---

[1] Soon after Francis I broke faith with the Emperor, Charles V challenged him to single combat; but Francis I deferred his reply and finally evaded acceptance. For the particulars, see Armstrong, *The Emperor Charles V*, I, pp. 180, 181.

[2] For the fluctuations of the policy of Clement VII, see Hellwig, *Die politische Beziehungen Clements VII*, pp. 56, 62.

confronted one another without recognizing any common authority, any basis of public law, or even any principle of nationality. International morals had sunk to the lowest ebb. Religion was never more ceremonious or ostentatious in its outward forms, but the emphasis placed upon its mere externals revealed the essential hollowness of the heart that could be satisfied with empty signs and symbols when the reality was wanting.

More than any other man of his time, Wolsey possessed an ecumenical quality of mind. A man of the world under the guise of an ecclesiastic, courtier and even sycophant though he was, he was inspired by a sense of catholicity that made him great. He had the intelligence to perceive that the chief need of England and of the world was peace. He proposed to secure it by so balancing continental interests that England would form the essential keystone in the arch of concord. Beyond this, except if possible to continue his system in the Papacy, of whose pacific function he had a high conception, he did not look. Only after a long and bitter experience did he fully realize that no single man, no single nation, no single institution can secure the stability of international relations; which can rest upon no other foundation than universal assent to fixed principles of good faith and equity.

The matrimonial project of Henry VIII and the Treaty of Westminster

Instead of such a public conscience, it was the doctrine of Machiavelli that now inspired the thoughts and deeds of princes; for, although the book on "The Prince" had not yet been published, the contagion of its principles was in the spirit of the time, and their bitter fruits had already begun to ripen.

In England, a fancy of the King was fatally pushing Wolsey from his policy of mediation to a policy of open partisanship with France against the Emperor. For eighteen years, Henry VIII and Catherine of Aragon had lived together in wedlock, and from their union children, dead and living, had been born. Then, just at the turning-point between a continued alliance with the Emperor and a closer intimacy with Francis I, the fascinating Anne Boleyn, returning from a residence in France, appeared at court; and her charms made a deep impression upon Henry VIII. Unlike others who before her had appealed to his fancy — including her elder sister, whom he had seduced — either because she was more virtuous or better advised, this lady refused to yield to the King's proposals except in the quality of Queen of England. Then, after all those years of tranquillity, the conscience of Henry VIII suddenly smote him with the intolerable thought that he had been living in sin with Catherine of Aragon, because the dispensation of Pope Julius II, by which he had been authorized to marry her, she having been the wife of his brother Arthur, was in principle uncanonical!

It cannot, indeed, be affirmed that the only reason for seeking a separation from Catherine of Aragon, against whose loyal love and spotless virtue there was no breath of suspicion in the King's mind, was his passion for Anne Boleyn, whose charms were in fact those of an attractive manner rather than of form or feature. Under the law of the Church there was the possibility of a doubt regarding the validity of the dispensation granted by Pope Julius II, and this had been raised by others,[1] though Henry himself appears never to have seriously entertained it while the marriage seemed advantageous. The problem of succession to the throne was complicated by the fact that the King's union with Catherine was not blessed with a living son, and by the further fact that England had never yet been ruled by a queen in her own right. Several years older than the King, the victim of a series of misfortunes in the birth of

---

[1] The supposition that this doubt was first raised by the Bishop of Tarbes in 1527, when negotiating a marriage between the Princess Mary and Francis I, is dismissed by Pollard, who says: "Doubts of the legality of Henry's marriage had existed long before the Bishop of Tarbes paid his visit to England. . . . They were urged, not only on the eve of the completion of the marriage, but when it was first suggested." — *Henry VIII*, pp. 173, 174.

her children, nearly all of whom had died in the first months of their existence, and already in the period of declining vigor, Queen Catherine was not likely to furnish England with a king. Real as these political considerations were, however, it is only by special pleading that they can be made to appear as the true motives of the King's conduct. While, for reasons of state, Wolsey approved his repudiation of Catherine, whom he cordially disliked, he feared the success of the court party which would be brought into power by the King's marriage with Anne Boleyn; and, therefore, favored the choice of a French princess as the Queen's successor. But Henry VIII, dominated by his one immediate thought of legalizing his union with the object of his fancy, was rapidly passing beyond the influence of his great minister. Between the certain displeasure of the King if Wolsey failed in securing the favorable action of the Pope, and the powerful influence of his enemies if the marriage with Anne Boleyn should be accomplished, the Chancellor could read a warning that made him tremble for his future.

So great an outrage as Henry VIII contemplated upon the rights of the Emperor's aunt and the honor of his house was certain not to be endured without opposition. Charles V could, however, defeat the purposes of Henry VIII only by destroying his influence with the Pope. To maintain that influence, a combination strong enough to outweigh that of Charles V was necessary; and this could be found nowhere except in a close alliance with Francis I. By an irresistible necessity, therefore, Wolsey was compelled to abandon his proud position as arbiter between Francis I and Charles V and seek aid of France.

On April 30, 1527, was signed the Treaty of Westminster, which provided that the Princess Mary should marry Henry, Duke of Orléans, the second son of Francis I; a perpetual peace was declared between the two kingdoms; and Henry VIII renounced for an annual pension of fifty thousand crowns all pretensions to the throne of France.[1] Thus united, the two monarchs agreed to force from Charles V the acceptance of a ransom of two million crowns for the release of the French princes and the payment of his debts to England. The mediatorial policy of Wolsey was thereby finally shattered, and England, without substantial benefit, drawn into the vortex of the Franco-Imperial quarrel.

Events were now rapidly bringing this conflict to an unexpected crisis. The union of a German army, composed largely of Lutherans, under the famous captain, George von Frundsberg, and the forces commanded by the Duke of Bourbon, at Milan, in February, 1527, gave the imperial cause preponderance in Italy; but it was the mutinous not the disciplined movements of this unpaid, starving, and badly organized host that now created a turning-point in history. Eager for pillage, the imperial army was determined to march to Rome. Restrained with difficulty by Frundsberg, who fell before his troops stricken with apoplexy in his efforts to restore order among them, this turbulent force passed to the nominal command of the Duke of Bourbon; and the lust for plunder, taking advantage of the perfidy of Clement VII in renouncing the truce with the Emperor and resuming his connection with the League, brought the unruly mob to the Eternal City.

What the real intention of the Duke may have been has furnished a subject for controversy; but his death on May 6, 1527, in attempting to scale the walls of Rome, has left the problem without solution.

Deprived of a commander, the wild host burst into the city to lay it waste. No palace, no cloister, no church, no tomb was spared in the orgy of violence and plunder. The crypt of the Holy Apostles was rifled, and a jewelled ring snatched from the dead hand of Julius II. In the midst of the assault, Clement VII, whose white robe was covered by the violet mantle of Paolo Giovio to conceal his identity in

---

[1] Dumont, IV, Part I, pp. 481 et seq.

his flight from the Vatican, found refuge behind the massive fortifications of the Castle of St. Angelo; but his asylum proved to be his prison, for Philibert de Chalon, Prince of Orange, — who succeeded to the command of the imperial forces at Rome, — held him captive in his stronghold while awaiting orders from the Emperor. Upon the results of that captivity turned, in great degree, the future destiny of Europe.

AUTHORITIES

Documents

The principal treaties of this period may be found in Dumont, Rymer, Léonard and Le Glay.

For the public acts of the Empire, the following are the most important: *Monumenta Habsburgica, 1473-1576*, published by the Kaiserliche Akademie der Wissenschaften, Vienna, 1853 et seq.; Lünig, *Das deutsche Reichsarchiv*, Leipzig, 1713 et seq.; Kluckhohn and Wrede, *Deutsche Reichstagsakten unter Kaiser Karl V*, Gotha, 1893 et seq.; Brieger, *Quellen und Forschungen zur Geschichte der Reformation*, Bd. I, Gotha, 1884; Kalkoff, *Die Depeschen des Nuntius Aleander vom Wormser Reichstage*, Halle, 1897; Neudecker and Preller, *Georg Spalatins historischer Nachlass und Briefe*, Jena, 1851.

For papal and Italian documents, see Martene and Durand, *Veterum Scriptorum et Monumentorum, Amplissima Collectio*, Paris, 1724; Molini, *Documenti di storia Italiana, 1522-1530*, Florence, 1836-1837; and Lämmer, *Monumenta Vaticana*, Freiburg, 1861. The Venetian records are largely reproduced in Sanuto's *Diarii*, Brown's *Calendar*, and Alberi, *Le relazione degli ambasciatori Veneti al Senato*, Florence, 1839 et seq.

An important French source is Vaissière, *Journal de Jean Barillon, secrétaire du chancellier Duprat, 1515-1521*, Paris, 1897. From the Netherlands we have Gachard, *Correspondance de Charles-Quint et d'Adrien VI*, Brussels, 1859. Robert, *Philibert de Chalon, Prince d'Orange, vice-roi de Naples*, Paris, 1902, contains interesting correspondence of the period.

The most important documents relating to England may be found in Brewer, *Letters and Papers*, and in the *Calendars* of Bergenroth and Gayangos.

Droysen, *Zeitgenossische Berichte über die Eroberung von Rom 1527*, Halle, 1881; and Orano, *Il sacco di Roma del 1527*, Rome, 1901, contain documents relating to the sack of Rome.

THE ASCENDENCY OF THE HOUSE OF HAPSBURG 403

The time-honored book, Robertson, *The History of the Reign of the Emperor Charles V*, London, 1769, — long admired for its comprehensive introduction, — even in the edition of Prescott, which contains an additional chapter, is now superseded by more modern works. Among these are De Leva, *Storia documentata di Carlo V in correlazione all' Italia*, Venice, 1862 et seq.; Baumgarten, *Geschichte Karls V*, Stuttgart, 1885 et seq.; and Armstrong, *The Emperor Charles V*, London, 1902, based on a wide use of documents and furnished with an excellent bibliography. Foronda, *Estancias y viajes de Carlos V*, Madrid, 1895, shows where Charles V was on every day of his life.

Mignet, *Rivalité de François Ier et de Charles-Quint*, Paris, 1875, is an elaborate study from original documents of the rivalry of Francis I and Charles V.

Turner, *The History of the Reign of Henry VIII*, London, 1826, is based on documents, some of which are reproduced by the author, but is now superseded by the more thorough investigations of Brewer, *The Reign of Henry VIII*, London, 1884; and Pollard, *Henry VIII*, new edition, London, 1902.

The relations of Maximilian I with Lewis II of Hungary are considered by Ulmann — already cited — and by Neuhaufer, *Kaiser Maximilians I Beziehungen zu Ungarn*, Vienna, 1865; and Liske, *Der Congress zu Wien im Jahre 1515*, in Forschungen zur deutschen Geschichte, Bd. VII, 1867.

The election of 1519 is specially treated by Rösler, *Die Kaiserwahl Karls V*, Vienna, 1868, but more fully and upon the basis of new documents by Weicker, *Die Stellung der Kurfürsten zur Wahl Karls V im Jahre 1519*, — which is a detailed digest of the "*Deutsche Reichstagsakten*" collected by Kluckhohn and other documents, — Berlin, 1900. The policy of Pope Leo X in relation to this election is specially discussed by Baumgarten, *Die Politik Leos X in Wahlkampf der Jahre 1518–1519* in the Forschungen zur deutsche Geschichte, Bd. XXIII, 1883, pp. 523, 570; and new light has been thrown upon the subject by Nitti, *Leone X e la sua politica*, Florence, 1892. Ehrenberg, *Das Zeitalter der Fugger*, Jena, 1896, has treated of the financial aspect of the election.

Two excellent summaries of Wolsey's diplomacy are given by Busch, *Drei Jahre englischer Vermittlungspolitik, 1518–1521*, Bonn, 1884; and *Cardinal Wolsey und die englisch-Kaiserliche Allianz, 1522–1525*, Bonn, 1886.

The position and influence of Luther are studied in Denifle, *Luther und Luthertum in der ersten Entwicklung quellenmässig dargestellt*, Bd. I, Mainz, 1904; Ranke, *Deutsche Geschichte im Zeitalter der Reformation*, Berlin, 1839–1847; and Bezold, *Geschichte der deutschen Reformation*, Berlin, 1890.

The captivity of Francis I and his deliverance are specially considered in the light of documents by Champollion-Figeac, *Captivité du roi François Ier*, Paris, 1847 ; and Gachard, *La captivité de François Ier et le traité de Madrid*, Brussels, 1860. The diplomacy of Louise of Savoy in this connection is fully examined from original documents by Jacqueton, *La politique extérieure de Louise de Savoie, relations diplomatiques de la France et de l'Angleterre pendant la captivité de François Ier*, Paris, 1892.

The political relations of Pope Clement VII are discussed by Grethen, *Die politische Beziehungen Clements VII zu Karl V*, Hanover, 1887 ; and Hellwig, *Die politische Beziehungen Clements VII zu Karl V im Jahre 1526*, Leipzig, 1889.

CHAPTER VI

THE INTERNATIONAL INFLUENCE OF THE REFORMATION

IN their effect upon Europe the sack of Rome and the capture of the Pope were the most impressive events of the sixteenth century, for they touched most deeply the interests and sentiments of the time. While the humanists lamented the wholesale destruction of precious books and manuscripts, which the ruthless soldiery wantonly used for fuel and to litter the beds of their horses, the disciples of Luther rejoiced in the humiliation of Clement VII, for whom many of them wished a fate more terrible than imprisonment. *Effects of the sack of Rome upon Europe*

The irreligion of the time was given shocking exhibition by the irreverence of Germans, Italians, and Spaniards alike in their treatment of the clergy and the sanctuaries. Before the Castle of St. Angelo, where the Pope and cardinals could behold their sacrilege, drunken soldiers clothed an ass with sacerdotal robes and compelled a priest to administer the sacrament to the animal upon its knees. "Babylon is fallen!" was the cry with which the enemies of the Papacy greeted the story of these insults to the Pope.

Even faithful Catholics regarded the misfortunes of Rome as a judgment of God for the sins of the Church. In England and France, while Clement VII received little personal sympathy, a great fear was felt lest the Emperor might use his advantage to depose the Pope or reduce him to impotence in his hands. Among the English people there was a strong anti-papal feeling; and Henry VIII, whose loyalty to the Papacy as an institution had won for him the title "Defender of the Faith," observed to Wolsey that the war between the Pope and the Emperor had no relation to matters of faith or religion, but was waged only for the sake of temporal possessions. It was chiefly because it was expedient to oppose the Emperor, and because Henry VIII needed the favor of the Pope, that England was disposed in any manner to come to the rescue of Clement VII. In France, a similar sentiment existed; but Charles V still held in captivity the French princes, and a union against him was, therefore, necessary.

When the Emperor, toward the end of June, received in Spain information of what had occurred at Rome, he was in the midst of festivities for the birth of his son Philip; nor did he, as many historians have declared, at once suspend them. Continued on the ground that they had been prepared at great expense, he not only personally participated in them, but they were not terminated until after the Archbishop of Toledo had remonstrated against them. Thus rebuked by public opinion, the Court went into mourning. Charles V hastened in a circular letter to the sovereigns to disavow all complicity in the sack of Rome and the capture of the Holy Father, for whose safety public prayers were then offered; but no step was taken to procure his deliverance.

The situation thus presented to Charles V was the most important crisis of his reign; for it offered him an opportunity to confine the Papacy to its spiritual functions, reform the Church by an ecumenical council, and restore the Empire by making Rome once more its capital and Italy the seat of its authority.

I. THE STRUGGLE OF CHARLES V FOR RELIGIOUS UNITY

The Emperor's valuation of religious unity

"Your Majesty is on the straight road to universal dominion," was the joyful cry of Gattinara upon learning of the course of events at Rome; but the Chancellor had not then estimated all the elements with which the Emperor had to deal.

The first practical consideration for Charles V was the

attitude of Spain. Rendered intensely papal and orthodox by the power of the Holy Inquisition, it was not to be expected that a country so profoundly under ecclesiastical influence would support an arbitrary deposition of the Pope. Both the Spanish and the Italian subjects of Charles V recognized the moral decadence of the Papacy, whose worldly policy had promoted strife among the nations and schism in the Church; yet the temporal power upon which the independence of the Pope was believed to rest could not be destroyed without the danger of still wider aberrations. If, under the control of Spain, Rome were made another Avignon, France, England, Germany, and other countries might establish national churches, and thus destroy forever the bond that had so long united Western Christendom. Without the Papacy, how could England, France, and Germany be held together as parts of the same system? Nay, confining himself to his own dominions, and leaving out of account the idea of a really universal monarchy in Europe, how could Charles V without that bond unite under his imperial rule Germany, Italy, and Spain?

While Catholicism was the sincere faith of the great mass of the Latin races, who would resent, and were already resenting, an outrage upon the Holy Father, Germany was permeated with Lutheranism. In that movement Charles V saw the greatest danger to his plans. Where he wished to impose uniformity it was already creating divisions. From tradition and authority Luther was appealing to the Bible and the individual judgment. The mystics had taken a still more dangerous step, and were resting their faith upon secret divine illumination. What divergences of belief might not result from the repudiation of Catholic doctrines? And how could the idea of imperial authority survive the destruction of the conceptions of divine ordinance and religious obligation upon which it had always rested? To the mind of Charles V — wholly lacking in constructive imagination, yet perfectly logical in the combination of abstract propositions — the unity of his empire seemed to rest upon the unity of religion; and to maintain it now became the great struggle of his remaining years.

Under the provocation of the perfidy of Clement VII, Charles V had said in 1525, "Either to-day or to-morrow Luther may be a man of worth"; but since that time the Emperor had learned many lessons. The Peasants' War of 1525 in Germany had been one of these. Partly economic and precipitated by physical distress, that movement had been tinged with religion also. Opposed to culture as well as to authority, it had deified the common man as the only true depositary of goodness and morality, in whom alone the Holy Spirit spoke. A theocracy of communists had threatened all established authority with extinction. Ignorant, as he was, of the actual conditions in Germany, the entire revolt had at first seemed to Charles V a mere expression of Lutheranism; although Luther himself had really disavowed and opposed it.

But the changed attitude of Luther, whose immense influence had sustained the cause of the princes as the only refuge of public order and security, soon taught the Emperor a still more important lesson. The reformer had seen in the social commotions of the Peasants' War the fruits of unrestrained individualism; and to prevent a total destruction of public authority, he was now invoking for his new doctrines the protection and support of the princes.

What was at first only a religious movement had, therefore, become for the Emperor a political danger of the greatest practical importance; for the local secular powers were perceiving their opportunity to profit by the destruction of the Roman system and the appropriation of its spoils. Enriched by the confiscation of the ecclesiastical estates, each Protestant prince, gathering into his own hands all the power that had been previously exercised by the Catholic prelates, might hope to become absolutely independent of outside authority.

In August, 1526, at the time of the Diet of Speyer, Charles V had probably not yet fully realized the danger that menaced him. Absorbed in his Italian campaign, and irritated by the attitude of the Pope, he would not have been able at that time, however earnestly disposed, to settle the Lutheran question. Accordingly, in the recess[1] of that diet, it was decided that the Edict of Worms should be suspended; that a general council should be summoned; and that, in the meantime, each religious party should so live, rule, and conduct itself that it should be prepared to answer to God and His Imperial Majesty. Thus, everything had been left in abeyance to await a future settlement.[2]

When, in May, 1527, Clement VII had fallen into the hands of the Emperor, events had revealed to Charles V the full significance of the Lutheran movement. On August 29, 1526, Lewis II, King of Bohemia and Hungary, had been slain by the Turks in the battle of Mohacs, together with the flower of his nobility and more than twenty thousand men. The event had presented the long expected occasion for the realization of the Archduke Ferdinand's claims through his marriage with Anna to the crowns of both kingdoms; but the decisive victory of the Turks, the ambition of John Zapolya, the Hungarian Woiwode or general, for the throne of Hungary, and the perturbed state of Germany with reference to the religious question invested the situation with peculiar difficulties.

Two conflicting interests now divided the Hapsburg policies; for Ferdinand was too closely engaged with the succession of the thrones of Bohemia and Hungary to be of aid to the Emperor, and Charles V was himself too much preoccupied with his Italian problems and his troubles with France and England to offer assistance to his brother. This embarrassment was made painfully evident when, having been elected King of Bohemia in October, 1526, Ferdinand sent

---

[1] The word "recess," — German *Rezess*, or *Abschied*, — as here applied, is equivalent to the expression "final act," or summary of conclusions reached by a diet.

[2] The transactions of this diet are fully given by Friedensburg, *Der Reichstag zu Speier, 1526*, Berlin, 1887.

an embassy to England to beseech aid from Henry VIII in sustaining his claims to Hungary against Zapolya.[1]

While Ferdinand was urging Charles V to make peace with France, even at the price of Burgundy, in order to come to his aid against Zapolya, the Emperor was exhorting the Archduke against exposing himself to new dangers through the alliance of Zapolya with the Infidel. Secretly rejoicing at the unhappy plight of the Hapsburgs, which Ferdinand's embassy only the more plainly revealed, Henry VIII listened with admiration to the eloquence of Ferdinand's orator, who described the woes of Christendom since the rise of Islam and exhorted the "Defender of the Faith" to come to his master's aid, but the appeal was answered with the excuse that it was not prudent for the King of England to offer aid to the Hapsburg cause in Hungary which would only add force to Charles V in Italy.

Had Henry VIII known that Ferdinand had sent an embassy to obtain for himself the Sultan's recognition, he could not have acted more discreetly. By the influence of Luigi Gritti, the natural son of a former Venetian ambassador to Constantinople, Zapolya's ambassador, Jerome Laszko, by the liberal use of money had won for his master not only the recognition of the Sublime Porte, but after difficult negotiations an offensive alliance against Ferdinand of Austria. By the same influence Ferdinand's overtures had ended in failure; and, after a period of imprisonment, his embassy had returned to inform him that an Ottoman army was preparing to march against him in Hungary.

In the meantime, Francis I had been in active negotiations both with Zapolya and with the Sultan. With the former he made an alliance in which it was provided that, in case Zapolya should die without a male heir, the second son of Francis I, Henry of Orléans, should succeed to the throne of Hungary. From the Sultan he obtained a renewal of com-

---

[1] See the account of this embassy in Kraus, *Englische Diplomatie im Jahre 1527*.

INTERNATIONAL INFLUENCE OF THE REFORMATION

mercial privileges in Egypt and the recognition of France as the protector of Christians in the Orient. By his relations with Zapolya and the Sultan, Francis I was preparing to curb the power of the Hapsburgs in the East.

While Henry VIII was indisposed to aid the Hapsburgs, and Francis I was actually plotting against them with Zapolya and the Sultan, Charles V was eager for both religious and political reasons to attack the Infidel. So anxious was he for this enterprise that a few months before the capture of Clement VII he was ready to abandon his claims to the Duchy of Burgundy and release the French princes for a payment of two million crowns, in the hope of being able to unite Europe in a holy war. The progress made by Ferdinand against Zapolya with the forces placed at his command by Bohemia and the capture of the Pope had, however, changed the situation; and in the autumn of 1527 the Emperor was resolved to press his good fortune in Italy, prepare to take up the suppression of heresy in Germany, and afterward throw the whole force of his empire into a campaign against the Turks.

To execute this threefold programme required the utmost concentration of all the forces at the Emperor's command. The first step forward was to settle his policy toward the Pope. To depose him without a general council would arouse against himself the hostility of the whole Catholic world. To secure a general council he must have the sanction of Clement VII himself and the consent of France and England. Even in his humiliation and imprisonment, the Pope was a factor indispensable to the imperial programme.

To these political considerations were joined others of great influence. As a sincere Catholic, Charles V could not conceive of religious unity without the Pope, and without religious unity he could not conceive of an empire. His religious zeal and horror of heresy not only found an echo but a powerful support in his Spanish environment. Practically every voice among his counsellors exhorted him to imitate his ancestors, to be a Catholic king in very truth, and to carry forward to a glorious victory all the sacred traditions of the orthodox faith. In earlier years his confessor had been the French Franciscan, Jean Glapion, whose influence had been exerted for large concessions in the pacification of the Church; but since 1523 the Spanish Dominican, Garcia de Loaysa, had been the director of the Emperor's conscience. It was he who now stood closest to his inner life at this most solemn moment of his career, and was to dictate the preamble of the testament in which Charles V exposed his political intentions.[1]

When, in August, 1527, Don Pedro de Veyre was sent to Italy to report upon the situation there, the Emperor's mood was to confine the captured pope to his spiritual functions, and to leave but little substance to his temporal power; but soon afterward Quinones[2] was instructed to release the Holy Father and restore his strongholds, upon condition that he supply a sum of money for meeting the demands of the imperial troops, deliver as security four fortified places, and pledge himself to neutrality between Charles V and his enemies. It was with great difficulty that the necessary funds were found in Rome, so completely had it been plundered and despoiled; and even the papal tiara is said to have been melted down and coined into money. By the treaty of November 26, nearly all the papal territory was remitted to the authority of Clement VII, certain cardinals and members of the Medici family being held as hostages for the execution of the Pope's engagements. On December 8, with the connivance of the imperial officers, Clement VII was allowed to escape from imprisonment in the Castle of St. Angelo and take refuge at Orvieto. The Emperor's experience with Francis I had taught him the futility of extorting promises, and he had perceived the danger of exciting the antagonism

---

[1] See Gossart, *Charles-Quint et Philippe II*, p. 17.

[2] The General of the Franciscan Order, who, under the name of Alvaro Perez, had been secretly sent to Charles V by Clement VII. See Hellwig, *Die politische Beziehungen*, pp. 56, 57.

of Christendom by imprisoning the Pope at a moment when the French and English were combining their forces against himself.

Apparently at liberty, yet really at the mercy of Charles V, Clement VII watched with eager interest the advance of Lautrec's French army on its march to Naples. For a time it appeared as if the Anglo-French alliance would result in establishing the French in Italy, and the Pope was preparing to renew his adherence to the league.

In England, hope was entertained that a favorable decision might be obtained from Clement VII in the matter of the King's divorce. In July, 1527, Wolsey had made an ostentatious journey to France, partly to stimulate efforts for the Pope's liberation if he were tractable, partly to threaten him with repudiation by England and France if he were not, and partly to secure his own future, in case the divorce proved successful, by arranging the King's marriage with a French princess.

The menace of Wolsey to create a schism and place himself in the position of an antipope sustained by a council to be called in France had, no doubt, affected the conduct of the Emperor toward the Pope. To meet the tactics of the Cardinal, Charles V had restored Clement VII to apparent liberty, thus removing the claim that he was the victim of coercion, at the same time intimidating Wolsey with a demand for the revocation of his legatine powers if he persisted in his course.

While Wolsey was playing his rôle in France, Henry VIII had taken advantage of his absence to remove all obstacles to his marriage with Anne Boleyn in spite of the Cardinal's craft in opposing it. His secretary, Dr. William Knight, had been despatched to the Pope to urge either (1) a dispensation for the King to marry a second wife without a divorce from Catherine, thus legitimating the issue of both marriages, — a proposition to which the Pope came near assenting;[1] or

---

[1] See Brewer, *Letters and Papers*, Nos. 6627 and 6705.

414   A HISTORY OF DIPLOMACY

Chap. VI
A. D.
1527-1559

(2) to declare the marriage with Catherine null and void.[1] As a result, Knight procured a secret dispensation for the King's marriage with Anne Boleyn; but it was not to become effective until the nullity of his union with Catherine of Aragon was decided.

The diplomatic duel over the divorce

While the Emperor was striving to disarm his enemies by the fiction of the Pope's freedom, Clement VII was negotiating to render his liberation complete and preparing to take sides with whosoever might ultimately prove to be uppermost in Italy. To this end, his policy was to temporize with all until the operations before Naples had decided who should be the victor.

Wolsey, who soon became aware of the King's negotiations, well understood that the secret dispensation granted by the Pope had no significance until the question of the legality of Catherine's marriage had been decided; and the King's personal diplomacy, therefore, proved a failure. Accordingly, Knight was sent back by Wolsey to ask of the Pope that the Cardinal himself, or some other proper person, be authorized to pronounce upon the validity of the marriage. If the Pope refused, pleaded Wolsey, the papal cause in England would be ruined forever; for the King would be driven to adopt measures injurious to the Papacy and ruinous to its legate. The Lutherans, it was intimated, were inciting the King to repudiate the papal authority in the question of the divorce, and to appropriate the temporal possessions of the Church.

To oppose the pressure of Wolsey, the representatives of Charles V protested to the Pope against the violation of the laws and honor of the Church, proclaiming the shamelessness of Henry's intentions, and emphasized the indignity to the Emperor implied in the action demanded.

Anxious to evade responsibility, Clement VII proposed at

---

[1] On the inconsistency of Henry VIII, who by his illicit relations with the sister of Anne Boleyn stood in the same relation to her that Catherine of Aragon did to him through her marriage with his brother Arthur, except that Henry's acts were illicit while hers were legal, see Pollard, *Henry VIII*, p. 208.

one time that Henry VIII should settle the question for himself by simply marrying another wife; at another, that Catherine should relieve the Head of the Church of so great an embarrassment by voluntarily retiring to a nunnery.[1]

At last, however, emboldened by the failure of the Emperor to check the advance of Lautrec, on June 8, 1528, a commission was issued to Wolsey and Campeggio to decide the case without appeal. But, while Campeggio was still on his way to England, Andrea Doria, the famous Genovese admiral, deserted Francis I and went over to the imperial cause; and, on August 15, Lautrec died before Naples, and the French army, weakened by disease and badly commanded, was defeated. By a sudden turn of fortune the Pope was once more at the mercy of the Emperor, and before Campeggio's arrival in England the whole character of the legate's mission had been changed. Instead of being in reality a judge, authorized with Wolsey to pronounce sentence in the matter of the divorce, he was thenceforth to play the part of a mere conciliator, endeavoring to persuade either the King or Catherine to yield, while announcing that the case would ultimately be referred to Rome.

The imperial victories thus soon put an end to the hope of securing a divorce sanctioned by the Holy See; for, on June 29, 1529, the Pope made his peace with the Emperor by the Treaty of Barcelona,[2] by which all the papal territories were restored to Clement VII, and the Medici reestablished at Florence, over which the Pope's nephew Alessandro, united in marriage to the Emperor's natural daughter Margaret, was placed as duke. No further mention was made at that time of a general council; the Emperor pledged himself to root out heresy; and, with the aid of a fourth of the ecclesiastical revenues in their dominions, he and his brother Ferdinand were to organize Christendom for a war upon the Infidel. Thus fortified, Clement VII, on

---

[1] See Brewer, *Letters and Papers*, Nos. 3802 and 6290.
[2] Dumont, IV, Part II, pp. 1, 7.

CHAP. VI
A. D.
1527-1559

July 16, transferred the divorce of Henry VIII to Rome. It was for England and the Papacy the parting of the ways. Henry resolved to repudiate the authority of the Pope, and Wolsey was thereby doomed to fall.[1]

Nature of the English separation

The separation of England from the ecclesiastical jurisdiction of Rome was not, as is often represented, due solely to the personal passion of the King. It was an act of political independence for which the nation had been long preparing, and for which the question of the divorce merely furnished the occasion. Since Wiclif's time a strong current of revolt against Rome had never ceased to be felt in England. The attitude of Luther had found numerous champions there, and the popular hatred of Wolsey had swollen the stream of hostility to the papal power. Without the King's support, the antipapal sentiment could, perhaps, not have found effective expression; but with it nothing was easier than the abandonment of Rome. Relying upon the people and the parliament, the King had no need to use arbitrary means to secure support. To many who could not morally approve of his treatment of Catherine the separation from Rome seemed justified as a measure of political expediency, and especially as an act of defiance to a system that was felt to be a fetter to the freedom of the nation. The apostasy was not to a great extent doctrinal, for neither Henry VIII nor his chief supporters were heretics as regards the substance of the ancient faith. Nor was the defection of England from the Papacy produced by the definite refusal of Clement VII to grant a dispensation for the separation of Henry VIII from Catherine of Aragon. It was caused rather by the determination of the English nation to leave the decision of the King's affairs to the judgment of Englishmen rather than to the verdict of a foreign prince in political alliance with the King's enemies.[2] Aside from the moral and canonical

---

[1] For further details of the divorce and of Wolsey's fall, see Pollard, as above.

[2] Campeggio was under orders from Rome that, if the legatine court reached a point where it was necessary to pronounce sentence, it

aspects of the case was the question of the papal jurisdiction. Clement VII was a temporal potentate, and he was in close alliance with Henry's enemy, the Emperor. If the action of Clement was governed by his political interests, why should not that of the King of England be guided by his political interests also? If a temporal sovereign could be the Head of the Universal Church, why might not Henry VIII be the Head of a national church? The time had come for the long threatened establishment of national churches to be carried into execution. England led the way, but others were soon to follow. It was the inevitable outcome of the modern national movement and the decay of universal rule.

Fortunately for the plans of Charles V in Italy, he quite unexpectedly found himself relieved from the opposition of the League of Cognac and the Anglo-French alliance. After the defeat of Lautrec's army and the family compact between Clement VII and the Emperor, the French had little prospect of success in Italy. The Emperor, on the other hand, having won over the Pope and obtained the ascendency at Naples, saw little advantage in carrying on a war with Francis I for the possession of the Duchy of Burgundy at a time when he wished to apply all his energies to the problems of Germany and the East. Accordingly, Louise of Savoy and Margaret of Burgundy, meeting at Cambray, in July, 1529, after previous secret negotiations, were able to arrange a series of interviews at which peace was finally concluded.

To avoid the comments of the curious, a subterranean gallery was prepared under the street which separated the Abbey of Saint Aubert, where Madame Louise was lodged, and the Hotel Saint Pol, occupied by Margaret of Burgundy. By this means the negotiations were personally conducted by the two ladies in perfect secrecy, with the result that the terms of the peace were entirely settled by them. Hand in

---

should be given against Henry VIII. See Brewer, *Letters and Papers*, Nos. 5732, 5734.

hand, the fair negotiators attended mass together, and afterward affectionately discussed the interests of Charles and Francis. The negotiations were not without their stormy moments, however, in which a rupture was threatened. When at last a reconciliation was effected, the peace was solemnly celebrated with religious ceremonies, followed by sumptuous banquets and general rejoicing. The conference terminated with a personal visit of Francis I, who promptly confirmed the transaction.

In the Peace of Cambray,[1] — or "Ladies' Peace," as it has been called, — dated August 5, 1529, Francis I abandoned all his allies and all his claims in Italy, accepted marriage with Eleanora, and agreed to pay a ransom of two million crowns for the release of his children. It was, in effect, a renewal of the Treaty of Madrid, except that the cession of the Duchy of Burgundy was no longer insisted upon by Charles V. To give the treaty special solemnity, it was provided that it should be registered and ratified by all the parliaments and chambers of account of the Kingdom of France and by those of Malines and Lille for the Netherlands.

After the arrival in Spain of a French agent to effect the deliverance of the French princes, eight months elapsed before they were finally released from their tedious confinement in the Castle of Pedrasse. One reason of this delay was the scheme, attributed to Duprat, to defraud the Emperor of forty thousand crowns by debasing the value of the coins with which the ransom was to be paid. The trick was discovered, and compensation was offered but, in the meantime, the princes were obliged to prolong an imprisonment whose severity had been sorely felt.

Unstable and mutually distrustful as the relations of Francis I and the Emperor were destined always to be, the diplomacy of Louise of Savoy was more permanently successful in prolonging the peace which she had so skilfully promoted between France and England. The English am-

---

[1] See Dumont, IV, Part II, pp. 7, 17.

bassadors had been excluded from the negotiations at Cambray, for the reason that England was not favorable to the reconciliation of Francis I with the Emperor; but care was promptly taken in effecting the peace with Charles V not to destroy the Anglo-French *entente*, which was newly confirmed by treaty, and continued to be maintained for the next fourteen years.

For Charles V the Peace of Cambray secured the great advantage of leaving his hands free for executing his plans in Italy and Germany; while France, for the moment, assumed the place which England had formerly occupied as conservator of the peace of Europe. Without serious opposition in Italy, therefore, allied by family ties to both the Pope and the King of France, who had promised to aid him in rooting out heresy and organizing an attack upon the Turks, and with England practically excluded from European influence, the Emperor seemed to occupy a position of power greater than any monarch of Europe had attained for many centuries.

Coronation by the Pope, which Maximilian had vainly sought during the long period of his struggles and negotiations, was now rendered possible for Charles V; but not in the manner nor upon the terms of a complete master of the situation. Prisoner and refugee as Clement VII had been, he was still able to impose conditions upon the Emperor. Eager to gather the fruits of his good fortune in the field and in the cabinet, on August 12, 1529, Charles V landed at Genoa with a resplendent retinue of Spaniards to celebrate the victories of his generals and diplomatists by receiving as Charles the Great had done the diadem of the Caesars from the Highpriest of Christendom.

With all the prestige and prerogatives of a German emperor, in undisputed possession of that Kingdom of Naples which had rendered Frederick II so powerful in Italy, in secure control of his once rebellious Spanish realm which he was about to flatter with the dream of world dominion, with France bound to him in a family alliance, and the Pope at

CHAP. VI
A. D.
1527-1559

last made subservient to his plans, this young monarch of less than thirty years seemed in a position to restore in full the old imperial power. Never before had the Latin and the Germanic peoples been so completely in the hand of a single ruler.

No mediaeval emperor had ever been a complete master in Italy. Charles the Great had not chosen to impose a despotic rule but had left the feudal and municipal powers a large measure of freedom. His successors, the German emperors, and especially the Hohenstaufen, had endeavored to unify the peninsula under their authority, but in vain. With this triumphal advent of Charles V, however, Italy, prostrate and defenceless, not only felt the approach of a new foreign domination, but of a new force and a new system; for the spirit of modern monarchy, armed with the powers of concentration developed in the service of the national states, gave to imperialism an absolute quality which the feudal empire had never possessed.

The progress of Charles V in Italy

Brought to the shore of Genoa by a galley bedecked with damask sails and silken cordage, and rowed by two hundred liberated slaves, because Andrea Doria thought it was not meet for so great a sovereign to be served by bondsmen; the Emperor, upon his arrival at the great mole erected for his landing, where he was welcomed by the Signory of the city, was hailed with cries of "Carlo, Carlo! Impero, Impero! God bless and preserve the King of the World!"

At Milan, Venice, and Florence — the great centres of Italian liberty — there were mutterings of discontent and forebodings of resistance; but they were silenced as the Emperor advanced. At Piacenza, the Treaty of Cambray was ratified. At Parma, he heard news of Ferdinand's victory over the Turks before Vienna. At Bologna, he met in person Clement VII, who had come thither to confer the imperial crown upon him.

It was originally intended that Charles V should land at Naples, proceed from there to Rome, and receive the crown, as Charles the Great had received it, in St. Peter's Church;

but the Pope was able to frustrate this design and fix the ceremony at Bologna.

Knowing that Ferdinand was clamoring for the Emperor's presence in Germany, and that it was there that he could be of most service to the Papacy, Clement VII was anxious to shorten the sojourn of Charles V in Italy, and as soon as possible to have him north of the Alps; where, as the Pope confidentially explained to the anti-imperialists, the Emperor would not only find enough to keep him busy, but would soon be stripped of his ready money, and thus incapacitated for further enterprises in Italy.

In only one direction was the Pope eager to have the Emperor act before his departure for Germany. When Clement VII was at war with Charles V, the Florentines had again expelled the Medici; and the Pope now demanded their restoration. For this a bitter war was necessary, since the brave republicans of Florence were resolved not to sacrifice their liberties without a desperate struggle. Bound by the Treaty of Barcelona, the Emperor was constrained to yield to the Pope's insistence, and Philibert de Chalon, Prince of Orange, was sent to compel Florence to accept the rule of the Medici.

Persuaded that it was the person of the Pope rather than the place of coronation that gave dignity and validity to that ceremony, the Emperor — having first received the iron crown of Lombardy — in the Cathedral of San Petronio, at Bologna, on February 24, 1530, accepted the crown of the Empire from the reluctant hands of Pope Clement VII.

An anachronism in every sense, the coronation of Charles V at Bologna was destined to be the last bestowment of the imperial crown by the hands of the Pope in Italy. The cope of Clement VII is said to have shaken with his emotion as he performed the act, while the Italians regarded it with fear and resentment. For the first time in history, the coronation procession was headed by artillery; while three thousand German *landsknechts*, three thousand Italian and three thousand Spanish soldiers, infantry and cavalry, followed the

Chap. VI
A. D.
1527-1559

Emperor as he marched to the sound of music into the great square of the Cathedral, guarded from approach on every side by the imperial troops.

Was it by force that the young emperor was to justify his imperial pretensions? He was not a soldier and had never in person won a battle. Was it by the prestige of the imperial idea? That had long been superseded by the national monarchies. Was it by the union of the papal and the imperial forces? The long tragedy of the Middle Ages had proved that the Papacy could never be permanently subordinated to the imperial will, and Clement VII was ready at any moment to betray the Emperor, as he had already resisted and baffled his pretensions. It was only in appearance, therefore, that, amid the pomp and splendor of that coronation scene, the dream of the Hapsburgs seemed for a moment to be already realized.

The condition and problems of Germany

Apparently on the point of successful reaffirmation in Italy, the imperial authority was exposed to extreme dangers in Germany. Since the Diet of Speyer in 1526, the impotence of the Emperor to unite the religious parties had been evident. Although not sanctioned by law, the principle *Cujus regio, ejus religio* had been accepted in actual practice. Each territorial prince had adopted the form of religion that pleased him best, and his people were subject not only to his influence but to his authority. If religious unity were ever to be restored, it was necessary that it be done at once.

Partly political, and partly an affair of conviction and conscience, the dissension of Germany in matters of religion presented a double problem.

As a political question it affected the independence of the princes, which they were able to fortify on the one side by utilizing the popular belief in the Lutheran doctrines for their own support, and on the other by appropriating to themselves the rich ecclesiastical properties of the Catholic prelates. Almost equal to kings in their respective principalities, by turning to their own account the advantages which the reform movement placed at their disposal, the greater German princes, if united in defensive leagues, were in a position to resist the will of the Emperor and to clothe themselves with a practically sovereign authority.

It would, however, be grossly unjust to infer that the real cause of the success of the Lutheran doctrines was the ambition of the princes. Promoted as it was in many cases by secular motives, the reform movement was a logical and necessary outcome of the constitution of the Germanic mind and nature in the presence of religious abuses which could no longer be tolerated.

The German discontent with the corruption of the clergy and the conduct of the Holy See dates from the Councils of Constance and Basel. A letter written to Aeneas Sylvius, afterward Pope Pius II, by Martin Mayer, on August 31, 1457, formulates all the essential *gravamina* of this movement. Nine complaints are enumerated, which may be briefly stated as follows: (1) The Pope neither regards the decrees of the Councils of Constance and Basel nor believes himself bound by the engagements of his predecessors, and appears disposed to annihilate and wholly exhaust our nation; (2) the elections of the prelates are here and there rejected; (3) benefices and dignities of each kind are reserved for cardinals and protonotaries; (4) predispensations are bestowed in great numbers; (5) annates and *medii fructus* are demanded without any postponement, and more than is due is demanded; (6) the guidance of the Church is not intrusted to the most deserving but to the most self-seeking; (7) in order to amass money, new indulgences are daily granted; (8) the tithe for the war against the Turks is enforced without consulting our prelates; (9) matters which should be considered and settled in our own region are, without distinction, required to be taken before the Apostolic Tribunal.[1]

To emphasize this list of grievances, it was summed up in the general indictment: — " A thousand artifices are devised whereby the Roman See may be able in a skilful way to

---

[1] See Gebhardt, *Die Gravamina*, pp. 27, 28.

empty our purses, as if we were mere barbarians. Our nation, once so renowned, which with its valor and its blood acquired the Roman Empire, and was the mistress and ruler of the world, is now plunged in poverty, become tributary and a slave, and these many years lies mourning in the dust its unhappy fate."

In the time that had elapsed since that arraignment of the Papacy, the catalogue of evils had increased in length, and the efforts of the popes to establish themselves as Italian princes at the expense of Christendom had intensified the hostility of Germany. The doctrines of Luther had, therefore, fallen upon willing ears; for they not only appealed to the individual conscience, the national pride, and the interests of the princes, they were the expression of all these slowly gathered into a deep and irresistible current.

The development of Lutheranism

When, therefore, in 1530, Charles V turned his face toward Germany, resolved to end its religious and political dissensions and to bring it into subservience to himself by rendering it obedient to the Holy See, he still underestimated the task that was before him. The necessity of reform in the Church was evident to all, except Clement VII and those who shared his conception of his position and his interests, and even the Emperor himself felt the need of a general council, which the Pope was skilfully obstructing; but the schism had already reached a point where reconciliation had become impossible.

With the progress of events, Luther himself had passed through a significant stage of evolution. The peasant revolt had created in him an aversion to democracy in the Church. In matters of faith, he thought, the people must have an authoritative head. In the cities, Zwingli's idea of congregational self-government had made progress. At Zürich, where the Swiss reformer had the seat of his propaganda, both State and Church drew their authority from their constituent members; and the example threatened to prove infectious for Germany as well. The bold apostle of democracy was, however, soon to fall in battle, and to furnish his rival re-

INTERNATIONAL INFLUENCE OF THE REFORMATION 425

former with a new argument against the danger of doctrines so radically revolutionary.

As early as November 22, 1526, Luther had written to John, Elector of Saxony, earnestly urging upon him to end all confusion in his principality by assuming over ecclesiastical affairs the same control that he exercised over "roads and bridges."[1] It was an emphatic appeal to realize the principle, *Cujus regio, ejus religio*. Doctrines and persons, as well as ecclesiastical property, were alleged to be within the proper jurisdiction of the ruling prince. The religion of the prince was the proper religion for his people, not by their choice but by his authority.

In July, 1527, the Elector had begun to apply this system. In place of one universal head the local prince was to rule in matters relating to cult, doctrine, and administration. Deprived of the guidance and protection of a universal superior, and sundered from the larger community of Christendom, the Christian believer was to be placed entirely under the authority of his immediate civil ruler. Instead of a separation of Church and State, both were to be united in the same hands; and that combination of powers against which the individual man had struggled for centuries was thus consummated in the person of a local prince, who was to assume the prerogatives of both pope and emperor.[2]

The diet held at Speyer in 1526 had adopted a policy of patience; but in that of 1529 the Emperor had annulled, of his "imperial and absolute authority," the agreement of 1526, under which the Lutheran churches had made progress. To prevent a further breach at a critical moment, Ferdinand had endeavored to soften the Emperor's action. The majority of the diet was content to prolong the existing situation, and only demanded tolerance for Catholics in the Lutheran countries until the decision of a general council. It was a "pro-

---

[1] See De Wette, *Luthers Briefe*, III, pp. 135, 137; and comments by Pastor, *Die kirchlichen Reunionsbestrebungen*, p. 4.

[2] Pastor, as above, applies to this union of political and ecclesiastical authority the expression "*Caesaro-papismus*."

test" against the revocation of rights already acquired that officially completed the rupture and, on April 25, 1529, gave to the party of dissent its name of "Protestants." Unwilling to accept mere temporary indulgence, and claiming the permanent right of existence by the recess of 1526, John of Saxony, the Landgrave Philip of Hesse, the Margrave George of Brandenburg, Dukes Ernest and Franz of Brunswick-Lüneburg, Prince Wolfgang of Anhalt, and the representatives of fourteen imperial cities signed this famous protest, and thus confirmed their determination to pursue their way and claim the rights accorded to them by the previous Diet of Speyer.[1]

The policy of the Emperor at Augsburg

Although soon after his arrival in Germany Charles V became aware of the difficulties in his path, he never wavered for an instant in his determination to crush out heresy, unite the Church, and attack the Infidel. Personally inclined toward a general council as the only solution of the religious problem, he nevertheless suffered himself to be influenced by Cardinal Campeggio, who accompanied him as papal legate, to make a trial of other measures.

The programme of Campeggio was, to hold steadily in mind the doctrinal unity of the Church as the ultimate goal, to win over the weaker adherents of the Lutheran movement by persuasion, and when all that could be accomplished by gentle and conciliatory measures had been effected, to drive the recalcitrant into the fold by "fire and sword."[2]

For many reasons the Emperor was opposed to the unnecessary use of force. Never really cruel by nature, experience had taught him the value of patience and moderation. Wishing to raise his brother Ferdinand to the dignity of "King of the Romans," in order that the Hapsburg authority might be permanently increased in Germany, which his position as a

---

[1] The argument of the Lutherans was, that the ordinance of 1526, having been unanimously enacted, could not be otherwise than unanimously abolished. It was not, however, for the individual, but for the "territorial" conscience that the plea was made.

[2] See Maurenbrecher, *Karl V*, p. 23.

crowned emperor now rendered possible, he was much more disposed to conciliate than to offend. In this policy he had the earnest support of Gattinara, an Erasmian in religious conviction, whose dominant idea was the consolidation of the Empire rather than the restoration of the Church.

At the Diet of Augsburg, which opened on June 20, 1530, the Emperor fully realized the delicacy of his situation. The disinclination of the Catholic princes to attack the Protestants in open war was evident, for a victory over the heretics would ultimately place themselves at the Emperor's mercy and destroy their political independence. Fearing that he would by an attempt at compulsion only expose his own weakness and render impossible the election of Ferdinand, the Emperor resolved, if possible, to win over the Protestants. For this purpose they were invited to present their case. Their answer was the famous confession of faith called the "Augsburg Confession," presented to the Emperor on June 25, as the standard from which their consciences would not suffer them to depart.

On September 23, the negotiations ended in an open breach, followed by the withdrawal of some of the Protestant princes. On November 15, the Emperor issued a decree ordaining the rigorous application of the Edict of Worms, which the Diet of Speyer in 1526 had practically suspended. Although three months' grace was given, it was a declaration of war against the Protestants.

Defeated in his efforts either to persuade or to overawe the Protestants, since the Catholic princes were at that time not disposed to declare war upon them, the Emperor was obliged to content himself for the time with civil processes against the Lutheran secularization of ecclesiastical property and a new effort to convoke a general council.

In his plan to elevate Ferdinand to the dignity of "King of the Romans," however, he was more successful. With the aid of three thousand ducats and the bestowment of new privileges upon the electors, he was able to secure Ferdinand's election at Köln, on January 5, 1531; but not in legal form, and not without a protest from the Elector of Saxony, who complained that the proceeding was in violation of the Golden Bull.

Foreseeing the dangers that threatened the Protestants, Philip, Landgrave of Hesse, had long been active in promoting a union for their protection. While the election was still in progress, the chief Protestant princes and the deputies of several cities met on December 22, 1530, at Schmalkalden, to discuss the Emperor's action in forcing the candidacy of Ferdinand, to consider the formation of a league for the defence of their political and religious rights against the Emperor and the Catholic princes, and to provide the ways and means to render it effective.

Although not immediately threatened with force, since the protest at Speyer in 1529 the Protestants had deliberated upon the question whether or not, in case it were applied, they should offer armed resistance. Luther was at first disposed to advise against it, at least so far as the Emperor was concerned, citing in support of his position the words of Christ, "Render unto Caesar that which is Caesar's"; but after the negotiations at Augsburg he expressed the view that, if the Emperor acted "not only against God and divine right, but also against his own imperial right, oath, duty, seal, and letters," resistance by armed force was justified.

When, therefore, on December 25, 1530, the Protestants at Schmalkalden sent to Köln their remonstrance against the election of Ferdinand, they were prepared to meet the consequences. On the following day they resolved to protect one another by a defensive league against any one who might attack them "on account of the Word of God, evangelical doctrine, or their holy faith."[1]

The international aspects of the Protestant movement In his letters to Rome, Campeggio dwelt upon the necessity of force; but the Emperor was better able to measure his resources. In Gattinara he had possessed a prudent

---

[1] The details may be found in Winckelmann, *Der schmalkaldische Bund*.

counsellor, but the Chancellor had died while on a journey, and had been succeeded by the Burgundian Granvelle, — a man of upright character, patient and moderate in temper, and devoted to his master's interests. It was he who was now to take up the burden of the complicated relations of Charles V to the powers of Europe, and to give counsel upon the affairs of Germany from this point of view.

It is, in truth, only in the light of international relations that it is possible to comprehend the conduct of the Emperor in his efforts to unify the Church. While the election of Ferdinand promoted the interests of the Hapsburgs in Germany to a degree that excited apprehension not only there but throughout Europe, the House had suffered a heavy loss in the death of its wisest member, Margaret of Burgundy. She had been succeeded in the government of the Netherlands by Mary, the widowed Queen of Hungary, whose early inclination toward Lutheranism had filled her brother with apprehension. Another sister, Isabella, wife of Christian II, the fugitive king of Denmark, had made an open profession of Lutheranism, afterward renounced; but that kingdom, under the rule of Frederick I, together with Norway, had become openly and officially Lutheran. In Sweden, matters had taken a still more decisive course. Under the vigorous rule of Gustavus Vasa, by the Treaty of Malmö of 1524 Sweden had become independent, and the Union of Kalmar had come to an end. This energetic monarch, from purely political motives, in order to break down the influence of the Catholic prelates and to obtain possession of the clerical revenues by the confiscation of ecclesiastical property, introduced and established Lutheranism by royal command, and constituted himself the head of the Swedish Church.

With Germany divided, the Scandinavian kingdoms committed to Protestantism, and the Ottoman Power planning a double attack, — upon Hungary from the South and East, and upon Mediterranean commerce from the coasts of Northern Africa, — the exposure of the Hapsburg interests was extreme.

430   A HISTORY OF DIPLOMACY

CHAP. VI
A. D.
1527-1559

In England, the alienation of Charles V was in every way past remedy. Henry VIII had appealed to the universities of Europe for an opinion favorable to his divorce from Catherine, and had obtained it from Paris and Orléans, Bourges and Toulouse, Bologna and Ferrara, Pavia and Padua, as well as Oxford and Cambridge.[1] In June, 1530, the lords of England, spiritual as well as temporal, had signed a letter to the Pope pressing him to comply with the King's request.[2] All the efforts of Clement VII to silence the clamor for the divorce had proved ineffectual. On the other hand, Henry VIII had obtained recognition as Supreme Head of the English Church, had decided to refer the question of divorce to the Archbishop of Canterbury, as the ecclesiastical primate of his realm, and the separation from Rome was already foredoomed; for, armed with the statutes of *praemunire*, the King of England was able to bid defiance to the Pope, and to impose his own will upon his kingdom.

The embarrassment of the Emperor's plans in Germany

Although the immense and varied dominions of Charles V rendered him, as it has been expressed, "a coalition in himself," in the divided state of Christendom he could hope for no ally except his old rival Francis I and his brother-in-law the King of Portugal. Even the Pope was but half-hearted in the enterprise of religious unity in Germany; for, as the French ambassador wrote from Rome, he not only feared that the Emperor was aiming at universal monarchy [3] but stood in still greater terror of a general council, which might easily depose him, either on account of his illegitimate birth

---

[1] Brewer, *Letters and Papers*, IV, Nos. 6332, 6448, 6491, 6632, 6636. For the manner in which the decision was obtained at Paris, see a very interesting account in Bourrilly, *Guillaume du Bellay*, pp. 92, 107.

[2] Brewer, as above, IV, No. 6513.

[3] If this ambition was not entertained by Charles V, it was proclaimed by others, as when the Spanish poet and soldier, Hermando de Acuña, sang that Heaven had promised

"Un monarca, un imperio, y una espada."

or the necessity of reform, or both combined. The threatened preponderance of the Hapsburgs, if they could succeed in uniting Germany, was equally serious for France and England; and neither Francis I nor Henry VIII could be indifferent to an enterprise of such far-reaching consequence. Not only so, but the new community of religious ideas which Protestantism was creating throughout Europe both favored a union between the enemies of the House of Hapsburg and furnished a basis of international alliances to render it effectual.

To meet the emergency thus created, Ferdinand proposed, as a first step, an attack upon the evangelical party in Switzerland by uniting and leading the Catholic cantons against it, thus making the downfall of the Zwinglians — who formed the most advanced wing of the reformers, and had acquired immense influence in the cities of Southwestern Germany — a point of departure for a similar movement against the Lutherans; but the Emperor perceived the danger of exciting the resentment of the King of France, who was in alliance with the Swiss, and hesitated to offend his German subjects by bringing Italian and Spanish troops north of the Alps. In truth, the Protestant Reformation had become an international question in which all Europe was soon to take a part.

The European importance of the movement was perceived by Charles V and the Protestants at the same time, and their discovery resulted in simultaneous action.

On her deathbed, Margaret of Burgundy had counselled a closer union between Charles V and Francis I, and even, if possible, a reconciliation of her nephew with England. Needing the aid of Francis I in his ecclesiastical projects, in pursuance of her last advice, the Emperor, on February 1, 1531, sent De Praet from Brussels to France with instructions to seek a closer alliance with Francis I, on the basis of a universal council for the reform of the Church, support of a war against the Sultan, the protection of Ferdinand's interests in the East, and the defence of Queen Catherine against the divorce proceedings of Henry VIII.[1] To secure the aid of Clement VII and his consent to the council, the two sovereigns should guarantee the security of the Pope and his family from any loss of authority or possessions. Finally, Francis I was urged to sever the connection of France with the evangelical party in Switzerland.

In the meantime, the Protestants at Schmalkalden had resolved to address the foreign powers, also urging them to aid in securing a council in the evangelical sense, and a special appeal was sent to France; but, when in March, their envoy, Matthias Reimbolt, reached Paris, Francis I, indignant with the selfish desire of Charles V to use him solely as an instrument for promoting the Hapsburg interests without any form of compensation, had resolved to oppose rather than further his designs. Perceiving his opportunity to frustrate the plans of the Hapsburgs, he announced the view that, if a council were convened, it should be held in a place where the participants would be free from every danger and able to express freely their convictions.

But the real answer of Francis I both to the Emperor and his opponents in Germany was the Treaty of Saalfeld of October 24, 1531, in which under the influence of a French envoy, Gervais Wain, the Dukes of Bavaria and the League of Schmalkalden were united in a coalition to which the King of France and the King of England might accede.[2] It was the point of departure for that policy of intervention in Germany by which France was to curb the power of the Hapsburgs.

Baffled once more in his efforts to secure a general council, Charles V not only realized that he was for the time powerless to effect the religious unification of Germany; but that, to avoid an open breach with France, he must pursue a conciliatory policy with the Protestants. At the same time,

---

[1] See Weiss, *Papiers d'état*, I, pp. 495, 496.

[2] On the missions of Gervais Wain, see Bourrilly, *Guillaume du Bellay*, pp. 124, 126.

Ferdinand's embassy to Constantinople returned with the news that his negotiations with Solyman the Magnificent had proved futile. For the moment, it seemed as if the Hapsburg claims to Hungary would have to be abandoned, and the Emperor even advised this course; for the truce with Zapolya was likely to terminate in a conflict in which Ferdinand would be confronted with overwhelming odds against him.

At the Diet of Nuremberg, therefore, in 1532, it was agreed that, until a general council was called, no one should be disturbed in the practice of his religion. It was only by a private personal understanding with Luther, made under the advice of the Emperor's confessor, Loaysa, that Charles V was able to maintain an illusory appearance of peace while preparing to attack the Sultan in North Africa.

But, although retrieved in part by later good fortune, the failure to curb the progress of religious reform in Germany was far more than a temporary arrest of the Hapsburg power; for, on the one hand, it gave fresh courage to the Protestant princes of Germany by revealing the impotence of the Emperor; while, on the other, it attracted the attention of all Europe to a possible revival of imperial domination which, if successful, would menace the liberties of every independent European state.

The designs of Charles V thus brought to a crisis the inherent conflict between mediaevalism and modernism, between the pretensions of universal authority and local freedom, between the conception of imperial supremacy inherited from ancient Rome and territorial rights and liberties as conceived by modern nations.

If Charles V had succeeded in suppressing Protestantism in Germany, he might have temporarily obstructed the course of history, but his success could not have been enduring; for his system was contrary to the laws of human development. Strange as it may seem to us, in all this struggle for religious unity, no voice made itself heard above the strife of princes in the name of the individual conscience and intelligence.

The absolutism which Luther conferred upon the territorial princes Zwingli conferred upon the congregation. Defeated in the larger field, the spirit of imperialism took refuge in rulers and theologians, to judge and to condemn with a narrower judgment and a more bitter condemnation than that of popes and emperors. But in the Church and in the State a great principle was on its way toward victory; and no emperor could prevent, as no power less than the combined energies of mankind can secure, its final triumph.

II. THE LIMITATION OF THE HAPSBURG POWER

Relations of Clement VII to France

In his efforts to unite Germany, Charles V had not been loyally supported by Clement VII, who feared a general council even more than the apostacy of the Protestants. In order to prevent the council, he had not only employed every subterfuge of evasion, he had sought to cultivate a close *entente* with Francis I, recently brought into relationship with his family by the marriage of Henry, Duke of Orléans, second son of the King of France, with Catherine de' Medici, — a union destined to exercise a tragic influence upon European history. The meeting of the Pope and Francis I at Marseilles, in October, 1533, had no other object than to celebrate, with all the pomp of the papal and royal courts united, the festivities of that fateful alliance. Connected by family ties with the King of France as well as with the Emperor, Clement VII seemed to have prepared the way for holding the balance of power in Italy by offsetting the one against the other.

The death of Clement VII in September, 1534, and the accession of Alessandro Farnese as Pope Paul III gave the Emperor some encouragement for the prosecution of his plans in Germany; for he hoped that the new pontiff, who had been favorable to a reform in the Church, would consent to convoke the general council which Clement VII had opposed.

Expedition of Charles V against Tunis

While this subject was under discussion, with the double purpose of protecting the exposed commerce of Spain in the Mediterranean and of inflicting a blow upon the Sultan, on

May 30, 1535, Charles V sailed with his fleet from Barcelona for an attack on the Moslem pirates of Tunis.

If the counsels and exertions of Cardinal Ximenes had proved fruitful, the corsair powers of North Africa might have been exterminated in their infancy; but, thriving and expanding during the inactivity of Spain, they had become a serious scourge to commerce and a menace to all the Mediterranean ports. As the first step in his long meditated attack upon the Sultan, Charles V now intended by a heroic enterprise to annihilate the pirate rulers of Tunis and Algiers and sweep the Moslem power from the coasts of Northern Africa.

As a military adventure the expedition proved highly successful, Tunis was captured, and Charles V thereby won a military prestige in Europe which he had never before enjoyed; but as a diplomatic triumph it was still more significant, for he was in reality facing not only the power of Solyman the Magnificent but the secret intrigues of Francis I, whose alarm and indignation at the growth of the Hapsburg power had led him to open negotiations with the Sultan.[1]

As early as 1525, and again in 1528, when engaged in war with Charles V, the King of France had been offered aid by the Sublime Porte; but these approaches had been unfruitful of results. When, however, the Emperor was endeavoring to unite Germany for a war upon the Infidel, Francis I, fearing that an attack upon the Hapsburgs at that moment by the Sultan might have the effect of favoring religious peace by engaging both Catholics and Protestants in a common cause, had sent Antoine Rincon as his ambassador to Solyman, in

Negotiations of Francis I with the Sultan and the Protestants

---

[1] The relations of Francis I with the Sultan were not so unprecedented as they have been represented. Diplomatic relations between the Sublime Porte and Venice had begun in 1500. In that same year, the King of Hungary had sent an ambassador to the Sultan. See Sanuto, III, 77, 117, 132, 453. In 1500, even the Emperor himself had sent an ambassador to him. See Sanuto, III, 180, 286. In 1509, Venice had formed an alliance with him against the Empire, France, and Spain. See Sanuto, IX, 356.

the hope of preventing aggressive action by the Sultan at that time.[1]

On the other hand, Zapolya had endeavored to attach the Protestants to his cause; but, although inclined to oppose Ferdinand, the Lutherans could not be induced to ally themselves with a prince already in alliance with the Infidel. Among the German princes, the most active opponent of the Hapsburgs was Philip, Landgrave of Hesse; but even he had declined the formal alliance with Zapolya proposed to him by Luigi Gritti in January, 1531; although he was earnestly seeking every support in procuring the restitution of Würtemberg to his cousin Ulrich, whom the Hapsburgs had dispossessed.

But Francis I was not so scrupulous in his hostility to the growth of the Hapsburg power, and was disposed to use any means likely to prove effective in abasing it. At the same time, therefore, that he was attempting to dissuade the Sultan from consolidating the union of the Germans by a premature attack, he was secretly negotiating with Philip of Hesse for a war against Charles V as soon as he had left Germany. In May, 1532, Guillaume du Bellay had been sent to Bavaria to complete an alliance with the opponents of the Emperor, which was intended to develop into a vast coalition against him, in which France, Hungary, England, Denmark, and the Duke of Prussia should be included.[2]

Having thus made provision to keep Germany divided, and in case of need to use the Emperor's own forces against him, three months before Charles V sailed for his North African expedition, Francis I had despatched an envoy, Jean de la Forest, to Barbarossa, Bey of Algiers, and to the Sultan, to propose that the Turks should attack Naples, Sicily, Sardinia, or Spain, while the King should advance through Savoy against Genoa. La Forest was further instructed to propose to the Sultan a peace with France, England, Scotland, the

---

[1] See Winckelmann, *Der schmalkaldische Bund*, p. 214; and Charrière, *Négociations*, I, pp. 198 and 207.

[2] See Winckelmann, as above, p. 213.

German princes, Denmark, and Switzerland, from which the Emperor was to be excluded unless he surrendered Milan to Francis I and recognized the suzerainty of France over the Netherlands.[1]

Before La Forest arrived at Constantinople, Tunis had fallen, and the scheme proved a failure; but it disclosed the determination of Francis I to arrest the progress of the Hapsburg power and share with Charles V in determining the destinies of Europe.[2]

While it is not probable that Charles V ever really aspired to a strictly universal domination, the titles of the House of Hapsburg, if everywhere made good, represented a union of powers that might well be regarded as a menace to the independence of other European states. As emperor, Charles V was "a temporal head for the world and for the Christian people," whose duty it was to represent and embody "the splendor and glory of the Holy Roman Empire." If he should possess the material force to make his authority respected, the Emperor, by virtue of his office, could claim in accordance with ancient law to be supreme over all kings and princes. Besides its hereditary estates in Austria, Styria, Carniola, Carinthia, and Tyrol, the House of Hapsburg now united under its nominal sway Germany, Bohemia, Hungary, Spain, the Two Sicilies, the Netherlands, a great part of Italy, and the resources of a vast colonial dominion.

Such immense possessions appeared to give substance to what without them would be only a titular pre-eminence. It was an aggregation of potentialities that might well awe the world, the apparent realization of the symbolic union of powers represented on the seal of Rudolf of Hapsburg, — the head of a man with five faces.

---

[1] The instructions of La Forest, dated February 1, 1535, are preserved in the Archives of Foreign Affairs at Paris, under "Correspondance de Turquie," II, folios 47 to 50.

[2] For the efforts of Charles V to secure peace with the Sultan for himself as well as for Ferdinand, see *Missions diplomatiques de Corneille Duplicius de Schepper*, pp. 55, 67.

It is true, that this multiple headship of the Hapsburgs possessed neither geographical, nor racial, nor religious, nor political unity; but who could say that the same skill and determination that had welded the once refractory and antagonistic elements of the Spanish kingdoms into a compact and subservient instrument of the sovereign will might not in time unify and consolidate all these diverse constituents of the Emperor's power into an equally harmonious and serviceable whole?

It was, therefore, not without reason, that France resented the assumptions of Charles V and his demands for aid in further augmenting the Hapsburg strength. Closed in between the power of Spain on the one hand and a united Germany on the other, with the Netherlands as a base of aggressive action and the Mediterranean under the Emperor's control, France would have been exposed to the risk of being reduced to the condition of an imperial province, as powerless as ancient Gaul under the dominion of the Roman Empire. The memory of the Emperor's scheme for the dismemberment of France was still in the minds of men; and Francis I, with a compact territory and a homogeneous people inspired by a fervid national sentiment, did not hesitate to enter the field once more against his old antagonist.

Attempt of Charles V to satisfy Francis I

Before the end of the year 1535, Francesco Sforza II, Duke of Milan, died; and the old contention over the possession of the duchy was reopened. Not being prepared for war, the Emperor offered the investiture of Milan to one of the sons of the King of France, upon condition that Francis I would agree to aid him in an attack upon Algiers, to sustain Ferdinand in his claim to the crown of Hungary, to exercise his influence with the Pope in favor of a general council, and to unite with him in forcing Henry VIII to abandon his separation from Catherine.

From one point of view this proposition seemed like a reasonable concession made in the interest of peace, but from another it was merely a bribe to the King of France to merge his interests with those of the Hapsburg

INTERNATIONAL INFLUENCE OF THE REFORMATION

dynasty and become an instrument for promoting its complete success.

In the previous adventures of France in Italy, imperial ambitions had been the motives for aggression; but now a new political principle was emerging into action. The national interests of France could not permit of its being encompassed by a power so preponderant as that of Charles V had become. Francis I, therefore, met the offer of Charles V with the suggestion that the investiture be conferred upon his second son, Henry, Duke of Orléans, whose succession to the throne of France was rendered probable by the feeble health of the Dauphin, Francis. Thus, France — whose future king might by this means occupy Milan, and through his union with Catherine de' Medici might eventually advance claims to the Duchy of Florence and the estates of his wife's father, the Duke of Urbino — would possess an effective counterpoise against the imperial supremacy in Italy.

To this arrangement the Emperor at first assented, then proposed the substitution of the third son of Francis I, Charles, Duke of Angoulême, who was not likely ever to be King of France. The refusal of Charles V to accord the investiture to Henry was regarded as clear evidence of his intention to retain exclusive control in Italy, and the negotiations ended without result. It was the crisis out of which was born a new movement in the international affairs of Europe. Francis I, whose own imperial ambitions had ended in defeat through the rising fortunes of the House of Hapsburg, was now to become the champion of a new system, — the security of territorial sovereignty through an equilibrium of the European powers.

It is from the closing years of the reign of Francis I that we must date the beginning of the modern political organization of Europe and of the motives and principles that underlie it. That period marks a complete break with the whole system of the Middle Ages. Before that time, the solidarity of Christendom — though long gradually dissolving under the influence of national sentiment, the schism in

The disappearance of religious solidarity

the Papacy, the *renaissance* movement, dynastic conflicts, and the development of Protestantism — was still a prevailing idea; but the alliance of Francis I with the Infidel, shocking as it was to a great part of Europe, practically ended it. From that time onward, national, as distinct from dynastic, interests became the mainsprings of international action. To defend those interests, new plans were soon to be formed and new agencies organized; but all was still in a rudimentary state.

The diplomatic methods of Francis I

Francis I had, as Louis XI had before him, secretaries to prepare his documents; but, as in the case of his great predecessor, all the weightier matters of diplomacy were in the hands of the monarch. His intercourse with ambassadors was so unconventional that it proved quite disconcerting to the grave and ceremonious diplomatists of Venice. Usually received in the King's apartments after dinner, they were led by him to a corner, or to the embrasure of a window, in the midst of a room full of company. "It has never been possible for me," says the Venetian ambassador Dandolo, "to converse with the King under other conditions, and it has rarely happened that His Majesty has ordered his suite to remain at a distance." Yet he well understood how to avoid discussing an untimely subject, and how to guard his own secrets. When disposed to throw off the ambassadors, he spent his time in hunting or moving rapidly from place to place, evading them by the swiftness of his movements. Regarding the King's negotiations with the Sultan, the same ambassador assures us that His Majesty always maintained the greatest secrecy, and that the envoys at his court were practically as far removed from him as if they had been at Milan.

It was only in the next reign that a department of foreign affairs was organized, but we find the King already surrounded with a secret council with which foreign relations were discussed, called the "Conseil des Affaires," composed of his talented sister Margaret, Queen of Navarre, — who was obliged to follow the King in his rapid journeys, sometimes accompanied by her husband, Henry d'Albret, — the Admiral de

Brion, Monseigneur d'Annebaut, the Cardinal of Lorraine, and the Dauphin. The council had no secretary; and, apparently, no records were kept.

In the same personal manner, Francis I organized his diplomacy, greatly augmenting the number of his envoys, whom he sent for the first time to Constantinople, Hungary, Poland, Denmark, and Sweden, and even to German states of the second class. These agents were rarely military men, but frequently high ecclesiastics, whom he could recompense with spiritual benefices without a heavy draft upon his treasury. The "Comptes des Trésoriers de l'Épargne" reveal the large sums spent by the King from 1526 to 1543 for the secret service of the kingdom in its relations with foreign countries.[1]

It was by diplomatic rather than by military agencies that Francis I now intended to carry on his conflict with the House of Hapsburg. His aggression upon Savoy was, however, a prelude intended to give him an advantage in negotiation. Believing that he could obtain a permanent path to Italy by wresting that duchy from its feeble duke, Charles III, whose chief offence was loyalty to the Emperor, Francis I laid claim to it through the alleged rights of his mother, Louise of Savoy, as well as to the Counties of Asti and Nice. Having obtained the reluctant sanction of the Parliament of Paris to a scheme well known to be illegal, but which that body had not the courage to resist, while the Bernese — marching nominally for the relief of the free city of Geneva from threatened absorption by Savoy — annexed the Pays de Vaud, in March, 1536, Francis I invaded the duchy, captured Turin, and took possession of Piedmont. Thus, by one blow, the King of France reappeared as a rival to the Emperor in Italy to present his claims to the Duchy of Milan.

The prompt arrival of Charles V at Rome indicated his

---

[1] See, for the diplomacy of Francis I in this period, Zeller, *La diplomatie française*, pp. 3, 8.

realization of the danger that now beset him; and his discussion of the situation with Velli, the French ambassador, affords an interesting illustration of his skill in diplomacy. When Velli complained to him that he had just concluded a treaty with Venice contrary to his engagements with France, he explained that it was not a new one but only a prolongation of previous treaties; "but," he replied, "it is not the same with regard to the conduct toward the Duke of Savoy, my brother-in-law and my vassal. That is not only an innovation but a hostility." When the ambassador reminded His Majesty that, notwithstanding his earlier promises, he had replaced the name of the Duke of Orléans in documents already agreed upon with that of the Duke of Angoulême, the Emperor replied that he had been willing to invest Henry with the Duchy of Milan on condition that sufficient sureties were given, that these could not be furnished, and that his offers had not been accepted in time. When Velli affirmed that they had been accepted on the eighth day of the preceding month, as was proved by his despatches; that, further, Francis I had offered reasonable sureties, and that others could not be demanded of him, the Emperor replied that he had not intended to require anything unreasonable, and that he was ready to refer that matter to the Pope and the Venetians.

"There is no question," retorted Velli, "in the engagements of Your Majesty either of the Pope or the Venetians. This change of names in articles agreed upon, the secret practices begun with the court of England, the offers made to the King of Portugal, are facts which I cannot be dispensed from bringing to the knowledge of my master. The rumor runs that negotiation with me is only a ruse to disarm our preparations for defence, in order to take us unawares. Have I, then, to reproach myself with having contributed to deceive him by confiding in the word of Your Majesty?"

"You, who speak in this fashion," replied the Emperor, "have you full powers to conclude?" "No," returned Velli, "but . . ." "It is you, then," was the Emperor's quick retort, "who amuse me; when you have full powers, I will listen to you."[1]

On the following day, in the presence of the Pope and the Consistory, the Emperor declared that he had come to Rome for two purposes: (1) to implore the Holy Father to convoke a general council to remedy the disorders in the Church; and (2) to prevent, if possible, the breaking out of war between the King of France and himself. With regard to the first, he had found the Holy Father and the Sacred College so favorably disposed that he had only to ask that they persevere in their course regardless of obstacles; as to the second, he wished to refer his conduct to that august assembly, in order that it might judge in the light of the facts who had ground of complaint, he or the King of France, and who should be regarded as author of the evils that threatened to desolate Christendom.

Recounting from the beginning the deceptions he had endured in his relations with France, he touched upon the rivalry for the Empire, the war which Francis I had incited in revenge for his defeat, the victory of Pavia, the Treaty of Madrid, the King's violated promises, and the renewed conspiracies against himself made effectual by frightening Europe with the phantom of universal monarchy.

With earnestness he presented his more immediate indictment, asserting that, having lost two armies, Francis I had asked for peace at Cambray; and, after obtaining it, had not observed it. "Although," he continued, "he had declared himself without the right to meddle with the affairs of the Empire, it was at his solicitation and with his money that the Landgrave of Hesse raised an army to wrest from my brother the Duchy of Württemberg. When he saw that I was turning my arms against the Infidel, he believed he had found a new pretext for a quarrel in an act of justice which the Duke of Milan exercised upon a wretched vagabond con-

---

[1] See Du Bellay, *Mémoires*, pp. 148, 149.

444   A HISTORY OF DIPLOMACY

CHAP. VI
A. D.
1527-1559

victed of assassination, whom it pleased the King to decorate after the execution with the title of ambassador." [1]

Then taking up the question of Milan, the Emperor explained that he would have been willing for the sake of peace to accord the investiture to the Duke of Orléans, " if sufficient security had been given that, once established in the Duchy of Milan, he would not trouble Italy by urging the pretensions of Catherine de' Medici, his wife, to the Duchies of Florence and Urbino"; but, he complained, "at the very time when the King of France was trying to bewilder me with negotiations, he was attacking with armed force and was despoiling, in violation of treaties, the Duke of Savoy, my brother-in-law and vassal of the Empire." [2]

Alternatives proposed by Charles V

In closing his allocution, the Emperor said: "Such, Most Holy Father, and you, most reverend cardinals, is the conduct I have maintained toward the King of France. In the present circumstances, there remain for me three propositions to make to him, and I protest in the presence of this august assembly that, whichever he may accept, he will find me disposed to give him satisfaction.

"The first is to fulfil my promise by according the investiture of the Duchy of Milan to one of the sons of France; but I wish that this may be a pledge of peace and not of war; and from now on this cannot apply to the Duke of Orléans, husband of the heiress of the Medici. In vain does the King offer acts of renunciation of the Duchies of Florence and Urbino; he has taught me too well what I must think, for what renunciation could be more authentic than that which he has made of the Duchy of Burgundy? There can,

---

[1] The reference is to one Merveilles, a Milanese supposed to be in the service of Francis I as secret agent near Francesco Sforza II. Having been implicated in a murder, he was tried, convicted, and executed with a speed that implied a sinister design. The affair created a great sensation; for Francis I claimed that the Duke of Milan had violated the immunity of his ambassador, while the Emperor and the Duke held that he was only a private person.

[2] See Du Bellay, *Mémoires*, pp. 150, 152.

therefore, be a question of the Duke of Angoulême only; and I will accord to him that favor on the following two conditions: (1) that the King will declare in what and how he intends to aid in the extirpation of heresy and a war against the Infidel; and (2) that he will commence by withdrawing his troops from the whole extent of the Duchy of Savoy, and that he will repair the damages they have done; for, until that shall be executed on his part, my honor does not permit me to yield to any agreement.

"If this course does not suit him, I am going to present to him a second, which goes to the heart of the matter; and I will give him twenty days to respond. Let us cease to inundate Europe with blood, it has already suffered too much from our fatal discords. Why should thousands of innocents be slaughtered for the quarrel of two individuals? For all the titles with which flattery decorates us, — kings, emperors, potentates, — we are only men, a little more elegant, perhaps, more richly arrayed, but often more avaricious and unjust than ordinary men. Since the quarrel is ours, and is our fault, if we cannot agree, *let us settle it body to body and with equal arms!* . . . It is easier to find a suitable place than one for a congress, — a bridge, an island, a boat anchored in the middle of a river. As to arms, I leave to him the choice, — a sword, a dagger, in a shirt only. I require only that he deposit in the hands of a third person, as the prize of the combat, the Duchy of Burgundy, as I will deposit that of Milan, and that he swear between the hands of His Holiness, as I to-day take solemn oath, that, if he issues victorious from the battle, he will turn all his forces against the heretics and the Infidel.

"Finally, if a war is necessary, — and I protest anew that it is with extreme repugnance that I propose this third alternative, — it is fitting that it should be the last; and that the issue should be such that one of us will find himself henceforth the poorest gentleman in Europe. . . . If, then, I do not cease to offer peace, it is not the issue that constrains me, it is the cry of humanity which resounds at the bottom of my heart; it is the desolation of fields, the sack of cities, the slaughter of old men, women, and children,—the unhappy victims of our passions."

The Emperor's explanation of his attitude

When the French ambassador attempted with an embarrassed air to reply to this outburst, the Emperor interrupted him with the impatient remark, that he was weary of the same excuses, and wished fewer words and more results.

The Pope was disturbed by the incident and dismissed the French plenipotentiaries till the following day. While at the next audience he was discussing with them what had occurred, the Emperor, who had come to take leave of His Holiness before departing from Rome, arrived at the Vatican. Taking advantage of the occasion, the French ambassadors begged His Majesty to declare if he really intended to challenge their master, and if he thought he had reason to do so.

Speaking in Italian, and in a loud voice, in order that all might hear him, he remarked that he was pleased to have an opportunity to explain his thought, as he feared he had been misunderstood. " In giving an account of my conduct since the moment when I began to govern the Netherlands by myself," he said, " I have wished to justify my course without inculpating any one. If any complaints have escaped me regarding the King of France, my brother, they only prove how much I have regretted not to hold in his heart the position I believe myself to have merited, and they imply no reproach from which he can take offence. No one more than I renders justice to his eminent qualities; I regard him not only as a magnanimous prince, but as a brave knight. If I have proposed to fight with him, this was on my part only a proposal to avoid the effusion of Christian blood. If also I have named twenty days for his reply, this was only a simple precaution; for I have calculated that after that period our armies would be so near each other that it would be very difficult to separate them without an engagement."

The Pope and the ambassadors seemed to approve of the Emperor's moderation, but Velli, having expressed his satisfaction that his master was not formally challenged and that his honor was not involved, requested of His Majesty to say whether or not he had promised the investiture of Milan for the Duke of Orleans; adding, " I have informed my master that you have promised it; if this is false, I merit an exemplary punishment."

" I have promised it," replied the Emperor, with an air of embarrassment; " but upon conditions impossible to fulfil."

" If you considered these conditions impossible," retorted Velli, " why then did you promise that which you could not perform ? "

" One of these conditions," replied the Emperor, " was the consent of my allies, who will never accept an arrangement so prejudicial to Italy."

Velli repudiated the idea that the consent of the Emperor's allies had ever been mentioned, and started to narrate the course of the negotiations, when the Emperor burst out with reproaches regarding the treatment of the Duke of Savoy; then, in a lower tone, and with a sarcastic smile, he said: " Is it not rather amusing that any one should beseech the King of France to be graciously pleased to receive Milan for one of his children, who, after all, are nothing to me; for even if they were my nephews, sons of my sister Eleanora, it seems that one might still reasonably contend with me concerning the choice of the one upon whom I might wish to bestow an establishment ! "[1]

In spite of the pacific language of the Emperor, his inflexibility regarding Milan and Savoy, in the presence of the animosity and settled policy of the King of France, could have no other termination than open war. To drive the French from Savoy, he invaded Provence, while Henry of Nassau attacked Picardy. The plan of devastating the country before the advance of the enemy left the imperial army in the midst of a wilderness without supplies; and, after the loss of twelve thousand men, the Emperor evac-

Invasion of France and mediation of Paul III

---

[1] See Du Bellay, *Mémoires*, pp. 154, 156.

uated France. Without glory and without result, the war left the quarrel exactly where it had begun.

After several short truces, Paul III undertook to mediate a peace. Neither side was disposed to abate its terms of settlement. In May, 1538, the aged pontiff proceeded by sea to Nice, the Emperor appeared at Villafranca, and the King of France at Villanuova. With admirable tact and industry, the Pope visited almost daily the two monarchs, aided by Queen Eleanora, who seconded all the efforts of the Holy Father with her husband and her brother; but all was in vain. Francis I was willing to surrender Savoy, if Milan were immediately given to the Duke of Orléans; Charles was ready to invest the Duke of Orléans with Milan after a delay of three years, if the King of France would at once restore Savoy. The expedient of a temporary depositary was proposed, but Francis I was suspicious that Milan would never really be delivered, and in this he no doubt correctly divined the Emperor's secret intention.

After a month of strenuous negotiation, Paul III perceived that a definitive peace was impossible, and resorted to the conclusion of a truce for ten years, signed on June 18, 1538, with provision for carrying on further conferences at Rome, whither both the Emperor and the King of France should send plenipotentiaries for that purpose.[1]

The truce was a victory for Francis I, since it legalized the *status quo*, and left him in possession of Savoy, with his claim to Milan still pending. On July 15, a storm drove the galley of Charles V upon the coast of Provence, and at Aigues-Mortes Francis I visited the Emperor upon his own vessel. Afterward, arm in arm, in the most affectionate intercourse, the two monarchs pledged to each other a loyal friendship. "Sir," said the Emperor after a long conversation, "servitors are often the cause of misunderstandings between their masters. We should have been in accord a long time ago, if we had ourselves discussed our affairs together; but better late than never."

---

[1] See Dumont, IV, Part II, pp. 169, 172.

But the Emperor was mistaken. It was not the passions and ambitions of two men that were now in collision, it was two political systems. Charles V and Francis I were only their representatives. One stood for the extension of imperial rule, the other for territorial sovereignty and national independence. Long after both the actors had left the scene, the great world drama of whose contending forces they were only temporary personifications, was to move forward from act to act until its *dénouement* in the triumph of local liberty.

Notwithstanding the amenities of Aigues-Mortes, neither of the two monarchs trusted the other; and their reason was excellent, for their quarrel remained unsettled. It was in these conditions of apparent peace and impending war that both prepared to gain by diplomacy what could not be obtained on the field of battle.

On February 3, 1539, Guillaume Pellicier, Bishop of Montpellier, but far more practised in affairs of state than in the offices of religion, was designated as the ambassador of Francis I at Venice. This post of observation, which a writer of the time called "the eye of all the West," — *oculus totius Occidentis*, — commanded the most central position for the prompt knowledge not only of the affairs of Italy but, through the commercial and diplomatic interests of the Republic, of all Europe and the Orient.

To avail himself of all the resources of information possessed by the Venetian "Inquisitori de' Secreti," — a commission of three persons organized expressly to guard the secret negotiations of the Republic, whose very existence depended upon wisdom rather than force, — Pellicier organized a well paid corps of informers, of whom the principal was Niccolò Cavazza, Secretary of the Senate, aided by other officials and members of Venetian society, lay and ecclesiastic.

For the affairs of the empire, Tassino da Luna, an agent residing at Lonato in Northern Italy, near the great routes of travel, was in constant communication with sources of information in Germany, and was able to carry on without suspicion relations with the German princes hostile to Charles V.

By means of these agents, the French ambassador at Venice was daily informed of the deliberations of the Venetian government, of the intelligence received from its ambassadors and other envoys, of the proceedings of the Emperor, and the actions of the German and Italian princes. "Not a company was raised in Germany of which he did not have foreknowledge, not an intrigue was spun in Italy of which he was not informed. Every day he sent to the Constable Montmorency a half dozen letters to acquaint him with the dispositions and humors of the chiefs of this world." His sources of information were so numerous, so diverse, and so exact, that sometimes forgetting the precise origin of his impressions, he imagined himself to be endowed with a mysterious gift of diplomatic prescience, and spoke of his power of divination as analogous to the instinct of birds of prey, hovering over a camp in expectation of the impending carnage. The defeat before Buda and the catastrophe at Algiers were predicted by him before they came to pass.

Entente of Francis I with the Sultan

Such was the instrument by which Francis I now intended to encompass and defeat the stratagems of Charles V. During the whole of the short period of professed amity that followed the interview at Aigues-Mortes, Francis was active in maintaining close relations with the "Sultan of sultans, the Sovereign of sovereigns, the Distributor of crowns to the monarchs of the globe, the Shadow of God on Earth," — as Solyman the Magnificent styled himself in his protocols.

An armed camp rendered permanent on conquered soil, a body of soldiers dominating over a population of slaves under the command of an absolute sovereign ruling as a religious and military chief, — such was the Ottoman Empire. That the Sultan was mild, just, faithful, and humane beyond most of his predecessors, and, indeed, beyond most Christian rulers of his time, did not render his power less formidable to his enemies.

In February, 1536, La Forest had concluded with him a commercial and defensive treaty, in accordance with which Barbarossa had made vast preparations for a naval assault upon the Emperor, and the Sultan's army of two hundred thousand men had been mobilized to attack Ferdinand in Hungary.

While, therefore, the apparent reconciliation of Charles V and Francis I excited alarm in Europe, and especially in England, at Constantinople it fell like a thunderbolt. When, soon afterward, the Emperor made his journey through France on his way to the Netherlands for the pacification of his native city of Ghent, this alarm was heightened. To the Sublime Porte it appeared, at first, clear evidence that the Sultan had been deceived and abandoned by the King of France; and all the skill of Antoine Rincon, then French ambassador at Constantinople, was necessary to quiet the Ottoman suspicions. The report that Francis I was not only reconciled with the Emperor, but intended to enter into a conspiracy with him to ruin the Ottoman Empire, which the partisans of Charles V did not hesitate to spread abroad, nearly caused the massacre of the ambassador and all the French in the Orient.

To meet this rising tide of anger, Rincon had but one expedient, — he simply told the truth. Only by solemnly insisting that the reconciliation was not real, by making lavish gifts to the Ottoman officials, by diligently keeping before the attention of the Sultan the evasive excuses of the Emperor for not restoring the Duchy of Milan to Francis I, and by generously furnishing aid and information in securing an advantageous peace between the Sublime Porte and Venice, did the ambassador at last succeed in allaying the suspicions of the Turks and winning the confidence of Solyman.

In the East and in the West, the diplomatic battle was now fairly on. The policy of France was directed toward four main objects: (1) to preserve, if possible, the alliance with England; (2) to maintain good relations with the Sultan; (3) to detach Venice from its alliance with Charles V;

and (4) to weaken the resources of the Republic for future opposition to French designs in Italy. To the accomplishment of this fourfold task the whole mechanism of the secret diplomacy of France was now directed.

The changed attitude of England

The long standing *entente* between France and England had for some time hung upon a slender thread; for events had essentially changed the conditions existing before the fall of Wolsey. The marriage of the King to Catherine of Aragon having been annulled in 1533, she had died a natural death in 1536; and a few months afterward Anne Boleyn, having failed to bear the King a male heir, had been decapitated by the unanimous verdict of twenty-six peers upon a charge of incest and adultery. On the very day of Anne Boleyn's execution the King had obtained from Archbishop Cranmer a license to remarry, had been betrothed to Jane Seymour on the following morning, and on October 12, 1537, her son, the future Edward VI, had been born. Twelve days later, Jane Seymour had died; but the Act of Succession made Edward heir to the throne. By the same act Anne Boleyn's daughter, Elizabeth, was declared to be a "bastard"; while no attack was made upon the legitimacy of Mary, the child of Catherine of Aragon.

In some degree, therefore, the cause of hostility between the Emperor and the King of England had disappeared. In June, 1538, Charles V had proposed to Henry VIII the marriage of the Princess Mary of England with the Infante of Portugal, to whom he had proposed to offer the Duchy of Milan, with a league between himself, the King of England, and the King of Portugal for its defence; but the Truce of Nice and the interview of Aigues-Mortes had excited the suspicions of Henry VIII, who feared a compact between Charles V and Francis I directed against England. When, therefore, in April, 1539, Marillac arrived in London as the ambassador of France, the situation was not only equivocal but the country was arming against a possible French invasion.

The marriage of Henry VIII on January 6, 1540, with

Anne of Cleve — who was so repugnant to the King that, if possible, he would gladly have found a means of avoiding the union after she had arrived in England — was, however, for the French an assurance that he would not go over to the Emperor; for her father, William of Cleve, was a powerful ally of the Lutheran princes, whom the King of England could not then afford to alienate. But his chief minister, Thomas Cromwell, whose urgency of the marriage and whose ultra-Protestant policy were displeasing to the King, was already in the balance and approaching his inevitable fall.

The moment that Henry VIII perceived with certainty that the *rapprochement* of the Emperor and Francis I was illusory, all was suddenly to change. In April, 1540, this became evident; and the King resolved to free himself from the "yoke," — as he termed his reluctant marriage with Anne of Cleve, — which he declared had been imposed upon him by Cromwell's representation that, being defenceless against the union of the Emperor and Francis I, he was in need of an ally upon the continent.

In July, 1540, therefore, Henry's marriage with Anne of Cleve was declared null and void, and Thomas Cromwell was beheaded. The Catholic reaction had already set in, and a friendly notice of these events was sent to the Emperor; who replied that the King of England would always find him a loving brother and a faithful friend.[1]

While the German Protestants lamented the loss of a powerful ally, Francis I promptly realized that he was now exposed to isolation in Western Europe. The hurried journey of Charles V through France in December, 1539, on his way for the pacification of Ghent, his evident intention not to settle the question of Milan advantageously to France, and his refusal to replace Isabella of Portugal — who had just died — with a French princess combined to confirm Francis I in the belief that the friendship of the Emperor was not real. It is not improbable that Francis I already knew, through

---

[1] Brewer, *Letters and Papers*, XV, No. 863.

his watchful agents at Venice, that Charles V had in 1539 secretly sought relations of amity with Barbarossa, and had proposed to deliver to him Spanish possessions in North Africa, including Tripoli and Tunis, in exchange for his alliance.[1] While still at Ghent, in March, 1540, the Emperor wrote directly to the Bey.[2] It was evidently a first step toward an intended neutralization of the French alliance with the Sultan; which, had it proved successful, would have placed both Francis I and the Venetian Republic at the Emperor's mercy.

All the more desperately, therefore, did the King of France struggle to prevent this result. With consummate art, the Emperor had in 1539 asked to be comprehended in the negotiations for peace with the Sultan in which Venice was engaged, and had solicited the mediation of Francis I with the Sublime Porte for this purpose; but the sagacity of Rincon had been equal to the occasion, and the Sultan had replied that the first condition of peace with the Emperor was the restitution of all the possessions which he had taken from the King of France!

Having thus demonstrated the solidity of the Ottoman alliance, the next step was to detach Venice from the Emperor by promoting a peace between the Republic and the Turks. This also was accomplished, and by Pellicier's revelation to Rincon of the secret instructions of the Venetian ambassador charged with the conclusion of the treaty the Sultan was able to deprive the Republic of its strongholds in Dalmatia and most of the Greek islands, and to impose a war indemnity of three hundred thousand ducats.

Thus, in the East, the diplomacy of France was successful in all its aims: the Ottoman alliance was preserved, Venice was separated from the Emperor, and the powerful Republic was so reduced in the Orient as to offer little prospective opposition to the ally of Francis I.

---

[1] See Zeller, *La diplomatie française*, pp. 183, 184.
[2] See Navarette, *Coleccion de documentos ineditos*, I, pp. 209, 216.

But a still more effective blow to the Hapsburg power was soon to be struck. In 1538, exhausted by their rivalry, Ferdinand and Zapolya had composed their quarrel by the temporary partition of Hungary, with the understanding that, during the Woiwode's life he should continue to rule in his part of the kingdom, and afterward the whole should pass to Ferdinand. The death of Zapolya, on July 20, 1540, reopened the entire question, and Hungary became once more the pawn of war and diplomacy. Three parties sprang up, of which one favored the rule of Ferdinand; a second, that of John Sigismund, the young son of Zapolya; and a third, that of Solyman the Magnificent.

Pellicier hastened through Rincon to urge the active intervention of the Sultan, but his pressure was superfluous; for Solyman had already determined to take advantage of the situation. The proposal of a French prince for the Hungarian throne was quietly brushed aside. Ferdinand, availing himself of the services of the veteran Hungarian diplomatist Jerome Laszko, sent him to Constantinople to press his case by offers of friendship and tribute "not only for Hungary but for the whole of Austria."[1] But Rincon was forewarned from Venice of Laszko's mission, and prepared for him a cool reception. In vain he offered in Ferdinand's name a higher tribute than the son of Zapolya could pay; in vain he proposed that even Austria itself should be held as a fief of the Sultan.[2] Solyman replied with lofty disdain, and cast the unhappy ambassador into prison.

On June 20, 1541, the Sultan departed from Constantinople to lead his army into Hungary, with the intention of driving Ferdinand not only from that kingdom but from his Austrian dominions also. Vienna soon trembled at his approach; but in September he halted at Buda, whose principal church was converted into a Mohammedan mosque.

Thus, the Kingdom of St. Stephen fell into three parts:

---

[1] See Charrière, *Négociations*, I, p. 445.
[2] See Charrière, as above, I, p. 494.

Western Hungary, under the uncertain rule of Ferdinand; Eastern Hungary, forming the independent principality of Transylvania; and Central Hungary, the greater part of the kingdom, governed from Buda by an Ottoman pacha.

The project of a Hapsburg-Valois middle state

In 1540, there had been for a moment a hope of reconciliation between the Emperor and the King of France by the organization of a middle kingdom, to be composed of the Netherlands and the Counties of Burgundy and Charolais, under the rule of Charles, the second living son of Francis I, and Mary, daughter of Charles V. By this plan a "buffer state," under a Hapsburg-Valois dynasty, would have been interposed between France and Germany; — an expedient for separating two powerful contestants whose principle has played an important rôle in subsequent history. But, as we have seen, two systems rather than two personal ambitions were now in conflict. While the Emperor refused to renounce his imperial supremacy over the projected kingdom, Francis I demanded "exclusive and entire dominion" over it. With a fatal necessity, the two systems were thus once more brought into violent collision.

The murder of the French ambassador

A tragic episode was soon to terminate the fictitious amity between the two monarchs. Returning to Constantinople from a visit to France, on July 3, 1541, near Pavia, the French ambassador to the Sultan, Rincon, and his companion, Fregoso, were led into ambush and assassinated on their journey. They had been warned by Guillaume du Bellay, Seigneur de Langey, the French governor of Piedmont, of evil intentions by the imperialists; but had continued on their way, although they had been induced to send to him for safe transmission to Venice their instructions, letters of credence, and other papers. It was these, no doubt, which were the object of the assassins; for it was natural to believe that Rincon, returning to his post, carried documents relating to the transactions of Francis I with the Sultan. In fact, after the murder, and in justification of it, copies of pretended instructions were spread broadcast representing the King of France in the most odious light.

That the plot was deliberate and authorized by high authorities cannot be doubted. On July 7, before the news of the assassination could reach Venice, the ambassador of Charles V had the indiscretion to send word to Pellicier to "prepare his lodgings for his coming guests"; which aroused the suspicions of the French envoy. That Del Vasto, Governor of Milan, was lying in wait for the travellers is believed to be proved by his remarks and conduct.[1] If the Emperor himself was not a party to the conspiracy, he did not hesitate to approve the murder of Rincon, who was a Spanish renegade in the service of the King of France. "If the persons in question had fallen into our hands," wrote the Emperor to his ambassador to France, "we should have asked nothing of Fregoso; but, as to the said Rincon, he would have ended his days in conformity with his temerities and offences."[2]

When Francis I learned of the outrage, he exclaimed, "I shall never be the friend of the Emperor until he accords me reparation. If he refuses, I shall declare to the whole world that I will not endure such an insult, and I shall show him that I am still King of France."

War was now inevitable, but Francis I was not yet fully prepared to declare it. While Charles V was pursuing his disastrous adventure of a winter attack upon Algiers, by which he lost his entire fleet and barely escaped with his life, Francis I was renewing his relations with the Sultan by the mission of Antoine Polin, — the Piedmontese successor of Rincon at Constantinople, — and recruiting his army with Italian *condottieri* by the agency of his embassy at Venice.

But it was not upon the field of battle alone that war was to be waged. In the Netherlands, the emissaries of France were exciting the municipalities against the rule of Spain, while Francis I entered into an offensive and defensive alliance with the Duke of Cleve. In Germany, the religious

---

[1] See Zeller, *La diplomatie française*, pp. 260, 261.
[2] See Lanz, *Correspondenz*, II, pp. 316, 317.

CHAP. VI
A. D.
1527-1559

differences furnished a basis for the creation of discord, and wherever Charles V sought to unite the princes Francis I endeavored to separate them. In Italy, the French diplomatists carried on their ceaseless anti-imperial propaganda, sowing the seeds of treason at Naples, tempting the Duke of Savoy to exchange Nice for a fief in France, and fanning into a flame the spirit of independence in the cities once republican. When, in July, 1542, open hostilities actually began, the Emperor bitterly complained of the Pope's neutrality, which seemed to place him, the champion of Catholic unity, upon a level with a Christian prince in alliance with Protestants and the Infidel to destroy the solidarity of Christendom; but Paul III replied by promising to convoke the long desired general council and summoning the belligerents to cease their conflict and submit their grievances to its decision.

It was not until the spring of 1543 that the Emperor left Spain to throw his whole force against Francis I. In the meantime, Solyman had marched in person upon Vienna; Barbarossa had ravaged the Neapolitan and Tuscan coasts with a fleet of more than a hundred galleys and an army of fourteen thousand men; Nice had been besieged; a French army had invaded the Netherlands; and, after the Emperor's refusal to bestow the investiture of Milan upon Ottavio Farnese, the Pope's neutrality suddenly changed into evident sympathy with France.

Isolation of Francis I and invasion of France

The emergency was great, and it called forth all the Emperor's powers as a statesman and diplomatist. Fortunately for his cause, the marriage of his son Philip with the Infanta of Portugal had just brought to his treasury an ample dowry, and the rich treasure ships of Mexico augmented his resources for the war. To hold the Pope in check, he conferred new favors upon Cosimo de' Medici, Duke of Florence, who was most able to bring pressure upon Rome. England, made more favorable to Charles V by the King's reaction toward Catholicism and exasperated by the intrigues of France to prevent the union of Scotland with England by the marriage of young Edward, Prince of Wales, with the infant queen of the Scots,[1] and to secure her betrothal to a French prince, joined with the fear that the success of Francis I might result in his annexation of the Netherlands and the destruction of English trade, had once more fallen into the arms of her old ally, and was ready for a joint invasion and partition of France.[2]

But it was in Germany that the Emperor won his greatest diplomatic victory at this time. The advance of the Sultan had at last aroused a sense of German patriotism to which Charles V now made an effective appeal. Allied with both the Schmalkaldic and the Catholic princes, he was able to keep even Philip of Hesse neutral while he subdued the refractory Duke of Cleve, the only German ally of Francis I, and divested him of Gelderland and Zutphen. At the Diet of Speyer, held in February, 1544, he denounced the alliance of Francis I with the Infidel, disclosed the previous offers the King had made to oppose the Protestants on condition that he be rewarded with Milan, and promised a free general council to be held on German soil and an early diet for the definite settlement of the religious question. At the same time, Denmark also deserted Francis I. Only the Pope and the Sultan were now friendly to the King of France; but Paul III could do nothing more than protest against the Emperor's surrender to the heretics and express his displeasure by postponing the council, while the Sultan could offer no immediate aid to his ally.

Thus supported by a united Germany, the Emperor planned with the King of England a joint invasion of France for June, 1544; and Henry VIII — who had sent Catherine Howard to the block, and was newly married to his sixth and last wife, Catherine Parr — crossed over to Calais in person. By September 12, the Emperor's army was threatening Paris from Soissons; but Henry VIII, intent upon the capture of Bou-

---

[1] See the draft of a treaty, dated July 1, 1543, for this marriage in Dumont, IV, Part II, pp. 261, 263.
[2] See Dumont, IV, Part II, pp. 252, 257.

logne, failed to support his further advance. Opportunity was thereby given to Francis I for separate negotiations with Charles V; and, on September 18, 1544, was concluded between them the Peace of Crépy.[1]

The Peace of Crépy

Consisting of mere temporizing alternatives, to be executed at the Emperor's discretion, the Treaty of Crépy, which seemed to concede all that Francis I had insisted upon, was, in reality, entirely nugatory, and left the conflict exactly where it had been at the Truce of Nice. Francis I was to retain his conquest of Savoy until his son Charles, who then bore the title of Duke of Orléans, was married to the Emperor's daughter with the investiture of the Duchy of Milan, or to his niece with a kingdom to be formed for him out of the Netherlands.

The death of the young duke within a year made it impossible to execute the treaty;[2] and it, therefore, had only two results: to occupy Francis I with the recovery of Boulogne from Henry VIII, and to leave the Emperor free to carry out his designs in Germany. Spain was already at his feet, Italy was within his grasp, but in Germany the Reformation, sheltered from the Hapsburg power by the earlier diplomacy of Francis I, had grown to manhood. It was a giant, therefore, and not a dwarf, with which Charles V was now to struggle for mastery.

III. The Rise of Independent Protestant States

Nature of the Protestant movement

If the Protestant Reformation had been merely a religious movement, it could not have survived the lifetime of the reformers who brought it into being. What rendered it triumphant was its political motives and influence, and pre-eminently its diplomacy.

---

[1] See Dumont, IV, Part II, pp. 279, 287, for the treaty; for the negotiations, Gachard, *Trois années*.

[2] On the futile efforts to execute the treaty, see the report of the Venetian ambassador, Marino Cavelli, in Tommaseo, *Relations*, I, pp. 342, 354.

In the sixteenth century, religion had no safeguard except the state, and every form of it which did not manage to procure state protection was persecuted to the death. The Anabaptists, who repudiated the supremacy of civil authority over the spiritual life, were doomed to extinction by Zwingli in Switzerland as well as by the disciples of Luther in Germany. The Waldenses in Italy were practically exterminated for the same reason. In France, after a desperate political struggle, the Huguenots ultimately failed to maintain their religious liberties because they lost their influence in the state. Only by foregoing the right of propaganda and public worship, has any religious body anywhere in Europe, until recent times, been able to preserve its existence without the exercise of political power; and in the social development of every country the spirit of religious toleration has been the most belated fruit of human culture.

It was only by the formation, combination, and co-operation of Protestant states that the reform movement won a final victory. On its political as on its religious side, the struggle was between local liberty and universal authority. As the greater implies the less, the right of territorial freedom in matters of religion became the vital issue not only for those who were prompted by their conscientious convictions but for those whose private interests were better served by their own autonomy. In no case was there a question of purely personal freedom. The Middle Ages had completely sunk the individual in the corporation; and the reformation of the Church, as well as the transformation of the State, could proceed only along the lines of corporate development. *Cujus regio, ejus religio* was, therefore, the formula which expressed the general conception of the time and the principle of its activity.

The intimate association of political interests with the new doctrinal movement is the more important to understand because it furnishes the only explanation of the course of events. The religious consciousness of that time has too often been made to bear the odium of narrowness

CHAP. VI
A. D.
1527–1559

Attitude of the German princes toward peace

Chap. VI
A. D.
1527-1559

and oppression which really sprang from a conception of political necessity. For the new faith and for the old it was a battle for existence, and only by alliance with political power could that existence be maintained.

The negotiations between the Pope, the Emperor, and the Catholic and Protestant princes of Germany at Hagenau and Worms in 1540-1541, and at Regensburg in 1541 and 1546, were political as well as religious in their character.[1] To enter into the details of these transactions, which, in the light of newly discovered documents, are only now emerging from the realm of theological controversy into the field of exact and dispassionate historical analysis, would lead us too far from the main current of international events; but the significance of their negative results must not be overlooked.

If the pacific temperament of Philip Melanchthon, who represented at Regensburg the doctrinal interests of the Lutherans, and the mild and moderate manners of the patient and accomplished papal legate, Gasparo Contarini, schooled from his youth in the arts of Venetian diplomacy, could not effect a reconciliation, it was not only on account of the wide divergence of theological creeds but in a large degree because an agreement was opposed by both Catholic and Protestant princes, who found it to their interest to widen rather than to close the breach. Not only were the Protestant rulers determined to preserve their autonomy in religious matters but, according to a Catholic authority of the highest order, the intentions of the leading Catholic princes were not wholly loyal to the cause of religion. They, it is affirmed, wished by becoming the leaders of the Catholic party to obtain advantages such as the Landgrave of Hesse and the Elector of Saxony had

---

[1] See Moses, *Die Religionsverhandlungen zu Hagenau und Worms, 1540-1541*, Jena, 1889; Vetter, *Die Religionsverhandlungen auf dem Reichstage zu Regensburg, 1541*, Jena, 1889; and Pastor, *Reunionsbestrebungen*.

acquired; and, "because they had no money, to wage war with the money of the Pope and the German clergy."[1]

At the time of the Peace of Crépy, nearly the whole of Northern Germany had gone over to the Protestant faith, and was under the control of Protestant princes. Only the South remained strongly Catholic, and even there the reformed faith had made considerable progress.

Defensive measures of the Protestant princes

It was, however, only by a close defensive union that the dissenting principalities could hope to maintain their position in case of a vigorous assault by the Emperor. Such a union was the League of Schmalkalden, but it was far from being a compact and effective combination. Only a few of the princes were prepared to resist Charles V in open war, partly on account of insufficient means and partly because of their feeling of obligation to maintain a certain loyalty to the Emperor.

When the news of the Peace of Crépy reached Germany, its full significance had been at once understood; for the Protestant princes perceived that Charles V was then free to turn all his energies against them.[2] Philip of Hesse had promptly sought to form an alliance with Henry VIII, but John Frederick of Saxony was so hostile to that "atrocious man,"—whom he placed on the same level with the Pope—that he would not even join in the attempt.

The sudden readiness of the Pope to call a general council,—shown in his bull of December 20, 1544, convoking it at Trent for March 18, 1545,—the negotiations of the Emperor

---

[1] Pastor, *Correspondenz des Cardinals Contarini*, pp. 22, 23.

[2] The Venetian ambassador, Bernardo Navagero, thus reports the anxiety felt in Germany regarding the success of Charles V in France: "If his enterprise in France succeeds according to his desire, he will be so formidable that those who oppose him to-day in the matter of religion will not dare to resist his will; if, on the contrary, he fails in that enterprise, it is believed he will yield to all the pretensions of the Protestants, for the majority of the princes, and the most powerful, belong to that sect; and, in order to obtain their aid, he will be favorable to them."—See Gachard, *Trois années de l'histoire de Charles-Quint*, p. 38.

CHAP. VI
A. D.
1527-1559

and Ferdinand for peace with the Turks, supported by the King of France, and the belief that a secret article bound the Emperor's new ally to aid him in rooting out Protestantism in Germany, had tightened the cords of the confederates of Schmalkalden, and had rendered them active in mediating a peace between France and England, with a view to neutralizing the influence of Charles V.[1] It was evident that when the storm should burst, the League would be prepared to oppose its fury with every means of resistance within its power.

Opening of the Council of Trent

If, at the time when Charles V first joined with the German reformers in demanding a general council, their wishes could have been fulfilled, and a thorough practical reformation of the Church carried into effect, the Protestant movement might, perhaps, have been arrested; but when, on December 13, 1545, the Council of Trent began its eighteen years of troubled existence, a reconciliation had become impossible.

Every circumstance seemed to conspire to defeat the success of the Council. Of the papal legates charged with representing the Roman See, Cardinal Del Monte, who held the first place, was an aged man of very ordinary mental endowments, appointed because he had been present at the last Lateran Council; Cardinal Cervino was famous chiefly for high theological scholarship; and Cardinal Pole, an English exile of royal blood, was wanting in practical efficiency and influence. When to the fact that they were instructed to do nothing without explicit reference to Rome, strife and disunion between the legates themselves were added, the probability of the Council's early fruitfulness entirely disappeared.

But the greatest impediment to the Council of Trent was the divergent, and even conflicting, interests of the Pope and the Emperor. For Paul III the support of the papal authority by a reaffirmation of Catholic doctrine was the chief end to be accomplished. For Charles V, on the contrary, an

---

[1] See Hasenclever, *Die Politik*, pp. 52, 96.

early doctrinal discussion was almost certain to widen the breach in Germany and prevent the success of negotiations with the Protestant princes and theologians, while a vigorous practical reform movement by the Council would go far toward weakening the Protestant cause and hindering its further development.

The Council became, therefore, a centre of active competition between the political interests of the Pope and the Emperor rather than a purely religious conference; and this opposition was rendered the more intense and the less decisive because, at the same time, the Emperor was negotiating with the Protestants in the imperial diets. In opposition to the wish of Charles V to employ the Council as an aid in his transactions with the German princes, — and, therefore, to postpone for a time definitive decisions that would only alienate them, — Paul III was determined to prevent any modification either of the ancient faith or of the traditional supremacy of Rome.

While, therefore, the papal delegates strove to maintain the idea that the authority of the Pope was above that of the Council, the representatives of the Emperor — the experienced diplomatists Don Diego Hurtado de Mendoza, and Francisco de Toledo — held that the Council was superior to the Sovereign Pontiff. The decision to vote as individual prelates, and not by nations as in the great councils of the preceding century, was highly favorable to the predominance of the papal influence, on account of the great number of Italian prelates present. It was, however, the Spanish theologians, who, although fewer in number, aided by the zeal and superior organization of the Society of Jesus, — which Ignatius Loyola had founded and Paul III had approved by a bull of September 27, 1540, — gave to the Council of Trent an impress so effective that its decisions were in the end a complete triumph for the theology and influence of Spain.[1]

---

[1] An important collection of sources for the Council of Trent has been undertaken by Merkel under the auspices of the Görresgesellschaft.

The Diet of Regensburg, 1546

With the long wished for general council finally summoned and in part assembled, the problem of Charles V was to induce the Protestants to accept its decisions. After the repeated failure of his plans for conciliation, the prospect was not encouraging; and the Diet of Regensburg, held in the spring of 1546, seemed to offer the last hope. For months previous to the Emperor's appearance there on April 10, 1546, it was reported, he had resolved to arrest the Elector of Saxony and the Landgrave of Hesse, if they attended the Diet; and, if they did not obey his summons, to make war upon them.[1]

In common with the Emperor's other chief political advisers, Granvelle had persistently opposed a war against the Protestants; but the Emperor's Spanish confessor, Pedro de Soto, became so zealous in his urgency of summary action that he threatened to return to Spain and enter a convent if his counsels were not followed.

The situation had, indeed, become acute; since, on the one hand, the Lutheran doctrines were rapidly spreading, and, on the other, the imperial authority was declining wherever they were accepted. "If," wrote the Venetian ambassador, Navagero, "the Emperor does not succeed in bringing the Protestants to reason, it will be necessary for him to remain in Germany or the Netherlands; for, in case he withdraws, the common opinion is that novelties prejudicial to him may be introduced into these last named provinces, which are already to a great extent infected with Lutheranism."

To what extent relations were now strained, was evident from the fact that, when the Diet opened, no one of the princes belonging to the League of Schmalkalden was present. Still, the Emperor hesitated to give the contest with the League the title or character of a religious war. Not without ostentation, therefore, when he had finally decided to destroy the League, he announced that it was only for the purpose of enforcing political obedience.

---

[1] See Gachard, *Trois années*, p. 105.

Notwithstanding the differences between the Pope and the Emperor, in one great purpose they were united. On June 7, 1546, a close alliance was formed between them, in which Paul III pledged the support of the Holy See with troops and money for the subjugation of the Protestants. At the same time, Albert, son of Duke William of Bavaria, was promised the eldest daughter of Ferdinand of Austria, with provision for succession to the crown of Bohemia in case Ferdinand's line should fail of male descendants; and thus the Houses of Hapsburg and Wittelsbach were at last united in a common cause. In case the Count Palatine Frederick III should not prove tractable, the Palatine electorate, it was further agreed, should pass to the Bavarian branch. To these alliances was added that of the vigorous and impetuous soldier, Albert Alcibiades, Margrave of Brandenburg-Kulmbach.

The Emperor's diplomacy at Regensburg

But the Emperor's greatest stroke of good fortune was his success in securing first the neutrality, and afterward the active assistance, of Duke Maurice of Saxony, who represented the Albertine branch of the Saxon dukes, and had long been in conflict with his cousin the Elector John Frederick. A Protestant in his religious faith, he was yet ready to promote his own personal ambition by serving the cause of Charles V against his co-religionists. Granvelle perceived in the ambition of Maurice the necessary instrument for the triumph of the imperial policy; but with keen perception of his own value, the young duke, who had refused to stand with the League, now negotiated with both sides, as if he possessed, and he soon proved that he did possess, the balance of power in Germany.

The sudden seizure of territory belonging to the Bishop of Augsburg by the Protestant forces of that city and of Ulm, on July 9, decided the Emperor to immediate action, and, although not fully prepared for war, on July 20, he placed the Elector John Frederick and the Landgrave of Hesse under the ban. On October 27, while the war was in progress, he signed a document which transferred the lands and

War against the League of Schmalkalden

dignity of the Saxon electorate from John Frederick of the Ernestine line, — which had held them since 1464, — to Maurice, as a reward for executing the ban against his kinsman.

Under the command of the Spanish Duke of Alba, the united papal, Italian, and Spanish troops soon brought South Germany under control. In the North, however, the conflict was more stubborn, and it required the presence of the Emperor himself and the concentration of all his forces to curb the resentful elector, whose people had risen in their might against the treachery of Maurice. At Mühlberg, on April 24, 1547, by the combined exertions of Alba and Maurice, John Frederick, his forehead streaming with blood, was taken prisoner; and, on June 19, the Landgrave Philip, having surrendered under the persuasion of Maurice and Joachim of Brandenburg, had a painful audience of the Emperor, by whom he was condemned to imprisonment.

Death of Henry VIII and Francis I, and position of Charles V

At last, it seemed, Charles V had risen to the summit of power, and by dividing the Protestants was in a position to enforce his will. Events of international importance seemed favorable to his designs. Francis I and Henry VIII had made peace on June 7, 1546, by the Treaty of Ardres, which provided for the return of Boulogne to France after eight years in exchange for a sum of money and a pension to the King of England, and the Emperor had conducted his war against the League in the constant fear of their intervention; but, on January 28, 1547, Henry VIII had passed away, and on March 31 Francis I had followed him. Of the three great monarchs who had so long controlled the destinies of Europe, Charles V was now left alone at the moment when he seemed to have attained a greater height of power in Germany than any Hapsburg had yet possessed.

The instruction to his son Philip, sent by the Emperor on January 18, 1548, at a time when his health gave indications that his own death might not be far distant, has been regarded as conclusive evidence of his extreme moderation in this period of his highest elevation and of the imaginary character of the ambition for world supremacy so often attributed to him.[1] In estimating the true significance of this document, however, it is necessary to remember that his imperial authority was even then far from an absolute triumph, that Philip was not designated as his successor in the imperial office, that the prince was still a young man, and that he would be placed by his father's death in a very difficult position. Pope Paul III had already shown his jealousy of the Emperor's success in Germany, had transferred the Council from Trent to Bologna, and was endeavoring to limit the Spanish power in Italy. Charles V had, moreover, failed to organize the Pan-German League by which he hoped to centralize the control of Germany in his own hands outside of the Diet. In promulgating the "Interim," he was not only adopting a last expedient, but was making a compromise of a nature difficult to enforce upon either Protestants or Catholics. When, finally, on June 30, 1548, that mandate was published, at the same time with the recess of the "Armed Diet," as that of Augsburg in 1548 was called, the Emperor evaded open disobedience to the Pope only by securing its acceptance by that body before receiving the refusal which he knew had been sent to the papal nuncio from Rome.

The purpose of that action was simply to maintain the *status quo*, by preventing further innovations and creating a temporary peace until the conclusions of a general council could be obtained. The essential correlate of the "Interim" was reform; for even Charles V did not believe that without reform the Church could ever be reunited. But what reform was to be expected? In dictating the conditions to be temporarily imposed, the Emperor was superseding both Pope and Council; in admitting a modification of the sacramental nature of the mass, in recognizing the authority of bishops, and in permitting priests to marry, the "Interim" aroused the indignation of Catholics while it did not satisfy the demands of Protestants; and in defending it the Emperor was placed in the position of having to prove to the Catholics

The Interim

---

[1] For this instruction, see Weiss, *Papiers d'état*, III, p. 263.

Chap. VI
A. D.
1527-1559

that they had won a victory, and to the Protestants that they had not suffered a defeat.

Ambition of Charles V for Philip and its failure

The attempt of Charles V to secure for his son Philip the succession to the Empire indicates his deep anxiety to concentrate all the Hapsburg power in the hands of a single monarch of his house; for only thus, it seemed, could the chief aims of the Emperor's life be realized. When, however, with great difficulty, by the mediation of their sister, Mary of Hungary, it was arranged with Ferdinand that Philip should become King of the Romans, and that Ferdinand's son Maximilian should follow him, the temper of Germany was found to be strongly against it.

Although the number of Spanish troops in Germany was never great, the victories of the imperial armies had aroused a feeling of hostility to their presence, and resentment that a foreign ruler had invoked them to combat German liberties was intense. Personally unattractive and unsympathetic, Philip was, moreover, in every sense repugnant to German tastes and sentiments. Weary of the influence of the Emperor's Spanish counsellors and officers, and on every ground preferring to divide rather than consolidate the Hapsburg power, the electors met the overtures in behalf of Philip's succession with a cold refusal; and the Emperor, deeply grieved and mortified, was obliged to dismiss unrealized his dearest dream.

The growing hostility to Charles V

Although the power of Charles V was never absolute in Germany, it had reached a point of apparent predominance where not only the German princes but the whole of Europe might easily become alarmed. The Spaniards in the Emperor's train, accustomed to absolutism at home, spoke insolently of Germany and boasted of a Spanish world monarchy. The irritation of the Emperor under the defeat of his ambition for Philip, the gruesome spectacle of two electors of the empire kept in what promised to be perpetual imprisonment, and the sympathy of the Protestants for their humiliated leaders all tended to stir the German blood.

But, while the apparent power and alleged tyranny of the

Emperor were capable of being used to excite Germany to resistance, the more penetrating intellects well understood that, in reality, he was not so formidable as he seemed. His Spanish possessions were far away, and his hold on Italy had been seriously shaken by the hostility of Paul III. The death of that pontiff in 1549 and the accession to the Papacy of Cardinal Del Monte as Julius III in the following year now ameliorated the Emperor's relations with the Holy See; but France, under Henry II, was already reviving the claims for which Francis I had so long contended.

As Dauphin, Henry II, soon after the Peace of Crépy, had signed a protest against the terms of that treaty, particularly the renunciation of the sovereignty of Flanders, the right to the Kingdom of Naples, the Duchy of Milan, and the County of Asti, and the restitution of the territories of Piedmont and Savoy.[1] With the accession of a new king to the throne, therefore, France once more resumed the national policy of curbing the power of the Hapsburgs. This fact furnished a new basis of international action and the occasion for a new order of the day in Germany.

Quick to see the advantage offered by the attitude of Henry II, the two restless and ambitious German princes, Maurice of Saxony and Albert Alcibiades, were ready to take advantage of it;[2] for Maurice felt that he had not obtained all that was his due for his services to the Emperor, and Albert Alcibiades wished to create a turmoil in which he might gain possession of church lands and endowments; while the imprisonment of Philip of Hesse, the father-in-law of Maurice, offered a sufficient *casus belli* against the Emperor. In the course of the year 1550, therefore, a plot was formed between Maurice, his brother Augustus, his brother-in-law William of Hesse, and Duke

---

[1] See Dumont, IV, Part II, pp. 288, 289, for the protest made by the Dauphin on December 12, 1544.

[2] On the earlier project of John of Brandenburg-Küstrin and Duke Albert of Prussia against the Emperor, see Barge, *Die Verhandlungen*, pp. 2, 3.

John Albert of Mecklenburg, to obtain the support of France against the Emperor; and, on October 5, 1551, as the fruit of these intrigues, a French envoy, disguised as a merchant, made an engagement with them by which Henry II entered into their coalition. Through the activity of Albert Alcibiades, a formal treaty was signed at Chambord by the King on January 15, 1552. The three imperial bishoprics of Metz, Toul, and Verdun — the strategic strongholds of Lorraine — were to be the spoils of Henry II, who was also to have Franche-Comté, recover the lost territories of France in the Netherlands, and have a voice in the selection of the next Emperor.

Diplomatic activity of Henry II

The movement appears in the narration of its origin like a rather petty conspiracy for the overthrow of a great emperor; but in its results it was destined to be one of the most important coalitions in the history of Europe. By giving Henry II an opportunity to pose as the defender of the Germanic liberties, it introduced into Germany the most powerful enemy of the House of Hapsburg; by striking boldly on the Rhine frontier, instead of laying the chief stress upon Italy, France was adopting an intelligent national policy; and by setting in motion against the Emperor the most active military commanders in the Empire, Charles V was deprived of a secure base of action.

But his conspiracy with the German princes was only a part of a great system by which the King of France intended to accomplish the abasement of the Hapsburg power. For the first time, French diplomacy was placed upon a strictly scientific basis. Francis I had been in person his own minister of foreign affairs, and with his personal decline the national policy had lapsed into irresolution and impotence. But Henry II, although possessing less talent than his father, not only recalled to power as his first adviser the Constable de Montmorency, whom Francis I had dismissed, but organized a regular department of foreign affairs under the immediate charge of four secretaries, of whom Bochetel directed the relations of France with England and Scotland;

INTERNATIONAL INFLUENCE OF THE REFORMATION 473

L'Aubespine, those with Germany, Savoy, and the Swiss Cantons; Clausse, those with Spain and Portugal; and Du Thier those with Rome, Venice, Piedmont, and the Orient; while Montmorency gave unity to the system by superintending its operation.[1]

It was the organized intelligence of France in alliance with the most vigorous element in Germany with which Charles V had now to contend. Jacques Mesnage, Sieur de Cagny, and Guillaume du Plessis, Sieur de Lioncourt, were sent to Switzerland to re-establish the old alliance with the Cantons; Gabriel d'Aramon was accredited anew to Solyman the Magnificent, with the view of bringing to an end the truce which the Sultan had made with the Emperor and Ferdinand, and to menace them with war on the Mediterranean and in Hungary; peace was confirmed with England by a treaty of March 24, 1550, with the young king, Edward VI; in Italy, Ottavio Farnese, Duke of Parma, was taken under the protection of France in his dispute with the Pope and the Emperor; and at the Papal Court, the French ambassador protested against the continuance of the Council of Trent, and finally succeeded in procuring its suspension for two years. In all these movements, France now skilfully played the rôle not of a conquering but of a liberating nation, protecting the rights of others against the Emperor as aggressor.

It is needless to linger upon the progress of events already pre-determined. While the carefully woven net of French diplomacy was being relentlessly closed in upon the Emperor, broken in health, divested of his illusions by his failure to secure the succession of Philip to the Empire, and despairing of the realization of his cherished ideals, he fell into a state of gloom and melancholy which left him without courage for resistance. Really almost defenceless in Central Ger-

CHAP. VI
A. D.
1527–1559

The defencelessness and peril of Charles V

---

[1] See Flassan, *Histoire*, II, pp. 20, 21. These secretaries were also charged with the financial and administrative affairs of certain French provinces.

CHAP. VI
A. D.
1527-1559

many, in the winter of 1551 he retired to Innsbruck, where, as he thought, he could best watch the proceedings at Trent, remain in touch with Italy, and in case of need retreat to Spain. His confidential letters to his sister Mary reveal the burden of his cares and the weakness of his position. "I do my best," he says in his letter of January 28, 1551, "to make a brave show of upholding my reputation, and not to let people understand that they can force me by fear to do what I do not wish. . . . I find myself at such a pass that, if the Germans, out of pure rascality, should choose to attack me, I should not know what else to do than to throw the handle after the hatchet; and even so, God only grant that I may have the strength to do it. . . . This war of Parma, the devil take it, is causing my ruin; for all the money that has come from the Indies is almost at an end, and I do not see wherewith I am to hide my nakedness."

For several months his sister Mary and his faithful emissary Lazarus von Schwendi[1] had been warning Charles V that Maurice of Saxony could not be trusted and was plotting mischief against him with the King of France, but both the Emperor and Granvelle were incredulous, and no effective steps were taken to counteract the hostile movements. Even as late as the end of February, 1552, the Emperor believed all could be arranged in an interview with Maurice, who was expected as a visitor at Innsbruck; but on March 13 the campaign was opened by the French in Lorraine, and on April 1, the German allies, having joined their forces at Rothenburg, in the very heart of Germany, were already at Augsburg.

Relation of Protestantism to the Emperor's misfortunes

The coalition between France and the German princes was in reality only an international combination for merely political purposes. When, however, the German allies issued their proclamations at Augsburg, they took the form of an appeal to the German nation against the Emperor's foreign

---

[1] For the activities of this agent of the Emperor, see Warnecke, *Diplomatische Thätigkeit des Lazarus von Schwendi*.

rule and alleged oppression in matters of religion. The Protestant princes had not generally favored the war, but since the Emperor was at bay the occasion seemed opportune for profiting by it, and he was left without defence. Only the slenderly protected pass of Ehrenberg now stood between Charles V and captivity, and he suddenly made a futile attempt at flight.[1] By Ferdinand's mediation at Linz, through which arrangements were made for a conference at Passau, time was gained; but the Emperor's retreat over the Brenner to Villach in Carinthia, begun on May 19 amid mountain storms, was hardly less humiliating than surrender. His last act before his departure was the liberation of the captive elector, John Frederick; but Philip of Hesse, whose deliverance was one of the alleged objects of the campaign of Maurice, was still held in the Netherlands.

When once safe from the pursuit of his enemy, although his situation was still perilous, the Emperor regained something of his old self-confidence, and felt once more — the more keenly, perhaps, because it had been so deeply wounded — the full sense of his imperial dignity. His first thought was to turn the popularity and influence of John Frederick, who still voluntarily remained in his company, to a good account; but the Elector, firm in his religious convictions, demanded as the condition of his alliance with the Emperor against Maurice, free evangelical preaching in the camp, the restoration of Hermann von Wied — who had been deprived of his archbishopric for turning Protestant — to his electorate of Köln, amnesty for all found in rebellion on account of religion, and the departure of all Italian and Spanish troops from Germany.[2]

The indignation of Henry II that his allies should without his concurrence begin negotiations with the Emperor, joined with a foreboding that Germany might be further

The transaction of Passau

---

[1] An interesting account of this attempt and its failure is given by Armstrong, *The Emperor Charles V*, II, pp. 252. 255.
[2] See Druffel, III, pp. 429, 437.

unified by his invasion, led him to terminate his campaign with the possession of Metz, Toul, and Verdun. The problem to be solved at Passau, therefore, became strictly national; and it was only by standing for what the majority of the princes demanded that Maurice, as an elector, could justify his position and profit by it. While Albert Alcibiades, whose motives were more mercenary, was busily engaged in secularizing Franconian bishoprics, Maurice, therefore, now posed as the champion of religious liberty.

On June 1, 1552, the negotiations of the princes began at Passau, where Ferdinand and Maurice were present in person. The two chief propositions of the Elector were complete tolerance in matters of religion, and the assembling of a national congress to adjust the relations of the two confessions. Subsidiary to these, were demands for the liberation of the Landgrave of Hesse, security in the possession of lands and properties already secularized by the Protestant princes, the abrogation of the "Interim," and certain acts of amnesty; in which, however, John Frederick was not to be included.[1]

As mediator in these negotiations, Ferdinand — who, as a German prince and as King of Bohemia and Hungary, had interests different from those of his brother, and on this account suffered unjustly from the Emperor's suspicions of his loyalty — was placed in extreme embarrassment. Only with the utmost persuasion, could Charles V be brought to realize the position of impotence in which he was placed. Unmoved by argument and entreaty, he resisted ratification of the articles brought to him by Ferdinand from Passau, and insisted upon making important modifications. Even in his condition of helplessness, he would neither consent to a perpetual peace with the rebels nor admit the right of the princes to settle their religious differences by themselves. While he remained emperor, he was resolved to guard as a sacred trust the proud prerogatives that belonged to him as Caesar.

---

[1] For the negotiations, see Barge, *Verhandlungen*.

On the other hand, although triumphant in the field, the whole future of Maurice hung upon the conclusion of a treaty. Practically abandoned by the King of France, he might, perhaps, if he went too far, be entirely isolated in Germany. On August 6, the ratification of the modified treaty by Maurice was announced with joy at Passau; but on the seventh, Charles V sent from Innsbruck his refusal to ratify it, even as modified by himself. On the eighth, before the messenger arrived, Ferdinand had dissolved the conference. What, then, remained to be done? To the eloquent appeals of his brother not to destroy the work of peace, the Emperor, for "the repose of the Holy Empire of the German Nation," on August 15, at Munich, sadly signed his name to the Peace of Passau. On September 3, the Landgrave Philip was liberated, and in the same month Maurice of Saxony set out with his army for Hungary, ostensibly to aid Ferdinand against the Turks.[1]

Although the Emperor signed a secret protest against the Treaty of Passau, it was against France and for the recovery of the three bishoprics that he now endeavored to unite Germany. By treating directly with Albert Alcibiades, who had offered his troops to France, that unscrupulous *condottiere* was again attached to the imperial cause, much against the Emperor's conscience; but, as he wrote to his sister, "Necessity knows no law." With obstinate courage he flung himself into the war against France, but the ramparts of Metz frowned grimly upon the Duke of Alba's assaults till Charles V cried out in despair, "I must leave the world and get me to a monastery; for I am betrayed, or at least as badly served as no other king can be."[2]

___

[1] His real intention, according to Barge, *Verhandlungen*, p. 156, was the foundation for himself of a Hungarian kingdom under Turkish suzerainty.

[2] On the attitude of the German princes during and after the war, see Haidenhain, *Die Unionspolitik*, pp. 166, 167. When Henry II died, the Landgrave of Hesse mourned his death as that of a great friend of the German nation.

There was purpose in this lamentation. In mind and body he was in a sadly morbid state; and in January, 1553, the English ambassador describes the death-like pallor of his face, the leanness of his hands, the dullness of his eyes, and his general physical weakness. And these were only the outward signs of the despair that consumed his soul. The illusions of power were at last fading into the night, and he was already longing for the quiet and repose of retirement at Yuste.

Marriage of Philip of Spain and Mary of England

The Emperor's dominating thought from this time forward was the future of his son Philip. Excluded from the Empire by the will of the German nation, Philip might nevertheless be left in a position of advantage to carry on the work in which the Emperor had failed.

In his war with Henry II, Charles V had endeavored to renew the English alliance, but in vain. To his request for aid, the English ambassador, Morrison, had been instructed to reply neither "Yes" nor "No," but that England was ready to aid him against — the Sultan!

On July 6, 1553, the young King Edward had passed away, and on July 10 Lady Jane Grey had been proclaimed; but the nation had rallied round the Princess Mary as having the better title, and the daughter of Catherine of Aragon became Queen of England.

Raised to the throne by a really national party, and loyally sustained by it so long as she stood for the independence of England, Mary herself was, nevertheless, personally resolved upon a reconciliation with Rome, and a restoration of Catholicism began almost at once. As the creature of the Duke of Northumberland, Lady Jane had naturally looked for support from France, while Mary inclined toward closer relations with her cousin the Emperor; and thus for a time the destiny of England became involved in the Franco-Imperial conflict.

The Hapsburg instinct for conquest by marriage was at once revived. Charles V even thought of offering himself to the new queen, but his age and state of health deterred him. Although negotiations were far advanced for the marriage of Philip — whose Portuguese wife had died four years before — to another Portuguese princess, and the Portuguese Infante was a suitor for Mary's hand, the Emperor seemed to renew his youth in his enthusiasm for the union of his son with the Queen of England; and the Portuguese envoy was detained in the Netherlands while Philip's suit was urged at London. From the wealth of his experience the Emperor counselled the Queen to win the Parliament, not to press religious change too rapidly, and to reinforce her position by a speedy marriage with Philip. The presence of the Princess Elizabeth in England, which contained the danger of a Protestant revolt against Mary, was to be averted by wedding her to the Duke of Savoy, thus doubly utilizing her in the Hapsburg interest. The Queen listened to the Spanish counsels; Parliament, though at first fearful of evil consequences to England, — after a short civil war which ended in suppressing the revolt of the country against the marriage, and a desperate diplomatic duel between Simon Renard, the Spanish ambassador, and Antoine de Noailles, who represented the interests of France, — in April, 1554, sanctioned the union, so fertile in misfortune; and in the following July the unpopular bridegroom came to England to find an eager but unattractive wife.

The policy of Charles V in Germany had been to unify the Church by localizing the Lutheran movement until he could find a means of defeating it altogether. In this he had signally failed, and he fully recognized his failure. On September 25, 1555, after long negotiations, ended the great national assembly that Maurice of Saxony had demanded.[1] With greater practical wisdom than Charles V had shown, Ferdinand brought to a successful issue the Religious Peace of Augsburg, — a compromise that gave to Lutheranism an unlimited right of peaceable existence in

___

[1] Maurice of Saxony had, in the meantime, fallen at Sievershausen in 1553.

the future, while nominally guarding through Ferdinand's decree called the "Ecclesiastical Reservation" the property rights of Catholics.[1]

The concessions of Ferdinand were, in effect, the virtual abdication of Charles V in Germany. The territorial autonomy which he had never ceased to resist had at length triumphed, and Luther's conception of Germany as in reality a confederation of sovereign princes, rather than an empire in the Roman sense, was vindicated by the recognition of the principle *Cujus regio, ejus religio*.[2] Thenceforth, Saxon Protestants and Austrian Catholics were to form coequal parts of the same system; but its basis was no longer a supreme and universal authority vested in the Emperor but a mutual and voluntary alliance for common purposes. The reality and significance of the change are indicated by the fact that the three bishoprics which Charles V had vainly sacrificed so much to recover were now quietly allowed to remain in the hands of France. Austria was still to be honored with the imperial title and the chief place in the conduct of imperial affairs, but it was toward the East rather than toward the West that the Austrian Hapsburgs thenceforth looked for their principal field of influence and expansion.

But a relinquishment of power more formal than the abandonment of Germany to Ferdinand by Charles V was soon to occur. On October 25, 1555, mounted on a little mule, for the Emperor could no longer ride a charger, Charles V entered Brussels; and, leaning on the shoulder of William, Prince of Orange, climbed to a high dais in the hall

---

[1] This decree required that prelates of the Catholic faith who went over to Protestantism should forfeit their ecclesiastical fiefs. In spite of this provision, the process of secularizing church property went steadily on, however, until it became a cause of further conflict.

[2] The right of migration from a state holding one form of faith to another state holding a different form of faith was conceded. While adhering to the idea that religious unity is necessary to the well being of a state, this compromise abandoned the notion that constraint is a duty owed to the soul of the heretic.

of the Order of the Golden Fleece. There, seated before the members of that order and other nobles, with his sister Mary on one side and his son Philip on the other, the broken monarch caused to be read a document stating the reasons for his abdication; then, in a brief address, the Emperor reviewed his past, recalled his long and numerous journeys, drew attention to his declining powers, commended Philip to the love and obedience of the Netherlands, exhorted those present to root out heresy, and closed with the words: "I can testify that I have never done violence, wrong, or injustice wittingly to any of my subjects; if any I have done, it has not been to my knowledge, but in ignorance; I am sorry for it, and I ask pardon for it." Then having formally conferred the Netherlands upon Philip, the emotion of the Emperor was answered by the sobs of the assembly as he concluded: "Gentlemen, you must not be astonished if, old and feeble as I am in all my members, and also from the love I bear you, I shed some tears."[1]

On January 16, 1556, in the presence of their deputations, the kingdoms of Spain and Sicily were also resigned to Philip, who together with his successors was further secretly charged with the perpetual vicariate of the Empire in Italy. Finally, after his return to Spain, a few months before his death, Charles V learned that his resignation of the Empire, which Ferdinand had begged him to delay in order to secure the succession, had been accepted.

Thus the vast power of the House of Hapsburg, which had threatened Europe with the revival of a universal monarchy, was at last divided into two parts, still to intimidate the world with the possibility of their reunion, but never in fact to be reunited.

In the retirement of his house connected with the monastery at Yuste, the dying emperor had one blow to bear which might well have shaken his faith in the system of ideas

---

[1] The scene is vividly described by Armstrong, *The Emperor Charles V*, II, pp. 349, 353.

CHAP. VI
A. D.
1527-1559

Prospects and
purposes of
Philip II

which he had so heroically struggled to impose upon the world. The Neapolitan Cardinal Caraffa, who had become pope as Paul IV, in his hatred of Spanish rule in Italy, poured upon the Emperor his maledictions for his contempt of religion in compromising with heretics, for which, he declared, God had accursed and smitten him with premature decay. With the crucifix before his gaze in the hand of the Archbishop of Toledo, when he himself could no longer hold it, unmoved in his faith but without the papal benediction, on September 21, 1558, Charles V was released from the burden of life.

Loyal to his father's principles and unselfishly devoted to their triumph in the world, Philip II now entered upon the scene as the heir and champion of the Hapsburg traditions. What had been lost in Germany seemed to have been gained in England. With studied prudence Philip II had avoided the appearance of dictating in the government of that kingdom, but his marriage to Mary and the return of the dynasty to the Catholic faith had inevitably allied it with the Hapsburg system; and for a time it had appeared that an Anglo-Spanish *régime*, with Spain as the predominant partner, was about to unite the Spanish kingdoms, England, the Netherlands, and Italy under a common rule; thus rendering that system supreme on the sea as well as on the land, while the Austrian Hapsburgs would hold the balance between the disunited princes of Germany, and France would be reduced to a condition of impotence and isolation. With the riches supplied by the American colonies, with a reasonable expectation of ultimate succession to the crown of Portugal, and with England as his partner, Philip II seemed likely to realize a domination more real and more extended than Charles V had ever possessed.

The alliance of Paul IV and Henry II, in December, 1555, to expel the Spanish from Italy; the Truce of Vaucelles of February 5, 1556, by which Henry II for a time abandoned the Pope; the renewal of the war and the intrigues to drag England into it, against the wishes of Cardinal Pole, who as papal legate in England was eager first of all to destroy the Protestants;[1] the battle of St. Quentin, in which Philip's forces won a famous victory; and even the fall and loss of Calais by the English on January 8, 1558; were all of secondary importance compared with the death of Mary Tudor on November 17 of the last named year, without leaving an heir to bind England to the Hapsburg system.[2]

The news of the Queen's death reached Philip II in the Netherlands; but Count de Feria, who had been sent by him a short time before to represent his interests in England, in the hope of winning the favor of Anne Boleyn's daughter, Elizabeth, the only natural claimant to the succession, summoned the council, proposed her name as with the authority of his master, and hastened to seek and salute her. The chance still remained of retaining the Hapsburg hold on England by a new marriage; but when De Feria insinuated that the young queen, whose legitimacy might easily be questioned, was indebted to Philip for her crown, she answered brusquely that she would "owe it only to her people."

Although Philip II had been victorious in the field, his treasury was exhausted, and since October he had been engaged in negotiations for peace with France, which the uncertain attitude of England now rendered still more imperative.

In a dilapidated castle belonging to the Bishop of Cambray, whose windows were patched up with paper to keep out the winds of winter, the plenipotentiaries of Spain, France, and England assembled to make peace. Among the negotiators

---

[1] For the tribulations of Cardinal Pole in his futile efforts to repeat the rôle of Wolsey, and for a graphic picture of the relations of Philip II and Mary, see the admirable *Dépêches de Giovanni Michiel.*

[2] How close the union between England and Spain was at the time of Queen Mary's death is evident from the fact that the English ambassador to Venice, Peter Vannes, had been recalled by Mary and the affairs of England intrusted to the Spanish ambassador, while at the same time the Venetian representative to England was accredited to Philip at Brussels, where he resided.

of Spain were Antoine Perrenot, the younger Granvelle, Bishop of Arras, the soul of the Spanish diplomacy; the Duke of Alba; William, Prince of Orange; and Count de Melito, the complaisant husband of the beautiful Duchess d'Eboli, mistress of Philip II. The French plenipotentiaries were Montmorency, the resourceful Cardinal de Lorraine, Marshal de Saint-André, and Claude de l'Aubespine, one of the secretaries of state. For the English appeared Thomas Thirlby, Bishop of Ely; Thomas Howard of Effingham, First Gentleman of the Chamber; and Nicholas Wotton, Dean of York.

For a time, the determination of the English to recover Calais and the obstinate refusal of the French to surrender it threatened to produce a permanent rupture, notwithstanding the ingenious proposal of the Cardinal of Lorraine that the prospective eldest daughter of the Dauphin should some day receive and return to England the town and territory of Calais as a dowry upon her marriage to the prospective eldest son of Queen Elizabeth!

In December, Henry II had learned that Philip II, who with his own hand had written two letters urging his suit upon the Queen, was seeking to marry Elizabeth of England, and the King of France had lost no time in asking the Pope not to grant the necessary dispensations. The attitude of Elizabeth herself and the improbability that Paul IV, who hated Philip and regarded Elizabeth as illegitimate, would grant them rendered more easy the *rapprochement* of Spain and France. When, therefore, Montmorency proposed the marriage of Philip II with the young princess Elizabeth of France, daughter of Henry II, England was obliged to accept the suggestion of the Duchess of Lorraine that Calais be retained by France for eight years, when it should either be surrendered or redeemed by the payment of five hundred thousand crowns; if, in the meantime, the English made no attack upon France or Scotland.[1]

---

[1] The treaty between France and England was signed on April 2, 1559. See Dumont, V, Part I, pp. 31, 34.

On April 3, 1559, a treaty was signed by Spain and France by which the marriage of Philip II and Elizabeth of France was arranged; Italy was practically abandoned by Henry II; Savoy and Piedmont were restored to the Duke of Savoy, Emmanuel Philibert, who was to marry the French princess Margaret; while the tacit retention of Metz, Toul, and Verdun, without imperial interference, and the autonomy of Lorraine gave a new security to France.[1] Although England did not cease to lament the loss of Calais, there was compensation in her liberation from foreign entanglements.

On the whole, therefore, the treaties of Cateau-Cambrésis, although condemned in France and England, were a long step in advance toward the affirmation of sound national policies and the delimitation of natural frontiers. That peace was not only a liquidation of the old conflict between France, Spain, and Germany for primacy in Italy; it was, as a recent historian has said, "the fundamental charter of Europe until the Treaty of Westphalia."[2]

In celebrating the marriage fêtes of his daughter, Henry II received a wound from which he died on July 10, 1559. Thus passed away the last of the great antagonists of Charles V, and thus ended a period of vast importance for the international development of Europe. The rise of independent Protestant states had brought in a new age, with new motives and new actors. Besides Sweden, Denmark, and the principalities of North Germany, England, Scotland, and the Netherlands were soon to throw their weight into the scale, and give to Europe a new basis of international relations and a new form of political equilibrium.

---

[1] See Dumont, V, Part I, pp. 34, 41.
[2] De Ruble, *Le traité de Cateau-Cambrésis*, Introduction.

AUTHORITIES

Documents

To the collections of treaties already named may be added for the present chapter, Testa, *Recueil des traités de la Porte Ottomane avec les puissances etrangères*, Paris, 1864–1896. The most important correspondence of the time not contained in works already mentioned may be found in the following: Charrière, *Négociations de la France dans le Levant*, Paris, 1848 et seq.; Lanz, *Correspondenz des Kaisers Karl V*, Leipzig, 1844–1846, and *Aktenstücke und Briefe zur Geschichte Karls V*, Vienna, 1857; Bradford, *Correspondence of the Emperor Charles V and his Ambassadors at the Courts of England and France*, London, 1850; Weiss, *Papiers d'état du cardinal de Granvelle*, Paris, 1841 et seq.; Gairdner's, Brodie's, and Turnbull's continuations of the Calendars of State Papers, London, 1861–1880; Tausserat-Radel, *Correspondance politique de Guillaume Pellicier, ambassadeur de France à Venise*, Paris, 1900; Winckelmann, *Politische Correspondenz der Stadt Strassburg im Zeitalter der Reformation*, Strasburg, 1887 et seq.; Lefèvre-Pontalis, *Correspondance politique de M. Odet de Selve, ambassadeur en Angleterre, (1546–1549)*, Paris, 1888; Bourrilly and Vaissières, *Correspondance politique de Jean du Bellay*, Paris, 1900; and Vertot, *Ambassades des Noailles en Angleterre*, Leyden, 1763. To these should be added the contemporary accounts preserved in Martin du Bellay's *Mémoires*, Paris, 1569, which contains also fragments of his brother Guillaume's *Ogdoades*.

The Venetian documents continue to afford valuable information. Besides Brown's *Calendar*, may now be mentioned Tommaseo, *Relations des ambassadeurs vénitiens sur les affaires de France au XVI*e *siècle*, Paris, 1838; Albèri, *Relazioni degli ambasciatori Veneti al Senato*, Florence, 1839–1846; Gachard, *Trois années de l'histoire de Charles-Quint (1543–1546) d'après les dépêches de l'ambassadeur vénitien Bernardo Navagero*, Brussels, 1865; Friedemann, *Les dépêches de Giovanni Michiel, ambassadeur de Venise en Angleterre, 1554–1557*, Venice, 1869; and Turba, *Relationen venetianischer Botschafter über Deutschland und Oesterreich*, Vienna, 1870.

From the Archives of the Vatican we have new light on the divorce of Henry VIII and Catherine of Aragon in Ehses, *Römische Documenta*, Paderborn, 1893; Friedensburg and Kupke, *Nuntiaturberichte aus Deutschland*, Abt. I of the first series, beginning in 1533, Gotha, 1892; Pieper, *Die päpstlichen Legaten und Nuntien in Deutschland, Frankreich, und Spanien seit der Mitte des 16ten Jahrhunderts*, I Teil, Münster, 1897.

Druffel, *Beiträge zur Reichsgeschichte (1546-1551)*, Munich, 1873-1896, contains important correspondence between Charles V and Ferdinand. Meinardus, *Der Katzenelnbogische Erbfolgstreit*, Wiesbaden, 1898-1902, throws new light on the imprisonment of Philip of Hesse.

Besides the works already named, Balan, *Clemente e l'Italia de suoi tempi*, Milan, 1887, deals with the condition of Italy at the time when the present chapter opens, and Bucholtz, *Geschichte der Regierung Ferdinands des Ersten*, Vienna, 1831-1838, with the state of Germany and its relations to the East. The struggle of Charles V for religious unity is discussed from a Catholic point of view by Pastor, *Die kirchlichen Reunionsbestrebungen während der Regierung Karls V*, Freiburg, 1879; the grounds of the German hostility to Rome are stated by Gebhardt, *Die Gravamina der deutschen Nation gegen den römischen Hof*, Breslau, 1895; the transactions leading to the War of Schmalkalden, by Hasenclever, *Die Politik der Schmalkaldener vor Ausbruch des schmalkaldischen Krieges*, Berlin, 1903, and Winckelmann, *Der Schmalkaldische Bund, 1530-1532, und der Nürnberger Religionsfriede*, Strasburg, 1892; and Bourrilly, *Guillaume du Bellay, Seigneur de Langey*, Paris, 1905.

For the relations of Francis I with the Sultan, see Zinkeisen, *Geschichte des osmanischen Reiches in Europa*, Hamburg and Gotha, 1840-1863; the Introduction to Charrière, *Négociations*; Zeller, *La diplomatie française vers le milieu du XVIe siècle, d'après la correspondance de Guillaume Pellicier*, Paris, 1881; and Vaissière, *Charles de Marillac, ambassadeur et homme politique, 1510-1560*, Paris, 1896. De Saint-Genois and De Schepper, *Missions diplomatiques de Corneille Duplicius de Schepper*, Brussels, 1856, gives an account of the activities of a prominent envoy of Charles V.

On the later efforts of Charles V to deal with the Protestants, see Pastor, *Die Correspondenz des Cardinals Contarini während seiner deutschen Legation, 1541*, Münster, 1880; Maurenbrecher, *Karl V und die deutschen Protestanten, 1545-1555*, Düsseldorf, 1865, based on the Archives of Simancas; Turba, *Verhaftung und Gefangenschaft des Landgrafs Philipp*, Vienna, 1896; Voigt, *Moritz von Sachsen*, Leipzig, 1876; Brandenburg, *Moritz von Sachsen*, Leipzig, 1898; Schlomka, *Die politischen Beziehungen zwischen Kurfürst Moritz und Heinrich II von Frankreich*, Halle, 1884; Warnecke, *Die diplomatische Thätigkeit des Lazarus von Schwendi*, Göttingen, 1890; Barge, *Die Verhandlungen zu Linz und Passau und der Vertrag von Passau im Jahre 1552*, Stralsund, 1893, based on Druffel's *Briefe und Akten*; Wolf, *Der Augsburger Religionsfriede*, Stuttgart, 1890.

The Council of Trent is fully treated in the great works of Sarpi and Pallavicini, in several editions, and more briefly by Froude,

Lectures on the Council of Trent, London, 1896; and Sickel, *Zur Geschichte des Concils von Trent*, Vienna, 1872.

On the plans of Charles V for his son Philip, see Gossart, *Charles-Quint et Philippe II, étude sur les origines de la prépondérance politique de l'Espagne en Europe*, Brussels, 1896. Meyer, *Die englische Diplomatie in Deutschland zur Zeit Edwards VI und Mariens*, Breslau, 1900, gives an analytical account of the nature and functions of English diplomacy in this period, with short biographies of the leading English diplomatists, and corrects certain dates in the Calendars of State Papers of the time. De Crue, *Anne duc de Montmorency*, Paris, 1889, is useful for the policies of France in this period. De Ruble, *Le traité de Cateau-Cambrésis*, Paris, 1889, is a valuable monograph, particularly as regards the execution of the treaty, to which the author assigns a greater importance than has been previously accorded to it.

CHAPTER VII

THE DEVELOPMENT OF A SOVEREIGN STATE SYSTEM

THE ferment of the Protestant revolt against universal central authority in matters of religion not only completed the movement toward separatism that the formation of national states had promoted but created within their own borders opposing parties which involved most of them in civil wars. The domestic conflicts thus engendered belong to the history of the separate nations rather than to the development of Europe as a whole; but their effect was so wide-spread and far-reaching as to be of the greatest international importance.

The moral disintegration of Europe

At a time when the European nations were ruled more extensively than at any earlier period by women and children, and therefore were practically governed by political parties, religious dissension tended to disintegrate the greatest national states by the double process of dividing their forces and creating dynastic questions. In the period immediately following the Council of Trent, known as the "Era of Religious Wars," when the principal strength of Europe was absorbed in the conflict between Protestantism and the Counter-Reformation, co-religionists abroad seemed dearer than compatriots at home. As a consequence, national policies were for the time to a great extent lost sight of in the struggle; but, for this very reason, the period was fruitful in new ideas regarding the nature of the State and of the relations between states. In Germany, the Protestant movement had been a conflict between powerful princes and a common superior; but in the more centralized and unitary states, like France, it involved the relation of the individual

CHAP. VII
A. D.
1559-1576

to the public powers, and led to new theories of the State. In order to escape constraint in matters of religion, dissent was compelled to seek a *modus vivendi* either in the control of the dynasty or in acquiring a degree of freedom that would diminish the power of the sovereign to impose religious uniformity. In practice both expedients were attempted, and both were in part successful; but they exposed the State to a new peril, the loss of its unity. It was because religious liberty implied political liberty, rather than from a passion for particular dogmas, that the wars of religion were fought. The primary question was, who should control the State, the Protestants or the Catholics? Liberty to teach and practise a particular form of religion implied the right to create a party to make it universal. To each side, therefore, the liberty of the other implied its own possible defeat. Wherever a party was already in control the disposition was so to conceive the nature of the State as to make its power absolute.

During the Middle Ages, a sense of moral solidarity had been imposed upon nearly the whole of Europe by the idea that the authority of the Roman See was by divine ordinance universal. With the rise of Protestant states, Europe was broken up into groups of powers which no longer possessed a common bond, and in which religion was beginning to be considered as a function of the individual state. What, then, were the normal relations of independent states recognizing no common spiritual superior?

This question might have been asked earlier if its conditions had existed; but it was, in effect, entirely new. Before it could be answered, it was necessary that jurists should elaborate more clearly the conception of the State and the principles of jurisprudence affecting the relations of political communities, that experience should demonstrate the necessity of applying them in practice, and that the nations should agree to accept them as governing international intercourse and conduct.

The present chapter is principally concerned with showing

under what conditions these questions received attention, and in what manner the great jurists of the sixteenth and seventeenth centuries attempted to answer them, how the bitter experience of the Thirty Years' War pressed the new doctrines upon public attention, and how by the application of these principles the Congress of Westphalia completed the organization of Europe as a system of sovereign states.

*Chap. VII
A. D.
1559-1576*

I. The Conception of the State as Sovereign

It is a noteworthy fact that, in the middle of the sixteenth century, there existed in Europe neither a clear conception of the State nor any defined principles of public law applicable to a group of independent nations. The customs and traditions of each realm formed its only constitution, and the ancient sea codes and a few ill defined usages of war and commerce were all that could be designated as law international. The mediaeval lawyers continued to divide law, as it had been divided in the Roman Empire, into *jus naturale*, the dictate of right reason; *jus civile*, the law of a particular people; and *jus gentium*, or law universally observed. Of an organic law of the State, or of law mutually binding between different nations, — *jus inter gentes*, — they made no mention; and in this they were followed by John Oldendorp in his great work on jurisprudence, published at Köln as late as 1539.

The non-existence of public law in Europe

The reasons for these facts are obvious. For centuries, Christendom was conceived of as one great state, in which the nature and relations of the feudal, and afterward the national, monarchies were obscured by their acknowledged dependence upon a common superior, the Holy Roman See. Within the circle of Christendom, authority, both civil and spiritual, was conceived of as descending from a divine source through the rulers whom God had established. Of the territorial state possessing sovereignty in itself there could, therefore, be no conception. Nor was any code needed for the regulation of the intercourse between monarchs; for the

Reasons for its non-existence

Law of Christ was considered a sufficient guide for temporal rulers, and the Pope, supreme in all moral and spiritual matters, was recognized as their rightful judge.

When, however, the Great Schism created a division of allegiance by presenting conflicting claims to papal authority, the influence of the Papacy was much impaired. Then began that accentuation of dynastic ambition, that struggle for supremacy in Italy, and finally that conflict between France, Spain, and Germany in which the Pope as an Italian prince became merely the ally of one or more of the contestants, and thus a political partisan rather than an international judge.

With the Protestant Reformation the moral solidarity of Christendom was still further weakened. Left without a common bond, the rulers of Europe, while ostensibly claiming to be Christian princes, in reality, as we have seen, pursued what they conceived to be their dynastic interests without reference to any fixed principles whatever. The will of the prince, therefore, became the source of law both for his own people and in his relations with other rulers.

The gradual recognition of territorial sovereignty

Although territorial states had for a long time existed, the association of definite legal jurisdiction with exact boundaries in space was only gradual. The impediments were twofold. On the one hand was the obstruction of feudal relations, on the other the claim of a world lordship. The persistence of this latter idea is surprising. The celebrated jurist Bartolus of Sassoferrato had declared it heresy to deny the right of the Emperor to rule the world. It was considered a great concession when Conradus Brunus, a German jurisconsult employed by Charles V and Ferdinand of Austria, said in his "De Legationibus," published in 1548: "To-day, moreover, the authority of the kings of France is so great, that many persons maintain their entire exemption from the jurisdiction of the Roman Empire."[1] In the time of Charles V it was considered very bold of Franciscus a

---

[1] *De Legationibus*, V, c. 19.

Victoria to deny the right of the Supreme Pontiff to exercise jurisdiction over kings; but now Fernando Vasquez claimed exemption from imperial supremacy for Philip II, disputed the existence of any *orbis dominus* whatever, and declared that neither Pope, nor Emperor, nor any man since Adam was, or at any time had been, *de jure* the lord of the whole world.[1]

But these declarations were only negative and merely preliminary to the conception of the territorial state as sovereign. The maxim *Jurisdictionem nemo habet extra territorium*, which accords full sovereignty to a territorial ruler and denies the right of foreign interference, had not yet been accepted or even proposed as a legal principle. It was still considered proper for a monarch, when it appeared to be either a duty or an advantage, to impose a particular religious creed upon the subjects of another, to form conspiracies and excite rebellion for this purpose, and even to appropriate whole kingdoms when it seemed possible to do so.

It was a revulsion from the anarchy produced by these causes rather than abstract speculation that brought into prominence the conception of the State and the idea of normal relations between political communities. Receiving their inspiration from the moving current of events, so replete with crime and tragedy, the jurists of the sixteenth and seventeenth centuries in the midst of warring elements spoke to the intelligence of kings and peoples, and from the

---

[1] Although Philip II had failed to obtain the imperial honor, he regarded himself as the greatest monarch in Europe. In 1558, at Venice, his ambassador, Vargas, claimed precedence on this ground. The French ambassador, Noailles, contested this position and the Senate, unwilling to discuss who was the greater monarch, decided that, as France had always preceded Spain upon its registers, France should have the first place. At the Council of Trent, Philip II had opened the same question and obtained the privilege of seating his ambassador on an eminence opposite the papal legates, instead of in the third place. For the bitter conflict on this question at Venice, the Council of Trent, and afterward in England, see Ward, *An Enquiry into the Foundation and History of the Laws of Nations*, II, pp. 454, 459.

heat and turmoil of an apparently interminable conflict pointed the way to a region of repose. It is this development of thought and its effects upon the future of Europe that give to the period we are now about to traverse its most abiding interest.

The Counter-Reformation and the Protestant resistance

All the more important movements of the time were mere incidents in the operation and conflict of two great forces. One of these was the Counter-Reformation,— a vigorous, systematic, organized movement, set in motion by the Jesuit influence in the Council of Trent and the earnest character of Pope Paul IV, — appealing to good Catholics everywhere by its religious zeal and moral aggressiveness, and backed by all the forces of Philip II; who, notwithstanding his personal differences with the Pope, was as eager as he to extirpate heresy everywhere and reunite the Church. The other was the Protestant struggle for existence, rendered the more desperate by the danger to which the new faith was now exposed, and inspired not only by conscientious convictions too deeply seated to be eradicated but by dynastic interests that depended upon Protestant support.

Although Queen Elizabeth was a Catholic at the time of her accession, and might have found shelter in a marriage with Philip II and a political alliance with the Hapsburg interests, she had the discernment to perceive that such a course would involve her own subordination to a foreign power, the sacrifice of English independence, and the probability of continued civil wars in England. She saw that the nation was at heart Protestant, — at least in the sense her father, Henry VIII, had been, — that a marriage and alliance with Philip II involved great risks, and that any marriage whatever would be for her and her kingdom an entanglement. With clear insight into the conditions of a problem of vast complexity, she made the double and heroic choice upon which her greatness and that of her country were to rest. She decided to become a Protestant, and to remain unmarried. In choosing against the supremacy of Rome and a partnership with the House of Hapsburg, she appealed to what was most fundamental in the instincts and character of her people. In deciding to repudiate marriage, "as marriage in that age so often meant conquest, her virginity became a symbol of national independence"; for, in the minds of her people, as in the realm of national policy, an English historian has truly said, "the virginity of Elizabeth was the virginity of England."[1]

With the Protestant forces of Germany balanced by the inertia or opposition of the German states that still remained Catholic, with the Scandinavian kingdoms too remote from the centre of conflict to feel that their religious interests were in peril, and with France divided by the hostility of Catholics and Calvinists in their struggle to control the destiny of the monarchy, it was to Elizabeth that the championship of Protestantism naturally and inevitably fell. In the last forty years of the sixteenth century, it is the contest between Philip II of Spain as the protagonist of Catholic predominance in Europe, and Elizabeth of England as the enforced representative of opposition to his schemes, that gives unity to the drama of international development. In that most tragic period of modern history, crowded with passionate characters and desperate deeds, nearly every European nation was called to take a part. As in the plays of the great dramatist whose comprehensive mind is the most typical product of the Elizabethan Age, in that period every impulse finds its embodiment every purpose its original device, every thought its expression, and every principle its impersonation. Were it not for this reason the best known period of European history, its complexity would render the exposition of its diplomacy a most formidable task; but in the midst of its intricate plots and conspiracies runs the broad current of one central movement, — the effort of the nations to assert their inherent powers, realize their unity, and establish their independence upon the basis of their deepest convictions in opposition to foreign rule. Out

---

[1] Seeley, *The Growth of British Policy*, I, p. 37.

of the fiery crucible of their internal strife and their desperate rivalry, we shall see emerging the bold outlines of their true individuality and national character. Regarded in their details, the "Wars of Religion" present a scene of violence and anarchy unparalleled in history; but contemplated in their effect upon human intelligence, they disclose in clear outlines the fundamental principles upon which reposes the permanent political order of the modern world.

The relations of England and Scotland

With all the advantages of physical insularity that gave to England security against foreign aggression, that kingdom was exposed to one constant danger. Even as a merely neighboring state, over which England had once exercised a precarious suzerainty, Scotland had been a source of frequent menace and constant disquietude. But at this time, the traditional ally of France had by the marriage of the Queen of Scotland, Mary Stuart, with the French Dauphin, Francis, on April 19, 1558, not only frustrated the plans of the English to unite the two kingdoms by marriage, but had pledged the transfer of the crown of Scotland to the kings of France in case the union should fail of direct heirs. The Dauphin of France had taken the title and the arms of the King of Scotland, and without action on the part of England it seemed probable that the Scotch crown would ultimately pass to the House of Valois.

But this was only the least of the impending dangers. Not only was Scotland likely to be permanently united to France, but a son of Mary Stuart — or, in circumstances not difficult to imagine, the Queen of Scots herself — might lay claim to the throne of England. Thus, as it appeared, England had only just escaped absorption by the House of Hapsburg to be exposed to a similar possibility by the House of Valois.

The Treaty of Cateau-Cambrésis, by which England had lost Calais, seemed almost like a league against Elizabeth. Among its secret pledges was the union of Spain and France for the extinction of heresy. The vengeance of Philip II on account of Elizabeth's rejection of his suit and his wish to render England Catholic now appeared to be offered an inviting opportunity of gratification in promoting the claims of Mary Stuart, whose Tudor blood made her a possible rival for the throne of England.

Before the alliance of Spain with France, there had been, indeed, a chance of balancing the Valois ambitions with Hapsburg jealousy; but, now that the two families were so closely united, that possibility seemed to have been removed. To meet the animosity of Spain and the pretensions of France, therefore, only one course was open to Elizabeth: to base her policy solely upon the national interests of her people, their independence of a foreign power, and the safety of their northern frontier.

Fortunately for England, if the government of Scotland was French, the Scotch people were far from being docile subjects of foreign rule; and for the first time in their history, England and Scotland found themselves animated by two sentiments in common. The first and most fundamental of these was hostility to the designs of France; the second, opposition to the system of Rome in religion. Widely different as they were in their tastes and opinions, Anglicans and Calvinists possessed these two grounds of affinity. It was the first emergence above the sea of strife of a basis of united action, which was soon to furnish solid ground for the formation of a closer union between the two kingdoms.

The preaching of John Knox, whose fervid nature was fired by the memory of a bitter captivity in France as well as by the religious doctrines of John Calvin, brought to an open revolt the spirit of rebellion that had long existed in Scotland; and, in October, 1559, the Queen Regent, Mary of Guise, was deposed from the regency. With prudent respect for the principle of royal legitimacy, Elizabeth now offered aid to the Scotch in expelling the French, on condition that they would acknowledge Mary Stuart as their lawful queen. Through the aid of the English ships the struggle was soon finished, and by the Treaty of Edinburgh, of July 6, 1560, the French rule in Scotland was brought to an end.[1]

---

[1] See Dumont, V, Part I, pp. 65, 67.

CHAP. VII
A. D.
1559-1576

The international effect of the religious conflict

The action of Elizabeth had seemed dangerously bold, but events soon justified her course. The refusal of the Guises to ratify the Treaty of Edinburgh foreboded war, for the brothers of the deposed Regent, the Cardinal of Lorraine and Francis Duke of Guise, who then practically governed France, were eager to punish the Scotch rebels and their ally; but the conspiracy to seize the young king, Francis II, at Amboise and place him under Protestant control had already plunged France into civil war. On December 5, 1560, Francis II died childless at the age of sixteen, and the Guises temporarily fell from power at the accession of the eleven-year-old Charles IX, under the regency of his mother, Catherine de' Medici.

Thus preoccupied at home, the question now was, whether France itself might not repeat the experience of Scotland; for Calvinism, equally militant in that kingdom, was making a determined struggle for control of the monarchy. What rendered the conflict there and everywhere more intense was the fact that, under Pope Pius IV, Catholicism, which had become sincerely religious in the pontificate of Paul IV, was now in its own way earnestly pursuing the path of ecclesiastical reform and striving once more to accomplish a spiritual mission in the world. Upon one point it was, moreover, fully determined: the unity of Christendom must be restored, and to this end no heretic could be allowed to occupy a throne.

When, therefore, in 1563, the Council of Trent closed its labors, Catholicism was preparing to march with a solid front to a new dominion of the world. In Spain, the Holy Inquisition was employed for the double purpose of enforcing religious uniformity and royal absolutism; but in most other parts of Europe, Protestant doctrines were demanding tolerance, particularly in the countries north of the Alps. This conflict of religious opinions was soon to open a new era in European politics; for France was thereby deprived for a generation of all international initiative, while the Netherlands offered a convenient field for active opposition to the predominance of Spain. By the division of Germany into practically independent principalities and the dissensions of France, Italy was at last left free to pursue its course without the intervention of any foreign power except Spain, and the theatre of European diplomacy was transferred to another centre.

But the Protestant movement had changed the policies and the affinities of the rulers as well as the scene of their activities. "The Catholic princes must not in this age proceed as formerly," writes a diplomatist in April, 1565. "At other times, friends and enemies followed the distinction of frontiers and countries, and were called Italians, Germans, French, Spaniards, English, and the like; now we are called Catholics and Heretics, and the Catholic prince must have all Catholic countries for his friends, as the heretics have all heretics, whether their own subjects or not, for friends and subjects."

Upon this background of mortal strife between Catholicism and Protestantism two figures stand out in conspicuous contrast as representatives of opposing ideas and purposes.

The contrasted qualities of Philip II and Elizabeth of England

In his gloomy palace of the Escurial, Philip II, with the zeal of a fanatic and the methods and industry of a clerk, planned the consolidation of his enormous heritage and the universal triumph of the Catholic faith. With businesslike diligence, his cold, dry intellect mastered the details of the voluminous reports of his numerous agents and councillors, and with systematic patience he wrote out his instructions in reply. Never before, perhaps, had such diligent and tireless personal attention been applied to the task of government; but the universal absolutism in which Philip II believed could no longer govern the world, even though aided by a relentless application of the laws of logic and the most finished mechanism of administration. Philip II might have become a deeper psychologist, and thereby an abler ruler, if he had better known the springs of human action by closer contact and sympathy with mankind.

Queen Elizabeth, on the other hand, with less abstract intelligence, possessed the subtle art of discerning and utilizing the talents of others. If her enemy was an embodiment of the genius of Spain, she was the personification of that common sense and practical sagacity that constitute the chief talent of her race. Personally irreligious at heart, she nevertheless knew the value and the danger of religious sentiment. In morals, she was what her father had been, a public champion of the claims of conscience; though, like him, she was not always a loyal subject of its authority. For her, strength, beauty, and order were the real marks of human perfection, — the objects of her admiration where they existed, and of her lamentation where they failed. For truth as an abstraction she had no reverence, and for its martyrs no sympathy. Her thought was often veiled in its expression, in order that she might reserve the power to praise or to condemn the results of action. Her deepest aversion was to be duped by others; her highest joy to outwit her enemies. While Philip laboriously contrived vast schemes of intrigue and domination, Elizabeth looked first to her own immediate security, concealed her hostility, profited by the errors or misfortunes of her enemies, and secretly furnished aid against them without imprudence or extravagance. Despite the businesslike system of his methods, Philip belonged to an antiquated school of statesmanship founded partly on family traditions and partly on abstract ideas. Elizabeth was even more modern than Machiavelli; for, to his estimation of ends as more vital than principles she added the intuition that success lies more in acting prudently upon the susceptibilities of others than in the possession of superior faculties.

The dynastic question in England

While few periods are so poor in great treaties and important negotiations as the reign of Elizabeth, few are so crowded with plots and conspiracies. All Europe was divided into two great parties, whose constituent elements were bound together by common interests rather than by formal conventions.

In Great Britain, the prospects of Mary Stuart seemed at the beginning more brilliant than those of Elizabeth

Tudor, for the Queen of Scots was not only recognized by all within her own realm, as a Tudor heiress she had claims to the throne of England also. As a Catholic, she enjoyed from the first the aid of a strong party of supporters for the English crown; and, when by her marriage with Lord Darnley, another Tudor descendant, she became the mother of James VI of Scotland, she possessed the advantage of representing a branch of the Tudor dynasty that might unite the two kingdoms. With Philip II and the whole Counter-Reformation movement upon her side, it appeared not improbable that she might displace Elizabeth, restore Catholicism in England, and unite the two crowns in her own person.

At the bottom of all Elizabeth's diplomacy until Mary's death lurks the secret fear that England might once more become Catholic, drive Elizabeth from her throne, and place the crown upon the Queen of Scots. Had the course of Mary been governed by prudence rather than by sentiment and passion, England might easily have had a different history. Her favor for her Italian secretary, Rizzio,— whose assassination was considered by the Scotch an act of patriotism,[1]— her complicity in the murder of Darnley, and her infatuation for Bothwell all tended to destroy that hold upon her people which the natural gifts and accomplishments of the Queen of Scots might have enabled her to retain. Her enforced abdication on July 24, 1567, and the coronation of the infant James under a Protestant regency, if not entirely the fruits of her own folly, were at least immense advantages to the good fortune of Elizabeth. A fugitive in the kingdom of her rival, the ill-starred Queen of Scots had by 1568 sunk to the level of a discredited exile; and to this humiliation she added the fatal indiscretion of permitting herself to become the centre of conspiracies against her protectress while still within her power.

---

[1] He was charged with conspiring with the Pope and the King of Spain to bring foreign troops into the kingdom.

CHAP. VII
A. D.
1559-1576

William the "Silent"

These conspiracies would, no doubt, have had a more prosperous development had Philip II not been embarrassed by an unexpected preoccupation. In the Netherlands a condition of affairs had arisen which had been dimly foreseen as a possibility even in the time of Charles V. To arrest the progress of Lutheranism, that emperor had introduced the Inquisition into the Netherlands as early as the year 1522, and even in his lifetime a great number of persons had been put to death as heretics; but the comparative moderation of Charles V and the practical wisdom of his aunt and sister as regents had now been superseded by the resolute fanaticism of Philip II, who, to the discontent of nearly the whole population, had organized new ecclesiastical machinery for the purpose of destroying heresy root and branch.

By a strange indiscretion the purpose of Philip II in the Netherlands was known in time to permit of the organization of opposition to his plans. Among the hostages sent to Paris by the King of Spain to guarantee the execution of the Treaty of Cateau-Cambrésis, was William Count of Nassau, who from his titular principality in the heart of the papal territory of Avignon bore the name, the Prince of Orange. While hunting in the Bois de Vincennes, Henry II, forgetting for the moment that the Prince did not know of the secret compact between France and Spain to crush out heresy, had confidentially exposed to him his intention to purge his realm of the "accursed vermin," who, he declared, under the cover of religion, would some day try to overthrow his government, but whom by the aid of the King of Spain he hoped to exterminate, although they included some of his highest nobles and even princes of the blood. With respectful attention the Prince of Orange listened without reply, as if he knew of the agreement, until he had learned all the details of the plan to destroy heresy in the Netherlands, in whose prosecution the Spanish troops were to be employed; and it is from this incident that he acquired the name the "Silent."

"From that hour," he wrote in his "Apology" twenty years afterward, "I resolved with my whole soul to do my best to drive this Spanish vermin from the land; and of this resolve I have never repented." Rich, eloquent, popular, and powerful, the Prince of Orange, although a Catholic, a personal favorite of the late emperor, and a general and councillor of the King of Spain, flung his whole soul into the cause of preventing the massacres that had been planned by causing the withdrawal of the Spanish soldiers from the Netherlands and securing a just and humane government of the country by the States General. Loyal to the Regent, the half-sister of Philip II, Margaret of Parma, William the Silent, — having been commissioned Governor of Holland, Zeeland, and Utrecht, and placed with Count Egmont in command of the Spanish troops, — had by 1564 not only succeeded in obtaining the removal of the Spanish army but with the aid of Counts Egmont and Horn the recall of Cardinal Granvelle, who, as the first minister of Philip II in the Netherlands, had been the chief instrument of the King's new policies. But all this had not averted the impending disaster. Resolved to "spare neither money nor life to maintain the faith," the King of Spain, on October 17, 1565, had sent the order that his will should be enforced by the inquisitors and that all the heretics should be put to death.

Following soon after the celebrated interview at Bayonne, of June 14, 1565, between Catherine de' Medici, Queen Elizabeth of Spain, and the Duke of Alba, at which a compact for the joint extirpation of heresy by France and Spain was believed to have been concluded, the orders of Philip II had aroused a feeling of terror in the Netherlands.[1] Until that

---

[1] The instructions of Philip II to the Duke of Alba are found in the Paris Archives C. K. 1393, B. 192, and are printed by Hume, *Calendar*, I, page lv of his introduction. They show that the most rigorous extermination of new doctrines was to be undertaken in both kingdoms. That Catherine de' Medici actually negotiated with Philip II such a league is proved by her letter to De Fourquevault, her

CHAP. VII
A. D.
1559-1576

time, since the death of Francis II, Catherine de' Medici, whose passion was to govern France at any cost, had balanced the Protestants against the Catholics and found her advantage in a policy of toleration. Now, however, it was believed, Spain and France were to unite in executing the earlier agreement between Philip II and Henry II.

To meet this danger, in November, 1565, twenty confederates had met in the house of Count Culemburg in Brussels and formed a league to resist the Inquisition. The Prince of Orange had announced that he would resign his office rather than execute the edicts, and the Regent had informed her brother that since the provincial governors refused to burn fifty or sixty thousand persons she was unable to enforce his orders; but all was in vain, and in August, 1566, a wave of popular resentment had swept over the Netherlands, in which the churches were desecrated by angry mobs. Furious with rage, the King swore by the soul of his father that it should cost the rebels dear.

The statesmanship of the Prince of Orange

Under strict orders to repress the disturbances, William the Silent was averse to the use of violence when he knew that only a reasonable course was necessary, and urged the Regent to suspend the edicts for the punishment of heretics; but in doing so she registered a formal protest that her act was null and void, and secretly denounced the Prince of Orange to the King.

In the spirit of a loyal minister, the Prince had honestly endeavored to suppress disorder, but he clearly perceived the true reason of its origin. Dependent upon commerce and intercourse with foreigners for their prosperity, the States of the Netherlands, surrounded by Catholic and Protestant neighbors, could not, he thought, prevent diversities of religious opinion among their populations. Their prosperity, and even their existence, depended upon religious toleration. "There is no reason to be amazed," he writes in one of his

---

minister in Spain, after her return from Bayonne, preserved in the Bibliothèque Nationale at Paris, also cited by Hume.

manifestoes, "much less to fly to arms, because a large part of the inhabitants of this country embrace and profess opinions contrary to those of their rulers.... A very large part of our people have embraced the new views, and rather than forsake them they will give up their lives and homes. To crush them into orthodoxy by force is impossible or intolerable. If their opinions are false, if the Catholic faith be based on eternal truth, their doctrines will melt away in good time, like the snow before the sun."

Being neither Lutheran nor Calvinist, the Prince could not comprehend the bitterness with which the Protestant sects regarded one another. His scheme of "neutralizing" the Netherlands, — that is, in substance, the toleration of all creeds, — discloses the deep and far-seeing quality of his statesmanship. To realize it, he was eager to obtain aid from the Lutherans of Germany, the Huguenots of France, and the Anglicans of England; but his efforts soon revealed the difficulties of this course. In his endeavors to form a league of German princes, he found that unless the Netherlanders abandoned Calvinism and accepted the Augsburg Confession, no important aid could be expected from the Germans. Failing in his attempts to break down sectarian prejudice by appeals for Christian sympathy, in order to unite the Protestants he even brought Lutheran theologians from Germany in the hope of convincing the Calvinists by argument. Finally, when all had failed, unable to avert the storm about to burst upon the Netherlands, after calming the fanatical rising at Antwerp, in April, 1567, the Prince of Orange retired from the scene to organize resistance from without.

While William the Silent was departing from the Netherlands the Duke of Alba was leaving Spain with an overwhelming army for the extermination of the heretics. The tragic story of his terrible invasion is, perhaps, the most exciting chapter of modern history. Never before had arbitrary power been less restrained by law or reason. With pitiless cruelty the mere suspicion of heresy was visited with

The triumph of Philip II in the Netherlands

CHAP. VII
A. D.
1559-1576

immediate death, until the desolated provinces lay helpless at the feet of the conqueror. In vain the Prince of Orange and his brother Louis of Nassau impoverished themselves in raising armies to withstand the consummate military genius of Alba, before whose advance they steadily melted away. In vain succor was implored from France, from England, and from Germany. In the silent gloom of the Duke's victories, heresy and patriotism seemed at last to have been utterly extinguished.

During the next four years the Netherlands were dumb with terror. Margaret of Parma resigned her office, the "Council of Blood" was organized, Counts Egmont and Horn were executed, the Prince of Orange found safety only in exile, and the Duke of Alba reigned supreme until his exaction of the tenth penny on all commercial transactions carried his system of oppression to an extreme which even Philip II could not sustain. But, in the meantime, strengthened by his success in the Netherlands and his supposed *entente* with the Queen Regent of France, the King of Spain seemed to be in a favorable position to take a part in the affairs of England.

Attitude of Philip II toward England

The first offensive action of Philip II toward England was the summary dismissal of the English ambassador, Dr. Man, in the spring of 1568, because the King would not tolerate the reformed faith in Spain even in the person of a diplomatic agent. There were, in truth, better reasons for dismissing the English ambassador; for Spanish commerce had been cruelly despoiled by English pirates with the Queen's consent, if not by her direction. But there were reasons why the King of Spain preferred for the time to avoid open war with England. At home, he was embarrassed by the insurrection of the Moriscoes, whom the Inquisition had driven to desperation; in Italy, he had not yet settled his quarrel with Pope Pius V concerning the conflict of the papal and the royal authority over the prelates of his realm; and in the Mediterranean, he was menaced by the Ottoman ascendency. In case the Netherlands should again revolt and should receive aid from Elizabeth, he might yet be unable to retain possession of them.

If Philip II had been prepared for hostilities, the occasion would, however, have been favorable; for the agents of Mary Stuart were pressing hard for Spanish aid, while the Catholic nobles of England were eager to restore the exiled queen to her rights in Scotland, and even to dethrone Elizabeth and put her rival in her place.[1] Although instructed by the King to cultivate the friendship of the Queen, the Spanish ambassador, De Spes, was in close relations with the Duke of Norfolk,[2] who had conceived the bold design of marrying Mary, uniting England and Scotland, and making himself the ruler of both realms.

Even in these delicate circumstances, the English privateers continued to capture the ships of Spain. To escape them, some vessels carrying specie to pay the troops of Alba ran for security into English ports; when, on the pretence of protecting it from capture, Elizabeth took possession of the money and decided to borrow it herself from the Genoese bankers who were sending it.

The Spanish ambassador threatened vengeance, and urged the King to invade England and dethrone Elizabeth. But the methods of Philip II were slow and intricate, and he referred the proposition to the Duke of Alba; in the meantime contenting himself with the seizure of English property in Spain, which Elizabeth's government regarded as justifying a still further appropriation of Spanish spoils.

---

[1] The following table shows the claim of Mary Queen of Scots to the English throne:

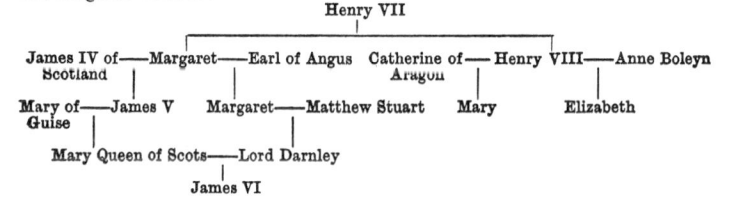

```
                          Henry VII
                              |
    ┌─────────────────────────┴─────────────────────────┐
James IV of—Margaret—Earl of Angus   Catherine of—Henry VIII—Anne Boleyn
 Scotland    |              |          Aragon      |              |
Mary of—James V    Margaret—Matthew Stuart         Mary      Elizabeth
 Guise    |
     Mary Queen of Scots—Lord Darnley
                    |
                 James VI
```

[2] See Hume, I, *Calendar*, No. 213.

In England, the Queen's chief minister, William Cecil, was anxious for war. As a Protestant, he knew that his own security and that of his co-religionists depended entirely upon Elizabeth's tenure of the throne, and he well understood that nothing would so rally the nation round her as an attack by the King of Spain; but Elizabeth herself, though willing to harass her enemy, wished above all to secure the peace of her kingdom, which she hoped to do by restoring Mary Stuart to her Scottish throne, maintaining thereby the doctrine of legitimacy, and thus ending the peril in which the presence of the Queen of Scots in England placed her.

On the Spanish side, the Duke of Alba and Philip II himself would have been pleased to aid both in the restoration of Mary to her Scottish throne and her plans to become Queen of England; but they feared a renewal of troubles in the Netherlands, suspected France, and dreaded a possible alliance between France and England. The prompt energy with which Elizabeth's government discovered the plots against her, took possession of Mary's person, arrested the Duke of Norfolk, suppressed the Catholic rising in the North, and thus rendered abortive the conspiracies that filled the summer and autumn of 1569 suddenly changed the situation, and the assistance that the conspirators had sought from Spain, and which, if it had been available a year earlier, might, perhaps, have been effectual, was then seen to be untimely.

The excommunication of Elizabeth by the bull of Pope Pius V, which the English Catholics had long desired, was finally published on February 25, 1570.[1] Like the aid ex-

---

[1] An English translation of this bull is printed by Brown, *Calendar*, VII, No. 475. The Queen is referred to as "that servant of all iniquity, Elizabeth, pretended queen of England, with whom as in a secure place, all the worst kind of men find a refuge." After reciting the charges against her as a heretic, the sentence of malediction is pronounced upon her adherents, she is " wholly deprived of her pretended right," her subjects are liberated from their oaths of alle-

pected from Spain, however, it had come too tardily to be of use to the English conspirators, and produced an effect quite contrary to their expectations. Even Philip II foresaw that its result would be to rally the nation round the Queen, and he urged the Pope to suspend it. In forbidding the English people to recognize Elizabeth as their sovereign, the Pope had forced them to regard Protestantism and patriotism as for them only different aspects of the same reality.

While England was thus resenting the papal interference and condemning the Catholic conspiracies, the Court of France was making its peace with the Huguenots by the Treaty of St. Germain, of August 8, 1570. Immediately Elizabeth reached out the hand of friendship. In previous years she had furnished aid to the Huguenots, and had received temporary possession of Havre as her reward, then suddenly lost it by the defeat of her allies; but now, for the first time since the beginning of her reign, a close defensive alliance with France against Spain was unexpectedly made possible. Charles IX, having reached his majority, had been favorable to the Huguenots, Catherine de' Medici was quite ready to use them against the hated Guises, and the growing power of Philip II, which the presence of Alba's army in the Netherlands rendered menacing to France, was exciting the alarm of French statesmen.

At no time during her tempestuous reign was Elizabeth exposed to greater danger, and at no time did she take more prompt or effective advantage of her opportunity. Even a brief delay might have been fatal to her, for Catherine de' Medici was considering a scheme to espouse the cause of the Queen of Scots, procure her hand in marriage with her third son, the Duke of Anjou — afterward Henry III — and thus renew the Valois claims to the crown of Scotland, and ultimately to that of England also.

The alliance of France and England

---

giance, and they are commanded not to obey her laws or commandments under the penalty of the sentence of malediction.

CHAP. VII
A. D.
1559-1576

But Elizabeth not only welcomed the *rapprochement* of France, with consummate skill she announced her own readiness to marry the Duke of Anjou, of which she had not the slightest intention, and thus encouraged the French advances. Although no formal treaty was concluded until April 29, 1572,[1] the benefits of the prospective alliance were immediately felt; for they went far toward rendering Elizabeth secure at home as well as safe from attacks abroad. When the proposed union with Anjou had served its temporary purpose, his younger brother, Alençon, succeeded him as a candidate for the hand of Elizabeth, and for eleven years she used this tender youth as a pawn in her negotiations.

The real value of the Anglo-French *entente* was apparent as early as July, 1571, when the Italian banker Ridolfi,— a secret agent of the Pope, of Mary Stuart, and of the Duke of Norfolk,— went from London to Madrid to urge upon Philip II a Spanish invasion of England, for which he promised the support of the English Catholics. The King of Spain was too well advised of the situation to lend himself to a scheme so chimerical, and the conspirator received little encouragement; for Philip refused to risk sending Spanish troops to England, unless Elizabeth were first assassinated or confined in prison.[2]

The general paralysis of international activity

During the remainder of his lifetime, Philip II never abandoned the hope of restoring the kingdom of which he had once been the titular king to its ancient faith and place in the papal system; but for many years, although Spain was apparently becoming the predominant power in Europe, no opportunity was presented for an effective attack upon England.

[1] See Dumont, V, Part I, pp. 211, 215.

[2] There is a passage in the instructions of Philip II to Medina-Celi, who in November, 1571, was sent to replace the Duke of Alba in the Netherlands, which proves that the King of Spain had at one time made up his mind to aid the Ridolfi plot. See Hume, *Calendar*, II, No. 289.

Apart from their effect upon the destiny of the ill-fated Queen of Scots, the chief historical importance of the intrigues promoted by papal and Spanish influences in England lies in the support which the English nation gave to the throne by its opposition to all foreign interference and its emphasis of its own supreme authority in the enactment of laws making it treason to deny that the succession could be determined by the Queen and the Parliament, consolidating the Church of England, and adopting the Thirty-nine Articles as the standard of its faith. The impact of foreign intervention had brought the English people to the full consciousness of their dangers and of their grounds of security as a nation.

It was fortunate for Elizabeth that she was asserting the sufficiency of her own people to regulate their own existence at a moment when no nation of Europe was in a position to execute a policy of opposition. Spain was still uncertain regarding the future of the Netherlands, in which the spirit of revolt, renewed by the Duke of Alba's cruelties, was soon to rise to a height of heroism almost unparalleled. France was divided into hostile camps by the question of religion, ruled by a succession of young monarchs under the influence of a woman of foreign birth and character, and directed alternately by counsellors of opposing parties. Germany, under the moderate and tolerant rule of the Emperor Maximilian II, was really a system of small states rather than a single state, in fact governed by its local princes, and kept in a condition of innocuous equilibrium by the balance of the Catholic and Protestant elements. The Scandinavian kingdoms were still in isolation from the general life of Europe, and Italy was comparatively tranquil under the predominant influence of the Pope and the King of Spain.

But if the period was one of relative impotence in the execution of great schemes of international readjustment, it was fertile in changes of thought more permanent in their results than the tragic incidents of conspiracy and assassination with which its records are crowded. Everywhere, but

The new theories of the State

CHAP. VII
A. D.
1559-1576

for different reasons, men were attaching a new importance to the State. In Spain, it was silently imposing its authority upon every faculty of the mind and crushing out every impulse of independent thought. In England, it was solidifying the royal power as the only safe refuge from anarchy, not by the elaboration of any new theory but under the guidance of practical necessity. In France, however, the rule of parties had opened a great debate regarding the ends, the nature, and the means of government, such as Europe had never known before. The rights of conscience, there so bitterly contested and so nobly defended, were seen to be bound up with the political fabric, and to have inseparable relations with the forms of civil society.

All these questions turn, in the last analysis, upon the source and nature of supreme authority. Where does it reside, and what is its origin?

Theories of royal power

In matters so practical as government, it is always conditions rather than theories that determine the course of historical events. In many ways, the circumstances of the time tended powerfully to confirm the royal authority in every European monarchy. In Spain, it was aided by the Holy Inquisition; in England, by a strong reaction against conspiracies for the overthrow of the existing monarch; in France, by the effects of the civil wars, which threatened to dismember the nation. What was most important to the international development of Europe is, that it was amidst these dangers that were elaborated those theories of the nature of the State and the prerogatives of the monarch upon which the political system of Europe has been erected.

Before the shock produced by the wholesale massacre of the Huguenot leaders on St. Bartholomew's Day, August 24, 1572, the absolutism which the Valois kings had imposed upon France had passed unquestioned, and even Calvin, who placed the authority of conscience above that of the king, commended submission to the royal power. While each of the religious parties had striven to control the royal authority, neither had raised objection to it; but when a crime so monstrous could be committed with the approval if not at the command of the king at the instance of his mother's passion for personal power, the aureole of sanctity seemed to vanish from the head of Charles IX, and earnest men thought chiefly of escape from a tyranny so revolting. As in the days of the Great Schism writers had ventured to review the prerogatives of the Holy See, so now men like François Hotman, Hubert Languet, Du Plessis-Mornay, and others began to discuss those of the Crown.

For a time, it seemed as if the revolutionary spirit would destroy France, as the Revolution two centuries later threatened to engulf it; but the death of Charles IX on May 30, 1574, and the accession of the Duke of Anjou as Henry III made it possible to defend once more the royal power as essential to the being of the State. It was then that Jean Bodin put his legal knowledge and ingenuity at the service of his king, and in 1576 offered to the world his famous work, "La République," the classic text-book on the nature of sovereign states.[1]

What is it, then, that serves as the foundation of a state? Inherent in the essence of an independent political community is the attribute of "Sovereignty," — absolute, indivisible, inalienable. He who represents it is the source of all law. There is no one above him or beside him to command or control him. Sovereignty, being absolute, admits of no limitation within the state; being indivisible, it cannot be shared or partitioned; being inalienable, it cannot be lost or taken away.

Such is the abstraction enthroned by Bodin. It is not, strictly speaking, a product of pure speculation but a result arrived at by historical analysis. It is the *majestas* or *imperium*, of the Roman law, no longer conceived of as uni-

---

[1] See Bodin, *Les six livres de la république*, Paris, 1576; and his own translation of it into Latin, Paris, 1591. The book soon ran through several editions in French and Latin, and was used as a text-book in the French and foreign universities.

versal, but as territorial; for it may exist in many forms and be represented in different ways. Of these Bodin considers an absolute monarchy the best, but historically he does not deny the existence of other modes of embodying sovereignty, which originally belonged to the members of the body politic in their totality, but without being effective until organized in some definite manner.

The sovereign is not, in Bodin's view, a wholly arbitrary being, as Machiavelli conceived him to be; for there are in the nature of man and of society certain natural and moral laws which ought to be obeyed; but, since the laws of the State emanate from the sovereign, he is absolved from obedience to them.

In offering to the world this conception, based on the omnipotence of French monarchs like Francis I, who furnished his ideal of a great sovereign, Bodin was well within the limits of historic facts. What he did was simply to disengage from its concrete setting the central, essential, and fundamental idea of sovereignty, upon which has been erected, with certain modifications, the present political system of Europe and the whole structure of modern international law. With the conception of the Sovereign State as a legal reality, jurisprudence had found a new field of labor, and diplomacy a domain in which it was soon to be supplied with new elements of practice.

Significance of the principle of sovereignty

That which gave to Bodin's conception a vital relation to the thought of his time was the fact that it satisfied a practical need. In an age when the State was so seriously threatened as an institution, a system of ideas so cogent, so logical, and so historical as that presented in Bodin's work could not fail to make a profound impression. Commending itself to sovereigns as a reasoned vindication of their rights, it proposed also to the disturbed states of Europe a refuge from the untried theories of neologists, from the horrors of civil war, and from the conspiracies and intrigues of factions and foreign powers.

The principle of sovereignty as enunciated by Bodin, by

placing the sovereign above and beyond the reach of all authority, made him the sole judge of his own rights and prerogatives. Within his realm, the sovereign prince was thus made absolute; but even beyond it he possessed, by virtue of his sovereignty, one exclusive privilege, — that of being represented by ambassadors.

In 1571, an incident had occurred in England that involved this attribute of sovereignty. Three years earlier, John Leslie, Bishop of Ross, had appeared at York as one of the representatives of the Queen of Scots to defend her before the commissioners appointed by Queen Elizabeth for the investigation of complaints brought against the deposed queen by her Scotch subjects, and afterward remained in London as her ambassador. Having been detected as an active agent in the plots which resulted in the execution of the Duke of Norfolk, he was brought to trial as a conspirator. In defence, he pleaded the immunity of an ambassador, whereupon, instead of judging him by English law, five persons learned in the Roman law were asked the following questions: (1) Whether an ambassador found in rebellion against the prince to whom he is sent may enjoy ambassadorial privileges, and may not be punished as an enemy? (2) Whether the representative of a deposed prince whose place is held by another may enjoy the privileges of an ambassador? (3) Whether a prince who has come into the kingdom of another prince, and is kept in custody, may be so represented? and (4) Whether, if denounced by the prince of the kingdom in which he is, such a representative may still claim ambassadorial privileges?

The answers to these questions were, that no prince lawfully deposed, or who does not have the absolute prerogatives of "majesty," can accredit ambassadors; that a prince who has not forfeited his principality may have an ambassador, even though in custody in another's kingdom, but whether or not his agent may claim ambassadorial rights depends upon that agent's credentials; finally, a prince may prohibit an ambassador from entering his kingdom, or command him to depart from it, if he "contain not himself within the bounds prescribed to an envoy"; yet in the meantime, he may enjoy ambassadorial privileges.[1]

In reply, the Bishop claimed that Mary was an absolute queen, that he had faithfully sought her deliverance and the safety of both kingdoms, that he possessed full authority as an ambassador, and that on this account he could not rightly be condemned. After further interrogation and a period of confinement in the Tower of London, he was ordered to leave the kingdom.

Nature of a sovereign state In rendering judgment in the case of the Bishop of Ross, the English experts in Roman law had employed as the basis of their decision a conception of the State similar to that of Bodin. According to that conception, the right of embassy does not belong to every great and powerful personage but only to a legal sovereign, the head of a sovereign state. It is only through the headship of an independent state that a prince is a sovereign, and only as such that he can accredit persons who may enjoy ambassadorial immunities.

What, then, is a state? Bodin began his great work with the definition, "A republic, *respublica*, is a rightful government of several households, and of that which is common to them, with sovereign power"; which is his fashion of saying that a community of families, not subject to a superior power outside of itself, when organized under a rightful government, constitutes a sovereign state. In a monarchy, the king has received by delegation the sovereign power; which, being absolute, indivisible, and perpetual, rests wholly in his hands. He alone, therefore, embodies in his person the representation of the State.

It is the State, however, and not merely the royal personage who constitutes its head, that now and henceforth will claim attention. In the feudal age, there was no conception of the State. Society was then composed of a hierarchy of

---

[1] Camden, *Historie of the Most Renowned and Victorious Princesse Elizabeth*, II, p. 26.

persons bound together in relations of vassalage and suzerainty. In the development of the national monarchies, the kings gradually concentrated in their own hands all public authority by absorbing in their own persons the prerogatives of the feudal lords. With the growth of national consciousness in the populations thus brought under royal control, modern states came into being; but the kings were still, in most cases, personifications of all the public powers. It was only when, at last, it became necessary to confirm the royal authority, threatened by rebellion, conspiracy, and civil war, by appealing to general principles, that the king was set forth as the legal representative of the State, thenceforth distinctly conceived of as an institution necessary to the peace and well-being of mankind.

Whether regarded as an institution brought into existence by contract or developed from divinely imposed natural conditions, the State was now represented as possessing inherent moral qualities. It was upon this ground that, in Bodin's theory, the dignity of the royal authority was made to rest. Thitherto, kingdoms and principalities had been treated very much as personal possessions, and were regarded as offering a legitimate field for conquest by those at war with the ruling prince. But in directing attention to the nature and origin of the State as a social organism a new realm of thought was opened. According to any theory, when it was once made the subject of analysis, the purpose of the State was seen to be the protection of the individuals composing it from injustice within its borders, and of the body politic as a whole from the attacks of foreign powers. As was soon pointed out, sovereignty is, therefore, for the person who represents it, "not an honor but a trust, not an immunity but a duty, not an exemption but a mission."[1] Kings are not irresponsible autocrats, they are the guardians and conservators of justice. The State

---

[1] The words of Hubert Languet in the *Vindiciae contra Tyrannos*, Paris, 1579.

is greater than its ruler, for the greatness of the ruler is derived from the sovereignty which he represents.[1]

A little later, the German jurist Althusius, while accepting Bodin's conception of sovereignty as the foundation of the State, under the influence of his observations in the Netherlands, defines it as "a right indivisible, incommunicable, and imprescriptible," belonging from its very nature, not to kings or princes, but to the whole body politic.[2] The State begins, therefore, to be conceived of as a moral being, possessing inherent rights; and, by deduction, charged with moral obligations.

By the force of circumstances, Queen Elizabeth was, more than any other ruler of her time, a champion of the conception of the State which the jurists were slowly working out in theory. The security of her throne depended entirely upon her representing the substantial interests of the English people, and this from the beginning she had resolved to do. Here was the key of her foreign policy, and while her ministers were often moved by party interests and sectarian passions, she steadily and unswervingly, sometimes in opposition to their will, stood for the well-being of the nation. She clearly perceived that too much aggression in Scotland would create new dangers at home, that the conquest and partition of the Netherlands in partnership with France, which were urged upon her by her ally and by her own ministers, would not only concentrate upon her kingdom all the power of Philip II but establish a traditional rival in a position of advantage; and that the advice of Cecil, in 1571 created Lord Burghley, that she should become the head of a great Prot-

---

[1] Similar doctrines are found in the work of the Scotch writer George Buchanan, *De Jure Regni apud Scotos*, published in 1580, who regards the king as created not for himself but for the people, — "*non sibi sed populo creatus.*"

[2] The title of the work of Althusius, published at Herborn in 1603, is *Politica Methodice Digesta et Exemplis Sacris et Profanis Illustrata*. See Gierke, *Johannes Althusius und die Entwickelung der naturrechtlichen Staatstheorien* for a full analysis of his work.

estant coalition against Spain, in which France was expected to join, was an imprudent proposition. She clearly perceived that, for political reasons, the French Court would finally remain Catholic; and that, so long as she could maintain a merely defensive alliance with that kingdom she would be able to secure England from attack by Philip II, while at the same time secretly aiding his opponents in the Netherlands and enriching her privateers by permitting them to prey upon Spanish commerce.

It was, it is true, only on the side of sovereign rights, not on that of international duties, that Elizabeth apprehended the conception of the State; but in this she was only following the general law of social development, in which duties are first discerned as the logical correlatives of rights. While robbing without compunction the Spanish merchantmen, she appealed, as we shall soon see, to a "law of nations" as an authoritative rule of conduct, and thereby contributed more than any other ruler before her to the recognition of principles of natural justice in the intercourse of sovereign states.

II. THE GENESIS OF INTERNATIONAL JURISPRUDENCE

Until the conception of the State was generally accepted, it was impossible that any principles of jurisprudence based upon it could obtain wide recognition. For Philip II, whose family had risen to power through a series of conquests by marriage, the relation of a sovereign to his subjects was merely a matter of hereditary right. To obtain that right over England he had married Mary Tudor. It was not unnatural, therefore, that a similar project should occur to his brilliant half-brother, Don John of Austria, the hero who had defeated the Turks at Lepanto on October 7, 1571, and one of the ablest generals of his time. On May 27, 1576, he wrote to the King of Spain just before going to the Netherlands as viceroy: "The true remedy for the evil condition of these Provinces in the judgment of all men is that England should be in the power of a person devoted and well

CHAP. VII
A. D.
1576-1610

affectioned to Your Majesty's service; and it is the general opinion that the ruin of these countries and the impossibility of preserving them to Your Majesty's crown will result from the contrary position of English affairs. At Rome, and elsewhere, the rumor prevails that Your Majesty and His Holiness have thought of me as the best instrument you could choose for the execution of your designs, offended as you are by the evil proceedings of the Queen of England, and by the wrongs which she has done to the Queen of Scotland, especially in sustaining against her heresy in that kingdom." [1]

To excite Catholic conspiracies in England, to put forward the claims of Mary Queen of Scots as rightful successor to the throne, to marry her, and thus become King of England, — such was the bold scheme of this natural son of Charles V; but both the prudence and the jealousy of Philip II were opposed to an adventure which England and France would combine to defeat, and which, if successful, would place the talented half-brother in a position too commanding for the King's advantage. Mary Stuart herself, however, appears to have been ready to support such a plan; for she afterward drew up a testament in which, if her son did not depart from heresy, she ceded all her rights in England and elsewhere to the Catholic king, or "others of his family at his pleasure."

The Pacification of Ghent

But, aside from the hesitation of Philip II to support the ambitious project of Don John, there were material difficulties in the way of its execution. In the Netherlands, the Duke of Alba had been succeeded by Requesens, who had died at his post; and the Prince of Orange, with indefatigable toil, was still opposing the King's policy of oppression. Three things he had persistently demanded, and these he continued to require: (1) the withdrawal of all Spaniards from the Provinces; (2) the free exercise of religion; and (3) the restoration of the ancient rights and liberties of the land. By the Union of Delft, of April 25, 1576, he had federated

---

[1] Cited by Seeley, *The Growth of British Policy*, I, p. 152.

Holland and Zeeland, — the slender beginning of the United Netherlands; and, on November 8, 1576, was concluded under the stimulus of the military excesses to which the Provinces had been subjected, a solemn treaty known as the Pacification of Ghent, by which the other fifteen Provinces leagued themselves with Holland and Zeeland to expel the Spaniards and establish religious toleration. By this compact Protestants and Catholics were at last united in a pledge to drive out their foreign oppressors.

When, therefore, Don John arrived in the Netherlands, it was to find them once more in open revolt, and this time united. To carry out his ambitious schemes in England, the difficulties of the Netherlands must be composed, and the new viceroy set about winning the confidence of the Provinces. His apparent clemency, his personal powers of fascination, and his moderate measures at first promised to disarm even the astute Prince of Orange; but that experienced statesman was not to be long blinded by the overtures of this new antagonist. Insisting upon the withdrawal of the Spanish troops and the acceptance of the Pacification of Ghent as necessary conditions of peace, the Prince drove Don John to sign the Perpetual Edict of February 17, 1577, which was, however, only a truce without guarantees which the Viceroy did not intend to observe longer than circumstances required. But William was the first to see that it was illusory, and Don John realized that without his consent no final settlement was possible. "He is the pilot who steers the ship; he alone can wreck it or save it," wrote the Viceroy to the King. To support Don John, Philip II even ratified the Perpetual Edict, the Spanish troops were temporarily again withdrawn, and the Viceroy set up his government in Brussels; but the Prince distrusted promises from which the Pope could easily dispense the King, and the people had such confidence in him as their leader that Don John wrote to Philip: "I see no other way to prevent the ruin of the State but the defeat of this man, who exerts such an influence over the nation."

CHAP. VII
A. D.
1576-1610

The civic spirit in the Netherlands

So far as the rule of Spain was concerned, the Viceroy had expressed the truth. The Prince of Orange, now himself a confessed Calvinist, had decided that the Netherlands should throw off the Spanish yoke, and his determination was unalterable. Nor was he unprepared for the conflict. Breda, Utrecht, Haarlem, and Amsterdam were soon in possession of his friends; and Antwerp and Ghent had already demolished their citadels. From the Zuider Zee to the Schelde, he was in command of the country, and his triumphant entry into Brussels in September, 1577, whence Don John had departed, proved how completely he was in the ascendency.

It was, beyond question, the distrust which William of Orange felt toward the Viceroy's promises which ended the long negotiations for peace, and his suspicions are evidence of his keen discernment; for Philip II had, as time revealed, already commanded the return of the Spanish troops.

Thus was resumed the struggle of the Netherlands with Spain, which was now to take the form of a battle for independence. In the Southern Provinces, the nobles were jealous of the Prince of Orange, whom they regarded as an ambitious heretic; but in the North, the spirit of autonomy was stronger, and the remembrance of the liberties formerly enjoyed awakened an intense civic consciousness which foreboded the formation of an independent state.

It was, in fact, in the Northern Provinces of the Netherlands more than anywhere else in Europe, except in Switzerland, that the whole population was permeated with the conviction that the State is a creation of the will of the people. The ancient privilege of being taxed only by their own representatives, the Calvinistic idea of the dignity of the individual, the terrible tyranny imposed upon them by foreign rule, and their native passion for personal liberty all combined to impel the inhabitants to rally round the Prince of Orange when he exhorted them "to let the King see that this is no revolt stirred up by men of influence, as he fancies, but that it is the general voice of the entire people, . . . who, without difference of age, sex, or condition, call aloud with one voice for justice. Let him know that, if he refuses it, you will throw yourselves into the arms of the ancient enemy of his house." Never before had the inherent prerogatives of a state been so clearly set before a reigning sovereign. It marked the entrance into practice of a new theory of the State as an embodiment of the sovereign will of a nation.

Negotiations of William the Silent for foreign aid

The Prince of Orange hoped at this moment that, if he could obtain the aid of England, he would be able to secure the independence of the Netherlands; but Elizabeth was too cautious to do more than guarantee a large loan of money to the rebels. Her policy was, not to enfranchise the Netherlands at once, for that would leave Philip II free to concentrate his forces upon herself; nor yet to allow the Provinces to pass under the protectorate of France, for that would have a similar effect with the added disadvantage of establishing the French preponderance. Her aim was, by keeping the revolt of the Netherlands alive to occupy and gradually enfeeble Spain, and at the same time to hold France as an ally by the fear of Philip's ultimate success.

The arrival in the Netherlands of his nephew, the great Italian general, Alessandro Farnese, Prince of Parma, in January, 1578, with a larger army than Alba had commanded, revealed the determination of Philip II to crush the revolt by force, and the victories of the Prince of Parma in the field and in winning over by negotiation the cities of the Southern Provinces soon changed the position of William the Silent to one of dire extremity. Without hope from England, and soon convinced that nothing could be expected from the Austrian Archduke Matthias, brother of the new emperor, Rudolf II, who had been invited by the Catholics to work out a compromise between the Prince of Orange and Don John, the Prince turned as a last hope to France; and in August, 1578, Alençon — now known also as the Duke of Anjou — was made " Defender of the liberty of the Netherlands." Broken in health and humbled in spirit, Don John passed away in the following October, and the Prince of Parma, the greatest military genius of his age, succeeded him as viceroy.

The Prince of Orange was now confronted with a double problem,—the securing of effective aid from without, and the maintenance of union within the Netherlands. The difficulty at the root of both was the question of religion. Alençon was a Catholic, but in France, although the next heir to the throne, he was considered an untrustworthy adventurer, and could not count upon serious official support. In the Netherlands, he was regarded with distrust, which he merited, and the remedy he might offer seemed as bad as the disease he was called in to cure. In sustaining him, which he thought it expedient to do, the Prince of Orange was risking his own popularity with his firmest supporters, who expected from the Duke the treason with which he finally betrayed all who trusted him. For Elizabeth, Alençon's presence in the Netherlands was a satisfaction; for it enabled her to prolong her marriage intrigue with him, by which she was accomplishing the double end of using the Netherlands as a guard against an attack upon herself by Philip II and of holding fast the French alliance.

But the real obstacle to the aim of William the Silent, the union of the seventeen provinces in an independent state, was the incompatibility of the Catholics and the Protestants, whose mutual hostility was the chief lever of the Prince of Parma in dividing the Provinces. In this he was so successful that the Pacification of Ghent was soon nullified, and by the Treaty of Arras the Southern Provinces agreed to maintain the Catholic religion, and in effect to submit to Philip II.

At the same time, by the Union of Utrecht, of January 23, 1579, Gelderland, Holland, Utrecht, Groningen, and Zeeland united to sustain the Protestant religion and to renounce allegiance to the King of Spain. Thus the great plan of the Prince of Orange for uniting all of the Netherlands was defeated, and the independent state which he had hoped to create was reduced to a union of the Northern Provinces.

To destroy this league, a price was placed upon his head, hired assassins were set upon his track, and in the famous ban issued by Philip II on March 15, 1580, the King of Spain offered to pay to any one who would " deliver him dead or alive, or take his life, the sum of twenty thousand crowns in gold, or in estates for himself and his heirs; we will pardon the successful person any crime if he has been guilty, and give him a patent of nobility if he be not noble; and we will do the same for all his accomplices and agents."

In striking thus directly at the person of William the Silent, Philip II was aiming a blow in the name of absolute and irresponsible despotism against the embodiment of the idea of the State as a self-constituted moral organism; for it was in the Netherlands that, both in theory and practice, that idea was being most clearly worked out. The doctrine which Althusius was formulating in his study was merely the reflex of the ideas involved in the desperate struggle of the principle of civil and religious liberty with that of absolute personal sovereignty.

William the Silent as a representative of the idea of the State

As between strictly absolute sovereigns, there never had been, and there never could be, an obligatory law of intercourse. If the will of the prince is law, there can be no binding law for the prince or his people except his own will. That was the principle which Machiavelli had disengaged from the political ideas and usages of his time, and that was the principle that had ruled Europe since the universal authority of the Holy See had been set aside. To find a law for the government of nations, it was necessary to discover a principle of obligation in the nature of the State. That principle the jurists of the time were slowly bringing to light, and events were directing their attention toward it in a multitude of ways.

In September, 1580, Sir Francis Drake returned from his voyage round the world laden with plunder taken from the capture of Spanish ships and raids upon Spanish colonies. His freebooting expedition was resented by Don Bernardino Mendoza, the Spanish ambassador at London, who appealed

The right of sovereignty based on occupation

to the Queen for the restoration of the plundered property. As usual, Elizabeth temporized, the ambassador became insistent, but other events intervened, and no reply was given. The answer prepared by her astute minister of foreign affairs, Sir Francis Walsingham, was lost; but its substance has been preserved by Camden.[1]

If Drake had violated any law, it was proposed to say, he was subject to prosecution in the courts of England. If found guilty there, restoration would be made; but, in reality, Spain had brought these evils upon herself by excluding the English from the commerce of the West Indies, "*contra jus gentium.*" No specific citation of any law is offered, but appeal is made to a principle of justice. England recognizes no right on the part of the Pope to make a donation of the lands discovered in or beyond the ocean, and admits no title of possession but actual occupation. All nations are free to navigate the high seas, and in denying this right and appropriating unoccupied lands, Spain has asserted proprietorship where it possessed no rights.

In appealing to a "law of nations," as yet unrecognized, the minister of Elizabeth, one of the greatest diplomatists of his time, was opening a long debate; and in resting rightful possession upon actual occupation, he was imposing upon sovereignty a territorial restriction of far-reaching consequence. Who, then, were the veritable occupants of the soil, if not its inhabitants; and that not by a title of sovereign decree but by vital relations to the land as its tillers and settlers? And if these rights were primarily vested in the occupants of a country, who could represent them but their own delegated agents? Thus, in opposition to the theory of personal absolutism, in the very first encounter, the principle of territorial sovereignty was advanced as the necessary foundation of international rights.

In order to comprehend the full significance of the conflict between imperialism and territorialism that was soon

---

[1] *Annales*, 1580, p. 309, edition of 1605.

DEVELOPMENT OF A SOVEREIGN STATE SYSTEM

to burst upon Europe, it is necessary to take note of the forces that were then preparing for the struggle.

In 1580, after the death of Henry the Cardinal, for a short time King of Portugal, Philip II put forth a claim to the crown of that kingdom; and, after a brief resistance, on June 29, 1581, took official possession of Lisbon, and Portugal was annexed to Spain. By this one stroke the whole colonial world, thitherto divided between the two powers, became the possession of a single monarch, and with it passed to Philip II the exclusive dominion of the sea.

Never before in the history of the world had this element of maritime supremacy been lodged in the hands of one ruler. It was, without doubt, the most portentous menace to the nations of Europe to which they had ever been exposed; for, as the battle of Lepanto by the defeat of the Turks had given the King of Spain preponderance in the Mediterranean, so the annexation of Portugal gave him the mastery of both the Atlantic and the Pacific oceans.

The war in the Netherlands thereby assumed a new character, since the triumph of Philip II in maintaining his sovereignty there would give him command also of the North Sea, and perhaps enable him to extend his conquest to France and the British Isles. Thus, by the power of his combined navies, the King of Spain might eventually exercise dominion over the greater portion of the earth.

Supported by the aid of the Holy See in its war on heresy everywhere, the Counter-Reformation, under the leadership of Philip II, now seemed assured of a final triumph. By sowing the seeds of rebellion in England and Scotland, by ruthlessly crushing out revolt in the Netherlands, and by taking advantage of the religious dissensions in France, the son of Charles V was planning to establish a monarchy more nearly universal than any of which his father had ever dreamed.

To meet this unprecedented combination of material and spiritual resources, there was no organized opposition. Elizabeth had never seriously prepared for war, had no wish to assume the position of a leader in forming a coalition against

Philip II, and no doubt correctly estimated that the forces at her command would prove far inferior to those of her antagonist. If based upon religion, a coalition formed by Elizabeth would have derived but little aid from France, which, though divided, was at heart loyally Catholic; and the Netherlands, whose aim was independence rather than the triumph of any creed, would have refused to act except in their own interest.

For Elizabeth, therefore, there was no course but to continue her previous policy of securing the peace and prosperity of her own people by thinking solely of their safety. It is only in the light of events that we can comprehend the prudence, the originality, and the perspicacity of her inaction. A more vigorous and aggressive line of conduct would, undoubtedly, have drawn upon her at an earlier date the concentrated forces of her opponent. By apparently aiming at nothing definite, by securing for her people through her self-restraint a long period of prosperous development, by withholding action until the nation had arrived at a full realization of its well-being under her moderate rule, by storing up and conserving its energies through her economies, and finally by making it evident that in attacking her her enemies were striking at the liberties of England, Elizabeth revealed a depth of insight that ranks her far beyond the wisest of her ministers. No other sovereign would have held fast to the French alliance and risked by seeming to be a participant in his schemes the final success of the wretched Alençon, apparently assured when, with the secret support of the King of France, by the Treaty of Plessis-les-Tours, of September 19, 1580, he received from the Provinces the formal sovereignty of the Netherlands. When at last, by his treachery in throwing off the constitutional checks which he had accepted and attacking Antwerp, the bubble of Alençon's adventure burst, no other ruler of England but Elizabeth would have refused to accept the sovereignty of the Netherlands; which, with the approbation of Henry III of France, was afterward urgently pressed upon her. Too wise to concentrate upon herself the forces of her great antagonist, as most of the kings of England probably would have done in the hope of obtaining possessions on the continent and perhaps even aspiring to the crown of France, she saw the advantage of holding back the aggressive instincts of her people and keeping her opponent occupied as far as possible from England.

But the conflict with Spain, however long it might be delayed, had now become inevitable. Two events, — the death of Alençon on June 10, 1584, and the assassination of the Prince of Orange by Balthazar Gérard a month later, — rendered it imminent. By the former circumstance Henry of Navarre, hated as a Huguenot, suddenly found himself separated from the throne of France only by the life of King Henry III. When the last of the Valois recognized the rights of this heretic, the husband of his sister Margaret, as his legitimate successor, the Counter-Reformation soon destroyed the remaining vestiges of unity in France by the formation of the "League" for preventing the succession of Henry of Navarre, and by its designation of his uncle Charles, Cardinal de Bourbon, as the future king of France. While the civil wars which followed rendered the French alliance useless to Elizabeth, the relations of Philip II with the "League" opened to him the prospect of French aid, or at least the absence of French opposition, in his efforts to crush the revolt of the Netherlands, whose great leader had now been destroyed. When this task should have been accomplished, he hoped to be free to invade England with the army of the Prince of Parma.

At no time had the conspiracies for the restoration of Mary Stuart to the throne of Scotland and her succession to that of England been wholly abandoned, but in the situation which had been created upon the continent nothing seemed simpler than to accomplish both results by an organized Scotch and English rising. In all these plans the moving spirit, in close association with the Guises in France, was the Spanish ambassador, Mendoza. But Walsingham had his spies everywhere, and the seizure of Francis Throgmorton, who had been used

Chap. VII
A. D.
1576–1610

Formation of the "League" and Elizabeth's loss of the French alliance

The expulsion of Mendoza

as a medium of communication, revealed the whole design, and papers found upon his person proved beyond question the ambassador's complicity. On January 19, 1584, Mendoza was summoned to appear before the Privy Council. When he saw that prevarication was in vain, he assumed an arrogant tone, and upon being informed that he must leave the country, he defiantly replied: "As I have apparently failed to please the Queen as a minister of peace, she would in future force me to try to satisfy her in war."

The Council, with a moderation as surprising as the ambassador's insolence, appealed at once to the "law of nations," and consulted two distinguished publicists for their opinions, the French jurist François Hotman, and Albericus Gentilis, an Italian lecturer on the civil law at Oxford.[1] Both advised the immediate expulsion of Mendoza from England, and this advice was carried into effect. William Waad was sent to Spain to explain this action to Philip II; but the King of Spain refused to see him, and he returned to England with his letters undelivered. That which gives most importance to the incident is that it led Albericus Gentilis to write his work "De Legationibus," published in the following year, in which he not only treats of the rights of ambassadors in the light of the principle of sovereignty, but foreshadows his later work as the first great writer on international jurisprudence by pointing out its basis in natural reason.

But it was Philip II who was now to gather into his own hand all the plans for the invasion and subjugation of Great Britain. A new motive was joined to his new opportunity, for the idea was germinating in his mind that he might claim the crown of England for himself through his descent from Edward III.[2] What then would be easier than to seek also

---

[1] In recognition of his knowledge of the Civil Law, Albericus Gentilis was made Regius Professor of that subject at Oxford in 1587, after some service as adviser to Elizabeth's envoy in Saxony, another Italian, Horatio Pallavicino.

[2] See the table of the descent of Philip II from Edward III of England through John of Gaunt, in Hume, *Philip II of Spain*, p. 263.

the crown of France, with the double advantage of King Edward's claims and the failure of male heirs in the Valois line upon the death of Henry III? The King of Spain was, therefore, resolved that "there must be no more wide-spread ramifications, no more of Guise's vague management, or of priestly blundering. The secret of how, when, and where, all the springs of action, must centre in one cell in the Escurial, and to that point all channels of intelligence must be blindly directed. Facts, information, pledges, were all that Philip demanded, while he communicated as little as possible in return. Mendoza was transferred to Paris, and the whole English 'enterprise,' so far as it was to be managed in England and France, was handed over to him."[1]

From this time forward, Philip II was determined to prevent a French invasion of England under the auspices of the Guises, in order to prepare one in his own interest. He was already recognized by the supporters of Mary Stuart as, after her, "the nearest Catholic heir of the blood royal of England." His policy was, therefore, to keep the Guises busy in France, to prevent Henry III and the Huguenots from offering aid to Elizabeth, to win the support of the new pontiff, Sixtus V, and to keep in close touch with the English Catholics. The first and second matters hardly required his serious consideration, for Henry III was fully occupied with the "League," which also demanded the chief attention of the Guises. In the third, he was so successful as to obtain, though with much misgiving on the part of the Pope, and only after the persistent efforts of Olivares, the Spanish ambassador at Rome, the pledge of a million crowns as a contribution to the invasion, to be paid when it was actually accomplished.[2] In the meantime, Mendoza at Paris was charged with the conduct of an intelligence bureau through which every event in England was promptly known to him, partly through his numerous spies in England and partly

---

[1] Hume, *Calendar*, III, p. xliii.
[2] Hume, *Calendar*, III, No. 426.

CHAP. VII
A.D.
1576–1610

Elizabeth's protectorate of the Netherlands

through the English ambassador in France, Sir Edward Stafford, who was in the pay of Spain.

For Elizabeth, isolated, the object of conspiracies, and betrayed by her own subjects, a new policy was now essential. By the death of William of Orange the revolted Spanish Provinces had been placed in desperate need of a protector, and the occupation of the Netherlands as an outpost for the defence of England was now seen to be important. In July, 1585, a deputation of the States General, in which the able Pensionary of Rotterdam, John van Oldenbarnevelt, was a prominent figure, appeared in England to negotiate for aid.[1] Although the sovereignty of the Provinces was urgently pressed upon her, the Queen positively refused to accept it; for her plan was to encourage her allies to use their own resources for the common defence rather than to render England responsible for their safety. Finally, it was agreed that five thousand English troops should be sent to occupy the Netherlands under the command of Elizabeth's favorite, Robert Dudley, Earl of Leicester, as lieutenant-general.[2] Soon after Leicester's arrival, Count Maurice, "born Prince of Orange," the second son and successor of William the Silent, having been chosen by the States General of Holland and Zeeland stadtholder, governor, captain-general, and admiral of those provinces with the view of preserving their autonomy, nevertheless expressed to Queen Elizabeth a wish that she would accept the sovereignty, which, however, she again refused. But the vain and ambitious Leicester was more easily persuaded. Received at The Hague with the honors of a sovereign prince, the Earl allowed himself so far to forget his instructions as to receive from the States General in the great hall of the Binnenhof the "absolute government."

The indignation of Elizabeth knew no bounds. Lord

---

[1] The reports of the envoys are found in Van Deventer, *Gedenkstukken*, I, pp. 78 et seq.

[2] For Leicester's instructions, see Bruce, *Correspondence*, pp. 12, 15.

Heneage was at once despatched to order her presumptuous "creature," as she called him, to renounce immediately the new dignity he had assumed, and to express to the States General her severe displeasure at their attempt to outwit her and impose upon her "subject" the sovereign responsibility which she had refused.

Leicester was allowed to remain in the Netherlands, but the war between his forces and those of the Prince of Parma though it served to maintain the *status quo* almost without change, did not cover him with glory. It did, however, lead Philip II to perceive that it was upon the conquest of England that the success of all his plans must eventually turn. To avert that calamity Elizabeth tried to keep him occupied upon the sea and in his colonies as well as in the Netherlands; and for this purpose Drake plundered Vigo on the coast of Spain, sacked and burned St. Domingo and Carthagena, and swept the Atlantic in search of Spanish treasure ships.

But so long as Mary Stuart lived, Elizabeth was as much exposed to danger within her own realm as to an open attack from Spain; and Mendoza, who at Paris continued to be the centre of conspiracy against her, considered that the assassination of the Queen, with whom his master was now at open war, would be the most effective step that could be taken. On May 12, 1586, he wrote to Idiaquez, the secretary of Philip II, that a priest named Ballard had been sent from England to inform him that four courtiers, — at the suggestion of one Anthony Babington, — had sworn to take the life of Elizabeth, and had asked for the King's support.

The Babington plot

Soon afterward, Mendoza received from Mary Queen of Scots a letter dated May 20, 1586, in which she declares that, in view of the great obstinacy of her son, James VI of Scotland, in his heresy, and the difficulty that would be presented for the triumph of the Catholic Church if he should succeed to the throne of England, she has resolved, unless her son should submit before her death to the Catholic religion, to cede and make over by will her right of succession to the English crown to the King of Spain, and she invites him in future to take her under his protection, and also the affairs of England.[1] In all this she enjoins great secrecy; for, should her action become known, it would cause the loss of her dowry in France, bring about an entire breach with the King of Scotland, and accomplish her total ruin in England.

Not failing to credit this resolution of the Queen of Scots to his own exertions, Mendoza enclosed to his king a copy of her letter, and pointed out to him that genealogists had shown that, if the rights of James VI could be set aside, the King of Spain would be the direct heir to the crown of England.

Some months later, the ambassador, — referring to the demand of the conspirators that, if they succeeded in killing the Queen, they should have assistance from the Netherlands and assurance of succor from His Majesty, — reported to Philip II, "This I promised them, in accordance with their request, upon my faith and word, . . . and urged them with arguments to hasten the execution." [2]

In his reply, while Philip II blames the indiscretion of his agent in sending such outspoken promises to the conspirators, he refers to the plot as so much "in God's service that it certainly deserves to be supported, and we must hope that our Lord will prosper it, unless our sins are an impediment thereto." Regarding Mendoza's letters to the conspirators, "it is to be hoped," he says, "that you did not sign them, and sent them by safe hands, so that God will protect them for the end in view; but, nevertheless, for the future, it will be best to confide such matters only to the credence of trustworthy persons who will convey them verbally rather than write them. I merely mention this point, *as everything else was well done.*" [3]

---

[1] Hume, *Calendar*, III, No. 442.
[2] Hume, *Calendar*, III, No. 476.
[3] Hume, *Calendar*, III, No. 477.

But the King's prudence was too tardy to be of service. Walsingham's spies had long been on the track of the conspirators, and Philip's studied secrecy in concealing the plot even from the Prince of Parma by sending him two letters, — the first directing him to prepare the forces under his command to embark, the second stating that England was their destination to be delivered only after the murder of Queen Elizabeth, — had no other result than to cost him the confidence of his general.

*Chap. VII
A. D.
1576–1610*

Discovery of the plot and execution of Mary Stuart

The priest Ballard was promptly placed upon the rack by Walsingham's inquisitors, and forced to make a full confession. Queen Mary's letters had been intercepted and copied, and her private papers were now seized. Although correspondence with Babington was found, her letter to him was in the handwriting of her secretary, and she persistently denied all knowledge of the plot to assassinate Elizabeth. In Mendoza's private communications to Philip II, however, the ambassador expresses the opinion that, judging from the contents of her letters to him, "the Queen of Scotland must be acquainted with the whole affair." [1]

Whatever the truth may be, the fate of the Queen of Scots was sealed. After a review of all the evidence, the court by which she was judged unanimously found her guilty of participation in a conspiracy to promote a Spanish invasion and to assassinate the Queen of England. Elizabeth professed to be reluctant to sign her death warrant, and appeared to hesitate to take this step; but public opinion rendered it necessary, and, after several months of wavering, on February 11, 1587, the document was signed. Even then Elizabeth refused to authorize the execution; preferring, as it would appear, to let the responsibility for it fall upon others. The Council as a body took the matter into its own hands without the Queen's direction, and on February 18, with protestations of innocence and carefully arrayed for the last act of her tragic existence, the Queen of Scots calmly and with dig-

---

[1] Hume, *Calendar*, III, No. 483.

nity met her fate; while Elizabeth, full of terror at the possible consequences of the act, blamed her ministers, disavowed her own responsibility, and even placed an unfortunate subordinate, Davison, upon trial for acting without orders.

The Protestant concert against Philip II

Previous to the revelations that disclosed the real purpose of Philip II, Elizabeth had been in secret negotiations with the agents of the Prince of Parma in the belief that she might secure the safety of England from an attack by Spain in return for her aid in obtaining the submission of the Netherlands.[1]

Her theory was, that, while it was desirable to prolong the conflict in order to distract and weaken her enemy, she might eventually show the King of Spain that peace with England was a necessary condition of peace in the Netherlands. For this purpose she had given to Leicester only enough support to keep the revolt alive, and had not encouraged serious military operations.

The death of Mary Stuart brought to an end this artful duplicity and placed the Queen of England in frank and irreconcilable antagonism with Philip II; who, as the heir of the late Queen of Scots, became a claimant for the throne of England. For Elizabeth, therefore, there was now but one course open, — to emphasize her advantage as the representative of England's independence, to unite sincerely with all of Philip's enemies, to array against him as far as possible a Protestant opposition, and to cripple his energies everywhere by all available means.

For this bold policy the condition of Europe was eminently favorable. James VI of Scotland could not seriously think of avenging his mother's death upon Elizabeth

---

[1] In carrying on these secret negotiations, Elizabeth was carefully concealing them from her own minister of foreign affairs. That Walsingham was, however, aware of them, is evident from his letters to Leicester. In one of April 11, 1586, he says: "Somewhat here is a dealing under hande, wherin ther is great care that I shold not be made acquaynted withall." — See Bruce, *Correspondence*, pp. 223, and 231.

DEVELOPMENT OF A SOVEREIGN STATE SYSTEM 537

when she was defending and Philip II was attacking his own right of succession to the throne of England; and Henry III of France could not make strenuous exertions in behalf of the rights of a Guise princess when the Guises in alliance with Philip II were preparing to rob him of his royal power. There was, therefore, no real danger for Elizabeth except from Philip II, or from a Guise triumph in France. Her course, then, became entirely obvious. Henry of Navarre had placed himself at the head of the Huguenots in France, the Protestant princes of Germany were being exhorted by him to aid in opposing the "League," and the revolted Provinces of the Netherlands if encouraged might still occupy the forces of the Prince of Parma. These, then, were her natural allies, and to them in her extremity Elizabeth was now ready to turn in good faith with such aid as she could offer to the common cause.

CHAP. VII
A. D.
1576–1610

On his side, Philip II perceived that he must either abandon the hopes he had so long cherished or invade and conquer England.

The "Invincible Armada"

It was the fruit of Elizabeth's national policy rather than the immediate action of the Queen herself that was now to save her country and her throne. During the long period of peace which her rule had secured, the energies and resources of her people had been enormously expanded, and England as a nation had acquired an unprecedented power of initiative. Although the royal navy was still small, the maritime resources of England had reached a high degree of development. While the Queen was still cherishing the illusion of a peaceful arrangement with Philip II, in the spring of 1587 Drake made his way into the harbors of Cadiz and Coruña, destroyed many Spanish ships and a great quantity of stores, and thereby considerably delayed the fitting out of the Armada with which Philip II designed to conquor England. When, at length, in July, 1588, the vast fleet of Spain intended for the invasion arrived in the Channel loaded with priests for the conversion of England and carrying an army of more than twenty thousand soldiers, who were expected to be reinforced by the army of the Prince of Parma, in spite of Elizabeth's frugality in preparing for defence, a practically equal English force was there to meet and to destroy it. Nor was it, as tradition has represented, chiefly the miscalculations and bureaucratic methods of Philip II, combined with a series of happy accidents ending in a destructive storm, that defeated the "Invincible Armada." It was rather the superiority of English sea-fighting off Gravelines on July 29, 1588, — "the crowning triumph of thirty years of good government at home and wise policy abroad," — that won the victory. It was the English nation, in full consciousness of itself, its dangers, and its responsibilities, that met and destroyed the invader on that day. It was there that the visible glory of the Elizabethan Age began. Thenceforward to the end of her reign, Protestants and Catholics alike identified the rule of Elizabeth with the life of England. In resisting the imperial spirit of Philip II, whose design was to become an emperor in fact if not in name, the English people well understood that they were battling for their independence as a self-constituted state.

The aspiration of Philip II to the crown of France

Thus checked in England, the passion of Philip II for universal dominion soon found another field. Expelled from his own capital by the population of Paris under the leadership of Henry Duke of Guise, Henry III of France, on December 23, 1588, sought to restore his authority as king by the murder of the Duke, followed by the execution of his brother the Cardinal and the imprisonment of the Cardinal de Bourbon. In the midst of these tragic events, Catherine de' Medici, who had introduced the system of government by assassination, passed away; and her guilty son, "a king without a kingdom," in the following August himself fell by the hand of Jacques Clément.

Thus, after ruling France for two hundred and fifty years, the line of Valois kings became extinct; and Henry of Navarre, the first of the Bourbon dynasty, as legitimate heir to the throne, assumed the royal title as Henry IV.

But the Counter-Reformation had laid down the doctrine that no heretic could be recognized as king, the Pope had declared Henry of Navarre to have forfeited by his heresy all right to the throne, and France was a Catholic nation.

Here, therefore, was a new opportunity for the King of Spain, whose daughter Isabella was the grandchild of Henry II through Elizabeth of France. Mendoza promptly proposed at Paris that his master be recognized as the "Protector" of France, and that Isabella should be accepted as queen and marry a French prince. Upon this condition, Philip II was to cede Flanders or Franche-Comté to France, carry on the war with Henry IV at his own expense, and open to the French the commerce of the South Seas, thitherto reserved as a monopoly of Spain.

Two French statesmen, Nicolas de Neufville Seigneur de Villeroy, and Pierre Jeannin, although good Catholics and attached to the "League," but believing in the doctrine of the "Politiques," who sought to preserve the independence of the State, now set their hands to the difficult task of securing the triumph of Catholicism without destroying France. In 1590, the agents of Philip II continued to press upon the "League" the rights of the Princess Isabella. Jeannin was sent to Madrid, where he discovered that behind the veil of religion was the ambition to render France an adjunct to Spain. In vain he pleaded the antiquity and sacredness of the Salic law. The Spaniards well understood its real nature as a principle of French nationality, and professed to treat it as a mere prejudice. In September, 1591, the leaders of the "League" went so far as to invite Philip II to assume the sceptre of France; but at that moment the King of Spain was too much preoccupied with the agitation in Aragon, which Catherine de Bourbon, sister of Henry IV and Regent of Navarre, had promoted, to take immediate action. In January, 1592, Jeannin continued his negotiations with the representatives of Philip II, and the project of a treaty was even drawn up in which the choice of Isabella was nominally agreed to; but the reluctance of

CHAP. VII
A. D.
1576-1610

Jeannin to place the kingdom in the power of a foreign potentate who was the hereditary enemy of France, joined with the indisposition of the Spanish agents to promise the immense subsidies required to carry on the war, caused the negotiations to end in failure. In the meantime, the Prince of Parma had been withdrawn from the Netherlands to aid the "League," and Philip II had endeavored to win support by gifts of money and promises; but an event of an unexpected nature was soon to change the situation by creating a new condition.

The conversion of Henry IV

"Now I am king," Henry III had written to the papal legate after the murder of the Duke of Guise; but events had shown that no king who did not represent the nation, however sustained by the theory of divine right, could hope to rule France. Possessing in an unusual degree the personal attributes which the French people have always admired in their sovereigns, even Henry of Navarre, who had so powerfully appealed to the popular love for a hero when his white plume led the victorious charge at Ivry, and of whose legitimate claim to the throne no man could doubt, was unable to unite France while he remained a heretic.

On April 29, 1593, at Suresnes, the deputies of the King and of the "League" met to deliberate upon the deplorable state of France. The Archbishop of Bourges, speaking for the royalists, saw no hope of saving the State unless there was submission to the legitimate royal authority. The Archbishop of Lyons admitted the necessity of obedience to the ruling prince, but could not see the possibility of concord in the kingdom without a king worthy of the title *Très-Chrétien* in name and in fact, and no heretic could claim this "highest and most excellent dignity in the world." If only Henry of Navarre would renounce his heresy and resume his confession of the Catholic faith, all objection to his supremacy would disappear.

On May 17, the Archbishop of Bourges announced the intention of Henry IV to become a Catholic. The declaration was soon known in every part of France, but the alleged conversion of the King was received with very different sentiments. Both Catholics and Huguenots found it difficult to believe in the King's sincerity, yet here was an expedient for the salvation of the State.

But the claims of the Infanta to the throne were not yet disposed of, and the "League" was not yet inclined to yield to Henry IV. The Spanish ambassador had already distributed twenty-four thousand crowns to procure a favorable vote for Isabella by the States General of France, and on May 29 her election was urged upon that body as the solution favored by His Holiness the Pope, His Most Catholic Majesty the King of Spain, and the good Catholics of the realm. Don Iñigo de Mendoza answered the arguments of those who sustained the authority of the Salic law by showing in a Latin speech that it dated only from the time of Louis X. The deputies then asked if Philip II would give his daughter in marriage to a French prince. In reply, it was proposed that, if they still clung to the Salic law, the Archduke Ernest of Austria, for whom the King of Spain had intended Isabella, might be elected King of France. As brother of the Emperor Rudolph II, who was unmarried, the Archduke, it was urged, might succeed to the imperial crown, and thus the future kings of France would be able to restore the Roman Empire!

At Hotman's suggestion it was answered that it was contrary to the laws and customs of France to choose a prince who was not of the French nation; but the deputies agreed that, if the King of Spain would give his daughter to a French prince whom they would choose as king, they would accept this solution. But that concession was not sufficient for the pride and ambition of Philip II. He wished, in truth, himself to choose the future king of France, and replied that, if the States General would make the Infanta Isabella and a French prince whom he would name "proprietary kings of the crown of France *in solidum*," he was willing to give his daughter in marriage to a prince of France.

The papal legate, in a plausible address, delivered in Italian, supported this proposition, as tending to the glory of God and worthy of the Most Catholic King, who was ready to devote his daughter to the cause of religion and the unity of France; but the real purpose of Philip II was now unmasked. On June 28, the Parliament decreed that the kingdom, which depended upon God alone, could not on the pretext of religion pass under the control of a foreign prince.

The reconciliation of Henry IV with the Pope

For a moment it seemed as if the "Politiques" had won a complete victory, and that France was now about to reassert itself against all foreign intervention; but the appearance was illusory, for it was only under conditions imposed from without that France could be reunited,

On July 25, in the old basilica of St. Denis, in the presence of crowds of Parisians who had gathered to behold the ceremonies, the kingdom once more found a king. At the door of the church, Henry of Navarre presented himself before the Archbishop of Bourges, surrounded by a group of ecclesiastics. "Who are you?" demanded the Archbishop. "I am the King," was the response. "What do you wish?" "I wish to be received within the pale of the Catholic, Apostolic, and Roman Church." "Do you wish it?" "Yes, I wish and desire it." Then, kneeling, the King renounced heresy and made his vows to live and die as a Catholic. The Archbishop raised him up, kissed him, and gave him absolution, after which he was led into the church, heard mass, confessed, and received the sacrament.

The joy of the people was unbounded, and shouts of "*Vive le roi!*" greeted him on every side; but the "League" still had motives for resistance, and it was not until March 22, 1594, that the King could enter Paris, until then occupied by his enemies and guarded by Spanish troops.

Now that Henry IV had become a Catholic and was in command of his capital, it appeared as if he might soon enter into undisputed possession of his entire kingdom; but Philip II hoped to win at Rome the battle he had lost in France, for if papal absolution could be withheld from the former heretic the "League" might still be kept alive and the allegiance of France in great part alienated.

The Spanish ambassador at Rome was, therefore, charged to urge the Pope not to receive an envoy from the King of France, and with the influence of twenty-two cardinals among the partisans of Spain this course for a time proved successful. In person, Clement VIII was more favorably disposed, and even sent his nephew, Giovanni Aldobrandini, to Spain to persuade the King to make peace and consent to the absolution; but Philip II was inexorable.

Unable to move the Pope otherwise, Henry IV despatched to Rome upon a secret mission Arnauld d'Ossat, afterward a famous cardinal and already an accomplished diplomatist.[1] At first the terms demanded of the new convert were that he should make war on the Huguenots, renounce his alliance with England, and enforce the Catholic faith in Navarre. Henry IV stoutly refused to admit the right of a foreign power to encroach upon his prerogatives as a sovereign in matters pertaining to the administration of his kingdom, and absolution was not granted until September 17, 1595. Even then, the pardon of the Holy See was obtained at a high price. On that day the procurators of the King of France were required to recognize in his name the insufficiency of the absolution at St. Denis, to promise the publication of the decrees of the Council of Trent, and to give the principal offices of state to Catholics. Then, in the presence of the whole papal court and several foreign ambassadors, they were required to prostrate themselves at the feet of Clement VIII, imploring his absolution as the only true and sufficient remission of their sovereign's sins, while the Pope administered with a rod a few stripes upon the shoulders of the vicarious penitents as a symbol of his divine authority to punish the former disobedience of their king.

If the Catholics were victorious in form, the Huguenots looked forward under Henry IV to toleration in fact, and the civil wars of France thus came to an end. Directed against

The Peace of Vervins

---

[1] The negotiations are found in the *Lettres du cardinal d'Ossat*, I, pp. 226 et seq.

CHAP. VII
A. D.
1576–1610

a united nation, the hostility of Philip II, who still continued the war against Henry IV, gave to the conflict with Spain a national character. Thus France as a nation was finally driven into open alliance with England and the Republic of the United Netherlands, in order to curb the pretensions of the King of Spain. Instead of a mere revolt in his own provinces, Philip II was now confronted with a coalition of a serious nature. The Netherlands had become independent, England was successfully contesting the supremacy of Spain upon the ocean, and France was united under a powerful enemy. Unless the conditions were changed, all of the great ambitions of Philip II were doomed to failure.

But, in truth, both France and Spain were now suffering from exhaustion. In a population of about twelve millions, the wars of religion in France are estimated to have cost four million lives, and the country was greatly impoverished. Spain also, in spite of its immense resources, was upon the verge of bankruptcy. Both England and the Netherlands were plundering the colonies, destroying the shipping, and even ravaging the coasts of Spain. In order to divide his enemies, Philip II was now ready to make peace with France.

Under the auspices of the Pope, negotiations were begun at Vervins, and a treaty of peace was finally signed on May 2, 1598.[1] It was, in effect, a reaffirmation of the Treaty of Cateau-Cambrésis. England and the United Netherlands, although Henry IV offered to include them in the peace, complained of desertion by the King of France, who had promised not to make a separate peace with Spain; but Henry IV justified his course as necessary to the interests of his kingdom. His important task was now to reconcile the nation to the Edict of Pacification signed at Nantes on April 13, 1598, declared to be "perpetual and irrevocable,"

---

[1] In the negotiations of Vervins one great embarrassment was the old question of precedence between France and Spain, but in this case also the French were able to hold their ground.

DEVELOPMENT OF A SOVEREIGN STATE SYSTEM 545

by which liberty of conscience was conceded to the French Protestants, together with the right of public worship and participation in the great offices of the State.

In every one of his most cherished purposes Philip II was, therefore, doomed to disappointment. England, Scotland, and the Netherlands had become officially Protestant, and were now beyond his power either to recover or to punish; and France, although still officially Catholic, by sacrificing religious uniformity to political unity, had baffled his intervention. All, in spite of his opposition, had maintained their right to regulate their affairs in their own way, and in his efforts to restrain them he had only confirmed their independence.

As he approached his end he saw the grandeur of Spain departing, her colonies in danger, her merchant marine disappearing from the ocean, her ports invaded and pillaged, and her military glory dimmed. His effort to retaliate by an invasion of Ireland ended in a disastrous failure, and, in the meantime, the colonial spoils that Spain had obtained with the conquest of Portugal were now being wrested away by the intrepid seamen of the Netherlands.

But it was a system rather than a man that was suffering defeat in the failures of Philip II. He had been the heir of the spirit of universal domination nourished in his ancestors and of the long and bitter struggle with heresy which had left so deep a mark on the history of Spain. Both by inheritance and by education he was the representative of a past that could not return and the enemy of a future which he could not comprehend. Essentially Spanish in his patience and perseverance, he was not wanting in the nobler qualities of personal devotion and self-consecration belonging to his race. Regarding himself as a chosen instrument of the divine will for rooting out false doctrine and restoring the universal authority of the Church, his whole life was a sacrifice upon the altar of his gloomy faith. When, racked with excruciating bodily tortures, he knew that his strength was rapidly ebbing away, his faith, his gentleness,

CHAP. VII
A. D.
1576–1610

and his patience surprised all his attendants. As the prayers and dirges in his cell-like chamber ceased for a moment, he exclaimed, "Go on, fathers; the nearer I draw to the fountain the greater grows my thirst." On September 13, 1598, without fear and without regret, his eyes fixed upon the same crucifix that had been held before his dying father, his face illumined with a smile of rapture, to the music of the choir that floated through the open window from the adjacent church, he passed away. The little cross that with his last movement he had pressed upon his bosom was buried with him in his great jasper tomb in the Escurial, which he had designed in the form of a vast grill, — like the instrument of torture used for the execution of martyrs, — the fitting symbol of his grim and cheerless existence and his hopeless battle.

The state of Europe at the end of the sixteenth century

Although Philip II as the champion of the Counter-Reformation had failed in his plans, the system which he represented had not been wholly vanquished. In many respects he had involuntarily done for Europe what the Emperor Charles V had previously done for Germany, — he had created among his opponents a combination so strong as to produce a temporary equilibrium. In France, as half a century before in Germany, the religious conflict had ended in a compromise by which Protestantism had obtained toleration. In the Netherlands, the Archduke Albert of Austria, as husband of the Infanta Isabella, was given the sovereignty of the Spanish Provinces, with the hope that those lost to Spain might yet be recovered, but the Dutch Republic had already become not only an independent state but a vigorous opponent.

Upon a larger scale, the whole of Europe had in like manner been brought into a state of equipoise. In Italy, Spain possessed in Naples and Milan the keys of assured preponderance. Thus, the greater part of Southern Europe was Spanish and Catholic. The North, however, had become almost entirely Protestant. Not only had England and Scotland been driven permanently beyond the Catholic pale, but the Scandinavian kingdoms had taken their final place in the ranks of Protestant powers. One of the last schemes of Philip II had been to promote the succession of an ardent Catholic, Sigismund III of Poland, to the crown of Sweden, with the purpose of securing to the Counter-Reformation the balance of power in the Baltic. Resistance of immense importance to the future of Europe in the year of Philip's death gave the victory to Charles of Södermanland, who was soon afterward crowned as Charles IX of Sweden; and thus perished the hopes that Spanish influence might be exercised in the Baltic, and that, with the aid of a great maritime power in the North, England might be conquered and the Netherlands recovered.

It was, therefore, in the intermediate region between the Catholic South and the Protestant North that the great battle between the Reformation and the Counter-Reformation was yet to be fought. The preponderance in this central region was still in the House of Hapsburg, and by the union of the Spanish branch at Madrid and the Austrian branch at Vienna, aided by the influence of the Papacy, the cause of the Counter-Reformation might yet be won. But in this movement France would be placed in extreme danger. On the east, the Austrian dominions and the Spanish possessions in the Netherlands and Franche-Comté, on the south the whole strength of Spain, with its maritime supremacy on the Mediterranean and the Atlantic, combined to menace the very existence of France. Practically surrounded by Hapsburg territories, and exposed to the renewal of civil war by a revival of the religious question, the future safety of France depended upon a limitation of the Hapsburg power.

After the internal pacification and rehabilitation of France, the most important problem for Henry IV was, therefore, to provide against the danger that might arise from the united aggression of the two branches of the House of Hapsburg. In this he was favored by the secret dread of the Holy See lest the excessive power of Spain in Italy might imperil its

Chap. VII
A. D.
1576-1610

independence, for the domination of Philip II had awakened in Clement VIII feelings toward him similar to those that had formerly caused the bitter struggle of the Papacy against imperial supremacy.

It is in the decision to remain Catholic and to continue anti-imperial, that we find the key to the future foreign policy of France. By this attitude Henry IV had already won a preliminary victory, for Clement VIII had finally granted him absolution in defiance of Philip II; and it was the wish to sustain France as a counterpoise to Spain that had prompted the Pope to offer his active aid in concluding the Peace of Vervins.

The central aim of French diplomacy was now, therefore, in co-operation with the Holy See, to keep divided and to limit the power of the House of Hapsburg. In Italy, the Pope was by French intervention able to secure the restoration of Ferrara. In the famous controversy between Pope Paul V and Venice, in which Fra Paolo Sarpi became the vigorous champion of the political rights of the Republic against the Pope, after Spain had failed to arrange a settlement, Henry IV became a successful mediator; and, although the cause of Venice was maintained in substance, the Pope was saved from complete humiliation. In his negotiations with Savoy, Switzerland, and the Grisons, old enmities were in great part removed, and progress was made toward closing the Alps to communication between Spain and Germany. In the Netherlands, France continued to furnish aid to the United Provinces when, after the death of Elizabeth on March 24, 1603, and the accession of James VI of Scotland as James I of England, the Republic could no longer hope for English support. After the peace between England and Spain in 1604, the friendship of France and the revolted Provinces became still more intimate until, on January 23, 1608, Jeannin concluded between them a close defensive alliance. As a result of this combination, Jeannin succeeded also in obtaining from the new king of Spain, Philip III, a suspension of the war between Spain and the Republic by the

Truce of Antwerp of April 9, 1609.[1] With England itself, now chiefly interested in discussing the King's prerogatives, yet always jealous of France as a powerful rival on the continent, Henry IV had at least the common bond of general antipathy to Spain. In Germany, in pursuance of the policy of Francis I and Henry II toward the Emperor Charles V, he sought to organize the Protestant princes among themselves, in order — to use his own expression — that he might " tune the German flutes to the music of France "; and openly intervened to prevent the succession of a Catholic prince to the vacant heritage of Cleve, Berg, Jülich, and Mark, which would endanger the United Netherlands, and actively supported the claims of the Protestant Elector of Brandenburg. With a clear prescience of a coming struggle, he did not suffer himself to be lulled into illusory security by the trivial character of the Emperor Rudolf II, nor by the indolence and self-indulgence of Philip III and the pacific programme of his minister, the Duke of Lerma, and the wishes of his own minister, Villeroy. Perceiving the weakness of the House of Austria in the East, when in Bohemia the Calvinists were organizing a national movement against the Hapsburg rule, and Hungary also — still a battlefield rather than a kingdom — was permeated with the same influence,[2] by the mission of Savary de Brèves he renewed the earlier relations with the Sublime Porte and established an *entente* with the Sultan that restored to France its former rôle of protector of the Christians in the Orient, and thus prepared the way for securing the future support of the Ottoman power when the time should come for a struggle with the Hapsburgs.[3]

---

[1] See *Les négociations de Monsieur le président Jeannin*, Amsterdam, 1695.

[2] Although the preaching of Calvinism did not begin in Hungary until 1558, in 1567 the country was so fully won for the Calvinistic doctrines that it was said: " *Calvinista hit, Magyar hit,*" — the faith of the Calvinist is the faith of the Magyar.

[3] For an elaborate account of the diplomacy of Henry IV, see Philippson, *Heinrich IV und Philipp III.*

CHAP. VII
A. D.
1576–1610

The "Great Design"

Such were the achievements of Henry IV, when, on May 14, 1610, the assassin Ravaillac struck him down, and he was succeeded by his nine-year-old son, Louis XIII, under the regency of his Italian mother, Maria de' Medici.

Plans far more systematic and pretentious have been attributed to Henry IV. Only within recent years, however, has the evolution of the legend of the "Great Design" been accurately traced from its origin in the ideals of the French Huguenots to its culmination in the utopian scheme portrayed in the "Mémoires" of the Duke of Sully, the great minister of Henry IV.[1]

According to Sully's representations, after the Peace of Vervins, Henry IV began with Elizabeth of England and continued with James I a plan to combine with Scotland, Sweden, and Denmark for enabling the United Netherlands to conquer the Spanish Provinces and the Swiss to acquire Franche-Comté, Tyrol, and Elsass; to liberate the German principalities from the domination of the Hapsburgs; to restore Bohemia and Hungary to the position of free elective monarchies; and to drive the Spaniards from Italy and confine them to their own peninsula.[2]

When these revolutions were accomplished, Europe was to be reorganized in fifteen states, as follows: (1) six hereditary monarchies, — France, Spain, England, Sweden, Denmark, and Lombardy, the last to be composed of Savoy and Milan; (2) six elective monarchies, — Rome with the kingdom of Naples, Venice, the German Empire, Poland, Hungary, and Bohemia; (3) three federal republics, — the Helvetic, to include Switzerland, Tyrol, Franche-Comté, and Elsass; the Belgic, to contain all the Netherlands; and the Italic, to be composed of Genoa, Lucca, Florence, Modena, Parma, and Piacenza, and thus to comprise a great part of Northern Italy.

---

[1] For the literature of this subject, see the authorities at the end of this chapter.

[2] For the true history of Sully's mission to London and his falsifications regarding it, see Laffleur de Kermaingant, *Mission de Christophe de Harlay*, pp. 112 et seq.

DEVELOPMENT OF A SOVEREIGN STATE SYSTEM 551

Taken together, all these were to constitute a great Christian Republic, in which the three types of Christianity, — Catholicism, Lutheranism, and Calvinism, — should be allowed perfect freedom. To avoid wars and to settle disputes among themselves, a General Council was proposed, in which the component states would be represented by a body of forty delegates, to meet annually in the most central cities of the different countries in rotation. Subsidiary to this Amphictyonic Congress, six special councils were to be established for the local affairs of each of the following groups: Northern Europe, the Empire, the Eastern Kingdoms, Southern Italy, Northern Italy, and Western Europe. From the decisions of these special councils appeal might be made to the General Council, which would have supervision over all the general interests. Thus federated and united, Christian Europe, pacified within, was to expel the Turks and realize the noble Christian ideal of European unity and universal peace.

Such was the "Great Design" attributed by Sully to Henry IV, but certainly never conceived by that monarch, and now believed to have been invented by the fallen minister as a means of procuring his own recall to the administration of the affairs of France. To give this invention the character of a sacred legacy from the great hero and pacificator who, it was represented, had confided his secret to his trusted counsellor, documents were altered and even fabricated; but these falsifications are now capable of complete refutation, not only from the absence of the corresponding pieces in the archives of the different governments concerned, but by the comparison of Sully's own manuscripts, in which the gradual development of the "Great Design" is recorded.[1]

It was not to Sully alone, however, that the events of the last decades of the sixteenth century suggested the need of

The work of the jurists

---

[1] For the evidence of this, see especially Kükelhaus, *Der Ursprung*, pp. 140, 177; and Pfister's articles in the Revue Historique.

great principles in the regulation of the states of Europe. The bitter wars of religion, the disappearance of all sense of community between the Catholic and the Protestant powers, the intervention of Spain in the affairs of England and France in alliance with domestic conspirators and religious partisans, and the unending war now begun upon the sea impressed all thoughtful men. The plain violation of every principle of right and justice was the one fact which appealed to the great jurists of the time, and it is their labors which were destined to be the most lasting fruit of this tragic period of international history.

As early as 1582, Balthazar Ayala, judge advocate of the Spanish army in the Netherlands, produced his work "De Jure et Officiis Bellicis," in which he discusses the nature of war and defines the proper method of conducting it. The normal state of mankind, he points out, is one of peace; but, in order to secure it, wars are necessary. The right to declare war and to make peace belongs exclusively to the sovereign. Rights exist, however, even in war; and there are, therefore, certain laws to which belligerents should be subject; but rebels have no claim to appeal to them, since their duty is to obey their prince. A just war is one which is waged publicly and lawfully by those who have the right to declare it, but it should be regulated according to fixed principles of justice both as to its causes and its conduct. Faith should be kept with the enemy, if he has a legal right to exact it; but not with rebels, whose envoys even, having no public character, are not inviolable.

A broader scope and a more elevated tone are found in the "De Jure Belli" of Albericus Gentilis, which first appeared in 1588.[1] War, in his opinion, is a painful necessity, arising from the fact that sovereigns have no superior to whose judgment appeal may be made. Disputes between sovereigns can be settled only by discussion or by force. When the former

---

[1] See Professor Holland's beautiful edition of the Latin text, Oxford, 1877.

DEVELOPMENT OF A SOVEREIGN STATE SYSTEM 553

has failed, war is the only alternative, and may be just on both sides. Religious differences, according to Gentilis, do not constitute a proper ground for war, since religion is a matter between each individual soul and the Creator. Only when the State suffers injury from a creed may a sovereign rightly suppress it. Self-defence is a natural right, and the Turk and the Spaniard, who aim at universal dominion, may rightly be resisted. In the largest sense, the whole world is one great republic, and aid may rightly be offered to any member of it who is wronged. Neutrality is, therefore, not a duty; still, in many cases it may be a right. While intervention in behalf of subjects against their rulers is ordinarily not defensible, when their cause is just and they revolt in great numbers, they may be aided; for kingdoms are not made for kings, but kings are chosen to secure justice to their subjects. The sea, like the air, belongs to all men in common, and arbitrary restriction of its use is a just cause of war. The jurisdiction of every sovereign is limited to the territory actually occupied by his subjects. States are responsible to one another and should be governed by principles of justice to be deduced from approved custom and the law of nature. The agreements of sovereigns should be regarded as sacred, and may bind their successors. Thus were laid down in bold outlines the foundations upon which the whole edifice of international jurisprudence has been erected, and it is upon them that Grotius and his successors were to build.

CHAP. VII
A. D.
1576–1610

But the time had arrived when in all nations men were beginning to perceive that it was upon such principles that Europe must be organized if the Germanic love of freedom were not to end in anarchy. In a passage of rare beauty of thought, the Spanish theologian Franciscus Suarez, called "the last of the schoolmen," wrote at the beginning of the seventeenth century: "The human race although divided into different peoples and kingdoms, has nevertheless a certain unity, not only as regards species, but moral and political. That unity springs from the natural precept of mutual

The idea of a society of states

love and compassion, a precept applicable to all, even to strangers, whatever may be their nation. Every state, republic, or kingdom, forms a member of this general body, which is the human race. None of these states is sufficient for itself: all have need of reciprocal support, association, and mutual relations to ameliorate their situation. For this reason some law is necessary to direct them and to govern correctly their relations and associations. Although much may be done by natural reason, still it is not in all respects sufficient; and more precise laws can be formulated from the usage of nations. As in a particular state or province law is formulated by custom, so in the human race as a totality legal rights may be formulated from the usages of nations." [1]

At last, the truth which the Roman world had so profoundly felt in the idea of empire was traced to its true origin in that community of nature which binds all men and all nations in one common whole. The Germanic conception of local liberty had created the independence of the Modern State, but without its complementary Roman truth of the subjection of the individual to the universal there could be no solid political system. It was only by fully recognizing the essential interdependence of states as members of a larger human society that the Germanic idea of national independence could vindicate its fitness to rule the world; for it was seen that, without the acceptance of an obligatory law securing the rights of nations, both great and small, independent states merely legalize among themselves the anarchy they were organized to repress.

III. THE DISTURBANCE OF EQUILIBRIUM IN GERMANY

The state of Germany before the Thirty Years' War

It is by interests and not by principles that the world is governed; and before the ideas of the jurists could be embodied in permanent institutions it was necessary that Europe

---

[1] Suarez, *Tractatus de Legibus ac Deo Legislatore*, Coimbra, 1612, Book II, chap. 19, No. 9.

DEVELOPMENT OF A SOVEREIGN STATE SYSTEM 555

should be devastated to a point that made an appeal to reason indispensable.

Since the death of the Emperor Charles V Germany had constituted a little world by itself, the balanced adjustment of whose inner mechanism rendered it of small international importance. This negative attitude of the German Empire did not result from any organic change in its constitution but only from a group of temporary conditions. The first of these was the personal disposition of the emperors. Ferdinand I, while remaining Catholic, made no attempt to repress reform. So little did he regard the Catholic tradition that he did not even seek to obtain the papal coronation. From this time forward the German kings assume the title of Emperor without reference to Rome, and the Pope has a correspondingly diminished influence in the affairs of Germany. Maximilian II, who succeeded to only a portion of the Austrian inheritance, was even less powerful and less decidedly Catholic than his father, and is reputed to have been "the first European prince of any religion who refused to persecute." He would neither obey the invitation of Pius V to attack the Protestants nor the request of the Lutheran princes to expel the Jesuits. In the early part of his reign he regarded Philip II with aversion on account of his former rivalry for the imperial crown, and in no way aided his plans for universal domination. Rudolf II, having been educated at the court of Spain, was more imbued with religious bigotry; but during his reign of thirty-six years he was so engrossed with astrology and alchemy that he took little interest in actual government. His brother Matthias, who succeeded him, was chiefly occupied in trying to reclaim Hungary and Bohemia from the Turks and the Calvinists.

Under these conditions, while in Germany the Catholic princes were working steadily for the Counter-Reformation, the Protestant princes were as steadily secularizing Church property. At first the Lutheran doctrines made rapid progress, and a Venetian ambassador estimated that in 1558 ninety per cent of the German population had accepted the

CHAP. VII
A. D.
1610-1625

reformed faith. But after the close of the Council of Trent, the Jesuits began to reclaim the people. The excellence of their schools, their zeal and industry in practical work, and their influence over the Catholic princes in the extirpation of heresy produced marvellous results, and by the end of the sixteenth century the greater part of Southern Germany had been won back to Catholicism.

But that which most of all tended to maintain peace within the Empire, and at the same time to render it impotent in international affairs, was the balance of the Catholics and Protestants in the Electoral College. Against the three ecclesiastical electors of Mainz, Köln, and Trier were poised the three temporal electors of Saxony, Brandenburg, and the Palatinate; while the Emperor himself, as King of Bohemia, held the remaining vote.

In the Diet also, Catholicism and Protestantism were so evenly balanced that it could rarely come to a decision; but the Catholics had a majority in the Imperial Chamber and the Aulic Council, which enabled them to impose their views in the interpretation of the laws.

Instability of the Peace of Augsburg

The Peace of Augsburg of 1555 was in reality merely a truce between the opposing creeds, which as soon as their balance was destroyed were certain to renew hostilities. For this there was a cause which sooner or later would become operative. This was the Ecclesiastical Reservation, which provided that, if Catholic bishops or abbots changed their religion, they were to vacate their offices and abandon to the Catholics their lands and endowments. The Protestants held, however, that this was designed merely to prevent dissension between bishops and their chapters; and that, therefore, in cases where the chapters themselves were Protestant and chose a Protestant bishop, the Ecclesiastical Reservation did not apply. In addition to this, the Peace of Augsburg in no way recognized the Calvinists, who had become a considerable party. The Palatinate, owing partly to its geographical position in proximity to France and the Netherlands, had gone over to Calvinism; which, rooting itself in the soil

DEVELOPMENT OF A SOVEREIGN STATE SYSTEM 557

of the older Hussiteism, had also made great progress in
Bohemia. The Peace of Augsburg, moreover, took no account
of the popular convictions but only of the views of the
princes, who were able to dictate the form of religion to be
practised in their respective states. Founded upon no principle whatever, either of freedom of conscience or of rule by
the majority, the religious peace of Germany, therefore, depended solely upon agreement between the princes. With
Lutheranism and Calvinism dividing the Protestant group,
and each detesting the other almost as much as the Catholics,
the equilibrium secured at Augsburg was essentially unstable
and liable to be disturbed by the slightest cause.

In 1606, in the free city of Donauwörth, in the midst of a
population almost wholly Protestant, a Catholic abbot organized a religious procession which provoked attack by the
populace and ended in a riot. By direction of the Imperial
Court, composed of Catholic members, the city was put under
the ban of the Empire without due form of trial, and Duke
Maximilian of Bavaria was appointed to execute the sentence. Taking possession of the place, he delivered the
parish church to the Catholic clergy and assessed the expenses of the expedition upon the city, which he refused to
vacate until they were paid.

This act aroused the indignation of the Protestants, and at
the diet of the following year the Elector Palatine took the
bold stand that the authority of the Empire had ceased to
exist in matters of religion and taxation. On May 15, 1608,
the formation of the Protestant Union[1] was completed under
the nominal leadership of the Count Palatine, Frederick IV,
but really inspired by Christian of Anhalt,[2] then the head of
the Calvinist party, who had resolved to set aside the authority of the Emperor and the Diet, and with the aid of
Henry IV of France to make war on the House of Austria.

---

[1] For the formation of the Union, see Ritter, *Die Gründung der Union*, being volume I of *Briefe und Akten*.

[2] For an account of his policy and negotiations, see Krebs, *Christian von Anhalt und die kurpfälzische Politik*.

Chap. VII
A. D.
1610-1625

Concealing his ultimate intentions, all who were hostile to the Emperor were invited to join the Union, which was on this account less coherent than the Catholic League formed soon afterward in opposition by Maximilian of Bavaria.

The succession to the estates of the Duke of Cleve came near supplying the spark needed to set all Germany in flames, but the death of Henry IV of France left the Protestant Union without the support necessary to an aggressive attitude, while the accession of John Sigismund, the Elector of Brandenburg, who was converted from Lutheranism to Calvinism, sufficiently strengthened the Union, to hold in check the zeal of the Catholic League. The territories in question were, therefore, divided between the Elector and Wolfgang William of Neuburg, who had appealed to the Catholic party, and war was thus postponed.

The Bohemian revolution

But the conflict so long preparing was soon precipitated in an unexpected way. On July 9, 1609, Rudolf II had been induced by the estates of Bohemia to sign the "Letter of Majesty" (*Majestätsbrief*), or royal charter, granting freedom of conscience to the people of that kingdom; leaving, however, the right to decide the form of public worship in the hands of the feudal nobles within their own jurisdictions, while in the royal domains public worship was made free to all confessions.

Repenting of this action, Rudolf II endeavored to revoke it; but violence followed, as the result of which in 1611 Rudolf was dethroned as King of Bohemia, and his brother Matthias took his place. In the following year Rudolf II died, and Matthias was chosen emperor.

The Protestants having built a church at Braunau on the lands of its Catholic abbot, and another at Klostergrab on those of the Archbishop of Prague, they were prohibited by the abbot and the archbishop from worshipping in them, but claimed the right on the ground that they were within the royal domain.

The King supported the views of the prelates, and the Protestants were obliged to submit in silence; but they resolved that, when Matthias should die, they would choose a Protestant king. When, however, in 1617, the Bohemian Diet met, they were informed that the crown of Bohemia was not elective but hereditary, and that Duke Ferdinand of the Styrian branch of the House of Austria had been designated by the renunciation of other heirs as the successor of Matthias to the throne. Although it was known that Ferdinand had been educated under Jesuit influences, and that he had wholly suppressed Protestantism in his hereditary estates, the Diet tamely renounced the right of election by recognizing Ferdinand as hereditary king.

Thus the perpetual rights of the House of Austria in Bohemia seemed to be legally admitted; but when the church at Braunau remained closed and that at Klostergrab was destroyed, a feeling of resentment was awakened which inspired a resolve to dethrone Ferdinand. A petition was prepared asking for redress, but it was declared illegal. Then, on May 23, 1618, Count Henry of Thurn with a band of followers burst into the room in the castle of Prague where the royal commissioners were seated, and, after an altercation, threw them bodily out of the window from a height of seventy feet above the moat, into which they dropped. "Jesus! Mary!" was the cry of Martinitz, as he fell. "Let us see if his Mary will help him," said one of the crowd. "By God, his Mary has helped him!" was the exclamation as he, his associate Slawata, and their secretary crept out of the moat unhurt.

Although this famous "defenestration" of Prague was, apparently, only an ill-considered local revolt, it was destined to begin a contest which raged for thirty years, and ultimately drew into its vortex nearly every important power in Europe.

The Bohemians were unprepared for the struggle they had precipitated, and obliged to appeal to their co-religionists for aid. Among these Christian of Anhalt was the most aggressive. Believing that the House of Austria was even weaker than it seemed, and that Hungary, Moravia, Silesia, and

Chap. VII
A. D.
1610–1625

probably Austria itself would join in a movement to throw off its rule, he entertained large plans for invoking the rest of Europe in a coalition for the humiliation of the Hapsburgs. Charles Emmanuel, Duke of Savoy, who had just concluded a conflict with Spain, had a considerable army in the field under the command of Count Ernest of Mansfeld, an energetic adventurer of the Italian *condottiere* type, who was sent to aid the cause of Bohemia. Everywhere behind the scene was the hand of Christian of Anhalt, who was flattering the Duke of Savoy with the prospect of the Imperial crown, if the Hapsburgs could be overthrown.[1] At the same time he was urging the young Elector Palatine, Frederick V, to cast in his lot with the Bohemians, who were already considering the idea of offering him the crown of their kingdom. This, it was supposed, would not only secure the active aid of the Protestant Union, but obtain the support of England, since Frederick had married Elizabeth, the daughter of James I. The Dutch also, it was thought, would send money to their Calvinistic friends. On the east, Bethlen Gabor, the Protestant ruler of Transylvania, was aiming to obtain with the aid of the Turks the supremacy in Hungary; and he was relied upon to keep the Hapsburgs occupied in Austria, at that time extensively permeated with Protestantism.

The subjection of Bohemia and expulsion of Frederick V

But all these expectations were soon to prove illusory. Matthias having died, through a disagreement on the part of the Protestant electors, on August 28, 1619, Ferdinand of Styria became emperor as Ferdinand II. Two days previously, he had been deposed as King of Bohemia, and the Elector Frederick V had been chosen in his place. Against the advice of many of his most faithful counsellors, the young elector accepted the crown of Bohemia, which he received at Prague on November 4. This action was the death-knell of the Bohemian cause; for, if an elector of the Empire could in this manner be made the beneficiary of a popular revolt against a recognized ruler, the door would be

---

[1] See Krebs, *Christian von Anhalt*, pp. 95, 100.

DEVELOPMENT OF A SOVEREIGN STATE SYSTEM 561

open to universal anarchy. The Bohemian revolution had thus ceased to be merely a question of the inherent rights of the Bohemian nation, and had become an attack upon the constitution of the Empire.

As might have been foreseen, the Protestant Union declined to sustain Frederick V. John George, Elector of Saxony, perceived in the combination of Bohemia with the already large and rich territories of the Palatinate a menace to his own dominions, and it was generally thought that two electoral votes in the hands of one person would give their possessor too much preponderance in the empire.[1] James I of England, who was engaged in trying to negotiate a Spanish marriage for his son Charles, and was, therefore, indisposed to offend the Hapsburgs, considered that the acceptance of the Bohemian crown by his son-in-law was an adventure of doubtful propriety, and offered no substantial support. The Dutch Calvinists sent some money, but their resources were limited. Bethlen Gabor found it impossible to take Vienna, his alliance with the Turks made even the Protestants recoil from his plans of conquest, and the pillage inflicted by his army like that practised by the greedy troops of Mansfeld made their presence equivalent to the destruction of the country.

But that which rendered hopeless the success of Frederick V was the union of the two branches of the House of Hapsburg in a common cause. In May, 1620, Spinola, the Spanish general in the Netherlands, was ordered from Madrid to invade the Palatinate in defence of the Emperor. Fearful of themselves becoming the prey to the Spanish army, the members of the Protestant Union, on June 3, concluded with the Catholic League the treaty of Ulm, by which they pledged themselves to neutrality; thus leaving Maximilian of Bavaria free to invade Bohemia without danger from attack in his rear. In defence of what he conceived to be the rights

---

[1] The vote of Bohemia joined to that already possessed by the Protestants would give them a majority in the Electoral College.

CHAP. VII
A. D.
1610-1625

of the Emperor, the Elector of Saxony actively espoused his cause, while the Bavarian army under Duke Maximilian, after imposing peace in Austria, where the estates were in revolt against Ferdinand II, proceeded to subdue the Bohemians. By the battle of the White Mountain near Prague on November 8, 1620, Frederick V, who had proved, as was predicted, only a "winter king," was driven from the country and sought refuge at The Hague. A terrible penalty for their revolt was paid by the defeated Bohemians, whose chiefs were executed and their lands confiscated, after which they were given by the Emperor to a new nobility composed of German Catholics.

The question of the Palatinate

The grievance now was that a Protestant electoral state had fallen into Catholic hands and was occupied by a Spanish army. This was a serious matter both from the German and from the international point of view; for not only was the balance thus destroyed between the religious confessions in Germany but the United Netherlands were menaced by the success of the Spaniards, France had cause for alarm from the active co-operation of Madrid and Vienna, and England was affected by the renewed aggressiveness of Spain and the indignity to the son-in-law of James I in excluding him from his electorate.

The pressing question, however, was, where was Frederick V to find effective assistance in recovering the Palatinate? The German princes, influenced chiefly by their local interests, were not disposed to risk their own fortunes in defending the rights of a Calvinist who had been so eager to abet and profit by revolution. The Landgrave of Hesse-Cassel was compelled by his people to make terms with Spinola. Several of the Protestant cities, such as Strasburg, Nuremberg, and Ulm, began to weaken; and, on April 12, 1621, the Protestant Union was dissolved and its troops were withdrawn from the Palatinate.

There was, therefore, no hope for Frederick V unless aid could be secured outside of Germany; for Mansfeld's unpaid mercenaries were no match for the well disciplined troops of

Tilly, the veteran general of the Catholic League, and the Spanish army under Spinola, and the local population found it more profitable to be dominated by Spanish and imperial officers than to be pillaged by irresponsible adventurers like Mansfeld's hungry troopers. Nor did such an ally as Christian of Brunswick, celebrated chiefly as a ruthless fortune hunter in search of spoils from secularized bishoprics, add much by his zeal and robberies to Frederick's cause.

On February 13, 1623, after his friends had been beaten in the field and the conference called in his behalf at Brussels at the instance of James I of England had ended in failure through the Elector's own mental instability, Frederick V was by imperial decree deprived of his electoral office and the electorate was transferred to Maximilian of Bavaria. To temper this act, it was announced that it did not exclude the just claims of the heirs of Frederick V after his death, and that if he would humbly ask for pardon and voluntarily surrender his electoral office the Emperor would consider the restoration of his lands. So far as Germany was concerned, therefore, it appeared that the war might thus be brought to an end by a compromise. The difficulty in the way was, however, that such a triumph would leave the House of Austria distinctly in the ascendency, and with it the cause of Catholicism for whose final predominance the Hapsburg influence was pledged.

The foreign power most directly affected by the condition of Germany after the Netherlands was France. The Truce of Antwerp having expired in 1621, the war between the United Netherlands and Spain had now been reopened, and as soon as the Hapsburg power should become sufficiently secure in Germany the whole force of Spain with the Emperor supporting it would be directed toward recovering the lost Provinces. Then, by the combination of the Spanish and Austrian strength, the Hapsburg ascendency would be more complete in Europe than it ever had been before.

For France, however, the moment was inauspicious for intervention. With the death of Henry IV the great preparations for attacking the House of Hapsburg had ceased, and Maria de' Medici, both during her regency and afterward, was chiefly interested in procuring Spanish marriages for her children. The kingdom possessed able statesmen and diplomatists, but none of sufficient force and influence to continue the policy of Henry IV; while the reopening of the wars against the Huguenots and the independence and rivalry of the great nobles so fully preoccupied the government that little notice was taken of the state of Germany.[1]

Through the inspiration of Pope Paul V, the interests of Ferdinand II as a champion of the Counter-Reformation were rather promoted than opposed by France. In 1614, Louis XIII, at the age of thirteen, had come to power, and his favorite and minister, the Duke de Luynes, became the virtual ruler of France. On April 15, 1621, through the negotiations of the Count de Bassompierre, this minister concluded the Treaty of Madrid, by which the control of the Valtelline, — the key to the passes across the Alps most necessary to secure communication between Italy and the Hapsburg domains in Germany, — was restored to the Grisons, from whom it had been taken by Spain;[2] but at the same time he also promoted the neutrality and dissolution of the Protestant Union, and induced Bethlen Gabor not to support the cause of the Bohemians. So long as the state of Germany was chiefly a question of religion, the Court of France, now intensely Catholic, had not been disposed to interrupt its newly resumed task of subduing the Huguenots and completing the unity of the monarchy by securing the absolute supremacy of the King; but now that the struggle in Germany was assuming a political aspect in which the preponderance of the Hapsburgs in Europe was involved, Louis XIII felt disposed to make terms with the Huguenots,

---

[1] For an admirable picture of the condition of France at this time, see Zeller, *Richelieu*, etc.

[2] For an account of the affair of the Valtelline, see Seehausen, *Schweizer Politik*, etc.

DEVELOPMENT OF A SOVEREIGN STATE SYSTEM 565

even offered aid to Mansfeld, and in 1624 began to seek the advice of Richelieu.

CHAP. VII
A. D.
1610-1625

It was, however, England that was to take the first step in trying to direct the course of affairs in Germany, but not without much hesitation and indecision. While the English people were moved by sympathy with the cause of Protestantism, King James I was touched by the indignity to his son-in-law and the appeals of his daughter Elizabeth to his family pride. But there were serious obstacles to effective intervention in behalf of Frederick V. The King had been most eager to secure the marriage of his son Charles to the Spanish Infanta Maria. To negotiate the match on the Spanish side, in 1613 Sarmiento, afterward the Count de Gondomar, had been sent to England as ambassador. From the Spanish point of view, the chief aim was to obtain a useful ally and to use the future Queen of England as an instrument for the restoration of Catholicism. For King James the object was also to secure an ally, but especially to obtain by means of the Infanta's rich dowry the money that Parliament would not grant him. Later, James I saw also in the enterprise a possibility of procuring as a wedding gift the return of the Palatinate to his son-in-law; and with this hope added to his former motive he was careful not to strain relations with the Hapsburgs.

The ambiguous position of England

But the personal visit of Prince Charles to Spain, accompanied by the Duke of Buckingham, in 1623 definitely settled the marriage question. The King of Spain received the young suitor with much friendliness, and was ready to use his influence with the Emperor for the restoration of the Palatinate, if Frederick's sons could be sent for their education to Vienna, where they would become Catholics. As for the hand of the Infanta, that would be given, with the consent of the Pope, upon condition that she have in the palace her private chapel, and that Catholics be allowed to hear mass in their own houses. The Infanta herself, however, went into hysterics, shrieked, and fell on the ground, when Charles, thinking to approach her as a lover, jumped over a wall into a garden where she was walking. Her confessor had reminded her how comfortable it would be to think of him who should lie by her side and be the father of her children as "certain to go to hell!"

The treaty was, however, prepared, and the necessary promises were made; but Charles returned to England so chilled and disgusted with the conduct of his intended bride and the exactions of the Spanish Court that the marriage, which had always been regarded with aversion by the English people, was never celebrated.

England's appeal to the Scandinavian powers

In the spring of 1624 the negotiations between England and Spain were broken off, and plans for intervention in Germany were discussed by the King and the Parliament. Both were now ready for war, but each had a different idea of its purpose, and therefore of its method. The King wanted to enforce the restoration of the Palatinate, and to accomplish this he thought it necessary to create a great European coalition against the Emperor, for which English money would be necessary. Parliament, on the other hand, thought of Spain rather than the Emperor as the natural enemy, and instead of invading Germany was disposed to send aid to the United Netherlands and to attack the Spanish coasts, commerce, and colonies. This divergence of aim and action, dynastic on the one side and national on the other, was destined to contribute in no small degree to that estrangement between the royal power and the parliamentary policy which ultimately overthrew the House of Stuart.

In the summer of 1624 James I began the formation of plans against the Emperor by sending Sir Robert Anstruther as ambassador to Christian IV, King of Denmark, and Sir James Spens to Gustavus Adolphus, King of Sweden, for the purpose of securing their co-operation in recovering the Palatinate. A similar attempt had been made by the King of England at the Conference of Sageberg in March, 1621, at which England, Denmark, and the United Provinces were represented; but the preoccupation of Gustavus Adolphus in his war with Poland and the dissolution of the Protestant

Union had proved sufficient reasons for abandoning the enterprise. In the meantime, Frederick V, through his agent Camerarius had in 1623 opened negotiations with the King of Sweden, who was in principle disposed to act in his interest but was waiting for greater security in his relations with Denmark and for better assurances of support from England. It was, in fact, the jealousy of the two Scandinavian powers which was now to stand in the way of concerted action.

Both Christian IV and Gustavus Adolphus had reasons for being interested in the affairs of Germany. The King of Denmark, as Duke of Holstein, was a member of the Lower Saxon Circle, and was anxious to extend his influence both on the Baltic and on the North Sea. One of his sons was Bishop of Verden and another expected succession to the archbishopric of Bremen, which gave the King a substantial interest in the Protestant cause in Germany.

Gustavus Adolphus, not less ambitious as a ruler than he was ardent as a Protestant, was engaged in establishing a great monarchy in the North. He had driven back the Danish armies, secured the independence of Sweden, pushed the Russians from the shores of the Baltic, and was engaged in a bitter war with Poland, whose king, Sigismund III, was still a claimant to the Swedish throne. The ambition of Gustavus Adolphus to make the Baltic a Swedish lake was now threatened with obstruction by the success of the Emperor, who both in a national and a religious sense was his most formidable foe. To stem the tide of the imperial advance in Northern Germany, to aid the cause of the Protestant princes, and to extend the borders of his barren and inhospitable country, whose chief product was hardy soldiers, were aims that could all be readily combined in the programme of this earnest, vigorous, and sagacious sovereign.

In Denmark, Anstruther, with the aid of the ambassador of France and the envoy of George William, the new Elector of Brandenburg, succeeded in inducing Christian IV to accept the English alliance against the Emperor, notwithstanding the efforts of the imperial ambassador to secure his neutrality; but the Royal Council was opposed to hostilities in Germany, and on July 27, 1624, the King decided to withdraw his promise.

When, in August, Sir James Spens arrived at Stockholm bearing secret instructions from Prince Charles of England and Frederick V in addition to his official orders from James I, he found Gustavus Adolphus willing to offer aid. His minister, Oxenstiern, even proposed a plan to form a coalition of all the Protestant powers and France against the House of Hapsburg, of which the King of Sweden was ready to take supreme command.

But the friction between Denmark and Sweden was too great to permit of their co-operation. Rivals for supremacy in the Scandinavian realm, it was at that time impossible for them to unite in any common action. As soon as the readiness of Gustavus Adolphus to join in a general alliance was known in Denmark, Christian IV began hostile negotiations with Poland and resolved in spite of his Council to place himself at the head of the movement against the Emperor.

The Danish intervention

It was England, therefore, that now became the centre of negotiations on the part of the rival powers of the North, each endeavoring to secure the leadership in the proposed attack upon the Emperor. In January, 1625, Anstruther was again sent to Denmark to secure the most favorable terms. They were, in fact, too favorable; for, while Gustavus Adolphus demanded fifty thousand men, of whom seventeen thousand should be paid by England with four months' pay provided in advance, Christian IV unwisely underbid him by offering to invade Germany with thirty thousand men, of whom only six thousand should be paid with English gold.

After a conference at London and much double dealing on the part of James I, by which the dignity of the Swedish king was deeply wounded, it was finally decided to confer the leadership upon the King of Denmark, and Gustavus Adolphus resumed his war in Poland.

An alliance was then concluded between England, the

DEVELOPMENT OF A SOVEREIGN STATE SYSTEM

United Netherlands, and Denmark, in which England undertook to pay monthly three hundred thousand and the Netherlands fifty thousand florins for the prosecution of the war; but from the outset the coalition was doomed to failure. On March 27, 1625, King James I died, and Charles I became King of England. The want of confidence in Buckingham as his chief minister, the marriage of Charles with Henriette Marie of France, and his secret concessions to the Catholics all combined to weaken him with Parliament; with the result that the English contingent of troops sent to the Netherlands was ill supplied and the subsidies promised to Denmark were not paid. Notwithstanding his marriage alliance with France and his urgent importunities, Charles I was unable to procure the participation of Louis XIII in the coalition against the Emperor; for Richelieu, who was at the beginning of his ministry and was eager first of all to consolidate the royal power by suppressing the Huguenots, hesitated to incur the combined hostility of Spain and the Emperor by open opposition. In Germany itself, little mutual confidence existed and every prince was thinking chiefly of his local interest. With the Netherlands mainly occupied in defending their own frontiers against a Spanish invasion, and England about to enter upon the bitter struggle between the King and the Parliament, Christian IV was left to bear the principal burden of a war of aggression for which he was not prepared.

IV. THE SIGNIFICANCE OF THE THIRTY YEARS' WAR FOR EUROPE

It was at this moment, so opportune for considering whether a conflict essentially German in its origin should become European in its development, that the traditional theory upon which wars had been so frequently undertaken was for the first time openly challenged.

Europe as it then existed was a complex product of race affinities, dynastic interests, and religious antagonisms, from which every bond of unity had disappeared. After a long struggle in which the idea of Christendom had been lost, the principle of political equilibrium had become the only guarantee of national security. Without alliances no independent state could hope to maintain its existence; and these, as experience had proved, were mere shifting sands. In Germany, the balance of forces was already destroyed, Ferdinand II was reasserting the imperial idea, and every Protestant principality was menaced. The union of the two branches of the House of Hapsburg threatened a revival of its preponderance in the whole of Europe. How, otherwise than by applying the principle of equilibrium, could the peace and safety of the nations be maintained?

In his "De Jure Belli ac Pacis," written in exile from his native Holland, and published at Paris in 1625, Hugo Grotius, continuing the work of Albericus Gentilis, points out that the misfortunes of nations arise from a disregard of justice, without which there is no real security. "If no community can subsist without observing some standard of right, as Aristotle proves by the example of brigands — who are obliged to recognize some principle of equity among themselves — with greater reason the human race, or a number of peoples, cannot dispense with it."[1] Even war itself has no other defensible object than justice, it should be undertaken only for a just cause, and it should be conducted in a just manner.[2] In the conflict of arms, he says, laws must, indeed, be silent, but only civil laws, not those perpetual laws inherent in the nature of man as man; for these, even in war, can never cease to possess authority.[3]

Far from being a sufficient ground of security, the principle of equilibrium, without justice, says Grotius, is a source of danger; for, being subject to constant changes, the condition of balance between opposing forces requires new conflicts to maintain it. Albericus Gentilis had held that war

---

[1] *De Jure Belli ac Pacis*, Preliminary Discourse, XXIV.
[2] The same, XXVI.
[3] The same, XXVI.

may be rightly undertaken to diminish the strength of a power whose growth implies a future danger to its neighbors;[1] but Grotius controverts this doctrine. "To enfeeble a prince of a state whose power increases day by day for fear that, if permitted to increase too much, it may upon occasion inflict injury, is," he says, "unjustifiable. . . . That one has a right to attack another because he has power to do harm, is contrary to all the rules of equity. Such is the constitution of human life, that one never exists in perfect security. It is not by the employment of force, but in the protection of Providence and by innocent precautions that one should seek resources of defence against the fear of uncertain danger."[2] It is in seeking what is just that treaties and alliances become really profitable, for all men recognize in justice a certain supremacy and obligation.

In an age whose ruling motives were dynastic interest, national aggrandisement, and religious bigotry, Grotius sought to discover the fundamental principles upon which international relations might securely rest. In doing so, he appealed to a source of authority more ancient and more universal than any dynastic right or any form of religious doctrine. Behind the political conceptions of his time he discerned the more august presence of man's rational intelligence, in whose norms of conduct he read the outlines of a law of nations. As reason is common to all men, and all men are kindred, not only the foundations of the State but of an organized Society of States are to be found in the constitution of humanity.

In opposition to the views of Machiavelli, Grotius holds that law is not the creation of a prince but an expression of a social need. Like the Florentine philosopher, he appeals to history and to the order of facts; but not in the same spirit nor with the same result. Machiavelli observes in the State nothing but the work of force under the guidance of

---

[1] *De Jure Belli*, Book I, chap. XIV.
[2] *De Jure Belli ac Pacis*, Book II, chap. I, section XVII.

the intelligence of one man; Grotius perceives in it a natural organism, existing apart from the will or purpose of the individual, of which every human being forms a part. Machiavelli limits his observation to that which happens in the order of political phenomena; Grotius traces these phenomena to their source in the passions of the human race, compares the objective act with the motive that inspired it, and perceives in the background of political action great principles of conduct that may, indeed, be violated, but which command obedience with the authority of all that most ennobles man.

It was the distinction of Grotius to work out in detail the application of the principle of equity to a society of sovereign states. To regard his system as a body of international law in the proper sense would be an exaggeration; for, notwithstanding his learned and ingenious endeavors to give his doctrines the support of a general consensus of opinion by the citation of passages from the whole range of literature, sacred and profane, and to found them as far as possible upon ancient custom and the precepts of the Roman law, his treatise as a whole is a vast mosaic of ideas built around the central idea of natural equity in the relations of independent states, rather than a digest of actually accepted principles.

But so great an enterprise did not fail to attract the attention of statesmen and sovereigns, and Grotius was soon invited to enter the public service of Poland, Denmark, Spain, England, and Sweden, and subsequently became the ambassador of Sweden to France. Gustavus Adolphus is said to have carried a copy of "De Jure Belli ac Pacis"—which he caused to be translated into Swedish—through all his subsequent campaigns, and to have slept with it under his pillow by the side of his Bible. Numerous editions and translations appeared, and before the author's death his work had become a classic which university professorships were soon afterward established to expound.[1]

---

[1] In Dr. Rogge's *Bibliotheca Grotiana*, The Hague, 1883, the whole number of titles in the bibliography of Grotius literature is four hun-

DEVELOPMENT OF A SOVEREIGN STATE SYSTEM 573

The value of the great work of Grotius was not, however, in furnishing to Europe a code which all nations could immediately adopt, but in presenting a new goal of international endeavor that appealed to the intelligence as well as to the real interests of mankind. His pre-eminent distinction was to show that behind the claims and pretensions of the imperial idea, which the nations of Europe had rejected and against whose revival they were at that moment contending, there was a reality more imposing than any of its embodiments had ever been, — the essential unity of all men and the universality of law as the basis of social existence. To this conception the faith and obedience of so many silent and submissive generations bore a more ample testimony than the fierce struggles of popes and emperors to impose their authority. Broader and deeper than the mighty heritage which civilization had received from Rome was the foundation upon which its true greatness had been erected,— an authority which senates could formulate but not create, which imperial decrees could ratify but not originate, whose source was in the fountain of existence and whose expression must be sought in the structure of mind and society.

Although Thomas Hobbes a generation later could say, "Every independent commonwealth has a right to do what it pleases to other commonwealths,"[1] and his picture of nations living "in a condition of perpetual war and upon the confines of battle, with their frontiers armed and cannons planted against their neighbors round about," has not ceased to be a faithful portraiture of the attitude of civilized states, the ideals proposed by Grotius created a new era in the history of Europe. In proposing the utility and even the neces-

---

dred and sixty-two, not including the writings of generations of jurists who have been inspired by his teaching or of the critics and biographers who have discussed his life and work. Before the close of the seventeenth century the Latin original was translated into Swedish, Dutch, English, French, and German. At Rome, it was put upon the Index.

[1] Hobbes, *De Cive*, chap. II.

CHAP. VII
A. D.
1625-1648

The schemes of Wallenstein and the project of Urban VIII

sity of the Christian powers forming "some kind of body in whose assemblies the quarrels of each one might be terminated by the judgment of others not interested," and that "means be sought to constrain the parties to agree to reasonable conditions," he was advancing ideas which down to our own time have been regarded as utopian.[1] It is, however, a sufficient honor to the name of Grotius that since the publication of his great work there has never ceased to exist a recognized science of international jurisprudence of which he is the accredited founder, developing in harmony with other branches of thought and knowledge, and which has slowly but impressively modified the relations of independent states.

The message of Grotius concerning the rights of war and peace was rendered timely by the fact that it was offered to the world when every principle of legality and of humanity was being openly violated. The lawlessness that then prevailed in Germany was hardly paralleled by the worst anarchy of the Middle Ages. To repel the Danish invasion, Ferdinand II was in need of an army, and Albert of Waldstein, generally known as Wallenstein, was proposing to furnish it upon a novel plan. Descended from an aristocratic family of Bohemia, and educated in his early years by the Moravian Brotherhood and afterward by the Jesuits, Wallenstein had become a brilliant soldier of fortune in whose mind principle was entirely subordinated to success. Profiting by the misfortunes of his countrymen, he had become the richest land-

---

[1] *De Jure Belli ac Pacis*, Book II, chap. XXIII. The idea of such a body was not, however, original with Grotius. In the *Nouveau Cynée, ou discours d'estat représentant les occasions et moyens d'establir une paix générale et liberté de commerce, par tout le monde*, written in 1623, a unique copy of which is in the Bibliothèque Nationale at Paris, Émeric Crucé proposed the choice of a city, — naming Venice as a suitable selection, — where the sovereigns should unite in maintaining a permanent corps of ambassadors who should by their votes settle all international differences. See the articles by Nys in the Revue de Droit International et de Législation Comparée, Brussels, 1890.

DEVELOPMENT OF A SOVEREIGN STATE SYSTEM 575

owner in Bohemia, and now offered to provide the Emperor with an army without expense. All he demanded in return was the privilege of obtaining support for his soldiers, not as Mansfeld had done by the general pillage of private property, but by enforced contributions from the legal authorities wherever his followers might be in need.

Armed with this authorization by the Emperor, he soon attracted about his person a formidable force of well paid adventurers, Catholics and Lutherans alike. With masterly prudence he coolly calculated when and where to strike. Mansfeld was defeated and expelled from Germany, recalcitrant princes and cities were stripped of their authority, Bethlen Gabor was neutralized by means of a peace between the Emperor and the Sultan, and the King of Denmark was driven from Schleswig and Jutland to his islands.

But the victories of Wallenstein were only a part of the vast movement that was at this time organized against the Protestants throughout Europe. As a result of disagreements over his French marriage, King Charles of England was now at war with France. At Rome, Pope Urban VIII had conceived the idea of a general attack on all the Protestant powers. Poland was to keep engaged the King of Sweden, and by a secret treaty of April 20, 1627, between Spain and France the naval power of England and the United Netherlands was to be destroyed.[1] Thus the Catholic powers were to resume command of the ocean and open communication between Spain and Germany by way of the Baltic. Denmark and ultimately Sweden were to be invaded, and Catholicism was to be universally restored.

On January 4, 1628, Christian IV was able to conclude a treaty with Gustavus Adolphus for the protection of their states; but in the following April Wallenstein was named Admiral of the Baltic and the North Sea, soon afterward received the investiture of the Duchy of Mecklenburg, formed a plan for a canal between the North Sea and the Baltic, de-

---

[1] See Ranke, *History of the Popes*, II, pp. 251, 253.

clared Wismar an imperial naval base, and began negotiations with the Hansa cities for the invasion and partition of Denmark. The Hansa fleets were to have a monopoly of the commerce with Spain. For the destruction of the English and Dutch sea power and for the subjection of Denmark a navy of twenty-five war vessels was to be equipped, toward which Philip IV of Spain was to contribute two hundred thousand crowns. But the Hansa cities were too wary to forward a scheme that threatened their own destruction, Stralsund resisted a long and cruel siege, and the vast plans of Wallenstein were not executed. On May 22, 1629, Christian IV, too jealous of his Swedish rival to cast in his lot with him, signed with the Emperor the Peace of Lübeck, by which he retained his hereditary possessions but renounced all right to interfere in Germany.

Both Ferdinand II and Urban VIII had now to learn the incompatibility of the papal and the imperial interests and the opposition to both in the spirit of the time. In France, the Huguenot rebellion had just been crushed by the fall of La Rochelle; but Richelieu's policy of religious toleration so long as the royal supremacy was recognized made it possible for every Frenchman, whether Protestant or Catholic, to be a patriot. This was also the idea of Wallenstein, whose great purpose was, regardless of religious uniformity, to consolidate the State. But in the mind of Ferdinand II political unity and religious unity were still identical; and on March 6, 1629, he issued the Edict of Restitution, by which two archbishoprics — Magdeburg and Bremen — and twelve bishoprics, with more than a hundred smaller estates, were reclaimed for the Catholic clergy. In these domains, under the principle of *Cujus regio, ejus religio*, the whole population, although it had been Protestant for half a century, was required to return to the Catholic faith or migrate to Protestant principalities.

This act would perhaps have had no other effect than to rekindle the religious war if it had not been attended with circumstances which gave it an important political bearing.

Wallenstein's army of a hundred thousand men, which was the Emperor's chief support, was a menace to the Germanic liberties, and from the Catholic as well as the Protestant point of view its existence was an assault upon the legal constitution of the Empire. Wallenstein himself was showing his contempt of the princes and electors and asserting that the Emperor should make himself supreme in Germany as the Kings of France and Spain had made themselves masters in their kingdoms. By the force of circumstances the situation in Germany was, therefore, assuming a political character which at the same time was provoking foreign interference to oppose the further development of the House of Hapsburg, now grown so threatening, and creating a division within the Empire itself which opened a new opportunity for diplomatic intervention.

Even before his accession to power as chief minister of Louis XIII, Cardinal Richelieu had outlined in his mind the double policy which was to give to France the first place in Europe: the King must be rendered absolute, and security against the foreigner must be obtained by dividing and abasing the House of Hapsburg. In 1626, he had shown his dexterity by obtaining "peace with the Huguenots through fear of Spain, and peace with Spain through fear of the Huguenots"; at the same time by the Treaty of Monzon of March 5, 1626, recovering the Valtelline for the Grisons, from which Spain had again taken it, and securing for France the exclusive right to use its passes.[1] In 1628, he had sustained the claim of the French Duke of Nevers to the succession of Mantua, — a possession vital to the Hapsburg supremacy in Northern Italy, — and in 1629, and again in 1630, he had in person assisted at the siege of Casale, a fortress in the Mantuan territory held by the Duke of Nevers, which the Spaniards were unable to reduce. But up to this time, although he had in secret opposed the Emperor, no opportunity had been offered to deal him a serious blow.

The policy of Richelieu

---
[1] See Dumont, V, Part II, pp. 487 et seq.

But the time was now ripe for a more effective move. Pope Urban VIII, notwithstanding the interest of the Church in having the Edict of Restitution executed, as a Florentine and as head of the Papal State, had become alarmed at the success of the Emperor, and especially at his disposition to assert his authority in Italy. The general discontent in Germany on the part of the Protestants because of the Edict of Restitution, and on the part of all the princes because of Wallenstein's army, afforded an exceptional opportunity for intervention; and the desire of Ferdinand II to secure the immediate election of his son as King of the Romans offered an additional advantage. By utilizing the inherent antagonism between the Papacy and the Empire, which a decisive imperial success never failed to call into action from the papal side, Richelieu was about to gain a diplomatic victory more brilliant than any he had ever won.

The Diet of Regensburg of 1630

With Wallenstein's great army in the field, the King of Denmark reconciled, Gustavus Adolphus preoccupied in Poland, and the more than three hundred mutually distrustful small states of Germany unable to resist him, Ferdinand II seemed in reality a formidable sovereign; and, had he possessed the qualities of Wallenstein, might have become the most powerful emperor who had ever ruled in Germany. Notwithstanding the interest of the Pope to employ the prestige of the Emperor to promote the Counter-Reformation, as an Italian prince, Urban VIII entertained the same suspicion of Ferdinand II that Clement VIII had cherished with regard to Philip II of Spain, and once more the Pope was to be the principal agent in humiliating the Emperor.

As the Jesuits had been the important factor in the Council of Trent, so now the Capuchin Brotherhood was to take the first place in the diplomacy of the Diet of Regensburg of 1630. Among the adherents of Richelieu — so close to him and so esteemed as to be called his "right arm" — was the Capuchin friar Père Joseph, born François Leclerc du Tremblay, son of a former French ambassador at Venice and President of the Parliament. After a brilliant course of education, in which he mastered Italian, Spanish, German, and English, as well as Latin, Greek, and Hebrew, Père Joseph travelled extensively over Europe, and in the guise of a missionary visited Spain as a secret agent of France. Without official rank either political or ecclesiastical, "*Son Eminence grise*," as Père Joseph was called, became the confidant and sometimes the adviser of Richelieu. For a considerable period, Capuchin friars quietly circulated between Vienna, Munich, and Paris, and Père Joseph was more thoroughly informed of the condition of Germany than the Emperor himself.

Following the rule that "when Richelieu wished to make a particularly good, not to say a bad, stroke he always employed pious persons," Père Joseph was sent to Regensburg with the accredited ambassador, Brulart de Léon. When, on July 30, they arrived at the Diet, so well had the ground been prepared that the members of the Catholic League had demanded the dismissal of Wallenstein, and he was already discharged from the Emperor's service.

It now remained to settle with Ferdinand II, who claimed the right of investiture, the succession of Mantua, and thereby relieve the siege of Casale by the Spanish general Spinola. But in spite of Père Joseph's protestations of the pacific intentions of France, the Emperor was suspicious, and proposed to include in the negotiations the question of the three bishoprics, — Metz, Toul, and Verdun, — which since they had been taken from the Empire by Henry II had been retained by France. To settle all outstanding differences and to conclude a general peace and alliance between France and the Empire was now the desire of Ferdinand II.

The embarrassment of the French envoys was extreme, for Richelieu had no thought of a general peace with the Emperor, and his design was merely to free his hands in Italy, in order that he might concentrate upon Germany all the strength he possessed in opposing the House of Hapsburg.

For this purpose, in 1629 he had sent to Sweden the Baron de Charnacé to enlist the co-operation of Gustavus Adolphus; and, in order to liberate him from his war with Poland, this envoy had mediated the Truce of Altmark of September 26, 1629, by which Sigismund III left the Swedes in possession of the whole of Livonia and parts of Prussia. Gustavus Adolphus was eager to try his fortunes in Germany, for he had perceived that, if the plans of Wallenstein were carried out, after Denmark had been conquered Sweden would be invaded. His sympathy with the Protestant cause was strong, and he believed that, if he invaded Germany, he would receive a powerful support from the Protestant princes. But the offers now made to him by France were felt to be deceptive. In January, 1630, Charnacé was directed to promise an annual subsidy of six hundred thousand livres if the King would invade Germany in defence of the Germanic liberties, drive the Spanish troops out of the Empire, and require the destruction of the imperial fortresses; but he must engage not to deprive the princes of the Catholic League of their possessions, nor disturb the Duke of Bavaria in his electorate, nor suppress Catholic worship where it was established. As these restrictions were not in harmony with his purposes, Gustavus Adolphus proudly declined the offer, which would have made him only the tool of Richelieu, and on July 4, 1630, his troops landed on the coast of Pomerania for the invasion of Germany on his own account.

The diplomacy of Richelieu regarding Mantua

Although there was at that time no treaty between France and the King of Sweden, Richelieu regarded him as effectively an ally, and his presence in Northern Germany was quickly utilized. The main point was to relieve the siege of Casale by a treaty with the Emperor and yet to avoid a general peace with him. Closely pressed at Regensburg, Brulart and Père Joseph dared neither sign the treaty of alliance which the Emperor demanded nor break off the negotiations. Equivocally instructed, with the apparent purpose of subsequent disavowal, on October 13, 1630, the French plenipotentiaries finally signed a treaty in which the King of France engaged neither to attack the Emperor or the Holy Roman Empire nor to aid their enemies with force or counsel; the Duke of Nevers, on condition that he ask for the clemency of the Emperor, was to receive the investiture of Mantua and Montferrat; and it was agreed that commissioners should be named to examine the question of the three bishoprics.

When Richelieu received the text of the treaty his wrath, real or dissembled, was so intense that he assured the Venetian ambassador, Contarini, that he felt like retiring to a cloister. But his anger was rather at being unmasked than at the action of his plenipotentiaries, whose instructions directed them to appear to yield all the points which they had finally conceded, but to do so by verbal promises only, and to avoid inserting them in the treaty. This evasion had, however, proved impossible even for the plausible Père Joseph; for the Emperor's negotiators had simply taken him at his word and insisted upon recording his protestations of his master's friendship in the written text.

But the situation was not too difficult for the genius of Richelieu. Directing his envoys to remain with the Emperor and propose some modifications in the treaty before it was ratified, he resolved to regulate the affairs of Italy in Italy, and to evade the general peace by using it as a cover for his Italian negotiations. In these he had a powerful ally, for Pope Urban VIII had decided that he needed the French in Italy to offset the growing power of the Hapsburgs. With the aid of the papal nuncio, Giulio Mazzarini, better known in the later history of France as Mazarin, on March 31, 1631, Richelieu was able to negotiate with the Duke of Savoy, Victor Amadeus, two secret treaties concluding an offensive and defensive alliance between France and Savoy, and in return for certain guarantees ceding to France perpetual possession of the fortress of Pinerolo in Piedmont, thus opening once more a gate into Italy "for the protection of Italian liberties."

But this was not the whole of Richelieu's success. Abel Servien was sent to Italy to settle the affair of Mantua, and

CHAP. VII
A. D.
1625-1648

to take advantage of the Treaty of Regensburg without ratifying it. This, again with the aid of Mazarin, was so well done that the imperial general and commissioner, Baron Gallas, signed with Servien at Cherasco on April 6, 1631, a treaty by which the Duke of Nevers was put in immediate possession of Mantua and Montferrat, and it was arranged that the imperial troops should evacuate the Valtelline and the French troops Piedmont. Then the secret treaties with Savoy were publicly confirmed. Pinerolo continued to be held by the French, who thus secured in Italy a firm base for dividing and checking the two branches of the House of Hapsburg. An almost equal diplomatic victory was the Treaty of Fontainebleau of May 30, 1631, a project of which Père Joseph brought back with him from Germany as the result of his negotiations with Maximilian of Bavaria, by which the Catholic League was detached from the dictation of Spain.

The plans of Gustavus Adolphus in Germany

While the astute cardinal was deluding the Emperor with the belief that a peace with France was substantially concluded, Charnacé had resumed his negotiations with Gustavus Adolphus, and, on January 23, 1631, had concluded with him the Treaty of Bärwald, in which the King of Sweden engaged to maintain in Germany thirty thousand infantry and six thousand cavalry, to respect the neutrality of the Catholic League, and to permit the exercise of the Catholic religion in places occupied by him wherever it was already established. In return he was to receive an annual subsidy of a million livres.

The invasion of Germany by Gustavus Adolphus was, from the Swedish point of view, primarily a measure of defence against the aggressive plans of the Emperor; or more strictly, perhaps, of Wallenstein. By landing an army on German soil the King of Sweden hoped to obtain the support of the Protestant princes, form a body of mutual defence in Northern Germany, obtain ports and fortresses on the Baltic, like Wismar and Stralsund, which would complete his mastery of that sea, and thus render secure his Swedish kingdom.

DEVELOPMENT OF A SOVEREIGN STATE SYSTEM 583

Whether or not he would have been finally content with a protectorate over the Protestant princes or really aimed, as Richelieu affirmed, at the crown of the Empire, is, perhaps, debatable.[1] His idea of a "*Corpus Evangelicorum*," modelled after the organization of the United Netherlands, governed by States General and presided over by a Stadtholder, may have been in his own mind a permanent institution, or it may have been only a temporary instrument with which to wage war upon the Emperor; but, in any case, it is evident that this body was designed to be absolutely under his control for purposes of war and peace. Although professing to be in imitation of the constitution of the Netherlands, it was so devised that its head would possess powers superior to those of the Emperor. If Gustavus Adolphus had carried out his plans, no merely ornamental diadem would have satisfied his mind. It was at a real power, not at a shadow, that he was aiming.[2]

It is not to be doubted that in his battle for the Protestant cause Gustavus Adolphus was sincere, for with the success of Protestantism in Germany was bound up his tenure of the Swedish throne. But the Protestant princes of the Empire were not eager to welcome his intervention. If by alliance with him they should bring upon themselves the vengeance of the Emperor, whose power had been shown by his victory over the King of Denmark, their position would be worse than before. If, on the other hand, Gustavus Adolphus should be victorious, their independence might be endangered by him.

In this equivocal situation, although the King of Sweden was hailed as a Messiah by the evangelical population, the princes were thrown into a state of alarm. Only William V, Landgrave of Hesse, and William of Weimar, were disposed to respond to his call.[3] The King's own brother-in-law,

---

[1] Richelieu, *Mémoires*, VIII, p. 76.
[2] See Kretzchmar, *Gustav Adolfs Pläne und Ziele in Deutschland*, pp. 152 et seq.
[3] See Struck, *Das Bündnis Wilhelms von Weimar mit Gustav Adolf*, pp. 21 et seq.

584   A HISTORY OF DIPLOMACY

CHAP. VII
A. D.
1625-1648

George William, Elector of Brandenburg, trembled for his Prussian possessions, and wrote to John George of Saxony that it would be dangerous for them if Gustavus set foot upon German soil. Had Ferdinand II promptly withdrawn the Edict of Restitution and offered the electors his protection, all the Protestant princes would probably have joined with him to expel the foreigner; but the obstinate refusal of the Emperor to withdraw the Edict on the one hand, and the persistence of Gustavus Adolphus in demanding their support on the other made a choice between the belligerents necessary. The Swedish army of thirteen thousand men furnished with six hundred cannons could be made either a friend or a foe, but neutrality was impossible; still, it was not until Tilly had been allowed to destroy Magdeburg, from exposure to whose terrible fate only Gustavus Adolphus could defend them, that Saxony and Brandenburg cast in their lot with him.

Before the battle of Breitenfeld, fought near Leipzig on September 17, 1631, Gustavus Adolphus had secretly negotiated with Wallenstein, who was then ready to join him in driving the House of Austria out of Germany, hoping thereby to obtain the crown of Bohemia for himself; but after that victory the King of Sweden was not disposed to share his success with so doubtful an ally.[1]

Victories and death of Gustavus Adolphus

It is unnecessary for our purpose to follow in detail the wonderful march of Gustavus Adolphus through the heart of Germany, first to the Rhine, where his presence in that "lane of priests" filled the ecclesiastics with terror lest their lands be immediately confiscated, and even excited the alarm of Richelieu; then, after creating for his general, Bernard of Saxe-Weimar, a duchy of Franconia out of the bishopric of Würzburg, to South Germany, amid the acclamations of the people, who hailed him as a deliverer; and finally northward to Lützen, where, on November 16, 1632, his army

---

[1] For a full discussion of the Wallenstein question, see the literature cited at the end of this chapter, particularly the documents collected by Irmer.

defeated the Imperial troops, once more commanded by Wallenstein, while the King himself fell, pierced with bullets, upon the field of battle.[1]

Thus, at the age of only thirty-eight, passed away the great "Snow King," and with him the plans that might have changed the history of Europe. Around his name are gathered many speculations. What might have happened if he had lived and continued to be victorious, it is impossible to say; but it is not improbable that a great Protestant confederation would have been formed in the North, which in the next generation might have passed under the leadership of the House of Hohenzollern through the marriage of the Princess Christina, who became Queen of Sweden, with Frederick William of Brandenburg, who became the Great Elector; and thus have effected three centuries earlier the transfer of predominance in Germany from Austria to Prussia.[2]

After the death of Gustavus Adolphus the Thirty Years' War at once changed its character. With him perished the hope of a great "*Corpus Evangelicorum*" able to resist the Emperor, and the problem for each of the contestants thenceforth was how to obtain from the conflict the greatest immediate advantage. Richelieu was aiming to extend the frontiers of France on the Rhine; Oxenstiern was thinking of territorial satisfaction for Sweden on the Baltic; Bernard of Saxe-Weimar, the greatest of the German Protestant generals, — whose army had already become like that of Wallenstein a mere band of professional soldiers and adventurers, — was solicitous for his Duchy of Franconia and its enlargement; while Wallenstein, now Duke of Friedland and imperial generalissimo, was reading in the stars mysterious prognostications of his future. More and more as the years went by the purposes for which the war had been originally undertaken were vanishing from view, and plunder and devastation

---

[1] For the march of Gustavus Adolphus through Germany, consult Map IV at the end of this volume.

[2] On the plans of Gustavus Adolphus for this marriage, see Engelhaaf, *Gustav Adolf in Deutschland*, p. 103.

were becoming almost its sole excuse. Even in matters of religion, it was not for toleration but for ecclesiastical property that men were contending, and for the power to dictate the religious faith of others. In this respect there was but little discrimination between Catholic, Lutheran, and Calvinist. When Gustavus Adolphus offered to restore to the Elector Palatine his ancestral territories on condition that he would permit Lutheran and Calvinist forms of worship on equal terms, Frederick V had stiffly rejected the proposition and died in exile. Of all the leaders on both sides only Gustavus and Wallenstein were in favor of religious liberty.

Attitude of France toward Protestantism

Thus denuded of great motives and great principles, the remainder of the Thirty Years' War possesses little general human interest except as a scene of suffering, intrigue, and tragedy, until the tide set in for peace.

The alliance between France and Sweden was only a part of Richelieu's policy to weaken the House of Austria, and was not intended in any way, so far as France was concerned, to aid the cause of Protestantism. When Gustavus Adolphus had invited France to enter with him upon the conquest of the territories of the Catholic princes along the Rhine, the temptation was strong; but Richelieu, who was a sincere believer as well as a patriot, was unwilling to abandon the Catholic electors and the Catholic League, and to permit the King of Sweden to ensure the success of the Protestants in the Empire. From first to last, the policy of France was to hold the balance between the antagonists; and when Gustavus was devastating Bavaria, Louis XIII not only sent the French resident at Munich to intercede for Duke Maximilian, but on hearing the news of the King's victory at the Lech said to the Venetian ambassador, " It is time to put a stop to the progress of this Goth," and discontinued the payment of his subsidies.

But now that the King of Sweden was dead, it was considered to be to the interest of France that the war should continue, and the Marquis de Feuquières was despatched to Germany to encourage Oxenstiern to prolong it. As a result, on April 13, 1633, the four circles of the West signed at Heilbronn a treaty of confederation with the Swedish chancellor for the defence of the Germanic liberties. Oxenstiern became the head of the alliance, and Sweden was promised a suitable territorial compensation. On September 5, 1633, at Frankfort, the King of France joined the coalition; but Feuquières was not able to secure the adhesion of the electors of Saxony and Brandenburg, with whom Wallenstein was now attempting to negotiate a peace.

Whatever his ultimate designs may have been for his own aggrandisement, it was Wallenstein who was now the master on the imperial side, and he was anxious to conclude a peace. The unlimited power which he possessed amounted almost to the abdication of the Emperor. From the beginning a champion of religious toleration, he was anxious to satisfy the Protestants by cancelling the Edict of Restitution and restoring the son of Frederick V to a portion of the Palatinate, and ready to offer security to Sweden by the cession of territories on the Baltic. Such a peace would have at least given repose to Germany and might have restored its unity upon the principle of toleration; but, if the Swedes and German Protestants were being used as the tools of France, Ferdinand II was not less the instrument of Spain, and Wallenstein's plans for peace were now to be turned against him.

From the Spanish point of view, concessions to the Protestants were not to be thought of, the co-operation of the Austrian power with Spain was considered necessary in the war with the Netherlands, and Wallenstein's position and schemes in Germany were full of danger to the Spanish influence. The secret negotiations of the Duke of Friedland with Sweden, Saxony, and Brandenburg, his coolness toward the Emperor's eldest son, Ferdinand, and his indifference toward the Cardinal-Infante of Spain, who had been appointed Governor of the Spanish Netherlands and desired to lead an army from Italy through Germany to Brussels, were further occasions of suspicion, while his endeavors to strengthen the bonds between himself and his army in order

588   A HISTORY OF DIPLOMACY

CHAP. VII
A. D.
1625–1648

to enable him to act independently of the Emperor, and even apparently against his will, gave color to the charge of treason. Seizing upon all these elements of distrust, the Spanish ambassador, aided by the enemies of Wallenstein at Vienna, was able to destroy his influence over Ferdinand II, and the Duke of Friedland was first officially deprived of his authority over his troops, and then betrayed and assassinated by his officers. The rewards and honors heaped upon the chief conspirators by the Emperor give evidence of the jealousy with which he had been inspired toward his ablest general.

The Peace of Prague

With the imperial forces reorganized and placed under the command of the Emperor's son Ferdinand, and the Spanish army of the Cardinal-Infante now upon German soil, the Hapsburg power was again consolidated, and after the victory at Nördlingen of September 6, 1634, South Germany was once more under the Emperor's control. On May 30, 1635, the Peace of Prague was signed by the plenipotentiaries of Ferdinand II and the Elector of Saxony, and on September 6 adhered to by the Elector of Brandenburg, and thus a new opportunity to end the war was offered.[1] But, although the Emperor was now ready to mollify the Edict of Restitution and establish relations upon the conditions that existed in 1627, confidence in his promises was wanting. Most of the princes and cities were, however, induced to accept these terms; for all Germany was weary of the war, and only the shattered remains of the League of Heilbronn formed a rallying point for its continuance.

The open intervention of France

Then it was that Richelieu entered upon that final series of negotiations with which he was to crown his career and lay the foundations for the predominance of France in Europe. It was the intervention of Spain to secure the greatness of the House of Austria in Germany that had turned the tide in the Emperor's favor, and the recovery of the United Netherlands was now the goal toward which the march of the

---

[1] See Dumont VI, Part I, pp. 88 et seq.

DEVELOPMENT OF A SOVEREIGN STATE SYSTEM 589

victorious Spanish army was directed. The old middle kingdom of Lothair, whose great artery was the Rhine, was in danger of falling entirely into Hapsburg hands. Italy was already in the grasp of Spain, Franche-Comté was its possession, the Lower Palatinate was its conquered province, on the Atlantic and the Mediterranean the maritime power of Spain was superior to that of France, and if the whole highway of the Rhine, flanked on the east by a Hapsburg Germany, should become a Spanish possession, France would be almost literally surrounded by its circle of fire.

With foresight of the situation, Richelieu had occupied Lorraine and forced the abdication of its duke. Numerous posts upon the Rhine had been quietly appropriated, and Coblenz, Ehrenbreitstein, and Philipsburg were in French possession. The main object now was to maintain a Rhine frontier. To secure this advantage, Richelieu had secretly promised that, if Elsass were ceded to France, all the Protestant alliances would be abandoned. But Ferdinand II was now too strong to make concessions, and Richelieu began that elaborate system of treaty relations by which a check was placed upon the Hapsburg power. On February 8, 1635, by the Treaty of Paris, the United Provinces were engaged for a partition of the Spanish Netherlands. On April 28, a new treaty was concluded with Sweden at Compiègne. On May 19, war was openly declared by France on the Cardinal-Infante and the King of Spain, but Richelieu did not cease to negotiate. On July 11 was concluded the Treaty of Rivoli, by which the Duke of Savoy was attracted with a project for the partition of Milan; and on October 26, by the Treaty of Saint-Germain-en-Laye, Bernard of Saxe-Weimar was promised four million livres a year for the service of eighteen thousand soldiers. The danger of France was not imaginary. In 1636 its territory was invaded by the Spanish from the Netherlands, but Richelieu's tolerance had united the monarchy within while his diplomacy had strengthened it from without, and the invasion was soon repelled.

It does not fall within the scope of this work to follow

Chap. VII
A. D.
1625-1648

the campaigns in the Netherlands, on the Rhine, in Saxony, Italy, and Spain, and finally in Bohemia and Bavaria, by which the ruin of Germany was completed and all Europe exhausted, and from whose fiery crucible finally came forth a new political order and a new conception of international relations. In December, 1640, Portugal threw off the sovereignty of Spain, and by the Treaty of Paris of February 1, 1641, the Duke of Braganza, who had assumed the crown, was accorded the assistance of a French fleet in return for his alliance. Both at home and abroad the great cardinal won triumph after triumph in the field and in the cabinet, until upon his death on December 4, 1642, Richelieu saw France upon the highway to that primacy in Europe which had been the dream of his tireless existence; and when, after the death of Louis XIII five months later, Anne of Austria assumed the regency of France during the minority of Louis XIV, although she was a sister of the King of Spain and a sister-in-law of the Emperor, the French monarchy under the ministry of Cardinal Mazarin could pursue no other course than to follow out the policy upon which the greatness of France had been established. That policy had been to unite the nation within, to crush out all local despotisms by substituting for them the more generous and enlightened despotism of the King, to break down the powerful dynastic combination by which France and Europe had been menaced, and to secure to the monarchy those "natural limits" — the Alps, the Pyrenees, and the Rhine — which would render it invulnerable to foreign aggression.

The great need of Germany and of Europe had long been peace, but how was peace to be attained when so many interests were involved, when a generation had passed since men had known anything but war, and when fighting had become the sole means of subsistence of those who had made it their only occupation? With the hardships, the poverty, and the social degradation of war had come also its moral consequences, the laxity of discipline and the disregard of rights. Multitudes of homeless people, men plundered of

DEVELOPMENT OF A SOVEREIGN STATE SYSTEM

all they possessed and punished because they possessed no more, and women abandoned to vice as a last resort, hovered hungry and miserable about the camps and followed the armies on the march. In some of the best parts of Germany two thirds of the houses had been destroyed, and so great was the loss of population that only half the remainder were occupied. Art, literature, and culture had practically ceased. For more than a hundred years after this period of desolation Germany did not regain her previous level of prosperity.

The Peace of Prague would have ended the misery of the Empire if it had not been for foreign interference, but it was Europe and not Germany only that was now involved, and neither France nor Sweden was disposed to permit a conclusion of the war that would leave the House of Hapsburg predominant in Europe.

A few months before the death of Ferdinand II on February 15, 1637, Pope Urban VIII had proposed a congress at Köln to which he invited the belligerents with the view of negotiating a peace; but the Protestant powers would not submit to the mediation of the Pope, and France was not willing to negotiate apart from her allies. Venice had offered to mediate in behalf of the Netherlands and Sweden; but, although the Netherlands accepted this proposition, Sweden would neither accept nor refuse it, ostensibly because the Republic had addressed Queen Christina merely as "*Sérénissime*" and failed to add "*Très-Puissante.*" Although the Venetian ambassador at Paris humbly apologized for the omission to Grotius, then the Swedish ambassador to France, the war was resumed and the attempt to mediate proved abortive.

Ferdinand III, who succeeded his father as Emperor, hoping to compose the affairs of Germany from within and thus remove all ground for foreign intervention, in 1640 had convened a diet of the Empire at Regensburg; but, although its deliberations lasted a year, the assembly brought forth no definite result except to prepare the way for negotiating a general peace. The fact which it made most evident was that the Empire was now thoroughly weary of the war.

Even France had sent no envoys to the Pope's proposed congress at Köln, but at Hamburg, where the Emperor was endeavoring to make a separate peace with Sweden, Count d'Avaux was present with the determination to prevent the isolation of France. Finally, after a long contest, on January 30, 1641, the alliance between France and Sweden was renewed,[1] and on December 25, the Emperor was constrained to accept an arrangement which provided for the assembling of a general congress for the negotiation of peace.[2]

It is difficult to exaggerate the obstacles to a general settlement. The war was still in progress, and no one of the belligerents had the slightest confidence in the good faith either of his enemies or of his allies. Much labor was expended in selecting a place where the Congress might convene. The Swedes would not consent to send their plenipotentiaries to Köln, nor to any city where the Pope was recognized as mediator, nor were they willing to grant precedence to the French wherever they might meet. France was opposed to the choice of two cities widely separated in space, for fear the Emperor might succeed in making peace with the Swedes without conceding the French demands. At last, Count d'Avaux proposed that the plenipotentiaries of the Emperor should meet the French at Münster and the Swedes at Osnabruck, two towns of Westphalia only thirty miles apart. After much difficulty this proposition was accepted, and the opening of the Congress was fixed for March 25, 1642.

Arrangements for the Congress of Westphalia

Thus, after six years of endeavor to settle the affairs of Germany without submitting to the restrictions that he feared would be imposed upon him by foreign powers, the Emperor had finally consented to treat with them unitedly on German soil. It was, in truth, nothing less than the

---

[1] See Dumont, VI, Part I, pp. 207 et seq.
[2] See Bougeant, *Histoire*, II, pp. 222 et seq.

reorganization of Germany and the restoration of the equilibrium of Europe that were now in question.

At last there was a prospect that instead of brute force some principle of justice might be invoked, but the same greed and suspicion that had so long embittered the war were now to embarrass and in part to characterize the efforts of diplomacy.

In order to afford security to the persons of the plenipotentiaries and their suites, Münster and Osnabruck were neutralized, and the foreign powers agreed to respect their religion and customs. Freedom of communication was also ensured between the two towns by neutralizing the route between them. Thus was set apart a small area of peace and security where the voice of reason might be heard.

But how was this charmed circle to be entered? In order to execute safe conducts, questions of precedence had first to be settled; for the plenipotentiary of France, Count d'Avaux, would not accord to Ferdinand III the title of Emperor, and Salvius, the representative of the Queen of Sweden, would not suffer his monarch to be named after the King of France. Thus months were wasted before a compromise was reached. It was finally decided that each plenipotentiary in his acts or communications should give his own ruler the first rank.

When these first obstacles had been thus ingeniously surmounted, the Emperor, who still wished if possible to exclude the foreign powers from regulating the affairs of the Empire, refused to ratify the treaty on the grounds that his representative, Lutzau, had treated with France and Sweden as if their rulers were equals of the Emperor; that in the copies of the treaty signed by France and Sweden his own name did not appear first; and that the neutralization of the Westphalian cities was derogatory to his dignity, since his safe conducts should be esteemed sufficient. For these reasons Lutzau was disgraced and his work repudiated. Anxious, however, not to appear the sole cause of the continuance of the war, Ferdinand III, nevertheless, while refusing to ratify the treaty in solemn form, wrote a letter in which he in-

CHAP. VII
A. D.
1625–1648

formally accepted its general terms; but, in promising the security of the plenipotentiaries, he omitted to name Münster, so that his promise applied only to Osnabruck, and to this place only after the ambassadors should have arrived there.[1] These omissions, which were construed by D'Avaux and Salvius as evasions, awakened new suspicions, and the Emperor's renewed attempt to isolate France by negotiating separately with Sweden still further impeded progress. It was, therefore, not until July 22, 1642, that the arrangements for the Congress of Westphalia were ratified.

Ceremonial impediments to negotiation

In the meantime, the war continued spasmodically, and the efforts for peace followed the fluctuations of its fortunes. The date for the opening of the Congress was already past, but the first representatives of the powers did not arrive in Westphalia until August, 1643. As late as October, 1644, several of the plenipotentiaries had not produced satisfactory full powers, and no serious business was done until June 1, 1645, when the French and Swedish propositions were handed in. "If," wrote Ogier, who accompanied the French plenipotentiary Abel Servien to Münster, "they create in the substance of the business delays proportioned to those hitherto, I do not know that the unborn child Madame Servien is expecting can hope to see the end of a treaty to which our adversaries create such extraordinary obstacles."[2]

The plenipotentiaries of the Netherlands did not arrive at the Congress until January 11, 1646. The time had been chiefly occupied in separate negotiations with France regarding the terms of their alliance, the position of the Republic in the Congress, and particularly as to whether or not its deputies were to be accorded the title of "Excellency," thitherto reserved for the representatives of kings and conceded only by exception to the ambassadors of Venice.[3]

---

[1] See Le Clerc, *Négociations*, I, pp. 113 et seq.
[2] See Boppe, *Journal du Congrès de Munster*, p. 88.
[3] These differences were finally settled by special treaties. See Bougeant, *Histoire*, II, p. 364.

Among the chief impediments to the negotiations at Münster were the questions of rank and precedence and the disputes which they elicited. Who should make the first visit; how far a host should accompany his guest, whether to the door or to his carriage; how the ambassadors should be seated; what titles should be employed in addressing the different plenipotentiaries, — these were the momentous questions upon which the diplomatists spent months of anxious thought.

Before the Congress began its business, the King of Denmark, who had been named as mediator between the Emperor and Sweden, had been provoked by the aggressive action of the Swedes, and was now engaged in open war with them.

Serious embarrassments might have arisen with the other mediators also had it not been for the good sense of Monsignore Fabio Chigi, the papal nuncio, — afterward Pope Alexander VII, — and Luigi Contarini, the Venetian ambassador, to whom the function of mediation for the Catholics and Protestants respectively was confided. The nuncio had caused a dais to be prepared for himself in the church, to be occupied by him after the procession should have entered. The French ambassadors, having been informed of this, declared that if the nuncio intended to officiate in pontifical vestments, this might be permitted; but, otherwise, the dais must be removed, and he must take his seat with the ambassadors, among whom he would have, however, the first place. To this he readily assented, and having carried the sacrament to the church he gave it to the suffragan, and then in his usual attire took his place as an ambassador.

But the French plenipotentiaries having next learned that the imperial representatives had arranged for their chairs to be stationed in advance of their own, they insisted that all the seats be placed in the same line at the left of the choir; the first for the nuncio, the next two for the Imperials, the next two for themselves, and the last for Contarini, to which he made no objection. But the formation of the procession raised a new difficulty. The Imperials insisted upon having the first places, against which the French protested. With much effort it was finally arranged by the nuncio that the Count d'Avaux should walk beside the imperial plenipotentiary, the Count of Nassau, and Servien beside his imperial colleague, Doctor Volmar; and this was considered a great victory for France. The Spaniards, unwilling to yield precedence to the French, remained at home. But the solution was received with joy by the people, who now for the first time believed that peace might be concluded.

Organization of the Congress The envoys of different grades at Münster and Osnabruck were so numerous that, according to the representative of Mantua, "it would require six hours to enumerate them." The houses were not sufficient for their accommodation, and "one could not look out of the door without seeing ten ambassadors."[1]

The Emperor's plenipotentiaries at Münster were Count Trauttmannsdorf, the Count of Nassau, and Doctor Volmar; at Osnabruck, Count Lamberg and John Crane.

The King of France sent Count d'Avaux and Servien to Münster, who were afterward supplemented by Henry Duke de Longueville, and later by De la Court, besides the French resident, De Saint-Romain. At Osnabruck also France had a minister resident, this office being filled in succession by Baron Rorté, Monsieur de la Barde, and Monsieur de la Court.

The Queen of Sweden was represented at Osnabruck by her great chancellor, Oxenstiern, in person, accompanied by John Salvius, one of the most experienced diplomatists of his time.

Spain had a delegation of four ambassadors and three envoys at Münster, headed by the Count de Peñaranda.[2]

---

[1] See the list of plenipotentiaries in De Garden, *Histoire*, I, pp. 80, 87.

[2] The rôle of Spain in the Congress was not prominent and ended with the reconciliation with the Netherlands soon to be noted. The war between Spain and France continued after the Peace of Westphalia was concluded.

DEVELOPMENT OF A SOVEREIGN STATE SYSTEM 597

There were present also at Münster the two ambassadors of Portugal, the eight deputies of the Netherlands, and four representatives of the Electoral College, besides the special delegates of the German electors, all of whom, except the Elector of Saxony, were represented at both Münster and Osnabruck. To these must be added the deputies of all the other principal German magnates and the free imperial cities and of several important personages in Italy, including the Princes Palatine, the Grand Master of the Teutonic Order, and various dukes, bishops, and counts of the Empire, the Duke of Savoy, the Grand Duke of Tuscany, and the Duke of Mantua.

CHAP. VII
A. D.
1625–1648

England, then in the throes of the Puritan Revolution was too divided and two much absorbed in the bitter contest between the King and the Parliament to take an active part in the affairs of Europe, and with Russia and the Ottoman Empire sent no delegates to the Congress.

Of organization, according to the modern idea of an international assembly, there was strictly speaking none; for in the Congress of Westphalia there were neither presiding nor recording officers, nor plenary conferences, nor committees of reference, nor reports of recommendations, nor formal sessions, nor voting of any kind. In truth, there was nothing in its mode of discussing the questions before it to distinguish its business from ordinary diplomatic negotiations except the proximity of the negotiators, their occupation of a neutralized area, and at Münster the presence of mediators.

Of these, the papal nuncio, Chigi, Bishop of Nardo, was the centre of the Catholic group, while the Chevalier Contarini, senator and ambassador of the Republic of Venice, mediated between the Emperor, the Netherlands, and the German Protestants. Sweden had also finally accepted the Venetian mediation, but this was found to be ineffectual in practice; for Contarini was fully occupied at Münster, fear was entertained that it might offend him to appoint a colleague, and the Swedes could not be persuaded to accept the services of a mere secretary. The result was, therefore, that at Osnabruck

Method of procedure

the plenipotentiaries of the Emperor and of the Queen of Sweden carried on their negotiations directly by exchange of notes.

At Münster, it had been intended that Cardinal Rosetti should represent the Pope, but Mazarin regarded him as too much inclined toward the interests of Spain, and imagined that by excluding him the person named in his place would be more favorable to France through indebtedness to the French for his nomination. Urban VIII, to express his dissatisfaction with the conduct of France in opposing Rosetti, who was to have been empowered as a legate *a latere*, sent Chigi with only the rank of nuncio. His instructions, if taken literally, rendered him little more than a letter box for the reception and exchange of notes between the negotiators; for he was forbidden to make any proposition on his own account, and not even to express an opinion upon the proposals made by the plenipotentiaries. His function was, therefore, reduced to listening to the reasons presented by each side and repeating them without prejudice to the other. The Pope, notwithstanding his apparent reduction of the nuncio to a monument of neutrality, intended in no respect to neglect any opportunity to guard the papal interests in Italy, to favor the Catholic princes against the Protestants in Germany, and to preserve to the prelates the properties of the Church.

Contarini, whose experience as ambassador of Venice at The Hague, in England, in France, and at Constantinople had won for him a great reputation as a cool, subtle, and capable negotiator, had also to protect the interests of his republic by maintaining as far as possible the equilibrium of the powers. Apart from this, no just complaint could be brought against his perfect neutrality, although the French at first flattered themselves that he was favorable to France and afterward complained when they found that he was not subject to their wishes.[1]

With such a system of mediation, the business of the Con-

---

[1] See Bougeant, *Histoire*, III, p. 11.

DEVELOPMENT OF A SOVEREIGN STATE SYSTEM 599

gress resolved itself into the presentation of manifestoes, written and oral, in which all the plenipotentiaries endeavored to emphasize the interests they represented. To present effective briefs, to answer the claims of opponents, to offer counter arguments, to make an impression upon the mediators in every conceivable manner, to create by conversation a favorable current of opinion, — such were the means by which the work of the Congress was tediously conducted.

CHAP. VII
A. D.
1625–1648

But the labors of the mediators were, in reality, not confined to the passive transmission of communications. Both Chigi and Contarini faithfully strove by every means to bring the plenipotentiaries to an understanding. The nuncio not only diligently presented to all the Catholic powers the arguments of the others, but he employed the papal resident at Vienna to influence decision at the imperial court, and attempted a similar course at Paris. Contarini also wrote with the same purpose to the Venetian residents at the different European capitals.

But it is unnecessary to dwell upon negotiations so long and so complicated as to fill whole volumes, and whose details should be more leisurely followed by those to whom they are of special interest. That which chiefly concerns us here is the bearing of the Congress upon the international development of Europe. Regarded from this point of view, the Peace of Westphalia was the most important, and in its results the most enduring, public act of modern history, for from it dates the present political system of Europe as a group of independent sovereign states.

As a question of international politics, the object of France and Sweden was to destroy forever the imperial pretensions by the abasement of the House of Hapsburg, and to establish their own security by giving solidity to the system of coequal powers. The safeguard of this system was the equilibrium of its component states. The preponderance of Spain, the threatened restoration of the Empire in Germany, and above all the union of both under the Hapsburg domina-

The political settlement

tion,— these were the perils to which Europe had been exposed, and these were the dangers which were now to be terminated.

To accomplish this object, the essential point was to enfeeble and reorganize the Empire. This transformation, turning chiefly upon the question of religion, will be considered by itself; but, to give stability to the new system, were demanded certain "satisfactions" for France and Sweden and certain "guarantees" for the future.

To this programme of despoiling and permanently subjecting the Empire Ferdinand III was disposed to offer a stout resistance. In this he had the support of Spain, and in Germany he still counted upon the loyalty of the Catholic princes. Of these Maximilian of Bavaria was the most important, but he also had suffered most heavily from the war, from which his duchy was still in peril. After long negotiations, Maximilian was finally wholly separated from the cause of the Emperor, and the Treaty of Ulm of March 14, 1647, proved the turning point in the efforts for peace; for whose conclusion on the basis of a general amnesty, "satisfactions," and "guarantees," Maximilian in alliance with France and Sweden thereafter earnestly strove.[1]

The "satisfaction" of France was urged on the ground of an indemnity for the expenses of the war. It was, without doubt, the gold of France that had conquered the House of Austria. Its seductions had undermined the loyalty of princes and cities, and Feuquières wrote with truth: "They love so well the sound of our pieces of gold that it depends only upon the King to place his money at a good rate." Denmark and Sweden as well as the German princes had

---

[1] The negotiations between France, Sweden, and Maximilian are thoroughly treated by Egloffstein, *Baierns Friedenspolitik*. The importance of Maximilian in the estimation of both sides is evident from the fact that his plenipotentiary, Hasland, was received at Münster as the ambassador of a "sovereign prince" and styled "Excellency" by both parties. See Boppe, *Journal*, p. 104.

enjoyed large subsidies from France, almost impoverished in consequence of the cost of the war.

But behind the plausible demand for indemnity was the dream of territorial expansion. "To give to Gaul the frontiers which nature has designed for it, to secure to the Gauls a Gallic king, to identify Gaul with France, and wherever ancient Gaul was there to establish the new," wrote Richelieu in his political testament, was the duty and the right of France. But Mazarin was not less truly a loyal Frenchman. Knowing how weary the German princes were of war, he combined with their interests the claims of France in such a manner as to convince them that without the Emperor's satisfaction of France peace could not be made. With splendid assurance he insinuated that the nearer France was to them the more useful would be its protection of the Germanic liberties against the House of Hapsburg. Thus, to the end of the negotiations Germany was divided against itself, and France obtained in full sovereignty from the spoils of the Empire the three bishoprics, Metz, Toul, and Verdun "with their districts," the landgraviates of Upper and Lower Elsass and the Sundgau, with the ten imperial cities of Elsass, although the treaty contained certain ambiguities regarding the cities of Strasburg and Brisach.[1] In addition, the Emperor renounced his sovereignty over Pinerolo, ceded to France the right to maintain a garrison in Philipsburg, granted to France freedom of commerce upon both banks of the Rhine, with the right to navigate that river throughout its whole length, and bound himself to erect no fortress on the right bank from Basel to Philipsburg.

If France had been prodigal in gold, Sweden had been not less so in the blood of its people, having lost in the war, it is estimated, half of its population. Behind the claim for indemnity for these losses was, however, another dream of ambition: Sweden aimed to protect itself by controlling the

---

[1] Expressions destined to occasion disputes when later Louis XIV attempted his policy of "reunion."

Baltic. To hold Germany in check, it demanded and obtained possession of Western Pomerania with the Islands of Rügen, Wallin, and Usedom, and the port of Wismar on the Baltic, and the secularized bishoprics of Bremen and Verden on the North Sea. These accessions of territory Sweden preferred to receive as fiefs of the Empire, which gave the right of appearance at the Imperial Diet under the titles of Dukes of Bremen, Verden, and Pomerania, Prince of Rügen, and Lord of Wismar.

As a guarantee of faithful execution, the Treaties of Westphalia were accepted as a fundamental law by all the contractants, who were empowered and bound to defend their provisions. Thus, for the first time, Europe received what may be fairly described as an international constitution, which gave to all its adherents the right of intervention to enforce its arrangements.[1]

The religious settlement

As it was dissension in matters of religion that had first introduced discord and division in the Empire, advantage was to be taken of it to perpetuate the political impotence of the Emperor. Under the guise of protecting the rights of religion, the definitive destruction of religious unity being now officially recognized, each territorial potentate in Germany practically became a sovereign not only in ecclesiastical affairs but in political matters also. The Transaction of Passau and the Peace of Augsburg were confirmed, and their privileges extended to the Calvinists. The date fixed as the limit for the restitution of ecclesiastical property was January 1, 1624. Whatever had been in Catholic possession before that time was to remain undisturbed, whatever had been acquired since was to be restored, and there was to be no future secularization. But the essentially political character of the religious settlement is evident from the limita-

---

[1] See Article XVII of the Treaty of Osnabruck, reproduced in the Treaty of Münster, which in the fifth paragraph reads: "All and each of the contracting parties of this treaty shall be held to defend and maintain all and each of the dispositions of this peace, against whomsoever it may be, without distinction of religion."

DEVELOPMENT OF A SOVEREIGN STATE SYSTEM 603

tion of liberty of conscience to the Catholic, Lutheran, and Calvinist confessions, according to the predilections of the territorial princes.

Each of the three hundred and forty-three states of the Empire was accorded the right of suffrage in the Imperial Diet on questions of general legislation, war and peace, taxation, the levy of armies, and measures for the common defence. In addition, each was authorized to make separate alliances with foreign powers, if not directed against the Empire or the Emperor; whom it was, however, still possible to oppose if necessary in his quality of King of Hungary.

Thus disappeared the last traces of imperial power. With the Diet charged with all legislation and automatically meeting every six months, the Imperial Chamber composed of an almost equal number of Catholics and Protestants, and six Protestants in the Aulic Council, the Emperor remained really a sovereign only in the domains of the House of Austria, and these were so hedged in as to exclude the possibility of westward expansion.

The importance of the Emperor was still further diminished by the territorial accessions acquired by three of the German electors. In compensation for the loss of Western Pomerania, the Elector of Brandenburg received, besides Cleve and Mark, the secularized bishoprics of Halberstadt, Minden, and Camin, with the expectation of the entire archbishopric of Magdeburg, — possessions which were destined to promote the future expansion of that electorate and the formation of the powerful state of Prussia. To the Elector of Saxony in 1635 had been ceded by Ferdinand II the whole of Lusatia. The Elector of Bavaria not only retained his electoral office but also the Upper Palatinate, while the Lower Palatinate, with an eighth electorate, was restored to the son of Frederick V as Count Palatine of the Rhine.

From every point of view, therefore, the Congress of Westphalia marks the arrest of that revival of imperialism which had been the dream of the House of Hapsburg. The definitive acts signed at Münster and Osnabruck on October 24,

CHAP. VII
A. D.
1625–1648

Effect of the Congress upon Europe

CHAP. VII
A.D.
1625-1648

1648,[1] opened a new era by officially establishing territorial sovereignty both political and religious in the public law of Europe. Hardly less serious than the overthrow of the Emperor was the defeat of the Pope, whose representative was called by the irony of fate to mediate a reconciliation that was in effect the final interment of mediaeval ideals. When the peace was about to be signed, the papal nuncio, realizing that it officially recognized the legitimacy of heresy within the Holy Roman Empire, protested against it with all his energy. His opposition having failed, Pope Innocent X issued a bull of formal protest against the treaties as "perpetually null, vain, invalid, wicked, and . . . without force and effect." But these fulminations were unavailing, and the Treaties of Westphalia were accepted by Catholics and Protestants alike as forming the fundamental law of Europe.[2]

[1] For the best editions of the text, see authorities at the end of this chapter.

[2] The scope of the Peace of Westphalia is shown in the tenth and eleventh paragraphs of Article XVII of the Treaty of Osnabruck as follows : —

"On the part of the Most Serene Emperor are included in this peace all His Majesty's allies and adherents, namely the Catholic King (Spain), the House of Austria, the Electors of the Holy Roman Empire, and with them the Duke of Savoy and the other States including the free and immediate Nobility of the said Empire and the Hanseatic cities, also the King of England, the King and Kingdoms of Denmark and Norway with the annexed provinces together with the Duke of Schleswig, the King of Poland, the Duke of Lorraine, and all the Princes and Republics of Italy, the States of the United Provinces and the Swiss Cantons, the Grisons, and the Prince of Transylvania.

"On the part of the Most Serene Queen and Kingdom of Sweden all their allies and adherents, namely, the Most Christian King (France), the Electors Princes and States including the free and immediate Nobility of the Empire and the Hanseatic cities, also the King of England, the King and Kingdoms of Denmark and Norway with the annexed provinces together with the Duke of Schleswig, the King of Poland, the King and Kingdom of Lusitania (Portugal), the Grand Duke of Moscovy (Russia), the Republic of Venice, the United Provinces, the Swiss, the Grisons, and the Prince of Transylvania."

Thus practically the whole of Europe was included in the peace, except the Ottoman Empire.

DEVELOPMENT OF A SOVEREIGN STATE SYSTEM 605

But, like many other agents in the performance of historic tasks of far-reaching consequence, the negotiators of the Peace of Westphalia had in mind no permanent results and no great principle. National interest and ambition were the mainsprings of all their work.[1] None the less, and perhaps even all the more, their enforced agreements have value as recording the progress of political evolution; for treaties are not purely voluntary compromises, they are acknowledgments of material conditions engendered by the state of human society. Those which have anticipated most have been doomed to the most humiliating failures. The importance of the Treaties of Westphalia lies in their frank recognition of the facts which rendered the Empire a menace to Europe, without proposing to reorganize the existing system upon any fantastic plan.

Two achievements were too obvious to dispute. The independence of the Swiss Confederation, which had been real since the fifteenth century, was officially recognized by the Congress and accorded the benefit of its guarantees. The independence of the United Provinces was also recognized by Spain. The Republic was bound by treaty with France not to make a separate peace, but the exhausted condition of Spain rendered it impossible to continue the war with both the allies. Taking advantage of this fact, Mazarin sought to make exorbitant demands. The resistance of Spain to concessions which would involve its abasement on the one hand and the fear of the Netherlands that Mazarin was about to abandon them in order to secure advantages for France on the other led to the conclusion of a secret treaty of peace between them on January 30, 1648.[2] By the terms of this treaty all the colonies taken from Spain in the Indies, Africa, and America — most of these being really at the expense of Portugal, now again independent — were ceded to

---

[1] Mathieu Molé, in an address to the King of France, referred to the Peace of Westphalia as "*l'ouvrage du ciel et non des hommes.*" — *Mémoires*, III, p. 293.

[2] Dumont, VI, Part I, pp. 365 et seq.

the Republic. In addition, the Schelde was closed from communication with the sea, which built up the prosperity of Amsterdam by the ruin of Antwerp through the transfer to Holland of all the commerce of the Spanish Netherlands.

Thus two self-constituted republics, representing new principles of civic life, were admitted to the society of European states; but the Peace of Westphalia was in no sense the triumph of either civil or religious liberty, or of justice as an international principle. It was, in truth, the consecration of territorial absolutism.[1] The question at issue in the Thirty Years' War was not the nature but the distribution of political power. The Empire was, indeed, destroyed; and with it disappeared that moral solidarity and that benignant restraint of local despotism by superior authority for which the imperial idea had always stood. In Germany, provincial egoism and petty tyranny were to flourish without control. In Europe as a whole, except in England, then in the travail of its political revolution, passive populations sought peace at the feet of rulers who had been rendered absolute by the efforts to save the State from dissolution.

It was, in fact, a new despotism that was thus imposed upon Europe, based like the old upon the use of force, regardless like the old of the rights of the individual man, but more firm in its grasp of power, more definite in its immediate ambitions, and rendered more intense by the sense of its limitations. Anarchy had given place to order, and religion had found refuge in the protection of the State; but the State had become so identified with its ruler that it was but

---

[1] In a sermon preached at Münster by Ogier during the Congress, he puts into the lips of Christ as King of kings the following words addressed to the princes of that time: "I have made you my lieutenants in this world, to be dispensers of my justice upon other men. I have placed you in a state that is hardly lower than that of my angels: they give impulsion to the heavenly bodies, you give motion to the mechanism of the earth. I have crowned you with honor and glory, and I have established you over the most beautiful works of my hands. Finally, I have put under your feet all other mortals." — Boppe, *Journal*, p. 223.

DEVELOPMENT OF A SOVEREIGN STATE SYSTEM 607

natural to impute to Louis XIV the aphorism, probably never uttered by him but expressing the most salient truth of his time, "*L'état, c'est moi !*" The Age of Absolutism had already entered upon its course, and with it a new conception of international life.

AUTHORITIES

In addition to the collections of documents previously cited, the following are the most important for the present chapter.

For the international relations of England, Spain, France, Scotland, and the Netherlands during the time of Philip II and Elizabeth, Camden, *The Historie of the Most Renowned and Victorious Princesse Elizabeth*, London, 1630; Thorpe, *State Papers relating to Scotland*, London, 1858; Hume, *Letters and State Papers, preserved principally in the Archives of Simancas*, London, 1892–1899; the Foreign Series of Calendars of State Papers, I–XV, edited by Stephenson (1558–1565), Crosby (1566–1577), and Butler (1577–1580), begun in 1863 and still in progress; Teulet, *Relations politiques de la France et de l'Espagne avec l'Ecosse*, Paris, 1862; Vertot, *Les ambassades de MM. de Noailles en Angleterre*, Paris, 1763; Bruce, *Correspondence of Leicester during his Government in the Low Countries*, London, 1844; Tommaseo, *Relations des ambassadeurs vénetiens sur les affaires de France au XVIe siècle*, Paris, 1838; Barozzi and Berchet, *Relazioni degli stati europei lette al Senato dagli ambasciatori veneti nel XVII secolo*, Venice, 1856.

For the relations of Spain and the Netherlands the most important are Groen van Prinsterer, *Archives ou correspondance inédite de la maison d'Orange-Nassau*, Leyden, 1841–1847, and Second Series, Utrecht, 1857–1861; Gachard, *Correspondance de Philippe II sur les affaires des Pays-Bas*, Brussels, 1848–1879, and *Correspondance de Guillaume le Taciturne*, Brussels, 1847–1857; Didier, *Lettres et négociations de Claude de Mondoucet*, French resident in the Netherlands 1571–1574, Paris, 1891.

For Henry IV, see Berger de Xivrey, *Lettres de Henri IV*, Paris, 1843–1858; Galitzin, *Lettres inédites de Henri IV*, Paris, 1860; Rommel, *Correspondance inédite de Henri IV avec Maurice le Savant*, Paris, 1840; Ritter, *Die Union und Heinrich IV (1607–1609)*, Munich, 1870–1874; and the memoirs, letters, and negotiations of Du Plessis-Mornay, Cardinal d'Ossat, Cardinal Du Perron, Villeroy, Bellièvre and Sillary, Jeannin, Boderie, Bassompierre, and especially the *Mémoires des sages et royalles oeconomies d'Estat* of Sully, Amsterdam,

1638; also important original documents in Laffleur de Kermaingant, *L'ambassade de France en Angleterre sous Henri IV: Mission de Jean de Thumery, Sieur de Bossise, 1598-1602*, Paris, 1886; and *Mission de Christophe de Harlay, comte de Beaumont, 1602-1605*, Paris, 1895. A collection of the *Lettres missives* of Henry IV is in course of publication by the Minister of Public Instruction of France.

For the affairs of France during the period 1616-1621 and for interesting information concerning diplomatic ceremonial, see *Lettere diplomatiche di Guido Bentivoglio, nuncio in Francia, etc.*, Turin, 1852.

Much interesting information regarding the condition of Germany prior to the Thirty Years' War may be found in Fiedler, *Relationen venetianischer Botschafter über Deutschland und Oesterreich im sechzehnten Jahrhundert*, Vienna, 1870.

For negotiations during the Thirty Years' War, see Gardiner, *Letters and other Documents illustrating the Relations between England and Germany at the Commencement of the Thirty Years' War*, London, 1865-1868; Ritter, *Briefe und Akten, etc.*, Munich, 1870-1903; Hildebrand, *Wallenstein und seine Verbindungen mit den Schweden*, Frankfort, 1885, from the Archives of Sweden; Irmer, *Die Verhandlungen Schwedens und seiner Verbundeten mit Wallenstein*, Leipzig, 1888-1891, from the Prussian Archives; Avenel, *Lettres, instructions diplomatiques et papiers d'état du cardinal de Richelieu*, Paris, 1853-1856; memoirs and negotiations of Richelieu, Mazarin, D'Avaux, Estrade, Feuquières, and Brienne. The *Testament politique* of Richelieu has been attributed to the imagination of Paul Hay, Marquis du Châtelet, but this applies only to the third part, published in the Amsterdam edition of 1689. The Amsterdam edition of 1687, containing only the first and second parts, is believed to be authentic. A new edition of Richelieu's *Mémoires* is about to be undertaken by the Société de l'Histoire de France.

The documents relating to the Peace of Westphalia may be found in Le Clerc, *Négociations secrètes touchant la paix de Munster et Osnabrug*, The Hague, 1725; Meiern, *Acta Pacis Westphaliae Publica*, Hanover and Göttingen, 1734-1740; Adam Adami, *Arcana Pacis Westphalicae*, Frankfort, 1698, and a later edition by Meiern under the title *Relatio Historica, etc.*, Leipzig, 1737. The Treaty of Münster is contained in Vast, *Les grands traités du règne de Louis XIV*, Paris, 1893-1899, with good bibliography. Carefully edited texts of the two treaties in full are given in Philippi, *Der Westphälische Friede*, Münster, 1898, which also contains interesting illustrations of the great paintings of the Congress and prints of commemorative medals with interesting text. Contarini's report of the Congress is printed in Fiedler, *Die Relationen der Botschafter Venedigs*, II, pp. 293, 366.

Boppe, *Journal du Congrès de Munster par François Ogier*, Paris, 1893, is a contemporary diary. See also *Correspondencia de los plenipotenciarios españoles en congreso de Munster*, Madrid, 1885, for the Spanish account.

Of special importance on the Counter-Reformation are Gothein *Ignatius von Loyola und die Gegenreformation*, Halle, 1895; Ritter, *Deutsche Geschichte im Zeitalter der Gegenreformation und des dreissigjährigen Krieges*, Stuttgart, 1901.

On the relations of Queen Elizabeth and Philip II of Spain, besides the histories of Ranke, Froude, and Prescott, see Beesley, *Queen Elizabeth*, London, 1893; Creighton, *Queen Elizabeth*, London, 1896; Hume, *The Courtships of Queen Elizabeth*, London, 1906, and *Philip II of Spain*, London, 1899; Philippson, *Westeuropa im Zeitalter von Philipp II, Elizabeth, und Heinrich IV*, Berlin, 1882; and Seeley, *The Growth of British Policy*, Cambridge, 1895.

On the revolt of the Netherlands and the international relations growing out of it, besides Motley, *Rise of the Dutch Republic*, in many editions, see Marx, *Studien zur Geschichte der Niederlandischen Aufstandes*, Leipzig, 1902; Blok, *Geschiedenis van het Nederlandische Volk*, Groningen, 1896, translated by Ruth Putnam, New York and London, 1900; Ruth Putnam, *William the Silent*, New York and London, 1895; Harrison, *William the Silent*, London, 1898; Brugmans, *Engeland en de Nederlanden in de eerste jaren van Elizabeth's regeering, 1558-1567*, Groningen, 1892; Philippson, *Ein Ministerium unter Philipp II, Kardinal Granvella am spanischen Hofe*, Berlin, 1895.

For the work of the jurists, see Janet, *Histoire de la science politique*, Paris, 1887; Weill, *Les théories sur le pouvoir royal en France pendant les guerres de religion*, Paris, 1892; Baudrillart, *Bodin et son temps*, Paris, 1853; Hancke, *Bodin, eine Studie über den Begriff der Volkssouveränetät*, Breslau, 1894; Dock, *Der Souveränetätsbegriff von Bodin bis zu Friedrich dem Grossen*, Strasburg, 1897; Gierke, *Johannes Althusius und die Entwickelung der naturrechtlichen Staatstheorien*, Breslau, 1880; Saffi, *Alberico Gentile e del dirrito delle genti*, Bologna, 1879; Professor Holland's Preface to his fine edition of. *De Iure Belli*, Oxford, 1877; Kaltenborn, *Die Vorläufer von Hugo Grotius*, Leipzig, 1848; Nys, *Le droit de la guerre et les précurseurs de Grotius*, Brussels, 1882; and *Les origines du droit international*, Brussels and Paris, 1894; and Walker, *A History of the Law of Nations*, Cambridge, 1899.

For the diplomacy of Henry IV of France and his alleged "Great Design," see Mercier de Lacombe, *Henri IV et sa politique*, Paris, 1861; Philippson, *Heinrich IV und Philipp III, die Begründung des französichen Uebergewichts in Europa*, Berlin, 1873; Petresco, *Henri IV et la Ligue Évangelique*, Paris, 1903; Rott, *Henri IV, les Suisses et la Haute Italie, la lutte pour les Alpes*, Paris, 1882; Couzard, *Une am-*

bassade à Rome sous Henri IV, Paris, 1900; De Crue, Relations diplomatiques de Genève avec la France, Paris, 1901; Cornelius, Ueber den Grossen Plan Heinrichs IV in the Münchener Hist. Jahrbuch, 1866; Ritter, Die Memorien Sullys in the Abhandlungen der Münchener Akademie, Hist. Class., 1871; Pfister's articles in the Revue Historique, LIV, LV, and LVI, 1894; Kükelhaus, Der Ursprung des Planes vom ewigen Frieden in den Memorien des Herzogs von Sully, Berlin, 1893.

On Richelieu and his policy, Hanotaux, Histoire du cardinal Richelieu, Paris, 1893 et seq., incomplete, vol. II ending with 1624; Zeller, Richelieu et les ministres de Louis XIII de 1621 à 1624, Paris, 1880; Avenel, Richelieu et la monarchie absolue, Paris, 1884–1887; Fagniez, Le Père Joseph et Richelieu, Paris, 1894; and La mission du père Joseph à Ratisbonne en 1630, Revue Historique, 1885; Lodge, Richelieu, London, 1896; Ranke, Französiche Geschichte, II, Leipzig, 1876, gives the German point of view. A recent brief biography of Mazarin is Hassall, Mazarin, London, 1903. The general history of France during the period is well presented by Perkins, France under Richelieu and Mazarin, Boston, 1887. The policy of Richelieu and Mazarin and the events leading up to the Thirty Years' War are very clearly stated by Bourgeois, Manuel historique de politique étrangère, I, Paris, 1897.

No adequate bibliography of the Thirty Years' War is possible within the limits compulsory here, nor is it deemed necessary to state the widely differing points of view of the leading historians of that period, Gindely, Prague, 1869–1880; Winter, Berlin, 1893; and Klopp, Paderborn, 1893–1896. A good brief outline may be found in Gardiner, London, 1903. Important studies of special questions are Krebs, Christian von Anhalt und die kurpfälzische Politik, Leipzig, 1872; Droysen, Gustav Adolf, Leipzig, 1869–1870; Engelhaaf, Gustav Adolf in Deutschland, 1630–1632, Halle, 1901; Kretzschmar, Gustav Adolfs Pläne und Ziele in Deutschland, Leipzig, 1904; Struck, Das Bündnis Wilhelms von Weimar mit Gustav Adolf, Stralsund, 1893, and Johann Georg und Oxenstierna, Stralsund, 1899; Waddington, La République de Provinces-Unies et les Pays-Bas espagnols de 1630 à 1650, Paris, 1895–1897; Die Boer, Die Friedensunterhandlungen zwischen Spanien und den Niederlanden in den Jahren 1632 bis 1633, Groningen, 1898; Droysen, Bernard von Weimar, Leipzig, 1885; Seehausen, Schweizer Politik während des dreissigjährigen Krieges, Halle, 1882; Bühring, Venedig, Gustav Adolf und Rohan, Halle, 1885, from the Venetian Archives; Zwiedineck-Südenhorst, Die Politik der Republik Venedig während des dreissigjährigen Krieges, Stuttgart, 1885; Odhner, Die Politik Schwedens im westphälischen Friedenskongress, Gotha, 1877; Egloffstein, Baierns Friedenspolitik von 1645 bis 1647, Leipzig, 1898; Jacob, Die Erwerbung des Elsass durch Frankreich im westphälischen

Frieden, Strasburg, 1898; Reuss, *L'Alsace au XVIIe siècle*, Paris, 1897-1898; Overmann, *Die Abtretung des Elsass an Frankreich im westphälischen Frieden*, Karlsruhe, 1905.

On the negotiations and results of the Peace of Westphalia, see Bougeant, *Histoire des guerres et des négociations qui précédèrent le Traité de Westphalie*, Paris, 1727; Koch and Schoell, *Histoire abrégée des traités de paix entre les puissances de l'Europe depuis la paix de Westphalie*, Brussels, 1837; De Garden, *Histoire générale des traités de paix*, Paris, 1848-1859, principally an amplification of Koch and Schoell; and Putter, *Geist des westphälischen Friedens*, Göttingen, 1795, an analysis of the contents of the treaties.

TABLE I

A LIST OF POPES AND EMPERORS FROM 1313 TO 1648, AND OF OTTOMAN SULTANS FROM 1453 TO 1648

Year of Acces- sion	Popes At Rome	Popes At Avignon	Emperors German	Emperors Eastern
1313		196. Clement V[1] since 1305		Andronicus II, since 1282
1314			‡ Lewis IV, of Bavaria[2] (Frederick of Austria)	
1316		197. John XXII		
1325				Andronicus II, with his grandson, Andronicus III, Palaeologus
1328	(Nicholas V)			Andronicus III, alone
1334		198. Benedict XII		
1341				John V, Palaeologus alone under regency[2]
1342		199. Clement VI		
1346			House of Luxemburg ‡ Charles IV	John V, with John VI, Cantacuzenos[2]

[1] The Avignon popes are recognized by the semi-official *Gerarchia Cattolica* down to and including Gregory XI, who returned to Rome in 1377. The number placed before a pope's name indicates his place in the recognized succession. Those without numbers prefixed are regarded as antipopes.

[2] The numeration of these emperors named John is variously given by different authorities. That adopted has seemed the least confusing.

‡ In this list the German emperors marked thus ‡, and no others, were crowned at Rome. Those in marks of parenthesis were rivals.

TABLE I

Year of Accession	Popes At Rome	Popes At Avignon	Emperors German	Emperors Eastern
1348			(Günther of Schwartzburg)	
1352		200. Innocent VI		
1355				John V (Matthias Cantacuzenos)
1356				John V, alone
1362		201. Urban V		
1370		202. Gregory XI		
1377	202. Gregory XI			
	Beginning of the Great Schism			
1378	203. Urban VI	Clement VII	Wenzel	
1389	204. Boniface IX			
1391				Manuel II, Palaeologus, alone
1394		Benedict XIII		
1399				Manuel II, with his nephew John VII, Palaeologus [1]
1400			(Rupert, of Bavaria)	
1402				Manuel II, alone
1404	205. Innocent VII			
1406	206. Gregory XII			
1409	(Alexander V) [2]			
1410	(John XXIII) [2]			
1411			‡ Sigismund (Jobst, of Moravia)	
1417	207. Martin V			
1423		Clement VIII		

[1] See note 2, p. 612.
[2] These popes were chosen by the Council of Pisa, but were not generally recognized.

Year of Accession	Popes		Emperors	
	At Rome	At Avignon	German	Eastern
1425		Benedict XIV		John VIII, Palaeologus [1]
1431	208. Eugenius IV			
1438			House of Austria	
1439		Felix V, at Basel and Lausanne	Albert II	
1440			‡ Frederick III, the last emperor to be crowned at Rome	
	End of the Great Schism			
1447	209. Nicholas V			Constantine XII or XIII, Dracoses, the last of the Greek emperors, killed in the siege of Constantinople, 1453 [2]
1448				

	Popes	Emperors	Ottoman Sultans
1453			Mohammed II, since 1451
1455	210. Calixtus III		
1458	211. Pius II		
1464	212. Paul II		
1471	213. Sixtus IV		

[1] See note 2, p. 612.

[2] The number of this Constantine is generally given as XIII, although no emperor called Constantine XII appears in the usual lists, the person who should properly have that number having had a merely nominal reign in 1067.

TABLE I

Year of Accession	Popes	Emperors	Ottoman Sultans
1481			Bajazet II
1484	214. Innocent VIII		
1492	215. Alexander VI		
1493		Maximilian I	
1503	216. Pius III, Sept. 22–Oct. 18		
"	217. Julius II		
1512			Selim I
1513	218. Leo X		
1519		Charles V [1]	
1520			Solyman, the Magnificent
1522	219. Adrian IV		
1523	220. Clement VII		
1534	221. Paul III		
1550	222. Julius III		
1555	223. Marcellus II, Apr. 9–30		
"	224. Paul IV		
1558		Ferdinand I	
1559	225. Pius IV		
1564		Maximilian II	
1566	226. Pius V		Selim II
1572	227. Gregory XIII		
1574			Amurath III
1576		Rudolf II	
1585	228. Sixtus V		
1590	229. Urban VII, Sept. 15–27		
"	230. Gregory XIV		
1591	231. Innocent IX		
1592	232. Clement VIII		
1595			Mohammed III
1603			Ahmed I
1605	233. Leo XI, Apr. 1–27		
"	234. Paul V		
1612		Matthias	
1617			Mustafa I
1618			Osman II
1619		Ferdinand II	
1621	235. Gregory XV		
1622			Mustafa I, again
1623	236. Urban VIII		Amurath IV
1637		Ferdinand III	
1640			Ibrahim
1644	237. Innocent X		
1648			Mohammed IV

[1] Charles V was crowned by the Pope at Bologna. No subsequent German emperor was ever crowned by the Pope.

TABLE II

Kings of France, England, and Scotland from 1313 to 1648

Year of Accession	France	England	Scotland
1313	Philip IV, the Fair, since 1285	Edward II, since 1307	Robert I, Bruce, since 1306
1314	Louis X		
1316	John I, lived only a few days		
"	Philip V		
1322	Charles IV		
1327		Edward III	
	House of Valois		
1328	Philip VI		
1329			David II, Bruce
1332			Edward I, Baliol
1342			David II, again
1350	John II		
1364	Charles V		
			House of Stuart
1370			Robert II
1377		Richard II	
1380	Charles VI		
1390			John, called Robert III
		House of Lancaster	
1399		Henry IV	
1406			James I
1413		Henry V	
1422	Charles VII	Henry VI	
1437			James II
1460			James III
		House of York	
1461	Louis XI	Edward IV	
1483	Charles VIII	Edward V, Apr. 9–June 25	
"		Richard III	
		House of Tudor	
1485		Henry VII	
1488			James IV
	House of Valois-Orléans		
1498	Louis XII		

TABLE II

Year of Accession	France	England	Scotland
1509		Henry VIII	
1513			James V
	House of Orléans-Angoulême		
1515	Francis I		
1542			Mary Stuart
1547	Henry II	Edward VI	
1553		Mary	
1558		Elizabeth	
1559	Francis II		
1560	Charles IX		
1567			James VI
1574	Henry III		
	House of Bourbon		
1589	Henry IV		
		Personal union in the House of Stuart	
1603		James I = James VI	
1610	Louis XIII		
1625		Charles I	
1643	Louis XIV		

TABLE III

Rulers of the Spanish Monarchies and Portugal from 1313 to 1648

Year of Accession	Castile	Aragon	Navarre	Portugal [1]
1313	Alfonso XI, since 1312	Jayme II, since 1291	Louis, Louis X of France, since 1305	Denis, the Worker, since 1279
1316			John I, John I of France	
"			Philip I, Philip V of France	
1322			Charles I, Charles IV of France	
1325				Alfonso IV
1327		Alfonso IV		
			Of Navarre alone	
1328			Jeanne II	
1336		Peter IV, the Ceremonious		
1349			Charles II, the Bad	
1350	Peter, the Cruel			
1357				Peter I
1367				Ferdinand
	House of Trastamara			
1369	Henry II			
1379	John I			
1383				Interregnum
1385				John I
1387		John I	Charles III	
1390	Henry III			
1395		Martin		
1406	John II, with Ferdinand I as Regent			
		House of Castile		
1412		Ferdinand I		

[1] Portugal was conquered from the Moors by Alfonso IV of Castile in 1095, and constituted an independent kingdom under his son, Alfonso I, in 1139.

TABLE III

Year of Accession	Castile	Aragon	Navarre	Portugal
1416		Alfonso V		
1425			Blanche (Queen) and John of Aragon	
1433				Edward
1438				Alfonso V
1441			John of Aragon, King as John II	
1454	Henry IV			
1458		John II		
1474	Isabella			
1479		Ferdinand II, the Catholic	Eleanore, and her son, Francis Phoebus, by Gaston de Foix	
1481				John II, the Perfect
1484			Catherine de Foix, (Queen) with Jean d'Albret	
1495				Emmanuel
1504	Philip of Burgundy [1]			
"	Regency of Ferdinand the Catholic			
1512			Dismemberment of Navarre by Ferdinand the Catholic	
	Union of Castile and Aragon in the Kingdom of Spain			
1516	Charles I, later Emperor Charles V			
1517			Henry II [2]	
1521				John III
1555			Jeanne III, (Queen) and Antoine de Bourbon	
1556	Philip II			
1557				Sebastian

[1] Juana, wife of Philip of Burgundy, was the legitimate sovereign but incapable of ruling.

[2] French Navarre comprised the small territory recovered from Ferdinand the Catholic. The remainder of Navarre went permanently to Spain.

Year of Accession		Navarre	Portugal
1572		Henry III, afterward Henry IV of France	
1578			Henry, the Cardinal
1580			Portugal becomes subject to Spain
1589		French Navarre is united with France [1]	
1598	Philip III		
1621	Philip IV		
1640			Portugal again independent under the House of Braganza John IV

[1] See note 2, p. 619.

TABLE IV

RULERS OF THE SCANDINAVIAN KINGDOMS, POLAND, AND HUNGARY FROM 1313 TO 1648

Year of Accession	Sweden	Denmark	Poland	Hungary
1313	Period of Anarchy	Eric VIII, since 1286	Ladislas IV, since 1304	House of Anjou Charobert, or Charles Robert, since 1308
1320		Christopher II		
1333			Casimir III, the Great	
1340		Waldemar III or IV, Atterdag		
1342				Lewis, the Great
1363	Albert of Mecklenburg			
1370			Lewis, the Great, of Hungary	
1376		Olaf V		
1382			Maria and Hedwig	Maria
1384			Hedwig, alone	
1385				(Charles, of Durazzo)
			House of Jagellon	
1386			Ladislas V, with Hedwig till 1390, afterward alone	Sigismund, of Luxemburg
1387		Margaret [1]		
1388	Margaret			
	The Union of Kalmar, including Norway			
1397	Eric, called the IXth in Denmark, the XIIIth in Sweden, with Margaret till 1412, afterward alone			
1434			Ladislas VI	
1437				Albert, of Austria
1439	Christopher III			Elizabeth

[1] Margaret was also Queen of Norway, and afterward of Sweden.

Year of Accession	Sweden	Denmark	Poland	Hungary
1440				Ladislas IV, Ladislas VI, of Poland
1445			Casimir IV	Ladislas V, Postumus, and regency of John Hunyady
1448	Revolt from Denmark Regency	House of Oldenburg Christian I[1]		
1457	Christian I			
1458				Matthias Corvinus, after 1469 also King of Bohemia
1464	Regency			
1481		John I		
1490				Ladislas VI, also King of Bohemia
1492			John I, Albert	
1497	John I			
1501	Regency		Alexander I	
1506			Sigismund I	
1513		Christian II, the Cruel		
1516				Lewis II, also King of Bohemia
1520	Christian II			
	House of Vasa			
1523	Gustavus I	Frederick I		
1526				House of Austria
				Ferdinand I, also King of Bohemia (John Zapolya)
1534		Christian III		
1540				Ferdinand I, alone
1548			Sigismund II, known as Augustus I	

[1] Christian was unable to hold Sweden to the Union of Kalmar, and that country was ruled by regents, with occasional efforts by the kings of Denmark to regain their authority until 1523, when the House of Vasa accomplished the complete independence of Sweden.

TABLE IV

Year of Accession	Sweden	Denmark	Poland	Hungary
1559		Frederick II		
1560	Eric XIV			
1564				Maximilian II, also King of Bohemia
1568	John III			
			Elective Monarchs	
1573			Henry of Valois	
1575			Stephen Bathory	
1576				Rudolf II, also King of Bohemia
1587			Sigismund III, Vasa	
1588		Christian IV		
1592	Sigismund, Vasa, King of Poland			
1604	Charles IX			
1611	Gustavus II, Adolphus			
1612				Matthias, also King of Bohemia
1618				Ferdinand II, also King of Bohemia
1627				Ferdinand III. also King of Bohemia
1632	Christina		Ladislas VII	
1648		Frederick III	John II, Casimir	

TABLE V

A CHRONOLOGICAL LIST

OF

TREATIES AND OTHER PUBLIC ACTS

Date a. d.	Subject	Page
June 5, 1316.	The death of Louis X without a male heir raises the question of female succession to the crown of France	5
June 29, 1320.	Edward II of England does homage to Philip V of France at Amiens	7
May 31, 1325.	Treaty of peace between Edward II of England and Charles IV of France	8
Jan. 20, 1327.	Deposition of Edward II by the English Parliament	10
March 31, 1327.	Treaty of peace between Edward III of England and Charles IV of France	10
June 6, 1329.	Edward III of England does homage to Philip VI of France at Amiens	11
May 1337.	Conferences at Valenciennes for the formation of a league against Philip VI of France . .	18
May 24, 1337.	Confiscation of the Duchy of Guyenne by Philip VI of France	18
Aug. 26, 1337.	Anglo-Imperial Alliance against Philip VI of France	18
Oct. 7, 1337.	Edward III of England announces his claim to the French throne	19
July 15, 1338.	The electors of the Empire assemble at Lahnstein to assert their prerogatives against the Holy See	21
July 16, 1338.	Edward III of England sails with his fleet to attack Philip VI of France	21
Sept. 5, 1338.	Edward III of England appointed Imperial Vicar for Western Germany	22
Feb. 21, 1340.	The English Chancellery officially styles Edward III " King of England and France " .	26

A CHRONOLOGICAL LIST OF TREATIES, ETC. 625

Date A.D.	Subject	Page
March 29, 1340.	Alliance of Edward III of England with Flanders against Philip VI	26
April 13, 1340.	Abduction of the English ambassador at Avignon	28
Aug. 25, 1340.	Pope Benedict XII endeavors to impose peace on England and France through ecclesiastical action	28
Jan. 10, 1356.	The Golden Bull, of the Emperor Charles IV	38
May 8, 1360.	The Treaty of Brétigny	56
Nov. 20, 1368.	Treaty of alliance between Charles V of France and Henry II of Castile against England	57
May 14, 1370.	Declaration of Charles V of France confiscating the Duchy of Guyenne	57
May 24, 1370	The Treaty of Stralsund	48
Oct. 28, 1371.	Treaty of alliance between Charles V of France and Robert Stuart, King of Scotland, against England	57
March 9, 1396.	The Truce of Paris confirmed by marriage of Richard II of England to Isabelle of France	66
1397.	Union of Kalmar	50
March 1409.	Assembling of the Council of Pisa	59
Nov. 5, 1414.	Assembling of the Council of Constance	60
July 28, 1415.	Citation of the King of France by Henry V of England to execute the Treaty of Brétigny	66
Aug. 15, 1416.	The Treaty of Canterbury concluding an alliance between the Emperor Sigismund and Henry V of England	67
Dec. 2, 1419.	Treaty of alliance between Henry V of England and Philip the Good, Duke of Burgundy	68
May 21, 1420.	The Treaty of Troyes delivering France to the English	69
July 1431.	Assembling of the Council of Basel	75
Sept. 21, 1435.	The Peace of Arras between Charles VII of France and Philip the Good, Duke of Burgundy	71
Jan. 1438.	Assembling of the Council of Ferrara	78
Jan. 24, 1438.	Decree of the Council of Basel suspending Pope Eugenius IV	75
June 7, 1438.	The Pragmatic Sanction of Bourges	75
Jan. 1439.	Transfer of the Council of Ferrara to Florence	79
March 26, 1439.	The Pragmatic Sanction of Mainz	75

Date A. D.	Subject	Page
July 5, 1439.	Decree of union of the Eastern Church with Rome	79
Nov. 5, 1439.	Election of Amadeus VIII, Duke of Savoy, as Pope Felix V by the Council of Basel	76
June 14, 1443.	Treaty between Pope Eugenius IV and Alfonso V of Aragon regarding Naples	76
May 28, 1444.	The Truce of Tours	72
July 12, 1444.	Treaty of Szegedin	78
Feb. 1447.	The Concordat of the Princes	77
Oct. 18, 1448.	Treaty of Rivoltella between Venice and Francesco Sforza	89
Feb. 21, 1452.	Treaty of Montils-les-Tours between Charles VII of France, Florence, and Milan	90
March 18, 1452.	Coronation of the Emperor Frederick III by Pope Nicholas V; the last ceremony of imperial coronation ever performed in Rome	79
April 11, 1453.	Treaty between the Republic of Florence and René of Anjou respecting Naples	91
May 29, 1453.	End of the Eastern Empire by the fall of Constantinople	79
April 9, 1454.	Treaty of Lodi forming a league for the protection of Italy	92
March 1456.	Establishment of a French protectorate over Genoa	93
July 12, 1458.	Bull of Pope Calixtus III claiming Naples as belonging to the Holy See	94
June 1, 1459.	Assembling of the Congress of Mantua	96
June 27, 1459.	Alliance of Charles VII of France and John II of Aragon	95
Jan. 18, 1460.	The Bull "Execrabilis" issued by Pope Pius II	97
Oct. 6, 1460.	Treaty of alliance between Louis, Dauphin of France, and Francesco Sforza, Duke of Milan	98
Nov. 27, 1461.	Letter of Louis XI of France to Pope Pius II abolishing the Pragmatic Sanction	99
Dec. 22, 1463.	Treaty of Louis XI of France with Francesco Sforza, Duke of Milan, ceding to him Genoa and Savona	102
July 18, 1464.	Alliance of Louis XI of France with George Podiebrad, King of Bohemia	105
1465.	Formation of the "League of the Public Weal"	101

A CHRONOLOGICAL LIST OF TREATIES, ETC. 627

Date A. D.	Subject	Page
Oct. 5, 1465.	The Treaty of Conflans between Louis XI of France and the princes forming the "League of the Public Weal"	103
Oct. 27, 1465.	Refusal of the Parliament of Paris to register the Treaty of Conflans by Louis XI	103
July 24, 1467.	Revocation by Louis XI of his ordinances against the papal authority	104
Oct. 14, 1468.	The Treaty of Péronne between Louis XI of France and Charles the Bold	106
Sept. 23, 1470.	Treaty of friendship between Louis XI of France and the Swiss Confederation	110
Dec. 3, 1470.	Repudiation of the Treaty of Péronne by Louis XI	110
Nov. 3, 1472.	The Truce of Senlis between Louis XI of France and Charles the Bold	112
June 1473.	Treaty of alliance between Yolande, Duchess of Savoy, and Charles the Bold	119
Oct. 1473.	Conference between the Emperor Frederick III and Charles the Bold at Trier, ending November 25	113
March 30, 1474.	Signature of the "Eternal" Compact between the Archduke Sigismund and the Swiss cantons	120
Nov. 2, 1474.	Triple alliance of Florence, Milan, and Venice	136
Aug. 29, 1475.	The Peace of Picquigny between Louis XI of France and Edward IV of England	122
Sept. 13, 1475.	The Truce of Souleuvres between Louis XI and Charles the Bold	124
Feb. 11, 1477.	The "Great Privilege" of the Netherlands	129
Aug. 19, 1477.	Acquisition of the Netherlands by the House of Hapsburg by the marriage of Mary of Burgundy with the Archduke Maximilian	131
Jan. 9, 1478.	Treaty of friendship between Louis XI and the Republic of Venice	136
April 26, 1478.	Conspiracy of the Pazzi	138
Aug. 1, 1478.	Meeting of the ambassadors of France and the Triple Alliance demanding a general council for abolishing the abuses of the Roman court	139
Aug. 16, 1478.	Prohibition by Louis XI of France of sending money to the Holy See	140
Dec. 23, 1482.	The Peace of Arras between Louis XI of France and the Netherlands	134

Date a. d.	Subject	Page
Jan. 24, 1492.	Conclusion of a league between France and Milan	176
April 22, 1492.	Alliance between the Pope, Venice, and Ludovico Sforza, Duke of Milan	177
April 29, 1492.	Personal alliance between Charles VIII of France and Ludovico Sforza, Duke of Milan	177
Nov. 3, 1492.	Treaty of Etaples between Charles VIII of France and Henry VII of England	179
Jan. 19, 1493.	The Treaty of Barcelona between Charles VIII of France and Ferdinand of Aragon	179
May 23, 1493.	The Treaty of Senlis between Charles VIII of France and Maximilian, King of the Romans	180
May 4, 1493.	Bulls of Pope Alexander VI dividing the spheres of discovery between Spain and Portugal	186
June 7, 1494.	Treaty of Tordesillas between Spain and Portugal regarding their spheres of discovery	186
Sept. 6, 1494.	Act of cession by Andrew Palaeologus of his right to the Eastern Empire to Charles VIII of France	183
Nov. 22, 1494.	Manifesto issued by Charles VIII of France at Florence of his intentions in the invasion of Italy	186
Nov. 25, 1494.	Treaty between Charles VIII of France and the Republic of Florence	185
Jan. 18, 1495.	Treaty between Pope Alexander VI and Charles VIII of France regarding the invasion of Naples	195
March 31, 1495.	Formation of the League of Venice against Charles VIII of France	202
Oct. 10, 1495.	Treaty of Vercelli between Charles VIII of France and Ludovico Sforza, Duke of Milan	207
July 31, 1498.	Treaty of friendship between Louis XII of France and Ferdinand the Catholic	215
Aug. 24, 1498.	Treaty of friendship between Louis XII of France and Henry VII of England	215
Feb. 9, 1499.	Treaty of alliance between Louis XII of France and the Republic of Venice	221
March 16, 1499.	Alliance between Louis XII of France and the Swiss Confederation	217
June 6, 1499.	Treaty of Peace between Louis XII of France and the Archduke Philip of Burgundy	217

A CHRONOLOGICAL LIST OF TREATIES, ETC.

Date A.D.	Subject	Page
Sept. 1499.	Dispensation by the Emperor Maximilian I of the Swiss cantons from the payment of taxes to the Empire and from the jurisdiction of the Imperial Chamber	226
July 14, 1500.	Treaty of alliance between Louis XII of France, Ladislas VI of Bohemia and Hungary, and John Albert of Poland against their common enemies	226
Nov. 11, 1500.	Treaty of Grenada between Louis XII of France and Ferdinand the Catholic	229
June 25, 1501.	Bull of Pope Alexander VI deposing Frederick, King of Naples, and dividing the kingdom between Louis XII of France and Ferdinand the Catholic	229
Aug. 10, 1501.	Treaty signed at Lyons between Louis XII of France and the Archduke Philip of Burgundy, arranging for the marriage of their children	231
Oct. 13, 1501.	Treaty between Louis XII of France and the Emperor Maximilian I according to Louis XII the investiture of Milan and his renunciation of all claims to the imperial title	232
April 5, 1502.	Treaty, signed at Lyons, between Louis XII of France and the Archduke Philip of Burgundy, representing Ferdinand and Isabella, confirming the marriage of Charles of Burgundy and Claude of France	232
Sept. 22, 1504.	The Treaties of Blois between the Emperor Maximilian I, Louis XII of France, and the Archduke Philip of Burgundy	251
Oct. 12, 1505.	Treaty between Louis XII of France and Ferdinand the Catholic stipulating the marriage of Germaine de Foix and regulating the affairs of Naples	258
May 14, 1506.	Public request of the French States General for the marriage of the Princess Claude with Francis of Angoulême	261
June 1507.	Secret conference at Savona between Louis XII of France, Ferdinand the Catholic, and Cardinal d'Amboise	272
Feb. 4, 1508.	Assumption of the title "Roman Emperor-elect" at Trent by Maximilian I	274

Date A. D.	Subject	Page
Dec. 10, 1508.	Formation of the League of Cambray	276
March 23, 1509.	Adherence of Pope Julius II to the League of Cambray	278
Feb. 15, 1510.	Peace between Pope Julius II and the Republic of Venice	284
March 14, 1510.	Treaty of alliance between Pope Julius II and the Swiss cantons	287
July 3, 1510.	Investiture of Ferdinand the Catholic by Pope Julius II with the Kingdom of Naples	287
May 28, 1511.	Citation by eight cardinals summoning Pope Julius II to appear before a general council	288
Oct. 4, 1511.	Formation of the Holy League	291
Nov. 13, 1511.	Adherence of Henry VIII of England to the Holy League	291
Dec. 20, 1511.	Treaty between Henry VIII of England and Ferdinand the Catholic for a combined attack on France	291
Nov. 19, 1512.	Adherence of the Emperor Maximilian I to the Holy League	291
March 14, 1513.	Alliance between Louis XII of France and the Republic of Venice for the partition of Northern Italy	296
April 1, 1513.	Truce between Louis XII of France and Ferdinand the Catholic with cession of Southern Navarre to the King of Spain	296
Aug. 7, 1514.	Alliance between Louis XII of France and Henry VIII of England stipulating the marriage of Louis XII to the Princess Mary	298
July 20, 1515.	Secret treaty between Emperor Maximilian I and Lewis II of Bohemia and Hungary	324
Oct. 13, 1515.	Treaty of alliance between Pope Leo X and Francis I of France	303
May 17, 1516.	Proposition of Emperor Maximilian I to make Henry VIII of England King of the Romans	324
Aug. 13, 1516.	Treaty of Noyon between Francis I of France and Charles of Spain	305
Aug. 18, 1516.	Concordat between Pope Leo X and Francis I of France	303
Nov. 1516.	Beginning of negotiations between Francis I of France and the German electors for succession to the Empire	325
Nov. 29, 1516.	Treaty of "perpetual alliance" between Francis I of France and the Swiss Confederation	306

A CHRONOLOGICAL LIST OF TREATIES, ETC. 631

Date A. D.	Subject	Page
Dec. 3, 1516.	Treaty of Brussels between Emperor Maximilian I, Francis I of France, and Charles of Spain	306
March 11, 1517.	Treaty of Cambray between Emperor Maximilian I, Francis I of France, and Charles of Spain confirming their previous agreements	306
Aug. 27, 1518.	Compact of Emperor Maximilian I with five electors for the succession of Charles of Spain to the Empire	329
Oct. 4, 1518.	Treaties between Henry VIII of England and Francis I of France accepting the principle of a universal peace	307
Jan. 14, 1519.	Adherence of Charles of Spain to the universal peace	307
June 17, 1519.	Treaty between Pope Leo X and Charles of Spain permitting the latter to retain Naples even though elected emperor	345
June 28, 1519.	Election of Charles of Spain as Emperor Charles V	345
May 26, 1520.	First visit of the Emperor Charles V to England	352
June 6, 1520.	Treaty between Henry VIII of England and Francis I of France at "The Field of Cloth of Gold"	352
July 14, 1520.	Treaty between Henry VIII of England and the Emperor Charles V at Calais	354
Oct. 23, 1520.	Coronation of the Emperor Charles V at Aachen	347
April 16, 1521.	First appearance of Martin Luther before the Emperor Charles V at the Diet of Worms	356
May 8, 1521.	Treaty of alliance between Pope Leo X and the Emperor Charles V	361
Aug. 2, 1521.	Opening of the Conference of Calais	362
Aug. 12, 1521.	Journey of Wolsey from Calais to Bruges to negotiate with the Emperor Charles V	364
Aug. 25, 1521.	Secret treaty between the Emperor Charles V and Henry VIII of England against Francis I	364
Nov. 24, 1521.	The Treaty of Calais between Pope Leo X, the Emperor Charles V, and Henry VIII of England against Francis I	366
Dec. 28, 1521.	Treaty of alliance between Francis I of France and Scotland	369
May 28, 1522.	Declaration of war by the Emperor Charles V and Henry VIII of England against Francis I	369

Date A. D.	Subject	Page
June 19, 1522.	The Treaty of Windsor, definitive alliance between the Emperor Charles V and Henry VIII of England against Francis I	370
Dec. 12, 1524.	Secret treaty of Pope Clement VII and Francis I of France	373
Feb. 24, 1525.	Capture of Francis I by the army of the Emperor Charles V	374
June 10, 1525.	Transfer of Francis I from Italy to Spain	381
Aug. 30, 1525.	The Treaty of Moore between Henry VIII of England and Louise of Savoy, Regent of France	384
Jan. 14, 1526.	The Treaty of Madrid between the Emperor Charles V and Francis I of France	387
March 17, 1526.	Delivery of the children of Francis I, as hostages, to the Emperor Charles V, and liberation of Francis I	389
April 15, 1526.	Ratification of the Treaty of Moore by Francis I	393
May 22, 1526.	Conclusion of the League of Cognac	395
Aug. 1526.	Recess of the Diet of Speyer suspending the Edict of Worms	409
April 30, 1527.	The Treaty of Westminster between Henry VIII of England and Francis I of France	400
May 6, 1527.	The sack of Rome and capture of Pope Clement VII by the imperial forces	401
April 25, 1529.	Protest at Speyer against the reapplication of the Edict of Worms	426
June 29, 1529.	Treaty of Barcelona between Pope Clement VII and the Emperor Charles V	415
July 16, 1529.	Transfer to Rome of the question of divorce of Henry VIII and Catherine of Aragon	416
Aug. 5, 1529.	Peace of Cambray between the Emperor Charles V and Francis I of France	418
Sept. 23, 1530.	Breach between the Protestants and Catholics at the Diet of Augsburg	427
Nov. 15, 1530.	Decree of the Emperor Charles V renewing the application of the Edict of Worms	427
Dec. 26, 1530.	Conclusion of the League of Schmalkalden	428
Oct. 24, 1531.	Treaty of Saalfeld between the League of Schmalkalden and the Dukes of Bavaria, left open for accession of the Kings of France and England	432
June 1532.	Diet of Nuremberg ordaining that until a general council was called, no one in Ger-	

A CHRONOLOGICAL LIST OF TREATIES, ETC.

Date A. D.	Subject	Page
	many should be disturbed in the practice of his religion	433
Feb. 1536.	Conclusion of a commercial and defensive treaty between Francis I of France and the Sultan Solyman the Magnificent	451
June 18, 1538.	Truce of Nice between the Emperor Charles V and Francis I of France	448
Sept. 27, 1540.	Bull of Pope Paul III approving the organization of the Society of Jesus	465
Sept. 18, 1544.	The Peace of Crépy between the Emperor Charles V and Francis I of France	460
Dec. 12, 1544.	Protest of the Dauphin, afterward Henry II, against the treaty of Crépy	471
Dec. 20, 1544.	Bull of Pope Paul III calling a general council at Trent for March 18, 1545	463
Dec. 13, 1545.	Opening of the Council of Trent	464
June 7, 1546.	Alliance between the Emperor Charles V and Pope Paul III for the subjugation of the Protestants in Germany	467
June 7, 1546.	Treaty of Andres between Francis I of France and Henry VIII of England	468
June 30, 1548.	Promulgation of the Interim at Augsburg	469
March 24, 1550.	Treaty of peace between Henry II of France and Edward VI of England	473
Jan. 15, 1552.	Alliance of Francis I of France with the German princes by the treaty of Chambord	472
Aug. 15, 1552.	Ratification of the transaction of Passau by the Emperor Charles V.	477
Sept. 25, 1555.	Conclusion of the Peace of Augsburg	479
Oct. 25, 1555.	Abdication of Charles V in the Netherlands	480
Dec. 16, 1555.	Alliance of Pope Paul IV and Henry II of France to expel the Spanish from Italy	482
Jan. 16, 1556.	Abdication of the kingdoms of Spain and Sicily by Charles V	481
Feb. 5, 1556.	The Truce of Vaucelles between the Emperor Charles V, his son Philip II, and Henry II of France	482
May 3, 1558.	The Emperor Charles V informed that his resignation of the Empire has been accepted	481
April 2, 1559.	Treaty of Cateau-Cambrésis between Henry II of France and Elizabeth of England	484
April 3, 1559.	Treaty of Cateau-Cambrésis between Henry II of France and Philip II of Spain	485

Date A. D.	Subject	Page
July 6, 1560.	The Treaty of Edinburgh between Mary Stuart, Queen of Scotland, and Elizabeth of England	497
Dec. 4, 1563.	Close of the Council of Trent	498
June 14, 1565.	Interview at Bayonne between Catherine de' Medici, Queen Elizabeth of Spain, and the Duke of Alba	503
July 24, 1567.	Abdication of Mary Queen of Scots	501
Feb. 25, 1570.	Bull of Pope Pius V excommunicating Elizabeth of England	508
April 29, 1572.	Treaty of alliance between Elizabeth of England and Charles IX of France	510
April 25, 1576.	The Union of Delft	520
Nov. 8, 1576.	The Pacification of Ghent	521
Feb. 17, 1577.	The Perpetual Edict	521
Jan. 23, 1579.	The Union of Utrecht	524
May 17, 1579.	Treaty of Arras by which the Southern provinces of the Netherlands agree to maintain the Catholic religion and submit to Philip II	524
March 15, 1580.	Ban against William the Silent published by Philip II of Spain	525
Sept. 19, 1580.	Treaty of Plessis-les-Tours by which the Duke of Alençon received the sovereignty of the Netherlands	528
July 1585.	Deputation of the States General of the United Provinces offering the sovereignty of the Netherlands to Elizabeth of England	532
June 25, 1591.	Treaty of alliance between Henry IV of France and Elizabeth of England	537
May 24, 1596.	Renewal of the treaty of alliance between Henry IV of France and Elizabeth of England	544
Oct. 31, 1596.	Accession of the United Provinces to the treaty of alliance between Henry IV of France and Elizabeth of England	544
April 13, 1598.	Promulgation of the Edict of Nantes by Henry IV of France	544
May 2, 1598.	Treaty of Vervins between Henry IV of France, Philip II of Spain, and the Duke of Savoy	544
Aug. 18, 1604.	Treaty of Peace between James I of England and Philip III of Spain	548

A CHRONOLOGICAL LIST OF TREATIES, ETC. 635

Date a. d.	Subject	Page
Jan. 23, 1608.	Treaty of alliance between Henry IV of France and the United Provinces	548
May 15, 1608.	Formation of the Protestant Union in Germany	549
April 9, 1609.	Truce of Antwerp suspending the war between Spain and the United Provinces for twelve years	549
July 9, 1609.	The "Letter of Majesty" of the Emperor Rudolf II	558
March 1621.	Conference of Segeberg in which England, Denmark, and the United Provinces consider a coalition against the Emperor	566
April 12, 1621.	Dissolution of the Protestant Union	562
April 15, 1621.	Treaty of Madrid restoring control of the Valtelline to the Grisons	564
Dec. 9, 1625.	Treaty of alliance between Charles I of England, Christian IV of Denmark, and the United Provinces against the Emperor	568
March 5, 1626.	Treaty of Monzon between France and Spain	577
April 20, 1627.	Secret treaty of alliance between Spain and France for the destruction of the naval power of England and the United Provinces	575
Jan. 4, 1628.	Treaty of defensive alliance between Christian IV of Denmark and Gustavus Adolphus of Sweden	575
March 6, 1629.	Promulgation of the Edict of Restitution by the Emperor Ferdinand II	576
May 22, 1629.	Peace of Lübeck between Christian IV of Denmark and the Emperor Ferdinand II	576
Sept. 26, 1629.	Truce of Altmark between Gustavus Adolphus of Sweden and Sigismund III of Poland ceding Livonia and parts of Prussia to Sweden	580
Jan. 23, 1631.	Treaty of Bärwald between Louis XIII of France and Gustavus Adolphus of Sweden for the invasion of Germany	582
March 31, 1631.	Secret treaties between Louis XIII of France and Victor Amadeus, Duke of Savoy, ceding Pinerolo to France	581
April 6, 1631.	Treaty of Cherasco between the Emperor Ferdinand II and Louis XIII of France regulating the Mantuan succession	582

Date A. D.	Subject	Page
May 30, 1631.	Treaty of Fontainebleau between Louis XIII of France and Maximilian of Bavaria by which the Catholic League was withdrawn from the influence of Spain	582
April 13, 1633.	Treaty of Heilbronn between Sweden and the German princes against the Emperor Ferdinand II	587
Sept. 5, 1633.	Adherence of France to the Treaty of Heilbronn	587
Feb. 8, 1635.	Treaty of Paris between Louis XIII of France and the United Provinces for a partition of the Spanish Netherlands	589
April 28, 1635.	Treaty of Compiègne between Louis XIII of France and Christina of Sweden	589
May 30, 1635.	The Peace of Prague between the Emperor Ferdinand II and the Elector of Saxony	588
July 11, 1635.	Treaty of Rivoli between Louis XIII of France and the Duke of Savoy against the Emperor Ferdinand II	589
Oct. 26, 1635.	Treaty of Saint-Germain-en-Laye between Louis XIII of France and Bernard of Saxe-Weimar against the Emperor Ferdinand II	589
March 20, 1636.	Treaty of Wismar between Louis XIII of France and Christina of Sweden against the Emperor Ferdinand II	589
Feb. 15, 1637.	Proposal of a peace congress at Köln by Pope Urban VIII	591
Jan. 30, 1641.	Renewal of the alliance of Louis XIII and Christina of Sweden against the Emperor Ferdinand III	592
Feb. 1, 1641.	Treaty of Paris between Louis XIII and the Duke of Braganza, claimant of the crown of Portugal, against Spain	590
Dec. 25, 1641.	Arrangement for the assembling of the Congress of Westphalia	592
July 22, 1642.	Ratification of arrangements for the Congress of Westphalia	594
June 1, 1645.	The French and Swedish propositions for peace handed to the Emperor's plenipotentiaries	594
Jan. 30, 1648.	Secret treaty of peace between Spain and the United Provinces	605
Oct. 24, 1648.	Signing of the Treaties of Münster and Osnabruck composing the Peace of Westphalia	603

INDEX

AACHEN, 39, 347.

Abbeville, 301.

Acciajuoli, Angelo, sent to secure aid of Charles VII, 89; confers with Sforza, 90.

Acuña, Hermando de, 430.

Adorno, Antoniotto, 361.

Adria, Kingdom of, 86, 227.

Adrian VI, Pope, as cardinal appointed regent of Spain, 347; accession to the Papacy, 368; death, 371.

Adriano da Corneto, Cardinal, supper in the vineyard of, 243.

Adriatic Sea, source of its name, 86.

Africa, 429, 605.

Agincourt, the battle of, 67.

Agnadello, the battle of, 279.

Aigues-Mortes, 448, 449, 450, 452.

Ailly, Pierre d', urges ending the Great Schism, 58.

Alba, Duke of, commands in South Germany, 468; 477, 484; negotiations at Bayonne, 503; invades Netherlands, 505; 507, 508, 509, 510, 511; superseded by Requesens, 520; 523.

Albert II, of Austria, 34.

Albert, Archduke of Austria, 546.

Albert, of Brandenburg, 324.

Albert II, Emperor, (V of Austria) 77.

Albert, of Hohenzollern, 53.

Albert, of Mecklenburg, King of Sweden, 50.

Albert, of Prussia, 471.

Albertine line of Saxon dukes, 467.

Albornoz, Cardinal, 41, 42.

Albrecht, Archbishop of Mainz, 326, 333, 338.

Albret, Alain d', 224.

Albret, Charlotte d', 224.

Albret, Henry d', 440.

Albret, House of, 359.

Albret, Jean d', 224, 248.

Alcantara, the Order of, 257.

Alcibiades, Albert, 467, 471, 476, 477.

Aldobrandini, Giovanni, 543.

Aleander, papal nuncio at the Diet of Worms, 357.

Alemanni, Niccolò, 218.

Alençon, Duke of, 301.

Alençon, Duke of, son of Henry II, proposed marriage with Elizabeth, 510; in the Netherlands, 523, 524, 528; death, 529.

Alessandrino, Cardinal, 229.

Alexander the Great, 397.

Alexander V, Pope, 59.

Alexander VI, Pope, character, 167; as vice chancellor, 168; election to the Papacy, 169; personal attributes, ambitions, and methods, 170; attitude toward the expedition of Charles VIII, 178; reception of Perron de Baschi by, 181; his bull to Charles VIII, 181; plans to divert Charles from Naples, 183; his prestige, 185; decrees concerning discovered lands, 186; negotiations with the Turks, 187; dangerous position, 188, 189; refuses demands of Charles VIII, 190; belief in astrology, 191; efforts to corrupt the King's advisers, 192, 193; seeks safety in St. Angelo, 194; interview and treaty with Charles VIII, 195; influence and victory over Charles VIII, 195, 196; confers title of "the Catholic" upon Ferdinand of Aragon, 197, 198; fears the success of Charles VIII, 200; joins the League of Venice, 201; changed attitude, 205; leaves Rome, 206; seeks the advancement of his son Cesare, 208; loss of prestige, 212; transactions with Louis XII, 221; negotiations with Sforza, 223; joins the Franco-Venetian League, 224; plans to check Louis XII, 229; referred to, 233, 238; his idea of the protection of Italy, 239; assassination of the nobles at Sinigaglia, 240; raises money by sale of new offices, 241; his end, 241; treasures seized by Cesare, 243; question as to the manner of his death, 243; referred to, 275, 314.

Alexandria, 296.

638　INDEX

Alfonso V, King of Aragon, attitude toward the Pope, 74, 75; conquers Naples, 76; 85; captured by the Duke of Milan, 87; joins Venice in war against Sforza, 91; accedes to the Treaty of Lodi, 92; death, 93.

Alfonso of Bisceglia, 228.

Alfonso XI, King of Castile, 32.

Alfonso II, King of Naples, accession, 181; 183, 184, 187; welcomes the ambassador of the Sultan, 188; offers protection to Alexander VI, 190; proposes tribute to Charles VIII, 196; abandons his throne, 197.

Algiers, 435, 436, 438, 450, 457.

Alidosi, 289.

Alsace, see Elsass.

Althusius, German jurist, 518, 525.

Altmark, the Truce of, 580.

Amadeus VIII, Duke of Savoy, 70, 76, 88.

Amadeus IX, Duke of Savoy, 105, 111.

Ambassadors, rights of, as explained in the trial of Leslie, 515.

Amboise, Georges d', Cardinal, his cipher code, 156; restores cities to the Archduke Philip, 217; rebukes the Venetian ambassadors, 220; elevated to the cardinalate, 222; 225; his policy and aspiration to the Papacy, 230; aims at a general peace, 231; 233, 234; as virtual ruler of France, 235; candidacy for the Papacy, 243; his policy, 248; co-operates with Julius II, 249; his aspirations as an explanation of the treaties of Blois, 252; fails to secure adhesion of Ferdinand, 253, 254; loss of prestige at Rome, 254; visits Maximilian, 255; leads the coalition, 256; resentment in France at his policy, 256; changed attitude, 260; 269; again favored by Julius II, 270; leads in the conference at Savona, 272; revival of papal hopes, 272; at Cambray, 276; his designs exposed to England by Venice, 281; his death, 285; personal attributes, 286; 294, 295.

America, 179, 199, 211, 257, 605.

American Colonies, 323, 482.

Amiens, 123, 301.

Amsterdam, 522, 606.

Anabaptists, the, 461.

Ancona, 86, 188, 194.

Andrew II, of Hungary, 53.

Angevin claims to Naples, 149, 167, 169, 229. See also Anjou.

Anglicans, 497.

Anglo-Imperial alliance, 18, 368, 370.

Anjou, Duke of, granted subsidy for France, 42; Duke of, as a regent of France. 67; claims to Naples (see also Angevin), 90; House of, 99; estates pass to Louis XI, 167; claims to Naples, 171, 174; 377.

Anna, wife of Richard II of England, 61.

Anna, of Bohemia and Hungary, 324, 335, 358, 409.

Anne, of Austria, 590.

Anne de Beaujeu, regency of, 149, 150; victory over the nobles, 151; attends to the internal interests of France, 165; cedes rights to Naples to René of Lorraine, 174; end of authority over Charles VIII, 175.

Anne, Duchess of Brittany, marriage, 151; 175, 178; plan of marriage with Louis XII, 221, 223; hostility to Louise of Savoy, 252; death, 297.

Annebaut, Monseigneur d', 441.

Anstruther, Sir Robert, 566, 567, 568.

Antoine, Duke of Lorraine, 326.

Antwerp, bankers of, 340, 505, 522, 528; the Truce of, 549, 563; 606.

Appenzell, 226.

Aquitaine, 19, 56.

Aragon, 64, 179, 263, 305, 539.

Aragonese dynasty at Naples, 167, 200.

Aramon, Gabriel d', 473.

Ardres, 352, 468.

Arezzo, Angelus von, 39.

Arezzo, Johann von, 39.

Aristotle, 570.

Arles, Archbishop of, 43, 76.

"Armada, the Invincible," 537.

Armagnacs, the, 68.

Armersdorf, Paul von, 340.

Armies, standing, 2, 3.

Army, French, 83.

Arras, the Treaty of, 70, 85; 130; the Peace between Louis XI and Flanders of, 134, 150; the Treaty of, 524.

Artevelde, Jacob van, 20.

Arthur, brother of Henry VIII, 399, 414.

Arthur, Count of Richemont, 70.

Artillery, 2, 163.

Artois, 84, 129, 133, 134, 180, 383, 387.

Asia, 187, 211.

Asti, 182, 200, 205, 251, 261, 441, 471.

Aubusson, Pierre d', 227.

Augsburg, 116, 131; Venetians opposed at Diet at, 286; the Diet of 1518 at, 328, 333; the Diet of 1530 at, 427; the Diet of 1548 at, 469; 474; the Peace of, 479, 556, 602.

INDEX

Augsburg bankers, 341.
Augsburg, Bishop of, 467.
Augsburg Confession, the, 427, 505.
Augustus, brother of Maurice of Saxony, 471.
Austria, 107, 262, 322, 437, 455, 560, 562; House of, see House of Hapsburg.
Avaux, Count d', 592, 593, 594, 596.
Avignon, captivity of the Papacy at, 1; unsafe for ambassadors, 28; antagonism to Rome, 43, 44; residence of the popes at, 44; 164, 372, 407.
Ayala, Balthazar, jurist, 552.

BABINGTON, plot, the, 533, 535.
Badajos, the bishopric of, 355.
Baden, 322.
Badoer, Andrea, 282, 284, 298.
Bainbridge, Christopher, 283, 287, 288, 290.
Bajazet II, Sultan of Turkey, 187, 277.
Balkan realm, 209.
Ballard, priest, 533, 535.
Baltic, the, problem of, 211; attempt of Spain to control, 547; 567, 575, 582, 585, 587, 602.
"Bank for indulgences," 168.
Bannockburn, 5.
Barbarigo, Doge of Venice, 202.
Barbarossa, Bey of Tunis, 436, 451, 454, 458.
Barcelona, treaties of, 179, 198, 415, 421.
Bari, Archbishop of, 43.
Baroncelli, Bernardo, 138.
Bartolini, papal nuncio, 251.
Bartolus of Sassoferrato, jurist, 492.
Bärwald, the Treaty of, 582.
Basel, council at, 75, 76, 105; joins the Swiss Confederation, 226; council at, 423.
Baschi, Perron de, 180.
Bassompierre, Count de, 564.
Baudoche, Claudius de, 326.
Bavaria, 34, 130, 322; Dukes of, 327, 432, 467; Elector of, 603.
Bayonne, 389, 503.
Beaucaire, 175.
Beaufort, Pierre, Roger de, 32.
Bedford, Duke of, 69.
Belgium, 209.
Bellinzona, 225.
Benedict XII, Pope, election, 16; suspected by the English, 17; opposes Anglo-Imperial alliance, 18; efforts to arrange an Anglo-French *entente*, 19; aims to dissolve the Anglo-Imperial alliance, 22; opposes Edward III, 26; endeavors to impose peace, 28; rebukes Philip VI, 30; humiliation of, 31; death, 32.
Benedict XIII, Pope, question of deposing, 57; capture and release, 58; deposition of, 59; visited by Sigismund, 63; deserted by the Spanish, 64.
Bentivogli, the, 218, 289.
Bentivoglio, Giovanni, 269, 270.
Berg, 18, 549.
Bergamo, 277.
Bergen, 47.
Bernard, of Saxe-Weimar, 584, 585, 589.
Berne, 108, 118, 125.
Berry, the Duke of, 67; the Duchy of, 99, 301.
Bethlen Gabor, 560, 561, 564, 575.
Bible, the, 357, 358, 407.
Blanche, natural daughter of Filippo Maria Visconti, 88.
Blois, the treaties of, 251, 252, 255, 258, 259, 263.
Bochetel, 472.
Bodin, Jean, 513, 516, 517.
Bohemia, 37; religious agitation in, 68; 70; Hussite struggle, 74; 77; quarrel with the Papacy, 104; 107, 116, 322, 328, 329; the vote of, 334; delegation at imperial election of, 343; complications in, 409, 411, 437, 549, 550, 555, 556; subjection of, 560; 584.
Bohemia, the King of, 39, 121, 348.
Bohemian revolution, 558, 559.
Boisy, Arthus de, 301, 305.
Boleslav IV, King of Poland, 49.
Boleyn, Anne, Queen of England, 399, 400, 413, 414, 452, 483.
Bologna, subdued by Pope Martin V, 74; 86; captured by Pope Julius II, 269; 271, 288; retaken by the Bentivogli, 289; 292, 330, 420, 421.
Bologna, the Concord of, 303, 404.
Bona, the Duchess, 135, 176.
Boniface VIII, Pope, 8, 27, 54, 382.
Boniface IX, Pope, 57, 58.
Bonnivet, French envoy, 338, 342.
Bordeaux, 20, 72, 369, 391.
Borgia, the, palaces at Rome of, 169; diplomacy of, 227; policy and methods of, 239.
Borgia, Cesare, Duke of Valentinois and Romagna, 170; visits Charles VIII in Rome, 192; as papal legate, 194; abandons Charles VIII, 197; efforts for his advancement, 208; his ambitions endanger Alexander VI, 213; his secu-

larization and journey to France, 222; marriage project, 223, 224; as regarded by Machiavelli, 227; conquers Romagna, 228; becomes gonfaloniere of the Church, 228; 233; conquest of Central Italy, 238; his cruelty, 239; revenge upon the nobles at Sinigaglia, 240; dictates promotions to the cardinalate, 241; the murder of Troches, 242; his plans analyzed by Machiavelli, 243; endeavors to control the papal election, 244; his one mistake according to Machiavelli, 246; loss of his conquests and death, 248; 269.

Borgia, Giovanni, 227.

Borgia, Lucrezia, 228.

Borgia, Rodrigo, Cardinal, as vice chancellor, 168; election to the Papacy, 169. See Alexander VI.

Borgo San Sepolcro, 145.

Bosnia, 54.

Bosworth, 179.

Bothwell, Earl of, 501.

Bouchier, Robert de, 29.

Boulogne, 179, 459, 460, 468.

Bourbon, Cardinal de, 123.

Bourbon, Constable de, 301.

Bourbon, Duchy of, 151.

Bourbon, Duke of, his alliance with the Emperor, 371; 372, 373, 377, 382, 383; fêted in Spain, 386; 387, 388; attacks Rome, 401.

Bourbon, House of, 152, 538.

Bourdin, Jean, 204.

Bourges, Archbishop of, 540, 542.

Brabant, 18, 20, 22, 31, 84, 129, 150.

Bracciano, 139.

Braganza, Duke of, 590.

Brandenburg, 34, 63, 322.

Brandenburg, Elector of, 108, 116, 549, 556, 587, 603.

Brandenburg, Margrave of, 39, 348.

Brandenburg-Küstrin, John of, 471.

Braunau, 558, 559.

Breda, 522.

Breisgau, 108.

Breitenfeld, the battle of, 584.

Bremen, archbishopric of, 567, 576, 602.

Brescia, 277, 292.

Brétigny, the Treaty of, 56, 66, 67.

Brèves, Savary de, 549.

Briçonnet, Guillaume, Cardinal, 175, 193, 194, 196, 198, 208.

Bricot, Thomas, 261.

Brie, 6, 107.

Brindisi, 277.

Brinon, Jean, 375, 383.

Brion, Chabot de, 386, 440, 441.

Brisach, 601.

British Isles, 527.

Brittany, question of succession, 32; 84; conquered by France, 151; 179, 251, 255; secured to France as inheritance of Claude, 300; 377.

Brittany, Duke of, 99, 121.

Bruges, 20, 26, 47, 364, 370.

Brulart de Léon, 579, 580.

Brunus, Conradus, jurisconsult, 492.

Brussels, 131, 480, 521, 522.

Brussels, the Treaty of, 306.

Buchanan, George, 518.

Buckingham, Duke of, 565, 569.

Buda, 450, 455.

Bulgaria, 54.

Burchard, master of ceremonies at papal court, 191.

Burghley, Lord, 518. See Cecil.

Burgo, Andrea del, 255, 286, 334, 343.

Burgos, 263, 264.

Burgundian deputies, 129, 130.

Burgundians, the, 68.

Burgundy, revival of imperial rights in, 38; Duchy of, given to Philip son of John II of France, 67; extent of territories, 84; a menace to France and the Empire, 84, 85; struggle with France, 100; 103; at war with France, 111; exhausted condition, 128; the spoils of, 128; partition of, 132; 133, 251, 382, 383, 386; promised to Charles V by Treaty of Madrid, 387; 391, 392, 411, 417, 418, 444, 445, 456.

Burgundy, John the Fearless, Duke of, negotiates with England, 66; as a regent of France, 67.

Buzardo, agent of Pope Alexander VI, 187, 188.

Byzantine Empire, fall of, 267. See also Greek Empire.

CADIZ, 537.

Calais, capture by the English, 56; 72, 152, 179, 296, 351, 352; the conference of, 362; the Treaty of, 366, 370; 380, 459; lost by the English, 483; contest over, 484; 485, 496.

Calatrava, the Order of, 257.

Calicut, 267, 392.

Calixtus III, Pope, 94.

Calvin, John, 512.

Calvinism, in Scotland, 497; in France, 498; in Hungary, 549; 557.

INDEX   641

Calvinists, 495, 497, 505, 549, 555, 556, 561, 602.
Cambray, Bishop of, 483.
Cambray, the League of, 252, 267, 272, 275; real purposes of, 276 ; war with Venice of, 279; lack of moral solidity, 279, 280 ; its purposes revealed to England, 281, 282; abandoned by Pope Julius II, 284; the baseness of, 295; 300.
Cambray, the Peace of, 417, 418, 420, 443.
Camerarius, 567.
Camin, 603.
Camoëns, 268.
Campeggio, Cardinal, 306, 336, 368, 415, 416, 426, 428.
Campobasso, 128.
Campofregoso, Baptiste, 144.
Canossa, Ludovico da, 303.
Canterbury, 67, 352; Archbishop of, 430.
Cape Verde Islands, 187.
Capello Paolo, 171.
Capet, House of, 5.
Capino, 391, 392, 393.
Capponi, Piero, 185.
Capua, 198.
Capuchin, Brotherhood, 578.
Caraffa, Cardinal, 482.
Cardinal-Infante of Spain, 587, 588.
Cardone, Don Ramon de, 292.
Carinola, Bishop of, 243.
Carinthia, 262, 437, 475.
Carlovingian legend, 172.
Carmeliano, Pietro, 282.
Carniola, 437.
Caroz, 345.
Carretto, Carlo di, Marquis of Finale, 250, 254.
Carthagena, 533.
Carvajal, Bernardin, Cardinal, 273, 274.
Casale, siege of, 577, 579, 580.
Casimir III the Great, King of Poland, 51, 52.
Casimir, the Margrave, 345.
Castel Nuovo, 198.
Castile, 20; withdraws support from the Pope, 64; 70; union with Aragon, 179; conflict over government, 256; 260; honors Philip and Juana, 263; animosity toward Ferdinand the Catholic, 263, 264, 272, 305, 394.
Castracani, Castruccio, 14, 22.
Cateau-Cambrésis, Treaty of, 483, 485, 496, 502, 544.

Catherine of Aragon, Queen of England, marriage, 283; as Spanish ambassador in England, 299; greets the Emperor Charles V, 352; influences England against France, 369 ; 394; relations with Henry VIII, 398, 399; 400, 413, 414, 415, 416, 430, 431, 438 ; death of, 452.
Catherine de Bourbon, 539.
Catherine, Queen of Navarre, 306.
Catherine, daughter of Charles VI of France, 68.
Catherine, sister of Charles of Spain, 329, 330, 333.
Cavazza, Niccolò, 449.
Cavelli, Marino, 460.
Cecil, William, 508, 518.
Cerdagne, 179.
Cervino, Cardinal, 464.
Cesarini, Cardinal, 78.
Cesena, 228, 271.
Chalon, Philibert de, Prince of Orange, 402, 421.
Chambord, 472.
Champagne, 6, 84, 107.
Charles of Anjou, 174.
Charles the Bald, Emperor, 128.
Charles, Cardinal de Bourbon, 529, 538.
Charles, Duke of Angoulême, 439, 442, 445, 456, 460.
Charles, Duke of Berry, 99, 101, 103, 107, 111, 112, 113.
Charles, Duke of Burgundy, the Bold, as Count of Charolais, 99, 101; 102; isolation in France, 103; proposed marriage, 104 ; at Péronne, 106; relations to Germany, 107; sentiment against, 109; negotiates with Emperor Frederick III, 110; truce with Louis XI, 111; ambition of, 112; reopens negotiations with the Emperor, 113; triumph over the Emperor, 115; humiliation of, 117; overthrow of, 118 ; concerning Elsass, 120; alliance with Edward IV of England, 121 ; abandoned by Edward IV, 123; Truce of Souleuvres, 124 ; attacks the Swiss, 125 ; defeat at Grandson, 125, 126; ruin of 127; appeals to the States General, 128 ; slain at Nancy, 128; legend concerning, 128 ; 132, 133, 134, 135, 151, 305, 382.
Charles, Duke of Gelderland, 326, 334
Charles, Duke of Orléans, 87.
Charles III, Duke of Savoy, 441, 444, 447.
Charles of Durazzo, 55.
Charles Emmanuel, Duke of Savoy, 560.
Charles IV, Emperor, position of Germany under, 34; treaty with Clement

642 INDEX

VI, 34; character of his reign, 35; coronation at Rome, 36; relations to his kingdoms, 37; Golden Bull of 1356, 38; charters universities, 38; threatens papal property, 40; wish to render imperial office hereditary, 40; Hanseatic League, 48; 61.

Charles V, Emperor, table showing sources and extent of inheritance, 231; affianced in infancy, 231; 250; rights under treaties of Blois, 251, 258; 263, 264, 265; marriage renounced at Cambray, 276; 291, 292; declared of age, 300; affianced to Renée, 301; wide separation of his territories, 305; alliance with the Empire and France, 306; adherence to general peace, 307; as a student of Machiavelli, 312; imperial aspiration, 323; aroused by activity of Francis I, 327; financial resources, 328; qualities, 329; gains promises of electors, 330; possession of Naples an objection to his election, 331, 332; negotiates with Bohemia, 334, 335; favored by the financiers, 340; favored by Germany, 341; wins election, 345; official notification, 346; installation, 347; conflict with Francis I, 349; plan for meeting the sovereigns, 351; visit to England, 352; at Calais, 353; need of favors from the Pope, 355; meets Luther, 356, 357; confers Austrian provinces upon Ferdinand, 358; proposed marriage with Mary of England, 359; rumors of alliance with Francis I, 360; compact with Pope Leo X, 361; receives Wolsey at Bruges, 364; refuses demands of Francis I, 367; supports De' Medici for the Papacy, 368; alliance of Bourbon, 371; new proposals to Francis I, 372; victory at Pavia, 374; proposals of England, 376; attitude toward Henry VIII, 377; wish to marry a Portuguese princess, 378; his reply to Wolsey, 380; disregards plan of Gattinara, 381; his four demands on Francis I, 382, 383; relation of the English to his transaction with Francis I, 384; reasons for moderation with Francis I, 385; marriage with Isabella of Portugal, 388; ratifies the Treaty of Madrid, 388; attitude of his former allies, 390; demands of Henry VIII, 394; his exactions at Madrid condemned, 394; confronted with the League of Cognac, 396; challenges Francis I, 397; takes up the cause of Catherine of Aragon, 400; his struggle for religious unity, 406; period of hesitation, 408; unable to aid Ferdinand, 409; threefold programme, 411; negotiates with Clement VII, 412; peace with Clement VII, 415; plans in Italy, 417; his advantages under the Peace of Cambray, 418, 419; in Italy, 419, 420; coronation at Bologna, 421; his difficult task in Germany, 424; policy at Augsburg, 426; attempt to win the Protestants, 427; opposed by the Protestants, 428; opposed in England, 430; embarrassment in Germany, 430; appeal to Francis I, 431; failure in Germany, 432; expedition against Tunis, 434; compared with Francis I, 437; attempt to satisfy Francis I, 438; diplomatic colloquy with, 442; arraignment of Francis I, 443; explanation of his attitude, 446; his illusory reconciliation with Francis I, 448; Europe alarmed, 451; proposal to Henry VIII, 452; efforts with the Sultan, 454; concerning the Hapsburg-Valois proposition, 456; war with Francis I, 457; wins Germany, 459; the Peace of Crépy, 460; as regarded by the German princes, 463; in relation to the Council of Trent, 464, 465; his diplomacy at Regensburg, 467; his position at the death of Henry VIII and Francis I, 468; instruction to his son, 468, 469; his ambition for Philip and its failure, 470; growing hostility to, 470; his peril, 473; retires to Innsbruck, 474; relation of Protestantism to his misfortunes, 474; attempted flight, 475; disillusionment, 477; efforts in behalf of Philip, 478, 479; the abdications of, 480; death of, 482; 485, 492, 502, 527, 546, 549, 555.

Charles the Great, Emperor, 1, 16, 100, 172, 201, 348, 419, 420.

Charles I, King of England, 561, 565, 568, 569, 575.

Charles IV, King of France, 6, 7, 8, 11, 25.

Charles V, King of France, 44, 56, 57, 65, 67.

Charles VI, King of France, 38, 57, 58, 65, 66, 68, 69.

Charles VII, King of France, as Dauphin, 68; resists the English, 69; diplomacy of, 70; rises to power, 71, 72; his administration, 83; makes alliances, 85; recognizes Orléans claim to Milan, 88; intervention in Italy, 89; attitude toward René, 91, 92, 94; hostility of the Dauphin to, 97; death of, 98; 152, 164, 166, 171, 172.

Charles VIII, King of France, proposed marriage, 134; under regency, 150; affianced to Anne of Brittany, 151, 152; appeal of the Italians to, 164; 165, 166; personality of, 171; imperial aspirations and claim to Naples, 173, 174; release from regency, 175; alliance with Sforza, 175, 177; appeal of Savonarola to, 177; relations to the chief powers of Europe, 178; concludes the Treaty of Etaples, 179; cedes territory to Maximilian, 180; receives a bull

INDEX 643

from Pope Alexander VI, 181; his expedition into Italy, 182; obtains rights to the Eastern Empire, 183; at Florence, 184, 185, 186; opposition of Pope Alexander VI to, 187; before Rome, 188, 189, 190; his demands, 191; terms of settlement with the Pope, 193, 194; personal interview with the Pope, 195; 196, 197; results from his occupation of Naples, 199; surprised by the League of Venice, 203; appeal to Venice, 204; departure from Naples, 205; retreat to France, 206; concludes the Treaty of Vercelli, 207; 208, 218, 230, 233, 309.

Charles IX, King of France, 498, 509, 513.

Charles Robert, known as Charobert, King of Hungary, 54.

Charles IX, of Södermanland, King of Sweden, 547.

Charlotte, daughter of Louis of Savoy, 97.

Charnacé, Baron de, 580, 582.

Charobert, King of Hungary, 54.

Charolais, 133, 180, 456.

Chastellain, Georges, 100.

Chaumont, Sire de, 156.

Cherasco, 582.

Cheyney, Thomas, 391, 392.

Chiasso, 288.

Chigi, papal nuncio, 595, 597, 598, 599.

Chimay, Jean de, 101.

China, 211.

Christendom, 27, 44.

Christian of Anhalt, 557, 559, 560.

Christian of Brunswick, 563.

Christian II, King of Denmark, 364.

Christian IV, King of Denmark, 566, 568, 569, 575, 576.

Christina, Queen of Sweden, 312, 585, 591.

Church, the, corruption in, 167.

Churches, national, 62, 75, 76.

Cibò, Giambattista, Cardinal, 168.

Cibò, Franceschetto, 168, 169.

Cities, Imperial, 34.

City-states in Italy, 310.

Civita Castellana, 169.

Civita Vecchia, 194.

Claude, Queen of France, affianced in infancy, 231; 250, 251, 258; betrothed to Francis of Angoulême, 200, 202, 276, 300, 382.

Clausse, Foreign Secretary under Henry II of France, 473.

Clemence, wife of Louis X of France, 6.

Clément, Jacques, 538.

Clement V, Pope, 8.

Clement VI, Pope, 32, 33, 34.

Clement VII, Pope, (at Avignon) 43, 44, 45, 86.

Clement VII, Pope, (at Rome) 362; accession, 371; his efforts for a general peace, 373; 390, 391, 395, 397, 401, 405, 409; attitude of Charles V toward, 411; negotiations of Charles V and Henry VIII with, 412; his escape, 412; efforts to strengthen himself in Italy, 414; his reply in the divorce of Henry VIII, 415; peace with Charles V, 415; his authority repudiated by Henry VIII, 416; 419, 420; crowns Charles V at Bologna, 421; 422, 424, 430, 432; his relations to France, 434; death, 434.

Clement VIII, Pope, 543, 548, 578.

Clergy, marriage of, 469.

Clermont, Cardinal, 287, 288.

Cleve, 116, 549, 603.

Cleve, Anne of, 453.

Cleve, Arnold of, 113.

Cleve, Count of, 18; Duke of, 130, 453, 457, 459, 558.

Coblenz, 22, 589.

Code of Justinian, 25.

Cœur, Jacques, 83.

Cognac, the League of, 395, 396, 417.

College, Sacred, 141, 169, 243, 270, 271, 288, 443.

Colmar, 109.

Colonial question, the, 210.

Colonna, the, 74, 190, 212, 397.

Colonna, Cardinal, 169.

Colonna, Oddo, Cardinal, 62.

Columbus, Christopher, 179, 199.

Commines, Philippe de, bought over by Louis XI, 121; 134; at Florence, 138, 139; 140, 142, 153, 166; at Venice, 184, 188; describes reception of Charles VIII at Naples, 198; unaware of the secret opposition of Venice, 200, 201; his discovery of the coalition, 202, 203; 204, 206, 219, 309.

Como, 292.

Compiègne, the Treaty of, 589.

Conchillo, Lopez, 257, 258.

"Concordat of the Princess," the, 77.

Condottieri, 166.

Confederation, the principle of, 165.

Conflans, the Treaty of, 103.

Constance, the Council of, 60, 61, 62, 423.

Constance, diet at, 273.

Constance, the Union of, 120.

644   INDEX

Constantine, the donation of, 16.
Constantinople, the fall of, 2, 78, 79; 175, 433, 437, 441, 451, 455, 456.
Contarini, Gasparo, 358, 462.
Contarini, Luigi, 581, 595, 597, 598, 599.
Copenhagen, 47.
Cordova, Gonsalvo de, 207, 230, 232, 233, 264.
"*Corps Diplomatique*," 309, 310.
Corsica, 242.
Coruña, 352, 537.
Coucy, 261.
Council of Blood, the, 506.
Council of Ten, the, 239, 240, 311.
Counter-Reformation, the, 489, 494; aids Mary Stuart, 501; 527; opposes Henry of Navarre, 529, 539; 546, 547, 555, 564, 578.
Count Palatine, 13, 18, 22; as an elector, 39; claims Burgundian territory, 130; 326, 333, 338, 348.
Courland, 51.
Courteville, Jean de, 327, 329, 330.
Cranmer, Archbishop, 452.
Crécy, the battle of, 34.
Crema, 277.
Cremona, 221, 277, 371.
Crépy, the Peace of, 460, 463, 471.
Crèvecœur, Philippe de, 172.
Croatia, 54.
Cromwell, Thomas, 453.
Croy, Antoine de, 101.
Croy, Guillaume de, 305.
Cryptography, 156.
Culemburg, Count, 504.
Cuspinian, 334.
Cyprus, the island of, 277.

DALMATIA, 54, 70, 277, 454.
Dandolo, 440.
Dante, 13, 16, 36, 312.
Darnley, Lord, 501.
Dauphiné, 84, 372, 377.
Davison, 536.
"*Deambulatio*," the, 348.
De Chièvres, 358.
"Defensor Pacis" of Marsilius of Padua, 16.
De Ganay, President of the Parliament of Paris, 195.
"De Jure Belli" of Albericus Gentilis, 552.
"De Jure Belli ac Pacis" of Hugo Grotius, 570, 572.
"De Jure et Officiis Bellicis" of Balthazar Ayala, 552.
De la Barde, 596.
De la Court, 596.
De la Pole, Edmund, Duke of Suffolk, 259.
De la Pole, William, Earl of Suffolk, 72.
"De Legationibus" of Conradus Brunus, 492.
"De Legationibus" of Albericus Gentilis, 530.
Delft, Union of, 520.
Del Monte, Cardinal, 464, 471.
Del Vasto, Governor of Milan, 457.
Denmark, resisted by the Hanseatic League, 47; union with Norway, 50; 209, 368, 370; becomes officially Lutheran, 429; 436, 437, 441; deserts Francis I, 459; 485, 550; attitude toward Germany, 567; intervention in Germany, 568; 575, 576, 583.
De Praet, 373, 374, 377, 385, 431.
De Saint-Romain, 596.
"Design, Great," the, 550.
De Solliers, 153.
De Spes, 507.
De Vesc, Etienne, 175, 193, 199, 204, 208.
Diaz, Bartholomew, 187.
Diesbach, Nicholas von, 110, 118, 121.
Diet, German Imperial, its composition, 322.
Digest of Justinian, 172.
Diplomacy, the Anglo-French, 3; instruction of France in, 84; as employed by Louis XI, 152; Venetian, 153; influence of Louis XI upon, 155; subsequent importance of, 157; the Italian methods of, 295.
Diplomatic Missions, 84.
"Discourses" of Machiavelli, 312.
Djem, 187, 189, 191, 192, 193, 194, 195, 197.
Donato, Girolamo, 280, 285.
Donauwörth, city of, 557.
Doria, Andrea, 415, 420.
Doriolo, Pietro, 152.
Dover, 352.
Drake, Sir Francis, 525, 526, 533, 537.
Du Bellay, Guillaume, 436, 456.
Du Bois, Pierre, 172.
Dubouchage, 153.
Dudley, Robert, Earl of Leicester, 532, 533.
Du Plessis, Guillaume, 473.
Du Plessis-Mornay, 513.

INDEX 645

Duprat, Antoine, 262, 301, 363, 383, 418.
Dutch Republic, the, 546.
Du Thier, Foreign Secretary under Henry II of France, 473.

EAST, diplomatic situation in the, 410.
Eastern question, the, 211.
Eberhard, Bishop of Liège, 326.
Eboli, Duchess d', 484.
"Ecclesiastical Reservation," the, 480, 556.
Edict of Pacification, the, 544.
Edict of Restitution, the, 576, 578, 584, 587, 588.
Edinburgh, the Treaty of, 497, 498.
Edward I, King of England, 4.
Edward II, King of England, 4, 5, 7, 8, 9, 10.
Edward III, King of England, does homage as Prince of Wales to the King of France, 8; declared King, 10; his claim to the throne of France, 11; appeals to the Pope, 12; his quest for an ally, 13; appeals to the Emperor, 16; his system of alliances, 18; announces his claim to French crown, 19; his embargo on wool, 20; as Imperial Vicar, 21; justification of his claim to France, 24; legality of his claim, 25; his compact with Flanders, 26; ecclesiastical opposition to, 28; accepts a truce with France, 29; loses support of Brabant and Flanders, 31; offered the crown of the Empire, 34; surrenders his claim to France, 56; preparation for war, 57; death, 57; 530.
Edward IV, King of England, 110, 111; alliance with Charles the Bold, 121; invades France, 121; dissuaded from conquering France, 122; makes peace with Louis XI, 123; establishes postal service, 155.
Edward VI, King of England, 452, 458, 473, 478.
Edward, Prince of Wales and Duke of Aquitaine, 57.
Egmont, Count, 503.
Egypt, 268, 411.
Ehrenbreitstein, 589.
Eleanor, of Aquitaine, 56.
Eleanora, Queen of France, 371, 385, 387, 388, 389, 391, 394, 395, 418, 447, 448.
Election, imperial, of 1519, 342, 344.
Electoral capitulation, the, 345.
Electoral College of the Empire, 342, 343, 348, 556, 561, 597.
Electors of the Empire, 38, 39, 325, 326.
Eliano, Luigi, 286.

Elizabeth, of Brabant, 84.
Elizabeth, daughter of Edward IV of England, 134.
Elizabeth, daughter of James I of England, 560, 565.
Elizabeth, Queen of England, 452, 479, 483, 484; decides in favor of Protestantism, 494; contest with Philip II, 495; bases her policy upon national interests, 497; aids Scotland, 497; qualities contrasted with those of Philip II, 499; plan to dethrone, 507; her excommunication, 508; alliance with France, 509; proposed marriage, 510; investigates complaints against Mary Stuart, 515; 518, 520, 523, 524; action in the case of Drake, 526; policy of inaction, 527; refuses sovereignty of the Netherlands, 528; loses the French alliance, 529; opposition of Philip II, 530; her protectorate of the Netherlands, 532; plot against, 533; secret negotiations with the Prince of Parma, 536; seeks alliance against Philip II, 536, 537; death, 548; 550.
Elizabeth, Queen of Hungary and Poland, 55.
Elizabeth, Queen of Spain, 484, 485, 503, 539.
Elizabeth of York, 179.
Elizabethan Age, the, 495, 538.
Elne, 204.
Elsass, 108, 118, 120, 124, 129, 358, 550, 589, 601.
Emmanuel Philibert, Duke of Savoy, 485.
Emperor, use made of the title by the kings of Germany, 274.
"Emperor-elect," title assumed by Maximilian I, 180.
Empire, see Roman Empire, Byzantine Empire, Greek Empire, Holy Roman Empire of the German Nation, Ottoman Empire.
England, dynastic pretensions, 3; war with France, 25; agrees to renounce alliance with Flanders, 56; establishment of postal service in, 155; 158, 164; attitude toward France of, 178; 209, 211; treaty with France, 215; treaty with the Netherlands, 259; 276, 280; diplomatic relations with Venice, 282; 290, 297; peace with France, 298, 299; takes first place in the diplomacy of Europe, 308; 350, 351, 367, 369; changed attitude after the defeat of France at Pavia, 374, 375; makes proposals to Charles V, 376; 383, 384, 390, 393, 398, 400; attitude toward the Papacy, 405, 406, 407, 414; repudiates papal authority, 416; opposed to the

646 INDEX

Peace of Cambray, 419; complete separation from Rome, 430; 431, 436, 451, 452, 458, 459, 472, 473; restoration of Catholicism, 478; alliance with the Hapsburgs, 482; 485, 494, 495; relations with Scotland, 496; 500, 506, 508, 509, 510, 511, 512; its aid sought by William the Silent, 523; 527, 528, 529, 530, 537; victory over the Armada, 538; 543; supremacy upon the sea, 544; 546; peace with Spain, 548; 552, 560, 565; its appeal to the Scandinavian powers, 566; 575; not presented at Congress of Westphalia, 597; its political revolution, 606.

English Church, the, 430, 511.

Equilibrium, political, 158, 164, 165, 238.

Ernest, Archduke of Austria, 541.

Ernest, Duke of Brunswick-Lüneburg, 426.

Ernestine line of Saxon dukes, 468.

Escurial, the, 499, 531, 546.

Esquerdes, 153.

Este, Beatrice d', 175.

Este, Cardinal d', 244.

Esthonia, 51.

Etampes, 103.

Etaples, the Treaty of, 179.

"Eternal Compact," the, 120.

Eudes IV, Duke of Burgundy, 6.

Eugenius IV, Pope, 71, 75, 76, 77, 78, 85.

Europe, equilibrium of, 158; derives its methods from Italy, 164; the rise of modern, 209; effect of the contest for Italy upon, 294; effects of the sack of Rome upon, 405; modern political organization of, 439; moral disintegration of, 489; non-existence of public law in, 491; its state at the end of the sixteenth century, 546.

European problems, the emergence of, 210.

Euse, Jacques d', 8.

"Ewige Richtung" or "Eternal Compact," 120.

"Execrabilis," the Bull, 97.

FAENZA, 228, 247, 254, 269, 271, 277, 278.

Fano, 228.

Farnese, Alessandro, accession to the papacy as Pope Paul III, 434.

Farnese, Alessandro, Prince of Parma, 523, 533, 535, 536, 537, 538, 540.

Farnese, Ottavio, Duke of Parma, 458, 473.

Fécamp, the Abbé de, 282.

Felix V, Pope, 76, 78, 88.

Ferdinand I, Emperor, plan to form a kingdom for, 299; affianced to Anna of Bohemia, 324; as candidate for the Empire, 331; 335, 358, 409, 410, 415, 420, 421, 425; as "King of the Romans," 426, 427, 428; 429; proposes an attack in Switzerland, 431; fails in negotiations with the Sultan, 433; 436, 438, 451; his arrangement with Zapolya, 455; 464, 467, 470, 473, 475; at Passau, 476, 477, 479, 480; plans for succession to the Empire, 481; 492, 555.

Ferdinand II, Emperor, succeeds Matthias in Bohemia, 559; accession to Empire, 560; 564, 570; secures aid of Wallenstein, 574; makes peace with Christian IV, 576; 578, 579, 584, 587, 589, 591, 603.

Ferdinand III, Emperor, 587, 588, 591, 592, 594, 600.

Ferdinand I, King of Aragon, 65.

Ferdinand II, King of Aragon, called the "Catholic," his marriage with Isabella, 179; receives the title the "Catholic," 197, 198; 201, 202, 207, 208, 214; agreement with Louis XII, 215; divides Naples, 229, 230; 232, 234; interest in papal election, 243, 244; 248, 250, 251, 253, 255, 256; as regent of Castile, 257; betrothal to Germaine de Foix, 258; 260, 263, 264, 265, 266, 270, 271; secret conference at Savona, 272; concerning Venice, 275; 276, 279, 280, 283, 284, 285; invested with Naples, 287; asked to support Maximilian for the Papacy, 290, 291; takes Navarre, 292; his actions in Italy considered, 294; truce with Louis XII, 296; the scheme of, 299; 300, 301, 303, 304; his death, 305; 309, 314, 323.

Ferdinand, King of Naples, investiture, 94; compact with Sforza, 95; 100, 102, 104, 136; alliance with the Pope, 138; 140, 141; detached from papal alliance, 147; 167, 168, 169, 176, 177, 181.

Ferdinand II, King of Naples, 190, 191, 197, 198, 203, 206, 207, 212.

Feria, Count de, 483.

Fermo, Oliverotto, 240.

Ferrara, 86, 149, 285, 331, 361, 548.

Ferrara, Council at, 78.

Ferrara, Duke of, 175, 176, 218, 288, 303, 390.

Ferreyra, Miguel, 258.

Feudalism, 1.

Feuquières, Marquis de, 586, 587, 600.

"Field of Cloth of Gold," the, 352.

Fieschi, Nicolino, 28.

Fiesco, Genoese admiral, 93, 95.

Finale, Marquis of, 250, 254.

INDEX

Fitzwilliam, William, 376.

Fiume, 275.

Flanders, uprising of, 20; new compact with Edward III, 26; defection from Edward III, 31; Duchy of, goes to the Duke of Burgundy, 67; 84; revolt in, 120; 129; as part of the Empire, 132; concludes the Peace of Arras, 134; the Council of, 150; as a fief of France, 151; 352, 353; as the market for English wool, 367; 383, 387, 471, 539.

Flodden Field, the battle of, 297.

Florence, 37, 73, 75, 79; controls most of Tuscany under rule of the Medici, 85; appeals to Charles VII, 89; treaty of, 91; accedes to the Treaty of Lodi, 92; 102, 135; under the ban, 138; peace with Naples, 147, 148, 149; first permanent diplomatic relations, 154; holds balance of power, 164; under the influence of Savonarola, 177, 184; treaty with Charles VIII, 185; loses by alliance with the French, 208; at war with Pisa, 213; 238, 239; invites the Sultan to take oriental dominions of Venice, 277; again expels the Medici, 421.

Foix, Gaston de, 261, 291, 292.

Foix, Germaine de, 258, 263, 272, 388.

Fondi, 43.

Fontainebleau, the Treaty of, 582.

Forli, the Bishop of, 126; 228, 271.

France, dynastic pretensions of, 3; war with England, 25, 26; concerning Scotland, 56; civil strife in, 67; its state at end of the Hundred Years' War, 83; instruction in Italian diplomacy, 84; its struggle with Burgundy, 100, 111; national feeling in, 112; invaded by Edward IV of England, 121; peace with Venice, 134; influence of the diplomacy of Louis XI upon, 150; under Anne de Beaujeu, 150; its army, 152; its territorial unity, 152; a menace to the Papacy and the Empire, 157; imperial aspirations of, 163; 164; the centre of Italian intrigue, 165; confidence of Italy in, 166; imperial tradition in, 172; concludes a league with Milan, 176; suffers from the expedition of Charles VIII, 208; 209, 211, 214, 215; *rapprochement* to Venice, 219, 220; concerning Naples, 230; 232, 250, 258, 270; isolated by Venice, 284; opposition of Pope Julius II, 265, 267, the league against, 290, 291, 293; defeated at Guinegatte, 296; peace with England, 298, 299; renews alliance with Venice, 301; concludes alliance with the Swiss, 306; 346, 366, 369, 370, 371; the invasion of, 372; defeated at Pavia, 374; 383, 384, 394; 400, 405, 406, 407, 419; in danger of the Hapsburgs, 431; 434, 436, 438; invasion of, 447; secret diplomacy of, 449, 451; changed attitude of England toward, 452; its success in the East, 453; invasion of, 458; 480, 482, 483, 485, 489, 492, 493, 496, 498, 499; compact with Spain regarding heresy, 502, 503, 504; peace with the Huguenots and alliance with England, 509; after the massacre of the Huguenots, 512, 513; 518, 519, 523, 527, 528, 529; question of succession, 538, 539, 540; united under Henry IV, 543; reduced by the religious wars, 544; Protestantism obtains toleration in, 546; dangerous position of, 547; alliance with the Netherlands, 548; aims to limit the Hapsburg power, 548; 552, 562, 563; at war with Charles I of England, 575; negotiates with Sweden, 579; attitude toward Protestantism, 586; 588, 589, 590; its demands at Westphalia, 600, 601.

Franche-Comté, 20, 84; in revolt, 120; invaded by the Swiss, 121; 128, 130; falls to Louis XI, 132; 180; its surrender demanded by Margaret of Burgundy, 297; 300, 472, 539, 550, 589.

Francis II, Duke of Brittany, 100, 101, 103, 112, 123, 151.

Francis I, King of France, 187; as Count of Angoulême, 252, 260, 262; accession, 300; reception of Venetian ambassadors, 301; obtains Milan, 302; negotiates with Leo X, 303; coalition against, 304; treaty with Charles of Spain, 305; alliance with the Empire and Spain, 306; imperial aspirations, 322, 323, 325, 327, 329; his second electoral campaign, 332; the financial question, 339, 340; 341, 344, 346; his conflict with Charles V, 349; plan for his meeting with Henry VIII and Charles V, 351; Wolsey's pressure upon, 359; rumors of an alliance with Charles V, 360; 361, 363, 365, 366, 367; his alliance with Scotland, 369; 370, 371, 372; his capture at Pavia, 374; his captivity in Spain, 381, 382, 385, 386; signs the Treaty of Madrid, 387; his deliverance, 388; reveals his intentions, 391; 392, 393, 394, 395; repudiates the Treaty of Madrid, 396; challenged by Charles V, 397; 399; negotiates with Zapolya and the Sultan, 410; 412, 417; confirms the Peace of Cambray, 418; 430, 431, 432, 434; his negotiations with the Sultan and the Protestants, 435, 437, 438; his reign marks a break from the Middle Age system, 439; his diplomatic methods of, 440; aggressions upon Savoy, 441; arraigned by Charles V, 443; praised by Charles V, 446; illusory reconciliation with Charles, 448; his *entente* with the Sultan, 450; 451, 453, 454, 456; war against Charles V,

648 INDEX

457; isolation of, 458; concludes the Peace of Crépy, 460; death of, 468; 472, 514, 549.

Francis II, King of France, 496, 498, 504.

Francis, son of Francis I of France, 307, 354, 387, 389, 418, 439, 441.

Franciscans, the, 15.

Franconia, Duchy of, 584.

Frankfort, decisions of, 21; as the place of imperial election, 39; 131, 324, 335; assembly of the electors at, 342; 587.

Franz, Duke of Brunswick-Lüneburg, 426.

Frederick of Austria, 13, 14.

Frederick, Count Palatine, 345, 346.

Frederick III, Count Palatine, 467.

Frederick IV, Count Palatine, 557.

Frederick V, Elector Palatine, 560, 562, 563, 565, 567, 568, 586.

Frederick, Elector of Saxony, 330, 331, 335, 337, 339, 344.

Frederick I, Emperor, called "Barbarossa," 49.

Frederick II, Emperor, 37, 50, 419.

Frederick III, Emperor, election, 77; coronation, 79; his claim to Milan, 87; his opposition to Pope Pius II, 96; aids the Pope in Bohemia, 105; opposes Podiebrad, 107; annuls the treaty with the Swiss, 109; rejects terms for Burgundian alliance, 110; his negotiations with Charles the Bold, 113, 115, 116, 117, 118, 127; urges marriage with his son upon Mary of Burgundy, 131; 133, 134; opposed to actions of Louis XI in Italy, 141, 142, 143; proposed by Sixtus IV as a joint arbitrator, 145; death, 180; his prediction that Austria would rule the world, 232.

Frederick of Hohenzollern, 62, 63.

Frederick I, King of Denmark and Norway, 429.

Frederick, King of Naples, 212, 222, 224, 230, 250, 277.

Frederick, King of Sicily, 14.

Frederick William of Brandenburg, 585.

Fregoso, Doge of Genoa, 93, 95.

Fregoso, an envoy, 456, 457.

Fréjus, the Bishop of, 142.

French expansion, the diplomacy of, 83.

Friesland, 34, 84, 130.

Friuli, 275, 277.

Frundsberg, George von, 401.

Fugger, family of bankers, 291, 328, 341.

GABRIEL, Bertucio, 139.

Gaetani, the, 228.

Gallas, Baron, 582.

Gallican Church, 303.

Gallipoli, 277.

Gama, Vasco da, 267, 268, 269.

Gandia, Duke of, 223.

Gar, Signor, 243.

Gascony, 19, 377.

Gattinara del Arborio, Mercurino, his policy, 358; his opposition to France, 360; opposes Wolsey, 362; at the Conference of Calais, 363; advantages over Wolsey, 364, 365; another treaty with Wolsey, 370; his advice after the victory of Pavia, 380, 381; his claims, against Francis I, 382; 384; his advice concerning Italy and France, 385; opposes the Treaty of Madrid, 388; 406 427; his death, 428, 429.

Gaul, 438, 601.

Gelderland, 113, 115, 116, 117, 120, 129, 459, 524.

Gelderland, Count of, 18, 21, 22.

Geneva, 124, 441.

Geneva, Count of, 20, 111.

Genoa, its aid sought by Philip VI, 26; abandoned to Milan, 87; reoccupied by the French, 92, 93; peril and relief of, 95; as a military and naval base, 99; resists John of Anjou, 101; its independence demanded, 142; renewal of homage to France, 142, 143; again given to Milan, 176; its opposition to France, 270; intercession of Julius II for, 272, 273; again becomes free, 293; French suzerainty recognized by the Doge of, 302; withdraws financial aid in imperial campaign, 340; welcomes Charles V, 419, 420.

Gentilis, Albericus, 530, 552, 570.

George, Margrave of Brandenburg, 426.

George William, Elector of Brandenburg, 567, 584.

Gérard, Balthazar, 529.

German language, 346.

Germany, opposes papal pretensions, 21; its position under Charles IV, 34; affected by the Hanseatic League, 49; favors the Teutonic Order, 51; relations to Charles the Bold, 107; postal service in, 156; its danger from France, 211; the bankers of, 340; favors Luther, 357; relation to the Papacy and to Lutheranism, 407, 408; the condition and problems of, 422; the Emperor's plans embarrassed in, 430; progress of religious reform in, 432, 433; success of Charles V in, 459; Protestantism in the North and Catholicism in the South of, 463; anxiety regarding Charles V in, 463, 470; Luther's conception of, 480; as a system

INDEX

of small states, 511; its state before the Thirty Years' War, 554; attitude of Denmark and Sweden toward, 567; the situation created by Wallenstein in, 577; the discontent in, 578; invasion by Gustavus Adolphus of, 579, 582, 583; the desolation in, 590, 591.

Gerson, Jean, 58, 62.

Ghent, 20, 26, 129, 131, 150, 451, 453, 522.

Ghent, the Pacification of, 520, 524.

Ghiara d' Adda, 221, 277.

Ghibelline party, 27.

Ghinucci, papal nuncio, 354, 363.

Giac, Pierre de, 69.

Gié, Marshal, 221.

Giglis, Sylvester de, 355.

Giorgi, Marino, 302, 303.

Giova, Bernardino, 269.

Giovio, Paolo, 401.

Giustinian, Antonio, 239, 243, 248, 256, 280.

Giustinian, Lorenzo, 281.

Giustinian, Sebastian, 301, 337, 350.

Glapion, Jean, 412.

Golden Bull of Andrew II of Hungary, 53.

Golden Bull of Charles IV regarding imperial elections, 38, 39, 40, 330, 335, 342, 343, 346, 428.

Golden Fleece, Order of the, 481.

Gondomar, Count de, 565.

Gonfaloniere of the Church, 228, 244, 246.

Good Hope, Cape of, 187, 267.

Gradenigo, 136.

Grandson, 125, 126.

Granvelle, Chancellor of Charles V, 429, 466, 467, 474.

Granvelle, the Younger, 484, 503.

Grassis, Paris de, 289, 311.

Gratz, 131.

Gravelines, 353.

"Great Privilege," the, 129, 130.

Greece, 111.

Greek Empire, the, 54, 78. See also Byzantine Empire.

Gregory IX, Pope, 51

Gregory XI, Pope, 42, 43

Gregory XII, Pope, 58, 59, 63.

Greifenklau, Richard von, 305.

Grenada, 179, 264.

Grenada, the Treaty of, 229, 233, 245.

Grey, Lady Jane, 478.

Grimani, Cardinal, 249.

Grisons, the, 548, 564, 577.

Gritti, Luigi, 410, 436.

Grotius, Hugo, 317, 553, 569, 571, **572**, 591.

Guelf party, 27, 37.

Guinegatte, the battle of, 296.

Guines, 352.

Guise, the family of, 497, 498, 529, 531, 537.

Guise, Henry Duke of, 538, 540.

Guise, Mary of, 497.

Gunpowder, 2, 163.

Günther of Schwartzburg, 34.

Gurk, Cardinal of, 183.

Gustavus I, King of Sweden, 429.

Gustavus II, Adolphus, King of Sweden, appeal of England to, 566; war with Poland, 567; terms with England, 568; his estimation of Grotius, 572; treaty with Christian IV, 575; invasion of Germany, 580, 582, 583; his victories and death, 584; results of his death, 585.

Guyenne, 3, 8, 23, 107, 122, 292, 377.

HAARLEM, 522.

Hagenau, 326, 329, 462.

Hagenbach, Peter von, 109, 113, 118, 120.

Hague, The, 532, 562.

Hainault, 34, 84, 129, 130, 133, 150.

Hainault, Count of, 18, 20, 22.

Hakon, King of Norway, 49.

Halberstadt, 603.

Hamburg, 47.

Hampton Court, 379.

Hansa cities, 576.

Hanseatic League, the, 46, 48, 49, 50.

Hapsburg, the House of, regains the imperial office, 77; the Austria-Tyrol and Austria-Styria branches of, 107; its territories in Southern Elsass, 108; importance of the marriage of Maximilian and Mary of Burgundy to, 132, 133; part of its Austrian lands falls to Hungary, 134; prediction of its power by Frederick III, 232; prospect of its union with Valois disappears, 260; the ascendency of, 321; Maximilian aims to increase the power of, 323; the efforts of, 327; its battle with the House of Valois, 332; the partition of its territories into Austrian and Spanish, 358; its divided interests, 409; limitation of its power, 434; united with Wittelsbach, 467; its division, 481; union with England, 482; the opposition of France and the Papacy to, 548; the opposition

of Richelieu to, 577, 582; its possessions, 589.
Hapsburg-Valois middle state project, the, 456.
Hedwig, Queen of Poland, 52, 55.
Heilbronn, the League of, 587, 588.
Heneage, Lord, 533.
Henriette Marie, 569.
Henry II, Emperor, 180.
Henry VII, Emperor, 1, 13, 36, 37.
Henry II, King of Castile, 57, 65.
Henry II, King of England, 56.
Henry III, King of England, 4.
Henry IV, King of England, 66.
Henry V, King of England, 66, 67, 68, 69, 121.
Henry VI, King of England, 69, 72.
Henry VII, King of England, 178, 179, 207, 215, 259, 281, 282, 294.
Henry VIII, King of England, accession, 282; marriage to Catherine of Aragon, 283; intervention in Italy, 283; honored by Pope Julius II, 287; joins the "Holy League," 291; aims at the conquest of Guyenne, 292; defeats the French at Guinegatte, 296; his understanding with Margaret of Burgundy, 297; alliance with Louis XII, 298; perceives the designs of Ferdinand the Catholic, 299; Francis I acknowledges debt to, 300; opposes Francis in Italy, 304; his support of Wolsey, 307; the imperial campaign, 323, 324, 332, 335; as described by the Venetian ambassador, 337; efforts of Richard Pace for, 338; more absolute as a ruler than the Emperor, 349; disposed to contend for real supremacy, 350; his meeting with Francis I and Charles V, 351, 352, 353; demands a truce between France and Spain, 360; accords full powers to Wolsey, 362; receives the news of the battle of Pavia, 375; his plan to dethrone Francis I, 377; the disillusionment of, 378; his obligations under the Treaty of Moore, 384; his condemnation of the Treaty of Madrid, 391, 393; his aid to Francis I and demands on the Emperor, 394; as "protector" of the League of Cognac, 395, 396; his matrimonial project, 398; renounces pretensions to France, 400, 401; his aid sought by Ferdinand in Hungary, 410; his negotiations with Pope Clement VII, 412; efforts to arrange his marriage with Anne Boleyn, 413; question of his divorce, 414; repudiates Rome, 416; gains the support of the universities, 430; as head of the English Church, 430; his changed attitude, 452; his several marriages, 452, 453, 459; his invasion of France, 459, 460; his alliance sought by Philip of Hesse, 463; his death, 468.
Henry II, King of France, as a hostage in Spain, 387, 389; affianced to Mary of England, 400; provision for his obtaining Hungary, 410; arrangement for his release from Spain, 418; marriage with Catherine de' Medici, 434; proposal to confer Milan upon, 439; his attitude upon accession to the throne, 471; opposes Charles V, 472; his diplomatic activity, 472; angered at the action of his allies, 475; alliance with Pope Paul IV, 482; opposes the marriage project of Philip II, 484; his death, 485; his inadvertent exposure of his plans to William the Silent, 502; 504, 539, 549.
Henry III, King of France, as a student of Machiavelli, 312; marriage project, 509, 510; accession, 513; 528, 529; occupied with the "League," 531; 537; expulsion and assassination of, 538; 540.
Henry IV, King of France, (of Navarre) as a student of Machiavelli, 312; the league against, 529; as ally of Elizabeth of England, 537; accession to the throne, 538; his conversion, 540; reconciliation with the Pope, 542; his foreign policy, 547; his death, 550; 557, 558, 563, 564.
Henry, King of Portugal, called the "Cardinal," 527.
Henry of Nassau, 345, 447.
Henry the Navigator, 267.
Henry of Thurn, Count, 559.
Hesse, the Landgrave of, 462, 466, 467, 562.
Hobbes, Thomas, 573.
Höchst, 343.
Hohenstaufen, the, 164, 420.
Hohenzollern, House of, 322, 585.
Holland, 34, 84, 129, 130, 209, 503, 521, 524, 532, 606.
Holstein, the King of Denmark as Duke of, 567.
"Holy League," the, 291, 293.
"Holy Office," the, 266.
Holy Places, the, 175, 186.
Holy Roman Empire of the German Nation, the, 321, 322, 477.
Holy See, the, 165, 166, 167, 168, 186, 270. See also Papacy.
Homage of the English kings to France, 7, 11.
Honfleur, 67.
Horn, Count, 503.
Hotman, François, 513, 530, 541.
Howard, Catherine, 459.

INDEX

651

Howard, Thomas, 484.
Hugonnet, Guillaume, 114.
Huguenots, the, 461, 505, 509, 512, 537, 541, 543, 550, 564, 569, 576, 577.
Hundred Years' War, the, 26, 56, 71, 90, 178.
Hungary, as the bulwark of Europe, 53; its public institutions, 53; 77, 107; seeks aid of Burgundy, 115, 121; King of, plots with Louis XI, 131; 209, 323, 334, 368; the complications in, 409; 433, 436, 437, 438, 441, 451; the question of succession reopened, 455; its division by the Ottoman invasion, 455, 456; 473, 549, 550, 555, 559, 560.
Hunyady, John, 96.
Huss, John, 16, 60, 61, 63.
Hussites, the, 75.
Hussite Wars, the, 63, 70, 74.
Hutten, Ulrich von, 326, 357.

IDIAQUEZ, 533.
Imola, 137, 228, 246, 271.
Imperial alliances, the crisis in the, 372.
Imperial ambition, the revival of, 321.
Imperial dominion, 172, 173.
Imperial idea, transformation of the, 349.
Imperial power, 158, 159, 163.
"Imperium," 310, 349.
India, 211, 268.
Innocent III, Pope, 27.
Innocent VI, Pope, 40, 41.
Innocent VII, Pope, 58.
Innocent VIII, Pope, annuls marriage of Maximilian and Anne of Brittany, 152; character of, 167; independence in office, 168; death, 169; 181, 186.
Innocent X, Pope, 604.
Innsbruck, 108, 274, 477.
Inquisition, the, 266, 267, 407, 498, 502, 504, 506, 512.
"Inquisitori de' Secreti," of Venice, 449.
Instruments of defence, 2.
Interim, the, 469, 476.
International jurisprudence, 519.
Intervention, foreign, the principle of, 165.
Ireland, 545.
Isabella, Queen of Castile, wife of Ferdinand the Catholic, 179, 197, 256, 257, 263, 266, 323.
Isabella, Queen of Denmark, 429.
Isabella of Portugal, 388, 392, 453.

Isabella of Spain, daughter of Philip II, 539, 541, 546.
Isabella, wife of Gian Galeazzo Sforza, 176, 183.
Isabelle of France, wife of Edward II of England, 5, 8, 9, 10.
Ischia, 198.
Istria, 275.
Italian methods, 157; politics, 164.
Italy, unrest in, 41; condition of, 85; the prey of the foreigner, 89; efforts for French preponderance in, 134; intervention of Louis XI in, 138; the French mission in, 140, 143; peace and equilibrium restored in, 149; influence of the diplomacy of Louis XI upon, 150; beginning of permanent missions in, 153; as the central seat of power and primary school of politics, 164; its craving for foreign intervention, 165; its confidence in France, 166; expedition of Charles VIII into, 182; its state at the end of the fifteenth century, 212; as the battlefield of Europe, 238, 253, 293; the effect on Europe of the contest for, 294; lost to the Empire, 322; plans of Gattinara concerning, 380, 381; ready to oppose Charles V, 390; Charles V in, 419, 420; falls away from Charles V, 471.
Ivry, 540.

JAGELLON, 52, 55, 323.
James I, King of England, VI of Scotland, birth and coronation, 501; 533, 534, 536; accession to the throne of England, 548; 550, 560, 561, 562; endeavors to aid Frederick V, 563; his plans for the marriage of his son, 565; opposition to the Emperor, 566; alliance with Denmark and the Netherlands, 568; his death, 569.
James IV, King of Scotland, 297.
Jandun, Jean de, 16.
Jeanne d'Arc, 69, 70.
Jeanne, daughter of Louis X, 5, 6.
Jeanne, daughter of Louis XI, 221, 222.
Jeannin, Pierre, 539, 540, 548.
Jerome of Prague, 62.
Jesuits, the, 555, 556, 574, 578.
Jesus, the Society of, 465.
Jews, the, 266.
Joachim, Margrave of Brandenburg, 325, 326, 333, 338, 344, 468.
Jobst of Moravia, 00.
John Albert, King of Poland, 226.
John of Anjou, 92, 93, 95, 101, 103.
John of Austria, Don, 519, 521, 523.
John of Bohemia, 13, 19, 23.

652 INDEX

John V, Duke of Brittany, 70.
John, Duke of Burgundy, called the Fearless, 68, 106.
John, Elector of Saxony, 425, 426.
John Frederick, Elector of Saxony, 462, 463, 466, 467, 468, 475, 476.
John of Gaunt, 530.
John George, Elector of Saxony, 561, 584.
John II, King of Aragon, 95, 179.
John I, King of France, 6.
John II, King of France, 56, 57, 67.
John Palaeologus, Greek Emperor, 78.
John XXII, Pope, 8, 9, 12, 13, 14, 15, 16.
John XXIII, Pope, 59, 60, 61, 62.
John Sigismund, Elector of Brandenburg, 558.
Joseph, Père, 578, 579, 580, 582.
Jouffroy, 99.
Juana of Aragon, 250.
Juana, Queen of Castile, 231, 256, 257, 259, 263, 264, 265, 272, 305, 323.
Juana I, Queen of Naples, 174.
Juana II, Queen of Naples, 73, 74, 75, 76, 174.
Jülich, 549.
Julius II, Pope, accession, 245; attitude toward Venice, 247; disregards Borgia, 248; rewards D'Amboise, 249; his diplomacy, 250; action concerning Venice, 254; his embarrassment, 255; growing prestige of, 269; recovers territory, 269, 270; relations to France and Spain, 270; as a military leader, 271; attempts to meet Ferdinand the Catholic, 272; intercedes for Genoa, 272, 273; his relation to the League of Cambray, 276, 277; excommunicates Venice, 278; abandons the League, 284; rupture with France, 287; his plans and defeat, 288; summoned to appear before a general council, 289; forms the "Holy League," 291; his triumph and death, 292; 303, 311, 399, 401.
Julius III, Pope, 471.
Jurists, the, 493, 551, 552.
Jus civile, 491.
Jus gentium, 491.
Jus inter gentes, 491.
Jus naturale, 491.
Justinian, Digest of, **172.**
Jutland, 575.

KALISCH, the Treaty of, 51.
Kalmar, the Union of, 49, 429.
"King of the Romans," 180.

Klostergrab, 558, 559.
Knight, Dr. William, 413, 414.
"Knights of the Sword," 51.
Knox, John, 497.
Köln, Archbishop of, 13, 22, 39, 77, 121, 329, 334, 338, 348.
Köln, Elector of, 556.
Kunigunde, 116.

LADISLAS V, Postumus, King of Hungary, 96.
Ladislas VI, King of Hungary, 217, 226, 323.
Ladislas V, King of Poland, 52.
La Forest, Jean de, 436, 451.
Lahnstein, 21, 58.
La Marck, Robert de, 326, 359.
Lamberg, Count, 596.
Lancaster, House of, 97, 178.
Lang, Matthias, Cardinal, 276, 288, 289, 290, 345.
Languages used in diplomatic intercourse, 157.
Languedoc, 42, 377, 382.
Languet, Hubert, 513, 517.
Lannoy, Viceroy of Naples, 387, 389, 393.
La Palice, Marshal de, 292, 301, 363.
Lark, Thomas, 383.
La Rochelle, 576.
Laszko, Jerome, 410, 455.
Lateran Council, 292, 295, 297, **464.**
Latin language, the, 157, 346.
La Trémoïlle, Georges, 69, 71.
La Trémoïlle, Military chief, 297.
L'Aubespine, Foreign secretary under Henry II of France, 473, 484.
Lausanne, 76, 126.
Lautrec, 389, 413, 415.
Law, public, its non-existence in Europe, 491.
"League," the, 529, 531, 537, 539, 542.
League, the Catholic, 558, 561, 563, 579, 580, 582, 586.
"League of the Public Weal," the, 100, 103.
Learning, the Revival of, 246.
Leicester, the Earl of, 532, 533, 536.
Leo III, Pope, 16.
Leo X, Pope, accession, 296; reconciles the Emperor and Venice, 297; negotiates with Francis I, 302, 303; adheres to the general peace, 307, 308; attitude in the imperial campaign, 328, 331,

332, 336; sudden change of attitude, 344, 345; concerning Wolsey and England, 354; his advantage over Charles V, 355; his compact with Charles V, 361; 362, 365; death, 368.
Leon, the Kingdom of, 394.
Leopold of Austria, 305.
Lepanto, the battle of, 519, 527.
Lerma, Duke of, 549.
Leslie, John, Bishop of Ross, 515.
Lewis IV, of Bavaria, Emperor, 13, 14, 18, 22, 30, 31, 32, 33, 34.
Lewis of Brandenburg, 33, 34.
Lewis V, Count Palatine, 326.
Lewis the German, 128.
Lewis II, King of Bohemia, 323, 324, 334, 335, 343, 358, 409.
Lewis, King of Hungary, called the Great, 52, 55.
"Lex Feudorum," 7.
"Lex Salica," 7.
"Lex Voconia," 6.
Lichtenstein, Paul von, 291.
Lichtenstein, Ulrich von, 202.
Liège, 22, 116.
Limburg, 18, 84.
Lisbon, 268, 527.
Livonia, 51, 580.
Loaysa, Garcia de, 412, 433.
Lodi, the Treaty of, 92.
Lombardy, 86, 233, 234.
Lonato, 449.
London, 47, 375, 393.
Longueville, Duke of, 596.
Loredam, Antonio, 219.
Lorraine, 84, 115, 116, 124, 128, 129, 472, 474, 485, 589.
Lorraine, Cardinal of, 441, 484, 498.
Lorraine, Duchess of, 484.
Lothair I, Emperor, 84, 128, 158, 209, 589.
Lotharingia, 84.
Louis I, of Anjou, 86, 174.
Louis II, of Anjou, 74, 75.
Louis, Duke of Savoy, 88, 91.
Louis IX, King of France, 4, 10.
Louis X, King of France, 5, 6, 541.
Louis XI, King of France, as Dauphin opposes the crown, 71; seeks refuge in Burgundy, 85; his rule at Grenoble, 97; his accession to France, 98; attitude toward the Papacy, 99; his policy in Italy, 101; his diplomacy with his vassals, 102, 103; revokes ordinances against papal authority, 104; opposed by Philip of Bresse, 105; at Péronne, 106; 109, 110, 111, 118, 119, 123, 124, 125, 127; seizes territory at the death of Charles the Bold, 129; 130, 131, 132, 133; negotiates the Peace of Arras, 134; intervention in Italy, 138; forbids the sending of money to the Holy See, 140; frustration of his mission in Italy, 143; his opposition to Pope Sixtus IV and support of Sforza, 146, 147; wish for an *entente* with Venice and the Pope and repudiation of Sforza, 149; his death, 149; his influence upon Italy and France, 150; his use of diplomacy and preference for Italians as agents, 152; his principle of secrecy, 153; his influence on diplomacy, 155, 157; his moderate intervention in Italy, 166; his inheritance of the Angevin claims to Naples, 167; his anxiety for his son, 171; his idea concerning the Netherlands, 172; his slight regard for his rights to Naples, 173; 440.
Louis XII, King of France, as Duke of Orléans, 151, 176, 200, 202, 206, 207; accession, 208; his exploits in Italy, 208; his search for allies, 214; his treaty with Philip Archduke of Austria, 217; plan for divorce and remarriage, 221; his transactions with Pope Alexander VI, 221; his many allies, 225; protects Florence and Bologna against Borgia, 228; agrees to divide Naples with Ferdinand the Catholic, 229; defeated at Naples, 230; his treaty with the Archduke Philip concerning the marriage of their children, 231; renounces all conquests in Naples, 232; renounces claim to imperial title, 232; his many mistakes as pointed out by Machiavelli, 233, 234; supports Cardinal d' Amboise for the Papacy, 243, 244, 245; drawn into the plans of Julius II, 249; makes the treaties of Blois, 251; assumes the title of King of Naples, 256; alliance with Ferdinand the Catholic, 258; 260, 261, 262, 270; his conference at Savona, 272; 273, 276; invades Venetian territory and gains the battle of Agnadello, 279; his designs exposed to England, 281; 285, 286, 289, 292, 294; his misfortunes, 296; tenacious in his purpose to recover Milan, 297; his last days, 298; 302, 309.
Louis XIII, King of France, 550, 564, 565, 569, 577, 586, 590.
Louis XIV, King of France, 590, 601, 607.
Louis of Nassau, 506.
Louise of Savoy, 252, 300; furnishes money for the imperial campaign of her son Francis I, 340; her preparations for his coronation, 346; 361, 371; as

654 INDEX

regent of France, 375; her negotiations with Wolsey, 376; 382; her diplomacy, 383; rewards Wolsey for his services, 384; negotiates for the release of Francis I, 386; the fruits of her diplomacy, 389; negotiates the Peace of Cambray with Margaret of Burgundy, 417; her skill in maintaining the Anglo-French *entente*, 418, 419; 441.

Louvain, 131; the decisions of the doctors of, 262, 263.

Lower Saxon Circle, the, 567.

Loyola, Ignatius, 465.

Lübeck, 47; the Peace of, 576.

Lucca, 86, 208, 390.

Lucerne, 108, 217.

Luna, Tassino da, 449.

Lusatia, 603.

Lusignan family, the, 277.

Luther, Martin, 16; beginning of his work, 328; at the Diet of Worms, 356; his translation of the Bible, 357, 358; his changed attitude, 408; his followers in England, 416; his change with the progress of events, 424, 425; approves of armed resistance, 428; 433, 434, 461.

Lutheranism, 407, 408, 422, 423; development of, 424; among the Scandinavian kingdoms, 429; its spread, 466; its right under the Peace of Augsburg, 479; 502, 557.

Lutherans, the, 414, 431, 462, 505, 555.

Luxemburg, 84, 129.

Luxemburg, the House of, 13, 40, 55, 77.

Luynes, Duke de, 564.

Lyons, Archbishop of, 540.

MACAULAY, 315.

Machiavelli, Niccolò, 65, 153; his estimate of Cesare Borgia, 227; his criticism of French diplomacy, 233; describes the methods and plans of Cesare Borgia, 239, 240, 243, 246; at Rome, 247; his comment on Cardinal d'Amboise, 286; his political philosophy, 311; his writings, 312; his maxims, 313; his purpose, character, and influence, 315; his philosophy as affected by Grotius and Rousseau, 317; 369, 371, 398, 500, 514, 525; compared with Grotius, 571.

Madrid, the Treaty of, 386, 390, 391, 393, 396, 418, 443; the treaty of 1621 of, 564.

Magaloto, Alberto, 153.

Magdeburg, 576, 603.

Magna Charta, 53.

"*Magnus intercursus*," 259.

Magyars, the, 53.

Maine, 167, 377.

Mainz, Archbishop of, 22, 39, 108, 114, 116, 329, 332, 338, 344, 345, 348, 357, 556.

Mainz, the Pragmatic Sanction of, 75.

Majorca, 64.

Malipiero, Italian historian, 309.

Malmö, the Treaty of, 429.

"*Malus intercursus*," 259.

Man, Dr., 506.

Mansfeld, Ernest Count of, 560, 562, 563, 565, 575.

Mantua, 86, 218, 288, 390, 577, 579, 580.

Mantua, the Congress of, 95.

Margaret of Angoulême, Queen of Navarre, 382, 440.

Margaret of Anjou, 72, 97.

Margaret of Burgundy, daughter of Maximilian, 133, 134, 150, 151, 178, 180, at Cambray, 276; as regent of the Netherlands and ruler of Burgundy, 276; 286, 290; directs a military movement against France, 296, 297; her understanding with Henry VIII, 297; 335, 336, 361, 375, 376; negotiates the Peace of Cambray, 417; her death, 429; 431.

Margaret of Flanders, 67, 84.

Margaret of France, daughter of Francis I, 485.

Margaret of Parma, 503, 504, 506.

Margaret, Queen of Denmark, 49, 50.

Margaret of Tyrol, 33.

Margaret of Valois, wife of Henry of Navarre, 529.

Margaret of York, 104, 130.

Maria, Infanta of Spain, 565.

Maria, Queen of Hungary, 55.

Marie, daughter of Charles IV of France, 11.

Marignano, the campaign of, 302.

Mark, 18, 549, 603.

Marsilius of Padua, 16, 22.

Martin V, Pope, 62, 64, 70, 71, 73, 74, 85.

Mary of Burgundy, daughter of Charles the Bold, 108, 110, 113, 115, 116, 126, 129, 130, 131, 133, 305, 382.

Mary, Queen of England, daughter of Henry VIII, affianced to the Dauphin of France, 307; her proposed marriage with Charles V, 354, 359, 363, 364; 377, 378, 381, 394, 399; affianced to Henry, Duke of Orléans, 400; 452; marriage with Philip of Spain, 478; 479, 482; her death, 483; 519.

Mary, Queen of France, wife of Louis XII, 298.

Mary, Queen of Scots, 496, 500, 501, 507, 508, 509, 510, 515, 520, 529, 531, 533, 535.

INDEX 655

Mary, daughter of the Emperor Charles V, 456.

Mary, sister of the Emperor Charles V, 429, 470, 474, 481.

Matthias, Emperor, 523, 555, 558, 560.

Matthias Corvinus, King of Hungary, 96, 107, 108, 134.

Maurice, Count, son of William the Silent, 532.

Maurice, Duke of Saxony, 467, 468, 471, 474, 475, 476, 477, 479.

Maximilian, Duke of Bavaria, 557, 558, 561, 563, 582, 586, 600.

Maximilian I, Emperor, 108, 110, 113, 116, 126; marriage, 130; 131, 132, 133, 141, 143, 145; attempts to reassert authority in the Netherlands, 150; becomes King of the Romans, 151; endeavors to establish postal service, 156; 167; opposition to Charles VIII of France, 178; accession to the Empire, 180; 182, 189; his fears of Charles VIII, 201; family relations with Sforza, 213; displeased with Sforza, 215; war with the Swiss, 216; isolation of, 226; treaty with Louis XII, 232; negotiations of Pope Alexander VI with, 242; overtures of Pope Julius II to, 249, 250; the treaties of Blois, 251, 254, 255; invests the Archduke Philip with Milan, 255; seeks imperial coronation, 260; his evasive answers to the ambassadors of Louis XII, 262; his military weakness, 269; his negotiations with Julius II, 273; adopts the title "Roman Emperor-elect," 274; his attack upon Venice, 274; negotiations of Venice with, 279; concerning the League of Cambray, 285; calls a conference at Mantua, 288; his aspirations to the Papacy, 290; borrows money of the Fuggers, 291; joins the "Holy League," 291; his actions in Italy considered, 294; aids Henry VIII at Guinegatte, 296; leads an army to oppose Francis I, 304; adherence to the Treaty of Noyon, the Treaty of Brussels, and cession of Verona to Venice, 306; alliance at Cambray, 306; 308; his designs concerning the imperial succession, 323, 324, 327; his poverty, 328; again seeks coronation, 330, 331; his death, 332; 349, 419.

Maximilian II, Emperor, 470, 511, 555.

Mayer, Martin, 423.

Mazarin, Cardinal, 581, 590, 598, 601, 605.

Mecklenburg, Albert, Duke of, 472.

Mediaevalism, 45.

Medici, the, 85, 136, 213, 293, 303, 331, 332, 415, 421.

Medici, Alessandro de', Duke of Florence, 415.

Medici, Catherine de', as a student of Machiavelli, 312; marriage of, 434; 439, 444; as regent of France, 498; her negotiations at Bayonne with Spain, 503; her policy in France, 504; her plan regarding Mary Stuart, 509; her death, 538.

Medici, Cosimo de', ruler of Florence, 95, 104, 154.

Medici, Cosimo de', Duke of Florence, 458.

Medici, Filippo de', 138.

Medici, Giovanni de', Cardinal, 168, 296.

Medici, Giuliano de', 138.

Medici, Giulio de', Cardinal, 362, 368, 371. See Pope Clement VII (at Rome).

Medici, Lorenzo de', called the "Magnificent," 135, 136; opposes Pope Sixtus IV, 137; attempt to assassinate, 138; welcomes the mediation of Louis XI, 141; reconciled with Ferdinand of Naples, 147; a champion of the system of balanced power in Italy, 165; 168; his appeal to Savonarola, 177.

Medici, Maria de', 550, 564.

Medici, Piero de', 104, 165, 177, 181, 184, 185.

Medina-Celi, 510.

Mediterranean commerce, 267, 268.

Melanchthon, Philip, 462.

Melito, Count de, 484.

Mendoza, Don Bernardino, 525, 526, 529, 531, 533, 534, 539.

Mendoza, Don Diego Hurtado de, 465.

Mendoza, Don Iñigo de, 541.

Merveilles, 444.

Mesnage, Jacques, 473.

Metz, 472, 476, 477, 485, 579, 601.

Mexico, 458.

Michaelangelo, 293.

Micheletto, 242.

Michiele, 228.

Milan, extent and power in Italy, 86; gains control of Genoa, 87; appeals to Charles VII of France, 90; abandons Charles the Bold, 126; invites intervention of Louis XI, 139; in league with Florence and Naples, 149; the Orléans claims to, 149; establishes the first permanent diplomatic relations, 154; its efforts at the French court, 165; in league with France, 175; menaced by the Duke of Orléans, 200, 206; description of the Orléans claims to, 213; conquest of, 224; attacked by the Swiss, 288; 293, 296, 302, 372, 438, 439.

Minio, Marco, 336.
Minorites, 15.
Missions, permanent, 153, 308.
Mitylene, the island of, 227.
Modena, 86, 303.
Mohacs, the battle of, 409.
Moldavia, 54.
Moncada, Ugo de, 397.
Montdidier, 301.
Montepessulano, Raimondo Marco, 153.
Montferrat, 86, 581.
Montfort, 103.
Montils-les-Tours, the Treaty of, 90, 91.
Montmorency, Constable of France, 386, 392, 450, 472, 473, 484.
Montone, Braccio da, 74.
Montpensier, Charles de, Duke of Bourbon, 371.
Montpensier, the Count de, 198, 206.
Monzon, the Treaty of, 577.
Moore, the Treaty of, 384.
Moors, the, 64, 179, 266.
Morat, the Lake of, 127, 135.
Moravia, 60, 559.
Moravian Brotherhood, the, 574.
Moriscoes, the, 506.
Morlhon, Antoine de, 141, 145, 146.
Morone, Girolamo, 385.
Morrison, 478.
Mortimer, 10.
Moslem pirates, 435.
Mühldorf, the battle of, 14.
Mulhäusen, 108.
Münster, 592, 593, 594; the Treaty of, 602.

NAMUR, 84, 129, 133.
Nancy, 128, 132, 305.
Naples, conquered by Alfonso V of Aragon, 76, 85; question of succession to, 93, 94; in league with Florence and Milan, 147, 148, 149; the Angevin pretensions to, 149, 167; threatened by Innocent VIII, 169; claim of Charles VIII, 173, 174; 177, 189, 197, 199, 200, 205, 206, 209; conquest of, 229; 242, 251, 258, 259, 271, 331, 332, 344, 345.
Napoleon Bonaparte, 172.
Narbonne, Cardinal de, 261.
Nasi, Francesco, 154.
Nassau, the Count of, 596.
National churches, 407, 417.
National states, 210.
Nations, 62, 158.

Naturelli, Philibert, 252, 260.
Navagero, Bernardo, 463, 466.
Navarre, 6, 64, 152, 180; taken by Ferdinand the Catholic, 292, 296; attacked by France, 359; 361, 362, 363, 387, 543.
Necho, 268.
Negropont, the fall of, 111.
Netherlands, the, 150; lost to France, 152; their importance to France, 172; treaty with England, 259; under the regency of Margaret of Burgundy, 276; conferred upon Philip II, 481; the Inquisition in, 502; revolt of, 503; reason for religious toleration in, 504, 505; triumph of Philip II in, 505; again in revolt, 521; the civic spirit in, 522; struggle with Spain, 522 and 523; as effected by the Treaty of Arras, 524; under Elizabeth's protectorate, 532; plunder the Spanish colonies, 544, 545; the Spanish provinces under Albert of Austria, 546; in alliance with France, 548; renewal of war with Spain, 563; 575, 588, 589; at Westphalia, 594, independence recognized by Spain, 605.
Neuss, 120.
Nevers, 84, 133; the Duke of, 577, 581.
Nice, the Truce of, 448, 452, 460.
Nicholas V, Antipope, 15.
Nicholas V, Pope, 78, 92, 94, 186.
Nicodemus de' Pontremoli, 154.
Nisch, the battle of, 78.
Nitti, historian, 345, 355.
Noailles, Antoine de, 479, 493.
Nördlingen, 588.
Norfolk, the Duke of, 507, 508, 510, 515.
Nori, Francesco, 153.
Normandy, 103, 377.
Northumberland, the Duke of, 478.
Norway, 47, 50, 209, 429.
Novara, 292, 296.
Novgorod, 47.
Noyon, the Treaty of, 305, 361.
Nuremberg, 39, 433, 562.

OGIER, 594, 606.
Oldenbarnevelt, John van, 532.
Oldendorp, John, 491.
Olivares, 581.
Orange, Philibert de Chalon Prince of, 402, 421.
"Ordonnance sur la Gendarmerie," 83.
Orléans claims to Milan, 90, 149, 171, 176, 181, 207, 209, 213.
Orléans, the council at, 140, 141.
Orsini, the, 190, 212.

Orsini, Cardinal, 169.
Orsini, Paolo, 240.
Orsini, papal legate, 344.
Ortenau, 326, 329.
Orvieto, 206, 412.
Osnabruck, 592, 593, 594; the Treaty of, 602.
Ossat, Arnauld d', 543.
Ostia, 194.
Otranto, 149, 277.
Otto III, Emperor, 49.
Ottoman Empire, the, 175, 209; menaces the Hapsburgs, 429; description of, 450; danger to the French in, 451; menaces Philip II, 506 : 549; not represented at Westphalia, 597.
Oxenstiern, 568, 585, 587, 596.

PACE, Richard, 324, 325, 337, 338, 339, 345, 368, 370, 371, 372, 373.
Pacific islands, the, 211.
Padua, 276, 280, 285.
Palaeologus, Andrew, cession of his rights to the Eastern Empire to Charles VIII of France, 183, 196.
Palatinate, the, 34, 322, 556, 562, 565, 566, 587, 589, 603.
Pallavicini, Cardinal, 272.
Pallavicino, Horatio, 530.
Palmier, Pierre, 147.
Panicharola, 153.
Papacy, the, changed character of, 1, 3, 4; concerning the Anglo-French quarrel, 8; declining influence of, 27; believed to be in league with France, 28; concerning the Golden Bull of 1356, 39; at Avignon, 41; efforts to end the schism of, 57; as an Italian state, 72; relations with Louis XI. 99; its loss of power, 157, 158; its claims, 164; fluctuations of its policy, 167; its claims over newly discovered lands, 186; under Alexander VI, 238, 243; regains power under Julius II, 270; 293; moral degeneration of, 295; opposition of Germany to, 328; an ally of Charles V, 358; its situation after the sack of Rome, 406, 407; its cause in England, 414, 416; 421, 423, 440; its representation at the Council of Trent, 464; in the Middle Ages, 490; fears the excessive power of Spain, 547, 548; its protest against the action at Westphalia, 604. See also Holy See.
Papal State, 41, 85, 136, 161, 186, 227, 271, 284, 289, 293.
Paper, the use of, 2.
Paris, treaties of, referred to, 4, 66, 589.

Parliament, the English, 479, 511, 565, 566, 569, 597.
Parliament, the French, 124, 441.
Parma, 293, 303, 331, 361, 420, 474.
Parma, the Prince of, see Farnese.
Parr, Catherine, 459.
"Partition," the principle of, 229.
Pasqualigo, Pietro, 301.
Passano, Jean Joachim de, 375, 383.
Passau, the conference at, 475, 602.
Paul II, Pope, 104, 105, 107, 119.
Paul III, Pope, 434; mediation of, 447, 448 : 458, 459; convokes the Council of Trent, 463, 464, 465; unites with the Emperor, 467; transfers the Council of Trent, 469; his death, 471.
Paul IV, Pope, 482, 484, 494, 498.
Paul V, Pope, 548, 564.
Pavia, 183, 372; the battle of, 374, 390, 443.
Paynellus, Andreas, 39.
Pazzi, the conspiracy of the, 136; Francesco de', 137; Cosimo de', 250.
Peace, the project of universal, 306; preliminaries to a general, 590.
Peasants' War, the, 408.
Pellicier, Guillaume, 449, 450, 454, 455, 457.
Peñaranda, Count de, 596.
Peraudi, Raimund, Cardinal, 183.
Perez, Alvaro, 412.
Péronne, the interview and Treaty of, 106.
Perpetual Edict, the, 521.
Pesaro, the Bishop of, 285.
Pescara, general, 385, 390.
Peter of Aragon, Franciscan monk, 42.
Peter IV, King of Aragon, 23, 64, 65.
Peter, King of Castile, called the Cruel, 65.
Petrarch, the poet, 36, 37, 42, 43.
Philibert, Duke of Savoy, 216.
Philip, Archduke of Austria, son of the Emperor Maximilian, 133, 150; relations with Louis XII, 214, 217, 230, 231; makes the treaties of Blois, 251; is invested with Milan, 255; claims Castile, 257, 259; 260, 262; his death, 263; 276, 305, 323.
Philip of Bresse, 104, 105, 111, 125, 195.
Philip, Duke of Burgundy, called the "Bold," 67.
Philip, Duke of Burgundy, called the "Good," 68, 70, 71, 85, 101, 104.
Philip IV, King of France, 4, 40, 172.
Philip V, King of France, 5, 7.

658 INDEX

Philip VI, King of France, 11, 12, 13, 16, 17, 18, 19, 20, 21, 22, 23, 24, 25, 30, 31, 34, 84.

Philip II, King of Spain, as a student of Machiavelli, 312; 406; marriage with the Infanta of Portugal, 458; 468, 469, 470, 473; marriage with Mary of England, 478; 482; marriage projects of, 484, 485; claims precedence of other monarchs, 493; supports the Counter-Reformation, 494; his contest with Elizabeth of England, 495, 499; aids Mary Stuart, 501; discovery of his plans in the Netherlands, 502; his triumph in the Netherlands, 505; his attitude toward England, 506; his growing power excites alarm, 509; hesitates to invade England, 510; opposes the plan of Don John, 520; resolves to crush the Netherlands, 522, 523; annexes Portugal, 527; his relations with the "League" in France, 529; his claim to England, 530; designs on France, 531; approves the plot against Elizabeth, 534; the Protestant concert against, 536; purposes to conquer England, 537; aspires to the crown of France, 538, 539, 541; opposes Henry IV at Rome, 542; confronted with a coalition, 544; his failure and death, 545; 555, 578.

Philip III, King of Spain, 548, 549.

Philip IV, King of Spain, 576.

Philip Landgrave of Hesse, signs the "Protest," 426; concerning the League of Schmalkalden, 428; 436, 443, 459, 462; seeks alliance with Henry VIII, 463; opposed by the Emperor, 466, 467; taken prisoner, 468; 471, 475, 476; liberated, 477.

Piccolomini, Aeneas Sylvius, 77, 94.

Piccolomini, Francesco, 245.

Picquigny, the Peace of, 122.

Piedmont, 441, 456, 471, 473, 481, 485.

Pio, Albert, Count de Carpi, 285.

Pisa, 184, 208, 289, 292.

Pisa, the Archbishop of, 138, 142.

Pisa, the Council of, 59.

Pisani, Venetian Ambassador at Rome, 278.

Pius II, Pope, 94, 95, 97, 99, 102, 104, 181, 245, 423.

Pius III, Pope, 245.

Pius IV, Pope, 498.

Pius V, Pope, 506, 508, 555.

Pius IX, Pope, 78.

Plessis-les-Tours, the Treaty of, 528.

Podiebrad, George, King of Bohemia, 96, 105, 107, 108.

Poggio, Bracciolini, 73, 79.

Poland, the struggle with, 51; separation from Hungary, 52; 107, 209, 368, 441, 566.

Pole, Cardinal, 464, 482, 483.

Polin, Antoine, 457.

"Politiques," the, 539, 542.

Pomerania, 51, 602.

Pontremoli, Nicodemus de', 154.

Portugal, discrimination against, at Constance, 64; disputes over discoveries, 186, 187; rivalry with Spain, 210; its commerce, 238; advanced by the discoveries of Da Gama, 267, 268; close relations with Spain, 378; annexed to Spain, 527; frees itself from Spain, 590.

Portugal, the Infanta of, 458.

Portugal, the Infante of, 452, 479.

Postal system, the royal, 2, 155, 156.

"Pragmatic Sanctions" referred to, 75, 97, 99, 102, 303.

Prague, 60, 61, 562.

Prague, Archbishop of, 558.

Prague, the Peace of, 588, 591.

"Praguerie," the, 71, 99.

"Prandium," the, 348.

"Prince, The," work of Machiavelli, 233, 240, 243, 312, 398.

Printing, 2, 163.

"Privilege of Union," of Aragon, 65.

"*Processio*," the, 348.

Protestantism, international aspects of, 428; in the Scandinavian kingdoms, 429; in Germany, 433; 440; its relation to the misfortunes of Charles V, 474; 480, 489; its resistance of the Counter-Reformation, 494; Elizabeth as champion of, 495; its demand for tolerance, 498; 508; in France, 546; 556, 559, 560, 583, 586.

Protestants, the, origin of the term, 426; their answer to the Emperor at Augsburg, 427; negotiate with Francis I, 435; organize against Philip II, 536; the defensive measures of, 463; opposed by the Pope and the Emperor, 467.

Protestant states, the rise of independent, 460.

Protestant Union, the, 557, 560, 561, 562, 564, 566, 567.

Provence, 167, 372, 377, 382.

Prussia, 51, 52, 53, 580, 585, 603.

QUINONES, 412.

Quirini, 259.

RAVAILLAC, 550.

Ravenna, 86, 277; the battle, 292.

INDEX 659

Recess, explanation of the term, 409.
Reformation, the, international influence of, 405; nature of, 423; its strength in Germany, 460; 492, 547.
Regensburg, 462, 466, 578, 582, 591.
Reimbolt, Matthias, 432.
Renaissance, the, 163, 167, 295, 440.
Renard, Simon, 479.
René of Anjou, 76, 90, 91, 92, 167, 174.
René, Duke of Lorraine, 124, 128, 130, 133, 174.
Renée, daughter of Louis XII of France, 300, 301, 305, 326, 333.
Renners, imperial chancellor, 330.
Rense, the decisions of, 21, 39.
"République, La," work of Bodin, 513.
Requesens, 520.
Rhodes, the siege and fall of, 371.
Riario, Girolamo, 137, 145, 148, 167.
Richard II, King of England, 61, 66.
Richelieu, Armand-Jean du Plessis, Cardinal de, his esteem of Machiavelli's work, 312; his advice sought by Louis XIII, 565; aims to consolidate royal power, 569; his religious toleration, 576; his policy, 577; concerning the Emperor, 578, 579; his diplomacy regarding Mantua, 580; his treaties with Savoy, 581; 584, 585, 586, 588, 589; his work for France, 590; his death, 590; 601.
Ridolfi, 510.
Rienzo, Cola di, 35, 36.
Rimini, 228, 247, 254, 269, 271, 277, 278, 289.
Rimino, the murder of, 239.
Rincon, Antoine, 435, 451, 454, 455, 456, 457.
Ring, Hermann, 339.
Rivoli, the Treaty of, 589.
Rivoltella, the Treaty of, 89.
Rizzio, Italian secretary of Mary Stuart, 501.
Robert of Artois, 24.
Robert of Geneva, 43.
Robert of Naples, 13.
Robertet, 286, 287, 301, 382.
Rochechouart, François de, 262.
Romagna, 41, 137; plans of the Borgia in, 223, 224, 228, 233, 242; invaded by Venice, 246; 254, 260; invaded by Julius II, 269; 277.
Romagna, Duke of, see Borgia, Cesare.
"Roman Emperor-elect," 274.
Roman Empire, 172, 308, 424, 438, 491, 492, 541.

Roman law, 172, 513, 515, 516, 572.
Rome, under Pope Innocent VI, 41; return of the popes to, 42; compared with Avignon, 42, 43; its condition when entered by Martin V, 74; the pest at, 139; as the seat of moral authority, 158; welcomes Charles VIII, 191; again the centre of European interest, 239; honors Pope Julius II, 293; the sack of, 401, 405; abandoned by England, 416.
"Römersaal," the, at Frankfort, 343; at Aachen, 348.
Romont, the Count of, 111, 124, 125.
Rorté, Baron, 596.
Rosetti, Cardinal, 598.
Ross, the Bishop of, 515.
Rosso, Venetian secretary, 392, 393.
Rostock, 47.
Rothenburg, 474.
Rousseau, Jean-Jacques, 317.
Roussillon, 179.
Rovere, Giovanni della, Prefect of Rome, 188.
Rovere, Giuliano della, Cardinal, his intrigues in the papal election, 168; aspires to the Papacy, 170; urges Charles VIII to invade Italy, 182; 192, 193, 204, 220, 221; becomes pope as Julius II, 244, 245.
Royal power, theories of, 512.
Rudolf of Anhalt, 189.
Rudolf II, Emperor, 523, 541, 549, 555, 558.
Rudolf of Hapsburg, 437.
Rupert of Bavaria, 58, 60.
Russia, 52, 209, 597.

SAALFELD, the Treaty of, 432.
Sageberg, the Conference of, 566.
Saint Bartholomew's Day, massacre of the Huguenots on, 512.
Sainte-Croix, Cardinal, 71.
Saint-Germain, the Treaty of, 509.
Saint-Germain-en-Laye, the Treaty of, 589.
Saint James, the Order of, 257.
Saint Louis, see Louis IX of France.
Saint Malo, the Bishop of, 175.
"Saint Mary, the German Knights of," 50.
Saint Omer, the Treaty of, 109.
Saint Paul, 16.
Saint Peter, the Patrimony of, 277.
Saint Pol, Constable of France, 103, 121, 122, 124.

660   INDEX

Saint Pol, the Count de, 200.
Saint Quentin, the battle of, 483.
Saint Stephen, see Stephen, Duke of Hungary.
Salian Franks, the, 6.
Salic law, the, 6, 539, 541.
Saluzzo, Marquisate of, 86.
Salviati, Francesco, Archbishop of Pisa, 138, 142.
Salvius, John, 593, 596.
Salza, Hermann von, 50, 51.
Samogitia, 51.
Santa Croce, 229.
Santa Pressede, 229.
Sanuto, Benedetto, 268.
Sanuto, Marino, 268.
Saracens, the, 54.
Sardinia, 64, 201, 436.
Sarmiento, 565.
Sarpi, Fra Paolo, 548.
Saurer, 334.
Savelli, Cardinal, 169, 178.
Savona, the secret conference at, 271.
Savonarola, 177, 184, 185, 206, 213, 225.
Savoy, 20, 111, 116, 118, 119, 127, 216, 441.
Savoy, the Duke of, 368, 458, 589.
Saxony, electors of, referred to. 22, 39, 108, 330, 348, 357, 358, 428, 462, 466, 467, 556, 562, 587, 603.
Scandinavian kingdoms, 49, 158, 511, 547, 566.
Scarampo, Luigi, 75.
Schaffhausen joins the Swiss Confederation, 226.
Schinner, Matthias, 287, 288, 325.
Schism in the Empire, 58, 60.
Schism, the Great, 42, 57, 72, 78, 492, 513.
Schlick, Gaspard, 77.
Schmalkalden, the League of, 427, 432, 459, 463, 464, 466, 467.
Schomberg, Nicholas, 373.
Schwendi, Lazarus von, 474.
Schwyz, 108, 304.
Scotland, 12, 155, 214, 359, 369, 496.
Senlis, the Truce of, 112; the Treaty of, 180.
Servia, 54.
Servien, Abel, 581, 582, 594, 596.
"*Sessio*," the, 347.
Seville, Archbishop of, 267.
Seymour, Jane, 452.
Sforza, the, 167, 225.

Sforza, Ascanio Cardinal, 168, 169, 190, 194, 213, 225, 244, 253.
Sforza, Blanche, 180.
Sforza, Francesco, 75; becomes master of Milan, 85, 86, 88, 89; joins with Florence in alliance with France, 90; his negotiations with Venice, 91; his opposition to France, 93, 94; his support of Ferdinand of Naples, 95; admired by Louis XI, 98; his alliance with Louis XI, 102; his death, 104; 154.
Sforza, Francesco II, 361, 371, 395, 438, 444.
Sforza, Galeazzo, 102, 104, 111, 119, 120, 135, 137, 140.
Sforza, Gian Galeazzo, 147, 148, 175, 176, 183, 184.
Sforza, Ludovico, called "The Moor," his measures in Milan, 140; aims to retain possession of Milan, 146, 147; seeks the favor of Louis XI, 148; forms a confederation with Florence and Naples, 149; 168, 169; his alliance with Charles VIII, 175; 176, 177, 180, 181, 183; proclaimed Duke of Milan, 184; 190, 200, 206; concludes the Treaty of Vercelli, 207; his strength in Italy, 212; his family relations with Maximilian, 213; his diplomatic struggle, 215; seeks alliance with the Swiss, 217; his negotiations with Alexander VI, 223; his ruin, 225.
Sforza, Maximilian, 292, 293, 296.
Sicilies, the two, 305, 323, 437.
Sicily, 20, 65, 85, 197, 201, 242, 436, 481.
Sickingen, Franz von, 326, 342, 357.
Siena, 37, 86, 189, 206, 208, 361, 390.
Sigismund, Duke of Austria, 107, 108, 110, 120.
Sigismund, King of Hungary, Emperor, accession to Hungary, 54, 55, 56; election to the Empire, 60; his mission of conciliation, 63; position in the Council of Constance, 63; confers the Electorate of Brandenburg upon Frederick of Hohenzollern, 63; visit to France and England, 65; honors Amadeus of Savoy, 66; his alliance with Henry V of England, 67; failure of his mission, 68; alliance with Charles VII of France, 70; relations to Venice and Bohemia, 70; coronation at Rome, 76; death, 76.
Sigismund I, King of Poland, 324, 334, 335, 343.
Sigismund III, King of Poland, 547, 567, 580.
Silinen, Jost von, 121.
Sinigaglia, assassination of the nobles at, 240.
Sixtus IV, Pope, negotiates the Con-

INDEX 661

cordat of 1472 with Louis XI, 119; 135, 137; his war with Florence, 138; his relations with Louis XI, 139, 140, 141; refuses French arbitration, 142; acknowledges the independence of Genoa, 144; collapse of his negotiations, 145; the isolation of, 146; alliance with Venice, 148; treatment of the Holy See, 166, 167; concerning the Angevin claims, 167; his death, 168; 186; his sanction of the "Inquisition," 266.

Sixtus V, Pope, 312, 531.

Sluys, the naval battle of, 27.

Society of states, 553, 571.

Soderini, the, 104.

Solyman, the Magnificent, Ottoman Sultan, 433, 435, 450, 455, 458, 473.

Soto, Pedro de, 466.

Souleuvres, the Truce of, 124.

Sovereign state system, the development of a, 489.

Sovereignty, referred to, 48, 492, 513, 514, 525.

Spain, formation of, 179; its power, 179; contends with Portugal over discoveries, 186; the possessions assigned to, 187; rivalry with Portugal, 210; rivalry with France and England, 211; its treaty with France, 215; dispute over Naples, 230; its commerce, 238; truce with France, 250; relations of Pope Julius II to, 270; sends an envoy to Cambray, 276; revolts against Charles, 328; its opposition to his acceptance of the Empire, 346, 347; its close relations with Portugal, 378; importance of its attitude toward the Papacy, 407; influence at the Council of Trent, 465; resigned to Philip, 481; its claim of precedence, 493; its agreement with France, 496; compact with France concerning heresy, 502, 503, 504; its commerce despoiled by England, 506, 507, 519; struggle of the Netherlands with, 522; its monopoly of commerce with the West Indies, 526; makes peace with France, 544; its decline, 545; makes peace with England, 548; renews war in the Netherlands, 563; secret treaty with France, 575; at the Congress of Westphalia, 596.

Spens, Sir James, 566, 568.

Speyer, diets of, referred to, 408, 422, 425, 427, 428, 459.

Spinola, Spanish general, 561, 563, 579.

Squillaci, the Prince of, 228.

State, the, changed conception of, 310; conception of, as sovereign, 491; new theories of, 511; nature of a sovereign, 516; as a moral entity, 517; conception of, in the Netherlands, 522, 523.

State of the Church, see Papal State.

States General, of Burgundy, 128.

States General, of France, 83, 151, 261, 393, 541.

States General, of the Netherlands, 503, 532.

Stella, Venetian envoy, 219, 220.

Stephen, Duke of Hungary, called Saint Stephen, 53.

Sternburg, Ladislas von, 343.

Stralsund, 576, 582.

Stralsund, the Treaty of, 48, 49.

Stratford, John, 29.

Stratford, Robert, 29, 30.

Suabian League, the, 34, 322, 341.

Suarez de Mendoça y Figueroa, Lorenzo, 201, 202, 253.

Suarez, Franciscus, 553, 554.

Suessia, the Duchy of, 223.

Suez canal, project of a, 268.

Sully, Duke of, 550, 551.

Sulz, Rudolf von, 113.

"Super Potestate Summi Pontificis," work of William of Occam, 16.

Surian, Antonio, 360.

Sweden, 47, 50, 429, 547, 567, 579, 601, 602.

Swedish Church, 429.

Swiss, the, oppose Charles the Bold, 109, 113, 118; participate in the Union of Constance, 120; invade Franche-Comté and conquer Vaud, 121; attacked by Charles the Bold, 124, 125; their victory at Lake Morat, 127; endeavor to extend their territories, 130; abandon Franche-Comté, 133; at war with the Emperor Maximilian, 216; acquire Bellinzona, 225; alliance with Pope Julius II, 287; oppose the French in Italy, 292, 296.

Swiss Confederation, the, 108, 217, 226, 304, 306, 605.

Switzerland, 432, 437, 473, 522, 548.

Sylvester II, Pope, 53.

Syphilis, its spread in Europe, 199.

Szegedin, the Treaty of, 78.

TARBES, the Bishop of, 399.

Taylor, English ambassador, 389.

Teutonic Order, the, 50, 51, 52.

Tewkesbury, the battle of, 111.

Thirlby, Thomas, 484.

Thirty-nine Articles, the, 511.

Thirty Years' War, the, 491, 569, 585, 586, 606.

Throgmorton, Francis, 529.

Tibaldeschi, Cardinal, 43.
Tibaldo, Milanese ambassador, 93.
Ticino, canton of Switzerland, 225.
Tilly, 563, 584.
Toledo, Archbishop of, 406, 482.
Toledo, Francisco de, 465.
Tordesillas, the Treaty of, 186.
Torquemada, Thomas de, 266.
Toul, 116, 472, 476, 485, 579, 601.
Tournay, 306, 307, 370, 384.
Transylvania, 54, 456, 560.
Trastamara, the House of, 65.
Trauttmannsdorf, Count, 596.
Trent, the Council of, 463, 464, 469, 473, 489, 493, 494, 498, 543, 556, 578.
Trier, the Archbishop of, 22, 25, 39, 77, 113, 116, 324, 330, 332, 334, 338, 344, 345, 348, 556.
Triple Alliance against Venice and the Pope, 136, 139, 140, 141, 142, 143, 144, 145, 146, 147, 148.
Trivulzio, General, 225.
Troches (or Troccio), 241, 242.
Troyes, the Treaty of, 68.
Tudor dynasty, 179, 501.
Tunis, 434, 437.
Tunstall, Cuthbert, 66, 325, 376.
Turin, 216, 441.
Turks, the, 56, 76, 78, 79, 165, 187.
Tuscany, 37, 85.
Tyrol, 34, 437, 550.

ULM, the Treaty of, 561, 600.
Unification, the principle of, 165.
Universities referred to, 38, 58, 59, 60, 61, 66, 73, 430, 530.
Unterwalden, 108, 304.
Urban V, Pope, 42.
Urban VI, Pope, 43, 44, 45.
Urban VIII, Pope, 574, 575, 576, 578, 581, 591, 598.
Urbino, the Duke of, 397, 439.
Uri, canton of Switzerland, 108, 304.
Utrecht, 34, 116, 503, 522.
Utrecht, the Union of, 524.

VALENCE, the Comté of, 222.
Valencia, Cardinal of, see Borgia, Cesare.
Valenciennes, conference of, 18.
Valentinois, Duchy of, 222; Duke of, see Borgia, Cesare.
Valois, the House of, 232, 253, 260, 261, 262, 332, 496, 538.
Valpergi, the brothers, 152.

Valtelline, the, 564, 577, 582.
Vannes, Peter, 483.
Varna, the battle of, 78.
Vasquez, Fernando, 493.
Vaucelles, the Truce of, 482.
Vaud, 121, 124, 125.
Velli, 442, 446, 447.
Venice, its aid sought by Edward III of England, 25; commercial interests, 56; difficulty with Sigismund, 70; importance in Italy, 86, 87; relations to Alfonso V and Sforza, 88, 89, 91; its commerce threatened, 102; relations with Charles the Bold, 111, 112; peace with France, 134, 141; peace with the Sultan, 143, 145; 148, 149, 165, 177, 178, 187, 188; its secret operations against Charles VIII, 200, 202, 205; embroiled with Alexander VI, 213; its rapprochement to France, 219, 220, 221; loss of commerce, 238; its support sought by Alexander VI, 239, 242; invades Romagna, 246; concerning the Treaty of Blois, 251, 252; concerning Julius II, 254, 256; decline of commerce, 267; 269, 273; war with Maximilian, 274, 275; excommunicated by the Pope, 278; its war with the League of Cambray, 279; appeals to England, 280; beginning of permanent relations with England, 282; peace with Julius II, 284; proposes a league against France, 290; 291, 295, 296; renewal of alliance with France, 301; 371, 390; joins the League of Cognac, 395; as a post of observation, 449; peace with the Sultan, 451, 454; its controversy with Pope Paul V, 548; offers to mediate for the Netherlands and Sweden, 591.
Venice, the League of, 199, 203, 206, 207, 212, 213, 230.
Vercelli, the Treaty of, 207, 213, 218.
Verdun, 84, 116, 128, 158, 472, 476, 485, 579, 601.
Vervins, the Peace of, 543, 548, 550.
Veyre, Don Pedro de, 412.
Victor Amadeus, Duke of Savoy, 581.
Victoria, Franciscus a, 492, 493.
Vienna, Congress of, 50.
Villari, historian, 316.
Villeroy, Nicolas de Neufville, Seigneur de, 539, 549.
Villinger, imperial chancellor, 330.
Vio, Thomas de, Cardinal, 328.
Visconti, the, 36, 42.
Visconti, Filippo Maria, Duke of Milan, 60, 86, 87, 213.
Visconti, Gian Galeazzo, 213.

INDEX

Visconti, Robert, 37.
Visconti, Valentine, 88, 213.
Vitelleschi, 75.
Vitelli, Vitellozzo, 240.
Vivès, Gabriel, 139.
Volmar, Doctor, 596.
Voltaire, 294.

WAAD, William, 530.
" *Wahlcapitulation*," the, 41, 345.
Wain, Gervais, 432.
Waldemar III, King of Denmark, 47, 49.
Waldenses, the, 461.
Wallenstein, 574, 575, 576, 577, 578, 579, 580, 582, 584, 585, 587, 588.
Walsingham, Sir Francis, 526, 529, 535, 536.
War, discussed by the jurists, 552, 553, 570, 571.
Wars, of the Roses, 97, 179; of religion, 496.
Warwick, the Earl of, 110.
Welser, banking house of, 342.
Wenzel, Emperor, 41, 54, 58, 60, 61.
West Indies, the, 526.
Westminster, the Treaty of, 398, 400.
Westphalia, the Congress of, 491, 592, 594, 596, 597, 603.
Westphalia, the Peace of, 485, 599.
White Mountain, battle of the, 562.
Wiclif, 16, 60, 61, 74, 416.
Wied, Hermann von, 329, 475.
William of Occam, 16.
William, Prince of Orange, called the "Silent," at the abdications of Charles V, 480; 484, 502; his work in the Netherlands, 503; his statesmanship, 504; opposes Alba, 506; opposes Philip II, 520, 521; determines to end Spanish rule, 522; seeks foreign aid, 523; his embarrassments, 524; as a representative of the idea of the State, 525; his assassination, 529.
William of Weimar, 583.
Windsor, the Treaty of, 370, 378.
Wingfield, Sir Robert, 324, 376.
Wismar, 47, 576, 582, 602.
Wittelsbach, the House of, 13, 34, 467.
Wolfgang of Anhalt, 426.
Wolfgang William of Neuburg, 558.
Wolsey, Thomas, Cardinal, his pacific policy, 297; becomes cardinal, 306; his triumph, 307; recommendations concerning the imperial election, 336; aspires to the Papacy, 337; his indifference to the candidacy of Henry VIII, 338, 339; personal qualities, 350; his plan for a meeting of the sovereigns, 351; at Calais, 353; his pressure on Francis I, 359; obstructions to his mediation, 360; opposed by Gattinara, 362; visits the Emperor at Bruges, 364; his meeting with Christian II of Denmark, 364; the reasons for his failure, 366, 367; 368, 369, 370; his papal hopes again disappointed, 371; secret negotiations with France, 372; his apathy in the war against France, 373; his treatment of De Praet, 373, 374; 375, 379; his proposals to Charles V, 380; resumes negotiations with Louise of Savoy, 383; his opinion of the Treaty of Madrid, 391; revival of his mediatorial policy, 394; his aims for England, 398; loses control over the King, 400; his journey to France, 413; his pressure upon Pope Clement VII, 414; concerning the King's divorce, 415; his fall, 416; 452, 483.
Women, question of hereditary rights of, 5, 6, 11.
Woodville, Elizabeth, 110.
Wool, its exportation prohibited, 20; market for, 367.
Worms, the Diet of, 355, 357; the Edict of, 409, 427; 462.
Wotton, Nicholas, 484.
Würtemberg, 322, 358, 436, 443.
Würzburg, 584.

XIMENES de Cisneros, Francisco, Cardinal, 264, 266, 267, 270, 328, 435.

YOLANDE of Aragon, 69, 70.
Yolande, Duchess of Savoy, 111, 119, 125, 127, 135, 207.
York, the House of, 97, 179.
Yuste, 478, 481.

ZANTFLIED, Cornelius, 44.
Zapolya, King of Hungary, 409, 410, 433, 436, 455.
Zeeland, 34, 84, 129, 130, 503, 521, 524, 532.
Zevenbergen, Max von, 341, 345.
Zug, canton of Switzerland, 108, 304.
Zürich, 108, 304, 424.
Zutphen, 113, 117, 459.
Zwingli, 424, 434, 461.
Zwinglians, the, 431.

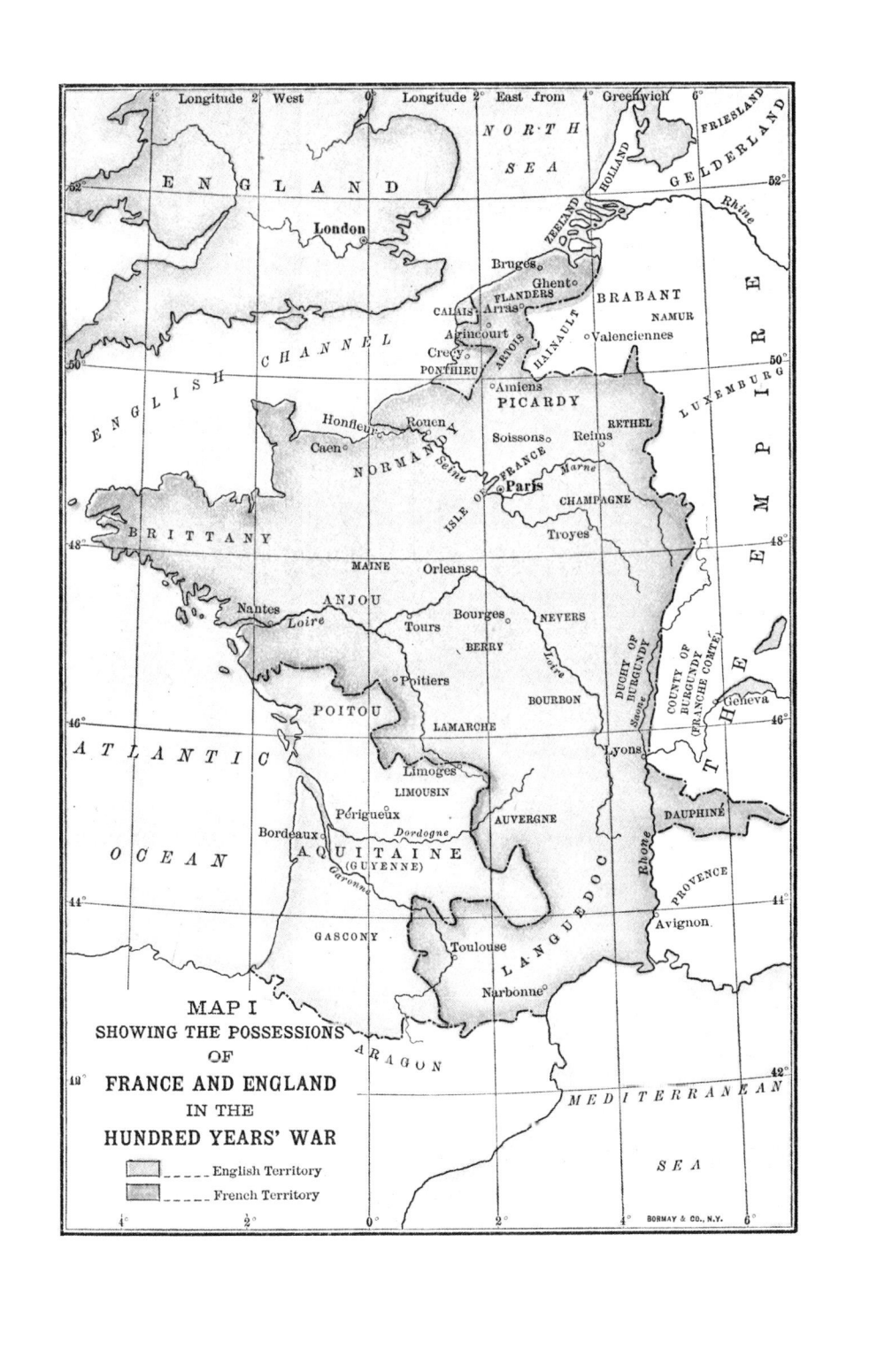

MAP I
SHOWING THE POSSESSIONS
OF
FRANCE AND ENGLAND
IN THE
HUNDRED YEARS' WAR

English Territory
French Territory

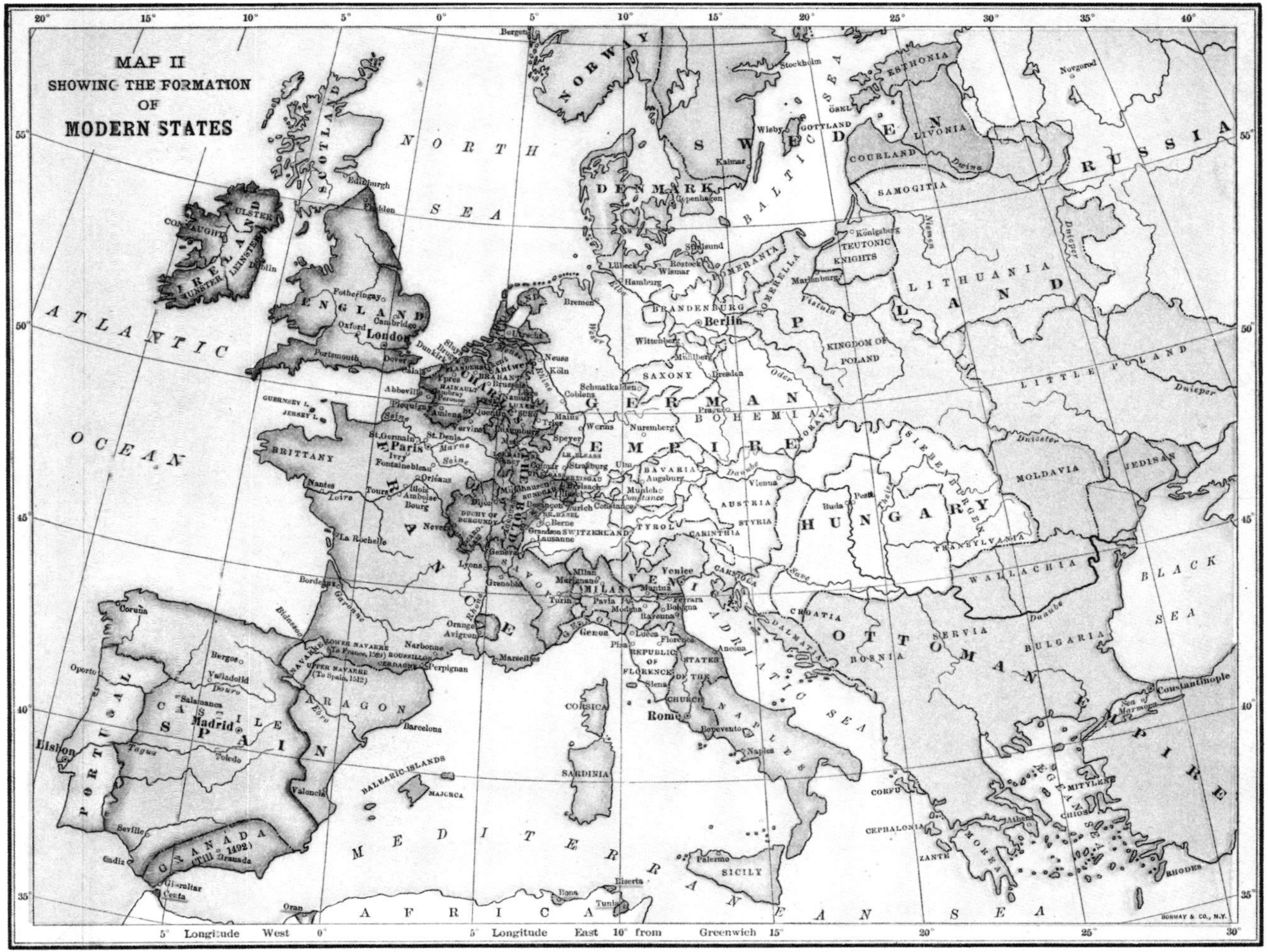
MAP II
SHOWING THE FORMATION
OF
MODERN STATES
NORTH SEA
ATLANTIC OCEAN
BALTIC SEA
BLACK SEA
ADRIATIC SEA
MEDITERRANEAN SEA
AFRICA
SCOTLAND
IRELAND
ULSTER
LEINSTER
ENGLAND
London
NORWAY
SWEDEN
DENMARK
RUSSIA
ESTHONIA
LIVONIA
COURLAND
SAMOGITIA
LITHUANIA
POLAND
KINGDOM OF POLAND
LITTLE POLAND
TEUTONIC KNIGHTS
GERMAN EMPIRE
BRANDENBURG
Berlin
SAXONY
BOHEMIA
BAVARIA
AUSTRIA
STYRIA
TYROL
CARINTHIA
SWITZERLAND
HUNGARY
TRANSYLVANIA
MOLDAVIA
WALLACHIA
JEDISAN
OTTOMAN EMPIRE
BULGARIA
SERVIA
BOSNIA
CROATIA
DALMATIA
FRANCE
BRITTANY
Paris
SPAIN
CASTILE
ARAGON
GRANADA
PORTUGAL
Madrid
Lisbon
Rome
NAPLES
SICILY
SARDINIA
CORSICA
MOREA
Constantinople
BORMAY & CO., N.Y.
Longitude West
Longitude East 10° from Greenwich

MAP III
ITALY
IN THE
SIXTEENTH CENTURY

MAP IV, SHOWING THE TERRITORIAL CHANGES EFFECTED BY THE PEACE OF WESTPHALIA.